A Summary of the Christian Faith

Also Available from LutheranLibrary.org

- *The Lutheran Confessions: A Brief Introduction* by Henry Eyster Jacobs
- *The Book of Concord: The Symbolical Books of the Evangelical Lutheran Church* by Henry Eyster Jacobs and Charles Krauth
- *The First Free Lutheran Diet Edited* by Henry Eyster Jacobs

About The Lutheran Library

The Lutheran Library is a non-profit publisher of good Christian books. All are available in a variety of formats for use by anyone for free or at very little cost. There are never any licensing fees.

We are Bible believing Christians who subscribe wholeheartedly to the Augsburg Confession as an accurate summary of Scripture, the chief article of which is Justification by Faith. Our purpose is to make available solid and encouraging material to strengthen believers in Christ.

Prayers are requested for the next generation, that the Lord will plant in them a love of the truth, such that the hard-learned lessons of the past will not be forgotten.

Please let others know of these books and this completely volunteer endeavor. May God bless you and keep you, help you, defend you, and lead you to know the depths of His kindness and love.

Dedication

To The
Candidates for the Ministry of the Gospel
Among Whom My Life Has Been Passed,
This Volume
Is
Affectionately Dedicated
By
Their Fellow-Student.

A Summary of the Christian Faith

by Henry Eyster Jacobs, D.D., LL.D.

Norton Professor of Systematic Theology Lutheran Theological Seminary at Philadelphia

Philadelphia

GENERAL COUNCIL PUBLICATION HOUSE

LutheranLibrary.org

Copyright Notice

This book was published 2019 by The Lutheran Library Publishing Ministry LutheranLibrary.org. Some (hopefully unobtrusive) updates to spelling, punctuation, and paragraph divisions have been made. Unabridged.

Originally published 1905 by the General Council Publication House, Philadelphia.

Image on imprint page is *Still Life With Bible* by Vincent Van Gogh.

109 – v5.2 2020-03-07

ISBN: 9781703710175 (paperback)

Summary Contents

Also Available from LutheranLibrary.org....ii
About The Lutheran Library....iii
Dedication....v
Copyright Notice....viii
Preface....lxv
What Does It Mean: "For Many Are Called; But Few Chosen!" (Matt. 22:14)....1
Luther On Speculations Concerning Predestination....5
1. Sources And Methods....9
2. The Being And Attributes Of God....25
3. The Trinity....51
4. Creation....73
5. Providence....85
6. Of Angels....99
7. Man As Created....109
8. Sin....121
9. The Grace Of God Towards Fallen Men....139
10. The Preparation Of Redemption....147
11. The Person Of Christ....151
12. The States of Christ....171
13. The Offices Of Christ, Christ As Prophet....193
14. Christ As Priest....203
15. Christ As King....219
16. The Mission Of The Holy Ghost....225
17. Faith in Christ....229
18. Justification....251
19. The Gospel Call....263
20. Illumination....271
21. Regeneration....281
22. The Mystical Union....299
23. Renovation Or Sanctification....303

24. The Word As The Means Of Grace....321
25. The Law And The Gospel....351
26. The Sacraments....367
27. Of Holy Baptism....381
28. Of The Holy Supper....399
29. The Church....427
30. The Ministry....473
31. The Church's Confessions....499
32. Church Discipline....511
33. The Christian Family....519
34. The State....529
35. Life After Death....541
36. The Resurrection Of The Body....551
37. The Return Of Christ....563
38. The General Judgment....577
39. Eternal Death....597
40. Eternal Life....603
41. The Divine Purpose As Interpreted By Its Contents And Results....615
Appendix: On The Spiritual Priesthood Of Believers. By Dr. Philip J. Spener (1677)....635
About the Author....653
How Can You Find Peace With God?....655
Benediction....656
Encouraging Christian Books for You to Download and Enjoy....657

Detailed Contents

Also Available from LutheranLibrary.org....ii
About The Lutheran Library....iii
Dedication....v
Copyright Notice....viii
Preface....lxv
What Does It Mean: "For Many Are Called; But Few Chosen!" (Matt. 22:14)....1
Luther On Speculations Concerning Predestination....5
1. Sources And Methods....9
Definitions....9
1. What is Dogmatic Theology?....9
2. Why is it a Science?....9
3. Why is this science called "Dogmatics" or "Dogmatic Theology"?....9
4. What is a "dogma"?....9
Scope....10
5. Is Dogmatic Theology a purely Biblical science?....10
6. State this distinction more sharply....10
Elements....10
7. With what three elements, therefore, has Dogmatic Theology to deal?....10
Relations....11
8. What, therefore, is the order of the chief branches of Theology that are here involved?....11
Presuppositions....11
9. What are the Presuppositions of Dogmatic Theology?....11
Process....12
10. Trace the process whereby the truths recorded in Holy Scripture attain scientific statement....12
Standard....13
11. Is Christian experience, then, a standard of doctrine?....13
Religion As A Life Proceeding From Faith....13
12. By what term is that habit, or state of mind and heart known which results from faith?....13
13. Is there, then, no religion or religious life where there is no faith in Christ?....13
14. Is "Religion" confined, then, to the designation of an inner spiritual life?....14
The Christian As Distinguished From Natural Revelation....14
15. Upon what does this claim of Christianity as the Absolute Religion rest?....14
16. But has not God revealed Himself to all men?....14
17. By what is the imperfection of this Natural Knowledge to be explained? 15
18. Of what are the truths contained in the Natural Revelation the foundation?....15

19. Is the Natural Revelation then useless?....15
20. Was there no supernatural revelation before Christ?....15
Holy Scripture As The Record of Revelation....16
21. What records were made of these earlier revelations?....16
22. What principle is to be observed in the determination of the meaning of the New Testament?....16
23. What does this imply?....16
24. Illustrate this?....17
25. Upon what is this principle based?....17
26. What term has been applied to this principle?....17
27. What further caution is needed in the study of the Holy Scriptures?....17
Relation of Reason to Revelation....17
28. Are Reason and Revelation, therefore, antagonistic?....17
29. What, then, is the first requisite for apprehending the meaning of Holy Scripture?....18
30. Has Reason, therefore, no office with respect to articles of faith?....18
31. How, then, is the proper relation between Faith and Reason maintained?....18
32. How is the so-called conflict between Science and Revelation to be explained?....18
Church Authority and Articles of Faith....19
33. Has the Church no authority to determine what are Articles of Faith?....19
34. Are the Church's declarations concerning Holy Scripture, the testimony of the Fathers, and the opinions of later theologians to be disregarded?....19
35. Repeat the confessional statements of the Lutheran Church on the relation of Holy Scripture to these testimonies....20
Clearness and Completeness of Scripture....20
36. But are the Holy Scriptures sufficiently clear and complete to dispense with supplementary revelations and the testimony of tradition as coordinate authorities?....20
Authority of Scripture....21
37. Is it proper to attach authority to the English, German or Latin Scriptures?....21
38. Should we not attach ultimate authority only to the original autographs?....22
Christian Experience and Scripture....22
39. Which is the more important aid to the knowledge of Scripture, acquaintance with the original languages, or Christian experience?....22
The Three Requisites of a Theologian....22
40. What rule has Luther formulated on this subject?....22
2. The Being And Attributes Of God....25
What is implied in Religion....25
1. What definition of Religion has been already given?....25
2. What kind of relation does this imply?....25
3. What does a personal relation involve?....25
4. What is meant by "a person"?....26
5. What, therefore, is essential to the very conception of religion?....26
Errors conflicting this conception....26
6. Against what errors is the conception of God as a personality arrayed?....26
Personality and Tri-personality....26

7. But is not the conception of God as a person in conflict with the Christian doctrine of the Three Persons in one Essence or Being? 26
8. Can God be defined? 27
9. What definitions then can be given? 27
10. Can such definition be further expanded? 27
Definition of God 28
11. Is this latter mode of definition widely adopted? 28
Name and Names of God 28
12. Why is "the Name of God" so frequently mentioned in Holy Scripture? 28
13. What then is the Name of God? 29
14. Explain Scripture passages in which the term occurs 29
15. Distinguish between "the Name" and "the Names" of God? 29
16. How are they classified? 29
Attributes of God 30
17. What are the attributes of God? 30
18. Are they then accidental? 30
19. Are they factors into which the essence of God has been resolved? 30
20. What then are they? 30
21. By what threefold method is the idea of the Divine Attributes gained? 30
22. State this more fully 31
23. How may the Divine Attributes be classified? 31
24. Define them 31
25. Enumerate the Absolute Attributes 31
26. What is meant by Independence? 31
27. What is meant by Simplicity? 32
28. What is meant by Infinity? 32
29. What is Infinity, when regarded with respect to temporal relations? 32
30. What is implied by Eternity? 33
31. What is Infinity, when regarded with respect to spatial relations? 33
32. What is the positive side of Immensity? 33
33. In how many ways is God omnipresent? 33
34. Which of these is Omnipresence in the proper sense? 34
35. But is not God described in Holy Scripture as coming and going? 34
36. How is this distinction designated? 34
37. But does not the omnipresence of God conflict with His simplicity? 34
38. What different modes of presence are there? 35
39. What is the Immutability of God? 35
40. But did not Creation imply or produce a change in God? 36
41. Did not Incarnation imply or produce a change? 36
42. Is not God sometimes described as repenting? 36
43. How about unfulfilled promises and conditions? 36
44. What distinction must be observed touching all such conditions? 37
45. What are the Relative Attributes? 37
46. What is the Life of God? 37
47. What Attributes are ascribed to the Divine Intellect? 38
48. What is Omniscience? 38
49. What is meant by "a simple act"? 38
50. What difference is there between God's knowledge of Himself and His knowledge of all beyond and besides? 39
51. Where is God's knowledge of future contingencies which never occurred

declared?.......... 39
52. What is the Wisdom of God?.......... 39
53. Before enumerating the Attributes or Perfections of the Divine Will, state whether there be a difference between the Divine Essence and the Divine Will.......... 39
54. Is the Divine Will determined by any process or succession of thought? 40
55. By what is the Divine Will characterized?.......... 40
56. What distinctions, however, have been made?.......... 40
57. We are now ready to hear an enumeration of the Attributes of the Divine Will?.......... 43
58. What is God's Power?.......... 43
59. Can God do what is wrong?.......... 43
60. Is not His power, therefore, limited?.......... 43
61. Against what further misunderstanding is God's Omnipotence to be guarded?.......... 43
62. What is the Justice of God?.......... 44
63. But does not this elevate the Law above God Himself?.......... 44
64. Is a thing then good because God has willed it, or has God willed it because it is good?.......... 44
65. But the question still arises: Is a thing good for no other reason than that it has been willed and commanded by God? Are Truth and Love, for example, virtues only because of God's command?.......... 45
66. But how in regard to matters of permanent and immutable morality, such as are declared in the Moral Law?.......... 45
67. In what different ways is the Divine Justice exercised towards men?.......45
68. Is God's Retributive Justice essential or accidental?.......... 45
69. What attribute is most closely connected with Justice?.......... 46
70. What is the Goodness of God?.......... 46
71. What does the Goodness of God include?.......... 47
72. What different forms are there of this love?.......... 47
73. What is the first form in which this love is known?.......... 48
74. Is the word used in Holy Scripture in any other sense?.......... 48
75. What distinction in grace was made by the Scholastics?.......... 48
76. What distinction with a better Scriptural foundation was also current? 48
77. In what other form is this Love known?.......... 49
78. Is there yet another form?.......... 49
79. What is the Holiness of God?.......... 49

3. The Trinity.......... 51

Peculiar to New Testament.......... 51
1. What knowledge of God is peculiar to Christianity?.......... 51
2. Is not this doctrine taught by Natural Revelation?.......... 51
3. Do not some non-Christian religions teach a triad or threeness in God?...51

Suggested in Old Testament.......... 52
4. Is it not taught in the Old Testament?.......... 52

Terminology.......... 52
5. Who is first known to have used the term "Trinity"?.......... 52
6. But why should non-Scriptural terms be employed?.......... 52

Not purely Speculative.......... 52
7. Is not the doctrine one of purely theoretical or speculative interest?.........52

Three Fundamental Propositions.......... 52

8. Upon what three propositions does the doctrine of the Trinity rest?........52
I. *The Unity of God*..53
9. What is meant when "unity" is ascribed to an object of thought?.............53
10. Apply this to God..53
11. Give Scripture proofs...53
12. Is not unity implied in the very conception of God?...............................53
13. But is not this unity contradicted when we say that there are three who are God?...53
II. *The Threeness of God.* (a) Divinity of Each Person proved from his having the Names, Attributes, Works and Worship of God; Coordination of the Three in same passage..54
14. What grounds are there for holding that there are three who are God?...54
15. How?...54
16. Apply this fourfold argument to the Father..54
17. Applying this same argument to the Son, give, first, passages in which the names of God are ascribed to the Son?...56
18. How is this argument from Divine Names ascribed to Jesus Christ further confirmed?...56
19. What attributes of God are ascribed to the Son?......................................57
He is Eternal...57
He is Immutable..57
He is Omnipresent...57
He is Omniscient..57
He is Omnipotent...58
20. What works peculiar to God belong to the Son?......................................58
21. What worship is claimed for the Son?...59
22. What adds especial force to these ascriptions of worship as an argument proving that the Son is God?..59
23. Where is the worship of the very highest of creatures reproved?.............60
24. Where are the Names of God ascribed to the Holy Ghost?....................60
25. What attributes of God are ascribed Him?...60
Eternity...60
Omnipresence..61
Omniscience..61
26. What works of God are ascribed to the Holy Ghost?...............................61
27. Where is divine worship addressed Him?...61
28. How can you prove the fact that the Holy Ghost is God by a comparison of Old and New Testament passages?...61
29. What is the chief point of attack concerning the divinity of the Holy Ghost?...62
30. What second class of arguments may be adduced for the doctrine of the Trinity?...62
III. *The Persons distinguished*...63
31. But may not Father, Son and Holy Ghost be only different forms or modes of manifestation of God?...63
The Holy Ghost a Person, not an Energy...63
32. How do you answer the proposed explanation, mentioned above (Q. 29) that the Holy Ghost is simply the divine energy or power?........................63
Explanation of the scientific formulation of the dogma: "Substance and"Essence," "Person," "Hypostasis," "Personal Acts," "Personal Peculiarities," "Generation," "Filiation," "Spiration," "the Double Procession," Order of

Persons, External Acts..64
33. What result has now been reached by this argument?.............................64
34. How is this doctrine taught by the Church?..64
35. What does the Athanasian Creed mean when it speaks of the "substance" and the Augsburg Confession, when it speaks of the "essence" of God?......64
36. How is this essence common to all three persons?....................................64
37. What is meant by "person"?..65
38. What are the distinguishing attributes of personality?..............................65
39. What is a brief definition of "person"?..65
40. What distinguishes "person" in Grammar?..65
41. For the popular statement of the subject, this is sufficient. What value, then, must be attached to the current Scholastic definition, as revised by the Reformers of both branches of Protestantism?...65
42. Repeat it...66
43. Why is "person" defined as substance?...66
44. Does this imply any contradiction with the formula of the Athanasian Creed that God is one in substance?...66
45. What is meant by the descriptive terms "individual", "intelligent" "incommunicable," "not sustained in another," "not the part of another"?66
46. How does "person" as used here differ from the same term as applied to men and angels?..67
47. By what term did the early Greek theologians designate the distinction which we indicate by "person"?...67
48. In what are the three persons alike or the same?.......................................67
49. In what are they distinguished?...67
50. What are these personal acts?..67
51. What is Generation?..68
52. From what conceptions must it be guarded?..68
53. Upon what Scriptural grounds does this rest?..68
54. What is Spiration?...69
55. Is it identical with the activity by which the Son is generated?..................69
56. What proof is there that the Holy Ghost proceeds from the Father?......69
57. Is our Lord's promise that He would send the Holy Ghost a proof that He proceeds from the Son as well as from the Father?..................................69
58. Why then did the Western Church maintain in opposition to the Greek Church that He proceeds not only from the Father but also from the Son? 70
59. What then are the five personal peculiarities founded upon these two acts?..70
60. Is there not then an order?..70
61. Is the term "Father" when applied to God always restricted to the First Person of the Trinity?...71
62. Besides the immanent acts, not common to all persons, but distinguishing them from each other (opera ad intra), what other personal acts are there?...71
63. What especially distinguishes them from the former class?.......................71
64. Name them..71
Old Testament Suggestions...72
65. What traces are there (see Q. 4) of this doctrine in the Old Testament?..72
Philosophical Arguments...72
66. What philosophical arguments for the Trinity hare been used and what is their value?...72

4. Creation... 73
Relation to what precedes.. 73
1. What is the relation of this chapter to what precedes?................................ 73
Definition.. 73
2. What is Creation?... 73
Source of doctrine.. 74
3. Whence do we derive our knowledge of this act?... 74
Mosaic account... 74
4. What is the purpose and scope of the Mosaic account?................................ 74
Trinitarian relations.. 74
5. Who created the world?.. 74
Father... 74
Son... 74
Holy Ghost... 75
6. But does not the Apostles' Creed ascribe this work in an especial sense to the Father?......... 75
7. Are Father, Son and Holy Ghost, then, associated causes of creation?...... 75
Origin of purpose.. 75
8. Whence came God's purpose to create?... 75
Immediate and Mediate.. 75
9. Does "create" always mean "to produce from nothing"?............................. 75
10. When creation is defined as "to produce from nothing," what is meant by "nothing"?......... 76
Relations to Eternity and Time... 76
11. Could the world have been created from eternity?..................................... 76
12. Was there time before the creation?... 76
How effected... 76
13. How was the world created?... 76
Result.. 77
14. What was the product of creation?... 77
Design... 77
15. What was the purpose of Creation?.. 77
16. What perfections?... 77
17. Show that the highest welfare of man was the subordinate end?............... 78
18. But does not the Epistle to the Hebrews (Chap. 2:7) declare that this refers to Christ?......... 78
19. Where else is the same doctrine taught?... 78
20. But does not the New Testament go still further?...................................... 78
21. Does this, however, depend upon the Order of Creation?.......................... 79
22. But is not the difficulty greater in regarding the lowest of creatures subservient to man's highest welfare?......... 79
23. For what various uses of man are creatures intended?.............................. 79
24. What proof of this can be found outside of Revelation?............................ 81
End.. 81
25. In what did Creation end?... 81
26. What is Optimism?.. 81
27. How must this theory be qualified?.. 81
28. What accompanied God's admiring contemplation of Creation?................ 82
29. Does this mean a cessation of God's activity?.. 82
Cautions concerning alleged conflict between Science and Revelation............. 82

30. What can be said of an alleged conflict between Science and Revelation on this article?....82
31. Explain this more fully....83
32. What other caution must be observed?....83
33. To what should this lead?....83
34. State some of the useless controversies that have been waged?....83
35. What method has been used to explain some apparent difficulties?....84
36. Does the occurrence of similar accounts in ancient Oriental literature, deciphered from inscriptions on tablets or otherwise preserved in any way affect the value and force of the Mosaic account?....84

5. Providence....85

Definition....85
1. What is Providence?....85
Relation to Creation....85
2. How is it related to Creation?....85
Against what Errorists to be maintained....86
3. Against what errors must it be constantly maintained?....86
Proofs....86
4. What proofs can be given from Scripture for the reality of Providence?. .86
5. Are there other arguments that might be cited?....86
Its Objects....87
6. With what objects is Providence occupied?....87
7. What error does this disprove?....87
Practical Application of its Universality and Particularity....87
8. What practical application of this universality and particularity of Providence is made by Holy Scripture?....87
9. Cite proofs....87
10. Does this mean that God has set limits to man's life and otherwise determined its details irrespective of any agency of man himself?....89
11. Is it, therefore, absolutely necessary that every one die at the particular time and by the particular disease which proves fatal?....89
12. But if Providence is occupied with all things, does this mean that it has something to do with the wicked deeds of men?....90
The Three Acts of Providence: 1. Foreknowledge 2. Predetermination 3. Execution by: (a) Preservation (b) Concurrence (c) Government (by Permission, Hindrance, Direction)....90
13. What acts are comprised in Providence? Three. Of these two are immanent, or occurring....90
14. But does not this imply succession in God?....90
15. How is the Foreknowledge to be distinguished from the Predetermination?....90
16. Can anything that God has foreknown occur otherwise than He has foreknown it?....90
17. Must not His foreknowledge, therefore, he the cause of the events foreknown?....91
18. How is the execution of what has been predetermined effected?....91
19. What is Preservation?....91
20. What is Concurrence?....92
21. What qualification must be attached to the explanation of this concurrence?....92

22. What is meant by Government? God's control of all acts of second causes. 92
23. In what different ways does this occur? 92
Special Providence 93
24. Is Providence occupied with all things in the same way? 93
Ordinary and Extraordinary Providence 93
25. What is meant by the distinction between Ordinary and, Extraordinary Providence? 93
"Law of Nature" 94
26. What other term designates Ordinary Providence? 94
27. What caution must be observed in the tracing of "laws"? 94
God not bound to His own laws 94
28. But if human experience were to haze all the details, so far as the past and the present are concerned, could God be bound in the future to the rules underlying such details? 94
The doctrine of Miracles: Miracle defined, Ground of its possibility, Ground of its necessity, Proof of its reality, Standpoints of its opponents, counterfeits, evidential value, distinctions, two classes of Miracles: (a) of Nature (b) of Grace
Practical Application: the correct estimate of Second Causes 95
29. What, then, is extraordinary Providence? 95
30. Upon what then does the possibility of a miracle depend? 95
31. Upon what does the necessity of a miracle depend? 95
32. What is the great proof of the reality of miracles? 96
33. From what standpoints is the possibility of miracles attacked? 96
34. Does the exposure of pretended miracles in any way affect the argument for the miracles recorded and prophesied in Scripture? 96
35. But have not miracles been wrought by Satan and his adherents? 97
36. Are miracles then evidences of the truth of the cause for which they are wrought? 97
37. What distinction was made by the Scholastics? 97
38. Into what two classes have miracles been divided? 97
39. What particular practical application is to be made of the doctrine of Providence? 98
6. Of Angels 99
Place and Estimate of the doctrine 99
1. Why is the doctrine of Angels treated at this place? 99
2. Why is so little prominence given it in the Confessions of the Church? ... 99
3. Is the doctrine, therefore, unimportant? 100
Definition 100
4. What are angels? 100
5. Why do we call them "pure" or "complete spirits"? 100
6. Are angels the only pure or complete spirits? 100
7. But are not angels sometimes described as having bodies? 100
Creation Attributes, Number 100
8. What do we know of their creation? 100
9. What are the attributes common to Good and Bad Angels? 101
10. How as to their number? 101
States 101
11. How many states of angels are there? 101
12. What differences in these three states with respect to the possibility of

sinning?.. 102
The Good Angels: Impeccability; Ground of Perseverance; Knowledge; Power; Works; Guardian Angels; Their service for the godly; Not to be invoked; Orders; Figurative Names.. 102
13. What ground is there for affirming the impeccability of the Good Angels? 102
14. But is such impeccability consistent with freedom of the will?..............102
15. What was the ground for the exaltation of the Good Angels to this higher stage?.. 102
16. What of the knowledge of angels?..103
17. What of their power?..103
18. What are the works of Good Angels?..103
19. Has each child of God a guardian angel?..103
20. Within what sphere do they serve the godly?..103
21. Where is their activity especially prominent?..104
22. Is this activity confined to individuals?..104
23. Are we to invoke angels for their aid?..104
24. But are there not several kinds of worship, one of which belongs to God alone, and another also to angels?.. 104
25. Are there no: instances where worship is actually accorded an angel?....105
26. What different orders of Good Angels are there?....................................105
27. What higher orders appear in the Old Testament?..................................105
28. By what figure is the brilliancy of their endowments indicated?............105
The Bad Angels: Problems concerning their Fall; Its order; Its effect on their endowments; Changed relation towards God; Their future; How now occupied; Demoniacal Possession.. 106
29. What problem meets us when we consider the fall of some angels?......106
30. Is it explicable?.. 106
31. Did the sin of the Bad Angels come from any external source?..............106
32. Did it come from any lack of divine grace which those who did not fall enjoyed?.. 106
33. What was the form of the sin whereby they fell?....................................106
34. What was the order of their fall?..106
35. What effect had their fall upon their angelic endowments?....................107
36. What disposition of God have they incurred?..107
37. What of their disposition towards God and His creatures other than themselves?.. 107
38. What of their future?..108
39. Do they know this?..108
40. Meanwhile how are they occupied?..108
41. What was demoniacal possession?..108
7. Man As Created.. 109
1. How many states of Man are there?..109
2. In which of these was man created?..109
3. What place does man hold in creation?..109
4. Of how many parts is man composed? Of two, viz., Body and Soul or Spirit.. 109
5. What is the Body?..109
6. But does not this imply some amount of impurity?..................................110
7. But cannot the soul exist without the body?..110

8. Is it not often taught, however, that the body is the prison of the soul, or its fetter, by which its heavenward flight is checked?....110
9. Do all theologians agree that mans nature has but two parts?....110
10. Upon what grounds is the distinction between "soul" and "spirit," as different parts of man's nature based?....111
11. By whom was such distinction taught?....111
12. Why is the theory unsatisfactory?....111
13. May not the two theories be reconciled?....111
14. What, then, is meant in Heb. 4:12 by "the dividing of soul and spirit"?..112
15. What then is the soul or the spirit?....112
16. May it not, then, be identical with the Spirit of God?....112
17. What mode of presence does the soul have in the body?....112
18. Do all men come from one ancestor?....113
19. Has this ever been questioned?....113
20. But were the old school of nineteenth century scientists the only opponents of the Unity of the Human Race?....113
21. Are there not other arguments for the Unity of the Human Race, beyond the Scriptural argument, which are just as strong as those now advanced by comparative zoologists?....113
22. What theories have been advanced to explain how, since Adam, souls enter the world?....114
23. What distinguished the state of Integrity from the state of Corruption which has succeeded?....115
24. As God is reported in Gen. 1:26 as saying, "Let us make man in our image, after our likeness," what difference is there between the "image" and the "likeness" of God?....116
25. But even though the application of the terms "image" and "likeness" to such distinction cannot be admitted, is not the distinction itself Scriptural? 116
26. What then is the image of God In the special sense?....117
27. How is this explained?....117
28. Knowledge was, therefore, one, of the constituents cf the image?....117
29. What other constituent is explicitly mentioned? Righteousness and holiness....117
30. What freedom was implied in this?....118
31. In what then does the original state of man differ from that which is at last attained by grace?....118
32. What external evidences of the presence of this image were there?....118
33. Was the image of God essential or accidental to mans nature?....119
34. Was it therefore a superadded gift?....119
35. Would you say, then, that the image was "supernatural"?....119
36. What estimate is to be placed upon the doctrine of mans first state?....120

8. Sin....121

Definition....121
1. What is sin?....121
2. What does this mean?....121
Place in Creation....121
3. What is the standard?....121
Two parts: Dichotomy vs. Trichotomy....121
4. Give (3) then, a somewhat fuller definition....121

Cause and Kinds.. 122
5. Who is the cause of sin?.. 122
6. How many kinds of sin are there?.. 122
Original Sin:: Confessional statement.. 122
7. What is Original Sin?... 122
Beginning... 122
8. Where then does Original Sin begin?.. 122
Origin and Application of term... 122
9. But is Original Sin a Scriptural term?.. 122
10. Does it always refer to the same thing?... 123
The First Sin and its significance.. 123
11. What was the significance of the prohibition in Paradise?........................ 123
12. What was involved in the disobedience?.. 123
13. What commandment was violated?... 123
14. Why is the sin known as "the sin of Adam"?... 123
Consequences of Fall.. 124
15. What were the consequences of the Fall?... 124
Punishments... 124
16. What was the Punishment?.. 124
17. How many forms of this punishment are there?.. 124
Unity of Race.. 125
18. How do these three unite?... 125
19. How was the warning, "In the day that thou eat est thou shall surely die," fulfilled?.. 125
20. You spoke of "the processes of temporal death." Explain this?................ 125
Extent of consequences... 125
21. But were this guilt and this punishment limited to our first parents?......125
Origin of Soul: Preexistence, Creationism and Traducianism.......................... 126
22. How can we be responsible for the sin of another?................................... 126
Image of God... 126
23. But have we not an express declaration, "The son shall not bear the iniquity of the father" (Ez. 18:20)?... 126
24. How then about Ex. 20:5, "Visiting the iniquity of the fathers upon the children upon the third and upon the fourth generation of them that hate me"?... 126
Immediate and Mediate Imputation... 126
25. What two terms have theologians used to explain the relation of Adam's sin to his descendants?.. 126
26. Which form of the doctrine is taught by Lutheran Church?...................... 127
Negative and Positive Elements.. 127
27. Into what elements does the Augsburg Confession resolve Original Sin? 127
Its Constituents... 127
28. How can the former be sin?.. 127
29. What is "concupiscence"?... 127
Universality of Original Sin... 128
30. How extensive is Original Sin?.. 128
31. Prove this universality... 128
External Evidences of Image... 129
32. But it is explicitly declared, "Where there is no law, there is no transgression' (Rom. 4:15). Does not Ms exempt infants who cannot know

the law?..129
Was it essential or accident...129
33. Beside infecting all men, what further statement can be made concerning the extent of Original Sin?...129
Effects on Man's Will...129
34. What is the consequence of this corruption of the highest powers?.......129
Error of Flacius...130
35. Is this corruption then so great as to justify the assertion that, since the fall, man's nature is sin?...130
36. Was such error ever taught?...130
37. Repeat the arguments by which his error was refuted...........................130
38. How did Flacius come to advocate such a manifestly extreme position?.131
Relative Power...131
39. Has Original Sin equal power in all?...131
Duration...131
40. How long does it remain?...131
41. What other opinion has been advanced?...131
42. How is this refuted?...131
Fruits...132
43. What are the fruits of Original Sin?...132
44. Where is this particularly taught?...132
Actual Sins: Definition,...132
45. When actual sins are spoken of, in what sense must "actual" be regarded? 132
46. Define Actual Sin?...133
Causes...133
47. What are the causes of Actual Sin?...133
Temptations...133
48. How does the devil tempt or stimulate mans inner depravity?...............133
49. How does the world stimulate man's inner depravity?...........................133
Inner Actions...134
50. What is meant by "an inner action"?...134
Effects...134
51. What effect has every actual sin?...134
Classification...134
52. How are sins classified?...134
53. What is a second mode of classification?...134
54. A third?...135
55. A fourth?...135
56. What of the distinction between Venial and Mortal sins?.........................135
Sin against the Holy Ghost...135
57. Is there any sin irremissible?...135
58. Why is it irremissible?...136
59. Is it referred to elsewhere in Holy Scripture?...136
60. What is here taught?...136
61. Are those who commit this sin ever troubled concerning it?..................137
9. The Grace Of God Towards Fallen Men.......................................139
The State in which Grace finds man...139
1. What is the natural fruit of sin?...139
2. But is not Eternal Death the result of a new act or volition of God?........139

3. All having sinned, we understand, therefore, that all would have eternally perished, unless God had interrupted the natural order of sin and death?..139
Not required by any consideration of Justice....140
4. God, however, had not interfered, and all had been left to the consequences of their sins, could man have complained?....140
5. If God had interfered to save one man, or a hundred, or a thousand, and had made no provision for the rest, would there have been any injustice?..140
6. But if He were to save the majority of the race, would the remainder be injured?....140
7. Was such a discrimination shown?....140
Motive....140
8. What moved God to interfere with the natural order of sin, and to provide for man's salvation?....140
9. What disposition of God is particularly manifest in this act of His will to save man?....141
Universality of Grace....141
10. What do you mean by the universality of Grace?....141
11. But may not the universality of Grace apply simply to the race as a whole? 141
12. What is the testimony of the Lutheran Church on this subject?....142
13. Explain somewhat more fully the text "God would have all men to be saved" (1 Tim. 2:4)....142
14. Recapitulate the arguments of our theologians in support of this position....142
Contents of God's Will....143
15. Is it right, then, to say that God willed that all should he saved provided they believe?....143
Why many are lost....143
16. If it be God's will that all should believe and be saved, how is it that many are lost?....143
Meaning of God's will....144
17. What is implied in saying that God wills man's salvation?....144
18. Why?....144
19. What then is God's saving will towards man?....144
Factors of the Plan of Redemption....144
20. What are included in this plan?....144
Where Predestination is to be treated....145
21. What is the proper place for the treatment of Predestination?....145
22. What has Luther said on this subject?....145
23. What has the Lutheran Church confessed concerning Predestination?. 145
10. The Preparation Of Redemption....147
When announced....147
1. When did God first reveal His purpose to redeem man?....147
Two-fold Preparation....147
2. What two-fold preparation at once began?....147
3. How was man prepared for salvation?....148
4. How was salvation prepared for man?....148
5. State the relation of the two parts of the human race to this two-fold preparation?....148
Heathenism and Judaism contrasted....148

6. Are we to understand, then, that the preparation through heathenism was entirely negative, and that through Judaism entirely positive?....................148
Salvability of those who lived before Christ....................149
7. Was there then no salvation for any who lived and died before Christ?...149
8. What ground is there for saying that the Old Testament saints had only a general promise concerning a salvation hereafter to be provided?..............149

11. The Person Of Christ....................151

Meaning of "Christ"....................151
1. In what relation is the Son of God considered at this place?....................151
2. What is His name with reference to this office?....................151
3. What is the meaning of "Christ" or "Messiah"?....................152
4. What other ideas are included in the name "Christ"?....................152
5. What, therefore, is a prominent subject of argument in the New Testament, and how is it proved?....................152
6. Is this, however, the exclusive line of argument by which the claims of Jesus are enforced?....................152
Topics included....................153
7. What topics are included in Christology, or that portion of Theology treating of the Mediatorial Office?....................153
Chalcedon Symbol....................153
8. How has the Church summarized its faith on this subject?....................153
The Divinity of Christ....................154
9. What is the first thing to be considered in treating of the Person of Christ? 154
The Humanity of Christ....................154
10. What is the second?....................154
Truth of the Humanity....................154
11. Why did the early Church lay such emphasis upon the word "true"?.....154
12. Upon what arguments did they base this error?....................155
13. How were they answered?....................155
Completeness of the Humanity....................155
14. What is implied in His true manhood?....................155
15. Who attacked this?....................155
Unity of Person....................156
16. What is meant by saying that there is but one Person?....................156
17. What proof have you of this unity?....................156
Relation of Person and Nature....................156
18. Is the person related in the same way to each nature?....................156
19. If we were to affirm that the human nature had a personality of its own, what would follow?....................157
Double Generation....................157
20. Since there are two natures, can we say there are two Sons, viz., a Son of God and a Son of Man?....................157
Incarnation....................157
21. By what term is the act of the Son of God in assuming human nature known?....................157
22. Was this peculiar to the Second Person of the Trinity?....................157
Consubstantiality of Humanity....................158
23. The conception of Jesus being so unlike that of others, was the human nature that resulted also unlike that of other men?....................158

Sinlessness of Humanity..158
24. How do you prove the sinlessness of Jesus?..158
25. But if Christ were impeccable, how do you explain His temptation? Is temptation possible, where a fall is impossible?...159
26. Was there any other particular in which the humanity of Christ was distinguished from that of others?...159
27. What was the purpose of the Incarnation?...159
28. Would the Son of God not have become incarnate if Adam had not sinned?..160
Personal Union...160
29. In what two senses is the expression, Personal Union, used?.................160
Attributes of Union...160
31. How has the Church guarded the statement of this doctrine?................160
32. How has the Athanasian Creed defined it?..161
Communion of Natures..161
33. What follows from this communion of the Person with both natures?..161
34. What analogy is there to this communion of natures?............................161
Personal Propositions...162
35. Because of this Personal Union and the Communion of Natures, is it proper to say, "God is man," and "man is God"?...162
36. What other result of the Communion of Natures is there?.....................162
Communicatio Idiomatum: Genus *Idiomaticum*..163
37. Classify or give the various kinds or genera of the *Communicatio Idiomatum*..163
38. Define more fully the first genus...163
39. What stress has been laid by the Lutheran Church on this point?..........163
40. Show how this thought of the first genus of the *Commnnicatio Idiomatum* underlies the entire theology of the Church and the religious experience of Christians...164
41. What controversy of the early Church centered about this genus of the Communication..164
42. Upon what Scriptural proofs does this rest?...164
Genus *Majestaticum*..165
43. Define the second genus...165
44. Does this mean that the properties of the divine become those of the human nature?...165
45. How has this doctrine been confessionally stated?.................................166
46. Upon what Scriptural grounds does it rest?..166
47. Do the Holy Scriptures particularize any divine attributes which are especially conspicuous in and through the assumed humanity?...................167
48. Are all the divine attributes imparted to the human nature of Christ?. 167
49. Were the imparted attributes always used?..167
Genus *Apotelesmaticum*...168
50. What is the third kind or genus of the *Communicatio Idiomatum*?.......168
51. How has this been confessionally expressed?..168
52. Are the natures then separate?...168
53. What Scriptural proofs are there for this Genus?...................................168
Estimate of doctrine..169
54. How in general is the doctrine of the *Communicatio Idiomatum* to be estimated?..169
55. Is this doctrine of the *Communicatio Idiomatum* offered as a sufficient

explanation of the mode in which the divine is related to the human in Christ? 169

12. The States of Christ 171

Basis of Distinction 171

1. Upon what is the distinction in the States of Christ based? 171

2. What is the origin of the terms? 171

Humiliation: Pertaining to which nature 172

3. Of what is the humiliation or emptying predicated, the divine or the human nature? 172

Not synonymous with Incarnation 172

4. But is not the humiliation synonymous with the incarnation? 172

5. Did they not coincide in their origin? 172

6. Why do we deny that the humiliation was of the divine nature? 172

Not a hiding 172

7. But might not the humiliation, or emptying, be a mere hiding (xputhis) of communicated power? 172

The *sedes doctrinae* 173

8. What passage of Scripture is the sedes doctrinae concerning the States of Christ? 173

Explanation, clause by clause of Phil. 2:5-11 173

9. Explain the first part of this passage 173

10. What then is the meaning of "form of God"? 173

11. What is the meaning of "emptied himself? 174

12. Explain "form of a servant." 174

13. "Being made in the likeness of man." 174

14. "And being found in fashion as a man." 174

15. "Humbled himself." 175

16. "Becoming obedient unto death, even the death of the cross." 175

Definition 175

17. How, then, is the State of Humiliation defined? 175

18. Why is this qualified by "according to His assumed human nature"? 175

19. Why is it limited by the word "full"? 175

What attributes conspicuously involved 176

20. What especially prominent divine attributes are not fully exercised? 176

Omnipotence 176

Omniscience 176

Omnipresence 176

His possession of all things 176

Duration 176

21. How long did the State of Humiliation last? 176

Stages, or grades, viz., conception and birth, circumcision, childhood, visible life among men, passion, death, burial 177

22. What various stages or grades are enumerated? 177

23. How is the humiliation manifest in the conception and birth? 177

24. What is involved in the controversy concerning the article of the Creed, "Conceived by the Holy Ghost, born of the Virgin Mary"? 177

25. How is the humiliation manifest in the circumcision? 177

26a. How in His childhood? 178

26b. How in His visible life among men? 178

27. How in His passion? 178

28. Were His sufferings only bodily?....178
29. What was the culmination of these sufferings?....179
30. How did this suffering differ from that endured by others, so as to add to its intensity?....179
31. What of His bodily sufferings?....179
32. What must be particularly observed in connection with these sufferings? 179
33. What was involved in the death of Christ?....180
34. What is the meaning of Christ's dying words, "It is finished"? (John 19:30.)....180
35. What place had the burial of Christ?....180
Exaltation: Definition....180
36. Define the State of Exaltation....180
37. Has it its stages or degrees?....180
When did it begin....181
38. When did the State of Exaltation begin?....181
39. What confessional difference is there on this point?....181
The *sedes doctrinae*....181
40. What determines this difference?....181
41. Why do we not regard the latter passage as referring to the descent?....181
42. What appears prominently in 1 Peter 3:18, 19? The fact that the descent occurred after the "quickening," or reunion of soul and body....181
Confessional statement....182
43. What is the confessional definition of this article? It is guarded with the greatest caution and earnestly warns against laying importance upon speculations as to details....182
Christ preaching to the spirits, not a preaching of the Gospel....182
44. Could the preaching to the spirits in prison have been a preaching of the Gospel?....182
45. But is there not a reference to a preaching of the Gospel to the dead in the immediate context to 1 Peter 3:18, 19, viz., in 1 Peter 4:6, "For to this end was the Gospel preached even to the dead"?....183
Why to antediluvians....183
46. Why is there a special allusion to the antediluvians as those to whom Christ preached?....183
Was there a preaching to Old Testament saints....183
47. Did this proclamation of Christ's victory extend also to the saints of the Old Testament, who died in faith of the promises fulfilled by His death and resurrection?....183
48. According to which nature did Christ make the descensus?....184
49. What, then, are the grades of the State of Exaltation?....184
Resurrection....184
50. What is the Resurrection?....184
52. When did Christ rise from the dead?....184
Characteristics of Christ's resurrected body....184
53. What were the characteristics of His resurrection body?....184
54. What is meant by "a glorified body"?....185
55. How do you explain the possession of these endowments as in Matt. 14:25, even before the resurrection?....185
56. Docs this same principle obtain in applying the terms "glorify" and "glorified"?....186

57. Why was the stone rolled away from the door of the sepulchre?............186
Place of doctrine of Resurrection in preaching of the Apostles........................186
58. Why has the resurrection of Christ such prominence in the preaching and teaching of the Apostles?..186
Its place in Apologetics..187
59. What place does the resurrection of Christ have in Apologetics?...........187
The Ascension...188
60. What is the Ascension of Christ?...188
61. May it not have been a mere disappearance as, in Gen. 17:22, God is said to have gone up from Abraham?...188
62. What is the heaven which Christ entered?...188
63. What was the end of the Ascension?...188
64. What exhortation and consolation are given by the Ascension?............189
The Session at the Right Hand of God...189
65. What is the Session at the Right Hand of God?......................................189
66. What is meant by referring various organs and parts of the human body to God?...189
67. Coming back to question 64, what, then, is meant by Christ's sitting at the Right Hand of God?...190
68. Is it synonymous with "reigning"?...191
69. How is this declared in our Confessions?..191

13. The Offices Of Christ, Christ As Prophet....................................193

Relation to what precedes..193
1. What relation has the contents of the two preceding chapters to what is now to be treated?...193
Three functions of Mediatorial Office..193
2. What three things belong to the Mediatorial Office?...............................193
3. What Scriptural ground is there for this distinction?..............................194
He is called Prophet..194
Priest..194
King..194
Meaning of "Prophet"...194
4. What is the meaning of "prophet"?...194
Prophetic Office defined and explained...195
5. What, then, is the Prophetic Office?...195
6. What does this imply?..195
Revelations before the Incarnation..196
7. But was there no revelation of God to men prior to the incarnation?.....196
8. Who is by preeminence the great prophet of the Old Testament, and how is the Old Testament prophetic office contrasted with that of Christ?........196
Christ's Preaching of the Law...197
9. What was the subject of Christ's teaching?..197
10. How did He teach the Law?..197
11. Where was this especially done?...197
12. In what words does Christ make most clear his relation to the Law?.....197
13. How was this further enforced?...197
14. Was the preaching of the Law by Christ merely a reaffirmation of its principles, or was it accompanied also by a reaffirmation of the authority of the Old Testament Scriptures?...198
15. But did not His leaching contain a criticism of the Law?........................198

16. Was the preaching of the Law the main object of this office?..................199
Christ's Preaching of the Gospel..................199
17. What is included in the Gospel?..................199
How Prophetic Office is continued; its two stages..................200
18. The Prophetic Office embraces, then, more than the function of teaching?..................200
19. What two stages of this office are there?..................200
Progress in Christ's teaching..................200
20. Was there progress in Christ's teaching?..................200
Miracles as seals of the Prophetic Office..................201
21. What were the seals of His Prophetic office? His miracles (John 3:2; Luke 24:19)..................201
22. What was their special function?..................201
23. What is meant by the promise (John 14:12) that greater miracles will be wrought by those who follow Him as preachers of the Gospel?..................201
14. Christ As Priest..................203
Defined..................203
1. What is the Priestly Office of Christ?..................203
According to which nature..................203
2. According to which nature is Christ our Priest?..................203
Old Testament types..................204
3. What Old Testament types were there of Christ's priesthood?..................204
The two functions of the Priesthood: 1. *Meaning of Satisfaction*;..................204
4. What are the two functions of this priesthood?..................204
5. Is the term "satisfaction' found in Holy Scripture?..................205
6. What other term is synonymous?..................206
7. Whom did Christ satisfy?..................206
8. In what relation did God receive satisfaction?..................206
9. But is not the rendering of satisfaction by one from whom it was not demanded a violation of law?..................206
10. Is it not an act of injustice to allow an innocent one to suffer for the guilt of another?..................206
11. What attributes of God are especially prominent in this provision for a satisfaction for sin?..................207
12. For whom was this satisfaction rendered?..................207
13. May not these passages be explained by the saying of Peter Lombard: Christ died sufficiently, but not efficiently for all"?..................208
14. For what sins was this satisfaction rendered?..................208
15. Has any other doctrine ever been widely taught?..................209
16. What is the consequence of the doctrine that the satisfaction of Christ is complete only with the respect to sins committed before baptism?..................209
17. What are the various punishments of sins, and How has Christ redeemed from each?..................209
The curse of the law (Gal. 3:13)..................209
The wrath of God..................210
Death..................210
Eternal condemnation..................210
18. By what means was the satisfaction of Christ rendered?..................210
19. How has this been confessionally stated?..................210
20. What two factors are comprised in this obedience?..................210

21. What is the Active Obedience?....211
22. What is the result of such complete conformity to the law?....211
23. Was this subjection to the Law rendered in order that He might Himself win the rewards?....211
24. What is the Passive Obedience?....212
25. Can the Active and Passive Obedience be separated?....212
26. Does righteousness, however, consist in deeds and sufferings?....212
27. How then did Christ's sacrifice differ from that of the Old Testament sacrifices?....213
28. When was the satisfaction rendered?....213
29. Does the resurrection belong to His satisfaction?....213
2. *The Intercession*; its stages and objects; its modes; its ground; its reality; its duration....213
30. What is the second function of the Priesthood of Christ?....213
31. How is this Intercession to be distinguished as to its stages and its objects?....213
32. But does He pray for the two classes of objects in the same way?....214
33. What is the ground of His intercession?....215
34. What is the mode?....215
35. How long does the Intercession continue?....215
36. But How can this Intercession profit those who are beyond the possibility of a fall, and partake of completed salvation?....215
37. But is not this explanation contrary to John 16:26, 27?....216
Moral Theories of Atonement criticized....216
38. What explanation can be given of the various Moral Theories of the Atonement, i.e., those which find the efficacy of Christ's work solely in the appeal which they make to us?....216
39. But are such theories entirely without foundation?....216
Refutation of the use of chief proof texts appealed to....217
40. But why, then, is reconciliation said to be, as in 2 Cor. 5:18-20, a reconciliation of men to God instead of God to men?....217

15. Christ As King....219

Definition....219
1. In what relation is the Kingship of Christ considered here?....219
2. Define it?....219
Stages....219
3. What stages belong to this Kingship?....219
Spheres....220
4. Within what spheres is this Kingship exercised?....220
Kingdom of Power....220
5. What is the Kingdom of Power?....220
6. How was this Kingship occasionally asserted even during His State of Humiliation?....221
7. Where does it culminate?....221
8. If the Kingdom of Power is Christ's dominion over all things, how can there be also a Kingdom of Grace and a Kingdom of Glory?....221
Kingdom of Grace....221
9. What then is the Kingdom of Grace?....221
10. Who are the subjects?....222
11. What is its peculiar sphere?....222

12. What are its characteristics?....222
13. How is it ruled?....222
14. To what privilege are its subjects admitted? They share in the rule....223
Kingdom of Glory....223
15. What is the Kingdom of Glory?....223
16. What different stages of this kingdom are there?....223
17. Is it eternal?....223
18. But is not this inconsistent with 1 Cor. 15:24-28?....223
16. The Mission Of The Holy Ghost....225
Place of doctrine....225
1. What is the second item in the Plan of Redemption?....225
2. Repeat a few passages of Scripture in which this is taught....225
Different Modes and Degrees of Presence....226
3. How are these passages to be explained?....226
4. But was He not present with the godly of the Old Testament, and was He not active also daring the ministry of Jesus?....226
Foundation of Mission....226
5. Upon what did this mission depend?....226
Relation to Pentecostal Miracle....227
6. Does not this refer, however, to the miracle of Pentecost?....227
Meaning of "Not yet given" (John 7:39)....227
7. How was this stated in the Reformation period?....227
Confessional statement....228
8. What is the Confessional declaration on this subject?....228
17. Faith in Christ....229
Instrument by which Christ's work is applied....229
1. How are the fruits of the Mediatorial Office applied by the Holy Ghost? 229
Confessional statement....229
2. How has the doctrine of Holy Scripture on this subject been summarized in the Augsburg Confession?....229
Distinctions between: (a) Subjective and Objective (b) Human and Divine (c) Direct and Discursive (d) As an act and as a habit (e) Explicit and Implicit (f) Crude and Energized....230
3. What distinctions have been made by theologians with respect to faith? 230
4. How do they distinguish between Subjective and Objective Faith?....230
5. What is Human Faith?....230
6. What is Divine Faith?....231
7. What is the distinction between Direct and Discursive Faith?....232
8. What is the distinction between faith as a habit and faith as an act?....232
9. What is the distinction between Explicit and Implicit Faith?....232
10. What is the distinction between "Crude Faith" and "Faith energized by Love"?....233
Distinction of prepositions "propter" and "per"....233
11. When you say that the fruits of the Mediatorial Office are applied through faith, what do you mean?....233
In what does the value of faith lie....233
12. In what then does the value of faith lie?....233
Various objects of faith enumerated, as distinguished from the proper object

here required.. 234
13. What then is the proper object of the faith through which the Holy Ghost brings salvation?.. 234
14. State some of these objects.. 234
15. Now we are ready to learn the proper object which faith apprehends, so as to obtain the fruits of Christ's Mediatorial Office?.......................................235
16. Cite a few of the many statements of our Confessions on this subject....235
17. What Scriptural proofs of this can be given?..236
18. Is it not an arbitrary matter, however, to restrict the faith, which receives the forgiveness of sins to the one article concerning the merits of Christ gratuitously given, and to ignore other articles of faith?...............................236
General and special faith contrasted...237
19. Are the acts of Justifying Faith, with respect to its object, of one kind?. 237
The elements of faith: Knowledge, Assent, Confidence...................................237
20. Analyze faith into its elements..237
21. What of the first?...237
22. What of the second?...238
23. What of the third?..238
24. What does this confidence imply?...238
Characteristics of Confidence — refers to a present good, a personal good, and that good as a means to an end..239
25. What are some of the characteristics of confidence with respect to its object?...239
How distinguished from Hope..240
26. How is confidence distinguished from Hope?...240
Scriptural argument for Confidence as belonging to Faith.............................240
27. Scriptural proofs that faith includes confidence?.......................................240
The Augustinian formula: *Credere Deum, Deo, in Deum*...............................241
28. How have the three elements of faith been sometimes distinguished?. .241
Degrees of faith, and relation to efficacy..242
29. Are there degrees of faith?...242
2 Thess. t:3. "Your faith groweth exceedingly."..242
30. Is the efficacy of faith in proportion to its degree?.....................................242
Double office of faith..242
31. Has faith, then, more than one office?...242
Relation to the New Life...243
32. How does the Augsburg Confession treat of the operative office or energy of faith?..243
33. What classical passage from Luther's Introduction to the Epistle to the Romans should be kept in memory?..243
34. What is the meaning of Gal 5:6, "In Christ Jesus, neither circumcision availeth anything, nor uncircumcision but faith working through love"?. .243
35. Where do we learn concerning the means employed by the Holy Ghost to work faith?.. 244
Faith may be lost; and if so, may be again recovered.....................................244
36. Can faith be lost?...244
37. Can faith, if lost, be restored?..245
Assurance of Faith... 245
38. Can one know whether he have faith?...245
39. Faith, then, must be more than mere probability?.....................................246
40. Upon what does this certainty depend?..246

Assurance dependent upon clearness of apprehension of the Gospel.............246
41. In what respect does the Gospel bring a certainty that cannot be found in the Law?...246
42. How do the Sacraments afford an argument for the certainty of faith? 247
Scriptural examples...247
43. What examples of certainty of faith are recorded in Holy Scripture?....247
The Witness of the Spirit...247
44. All this shows that one can and should have certainty of faith, but how is this obtained?...247
45. Explain this more fully...247
46. By what term is this witness of the Spirit sometimes designated?.........248
Faith and self-examination..248
47. Can the presence of faith be decided by self-examination?....................248
48. But what if such examination result in the revelation only of one's spiritual poverty, and faith itself be hidden?..249
49. Against what must we guard in every such self-examination, whether daily or before partaking of the Lord's Supper?...249
50. What was Luther's advice to Brenz when troubled by doubts concerning the assurance of faith?...249
Is salvation ever possible without faith...250
51. Is there salvation without faith?..250
18. Justification...251
Various meanings..251
1. In what senses is the word "justify" used in Holy Scripture?...................251
Proofs of Forensic sense at this place..252
2. In what sense is it used in the treatment of the justification of man, the sinner, before God?...252
Definition..253
3. Justification being used, therefore, in a forensic sense, how is it defined?.253
4. What Scriptural proofs are there for this?..253
What sins not imputed...254
5. Of what sins is there a non-imputation?...254
What righteousness of Christ imputed...254
6. What righteousness of Christ is imputed?..254
Meaning of "impute"...255
7. What is the meaning of the word "impute" or "reckon"?.........................255
8. Where is such distinction drawn?..255
9. Apply this to the article of Justification...255
Ground of imputation...256
10. But is there need of any foundation? Could not God have justified man without any ground whatever?...256
In what sense is faith imputed (Rom 4:5)...256
11. What is meant by the expression, "Faith is imputed" (Rom. 4:5)?..........256
12. What is meant by the expression, "Faith justifies"?.................................256
Denial of man's agency...257
13. Has man then no part in his own justification?.......................................257
Justification not an internal work...257
14. Is it a work of God within man?..257
15. Why cannot love justify or contribute towards justification?..................257
Faith does not justify as a root...257

16. May we not say that faith justifies because it is the root of good works? 257
Importance of the Exclusive Particles....258
17. In what formulas has this doctrine been expressed?....258
18. What is their force?....258
19. What then is the meaning of the formula:....258
20. What four reasons did Melanchthon urge for keeping these "exclusives" always in view?....259
1. The glory of Christ....259
2. The comfort of distressed consciences....259
3. The offering of true prayer....259
4. The difference between the Law and the Gospel....259
James 2:24....259
21. How is James 2:21-24 to be understood?....259
No degrees of Justification....260
22. Is Justification gradual?....260
23. May not some sins be forgiven, while others remain unforgiven?....260
24. But is not the righteousness of some believers much greater than that of others? For instance, is not that of Mary the mother of Jesus, the Apostle John, the Apostle Paul, etc., greater than that of the penitent thief?....261
19. The Gospel Call....263
The order of Salvation....263
1. What is meant by the Order of Salvation?....263
2. Where do we find a popular summary of this Order?....263
3. What are the acts belonging to this Order?....263
4. What difficulty is experienced in their treatment?....263
Definition....264
5. What is the Call?....264
Two elements....264
6. What two things concur in the call?....264
Is there a double word....264
7. Is it true, then, that there is a double Word of God, and that besides the outward Word which is offered to all, there is an inner Word which is offered to only a few?....264
Explanation of difference in results....265
8. Is there, therefore, an inner presence of the Holy Spirit with the Word wherever preached?....265
9. How has this been confessionally stated?....265
Rom 8:28....265
10. But does not Rom. 8:28, "Whom he predestinated them he also called," restrict the call to a class, viz., to those predestinated from all eternity, and ultimately "glorified"?....265
Attributes of Call....266
11. What attributes belong, therefore, to the call?....266
Subjects, Objects....266
12. To whom is the call addressed?....266
13. To what does it urge?....266
Relation of Law and Gospel to Call....267
14. By what means does the call come?....267
Inequalities....267
15. But does the Gospel come to all in the same form or degree?....267

16. What results from the consideration of this inequality?........................268
17. Does this mean that we are not to be concerned about the fact that there are many millions who have not heard the call?..268
Preparatory invitations..269
18. Is there not a preparatory work of the Holy Spirit even prior to and without the Gospel, which is sometimes termed a call or calling?..............269
Call under the Old Testament...270
19. Was the Gospel call addressed those who lived under the Old Testament? 270
20. Was there not a difference between the scope of the call in the Old Testament and the New Testament?..270
20. Illumination..271
Condition of Man to whom the Call comes..271
1. In what state does the Gospel call find man?...271
2. How is this taught in our Confessions?..271
3. Is this statement Scriptural?..272
4. What illustration of this can be cited?...272
5. Is man's natural condition simply one of ignorance?..............................273
6. Scriptural proofs?...273
7. What, therefore is necessary, in order that the Gospel call may reach the end for which it has been intended?...273
Definition..274
8. What is this activity?..274
Confessional statements..274
9. How is this stated in our Confessions?...274
Scripture Proofs..274
10. Give a few more Scripture texts referring to Illumination.....................274
Means..275
11. What are the Means of Illumination?..275
The Word of God...275
Both Law,...275
And Gospel,...275
Is there ever Immediate Illumination...275
12. Is there no immediate Illumination?..275
13. But is not Illumination to be sought in the abstraction of the mind from earthly things, and in awaiting silently a supernatural divine light?............276
Forms..276
14. Is the illuminating power of the Word restricted to the acts of hearing, reading and meditating?..276
Legal and evangelical..277
15. What two kinds of illumination are there?..277
16. What are the gifts communicated by this illumination, as referred to in our Catechism, "enlightened me with his gifts"?...277
17. Is Illumination limited to the intellect?..277
Gradual..278
18. Illumination, then, is gradual?..278
19. But was not the illumination of Paul on the way to Damascus sudden and complete?..278
20. What illustrations have been given?...278
21. What caution must be employed in the study of all such examples?......279

Different senses of the Term....279
22. Is the term Illumination always restricted to the particular stage of grace just explained?....279

21. Regeneration....281

Definition....281
1. What is Regeneration?....281
2. How is it related to Illumination?....281
3. What brief definition, then, can be given?....281
Confessional statement....282
4. How is this taught in our Confessions?....282
Scripture Proofs of Man's Inability....282
5. But is it not an extreme statement to maintain, that, even after man has been brought to see his sins, and to learn of the offered grace, he cannot, of his own powers, believe?....282
Illustrations given in the Confessions....283
6. What figures with respect to men's inability are employed by our Confessions?....283
The question of Responsibility....284
7. But does not this practically deny man's responsibility?....284
In what respect is man's will free....284
8. From this I understand that man's will has a certain freedom?....284
9. But does the resistance of the will to the grace of God ever entirely cease?....284
How is Regeneration wrought....285
10. How is Regeneration wrought?....285
Law, Gospel and Sacraments, in their relation to Regeneration....285
11. Is Regeneration wrought by all parts of God's Word?....285
12. How do the Sacraments regenerate?....286
Substantial or Accidental; Instantaneous or Gradual....286
13. Is Regeneration a "substantial ' or an"accidental" change, as was discussed in the Flacian controversy?....286
14. Is Regeneration instantaneous or gradual?....286
Subjects — Infant Faith....287
15. Who are subjects of Regeneration?....287
16. What cautions, therefore, are to be observed?....287
17. What proofs are there of the possibility of infant faith and regeneration?....288
18. How has the doctrine of infant faith or regeneration been guarded?.....289
18. Can Regeneration be lost?....290
19. Is not Regeneration as a theological term sometimes used in a wider sense than that which has thus far been considered?....290
Distinctions and Synonyms....291
20. How would you distinguish it from Justification and Sanctification?...291
21. What synonyms has it? The nearest equivalents are:....291
22. Are there any other terms that cover to a considerable extent the same ground?....291
23. What is the meaning of Repentance?....292
Repentance....292
24. What important result followed a revision of the definition?....292
25. How did this discovery influence Luther?....292

26. In what, then, does Repentance coincide with Regeneration?............293
27. What are the two parts of Repentance?............293
28. What inferences may be derived from this?............293
1. No true repentance without faith............293
2. Wherever there is faith, there is repentance............293
3. Contrition and faith act reciprocally upon each other............293
29. What was the first of Luther's 95 Theses?............293
30. How is this expressed in our Catechism?............294
31. In what, however does Repentance differ from Regeneration?............294
Conversion: Distinguished from Regeneration; can man cooperate; is the will passive; no encouragement of security. Errors of Pelagianism, Semi-Pelagianism, Synergism, Enthusiasm............294
32. How does Conversion differ from Repentance?............294
33. How does Conversion differ from Regeneration?............294
34. Can man in any way cooperate in his Conversion?............295
35. Is it right to say that in Conversion the will is purely passive?............295
36. Does this encourage men to be idle and secure with respect to their Conversion?............296
37. But suppose some one would object:............296
38. Against what errors has the Lutheran Church particularly guarded in the treatment of this article?............297

22. The Mystical Union............299

Defined............299
1. Besides the righteousness of Christ and the gifts which it has purchased what else does faith receive?............299
What it means............300
2. Does this mean no more than that the influence or the power or the gifts of Christ live in the believer, as a parent lives in a child, or a great teacher in his followers?............300
Confessional treatment............300
3. Is this doctrine treated explicitly in the Church's Confessions?............300
Luther's explanation............300
4. How does Luther treat it?............300
Treatment by Apostles............301
5. Who gives the most prominence to this doctrine?............301
Practical Application............301
6. What practical application has been made of this doctrine?............301
Caution............302
7. Is the term "Mystical Union' and its separate treatment in Lutheran Dogmatics entirely satisfactory?............302

23. Renovation Or Sanctification............303

Definition............303
1. What is Renovation or Renewal in its widest sense?............303
2. How is the term applied to spiritual things?............303
3. What does it mean in the stricter sense?............303
Distinctions............304
4. How is Renovation distinguished from Regeneration and Justification?............304
Two sides............304

5. What are the two sides of Renewal?....304
Condition of "the Old Man"....305
6. What is the condition of the old man?....305
7. Give a few Confessional statements?....305
As related to various parts of our nature....306
8. How does Renewal affect the various parts of our nature?....306
Its Active Principle....306
9. What is the active principle of Renovation?....306
The Divine Side....306
10. Under Question 4 it was stated that Renovation is a work of God and man cooperating. State this more fully....306
The Means: Word and Sacraments according, each, to its peculiar sphere; Modes in which the Means are applied....307
11. Through what means is Renewal or Sanctification wrought?....307
12. How are these means applied?....307
13. What follows the appropriation of the Word?....307
The Human Side....308
14. Has man no part to perform in Renovation?....308
Prayer and Renovation....308
15. In what act of man does this appear?....308
16. What, therefore, are the elements of Prayer?....309
17. Is prayer always an act?....309
Gradual....310
18. Is Renewal or Sanctification instantaneous?....310
Perfection and Perfectionism....310
19. Does it ever reach perfection in this life?....310
20. To what passages of Scripture do the advocates of Perfectionism appeal, and how are they answered?....310
21. Is there any disparagement by this of perfection itself?....311
22. How do the advocates of Perfectionism sometimes define their position?....311
Office of Good Works....312
23. What is the Relation of Good Works to Renovation?....312
24. What do you mean by calling them "instrumentalities"?....312
How Good Works are produced....312
25. How, then, does the Holy Spirit renew men?....312
26. What warning does Scripture give?....313
27. How are Good Works fruits of Renovation?....313
Good Works defined, and the definition explained clause by clause:....313
28. Give a definition of Good Works....313
29. Explain the term "free acts."....314
30. How has the principle here stated been paradoxically expressed?....314
31. But are there no Good Works before justification?....315
32. In saying that "Good Works are wrought according to the standard of the divine Law," what errors are rejected?....316
33. What favorite illustration was used by the Reformers?....317
34. Why does the definition add, "with the light afforded by true faith in Christ"?....317
35. Why does it conclude with the words "to the glory of God and the edification of men"?....317
In what sense any works are good....318

36. But can any works meet this standard?....318
37. How then can they be called "Good Works"?....318
38. How is this confessionally expressed?....318
The question of Rewards....319
39. Are Good Works rewards?....319
40. How has this been explained?....319
41. Do the Lutheran Confessions teach such doctrine?....319
42. But does not the Apology go too far in saying that they "merit" these rewards?....320
43. Give some Scripture proofs....320
44. But is there not a difference of rewards?....320
24. The Word As The Means Of Grace....321
Reference to previous statements....321
1. In the treatment of the various acts of the Applying Grace of the Holy Spirit, what has been a most prominent feature of them all?....321
Is the doctrine of Means a limitation of God's sovereignty....321
2. Is it not a limitation of God's sovereignty and power to affirm that these acts are accomplished only through means?....321
Are Means ever dispensed with....322
3. But in extraordinary cases, does He not dispense with means?....322
Relative position of the Word and the Sacraments....322
4. Are not these means variously designated?....322
5. How are these statements harmonized?....322
What is the Word....323
6. But what is the Word?....323
The Holy Scriptures as the Record....323
7. Where is it to be found?....323
8. In what senses are the Holy Scriptures inspired?....324
The Supreme Test of Holy Scripture....328
9. What, then, is the supreme test of the claims of Scripture, or of any portion or book of Scripture?....328
10. But how is this religious test effective?....329
11. Illustrate this....330
12. But is it possible for this test to be applied by any individual or by any age of the Church to all the details or even all the books of Holy Scripture?....331
Proper Place of Literary-historical criticism....332
13. Is no weight whatever, therefore, to be attached to literary-historical criticism?....332
14. Distinguish further between the religions use of literary-historical criticism and literary-historical criticism separated from religious criticism.333
15. Is there such criticism in the New Testament Scriptures themselves?....334
16. What principle should always be remembered in such studies?....334
Estimate of the human factor....334
17. But are not some of the most conservative defenders of traditional theories of inspiration also open to criticism?....334
18. Would you say then that some things in Scripture are unimportant, and may be readily surrendered?....335
Organic relation of parts....335
19. Upon what principle of interpretation has the Lutheran Church, therefore, always insisted?....335

20. In view of all that has been thus far presented in this chapter, would you say "The Bible is the Word of God," or "The Bible contains the Word of God"? 336
21. Why was such peculiar position ascribed to one book of the Bible, and one author? 337
No distinction between Inner and Outward Word 338
22. Is a distinction between an Inner and an Outward Word to be admitted? 338
23. What proofs for this can be given? 339
Scripture more than a "directory" 340
24. Is it the office of the Word simply to afford directions that are to be followed in order to obtain salvation? 340
Spirit and Word inseparable 340
25. What testimony is given to the presence of the Holy Spirit in and with the Word? 340
Efficacy of Word 341
26. Is the Word, then, always efficacious? 341
Explanation of Prayer for the Spirit as interpreter 341
27. But if the Holy Spirit is always in and with the Word, why do we constantly pray for the coming and presence of the Spirit? 341
The Church as the instrumentality for communicating the Word 342
28. How does the Word reach men? 342
29. But how is it apprehended? 342
The Preached Word 342
30. What is the special function of the preached and of the read Word? 342
The Read Word 344
31. How does the read Word differ? 344
32. How is this "daily exercise of reading" to be observed so as to derive from it the benefits for which the Scriptures have been given? 344
Preaching as a Means of Grace 345
33. Is the success of preaching as a means of grace conditioned by the observance of similar principles by the preacher? 345
34. What keeps preaching close to this center? 346
35. What especial provision has been an important aid in preserving the true proportion in preaching the Word? 347
36. How may this system be abused? 347
Antithesis of the Roman Catholic Church 348
37. How does the teaching of the Roman Catholic Church concerning the Word as a Means of Grace differ from that of the Lutheran Church? 348
Difference of the Reformed view 348
38. How does the teaching of the Reformed Church or Churches differ from the Lutheran in this respect? 348
25. The Law And The Gospel 351
Division of the Word 351
1. How is the Word of God divided? 351
Distinction explained 351
2. Does this distinction coincide with that between the Old and the New Testaments? 351
3. Where is this distinction briefly stated? 351
a. Between the Law, or letter 352

b. Between the Law as leading to despair....352
c. Between the Law, as except through Christ nothing but a letter, and the Gospel....352
d. Between the Law as containing much that is typical and unintelligible until its true interpretation is found in the Gospel, and the Gospel as the goal of all that towards which the Law is directed..352
4. What importance is attached to the distinction between Law and Gospel? 352
5. What, then, is the main point of difference?....353
Different senses of both terms....353
6. Are the words "Law" and "Gospel" used in Holy Scripture in but one sense?....353
Divisions of the Law....354
7. How has the Law been divided?....354
The Moral Law: Defined, distinguished, Office of the Natural Law, the Revealed Moral Law, where found, where repeated, test as to whether a precept belong to Moral Law, an organic whole, its sphere, nature of the obedience it demands, result of its preaching, because it cannot justify is it useless, the three uses of the Law, how should it be preached....354
8. What is the Moral Law?....354
9. How has the Moral Law been distinguished?....354
10. What is the office of the Natural Law?....355
11. What shows its feebleness in man's fallen estate?....355
12. What is the Revealed Moral Law?....355
13. Where is it summarized?....355
14. Where are the Ten Commandments repeated?....356
15. Where is their meaning fully explained and applied?....356
16. How can the perpetual obligation of particular precepts be determined, and their place in the Moral Law established?....356
17. Can we say that everything in the Ten Commandments as reported in Ex. 20 belongs to the Moral Law?....356
18. Is the Moral Law a code of coordinate and parallel precepts?....356
19. What is its sphere?....357
20. What obedience does the Moral Law demand? That which is the most perfect and complete:....357
21. What is the result?....357
23. What, then, is the use of the Law? It has a three-fold use:....358
24. Do not the sufferings of Christ belong to the elenchtical use of the law? 359
25. What, then, is the didactic or third use?....359
26. But why is this necessary, when the regenerate have the Holy Spirit who constantly impels them to do God's will?....360
27. What is necessary for fulfilling the duty of a true Christian pastor in preaching the Law?....360
Relation of Forensic and Ceremonial Laws to the Moral....360
28. What were the Forensic and the Ceremonial Law?....360
29. How were they related to the Moral Law?....360
30. How did the Forensic and Ceremonial Laws differ from the Moral?.....361
31. How do you prove the abrogation of the Forensic Law?....361
The Ceremonial Law: its contents, object, abrogation....361
32. What were the contents of the Ceremonial Law?....361

33. What was the chief object of the Ceremonial Law?....362
34. How is the abrogation of the Ceremonial Law proved?....362
Definition of Gospel....363
35. How is "Gospel" to be defined when contrasted with "Law"?....363
36. How does the Gospel regard Christ?....363
37. Can any doctrine concerning the goodness or the Fatherhood of God, which is not based upon a clear confession of the divinity and priestly work of Christ be termed "Gospel"?....363
The Gospel not a New Law....364
38. May it not be regarded a new law, offering salvation upon easier terms than were given by the former law?....364
In what Law and Gospel differ and in what they coincide....364
39. How do they differ?....364
40. In what do they coincide?....364

26. The Sacraments....367

Two modes of applying the Gospel....367
1. In what two ways is the Gospel applied as a Means of Grace?....367
2. What distinguishes the Sacraments from other means of individualizing the general word, of the Gospel?....367
Definition of Sacrament....367
3. Define a Sacrament?....367
4. Why do you call it an action?....368
Origin and history of term....368
5. Is the term "Sacrament" biblical?....368
6. Whence was it derived?....368
7. How was it employed by the Reformers?....368
8. How could Absolution be regarded as a Sacrament?....368
Peculiar office of a Sacrament....369
9. What, therefore, is the peculiar office of a Sacrament?....369
10. How do our Confessions describe them?....369
11. How is this thought amplified by our theologians?....369
Whose act is the Sacrament....370
12. Whose action is that of the Sacraments?....370
How a Sacrament differs from a sacrifice....371
13. How does a Sacrament differ from a sacrifice?....371
The three essentials of a Sacrament....371
14. What are the three essentials of a Sacrament?....371
Importance of the Sacramental "word"....372
15. Is this last point so explained in the Confessions?....372
16. How may this be summed up?....372
Confirmation and Ordination not Sacraments....372
17. Why is Confirmation not reckoned among the Sacraments?....372
18. But has not Ordination sacramental validity?....373
Not everything that God has instituted and commanded, a Sacrament....373
19. Does the rank of Sacraments belong to all objects having God's command?....373
When does the Sacrament exist....373
20. When does the Sacrament actually exist?....373
Where does the right to administer the Sacraments belong....374
21. To whom does the right to administer the Sacraments belong?....374

22. Are there no exceptions? 374
Upon what does their efficacy depend 375
23. Upon what does the efficacy of the Sacraments depend? 375
24. How do our Confessions stale this last point? 375
25. Is, therefore, their efficacy depended upon the faith of the recipient? 376
26. We repeat the question: Upon what does the efficacy depend? 376
In what sense are they necessary 376
27. Are the Sacraments necessary for salvation? 376
What is their chief purpose 377
28. What is the chief purpose of the Sacraments? 377
29. In saying that they 'are signs and testimonies of the will of God toward us' is it meant that these signs are the elements of the Sacraments? 377
30. Is their influence, then, merely of a didactic character? 377
What are their secondary ends 378
31. Such being the primary, what are the secondary ends of the sacraments? 378
The question as to Old Testament Sacraments 378
32. Were there Sacraments under the Old Testament? 378
The differences between Baptism and the Lord's Supper 379
33. Were there not other Old Testament acts that had a sacramental character? 379
34. But in what do the so-called Sacraments of the Old Testament differ from those of the New Testament? 379
35. How do the two Sacraments of the New Testament differ? 379
27. Of Holy Baptism 381
Definition 381
1. Define Baptism 381
2. How does Baptism meet the three requirements of a Sacrament above given (Chapter 26, 14)? 381
Institution 381
3. When was it instituted? 381
4. Where is the institution recorded? 382
5. But John certainly baptized before this? 382
Meaning of formula 383
6. What is Baptism according to the words of institution? 383
7. How is this established? 383
Who baptizes 383
8. Who is it that baptizes? 383
The Element 384
9. What is the earthly element? 384
10. Is there no prescription as to the quality? 384
11. Is there no prescription as to the quantity? 384
12. Is Immersion a valid method of baptism? 384
13. But does this prove that it was the only mode? 385
14. How early do we find the justification of Sprinkling or Pouring, as a mode of Baptism? 385
The Heavenly Gift 385
15. What is the heavenly gift? 385
The Minister 386
16. By whom is Baptism administered? 386

17. Does the validity of Baptism depend upon the regularity of the administrator's call?......386
18. Why did not our Lord administer Baptism?......386
19. How do we explain Paul's declaration that he was sent to preach and not to baptize (1 Cor.1:17)?......387
20. Can no one baptize except a regularly called minister?......387
21. How is the necessity of such departure from the rule safeguarded?......387
Subjects......388
22. Who are to be baptized?......388
23. The only persons concerning whose right to Baptism there seems to be any difference of opinion, are little children. Give, therefore, a somewhat fuller argument on this subject......388
24. Is this attested also by the practice of the Church in the earliest period after the Apostles?......389
25. But are not the children of Christian parents already in covenant relations to God, in virtue of their birth?......390
Effect......390
26. What is the effect of Baptism?......390
27. Are all the baptized saved?......390
Relation to Faith......391
28. Has Baptism the same relation to faith in all its subjects?......391
29. But how are the difficulties concerning the possibility of infant regeneration and infant faith met?......391
30. But cannot this doctrine be greatly abased?......392
Perpetuity......393
31. Is the importation of the efficacy of Baptism confined to the moment of its administration?......393
32. But what comfort does this afford, if we have broken its conditions?....393
Repetition......394
33. Can Baptism be repeated?......394
Relation of Confirmation......395
34. Is there not a renewal of the covenant in Confirmation?......395
Necessity......395
35. In what sense is Baptism necessary?......395
36. What does the Augsburg Confession mean when it condemns the Anabaptists for teaching that children are saved without baptism?......395
37. Has God anywhere promised His saving grace except in the observance of the provisions of the Order of Salvation which He has revealed to us?......395
38. What has been the prevalent opinion of Lutheran theologians on this point?......396
39. Is the same affirmed of the children of unbelieving parents?......396
Accidentals......396
40. In its administration, what are the essentials of Baptism?......396
28. Of The Holy Supper......399
Definition and *sedes doctrinae*......399
1. What is the Lord's Supper?......399
2. From what passages of Scripture is the doctrine of the Lord's Supper to be learned?......399
Elements......400
3. What are the elements?......400

Heavenly Gift..400
4. What is the heavenly gift?..400
Literal interpretation of Words...400
5. But are these words to be interpreted literally?...400
6. What warning does Scripture give concerning the effort to explain away what God has declared?...401
7. What example is commended for the opposite of this?................................401
8. What would follow from our rejection of a literal interpretation because of our inability to understand how this could be possible?...................................402
9. Are there no other arguments for the literal meaning of these words?...402
10. What is the argument from the testamentary character of the Holy Supper?..402
11. Is there any variation in which the words are reported?.............................403
12. What evidence is there corroborative of the literal interpretation?........404
Opposing arguments answered...404
13. What are the chief arguments on the other side?.......................................404
14. How many modes of the presence of the body of Christ are there?.......405
15. What is the second chief argument?..405
Sacramental Presence...406
16. How is the presence of the Body and Blood of Christ in the Lord's Supper defined?..406
Sacramental Union...406
17. You have shown thus far that in this Sacrament the heavenly gift is the Body and Blood of Christ. State now the relation which they have to the bread and wine..406
18. This doctrine seems to me to remove from the Lord's Supper one of the essentials of a Sacrament. (See Chapter 26, 14.)...407
19. What kindred doctrine is rejected?...407
20. How then is the doctrine of the Sacramental Union stated?.................408
21. Is the expression that the body and blood of Christ are "in, with and under" the bread and wine, an adequate statement of the doctrine?..........408
22. What is meant by the expression, "This cup is the new covenant in my blood"?..408
Sacramental Eating...409
23. In what manner are the Body and Blood of Christ received?.................409
24. May this not be simply by faith?...409
25. What is meant by the "Capernaitic mode"?..409
26. Discriminate the modes of "eating," and state their relation to the Lord's Supper...409
Sacramental Promise...410
27. Having considered the element, and the heavenly gift, the third factor of the Sacrament remains...410
28. How does the Catechism estimate the force of these words?..................411
29. But how can the assurance and promise of God's grace to us individually be the chief thing in the Sacrament, when the Body and Blood of Christ are also there?..411
30. Since, however, the promise is given also outside of the Sacrament, does not this involve a depreciation of the Lord's Supper?.....................................412
Sacrament as a Memorial...412
31. In what sense is the Lord's Supper a memorial service?...........................412
32. Explain this more fully..412

33. What is the main difficulty concerning the acceptance of the Real Presence?....413
34. Has the chief effect of the Lord's Supper throughout the nearly two thousand years of its use, been to proclaim Law and Gospel, as suggested under 31?....414
Not a sacrifice....414
35. Is the Holy Supper in any sense a sacrifice?....414
Sacrificial side....414
36. But is not the use of the Holy Supper sacrificial?....414
Ministers....415
37. Through whom is the Lord's Supper administered?....415
38. But is there no necessity that justifies the administration by a layman?..415
Administration in both kinds....415
39. In the administration is it essential that both the bread and the wine be given to all communicants?....415
40. Upon what grounds, therefore, has the withdrawal of the cup been defended?....416
To whom to be administered....416
41. To whom is the Holy Supper to be administered?....416
42. Are no doctrinal tests necessary?....417
43. Is the faith which is required for the profitable use of the Lord's Supper merely doctrinal correctness concerning this article?....417
44. Does the Sacrament bring condemnation where there is weak faith?....417
45. Does the Catechism mean that doubts should deter one from receiving the Sacrament?....418
46. Should a pastor administer the communion to himself?....418
Sacrament as a communion....419
47. Has the Lord's Supper any other purpose than that of individualizing the general promise of the Gospel?....419
48. What follows from this?....420
Prophetical side....421
49. Is there not also a prophetic element in the Lord's Supper?....421
Sacrament as an epitome of doctrine....422
50. What important practical result follows from these uses of the Lord's Supper?....422
51. What three parts belong to the sacramental action?....422
Consecration....422
52. What is the consecration?....422
Distribution....423
53. What is the distribution?....423
Reception....423
54. What is the reception?....423
How often....424
55. How often should the Lord's Supper be received?....424
56. What admonition concerning this does our Catechism give?....424
29. The Church....427
Relation to what precedes....427
1. Recapitulate the several stages in the Plan of Salvation already noted.....427
2. What remains to be treated?....427
3. What is this Organism?....427

Origin.. 427
4. When did the Church begin?.. 427
Definition.. 428
5. How is the Church defined?.. 428
6. How can it be proved that only regenerate and believing persons constitute the Church?.. 429
7. But is the term always restricted to the regenerate and believing?..........430
Organic structure.. 430
8. How is the Church properly so called divided? Into the Church Militant and the Church Triumphant.. 430
9. How is this assembly of believers united?.. 431
10. In what sense is Christ called "Head of the Church"?.......................... 432
Attributes.. 432
11. What are the Attributes of the Church?.. 432
12. What is meant by the Unity of the Church?....................................... 432
13. In what definition of the Church is this unity made prominent?..........433
14. What is meant by the Holiness of the Church?................................... 434
15. What is meant by the Catholicity of the Church?............................... 434
16. What is meant by the Apostolicity of the Church?............................. 435
17. What is meant by the Perpetuity of the Church?................................ 435
18. Is the lot of the Church one of uninterrupted progress?...................... 436
19. What index is there of its real prosperity or adversity?....................... 436
Intermingling with others.. 437
20. What scriptural foundation is there for the doctrine that hypocrites and wicked men are mingled with the true Church in the same outward assembly?.. 437
21. Are such persons to be regarded Members of the Church?.................. 437
Visible and Invisible.. 438
22. Is the distinction between a Visible and an Invisible church correct?....438
Marks... 439
23. How can the true Church be distinguished?....................................... 439
24. Show that the Preaching of the Word is a mark of the Church............440
25. What proof is there that the Sacraments are marks of the Church?......440
26. Are then all marks of the Church of the same importance?.................. 441
27. What is meant by "the pure Preaching of the Word"?.......................... 441
28. When it is said that the "pure preaching" is a mark, how is this to be interpreted?.. 441
29. What errors are here guarded against?.. 442
30. What is meant by "the right administration of the Sacraments"?.........442
Relation of Attributes and Marks... 443
31. Do the Attributes of the Church belong to it also as an external body?.443
Other Marks rejected... 444
32. Have not other marks been proposed besides those above given?.........444
33. To dwell upon but one of these marks, why cannot the succession of Bishops be admitted as a mark of the Church?.. 444
Membership... 445
34. Who are the members of the Church?... 445
No salvation except through Church.. 446
35. Is the declaration, "*Extra ecclesiam nulla salus est*," "Outside of the Church there is no salvation," correct?... 446
36. But would this justify one in saying that any are saved without the

instrumentality of the Church?.. 446
No Platonic State.. 447
37. What inference do we derive from this?.. 447
38. What estimate, therefore, should be placed upon the significance of the individual in the service and progress of the Kingdom of God?.. 449
39. Why does the Apology of the Augsburg Confession indignantly repudiate the charge that the Lutheran conception of the Church mas that of "a Platonic State"?.. 450
The Communion of Saints.. 450
40. But how does this agree with the doctrine that the Gospel deals with us not as a community but with individuals?.. 450
41. But is not Religion purely a matter between God and the individual?... 451
42. Where in the Holy Scriptures do we find the most extended argument to this effect?.. 451
43. What daily reminds us of the same principle of the Church as a community?.. 451
44. How is this common or community spirit of the Church maintained? 452
45. How do the Sacraments declare the importance of the community thought in the Church?.. 452
46. What two spheres, then, does this communion comprise?.. 453
The Lutheran, as a true Church.. 454
47. Is the Lutheran Church true and catholic?.. 454
48. But how can it be a true Church when it has so many divisions?.. 454
49. But how is Rome's objection concerning the recent origin of our Church to be met?.. 454
50. Is the Lutheran the true and catholic Church?.. 456
51. Where is this stated in our Confessions?.. 457
52. How is this consistent with the severe criticism and condemnation declared in portions of our Confessions against those who dissent from our doctrine?.. 458
Function and Authority.. 458
53. What is the special office and calling of the Church?.. 458
54. Whence has it this authority and commission?.. 458
55. Does not this power belong, however, to a class or order within the Church?.. 459
56. Can the Church, at its will, dispense with the ministerial office?.. 459
57. Explain the call or appointment by the Church?.. 460
External Organization.. 460
58. What inevitably results?.. 460
59. How is the organization effected?.. 460
Church Traditions.. 461
60. What matters may be particularly classed under the head of Church Traditions?.. 461
61. What general principles must guide their use?.. 461
62. But may not a rite or ceremony become the badge of a confession?...... 462
63. What notable illustration of this principle is found in Holy Scripture? 462
64. Is then one at entire liberty, according to his own judgment, to comply or not with the regulations concerning adiaphora which the Church, from time to time, may make?.. 463
65. What doctrinal principle should decide all liturgical regulations and practices?.. 463

66. What gives a Confession of Faith or a doctrinal decision of a synod its validity? ... 464
Open Questions ... 465
67. Are there then Open Questions? ... 465
Errors conflicting with doctrine of the Church — Heresy, Schism, Sectarianism, Syncretism, Secularism, etc ... 466
68. What forms of error are in conflict with the true doctrine and the practical efficiency of the Church? ... 466
69. What is Heresy? ... 466
70. What is Schism? ... 466
71. What is Sectarianism? ... 466
72. What is Syncretism? ... 467
73. Why is Syncretism to be condemned? ... 467
74. Does the rejection of Syncretism mean, therefore, that all Church fellowship with those who have not attained the same degree of light and knowledge with one's self is to be renounced and condemned? ... 468
75. Is this the principle and spirit of the Confessions? ... 469
76. How then is the line to be drawn, within which such charity is to be exercised? ... 470
77. What is Secularism? ... 470
78. In what does Secularism culminate? ... 471
79. Against what other tendencies must especial care be taken? ... 471
Leading types of doctrine and life ... 471
80. What are the three leading types of ecclesiastical doctrine and life? ... 471
81. How is this distinction modified? ... 472
30. The Ministry ... 473
Definition ... 473
1. Through what instrumentality does the Church chiefly administer the Means of Grace? ... 473
2. What is the Ministry? ... 473
Permanent and Temporary Elements ... 473
3. Is the designation of a special class of men to till this office simply a matter of convenience? ... 473
4. Is this classification of offices absolute for the Church of later times? ... 474
5. What was the ultimate result? ... 474
All pastors bishops ... 475
6. Is there no distinction in the New Testament between Presbyters and Bishops? ... 475
7. Is there any Confessional declaration on this subject? ... 475
8. Is there any serious dissent from this even among scholarly advocates of diocesan episcopacy? ... 475
9. If the distinction between bishops and presbyters be not made by divine right, is it admissible? ... 476
The Ministry and the Priesthood ... 476
10. Is it proper to call Ministers "priests"? ... 476
11. But is not the office of teaching and preaching and administering the Sacraments a prerogative of the spiritual priesthood? ... 477
12. Give the statement of our Confessions on this subject ... 477
13. Scripture proofs? ... 478
The Call to the Ministry. Immediate and Mediate Call distinguished; Mode of

Mediate Call; Preparatory factors; "Call" in special sense; Part of the Ministry and Laity in giving Call; Lay preaching; Limits of Ministry as determined by Call....478
14. Has the form of the Call to the ministry been uniform in all ages?....478
15. Is there any divinely-prescribed order according to which the Church proceeds in giving the Call?....478
16. What is the order as we now find it?....479
17. What prepares for the Call?....479
18. Is the Call to the ministry cm inner conviction of duty wrought by the Holy Spirit upon man's heart?....479
19. What other agencies may be mentioned as preparing the way for the Call?....480
20. What is the next stage in preparing the way?....480
21. What is the Call in the most special sense?....480
22. By whom is the Call given?....480
23. Is there, then, no true ministry except where the Call comes from both portions of the Church?....481
24. How is this accomplished?....481
25. But are all laymen, or all communicant members of churches competent to give a discriminating judgment as to the qualifications of a candidate?. .481
26. When is a modification of this principle justifiable?....482
27. Where a regularly called pastor cannot be had, is it never proper for a layman to preach or teach publicly in the Church?....482
28. How about the preaching of theological students?....482
29. Is the Call which constitutes the ministry limited to the pastorate of a local congregation?....483
30. If one called to the ministry ceases to discharge its duties is he any longer a minister?....483
Ordination: Definition; Not absolutely necessary; Ordinary form; Lutheran estimate of; Who is to ordain; Congregational or Synodical Ordination; Reordination; Ordination *sine titulo*....483
31. What is Ordination?....483
32. Does Ordination make one a minister?....484
33. Is not Ordination a divinely prescribed ceremony?....484
34. What is the ordinary form of Ordination?....484
35. What is the chief thing in Ordination?....484
36. What is the exact estimate of such ceremony in the Lutheran Church? 484
37. By whom is Ordination administered?....485
38. Can Ordination be administered by the authority simply of a congregation?....485
39. Should ministers who have been ordained in other communions be reordained on entering the Lutheran ministry?....486
40. Should one be ordained "*sine titulo*"?....486
Are there grades....487
41. Are there different grades of ministers of the Word?....487
Power of Ministers....488
42. What Power or Authority have ministers?....488
43. These seem to be functions whose exercise dare not be declined by ministers. Are there any, besides these, that are permitted them?....488
44. How are these two different spheres classified?....488
45. In what sense is "preaching" a prerogative of the ministry?....489

46. Are laymen absolutely forbidden to administer the Sacraments?.........489
47. Has an ordained minister the right to preach and administer the Sacraments everywhere?.........489
Preaching as a function of the Ministry.........489
48. What subjects are to be treated in the preaching of the Word?.........489
49. Has the congregation the right to prescribe the subjects that are to be included or excluded in the preaching of the Word?.........490
Administration of Sacraments of the Ministry.........491
50. What is required in the administration of the Sacraments?.........491
Administration of Power of Keys: Confession and Absolution, private and public, Part of Ministry in Discipline.........491
51. What is the office of remitting and retaining sins?.........491
52. By what terms is this individual dealing between a pastor and a parishioner known?.........491
53. What various forms of confession are there?.........492
54. How does Lutheran Private Confession differ from that of the Roman confessional?.........493
55. How are some of the advantages of such Confession and Absolution obtained?.........494
56. Can Church Discipline be exercised by a congregation independently of the ministry?.........494
External duties of Ministry.........494
57. Mention some of the matters comprised within the sphere of External Power.........494
Deacons and Deaconesses.........495
58. What other ministers are there beside the ministers of the Word?.........495
59. What were the Deaconesses of the early Church?.........495
The End of the Ministry.........495
60. What is the end of the Ministry?.........495
Comfort with respect to its duties.........496
61. What special comfort have ministers of the Word who recognize their office as coming to them from a clearly divine call?.........496
31. The Church's Confessions.........499
Necessity.........499
1. Why are Confessions of Faith necessary?.........499
2. But is not the Bible a sufficient confession?.........499
3. Within what spheres are such Confessions necessary?.........500
4. Why should such confessional obligation be exacted especially of a pastor?.........500
Precise Function.........500
5. But does not this assume that the conscience of the pastor must be determined by the judgment of the Church rather than by Holy Scripture?.........500
6. If, however, the judgment of the pastor or candidate should differ from that of the Church?.........501
Nature of Test.........501
7. What should be the nature of the confessional test?.........501
Confessional obligation analyzed.........501
8. What two things are involved in a confessional obligation?.........501
Precautions to be observed.........502

9. Are there no precautions, however, to be observed in subscribing to the Confessions? 502
10. May we not then subscribe to them, “in so far as” they agree with Holy Scripture? 503
The Lutheran Confessions classified 503
11. How may the Confessions of the Lutheran Church be grouped? 503
I. Practical handbooks for popular instruction 503
II. Theological Confessions 503
I. The Catechisms are symbols pertaining to the religious life of the individual Christian 505
II. The other Confessions are symbols pertaining to the ecclesiastical organization and define the principles that are to govern the Church in preaching the Word and administering the Sacraments 505
Abuse of Confessions 505
12. How may Confessions be abused? 505
Objections answered 506
13. But does subscription to Confessions produce absolute harmony among all who comply with this requirement? 506
14. Are not the controversies settled in our Confessions merely such as belonged to the Church in Germany over three hundred years ago, and, therefore, of no very great importance to us in America? 507
Rules for controversies 507
15. How are doctrinal controversies to be conducted? By carefully keeping in mind two scriptural principles: 507
16. Has any statement on this subject been made by our theologians? 508
17. What does this last statement mean? 508
18. What model of controversial composition may be mentioned? 509
32. Church Discipline 511
The two spheres 511
1. What two spheres are there for the exercise of Church discipline? 511
2. Have those who occupy the ministerial office any prerogative exempting them from the same discipline as other members of the Church? 511
The Object 511
3. What is the main object of the discipline of a member of the Church? 511
4. But is this the only object? 512
Indispensable 513
5 Has the Church, therefore, any authority to dispense with Church Discipline? 513
6. What do our Confessions declare on this subject? 513
7. What have our theologians to say on the subject? 513
Offenses noticed 514
8. With what offenses is this discipline occupied? 514
Grades 514
9. What grades of Church Discipline are there? 514
Divinely-prescribed order 514
10. Is there a divinely prescribed order for the process? 514
11. Is this limited to acts which are personally injurious or hostile to the person reproving? 515
12. What caution, however, is to be employed with reference to this private interview? 516

13. How in regard to public offenses?......516
Excommunication......516
14. When must resort be had to excommunication?......516
15. To whom does the decision as to excommunication belong?......516
16. Why is the presence and concurrence of the ministry so important?......517
17. What penalties are imposed by such discipline?......517
18. But what if the Excommunication be unjust?......518
Secret sins......518
19. Does not the Key of binding, as well as that of loosing refer to secret as well as to public offenses?......518
20. How is the discipline of pastors distinguished from that of other members of the Church?......518
Discipline of Pastors......518
21. What special provision does the New Testament make with respect to the discipline of pastors?......518
33. The Christian Family......519
Place of Family......519
1. What other institutions besides the ministry are there through which the spiritual welfare of man is promoted?......519
2. What is the office of the Family?......519
3. How does the Church exert its most effective influence?......520
4. What is a Christian Family?......520
Marriage with unbelievers......520
5. Is it wrong for one in the communion of the Church to marry an unbeliever?......520
6. May there not be a Christian home even with such defect?......521
Meaning of Marriage Ceremony......521
7. What is the significance of the ecclesiastical marriage ceremony?......521
Marriage indissoluble......521
8. Is marriage under any circumstances dissoluble?......521
When is Divorce permissible......522
9. What are the offenses that completely break the marriage covenant, and justify divorce?......522
Precautions to be observed in admitting persons to ceremony......522
10. What care is to be taken in regard to marriages?......522
11. But if it should be objected that these prohibitions belong to the Ceremonial Law, and have been abrogated since the coming of Christ, what answer shall be given?......522
12. What other precaution is to be taken?......523
13. Can a pastor perform the ceremony for those who are avowed atheists or otherwise defiant opponents of the Christian religion, or when one party professes to be such while the other claims to be a Christian?......523
14. Should the Church or pastors have anything to do with marriages that have been contracted in violation of God's law?......523
Relation of Family to other institutions......524
15. How does the Family, as a divine institution, enable us to estimate other institutions?......524
Celibacy......524
16. But is not Celibacy especially commended by Paul in 1 Cor. 7?......524
17. What is meant by Luke 18:29?......525

Family as a Religious Center......525
18. What of the Christian Family as a center of religions influence?......525
19. Is family religious instruction sufficient?......526
Education and Schools......526
20. What admonition does the Large Catechism give concerning Christian education?......526
21. How has Luther elsewhere discussed this?......526
22. Should the school be expected to afford all the religious instruction?......527
Summary......527
23. What is the sum and substance of the doctrine concerning marriage?......527
34. The State......529
Place of State......529
1. What has the State to do with spiritual things?......529
2. Does the Heavenly Citizenship of the Christian (Phil. 3:20) justify him in indifference to the prerogatives cf earthly citizenship?......529
3. What is the teaching of our Confession on this subject?......530
War......530
4. Passing by other acts that are here justified, we ask concerning going to war and serving as soldiers......530
Oaths......531
5. Give a summary of the doctrine of the Oath......531
Church and State......532
6. What errors have been prevalent concerning the relation of Church and State?......532
7. But has not the State also assumed authority over the Church?......532
8. Does not the reorganization of the Church at the time of the Reformation afford the precedent for such usurpation of power on the part of the State?......533
9. May we not derive the inference hence, that the precedents of Church government in Europe cannot be applied to the circumstances of the Church in America, except with great discrimination?......534
Limitations of power of the people and majorities......534
10. Has any particular form of government higher authority than another?......534
11. Is the declaration: "Government of the people, by the people, for the people," strictly correct?......534
12. Upon what principle of the Reformation is a government of God through the people and by God through the people founded?......535
13. Is it consistent with the Christian calling for one as a member of a nation of free rulers to cast his ballot and give his support in accord simply with the demands of conventions and caucuses, trusts or unions, employers or parties?......535
The Christian and Political Wrongs......536
14. Is the Christian to seek no remedy for manifest abuses in the State?......536
The Church and Political Wrongs......537
15. What responsibility has the Church in regard to laws enacted or crimes tolerated under the sanction of laws, that are clearly contrary to the Holy Scriptures?......537
Responsibility of one State for the wrongs of another......537
16. Has one State no responsibility with respect to wrongs that outrage

humanity continued for years by another State, and in the face of repeated protests? ... 537
The Sphere of Religious Liberty ... 538
17. Is it within the power of the State to punish heresy? ... 538
18. But cannot the State make religions tests? ... 538
19. Did Luther never advocate the punishment of heresy by death? ... 538
20. Is the State, therefore, without jurisdiction in regard to ecclesiastical affairs? ... 539
National Life in the service of the Kingdom of God ... 539
21. What can be said concerning the varied lots of Earthly Governments? ... 539
35. Life After Death ... 541
The Goal of Revelation ... 541
1. Towards what end are the entire Revelation of God in Christ and all the details of the Plan of Redemption which it announces, directed? ... 541
Definition of Death ... 542
2. What is Death? ... 542
What is peculiar to man's State ... 542
3. What is peculiar about man's death? ... 542
4. What is the relation of death to the two parts of mans being that are thereby separated? ... 542
Estimate of arguments for the Immortality of the Soul ... 543
5. Is the doctrine of the Immortality of the Soul peculiar to Christianity? ... 543
6. What estimate is to be placed upon these proofs? ... 543
7. How may this be illustrated? ... 544
Old Testament doctrine concerning it ... 544
8. Has there been no progress in the revelation of this doctrine? ... 544
Causes, Extent and Offices of death ... 545
9. What causes of this separation are enumerated in Scripture? ... 545
10. Is bodily or temporal death limited to the moment of separation of soul from the body and the state which succeeds? ... 546
11. What two-fold office does death serve? ... 546
12. Is this the only way in which the curse is changed into a blessing? ... 546
State of Souls after death. What they carry with them; A Provisional State; No Purgatory, neither Repentance nor Unconsciousness after Death taught in Holy Scripture, Distinction between State after Death, and that which follows the General Judgment; Temporal Standards inadmissible ... 548
13. Do the dead carry nothing with them? ... 548
14. Have they any knowledge of what is occurring on earth? ... 548
15. What is the general condition of souls after death? ... 548
16. Is the state one, then, in which the souls of believers are subjected to a process of purification and preparation for heaven? ... 548
17. Is there any possibility of saving repentance after death? ... 549
18. May not the state between Death and Resurrection be one of unconsciousness? ... 549
19. State briefly what is meant by "Life after Death." ... 550
20. Is the period between Death and Resurrection one that is to be reckoned according to the standard by which time is measured in this life? ... 550
21. What may be said concerning the very limited amount of details which Holy Scripture gives on the whole subject of Life after Death? ... 550

36. The Resurrection Of The Body....551
Definition and Scriptural Grounds....551
1. What is the Resurrection of the Dead?....551
2. What scriptural grounds are there for this doctrine?....552
3. Is the New Testament content with declaring the Resurrection as an irrefutable fact?....552
Old Testament Testimony estimated....553
4. What is the value of the Old Testament prophecies concerning the Resurrection?....553
Arguments from Nature estimated....553
5. Is this article known by the Light of Nature?....553
Misinterpretation of....554
6. What has been a frequent method of explaining away the Resurrection? 554
Source of....554
7. Whence does the Resurrection come?....554
Agents, Means, Subjects....555
8. Who will raise the dead?....555
9. By what means will they be raised?....555
10. Who will be raised?....556
The Resurrection of the Ungodly....556
11. Will the ungodly be raised again because of the merits of Christ?....556
Nature of the Resurrection Body....557
12. Will the Resurrection Body be a material body? It will be of the same nature as that which Christ had after His resurrection....557
13. Do you hold that there is necessarily an atomistic identity between the body that is buried and the one that is raised?....558
14. Do we know anything as to the stature of the Resurrection Body?....558
15. What are the Attributes of the Resurrection Body?....558
16. Enumerate, therefore, these Attributes....559
17. Explain them in detail....559
1. Immortality....559
2. Glory and Brilliancy....559
3. Perfection of Powers....560
4. Spirituality....560
18. What of the resurrection bodies of the godless?....561
19. What can be said of the last generation of believers on earth, who do not die, but are alive at the general resurrection?....561
The Resurrection not a Process....561
20. Will the Resurrection be a process continuing through a considerable period?....561
How to treat difficulties concerning it....561
21. If difficulties concerning the Resurrection occur, how are they to be regarded?....561
37. The Return Of Christ....563
Relation to the Resurrection....563
1. When will the Resurrection occur?....563
2. Is the Second Coming promised only with respect to its relations to the individual?....563

The Two States of the Church........564
3. What resemblance is there between the condition of the Church in this life and that of the individual believer?........564
4. But is not the power of evil gradually broken by the preaching of the Gospel and the wide diffusion of the principles of Christianity?........564
5. What estimate is placed, therefore, upon the Return of the Lord?........565
The Two States of Creation........565
6. Is there not even a wider scope for its decision?........565
The Time........566
7. When will this event, toward which all things tend, occur?........566
8. What may be said of such signs in general?........566
The Signs: 1. Universal Preaching of the Gospel; 2. Conversion of Israel; Decline and Oppression of Church, including the career of Antichrist; 4. Extraordinary Historical Events; 5. Supernatural Material Phenomena........567
9. What are these signs?........567
10. What of the first?........567
11. What of the second, the Conversion of the Jews?........568
12. What of the third, the Decline and Oppression of the Church?........569
13. In what will this spurious Christianity and its persecuting spirit be concentrated?........570
14. When can Christians know for a certainty as to who Antichrist is?........571
15. What warning concerning a premature decision concerning the fulfillment of the prophecy concerning Antichrist does Church History give?........571
16. Are there not antichristic principles in the Papacy?........572
17. Is not this enough to show that the Pope is Antichrist?........572
18. What of the fourth sign of the Second Coming, viz., the Extraordinary Historical Events?........573
19. What of the fifth?........573
The Chiliastic Interpretation examined........573
20. Will there be a two-fold coming or manifestation of Christ?........573
21. Why is such opinion rejected?........574
Characteristics of the Second Coming........575
22. What will be the characteristics of Christ's Second Coming?........575

38. The General Judgment........577

Scriptural and Confessional Declarations........577
1. What will follow the Second Coming of Christ?........577
Christ as Judge........578
2. Is judgment to be ascribed exclusively to the Son?........578
3. But does not Christ say that "the Father judgeth no man" (John 5:22)?...578
4. Is it not said also that it is not the office of Christ to judge?........578
5. Are Love and Justice mutually exclusive?........579
6. According to what nature will Christ be our judge?........580
In what sense Christians will be judges........580
7. Are not the faithful followers of Christ also to be judges?........580
Office of angels in the Judgment........581
8. What will be the office of angels at the judgment?........581
Who are to be judged........581
9. Who are to be judged?........581
10. But will the righteous both judge (7) and be judged?........582

What will be judged......582
11. What will be judged?......582
12. Are we, then, to infer that in the Final Judgment, no account is to be taken of works?......583
13. Will account be taken only of works in general?......584
The Sins of the Godly at the Judgment......584
14. Does this necessarily mean that every sin of the righteous will be examined and published on the Day of Judgment?......584
15. Will the godly recall their sins on the Day of Judgment?......586
The Norm of the Judgment: the Gospel for believers, the Law for unbelievers......586
16. According to what norm or rule will judgment be pronounced?......586
17. But is it not expressly said that the godless also will be judged according to the Gospel?......587
The Examination and "Books"......587
18. In how far are the details of the examination to be figuratively interpreted?......587
19. What is meant by "the Books"?......588
20. With what two things has the decree of the Judge to do?......589
Doctrine of Rewards to be guarded......589
21. Against what must the doctrine of rewards for the godly on the Day of Judgment be carefully guarded?......589
22. But is the awarding of these rewards postponed until the Day of Judgment?......590
Difference in Rewards......590
23. Will there be differences, then, in the rewards?......590
Salvation "without reward"......591
24. Will any be saved who will be without reward?......591
Incompleteness of Record at death......591
25. Are the works which are judged completed with the death of the person judged?......591
Degrees of Punishment and Incompleteness of Record of Wicked at death....592
26. In what will the sentence of the wicked agree with, and in what will it differ from that of the godly?......592
27. Is it true also of the godless that their works are not completed with their death?......592
No third class......593
28. Beside the godly and the godless, do the Scriptures permit us to admit the suggestion of any third class?......593
The Sentence......593
29. What important difference in the qualifications attending the sentence?......593
Events succeeding Judgment, particularly End of World, Final Conflagration and Change of Heaven and Earth......593
30. What will immediately follow the execution of the sentence?......593
31. What then?......594
32. For what purpose will the world be destroyed?......594
33. Will this be accomplished by the complete annihilation of the present world, and the substitution of a new creation, or simply by the purification of this present world by fire and its transformation into "new heavens and a new earth"?......595

34. How has the other side been stated?....596
35. What, however, is fixed?....596

39. Eternal Death....597

Defined....597
1. What is Eternal Death?....597
Both Place and State....597
2. Is it a place or a state to which the godless are to be consigned?....597
Important distinction....598
3. What care must be taken in the understanding of terms employed?....598
Literal or figurative "Fire"....598
4. When the place of punishment is described as "a lake of fire," is this to be understood literally or figuratively?....598
5. How have the punishments been classified?....599
Classification of punishments....599
6. Will there be an end to these punishments?....599
Punishments, without end; doctrine state, and objections answered....600
7. But will (here not be, according to this statement, a disproportion between sins as committed in a brief period of time, and their punishment throughout all eternity?....600
8. But must not allowance be made for the qualitative use of the word "eternal"?....601
9. What qualification, however, should always attend the preaching of this doctrine?....602

40. Eternal Life....603

Defined....603
1. What is Eternal Life?....603
2. What three things are included in the conception?....603
3. Explain the first?....604
4. Explain the second....605
5. Explain the third....605
"Salvation" and "Glory" distinguished; the former for the individual; the latter for the community of "the Blessed"....606
6. What distinction has been made by some of our theologians?....606
7. What relation do these two conditions have to each other?....606
8. But is salvation peculiar to the period after the General Judgment?....607
The Beatific Vision: its effects and attendants....607
9. What is a most prominent element of the blessedness of Heaven?....607
10. What does this mean?....607
11. But does this mean that with their bodily eyes the godly shall behold God?....608
12. What will be the effect of this sight of God?....608
13. What will accompany the sight of God?....609
The Community of the Blessed....609
14. Is the communion of the blessed with God one that isolates them from one another?....609
15. In what form is this social life of the blessed described as especially expressing itself?....610
16. Will all have the same glory?....611
The Home of the Blessed....612

17. What will be the home of the Blessed after the Final Judgment?............612
18. What argument concerning the nature of this abode has been made from the blessings of the present life?............612
19. Will the rest of heaven be inaction?............613

41. The Divine Purpose As Interpreted By Its Contents And Results 615

Order of Treatment............615
1. What is the sum and substance of God's revelation of Himself to man?. .615
Predestination defined, and definition explained clause by clause. Different senses of term, "Out of grace," "Out of Human Race," "Each Individual," Relation of Foreknowledge, In what senses "Absolute" and "Conditional," Condition presupposed in Decree, "In Christ," Is Faith a cause of Election, Parallel of Justification............616
2. What is the meaning of "Predestination"?............616
3. In what two senses is the word used?............616
4. What synonym is there for Predestination?............616
5. Define Predestination or Election............617
6. What is the force of the expression, "out of pure grace"?............617
7. What is meant by God's determination "to save out of the human race"? 617
8. What is declared by the words "out of the fallen, condemned and helpless human race"?............617
9. Why do you say "each individual"?............618
10. What is the force of the words "who from eternity he foresaw"?............618
11. Why cannot Predestination be identified with foreknowledge?............618
12. In what sense is Predestination dependent upon Foreknowledge?............619
13. Is the decree of Predestination, therefore, absolute?............619
14. Is it conditional?............620
15. What caution have our theologians shown in applying these terms?......621
16. State the condition upon which the decree which is not conditionate is based?............621
17. But does not the expression "in Christ" declare even more than that the merits of Christ have been provided for mans salvation?............621
18. Does not this introduce a synergistic error into the statement of Predestination by making faith a cause of election, and thus denying that it is an act of God's free will?............622
19. Can you cite the opinion of any Lutheran theologian generally recognized as worthy of consideration?............622
20. Can this be reduced to a tabular form?............624
The Four and the Eight Factors to be accounted in constructing the doctrine 624
21. What factors must always be kept clearly in mind in attempting to construct a satisfactory statement of this subject?............624
Faith sometimes a condition, sometimes a result............625
22. But is not faith the fruit and result of Predestination?............625
Important caution concerning Faith............626
23. Is there no need of caution, however, in stating the relation of faith to election?............626
The Elect: Are all who believe elect; can the elect fall; can one know whether he be elect............626

24. Are all who believe elect or predestinated to life?....626
25. Can the Elect fall from God's grace?....627
26. Can one know whether he be elect?....627
27. What is the remedy for doubt as to whether one be in the number of the Elect?....628
The Non-elect: Meaning of "Reprobation," Why Predestination is particular, Rom. 9:15 sqq explained....628
28. What of the disposition of God towards the Non-elect?....628
30. Is the state of the Reprobate precisely the same as though Christ had not died and the offers of the Gospel had not been made them?....628
31. What then is Reprobation?....629
32. Why is Predestination particular instead of universal?....629
33. But is not this contrary to Rom. 9:15 "I will have mercy on whom I will have mercy," "Whom he will he hardeneth'?....629
The doctrine of Predestination not to be ignored....631
34. As this article contains so many difficulties, would it not be better to entirely ignore it?....631
35. What consolation does the consideration of this doctrine in its true place and order afford?....631
How to be guarded....632
36. In what does the special peril lie in its treatment?....632

Appendix: On The Spiritual Priesthood Of Believers. By Dr. Philip J. Spener (1677)....635

1. What is the Spiritual Priesthood?....635
2. Is there any scriptural testimony concerning it?....635
3. Why is it called a Spiritual Priesthood?....635
4. Whence is this Spiritual Priesthood derived?....635
5. How do Christians become priests?....636
6. Does not anointing also pertain to the Priesthood?....636
7. Are all believers, then, partakers of the anointing?....636
8. But for what purpose was Christ anointed?....636
9. For what are those who believe on Him anointed?....636
10. Who are such spiritual priests?....636
11. But does not the name "priest" belong only to the preachers?....637
12. But are not preachers the only "spiritual" ones?....637
13. What are the duties of the Spiritual Priesthood?....637
14. What have spiritual priests to offer?....637
15. How have we to offer our bodies and their members to God?....637
16. Hew should we offer our souls to God....638
17. How have we, further, to offer ourselves as a sacrifice to God?....638
18. Should we not also sacrifice our old Adam to God?....638
19. What else have we to offer?....638
20. Is there nothing still further for us to offer?....638
21. But have we not also to bring such offering to God, in order to atone for our sins?....638
22. But are the above-mentioned sacrifices which we bring to God, entirely pure?....639
23. How often and when should we offer such sacrifices?....639
24. Beside the sacrifices, what else belonged to the office of Christ, as Priest?

.... 639
25. What is, then, the third office of priest?.......................................639
26. Are all Christians, then, preachers, and have they to devote themselves to the office of the ministry?...639
27. But what, then, have they to do with the Word of God?.......................640
28. How have they to use it for themselves?...640
29. Is it. then, the duty of all Christians to diligently read the Scriptures?..640
30. But would it not be better, if they would simply believe all that they hear from their pastor?... 640
31. Are the Scriptures, therefore, not too difficult for simple persons who are without education?.. 640
32. But is there not in the Scriptures much that is obscure, and. therefore, too high for the simple?... 641
33. Would it not, therefore, be better if plain persons would not read them?
.... 641
34. Can they then, in their simplicity, learn to understand them?...............641
35. But as they do not have the assistance of foreign languages and of sciences of various kinds, how is it possible for them to understand the Scriptures?
.... 642
36. Whence, then, do simple, godly Christians have the ability to understand the Scriptures?... 642
37. But what have they to do in the reading of the Scriptures, in order to be assured of their truth?... 642
38. Is it necessary, then, to the salutary and living knowledge of Scripture, that we should seek to be improved thereby?...643
39. But How can readers hinder this use of Scripture and thus do themselves injury?... 643
40. But would it not be better to leave the more diligent investigation of the Scriptures to the preachers, and for the rest to abide by their simplicity?...644
41. What, then, would one do who would commend such simplicity to the people?... 644
42. But where all would so diligently study the Scriptures, would not confusion result?... 645
43. But are Christians always to be occupied with God s Word, so as no longer to attend to their worldly business?..645
44. But have Christians to treat God's Word only for their own good?.......645
45. What is the preaching of which Peter speaks (1 Peter 2:9)?....................645
46. Has the Christian, then, an obligation with respect to the salvation and edification of others?.. 646
47. How is it shown in the Ten Commandments?.......................................646
48. What is taught us on this point in the Apostles' Creed?.........................646
49. What concerning this duty do we find in the Lord's Prayer?.................646
50. How does our Baptism refer to this?...646
51. Is the Lord's Supper directed towards the same end?...........................647
52. But how have believing Christians to use the divine Word among their fellow-men?.. 647
53. Is this then for all Christians?..647
54. How have Christians to teach?...647
55. How can they convert the erring?...647
56. What have they to do in admonition?..648
57. How do they exercise the office of reproving?.....................................648

58. How in consoling? 648
59. Do the offices mentioned belong to all Christians? 648
60. But do Christian women have any share in such priestly offices? 648
61. But are not women forbidden to teach? 649
62. But in what way have Christians to exercise such offices? 649
63. Is it proper for assemblies to be held for such purposes? 649
64. But should one be appointed in such assembly as a teacher of the others? 649
65. But is it right for those who have not studied to devote their attention to intricate questions and dark passages of Scripture, and to be intent upon discussing them? 650
66. Are any duties with respect to the Sacraments included in their office? 650
67. But are not disgraceful confusion and disorder in the Church to be apprehended from this? 650
68. What, then, has the ministry to do, in order that all disorder be avoided? 650
69. But how have Christian priests to conduct themselves so as to avoid disorder? 651
70. But have not spiritual priests the power to judge their preachers? 651

About the Author 653

Selected Bibliography 653

How Can You Find Peace With God? 655

Benediction 656

Encouraging Christian Books for You to Download and Enjoy 657

Devotional 657

Theology 657

Novels 657

Essential Lutheran Library 657

Preface

AN ATTEMPT is here made to restate the doctrines of the Christian Faith upon the basis of the Lutheran Confessions. Hutter's Compend, an English translation of which, a number of years ago, served a good purpose, suggested the mode of treatment as well adapted to the use of theological students, intelligent laymen, and active pastors. While no important technical theological term is ignored and the aim is to explain whatever enters into the form as well as the material of Theology, a scholastic treatment is avoided as far as possible. We have endeavored to gather results, and embody them in concise definitions, supported by condensed arguments, drawn largely from our Confessions and Luther, and our theologians, as well as, in not a few cases, from those of other communions.

The book, however, is not a mere compilation, but the matured expression of the convictions of the author, from the time when, as a child he was introduced to many of the problems treated, to the present.

On certain living questions, widely and hotly agitated, greater space and freedom of discussion was allowed, that a candid testimony might be given on every important topic, for which the book may be consulted. It is not offered as the final word of controversy on any point, but as a starting point and suggestion of earnest thought.

An injustice, we believe, is done some of the great dogmaticians of our Church, when their works are criticized because of the dryness and scholastic form of their treatment. Where the effort is made to condense the entire compass of Divine Revelation into the compact form of a brief volume, the book becomes little more than an index and guide. Men become theologians, not by committing such text-books; but by clothing the outline with flesh from their constant study of Holy Scripture and Christian experience, whether as read in Church History, or recognized in their own lives, and those nearest them. The living teacher makes the text-book -Only the thread of what he gives his students. In writing this volume, we have often felt condemned as though it were, wrong to hurry over themes that offered such rich suggestions for edifying treatment.

Material pertaining to the History of Doctrine has been introduced only to a very limited extent. The scope of this book is one of results. For the process, whereby those results have been attained, we have another book in prospect, if life and strength should be spared to undertake it.

The Scripture Proof Texts are intended to be accurate translations of the Original. No space is lost by discussing inaccuracies of translations. Except in only three or four passages, they are from the best English translation of the New Testament, the American Revised Version, which we cordially recommend to all students and pastors.

Acknowledgments are due my son, the Rev. Charles M. Jacobs, for valuable assistance not only in revising the manuscript, and in aiding me in seeing it through the press, but also in numerous important suggestions in almost every chapter, concerning the treatment that have been adopted. A number of pages were also read by President Haas, of Muhlenberg College, my associate on "The Lutheran Cyclopedia"; and his kind notes were highly valued, and have contributed to the result. We bear, however, full responsibility for all that is here found.

If this book will be of service in proving that the faith of our Fathers is capable of being expressed in the English language in what is not a mere translation, and in aiding in restatement of Lutheran doctrine in a form adapted to a new land and new age; if it will be the means of representing correctly the spirit of Lutheranism to the religious world and theological circles in America; if, even to a small measure, it will bring our separated churches and schools to a realization not only of what is contained in our common heritage, but of the sources of strength whence our life may be renewed; if it will in any way change controversies from mere wrangling concerning the terminology of dogmas to an earnest, serious, modest, chastened inquiry into the truth which underlies them; if it will lead students of Theology to become devoted scholars of the Holy Scriptures, and pastors to grow ever more profoundly into the contemplation of "the deep things of God," and their application to their people; if it will withdraw the attention of men from that which is merely outward and temporal, the incidental and changing, to that which is inner and eternal, the essential and permanent, its publication will not be in vain.

HENRY EYSTER JACOBS.

Lutheran Theological Seminary, Philadelphia, July 11, 1905.

What Does It Mean: "For Many Are Called; But Few Chosen!" (Matt. 22:14)

(From the "Harmony of the Four Evangelists," by Chemnitz, Lyser and Gerhard. The exposition here translated is by Gerhard.)

"The reason why few are chosen is not placed in any absolute decree of God, but in men themselves. From the Parable of the Wedding Garment, both these propositions can be most clearly established. That God is not responsible for the paucity of the elect, is apparent from all that is ascribed to God in the parable:"

"1. 'He made a marriage feast for his son.' By this, the eternal decree of God is meant, that, in the fullness of time, His Son should assume human nature, and personally unite it with Himself, and in it accomplish the work of redemption. For since God, from eternity foreknew that man whom He would create in perfect righteousness and holiness would transgress, by voluntary disobedience, the law which would be given, and, by this transgression would bring upon himself and all his posterity, eternal death, He also decreed from eternity to prepare a remedy for this fall in Christ as Mediator. This eternal decree of God clearly shows that God is not delighted by the death of any one, but desires, and that too, earnestly, that all be saved; for He decreed to send His Son as Mediator for all, and decreed to offer this salutary remedy to all."

"2. That in the fullness of time, He put this decree into execution, and 'prepared the marriage for His Son,' i.e., sent Him into the flesh. This work of God also shows that He desires the salvation of all, and has rejected no one from absolute hatred. For in giving His Son to the The Divine Purpose, in His Son He offered salvation to the whole world. Because since, by His assumed human nature, He is 'of one substance' with all men, God follows none of them with absolute hatred, but wants all to partake of His blessings."

"3. That He gave His Son to death for all men (Rom. 8:32). For we have shown above, that by 'oxen and fatlings' in this parable, the passion and death of Christ are mystically signified. He was slain on the altar of the cross, to prepare all things which are required for the celebration of this wedding feast. But from manifest declarations of Scripture written by the rays of the sun, it is evident that Christ died for all men (Rom. 5:8; 2 Cor. 5:14; 1 Tim. 2:6; Heb. 2:9). Wherefore the passion and death of Christ are evident testimony that God sincerely desires that all enjoy the blessings of the heavenly feast both in this world and the next."

"4. That He has called the human race, on account of its relationship to the assumed human nature of His Son, to participation in His blessings and association of eternal joys; for this is what is meant in this parable by the call to the marriage of His Son. But those to whom God in and through the call offers the blessings of His Son, He has not reprobated from any absolute hatred. From the call itself, therefore, we infer that it is no fault of God that only a few are chosen; otherwise election would be opposed to the call and condemnable hypocrisy would be ascribed God in calling to the wedding, by an external 'will of the sign,' those whom with the internal 'will of the purpose,' He wanted to be absolutely excluded from the wedding. A careful consideration of the manner in which this call is described, will make it the more manifest that the cause of the small number of the elect should be ascribed to the called themselves. The call is described as universal and serious. It is universal because pertaining to all people, times and places. . . . That it is serious is manifest from the fact that the King is wroth with those declining the invitation, and heavily punishes this contempt of His call. If God, therefore, seriously calls all to partake of His Kingdom, He undoubtedly rejects none from absolute hatred. Hence the cause why only a few are elected cannot be ascribed to God."

"5. Neither must the fact be passed by that it is through His servants, i.e., through ministers of the Church, He calls to the wedding. Whatever, therefore, they do according to His Word in giving the call, He ratifies. But they 'preach the Gospel to every creature' (Mark 16. 16); 'teach all nations' (Matt. 28:10); 'reprove every man and teach every man' (Col. 1:28), and that, too, according to Christ's instructions. This, therefore, God ratifies, and, thus, through these His ministers, He offers to all the word of the Gospel, and with the word of the Gospel, the blessings of His Son; and in His Son, life and eternal salvation. How, then, could He have rejected from absolute hatred some men, yea the greater part of the human race? That to all called to the marriage of His Son He offers gratuitously the wedding garment, in which they may appear in a worthy manner at the wedding, we have above shown. In the call, therefore, and the word of the call, it is His will that there be an efficacious means in the hearts of men for their conversion, illumination, regeneration, justification, renovation and sanctification; all of which may be understood in a certain way as the wedding garment. But if He desires to effect all these things by the Holy Spirit in the hearts of the called, undoubtedly the fault is not attributable to Him that some are without the wedding garment, and, therefore, are cast into outer darkness, i.e., that they are not of the number of the elect. As, further, by the The Divine Purpose word of the Gospel, it is His will to enkindle faith in the called, so also, by the same means, He wishes to preserve and increase it; and, hence, that some lose the wedding garment of true faith, cannot be His fault, neither can it be ascribed to Him; but they for themselves, and of their own accord, reject the garment that has been given them out of grace, and, on this account, deserve to be cast out of the wedding feast."

"6. That He is not angry, neither sends His armies to burn and destroy, nor calls others to the marriages, passing by the former guests, before those called decline coming, slay the servants who give the invitation, and make themselves unworthy of the royal wedding; and that He commands no guest to be expelled until one is found who has rejected the wedding garment, makes it clear that exclusion from this royal wedding depends entirely upon the consequent and judicial will of God, whereby, on account of obstinate contempt of the call, and on account of persevering unbelief, He has excluded from salvation some whom, by His antecedent will, He wished to save, and offered to them the means of grace (Acts 13:46)."

"All these circumstances testify more clearly than the light of noonday that the reason why there are only a few elect is not to be sought in any absolute decree of God. But that the cause is to be sought only in the men themselves, Christ teaches also in this parable in which he presents to us four classes of men who, by their own fault, are excluded from the joys of the wedding feast."

"Let us apply this, therefore, to our profit:"1. Theoretically, so as to oppose the truths above mentioned against perilous opinions concerning the absolute decree of Election and Reprobation, the distinction between the Will of the Sign and the Will of the Purpose, Election on account of Foreseen Works, the Merit of our works, doubt of grace and perseverance. For if God calls all, and, in the word of the Gospel, offers to all the blessings of His Son, He undoubtedly has reprobated none from absolute hatred. If the call is serious, we must not think that He calls some only with the external will of the sign, and externally. If both call and election are gratuitous, neither occurs on account of foreseen works. If our salvation depends upon gratuitous election, it does not come to us because of the merits of our works. If Election does not fail, true believers in Christ should never doubt concerning the grace of God and the perseverance of faith," etc.

Luther On Speculations Concerning Predestination

(From a letter to Caspar Aquila, Oct. 21, 1528, De Wette's Luther's Briefe, III, 391 sqq.)

"Why is it that we most miserable men who as yet are unable by faith to receive the rays of the divine promise or by our works to reflect the smallest sparks of the divine commands, notwithstanding our impurity and weakness, should assume to rise to the comprehension of the light of the sun, yea to the incomprehensible light of God's mysteries? Do we not know that He dwells in light unto which no man can approach? And yet we approach, or rather presume to approach! Do we not know that His judgments are past finding out? And yet we endeavor to find them out! This too we do, before we have been enlightened by the rays of the promise and the sparks of the commandments. With the eyes of moles we rush into the majesty of that light which cannot be described by words or signs; yea, is hidden and not revealed. What wonder if the glory stupefy us, while we look upon its majesty! What wonder, if, in a reverse order, we seek for the fullest light, before we seek for the day-star. Let the day-star first arise in our hearts (as 2 Peter 1.:19 says) then we will be able to see at last the light of noonday."

"We must teach, indeed, concerning the inscrutable will of God, in order that we may know that there is such a thing, but to endeavor to comprehend it is a most perilous precipice. Hence I am accustomed to confine myself to the word of Christ to Peter: 'If I will that he tarry till I come, what is that to thee? Follow thou me'; for Peter had asked concerning God's dealings with another, viz., as to what was to be the lot of John. So when Philip asked: 'Lord, show us the Father, and it sufficeth us He checked him with the words: 'Believest thou not that the Father is in me, and I am in the Father? He who sees me, sees also the Father.' For Philip wanted to see the majesty and secrets of the Father, as though God were far beyond the promises and commands concerning Christ. So too, the wise man says: 'Seek not the things that are too high for thee; but diligently think of what has been commanded thee' (Ecclesiasticus 3:22). Besides, only consider, I ask, what advantage would it be for you to know these secret judgments of God, beyond his commands and promises? Tell him, therefore, that, if he wants to have peace of heart and to avoid the perils of blasphemy and despair, he must abstain from such thoughts, since he knows they are clearly incomprehensible. Why does he permit himself to be tormented by Satan with things that are impossible; as though one were to be rendered anxious as to how the earth could stand upon the waters without sinking into them, or the like? First let him busy himself with the promises and commandments; and then he will see whether he ought to attempt impossibilities in addition. If he neglect this advice, let him beware lest he repent too late. There is no other remedy for such thoughts than to absolutely abandon them; although while Satan urges them, it is very difficult to do so, since he represents that they demand examination. For this reason, we must contend here no less with contempt, than with distrust, despair or any other heresy. The majority are deceived by not recognizing such thoughts as temptations of Satan; and for this reason almost every one despises them or tries to despise them although they are the fiery darts of the most wicked of the most wicked of spirits in heavenly places. For by them Satan fell from heaven, when he wanted to be like the Most High, to know all things which God knows, and was not content with knowing only what he ought to know. Here we must fight by fleeing; and must not try to be wiser than we should be, but be sober; for otherwise one will be overcome. For we cannot think of Christ, while such thoughts prevail. Adam fell, when the prohibition of one tree troubled him with questions concerning the wisdom and will of God. In short, this is the chief temptation and one that is peculiarly diabolical; it is enough for us to experience such as are common to man. This will furnish an answer also to the other question, viz.: that the preacher should discharge the duty with which God has entrusted him, without regard to what God has not commanded, viz.: as to the question why one hears and another does not. 'What is that to thee,' says Christ. 'Follow thou me,' me, me, me, not your questions, or speculations."

Every reader of Luther's writings knows the references he repeatedly makes to the aid afforded him by Staupitz when he was tormented by abstract speculations concerning Predestination. "Begin with the wounds of Christ," said Staupitz; "then all arguing concerning Predestination will come to an end....But when men follow their own thoughts, the Laudate ceases and the Blasphemate begins."

His final opinion is in the last of his works, his "Lectures on Genesis" (Opera Exegetica, 6:296, 300).

"Audi Filium incamatum et sponte se offeret Praedestinatio....When, therefore, the devil attacks thee, say only: 'I believe in our Lord Jesus Christ, of whom I have no doubt that He became incarnate, suffered and died for me, and that into His death I have been baptized.' At this reply, the temptation will cease and Satan will turn his back....This also must we do: we must cease our disputations, and must say: 'I am a Christian,' i.e., 'The Son of God was incarnate and born. He has redeemed me. He sits at the right hand of the Father, and is my Savior.' In the very fewest words thus repell Satan: 'Get thee behind me. God's Son came into the world, to destroy thy work and dispell all doubt.'...Through Christ and the Gospel, God reveals to us His will. This we reject with disdain, and, after the example of Adam, are delighted with the forbidden tree above all others. This vice inheres in our very nature. Paradise and heaven are closed. While the angel guards the entrance, in vain do we attempt to enter. For Christ has said truly: 'No man hath seen God at any time' (John 1:18), and, nevertheless, of His immense goodness, God has revealed Himself to us, in order to satisfy our desire. He has presented to us His visible image. 'Lo, thou hast my Son,' He says. 'He who hears Him and is baptized is in the Book of Life. This I reveal through my Son, whom thou canst touch with thy hands and gaze upon with thine eyes.'"

"These things I have desired to present thus carefully and accurately. For after my death, many will quote from my books, and attempt to establish errors and fancies of every kind. Among other things, I have written, it is true, that all things are absolute and necessary. But, at the same time, I have added that God is to be considered only as He has been revealed, as we sing in the Psalm:

"Ask ye, Who is this?
Jesus Christ it is,
Of Sabaoth Lord,
And there's none other God,'

"And I have taught thus in many other places. But they will pass by such passages, and will seize hold only of those concerning God as unrevealed (de Deo abscondito). You, then, who are now listening to me, remember that I have taught that we are not to inquire concerning the Predestination of an unrevealed God, but that we are to acquiesce in what is revealed through the call and the ministry of the Word. For there thou canst be certain of thy faith and salvation, and canst say: 'I believe in the Son of God who said, He that believeth in the Son, hath everlasting life (John 3:36). In Him, therefore, there is no condemnation or wrath, but the gracious purpose of God the Father.' This protest I have made elsewhere in my books, and now enter it once more with my living voice. Ideo sum excusatits."

1. Sources And Methods

Definitions

1. What is Dogmatic Theology?

The Science of the Christian Faith.

2. Why is it a Science?

Because the Christian Faith, with all its contents is an object of knowledge. It differs from other departments of knowledge in the nature of the facts, with which it has to deal. In common with every other branch of learning, its facts are capable of classification and systematic presentation. Facts so treated constitute a science.

3. Why is this science called "Dogmatics" or "Dogmatic Theology"?

Because it is the systematic arrangement of definitions of doctrine, known as "Dogmas." It is the science of Dogmas.

4. What is a "dogma"?

Properly a definition of doctrine made by an ecclesiastical organization. In a wider sense, it refers also to statements of principles involved in the consideration of the various articles of the Christian Faith.

Scope

5. Is Dogmatic Theology a purely Biblical science?

No. It deals not only with doctrines taught in Holy Scripture, but also with the forms which such doctrines have assumed in their treatment by the Church. In this it is distinguished from Biblical Theology, which, unlike Dogmatic Theology, is restricted to the contents of Holy Scripture.

6. State this distinction more sharply.

Biblical Theology is the science of the faith taught in Holy Scripture. Dogmatic Theology is the science of the definitions of the scriptural faith, made by the Church, or widely prevalent within the Church.

Elements

7. With what three elements, therefore, has Dogmatic Theology to deal?

[A.] In all Protestant Theology, the material of the dogma comes or professes to come from Holy Scripture.

[B.] The definition of the doctrine has been called forth by certain historical circumstances.

[C.] The definition inevitably is framed in technical terms, determined by current philosophy. Every dogma contains, therefore, a scriptural, an historical, and a philosophical element.

Relations

8. What, therefore, is the order of the chief branches of Theology that are here involved?

Biblical Theology lays the foundation. The History of Dogmas shows the process by which the material has been taken from Scripture, and then, after being discussed on its various sides, has attained a scientific formulation. Dogmatic Theology brings together the results, that are shown to have been attained by the History of Dogmas, and exhibits their scriptural foundations and their relation to each other.

Presuppositions

9. What are the Presuppositions of Dogmatic Theology?

[A.] The existence of God.

Dogmatic Theology no more undertakes to prove this, than Astronomy undertakes to prove the existence of stars, or Logic the reality of thought. The arguments usually considered in Natural Theology, viz., the Ontological, Cosmological, Teleological, and Moral, have their place, as attempts to analyze and express what exists in man's mind prior to all argument and even all thought. But God's existence is not a certainty because of these arguments, any more than a man has self-consciousness solely because of metaphysical processes that seem to him to demonstrate his own existence.

[B.] The ability of man to attain to some degree of knowledge of God.

Limited as the capacity of all finite beings is, man's knowledge is neither uncertain nor indefinite, within the sphere where God has imparted to him the means of knowing.

[C.] The Revelation of God in Christ.

The Christian Faith assumes the historical reality of Jesus Christ, and from this, as a center, derives all knowledge and reaches all conclusions. Dogmatic Theology is, therefore, the scientific statement of the truths taught by Jesus Christ, as received by faith and confessed by believers. It knows no revelation supplementary to that given by Christ, and estimates the value of preparatory revelations, such as in Nature, and in a still higher degree in the Old Testament, only as they are recognized and taught by Christ Himself. (Chapter 13, 5.)

[D.] The Holy Scriptures as the inerrant Record of Revelation.

The New Testament is the inerrant record of the revelation of Christ in word and deed, and of the truths and principles proceeding, under the guidance of the Holy Spirit, from that revelation. The Old Testament is in like manner an inerrant record, having the express and often repeated testimony and authority of Christ, of the preparatory and partial revelations made concerning Him before His coming. Heb. 1:1.

[E.] The Reception of this Revelation, and its confession by a community of believers.

There must be a Church, in order that there may be dogmas. No individual teacher or isolated believer can frame a dogma. It is a statement of Scriptural truth embodied in the public confession of a number of those professing faith in Christ's name. "Dogmatics deals not with the individual faith of the dogmatician, but with the common faith of the Christian Church to which he belongs, and which he confesses as his own by belonging to such communion" (Luthardt).

Process

10. Trace the process whereby the truths recorded in Holy Scripture attain scientific statement.

The Holy Scriptures are more than a textbook of doctrine. Each word of God is a seed of life intended to lodge within men's hearts, and therein to grow. By the presence of the Holy Spirit, a life-principle is conveyed, whereby man is quickened in all his powers and faculties, and all his views of truth and duty are transformed. This new life inevitably expresses itself in confession. Man translates into his own language the thoughts of God, and is ready to give free utterance to the relation of this new life to the world within and around him. As this one life is shared by many whose experience is the same, a common confession results, around which the Christian community, i.e., the Church, centers. This confession may be occasioned by the necessities of the inner life, the attacks or misrepresentations of enemies, or the misunderstandings of other Christians, calling for an accurate and discriminating statement of the faith as it has been received. The formulation of dogmas has been an unavoidable and progressive task of the Church, under the impulse of its divine life, in order to exclude from its teaching various errors. Its aim has been to guard the pure teaching of God's Word, by giving it a sharper expression, so as to leave no room for the protection of errorists beneath statements that are found to be ambiguous. Dogmatic Theology deals, therefore, not with the mere letter of Scripture, but with the truth of Scripture, as it has been assimilated into the life, and as this inner life may be known by its external confession. It is the science of the Christian Faith, whether the term faith be taken objectively (*fides quae creditur*) or subjectively (*fides qua creditur*). See Chapter 17, 4.

Standard

11. Is Christian experience, then, a standard of doctrine?

Never. While an important element in the interpretation of doctrines, in so far as it declares the presence and power of the Holy Spirit in applying God's Word, it must constantly be tested and adjusted by Holy Scripture. The spiritual sense of believing men is not to be depreciated (1 Cor. 2:15, "He that is spiritual judgeth all things"), nevertheless it is always to be recognized by its complete subjection to Holy Scripture (1 John 4:1,2; Gal. 1:8; Acts 17:11). A true and normal faith is one that holds implicitly and exclusively to the revelation of God in Christ contained in the Holy Scriptures. It is a faith that lives in communion with Christ; but Christ in the heart of the believer, and Christ in His Word are always one and the same.

Religion As A Life Proceeding From Faith

12. By what term is that habit, or state of mind and heart known which results from faith?

Religion, or "the communion of man with God."

13. Is there, then, no religion or religious life where there is no faith in Christ?

The term is used in a wider and a narrower sense.

In its wider sense, it refers to all the aspirations of man after God, such as those described by Paul to the Athenians (Acts 17:22), and, thus, is in a measure universal. Man is distinguished from other animals chiefly by the religious faculty, or the sense of dependence of God, however vague, indefinite or corrupt that conception of God may be.

But in a narrower sense, it refers to the realization of these ideas or conceptions, after which man has struggled. In the Old Testament, this realization began with the promises concerning Christ; in the New Testament alone, do they reach their consummation.

In its wider sense, it is applied to all foreshadowings of the communion of man with God; as where the existence of a Supreme Being and man's obligations to serve Him, are acknowledged. In the absolute sense, it is man's cheerful recognition and joyful service of a Supreme Personality, based upon the consciousness of reconciliation and a community of interests with Him.

14. Is "Religion" confined, then, to the designation of an inner spiritual life?

It is popularly used to designate also the various modes or systems which profess to lead man to communion with God. The communion of man with God is Religion subjectively so called. The statement of the principles underlying this communion is Religion objectively so called. In this sense, we speak of the Christian Religion, in which alone, religion in the subjective sense is fully attained; as well as the Jewish Religion, as, prior to Christ, Christianity in the germ, and the Zoroastrian, Confucian, Brahman, Buddhist and Mohammedan religions, which contain a common truth in their recognition in greater or less degree of a Higher Power, and man's helplessness by nature, but which distort and corrupt this truth (Rom. 1:20-23)

Christianity, therefore, is not, properly speaking, merely one religion, and that the best, out of many; that is, a species, coordinate with Zoroastrianism, Confucianism, etc., within the same genus; but the one, absolute and pure religion. The other religions show the various ways in which men seek after God. Christianity alone shows the way in which God is found.

The Christian As Distinguished From Natural Revelation

15. Upon what does this claim of Christianity as the Absolute Religion rest?

Upon the, fact that it is a supernatural divine revelation. The communion of man with God is possible only by God's revelation of Himself to man.

16. But has not God revealed Himself to all men?

Yes, as Creator, Lawgiver and Judge; but not as Redeemer, or loving Father in Heaven. (Ps. 8:1, 3; 19:1; Acts 17:26,27; Rom. 1:20; 2:15.)

This universal revelation is known, as the Natural Revelation of God, or revelation according to the Order of Creation.

17. By what is the imperfection of this Natural Knowledge to be explained?

It has become inadequate because of the enfeeblement and corruption of man's powers by sin (Rom. 7:10-12; Rom. 1:21; 1 Cor. 2:14; Eph. 5:8; Matt. 11:27; John 1:5). It is adapted to a condition of man's nature that no longer exists. The Natural Revelation is like writing that needs the intervention of a lens in order to be legible by one whose sight is failing. Some facts indeed are known, but they are misapprehended and viewed in wrong relations; and the most important are entirely wanting.

18. Of what are the truths contained in the Natural Revelation the foundation?

Of the various natural religions. None of them could have obtained its hold upon men and retained it for ages, if beneath their gross corruptions there had not been elements of truth. But even these few truths are diversely apprehended and constantly modified and misconceived. Thus the first chapter of Romans shows the process of religious deterioration, whereby the conception of God is brought down to the standard of that of corruptible man, and is at last lost in the multiplicity of his manifestations and works, so that "the truth of God is changed into a lie" (Rom. 1:21-25).

19. Is the Natural Revelation then useless?

By no means. It alone keeps man from becoming like the brutes which perish. It constantly reminds him of a higher standard than is attainable under the mere light of Nature. It renders all the prescriptions of merely natural religions unsatisfactory. It cannot answer the inquiries of the heart for certainty, but it impels man ever onward in his search for truth and for God. It prepares the way for the supernatural revelation of God in Christ, by its unwearied assertion of claims which man cannot meet in himself or by the aid of any other religions.

20. Was there no supernatural revelation before Christ?

Supernatural, as distinguished from "Natural Revelation," or "Revelation according to the Order of Redemption," as distinguished from "Revelation according to the Order of Creation," began immediately after man's fall. Before Christ, it consisted of a series of preparatory and partial revelations in word, deed and history. These were fragmentary and largely figurative, as distinguished from the one, full and complete revelation in Jesus Christ. "God who in many parts and in many ways spake of old to the fathers through the prophets, spake, at the extremity of these days unto us through his Son" (Heb. 1:1, 2). The chief distinguishing characteristic of the earlier revelation, therefore, was its "many parts." It could be understood only when taken as a whole, and with the end clearly in view upon which all these parts centered.

Holy Scripture As The Record of Revelation

21. What records were made of these earlier revelations?

The canonical books of the Old Testament are an inerrant record of all these preparatory and partial revelations concerning Christ (John 5:39; Acts 17:11). They are to be constantly read and judged in the light and according to the standard of the New Testament. The New Testament is not to be interpreted by the Old, but the Old is to be interpreted by the New. While historically the New Testament rests upon the foundations of the Old, and the appeal was constantly made to devout Jews in our Lord's time to accept Jesus as the Christ, because of the Old Testament testimony, with Christians the process is reversed, and with the ampler and plainer and complete testimony of Christ, as recorded in the New Testament in their hands, they accept the Old because attested by the New, and explain its types and shadows and promises and isolated statements, entirely with reference to the end towards which by Divine inspiration they were guided, and of which the New Testament clearly teaches.

22. What principle is to be observed in the determination of the meaning of the New Testament?

That of the organic relation of the various parts of Holy Scripture to one another.

23. What does this imply?

Not only that each passage must be interpreted in the light of the context in which it stands, but that the central and fixed point for the treatment of each doctrine is to be found in those parts of Holy Scripture which explicitly and fully discuss it. To such passages, termed by theologians the sedes doctrinae, or seat of the doctrine, all incidental allusions in other texts are to be subordinated.

24. Illustrate this?

In considering the doctrines concerning sin, grace, justification, the Epistle to the Romans is the starting point, with its extended and minute arguments. In the same way, the Relation of Law and Gospel, is to be learned from the Epistle to the Romans, the Relation of the New Testament to the Old from the Epistle to the Hebrews, and the doctrine of the Humiliation and Exaltation of Christ from the Epistle to the Philippians. When the meaning of these passages has been gathered, they form the guide to the interpretation of all other parts of Scripture.

> Obscuriora et pauciora explicanda sunt ex clarioribus ac pluribus.
>
> [Literally: Too obscure, and fewer of them explained one by one of more noble, and the majority of cases.]

25. Upon what is this principle based?

Upon the fact that there is no article of faith, i.e., no doctrine, knowledge of which is necessary for salvation, that is not set forth somewhere in Holy Scripture in clear and express terms, and that such clear and express statements then become the rule and standard according to which those which are less clear are to be decided.

26. What term has been applied to this principle?

The doctrine of the "Analogy of the Faith." It is that of the self-consistency or harmony of Scripture, an inevitable deduction from its inerrancy and inspiration.

27. What further caution is needed in the study of the Holy Scriptures?

As the records of a supernatural revelation, even when their language is clearest, truths and facts are declared beyond man's power to explain.

Relation of Reason to Revelation

28. Are Reason and Revelation, therefore, antagonistic?

Not in reality, for as a standard of truth, Reason has normatively to do only with what pertains to the sphere of the Natural, while Revelation has to do with what pertains to the sphere of the Supernatural. They can be no more really opposed to each other than a truth of Geometry can be opposed to one of Chemistry or Music. Rules deduced, therefore, from the observation of physical phenomena, can never be made the standard according to which to judge supernatural truths.

29. What, then, is the first requisite for apprehending the meaning of Holy Scripture?

Faith, or that state of mind which takes God at His word, even when it cannot explain difficulties inherent in the language of Scripture.

30. Has Reason, therefore, no office with respect to articles of faith?

Yes, when it is kept in subordination to faith. Starting with the assumption, that it cannot explain the mysteries of the supernatural from the standpoint of the natural world, sanctified reason becomes an important instrument for comparing spiritual things with spiritual, and, by the guidance of the Holy Spirit, reaching conclusions. This has been distinguished by theologians as "the instrumental use of Reason," as contrasted with "the normative use" with regard to matters of faith.

31. How, then, is the proper relation between Faith and Reason maintained?

Only by the illuminating presence and activity of the Holy Spirit (1 Cor. 2:14, 15).

32. How is the so-called conflict between Science and Revelation to be explained?

By the unscientific methods of those claiming to be representatives of science. To force the rules pertaining to one branch of knowledge into an entirely diverse department is unscientific. The fallacy has been illustrated by the Stoic philosopher, Epictetus:

> "When you want to write to a friend, Grammar will tell you what words you should write, but whether you should write or not, Grammar will not tell you. Music will inform you concerning sounds, but whether you should sing just now or play on the lute, Music will not tell."

The consequence of this error, is the disregard, to greater or less degree, of faith as a factor in the apprehension of all religious truth.

> "So ignorant, blind and perverted is man's reason or natural understanding, that when even the most able and learned men on earth read or hear the Gospel of the Son of God, and the promise of eternal salvation, they cannot from their own powers, perceive, apprehend, understand or believe and regard it true, but the more diligence and earnestness they employ, in order to comprehend with their reason these spiritual things, the less they understand and believe, and before they become enlightened or taught of the Holy Ghost, they regard all this as only foolishness or fictions" (Formula of Concord, 553:9).

Church Authority and Articles of Faith

33. Has the Church no authority to determine what are Articles of Faith?

The Church is only a witness; never a judge of what is truth. It cannot lay down a single article which Scripture has not previously taught. Neither can it disannul or modify what Scripture has determined.

34. Are the Church's declarations concerning Holy Scripture, the testimony of the Fathers, and the opinions of later theologians to be disregarded?

By no means. Scripture itself exhorts:

> "Despise not prophesyings" (1 Thess. 5:20).

The gifts of God in our fellowmen are bestowed for the edification of the Church, and as such are to be reverently acknowledged and used. Every testimony for the faith is to be prized. Every declaration that is the result of the Holy Spirit's work in applying Holy Scripture to the minds and lives of men, is to be considered.

> "Although faith depends not on human authority, but on the Word of God, nevertheless as Scripture wants the weak to be strengthened by those who are stronger, it is of advantage, in every kind of temptations, to have Church testimonies. For as we desire to consult living men who have had

> experience in spiritual affairs, so also those of old whose writings are approved" (Gerhard).

35. Repeat the confessional statements of the Lutheran Church on the relation of Holy Scripture to these testimonies.

[A.] "We believe, teach and confess:

"That the only rule and standard, according to which at once all dogmas and teachers should be esteemed and judged, are nothing else than the prophetic and apostolic Scriptures of the Old and of the New Testament as it is written.

> Ps. 119:105. 'Thy word is a lamp unto my feet, and a light unto my path': and Gal. 1:8. "Though an angel from heaven preach any other gospel unto you let him be accursed."

"Other writings of ancient or modern teachers, whatever reputation they may have, should not be regarded as of equal authority with the Holy Scriptures, but should altogether be subordinated to them, and should not be received other or further, then as witnesses as to in what manner and at what places, since the time of the apostles, the doctrine of the prophets was preserved."

[B.] "The Holy Scriptures alone:

"...remain the only just rule and standard, according to which as the only touchstone, all dogmas should and must be discerned and judged, as to whether they be good or evil, right or wrong.

"The other symbols and writings are not ... as are the Holy Scriptures, but only a witness and declaration of the faith, as to how at any time the Holy Scriptures have been understood and explained in articles in controversy in the Church of Christ, by those who then lived, and how the opposite dogma was rejected and condemned" Formula of Concord. "Introduction.").

Clearness and Completeness of Scripture

36. But are the Holy Scriptures sufficiently clear and complete to dispense with supplementary revelations and the testimony of tradition as coordinate authorities?

They are called "a lamp and a light." "a light that shineth in a dark place." and men are recalled from all professions of special revelations to their sure test. (Is.

8:20). While there is much in Scripture that is obscure and is intended throughout all ages to exercise the faith of believers, it is sufficiently clear and complete to bring salvation to the humble. "It is able to make wise unto salvation" (2 Tim. 3:15), and makes the man of God "thoroughly furnished unto all good works" (2 Tim. 3:17). It was because of the insecurity of the testimony afforded by tradition that the Holy Scriptures were written (Luke 1:3,4; Phil. 3:1).

Authority of Scripture

37. Is it proper to attach authority to the English, German or Latin Scriptures?

In giving the Holy Scriptures by divine inspiration, God used human language simply as a medium to convey divine thoughts and the statement of divine facts. There was such divine guidance and control of the inspired writers that the result was as perfect a statement of what God meant to communicate as was possible in human words. These words, however, were entirely subordinate to the thought not only of each particular sentence, but of each particular book, and of Scripture as a whole. As the Word of God, however, was for people of all languages, these thoughts are translatable into other tongues. It is the same divine, life-giving truth, whether it be stated in English or German, Greek or Hebrew. As, however, the original writers were inspired, while the translators were not, the translations are subject to constant revision according to the original language and text in which each book was written. As there are no two words of the same language that are precise equivalents, so a word loses some associations and shades of meaning and gains others by translation. Where a controversy or the decision of critical points turns upon a single word or sentence, a reference to the original will be needed in order to fully assure one of its meaning. But as to the general tenor and argument of Holy Scripture, there are very few who do not gain it, and that most properly, entirely from translations. The material remains the same, even though the form is changed.

38. Should we not attach ultimate authority only to the original autographs?

These autographs have probably long since perished. We know of no direct transcript from them. But while the oldest manuscripts of the New Testament show over 150,000 variations in the text, there are very few that make any important change in sense, and of these not one which in any affects or modifies any article of the Christian Faith.

Christian Experience and Scripture

39. Which is the more important aid to the knowledge of Scripture, acquaintance with the original languages, or Christian experience?

Undoubtedly the latter, first in one's own life, and then in the lives of others; but to be a competent and well-furnished teacher of the Christian religion, such as every pastor is called to be, one should have both. No one can understand the Psalms of David unless he has passed through spiritual struggles such as David experienced. No one can appreciate the Epistles of Paul, unless, with Paul, he knows the bitterness of sin, and the need of grace, and, like the Apostle, has failed in his efforts to be justified by the Law. It was the greater depth of Augustine's religious experience that made him the best interpreter of Paul in the Ancient Church, notwithstanding his limited knowledge of the original languages of both Old and New Testament. It was the thought of Holy Scripture as expressed in the Latin translation that guided Luther's religious experience through its critical stages. His knowledge of Greek was very limited until after the Reformation had begun, and he had the assistance of Melanchthon. His knowledge of Hebrew was not independent of specialists, whom he called in as advisers in his translation of the Old Testament. Augustine was a greater theologian than Origen or Jerome; Luther than Reuchlin or Erasmus, or even Melanchthon.

The Three Requisites of a Theologian

40. What rule has Luther formulated on this subject?

Haec tria theologum faciunt: Oratio, Meditatio, Temptatio.

These three things make a theologian: Prayer, Meditation, Trial.

[A.] Prayer refers not simply to an act, but to the spirit or temper in which all study should be begun, continued and ended.

1 Thess. 5:17, "Pray without ceasing."

It implies the constant sense of dependence upon the illuminating agency of the Holy Spirit, and the subjection of intellect and will to that of God. It means the laying aside of all prejudice, party spirit, and arbitrary judgments, the absence of all pride of opinion or learning, and the search for knowledge only to the end that God may thereby be glorified.

[B.] Meditation refers to the contemplative habit with respect to the truths of revelation recorded in Holy Scripture.

This finds its material first of all in the Scriptures themselves. They are to be read reverently, attentively, accurately, constantly, obediently, and with more regard to practical than to theoretical ends. Attention is to be given to their scope and purpose, rather than to their details; to their arguments, than to detached statements. An excessive occupation with details, is as if a surveyor who is commissioned to map out a district of country, forgets himself in the close examination of the leaves of a forest, or of the chemical constituents of the soil, and returns without having accomplished his task. The minutest details are important when judged in their relation to the whole. But the bearing of Scripture as a whole, and of each book, and each section of each book upon the whole must be appreciated, in order that each verse and each word be understood aright. Meditation is occupied not simply with the words and text and arguments of Scripture, but also with the facts and truths comprised in its study as a whole, and in their application in the lives of the Church and of individuals. We are not only to begin with Holy Scripture, and to go forth from this center to the application of its doctrines to human life, but all the occurrences of our daily lives should be interpreted in the light of Scripture. The history of the world is a treasury of material from which ever fresh illustrations of Scriptural doctrines may be drawn. While special hours and seasons are favorable for special exercises of this kind, the meditation here meant is constant. It is not confined to devotional hours, or to any particular efforts, but is inseparable from all mental activity of the true theologian (Ps. 1:2).

[C.] Trial or Practice.

For theology is directed to a practical end. The revelation of God in Christ has been made in order to re-establish the communion of God with man. Only he in whom this end of revelation has been reached, and who realizes it in his own experience, actually knows what it is (John 7:17; Rev. 2:17).

Such trial or practice is continuous and progressive. Man's knowledge of God in Christ is deepened and extended by the fruits of particular words and promises of God in his individual life, and by his close observation of similar results in the lives of others. What is otherwise general, is thus made special and individual. What is otherwise abstract, is thus made concrete. What is otherwise distant is brought home to the heart and deeply impressed there. It is in conflict with the trials and temptations of life, that God's grace is magnified (2 Cor. 12:9).

It is in the school of affliction that the riches of God's revelation are more fully prized.

2. The Being And Attributes Of God

What is implied in Religion

1. What definition of Religion has been already given?

We have said that it is "man's cheerful recognition and joyful service of a Supreme Personality, based on the consciousness of reconciliation and a community of interest with Him" (Chapter 1, Question 13).

2. What kind of relation does this imply?

A personal relation, an attitude or disposition of one person to another. It is not the mere acceptance of a certain number of principles, as when one learns a system of philosophy or commits to memory a list of axioms. Nor is it the experience of a particular class of emotions or delight in peculiar forms of sentiment. Nor is it the recognition of a certain number of rules of conduct, as obligatory. Religion has its intellectual, its emotional, and its ethical sides, because they are all involved in the personal relation, in which the very essence of religion consists.

3. What does a personal relation involve?

A certain identity or likeness between the objects which it comprehends, viz., personality. God is a person. Man is a person. Religion is a relation of man to God.

4. What is meant by "a person"?

Whatever can say "I." It expresses itself in self-consciousness and self-determination, or freedom. (See Chapter 3, 38-40.)

5. What, therefore, is essential to the very conception of religion?

Not merely reliance on some "great unknown," but a vivid conception of man's affinity with God, as the basis of all his relations to Him. As man was created in God's image, it is impossible to think of God except by beginning with what is implied in this image, and rising from this common basis to that in which God must be distinguished from man. As God has theomorphized man, man, within certain limits, cannot do otherwise than anthropomorphize God. Holy Scripture both follows this mode of presentation, and guards against its abuse.

Errors conflicting this conception

6. Against what errors is the conception of God as a personality arrayed?

Against Pantheism which teaches that God is the universal substance, and that man, as well as the universe is only one form of His manifestation, a mere phenomenon of God. Against all systems which would represent God as the mere force or thought of the universe. Against Polytheism which, on the one hand, by multiplying gods, denies a Supreme Being, and, on the other, abuses the anthropomorphic process by investing God with the limitations and infirmities of men, and even of lower creatures (Rom. 1:23). Against Agnosticism which denies the possibility of any knowledge of God, and Atheism which absolutely denies his existence.

Personality and Tri-personality

7. But is not the conception of God as a person in conflict with the Christian doctrine of the Three Persons in one Essence or Being?

No. For Natural Revelation knows nothing of the Son or Holy Spirit, and even the Father it does not know as "father"; but, nevertheless, all the teachings of natural religion point to God as person. Nor does the ampler and purer revelation made of God in Christ in any way disprove this. Religion is the communion of man with God the Father apprehended and reconciled through the Son; with the Son as Redeemer and Revealer of the Father's will; and with the Holy Ghost, as Teacher, Governor and Comforter. What natural religion gropes after as one Person, supernatural revelation declares to be not one Person, but Three Persons in one Being.

8. Can God be defined?

The answer depends upon what is meant by "a definition." If "a definition" be full and complete, it would be equivalent to circumscribing God, which is impossible. In this sense, to define is to trace limits or boundaries, which would conflict with God's infinitude. But if it be the condensation into a few words, of what Holy Scripture declares to be His essential and distinguishing properties or attributes, this can be done.

9. What definitions then can be given?

"God is an infinite spiritual substance." Here "substance" denotes the widest class or genus, while "spiritual" distinguishes this from "material" substances. The word "infinite" indicates the specific difference distinguishing God from other "spiritual substances." Angels are "finite spiritual substances." Nevertheless such definition is inadequate, as there is a form of Pantheism which would accept it. The term "intelligent" if inserted would partially guard against such misconception. So God may be defined as "an absolute substance," distinguishing Him from all substances that are dependent on Him.

Or enumerating the distinguishing qualities, relations and works of God, we have the definition of the Augsburg Confession:

"One divine essence, eternal, without body, without parts, of infinite power, wisdom and goodness; the Maker and Preserver of all things, visible and invisible."

10. Can such definition be further expanded?

Yes, as by Melanchthon, in his Loci Communes, which Chemnitz has admirably analyzed and grouped under four heads:

[A.] A clause referring to essential attributes:

"God is a spiritual essence, intelligent, eternal, true, good, just, holy, chaste, merciful, most free, of immense wisdom and power, different from the bodies of the world, and all creatures."

[B.] A clause referring to the relations or properties and notions of persons:

"One in substance and nevertheless three in persons, the Father Eternal, who, from eternity, has begotten from His own essence, the Son, His image; the Son, the coeternal image of the Father, begotten of the Father from eternity; and the Holy Ghost, proceeding from eternity from Father and Son."

[C.] A clause referring to the will of God, as manifested in a universal action:

"And that this Eternal Father, with His coeternal Son and the Holy Ghost, coeternal with the Father and the Son, has created and preserves heaven and earth, things visible and invisible, and all creatures."

[D.] A clause referring to the will of God, as manifested in a special action, viz., in favors towards the Church:

"And that this eternal, only one and true God, within the human race, which He created according to His image and for certain obedience, has chosen through this Son a Church that it may be holy and blameless before Him, on account of, through and in the Son, whom He has appointed Head of the Church, His body; and that the Son has sent from the Father and Himself, the Holy Ghost, as the Quickener and Sanctifier of the Church."

Such a description of God is a brief summary of all Theology.

Definition of God

11. Is this latter mode of definition widely adopted?

Yes. An example is found in the Westminster Large Catechism:

> "God is a Spirit, in and of Himself infinite in being, glory, blessedness and perfection; all-sufficient, eternal, unchangeable, incomprehensible, every where present, almighty, knowing all things, most wise, most holy, most just, most merciful and gracious, long-suffering, and abundant in goodness and truth."

Name and Names of God

12. Why is "the Name of God" so frequently mentioned in Holy Scripture?

Because no one can apprehend God in His essence or as He is.

> John 1:18. "No one hath seen God at any time."

Ex. 33:20. "There shall no man see me and live."

1 Tim. 6:16. "Dwelling in light, which no man can approach unto; whom no man hath seen, nor can see."

Deut. 4:12. "Ye heard the voice of the words, but saw no similitude; only ye heard a voice."

13. What then is the Name of God?

All that God wants us to know concerning Himself in this life. It is the sum and substance of God's revelation to man of what God is.

14. Explain Scripture passages in which the term occurs.

When the Psalmist sings (Ps. 8:1), "How excellent is thy name in all the earth," he celebrates the glory of the revelation of Himself which God has made. When he declares, "They that know thy name, shall put their trust in thee," he means, "they who have learned to know Thee as Thou hast condescended to reveal Thyself." "To remember and to praise God's Name" is to take to heart and proclaim what God has made known. The Name of God is hallowed "when the Word of God is taught in its truth and purity, and we, as children of God, lead holy lives, in accordance with it."

15. Distinguish between "the Name" and "the Names" of God?

"The Name" stands for God's entire revelation up to the time in which the word is used. "The Names" are particular designations, expressing either His being, or some prominent attribute, relation or work of God.

16. How are they classified?

[A.] Essential
Such as Jehovah, Jah, Adonai, Elohim, El, in the Old, and Theos in the New Testament. Their etymology is obscure, although often stated with a great degree of confidence. Jehovah, the incommunicable name of the Old Testament, is widely, although not with certainty, ascribed to the Hebrew verb meaning "to be," and interpreted according to Ex. 3:14, as "he who is what he is," implying the

independence, freedom, immutability, eternity and faithfulness of God, as contrasted with the dependence and mutability of creatures.

[B.] Attributive

As when God is designated by one of His attributes, as "The Almighty" (particularly frequent in Job).

[C.] Relative

Expressing certain relations, as "King of kings," "Lord of lords," the Creator," "Preserver," "the Searcher of hearts," etc.

Attributes of God

Definition

17. What are the attributes of God?

The various forms or modes in which the divine essence is expressed, or the various ways in which the one and simple divine Being has revealed Himself as subsisting.

18. Are they then accidental?

There are no accidents in God.

19. Are they factors into which the essence of God has been resolved?

This would conflict with the simplicity or impartibility of God.

20. What then are they?

Qualities inseparable from God's being.

How idea gained

21. By what threefold method is the idea of the Divine Attributes gained?

By Causality, Eminence and Negation.

22. State this more fully.

[A.] By way of causality

We reason from the effect to its source. All the perfections required for what He has done and is doing are ascribed to God.

[B.] By way of eminence

We ascribe to God in the highest degree all the perfections we see in creatures.

[C.] By way of negation

We deny to God the limitations and defects inherent in creatures.

Classification

23. How may the Divine Attributes be classified?

Into Absolute or Immanent, and Relative or Transient.

24. Define them.

Absolute or Immanent Attributes pertain to God as He is in Himself. They cannot in any form or measure, be ascribed to creatures, and, therefore, are absolutely incommunicable.

Relative attributes imply a relation of God to a created world. They are by analogy communicable, because they have their counterpart in creatures.

The former are sometimes called Negative, because they deny the imperfections found in creatures, and the latter Positive, because they affirm the existence in the highest degree of the excellent qualities found in creatures in a lower degree.

Absolute Attributes — Independence, Simplicity, Infinity, Immortality

25. Enumerate the Absolute Attributes.

Independence, Simplicity, Infinity and Immutability.

26. What is meant by Independence?

That God depends upon no cause outside of Himself, but that He is of Himself, and all-sufficient. This attribute is sometimes called "Aseity" (from Latin, a from, and se, himself).

Is. 43:10, 11. "I am he. Before me, there was no God formed, neither shall there be after me. I, even I, am Jehovah."

Ex. 3:14. "And God said unto Moses: I am that I am." Marginal Reading: "I am, because I am."

27. What is meant by Simplicity?

That God is without all composition, and cannot be resolved into parts. Whatever is in God, is God. There are no accidents. Neither can the attributes be regarded as other than the Essence of God, but only as the one essence variously expressed, or regarded. To regard the essence of God as the sum of the attributes, or to resolve the essence into the various attributes, would conflict with the simplicity of God. Simplicity includes spirituality (John 4:24) invisibility and incomprehensibility; since to see and comprehend an object, in this life, we must be able to consider it in its elements, part by part.

28. What is meant by Infinity?

That all of God's perfections are without end or limit.

Ps. 145:3. "His greatness is unsearchable."

Job 11:7, 8. "Canst thou by searching find out God? Canst thou find out the Almighty unto perfection? It is as high as heaven, what canst thou do? Deeper than Sheol, what canst thou know?"

Infinity is not so much a separate attribute, as a characteristic of all the divine attributes.

29. What is Infinity, when regarded with respect to temporal relations?

Eternity, i.e., God's absolute transcendence of time.

Ps. 90:1, 2. "Even from everlasting to everlasting thou art God."

1 Tim. 1:17. "Now unto the king, eternal, immortal, invisible, the only God, be honor and glory, forever and ever. Amen."

30. What is implied by Eternity?

Not only that God is without beginning and end, but also without succession, or differences of time. The attribute of simplicity shows that nothing of God's life passes away with time, but that, at every moment, He possesses whatever we have throughout our lives successively. What we have in parts, God has as a whole. To Him, past, present and future are one Now. Nothing can be past or future in One, whose life continues the same and unchanged. Possessio vitae tota simul.

31. What is Infinity, when regarded with respect to spatial relations?

Immensity, i.e., God's absolute transcendence of space. He can be neither measured nor enclosed by it.

> Jer. 23:24. "Do not I fill heaven and earth? saith Jehovah."
>
> 1 Kings 8:27. "Behold heaven and the heaven of heavens cannot contain thee."

32. What is the positive side of Immensity?

Omnipresence.

33. In how many ways is God omnipresent?

In three:
[A.] By His power.

> Acts 17:28. "In him we live and move and have our being."

[B.] By His knowledge.

> Heb. 4:13. "All things are naked and laid open before the eyes of him with whom we have to do."

[C.] By His essence.
Ps. 139:7-10. "Whither shall I flee from thy presence? If I ascend up into heaven thou art there: if I make my bed in Sheol, behold thou art there; if I take the wings of the morning, and dwell in the uttermost parts of the sea, even there shall thy hand lead me, and thy right hand shall hold me."

34. Which of these is Omnipresence in the proper sense?

Only the last. God's presence is more than that of the sun, which penetrates all things with its rays, while it is far remote, or that of one whose influence works long after he has died.

35. But is not God described in Holy Scripture as coming and going?

This does not imply any real absence of His essence, but refers only to different modes of presence. God is said to be present in a peculiar way, when He manifests His presence by certain works, especially when He confers and increases spiritual gifts, or otherwise makes known His providential care of the regenerate; or when by signal judgments He declares His wrath against the ungodly.

> Ex. 20:24. "In every place, where I record my name, I will come unto thee, and I will bless thee."
>
> John 14:23. "If a man love me, he will keep my word; and my Father will love him, and we will come unto him, and make our abode with him."
>
> Is. 66:15. "For behold Jehovah will come with fire, and his chariots shall be like the whirlwind, to render his anger with fierceness, and his rebuke with flames of fire."

The omnipresence of God considered relatively or with respect to creatures, is God's efficacious energy exercised in connection with His immensity. This energy admits of different degrees. But the relation of the substance of God to the substance of the creature is not nearer at one time, and more remote at another.

36. How is this distinction designated?

We distinguish between the essential and the operative omnipresence. Abelard, the Socinians and Deists have denied the former, and taught that God is in heaven as to His essence, and is on earth only potentially.

37. But does not the omnipresence of God conflict with His simplicity?

By no means. He is not present by extension or expansion, as a cloud may cover a valley or a province, with part shadowing part; but all God is everywhere. Nothing can be so small within which God is not; nothing so vast that He does not circumscribe.

38. What different modes of presence are there?

Firstly, that of a body in space, where each atom of the object corresponds to a point within a conceived area. This is known as Circumscriptive or Local Presence.

Secondly, that of a finite spirit, within space. As spirit or soul is simple, and not resolvable into parts, its presence at a place is not to be estimated according to spatial relations. This is known as Definitive Presence.

Thirdly, that of God, or the Infinite Spirit, like finite spirit in simplicity, but unlike all other spirit, in transcending every limitation. This is known as Repletive Presence. The omnipresence of God is repletive. "Totus in rebus omnibus, totus in singulis, totus in se."

39. What is the Immutability of God?

That attribute according to which He is subject to no change or variation, whether of essence, or of accident, of attribute or of purpose. There is no conversion into another essence, no passion or corruption, no decrease or increase, no alteration or local mutation.

> Rom. 1:23. "The glory of the incorruptible God."
>
> 1 Tim. 1:17. "The King eternal, immortal, invisible."
>
> James 1:17. "The Father of lights, with whom can be no variation, nor shadow that is cast by turning."
>
> Num. 23:19. "God is not a man that he should lie, neither the son of man that he should repent: Hath he said and will he not do it? Hath he spoken, and will he not make it good?"
>
> Mal. 3:6. "I, Jehovah, change not."
>
> Ps. 102:26, 27. "They shall perish, but thou shalt endure. Yea, all of them shall wax old like a garment; as a vesture shalt thou change them, and they shall be changed; but thou art the same."

40. But did not Creation imply or produce a change in God?

No. For from all eternity, it was His will to create the world. There was no change in God. The change was in the creature. What before was not then came into being.

41. Did not Incarnation imply or produce a change?

In like manner, this was what God had willed from all eternity. The Word became flesh, not by the change of divinity into humanity, but by the assumption of flesh by the person of the Word.

42. Is not God sometimes described as repenting?

This expression is used to declare not a change in God, but in a relation caused by a change in man. When a ship changes its course, the needle of its compass continues to point north, but, in order to do so, it necessarily assumes a different angle when regarded from the line of the ship's motion. The change is not in God's purpose, but in the event; not in His will, but in the object willed; not in God's disposition, but in the external work and result, where He has left a certain amount of free agency to man, or to other second causes. These second causes remaining unchanged, God is unchanged. The second causes varying, God's immutability requires what may seem to be externally, but in reality is not, a change.

43. How about unfulfilled promises and conditions?

They are not absolute, but adjusted to conditions which man has not met.

> Jer. 18:7-10. "At what instant I shall speak concerning a nation and concerning a kingdom, to pluck up and to break down and to destroy it; if that nation concerning which I have spoken, turn from their evil, I will repent of the evil that I thought to do unto them. And at what instant I, shall speak concerning a nation and concerning a kingdom, to build up and to plant it; if they do that which is evil in my sight, that they obey not my voice, then I will repent of the good, wherewith I said that I would benefit them."

44. What distinction must be observed touching all such conditions?

That it is one thing for God to change His will, and quite another for Him to will the change of anything. When He willed to change the Old Covenant for the New, and to abrogate Levitical rites and ceremonies, it was a change which He had determined and decreed from eternity, and instead of being a change of will, was the execution of that will and purpose.

Relative Attributes — Perfections of Life

45. What are the Relative Attributes?

Perfections of Life, Intellect and Will, in God existing in an infinite, and communicable to creatures in finite measure.

46. What is the Life of God?

The inner energy of His being, ever active within God, and imparting movement and efficacy to created things. Life as an inner principle is declared by

> John 5:26. "As the Father hath life in himself, even so gave he to the. Son also to have life in himself."
>
> Jer. 10:10. "He is the living God, and an everlasting king." 1 Tim. 6:16. "Who only hath immortality." Ps. 42:2; 84:2. "For the living God."

Life as imparted to others:

> Acts 14:15-17. "That ye should turn from these vain things unto a living God, who made the heaven and the earth and the sea and all that in them is" (i. e., Life in Nature), "who in the generations gone by suffered all the nations to walk in their own ways" (i. e., Life in History), "and yet he left not himself without witness in that he did good, and gave you from heaven rains and fruitful seasons, filling your hearts with food and gladness" (Life in Providence).
>
> Acts 17:28. "In him, we live and move and have our being."

Of Intellect (Omniscience, Wisdom)

47. What Attributes are ascribed to the Divine Intellect?

Knowledge and Wisdom. Since they are infinite the former is generally known as Omniscience, while the latter is expressed in the term "the All-wise God."

48. What is Omniscience?

That, by which God by a simple act knows Himself, and all things outside of Himself, whether present, past, future or possible.

> Matt. 11:21. "If the mighty works had been done in Tyre and Sidon which were done in you, they would have repented long ago in sackcloth and ashes." Cf. 1 Sam. 23:12.
>
> Ps. 139:1, 2, 3. "Thou hast searched me and known me. Thou knowest my downsitting and my uprising, Thou understandest my thought afar off. Thou searchest out my path and my lying down, and art acquainted with all my ways."
>
> Ps. 15:3. "The eyes of Jehovah are in every place, keeping watch upon the evil and the good."

49. What is meant by "a simple act"?

As there is no succession of thought or act in God, His knowledge is not derived by any process of reasoning, or discursive methods, as from effects to causes, or from particulars to generals. All the attributes of His being belong to His Omniscience. "It is an absolute, simple, eternal, infinite, simultaneous, unchangeable and perfect intuition" (Heppe).

> Is. 40:13. "Who hath directed the spirit of Jehovah, or being his counsellor, hath taught him." Cf. Rom. 11:34.

50. What difference is there between God's knowledge of Himself and His knowledge of all beyond and besides?

The former is natural and necessary, and could not have been otherwise; the latter is free, and dependent upon the determination of His will either causatively or permissively.

51. Where is God's knowledge of future contingencies which never occurred declared?

> John 3:20. "God is greater than our heart and knoweth all things."

52. What is the Wisdom of God?

His most exquisite skill in so adjusting causes to effects, and means to ends that the purposes of His good and gracious will are never thwarted.

> Rom. 11:33. "O the depth of the riches both of the wisdom and the knowledge of God! how unsearchable are his judgments and his ways past tracing out!"

> Job 12:13. "With God is wisdom and might; he hath counsel and understanding."

> Rom. 16:27. "To the only wise God, through Jesus Christ, to whom be the glory forever."

Of Will — What is God's Will, how determined, how characterized, distinguished into Natural and Free, Efficacious and Inefficacious, of Sign and of Purpose, Revealed and Secret, Absolute and Conditioned, Absolute and Ordinate, Antecedent and Consequent

53. Before enumerating the Attributes or Perfections of the Divine Will, state whether there be a difference between the Divine Essence and the Divine Will.

The Divine Will is the Divine Essence directed towards the Good, and against the Evil, known by the Divine Intellect.

54. Is the Divine Will determined by any process or succession of thought?

As the Divine Intellect by one, simple act knows all things (see above Question 49) so by one volition God from eternity wills all that He wills. Distinctions are made in accommodation to our comprehension, which do not exist in the will itself.

55. By what is the Divine Will characterized?

By the attributes pertaining to the Divine Essence, of which the Absolute Attributes above enumerated (Quest. 25 sqq.) are particularly to be regarded. It is independent, because God is independent; simple, because God is simple; eternal, because God is eternal; immutable, because God is immutable.

56. What distinctions, however, have been made?

Distinctions founded on the diverse classes of objects comprehended in God's will, or which express the diverse modes with which He wills them. They are:

[A.] Into Natural and Free.

The Natural Will is the expression of His Nature. He necessarily wills what is described by His attributes. The Free is that by which He wills what He might have willed otherwise, as the creation of the world, the incarnation, the redemption of the human race, the call of Paul as an apostle.

[B.] Into Efficacious and Inefficacious.

This is an Augustinian distinction, which must be most carefully guarded. The Efficacious Will is one that is inevitably fulfilled, as the will to reward the godly, and punish the wicked, the will of Christ to give Himself for lost men (John 10:18), and to rescue some souls from ruin. The Inefficacious, is one which is not fulfilled, since it has regard to conditions with which man does not comply, Thus it is the will of God that all should be saved (I Tim. 2:4). But it is not God's will that any man should be saved against his own will, or that the freedom of man's will to resist God's gracious will concerning Himself should be destroyed. There are barriers which even God does not will to overcome. Nevertheless when men perish, it is not because of lack of efficacy in the Divine Will, but because they do not appropriate the divine efficacy exerted upon them.

[C.] Into Will of the Sign and Will of the Purpose.

The former is in reality the expression or declaration of the Will; the latter is the Will in the proper sense. The former is God's Will as declared through outward signs; the latter, the Will, as it exists in God. The former, Luther, in his commentary on Genesis, refers to the Revealed Word of God; the latter, to God's pure Majesty, or hidden counsel. Examples of "will of the sign" are Matt. 6:10, 'Thy will be done, as in heaven, so on earth," where "will" means, "Whatever Thou commandest, or declarest that Thou wishest to be done," and 1 Thess. 4:13, "This is the will of God, even your sanctification," i.e., "This is the commandment or sign of the divine will, viz., your sanctification, that you abstain from fornication." In general it may be said, that "the will of the sign" is that by which God indicates to men what He wants them to do; and "the will of the purpose," that by which He has determined or decreed what He wants man to do, or what He wants to be done to men. Thus by the will of the sign, God wanted Abraham to make all preparations for slaying Isaac, while by the will of His purpose, He determined to preserve his life. The will of the sign has been distributed by the Scholastics into five spheres or modes: "With respect to evil: Prohibition and permission. With respect to good: Precept, advice and operation." God declares, they say, that He wills something either by Himself or through others. If by Himself, directly, it is when He effects something; this is called "operation." If by Himself, indirectly, it is when He does not hinder or prevent an operation; this is called "permission." But if God declares He wants something done by another, this occurs either by directly commanding what He wants done and prohibiting the contrary, or by a persuasive induction, viz., advice or counsel. Accurately speaking, however, "the will of the sign," is nothing more than "the sign of the will." For whatever God commands, prohibits, promises, threatens or does, is a sign of His will, although not of His entire purpose. The sign reveals what is nearest us, but not the remoter springs whence it flows. The will of the sign proceeds from the will of the purpose. The two can never be opposed to each other. The "will of the purpose" passes ultimately into "the will of the sign," when faith is replaced by knowledge, and what is obscure at one stage of revelation becomes clear at another (Eph. 3:5; 4:13; 1 Cor. 13:12; John 13:7).

[D.] Into Revealed and Secret.

This is only a better statement of the distinction which has just been explained. For the secret will:

> Rom. 11:33, "O the depth of the riches both of the wisdom and of the knowledge of God, how unsearchable are his judgments and his ways past tracing out."

For the revealed will:

> John 6:40, 'This is the will of my Father that every one that beholdeth the Son and believeth on him should have eternal life."

For both:

> Deut. 29:29, "The secret things belong unto Jehovah, our God, but the things that are revealed belong unto us and to our children forever."

[E.] Into Absolute and Conditioned.

The former is without; and the latter, with conditions. It was by His Absolute Will, that God determined to create the world; for He willed this without condition. It is also by His Absolute Will, that they whom He foresees as believing on Him until the end, shall be saved; for this also is without condition (Chapter 9, 15). But it is by His Conditioned Will, that He wills the salvation of all men; for the condition is faith (Chapters 9, 16; 41. 15, 16).

[F.] Into Absolute and Ordinate.

The former is without, and the latter with regard to second causes. The Ordinate, while at first sight, equivalent to the conditioned, is found, on reflection, to differ. God wills that man's physical life be nourished by food and drink, and that his spiritual life be quickened and sustained by the Means of Grace. In both cases there is an order of agencies through which God works. It is the conditioned will of God that men be saved if they believe; it is His ordinate will that they believe, viz., that from the Means of Grace rightly used, they obtain faith. God's will to create the world by His word was ordinate, but not conditioned. So also His will to raise the dead at the last day by the voice of the Archangel, is also ordinate. The meaning of "Absolute" must, therefore, be decided by determining whether it be the antithesis of "conditioned" or of "ordinate" (Chapter 41:15).

[G.] Antecedent and Consequent.

The former refers to a disposition of God determined without regard to any circumstances; the latter to one in which circumstances or conditions on the part of the creature, are regarded.

> Matt. 23:37. "O Jerusalem, Jerusalem, that killeth the prophets, and stoneth them that are sent unto her! how often would I have gathered thy children together, even as a hen gathereth her chickens under her wings, and ye would not."

Here man's will is represented as frustrating the will of God. By His Antecedent Will, God would save Jerusalem. But a condition intervenes and an order must be observed. Man retains the power to resist God's will, and not comply with the condition, and fall in with the order which God's will has arranged. Hence it is God's will both that Jerusalem should be saved, and that it should not be saved. According to His Antecedent Will, that it should be saved. According to His Consequent, that it should not be saved, but be left to its sins.

57. We are now ready to hear an enumeration of the Attributes of the Divine Will?

Power, Justice and Truth, Goodness and Love, and Holiness.

Omnipotence

58. What is God's Power?

He is Omnipotent, that is, He can do whatever He wills.

> Matt. 19:26. "With God, all things are possible."
>
> Luke 18:27. "The things which are impossible with men are possible with God."
>
> Ps. 115:3. "Our God is in the heavens; he hath done whatsoever he pleased."
>
> Ps. 135:6. "Whatsoever Jehovah pleased that hath he done."

59. Can God do what is wrong?

> Heb. 6:18. "It is impossible for God to lie."

60. Is not His power, therefore, limited?

No. For God does not will, and cannot will what is contrary to His nature, or what would imply any imperfection. Mortality or liability to death, fallibility or liability to deception, mendacity or the power of deceiving and defrauding men, instead of implying power imply the lack of power. Every attribute ascribed to God, is a declaration that its opposite cannot be conceived of as possible.

> 2 Tim. 2:13. "He cannot deny himself."

61. Against what further misunderstanding is God's Omnipotence to be guarded?

Against every form of contradiction, e. g., as if it could be His will to make the deeds of the past matters that had never existed. Nevertheless what may seem contradictory and may actually be such within the sphere of the natural world, often is not such within the sphere of the supernatural.

> Eph. 3:20. "Unto him that is able to do exceeding abundantly above all that we can ask or think."

Justice

62. What is the Justice of God?

That according to which God wills, approves, does and commands what is prescribed in His Law, and hates and punishes whatever conflicts with it.

> Deut. 32:4. "A God of faithfulness and without iniquity, just and right is he."

> Ps. 145:17. "Jehovah is righteous in all his ways."

> Ps. 119:137. "Righteous art thou, O Jehovah, and upright are thy judgments."

63. But does not this elevate the Law above God Himself?

No. For the Law is only the expression of God's nature. As declared to men in time, it is only the revelation of the immanent law, or standard, existing within God from all eternity.

64. Is a thing then good because God has willed it, or has God willed it because it is good?

This question may be otherwise stated as asking whether the will of God, or His essence and attributes are the standard of right and wrong.

For man it is enough to know that God has so willed a thing. For since there is complete harmony between the will and the attributes of God, whichever be regarded as the original, the result must be the same.

65. But the question still arises: Is a thing good for no other reason than that it has been willed and commanded by God? Are Truth and Love, for example, virtues only because of God's command?

Some things are good entirely because of God's will and command, as the rites and ordinances of the Ceremonial Law, which had only temporary validity, and whose observance was condemned after the period had transpired for which they were appointed (Gal. 5:2).

66. But how in regard to matters of permanent and immutable morality, such as are declared in the Moral Law?

They are rooted in God's own nature. Their ultimate standard, therefore, is not the will, but the very nature of God Himself. The highest grade of righteousness in man is the image of God, in which man was created.

> Eph. 4:24. "The new man that after God hath been created in righteousness and holiness of truth.

While therefore the observance of ceremonies and all positive commands are good and right only because God has willed them, other things God wills because they are right and good, as love to God and one's neighbor. Even though God had not prescribed them in any express commandment, they would not cease to be right and obligatory upon us.

67. In what different ways is the Divine Justice exercised towards men?

Either in prescribing or in executing laws. Laws are prescribed (Legislative Justice) both in conscience and in Scripture. They are executed (Distributive Justice) either by rewarding the good (Remunerative Justice) or by punishing the wicked (Retributive Justice).

68. Is God's Retributive Justice essential or accidental?

It belongs to God's very nature to hate and punish sin. No sin can permanently escape punishment, just as no good can fail of reward.

Ex. 34:6, 7. "A God that will by no means clear the guilty."

Ps. 5:5. "Thou art not a God that hath pleasure in wickedness; evil shall not sojourn with thee."

Ex. 23:7. "I will not justify the wicked."

Hab. 1:13. "Thou art of purer eyes than to behold evil."

Cf. 1 Tim. 5:24, 25.

Truth

69. What attribute is most closely connected with Justice?

Truth. For the Justice of God is God's being true to His nature. The truth of God is the conformity of His statements with reality, and His fidelity in fulfilling promises and threatenings.

See Deut. 32:4 (Quest. 62); Heb. 6:18 (Quest. 59).

Goodness

70. What is the Goodness of God?

[A.] On the one hand, His being absolutely perfect.

Luke 18:19. "None is good, save one, that is God."

Mark 5:48. "Your Heavenly Father is perfect."

[B.] His will to impart this perfection to others, the self-communication of all his moral excellences to creatures.

James 1:17. "Every good gift and every perfect gift is from above, coming down from the Father of lights."

1 Cor. 4:7. "What hadst thou, which thou didst not receive?"

Rom. 2:4. "Or despisest thou the riches of his goodness and forbearance and longsuffering, not knowing that the goodness of God leadeth thee to repentance?"

[C.] His attraction of men to Himself as to the Highest Good.

> Ps. 73:25, 26. "Whom have I in heaven but thee? And there is none upon earth that I desire besides thee. My flesh and my heart faileth; but God is the strength of my heart and my portion forever."

Love: (a) Benevolence, (b) Beneficence, (c) Complacency

71. What does the Goodness of God include?

His Love, i.e., His delight in His creatures, and His craving for their welfare, a reflection of a similar but higher relation between the Persons of the Trinity.

> 1 John 4:8. "God is love."

> 1 John 3:16. "Hereby know we love, because he laid down his life for us."

> John 17:24. "Thou lovedst me before the foundations of the world."

72. What different forms are there of this love?

[A.] Love of benevolence

God's disposition from eternity towards a creature, prior to any good that can move this love (John 3:16).

[B.] Love of beneficence

By which He carries this love of benevolence into effect, in working His good will for and in it (Eph. 5:25).

[C.] Love of complacency

By which He delights in the fruits of the love of beneficence as they are seen by Him in regenerate men.

> Heb. 11:5. "For he hath had witness borne to him that before his translation he had been well-pleasing unto God."

Grace

73. What is the first form in which this love is known?

Grace, i.e., God's love regarded as gratuitous; His favor shown without regard to man's merit, and in spite of man's demerit. Rom. 11:6. "But if it be by grace, it is no more of works; otherwise grace is no more grace."

> Rom. 3:24. "Being justified freely by his grace through the redemption that is in Christ Jesus." (Chapter 9:9 sqq.)

74. Is the word used in Holy Scripture in any other sense?

Yes, by customary figure of speech, for gifts bestowed by this grace. Of these, some are ordinary, as in I Cor. 15:10:

"I labored more abundantly than they all; yet not 1, but the grace of God which was with me."

Others are extraordinary and miraculous.

> Eph. 4:7. "But to each one of us was the grace given, according to the measure of the gift of Christ." 1 Cor. 12:4, 7, 8.

75. What distinction in grace was made by the Scholastics?

Into Grace gratuitously given (Gratia gratis data) and Grace making grateful or acceptable (Gratia gratum faciens). By the use of the former, man, it was taught, could gain relative merit, entitling him to the latter. As we shall see afterwhile, nothing recommends man to the consideration of God but the righteousness of Christ. The grace gratuitously given, and the grace making acceptable, cannot, therefore, be distinguished.

76. What distinction with a better Scriptural foundation was also current?

Into Prevenient, Operating and Co-operating Grace. "Prevenient" grace precedes man's desire or care for salvation; "Operating" grace works within man Repentance and Faith";"Co-operating," attends the exercise, by the regenerate, of the new powers which operating grace has implanted. It is readily seen that the distinctions are not of the grace itself but of man's various relations to this grace, and of the process whereby the Christian life within man begins and grows to perfection.

Mercy

77. In what other form is this Love known?

As Mercy, or God's disposition to relieve the miserable, the divine compassion.

> Luke 1:78. "The tender mercy of our God, whereby the Dayspring from on high hath visited us."
>
> Eph. 2:4. "God being rich in mercy, for his great love wherewith he loved us."
>
> Ps. 103:8. "Merciful and gracious, slow to anger and abundant in loving kindness."

Longsuffering

78. Is there yet another form?

Yes. God is long-suffering. By this, it is meant that He defers inflicting merited punishment, in order to afford an opportunity for repentance.

> Rom. 2:4. "Despiseth thou the riches of his goodness and forbearance and longsuffering, not knowing that the goodness of God leadeth thee to repentance?"
>
> 2 Pet. 3:9. "The Lord is long-suffering to you-ward, not wishing that any should perish, but that all should come to repentance."
>
> Rev. 2:21. "I gave her time, that she should repent."

Holiness

79. What is the Holiness of God?

That which separates and distinguishes Him from all that is not God; the conformity of His will with His nature; the sum of His moral attributes.

> Is. 6:3. "And one cried to another and said: Holy, holy, holy, is Jehovah of hosts." 1 Pet. 1:16. "It is written, Ye shall be holy: for I am holy."

3. The Trinity

Peculiar to New Testament

1. What knowledge of God is peculiar to Christianity?

That there is but one God; and yet that this one God is Father, Son and Holy Ghost.

2. Is not this doctrine taught by Natural Revelation?

It is neither taught by Natural Revelation, nor can it be demonstrated from that source, even when the fact has been made known from Holy Scripture. It is a "pure," not a "mixed" doctrine.

3. Do not some non-Christian religions teach a triad or threeness in God?

Yes, as particularly, Hinduism and the religion of the Ancient Egyptians; but such doctrine is entirely different from that of the Trinity, and not exclusive of Pantheism and Polytheism.

Suggested in Old Testament

4. Is it not taught in the Old Testament?

It is suggested there, but not expressly taught. When the doctrine has been learned from the New Testament, it can be faintly traced in the Old.

Terminology

5. Who is first known to have used the term "Trinity"?

Tertullian in "De Pudicitia," Chapter 21.

6. But why should non-Scriptural terms be employed?

In order to express in one word what Holy Scripture teaches in many words and in numerous passages.

Not purely Speculative

7. Is not the doctrine one of purely theoretical or speculative interest?

By no means. It is intensely practical. The burning point of all controversies concerning it has reference to the nature of Jesus Christ, and involves the truth of His declarations as the Revealer of the Father, and the efficacy of His work as the Redeemer of the human race.

Three Fundamental Propositions

8. Upon what three propositions does the doctrine of the Trinity rest?

Upon the following:

I. There is but one God. II. There are three who are declared to be God. III. The distinction between the three is not one of manifestation only, but is real and personal.

I. The Unity of God

9. What is meant when "unity" is ascribed to an object of thought?

Either that such object is undivided within itself (affirmatively) or that there is no other such object (exclusively).

10. Apply this to God.

He is one and but one, that is, He is the only God (Deus est unus et unicus).

11. Give Scripture proofs.

1 Tim. 2:5. "There is one God."

Gal. 3:20. "God is one."

Deut. 6:4. "Hear, Israel, Jehovah, our God, is one Jehovah."

Ex. 20:3. "Thou shalt have no other gods before me."

Is. 43:10, 11. "Before me, there was no God formed, neither shall be after me. I, even I, am Jehovah; and besides me, there is no Savior."

12. Is not unity implied in the very conception of God?

There cannot be more than one Supreme Being. For this reason, wherever among the heathen a plurality of gods in taught, the mind inevitably turns to one as supreme, and regards the rest as subordinate.

13. But is not this unity contradicted when we say that there are three who are God?

There would be a contradiction, if we were to teach that they are three in the same sense that they are one. If there are three who are God, and there be but one God, then the reference is to three distinctions within the one God. There cannot be three Gods.

II. The Threeness of God. (a) Divinity of Each Person proved from his having the Names, Attributes, Works and Worship of God; Coordination of the Three in same passage

14. What grounds are there for holding that there are three who are God?

The first ground is that Father and Son and Holy Ghost can each separately be proved to be God.

15. How?

Because to each separately are ascribed: (a) Divine Names; (b) Divine Attributes; (c) Divine Works; (d) Divine Worship.

16. Apply this fourfold argument to the Father.

The argument concerning the Father is so overwhelming that it has no opponents among those believing in the existence of God. The controversy is with those who deny that the argument belongs to the Son and the Holy Ghost. Nevertheless, to make the process complete, it is herewith recapitulated: To the Father are ascribed Divine Names:

[A.] Names:

> 1 Cor. 8:6. "To us there is one God the Father, of whom are all things, and we unto him: and one Lord Jesus Christ, through whom are all things, and we through him."

> 2 Cor. 1:3. "Blessed be the God and Father of our Lord Jesus Christ."

> Gal. 1:3. "Grace and peace from God the Father and our Lord Jesus Christ."

[B.] Attributes:
Omnipotence.

> Matt. 11:25. "I thank thee, O Father, Lord of heaven and earth."

> Mark 14:34. "Abba Father, all things are possible with thee."

Eternity.

Is. 9:6. "The Mighty God, the Everlasting Father."

Holiness.

John 17:11. "Holy Father, keep through thine own those whom thou hast given me."

Goodness.

Titus 3:5. "But when the kindness of God our Savior and his love appeared."

Mercy.

1 Peter 1:3. "Blessed be the God and Father of our Lord Jesus Christ, who, according to his great mercy, begat us unto a lively hope by the resurrection of Jesus Christ from the dead."

Glory.

John 17:3. "The glory which I had with thee before the world was."

[C.] Works:

Here it is sufficient to refer to those mentioned in 1 Peter 1:3 above cited, viz: Regeneration and Resurrection from the dead, and in 1 Cor. 8:6, viz: Creation and Providence.

[D.] Worship:

John 4:23. "The hour cometh and now is, when the true worshippers shall worship the Father in spirit and truth; for such doth the Father seek to be his worshippers."

Phil. 2:11. "That every tongue shall confess that Jesus is Lord to the glory of God the Father."

John 16:23. "Whatsoever ye shall ask the Father in my name."

Rev. 1:6. "Priests unto his God and Father."

17. Applying this same argument to the Son, give, first, passages in which the names of God are ascribed to the Son?

John 1:1. "And the Word was God." Cf. V. 14.

Rom. 9:5. "Christ who is over all God blessed forever."

Heb. 1:8. "Of the Son he saith: Thy throne, O God, is forever and ever."

John 20:28. "Thomas answered and said unto him: My Lord and my God."

1 John 5:20. "His Son Jesus Christ. This is the true God and eternal life."

Titus 2:13. "The appearing of the glory of the great God and our Savior Jesus Christ," or as in the margin, "of our great God and Savior Jesus Christ."

18. How is this argument from Divine Names ascribed to Jesus Christ further confirmed?

By a comparison between many passages in the Old with others in the New Testament.

[A.] Thus the theophany of Is. 6:1, is explained in John 12:41

"These things said Isaiah because he saw his glory; and he spake of him. Nevertheless even of the rulers many believed on him," i.e., on Jesus.

[B.] The sublime description of the immortality of Jehovah

In Ps. 102:25-27, is quoted in Heb. 1:8, 10, 12, as referring to the Son.

"Of the Son he saith: Thou Lord in the beginning didst lay the foundation of the earth," etc.

[C.] Isa. 7:14

"Behold a virgin shall conceive and bear a son, and shall call his name Immanuel," is quoted in Matt. 1:21, "And thou shalt call his name Jesus; for it is he that shall save his people from their sins."

[D.] Isa. 40:3

"The voice of one that crieth, Prepare ye in the wilderness the way of Jehovah," is interpreted by John 1:23,30 as referring to John the Baptist's relation to Jesus.

19. What attributes of God are ascribed to the Son?

He is Eternal.

Col. 1:17. "He is before all things, and in him all things consist."

John 1:2. "The same was in the beginning with God."

Rev. 1:8. "I am the Alpha and the Omega, who is and who was and who is to come the Almighty."

He is Immutable.

Heb. 1:12. "They shall be changed, but thou art the same, and thy years sball not fail."

Heb. 13:8. "Jesus Christ, the same yesterday and today and forever."

2 Cor. 1:19. "The Son of God, Jesus Christ, was not yea and nay, but in him is yea."

He is Omnipresent.

Matt. 28:20. "Lo, I am with you always even unto the end of the world."

Matt. 18:20. "Where two or three are gathered together in my name, there am I in the midst of them."

Eph. 1 123. "The fullness of him that filleth all in all."

He is Omniscient.

John 2:25. "He needed not that any should bear witness concerning man; for he himself knew what was in man."

John 1:48. "Before Philip called thee, when thou wast under the fig tree, I saw thee."

Rev. 2:18, 23. "Thus saith the Son of God, I am he that searcheth the reins and hearts."

John 21:17. "Lord, thou knowest all things, thou knowest that I love thee."

He is Omnipotent.

Matt. 28:18. "All authority hath been given unto me in heaven and on earth."

Rev. 1:18. "I have the keys of death and of Hades."

Phil. 3:21. "He is able even to subdue all things unto himself." Heb. 1:3. "Upholding all things by the word of his power."

Col. 1:17. "He is before all things, and in him all things consist." He is Life.

John 14:6. "I am the way, the truth and the life."

John 11:25. "I am the resurrection and the life."

John 5:21. "The Son giveth life to whom he will."

20. What works peculiar to God belong to the Son?

[A.] Creation

John 1:3; Col. 1:16; Heb. 1:10 (See above).

[B.] Preservation

Col. 1:1; Heb. 1 13 (See above).

[C.] Forgiving sins

Mark 2:9,10, and saving, Matt. 1:21.

[D.] Raising the dead

2 Cor. 1:9. "We trust in God who raiseth the dead."

John 6:39. "This is the will of the Father that of all that which he hath given me, I should lose nothing, but should raise it up at the last day."

[E.] Judging the world

John 5:22, 23. "For neither doth the Father judge any man, but he hath given all judgment unto the Son, that all may honor the Son, even as they honor the Father." For to exercise this office infinite knowledge, power and majesty are required.

21. What worship is claimed for the Son?

[A.] Equal honor with the Father
(John 5:23, as above).

[B.] Baptism is to be administered in the name of the Son, just as in that of the Father (Matt. 28:19).

[C.] We are bidden to believe in the Son, just as in the Father.

John 14:1. "Believe in God, believe also in me."

[D.] He is to be religiously adored.

Phil. 2:10. "That at the name of Jesus every knee should bow."

Rev. 5:12-14. "Worthy is the Lamb that hath been slain to receive the power and riches and wisdom and might and honor and glory and blessing. And every created thing which is in the heaven and on the earth and under the earth, and on the sea, and all things that are in them heard I saying, Unto him that sitteth on the throne, and unto the Lamb be the blessing and the glory and the dominion forever and ever."

22. What adds especial force to these ascriptions of worship as an argument proving that the Son is God?

The fact that God has revealed Himself as a jealous God, sharing His honor with none else.

Is. 42:8. "I am Jehovah; that is my name, and my glory will I not give unto another."

Cf. Ex. 20:3, 5

23. Where is the worship of the very highest of creatures reproved?

When John intended to worship an angel he heard these words:

> Rev. 22:9. "See thou do it not; I am a fellow-servant with thee and with thy brethren the prophets and with them that keep the words of this book; worship God."

24. Where are the Names of God ascribed to the Holy Ghost?

> Acts 5:3, 4. "Why hath Satan filled thine heart to lie unto the Holy Ghost Thou hast not lied unto men, but unto God."
>
> 1 Cor. 3:16. "Know ye not that ye are a temple of God, and that the Spirit of God dwelleth in you?"
>
> 1 Cor. 12:4-6. "Now there are diversities of gifts, but the same Spirit. And there are diversities of administrations, and the same Lord. And there are diversities of workings, but the same God who worketh all things in all."
>
> 1 Sam. "The Spirit of Jehovah spake by me," interpreted in V. 30: "The God of Israel said."

25. What attributes of God are ascribed Him?

Eternity.

> Heb. 9:14. "Christ who, through the eternal Spirit, offered himself without blemish unto God." So, in accordance with the ordinary mode of describing the eternal in the Old Testament, as that which preceded the creation, Ps. 90:2, the Spirit is mentioned in Is. 40:13: "Who hath directed the Spirit of Jehovah, or, being his counsellor, hath taught him?"

Omnipresence.

Ps. 139:7. "Whither shall I go from thy Spirit? Or whither shall I flee from thy presence?"

Omniscience.

1 Cor. 2:10. "The Spirit searcheth all things; yea the deep things of God."

26. What works of God are ascribed to the Holy Ghost?

[A.] Works of Power

As creation. Gen. 1:2; Ps. 33:6. "All the host of them by the breath of his mouth;" Ps. 104:30: "Thou sendest forth thy Spirit, they are created;"

Conception of Jesus, Luke 1:35;

Casting out of demons, Matt. 12:28;

Anointing of Jesus as Christ, Acts 10:38.

[B.] Works of Grace

As His activity in everything pertaining to the redemption and salvation of man.

[C.] Works of Justice

Culminating in raising the dead.

> Rom. 8:11. "If the Spirit of him that raised up Jesus from the dead, dwelleth in you, he that raised up Christ Jesus from the dead shall give life also to your mortal bodies through his Spirit that dwelleth in you"

27. Where is divine worship addressed Him?

[A.] According to Matt. 28:19, Baptism is to be administered in His name.

[B.] In 1 Cor. 6:19, the hearts of believers are said to be temples of the Holy Ghost.

[C.] He is joined with the Father and the Son in the Apostolic benediction (2 Cor. 13:13).

28. How can you prove the fact that the Holy Ghost is God by a comparison of Old and New Testament passages?

When what is ascribed to God or Jehovah in the Old Testament, is ascribed in the New to the Holy Ghost. Thus in Is. 6:8-10, words spoken by Jehovah, are quoted in Acts 28:25 as spoken by the Holy Ghost through Isaiah. If in Is. 1:2; Ez. 1:3; Jer. 1:2; Hos. 1:1, etc., Jehovah is declared to be speaking through the prophets, this is further interpreted in 2 Peter 1:21, when men of God are said to have spoken "as they were moved by the Holy Ghost' and 1 Peter 1:11,"Searching what time or what manner of time, the Spirit of Christ, which was in them did point unto."

29. What is the chief point of attack concerning the divinity of the Holy Ghost?

The force of the above argument is met by the assertion that the Holy Ghost is not distinct from the Father, but His Spirit, i.e., His intelligence, will and energy. This will be considered below. (Q. 32.)

30. What second class of arguments may be adduced for the doctrine of the Trinity?

Those passages of Scripture in which all three, Father, Son and Holy Ghost, are co-ordinated.

[A.] The Theophany at Christ's baptism

(Matt. 3:16, 17) where Jesus is baptized, the Holy Ghost is present in the visible form of a dove, and the Father speaks from the opened heavens.

[B.] The Baptismal Formula

> Matt. 28:19, "Go ye, therefore, make disciples of all nations, baptizing them into the name of the Father and the Son and the Holy Ghost."

[C.] The Apostolic Benediction

> 2 Cor. 13:13, 'The grace of the Lord Jesus Christ and the love of God and the communion of the Holy Ghost be with you all."

[D.] The Promises of Christ

> John 14:16, "I will pray the Father and he shall give you another Comforter even the Spirit of Truth." 15:26, "When the Comforter is come, whom I will send unto you from the Father, even the Spirit of Truth which proceedeth from the Father."

[E.] Similar formulas of St. Paul

> As 1 Cor. 12:4-6 (see above, Q. 24), Eph. 4:4-6.

III. The Persons distinguished

31. But may not Father, Son and Holy Ghost be only different forms or modes of manifestation of God?

No. For Father and Son are expressly distinguished as "other."

> John 5:32, 27. "It is another that beareth witness of me.... the Father that sent me, he hath borne witness of me."

The Father speaks of the Son, and the Son of the Father, the Father addresses the Son, and the Son addresses and prays to the Father. The Spirit is constantly carefully distinguished from both Father and Son. These statements are manifest throughout the entire New Testament, and particularly in John, Chapters Xiv-Xvii.

The Holy Ghost a Person, not an Energy

32. How do you answer the proposed explanation, mentioned above (Q. 29) that the Holy Ghost is simply the divine energy or power?

The names by which He is designated are personal, as in the Baptismal Formula and Apostolic Benediction. They cannot be a personification of God's power. Personal works are ascribed Him; He teaches, prays, speaks, governs the Church. Personal revelations are made, as at Christ's Baptism and at Pentecost. Personal occurrences are mentioned, e. g., He is blasphemed (Matt. 12:31), is tempted (Acts 5:9), dwells in the hearts of believers (1 Cor. 3:16), is resisted (Acts 7:51), is grieved (Eph, 4:30). The distinctions between Father, Son and Holy Ghost cannot, then, be modal, but are personal.

Explanation of the scientific formulation of the dogma: "Substance and"Essence," "Person," "Hypostasis," "Personal Acts," "Personal Peculiarities," "Generation," "Filiation," "Spiration," "the Double Procession," Order of Persons, External Acts.

33. What result has now been reached by this argument?

The establishment of the three propositions set forth under Question 8.

34. How is this doctrine taught by the Church?

In the Athanasian Creed it is thus stated: "We worship one God in Trinity, and Trinity in Unity, neither confounding the Persons nor dividing the Substance. For there is one Person of the Father, another of the Son, and another of the Holy Ghost. But the Godhead of the Father and of the Son and of the Holy Ghost is all one, the Glory equal, the Majesty co-eternal. Such as the Father is, such is the Son and such the Holy Ghost. . . „ The Father is God, the Son is God and the Holy Ghost is God; and yet there are not three Gods, but one God."

And in the Augsburg Confession: "There is one divine essence which is called and is God. . . . and yet there are three persons of the same essence and power, who also are co-eternal, the Father, the Son and the Holy Ghost."

35. What does the Athanasian Creed mean when it speaks of the "substance" and the Augsburg Confession, when it speaks of the "essence" of God?

That which makes God God, His very being, that of which all His perfections and attributes are the expression.

36. How is this essence common to all three persons?

Not as though it were divided among them, or each contributed to it a part; for this would be contrary to the Unity and Simplicity of God. But to each person, belongs the entire divine essence. The Father is not God without the Son or the Holy Ghost. The entire one essence is in the three persons collectively and individually. There are three who are God, and, nevertheless, there are not three Gods.

37. What is meant by "person"?

"Not a part or quality in another but that which properly subsisteth" (Augsburg Confession). Father, Son and Holy Ghost are not parts of God, as man's spirit is a part of his complex nature; neither are they qualities or attributes of God, as God's love, is God considered as loving, and God's omniscience is God considered as knowing. But they "properly subsist," i.e., they have a distinct and independent relation, apart from our thought or God's revelation. While "the Father is God, and the Son God, and the Holy Ghost God," the Father is neither the Son nor the Holy Ghost. "For there is one person of the Father, another of the Son, and another of the Holy Ghost." "We are compelled by the Christian verity to acknowledge every person by Himself to be God and Lord" (Athanasian Creed).

38. What are the distinguishing attributes of personality?

Self-consciousness and self-determination.

39. What is a brief definition of "person"?

A person is one who can say "I."

40. What distinguishes "person" in Grammar?

The personal pronouns. "I" and "thou" express personal relations. When the Father speaks of Himself as I and addresses the Son as "Thou," or when the Son refers to either Father or Holy Ghost as "He," there is a clear distinction of personality taught.

41. For the popular statement of the subject, this is sufficient. What value, then, must be attached to the current Scholastic definition, as revised by the Reformers of both branches of Protestantism?

Each term is carefully chosen with reference to both actual and possible controversies or misunderstandings.

42. Repeat it.

"A person is a substance, individual, intelligent, incommunicable, not sustained in another, or a part of another."

43. Why is "person" defined as substance?

To affirm (a) that it is not a mere subjective conception. It is more than an i.e., or matter of thought, (b) In contrast with what is accidental.

44. Does this imply any contradiction with the formula of the Athanasian Creed that God is one in substance?

Like the "persons," the "essence" of God, is neither a mere subjective conception, nor accidental. The Scholastic definition only attempts to define one species of substance from another. At every stage in the attempt to reduce the contents of divine revelation into the technical terms of philosophy, the inadequacy of these terms becomes apparent. Loqnimur de his rebus non ut debemus, sed ut possumus.

45. What is meant by the descriptive terms "individual", "intelligent" "incommunicable," "not sustained in another," "not the part of another"?

"Individual" is what distinguishes one from others of the same nature, the characteristic of what is separate and distinct. The individuality of each person is clearly presented in the declarations of the Schmalkald Articles: "The Father is begotten of no one; the Son, of the Father; the Holy Ghost proceeds from Father and Son. Not the Father, not the Holy Ghost, but the Son became man."

"Intelligent," having self-consciousness and thought. No tree or beast is a person.

"Incommunicable," i.e., incapable of imparting its individuality to another. The personality of one can never become the personality of another. No human father communicates his personality to the children whom he begets.

"Not sustained in another," to exclude any thought that the relation is analogous to that of the humanity of Christ to His divine nature. The one had a beginning in time, the latter was from all eternity; the one originated from the act of the latter, and exists only through that act.

"Nor a part of another." This is the statement of the Augsburg Confession, explained in Q. 37.

46. How does "person" as used here differ from the same term as applied to men and angels?

In the latter case, each person has an essence of his own; here there is but one essence for the three persons.

47. By what term did the early Greek theologians designate the distinction which we indicate by "person"?

"Hypostasis." They preferred this to "person," because they regarded it more irreconcilable with Sabellianism than the Greek word for "person," which means likewise "a mask," and could readily be perverted into the conception that the distinctions in God were not real, intrinsic and immanent, but only different economical and official manifestations assumed in time.

48. In what are the three persons alike or the same?

[A.] They have, as we have shown, the same undivided divine essence.

This was confessed by the Council of Chalcedon in the declaration that one Person is "consubstantial," or in Greek "homoousios" with the other.

[B.] They have the same Majesty

So that no preference is given one Person above another. "The Glory equal, the Majesty co-eternal." "In this Trinity, none is before or after other; none is greater or less than another" (Athanasian Creed).

[C.] Each of the three persons exists in the essence of each of the two others.

This was designated by the Greek Fathers as perichoresis, or the eternal and inseparable pervasion of one person by the other. John 14:10, "I am in the Father and the Father in me."

49. In what are they distinguished?

By certain modes, not of manifestation, but of simultaneous subsistence of the one divine essence. They bear a certain relationship to each other based upon two personal acts, which result in five personal peculiarities.

50. What are these personal acts?

They are immanent and eternal activities of God, known as opera ad intra, because they do not go out of God, but are wrought within Him. These are Generation and Spiration, when viewed with respect to the activity itself, or

Filiation and Procession, when viewed with respect to its results.

51. What is Generation?

That activity whereby one Person is Father and another Son. Or, more specifically, "the act, whereby God the Father, from all eternity, by the communication of His essence, begets the Son, His image, truly and properly, yet in a supernatural and inscrutable way."

52. From what conceptions must it be guarded?

From that of creation, as though there could have been a time when the Son were not. From that of completion, as though the activity were one act that has ended or is not continuous. From all i.e.s of succession, change, division or multiplication. From all attempts to explain it figuratively; for if the generation be figurative, then God is Father and God is Son only figuratively and not really. Yet literal as it is, it is raised above all the limitations of human relationships. It is the human relationship which is a feeble figure of the divine.

53. Upon what Scriptural grounds does this rest?

[A.] Ps. 2:7. "Thou art my Son, today have I begotten thee." Compare with this the New Testament passages which take it as a basis:

> Acts 13:33. "As it is written in the second Psalm, Thou art my Son, today have I begotten thee."
>
> Heb. 1:5. "But unto which of the angels said he at any time, Thou art my Son, this day have I begotten thee?"
>
> Heb. 5:5. "Christ glorified not himself to be made a high priest, but he that spake unto him, Thou art my Son, this day have I begotten thee." God's day is eternity.

[B.] Express declarations of the peculiar nature of Christ's Sonship:

> John 1:14. "We beheld his glory, the glory as of the only begotten from the Father."
>
> John 1:18. "The only begotten Son who is in the bosom of the Father he hath declared him."

Rom. 8:32. "He that spared not his own Son." The "his own" is not a simple possessive, but is the adjective "idios," meaning his own in a peculiar sense, a sense in which none other would be called his son. Compare with this John 5:18, where Jesus is understood, by calling God "his own Father," using "idios," and therefore claiming God as Father in a sense none else could claim, as "making himself equal with God."

John 3:16. "God so loved the world, that he gave his only begotten Son."

Heb. 1:3. "Who being the effulgence of his glory, and the very image of his substance."

54. What is Spiration?

The activity of the Father and the 'Son, whereby, from all eternity, the Holy Ghost proceeds from both.

55. Is it identical with the activity by which the Son is generated?

No. The Holy Ghost is nowhere said to be begotten; and if this had been so, He would be Son and not Holy Ghost.

56. What proof is there that the Holy Ghost proceeds from the Father?

John 15:26. "The Spirit of truth which proceedeth from the Father."

57. Is our Lord's promise that He would send the Holy Ghost a proof that He proceeds from the Son as well as from the Father?

Not of itself, for a distinction must be made between the gift of the Holy Spirit in time from the Ascended Savior. and a relation subsisting in God from all eternity.

58. Why then did the Western Church maintain in opposition to the Greek Church that He proceeds not only from the Father but also from the Son?

[A.] Because if He is called in one passage of Holy Scripture, as in Matt. 10:20, "the Spirit of the Father," He is called elsewhere "the Spirit of His Son" (Gal. 4:6) and "the Spirit of Christ" (Rom. 8:9).

[B.] Because in John 16:15, His relation to the Son is described as such that all that the Spirit teaches is derived through the Son.

[C.] The Son is sent equally by the Father and the Son (John 16:7; John 15:26).

[D.] Without the procession from the Son as well as from the Father, it would be difficult to distinguish the Spirit from the Son, or to hold that the Son would not be subordinate to the Father.

[E.] Our Lord's breathing upon His disciples with the words: "Receive ye the Holy Ghost," was regarded a figure of what occurs from all eternity.

[F.] Hence "the river of water of life, bright as crystal, proceeding out of the throne of God and of the Lamb," in Rev. 22:1, was widely applied to the double procession from eternity.

Without urging the complete decision of the question by each argument separately, taken together they indicate such a relationship, as to render any other inference very difficult.

59. What then are the five personal peculiarities founded upon these two acts?

Two belong to the Father alone: That He is unbegotten ("The Father is made of none, neither created, nor begotten." — Athanasian Creed), and Paternity. One belongs to the Son: Filiation, that He receives and has all His essence of the Father. One belongs jointly to Father and Son: Spiration, and one to the Holy Ghost: Procession.

60. Is there not then an order?

Undoubtedly, yet not of rank or of time, but of origin and operation.

When the Athanasian Creed confesses: "None is before or after other," the next clause interprets it: "None is greater or less than another." The order is: "The Father"; "the Son of the Father"; "the Holy Ghost, of the Father and the Son." Or: "The Father through the Son in the Holy Ghost."

Rom. 11:33. "For of him and through him and unto him are all things."'
John 5:19. "The Son can do nothing of himself, but whatsoever he seeth the Father doing."

61. Is the term "Father" when applied to God always restricted to the First Person of the Trinity?

It often refers to the essence of God, and thus belongs to all three persons alike. When in the Lord's Prayer we address, "Our Father which art in Heaven," no Trinitarian relation is expressed or implied. We pray to all three persons in the one essence. The entire being of God is Father to men both by creation and regeneration. Nor can we address one person of the Trinity in prayer without addressing all; for they are all and in all, since they are one in essence.

62. Besides the immanent acts, not common to all persons, but distinguishing them from each other (opera ad intra), what other personal acts are there?

The external activities proceeding from the power common to all three persons, and directed to an end outside of God (opera ad extra).

63. What especially distinguishes them from the former class?

They are common to all three persons. For this reason they are sometimes called "essential," while the immanent acts are called "personal." Nevertheless each person has manifested Himself in a peculiar way in a temporal work or act, which is ascribed to Him not exclusively or predominantly, but because of the prominence given to that person in the description of said act in Revelation.

64. Name them.

Creation., or the external work of the Father. Redemption, or the external work of the Son. Sanctification, or the external work of the Holy Ghost.

Old Testament Suggestions

65. What traces are there (see Q. 4) of this doctrine in the Old Testament?

It explains the passages where God speaks of God and the Lord of the Lord (Gen. 19:24; Ex. 16:7; 34:5,6; Num. 14:21); those in which the Son of God is explicitly mentioned (Ps. 2:7); those in which a plurality of Persons is mentioned (Gen. 1:1,2; Ex. 31:1,3; Ps. 33:6; Is. 61:1), as well as those in which God speaks of Himself in the plural number (Gen. 1:26; 3:22), or where the name of God or Jehovah is thrice repeated (Num. 6:23-26; Deut. 6:4, 5; Ps. 42:1, 2; 67:6, 7) .

Philosophical Arguments

66. What philosophical arguments for the Trinity hare been used and what is their value?

One from personality. Personality implies self-consciousness, and self-consciousness implies three things, a subject contemplating, an object contemplated and a subject conscious that that which contemplates and that which is contemplated are the same.

Another from love. This implies a subject loving, an object loved, and the communion of love in a third who unites the love of the one loving and the one loved.

Both have value as illustrations, but not as arguments.

4. Creation

Relation to what precedes

1. What is the relation of this chapter to what precedes?

We come now to the more specific treatment of God in relation to what is not God. This, of necessity, has been anticipated, to an extent, in considering the Divine Attributes. But what has been only incidentally mentioned, is now to be more fully examined. Recurring to the external activities of God (Opera ad extra) defined at the close of preceding chapter (Q. 62, 63), we may say that all that remains for us in this treatise, is to treat of the three themes, Creation, Redemption and Sanctification.

Definition

2. What is Creation?

The act by which God brought into being that which had no preexistence, except in His thought.

> Heb. 11:3. "By faith we understand that the worlds have been framed by the word of God, so that what is seen, hath not been made out of things which appear."

Source of doctrine

3. Whence do we derive our knowledge of this act?

Solely from Revelation. It is a pure, not a mixed doctrine. The heathen cosmogonies and modern scientific heathenism, with many divergent theories, some in a pantheistic, others in a dualistic, and still others in a purely materialistic way, exclude the free activity and will of a sole Eternal, Omnipotent, Supreme Being. The New Testament references of which Heb. 11:3 is central, presuppose the detailed description with which Holy Scripture opens in Gen. 1.

Mosaic account

4. What is the purpose and scope of the Mosaic account?

It has a religious and not a scientific end. Its aim is not so much to record a detailed cosmogony in opposition to the many elaborate hypotheses which had preceded, as to solemnly affirm the supremacy and omnipotent activity of God, and the goal of all creation in Man, as its summit, towards which each successive creative act was an advance.

Trinitarian relations

5. Who created the world?

The Triune God.

Father.

1 Cor. 8:6. "God the Father, of whom are all things, and we unto him."

Son.

1 Cor. 8:6. "One Lord Jesus Christ, through whom are all things."

Col. 1:15, 16. "Who is the image of the invisible God, the first-born of all creation; for in him are all things created in the heavens and upon the earth, things visible and invisible, whether thrones or dominions or principalities or powers, all things have been created through him and unto him."

John 1:3. "All things were made by him."

Holy Ghost.

Ps. 104:30. "Thou sendest forth thy Spirit; they are created."

Ps. 33:6. "All the host of them by the breath of his mouth."

Gen. 1:2. "The Spirit of God moved upon the face of the waters."

6. But does not the Apostles' Creed ascribe this work in an especial sense to the Father?

Yes, according to the order of the Persons of the Trinity, and because what the Father has of Himself, the Son and Holy Ghost have of the Father.

7. Are Father, Son and Holy Ghost, then, associated causes of creation?

There is but one Creator. The three Persons are one God, and one cause and Author of creation.

Origin of purpose

8. Whence came God's purpose to create?

All the external works of God proceed from His free will, and not from His natural will or any inner necessity, as do the immanent or personal works.

Immediate and Mediate

9. Does "create" always mean "to produce from nothing"?

Theologians distinguish between "immediate" and "mediate creation." The former is the proper sense of the term; in the latter sense, it refers to the producing of something from preexisting material, as in Gen. 1:11, the coming forth of grass and trees from the earth; and yet even here there is that which calls for an immediate creative act of God, for grass and trees could never be produced by mere matter. Man's soul was created immediately, and his body mediately. In Ps. 51:10, "Create in me a clean heart," the word refers to a change of properties or renewal. It is with immediate creation that we have to do here.

10. When creation is defined as "to produce from nothing," what is meant by "nothing"?

Absolute non-existence. Not "a relative nothing," as from matter without form and void.

Relations to Eternity and Time

11. Could the world have been created from eternity?

No. For eternity is an attribute of God alone. Ascribe eternity to a creature, and you ascribe infinity, for eternity is infinite duration.

12. Was there time before the creation?

With the creation, time began. For time implies succession, and, as before the creation, God alone existed and God is immutable, there was no succession.

How effected

13. How was the world created?

Not by the thought, but by the word of God.

> Ps. 33:6. "By the word of Jehovah were the heavens made."
>
> 9: "He spake and it was done; he commanded and it stood fast."
>
> Gen. 1:3. "God said: Let there be light, and there was light."

John 1:1-3 shows that this was none else than the Personal Word of God, or Second Person of the Trinity, expressing and revealing the thought and purpose of

God.

Result

14. What was the product of creation?

Heaven and earth. By the former is meant not only the visible heavens with their stars, planets, comets, meteors, etc., but the entire super-terrestrial world of spirits (2 Cor. 12:2; Rev. 4:1). By the latter, also all that earth contains. The physical insignificance of the earth is compensated by its destiny as the abode of the incarnate God, and the theater of Redemption.

Design

15. What was the purpose of Creation?

The manifestation of the perfections of God, as the ultimate end; the highest welfare of man as the subordinate.

16. What perfections?

The glory of His goodness, wisdom and power.

> Ps. 19:1, 2. "The heavens declare the glory of God, and the firmament sheweth his handiwork. Day unto day uttereth speech, and night unto night sheweth knowledge." Ps. 104; Ps. 106:4-9; 148; Rev. 4:11.
>
> Ps. 8:1, 3. "o Lord, our Lord, how excellent is thy name in all the earth, who hast set thy glory upon the heavens. When I consider thy heavens the work of thy fingers, the moon and the stars which thou hast ordained, what is man that thou art mindful of him?"

These attributes are specifically mentioned: Goodness, Ps. 145:9, 10; Wisdom, Ps. 104:24; Power, Is. 40:26; Rom. 1:20.

17. Show that the highest welfare of man was the subordinate end?

Ps. 8:4, 6. "What is man that thou art mindful of him or the Son of man that thou visitest him? Thou makest him to have dominion over the works of thy hands; thou hast put all things under his feet."

18. But does not the Epistle to the Hebrews (Chap. 2:7) declare that this refers to Christ?

Yes, as the Son of man, the ideal or representative Man, through whom the dominion over creation, lost by the fall, is more than restored.

1 Cor. 3:21. "For all things are yours."

19. Where else is the same doctrine taught?

Gen. 1 126. "And God said, Let us make man in our image, after our likeness; and let them have dominion over the fish of the sea, and over the birds of the heavens, and over the cattle, and over all the earth." Ps. 115:7. "The earth hath he given to the children of men."

20. But does not the New Testament go still further?

Yes, by declaring that all creatures, even angels, exist for the sake of men.

Heb. 1:14. "Are they not all ministering spirits sent forth to do service for the sake of them that shall inherit salvation."

1 Cor. 3:22. "The world or life or death or things present or things to come, all are yours."

Rom. 8:28. "We know that to them that love God, all things work together for good."

21. Does this, however, depend upon the Order of Creation?

No; but of Redemption, in which the superiority of Man appears in that the Son of God personally united Himself to a human nature, thus distinguishing it above all creatures. Nevertheless God had this exalted destiny of the human race and the Plan of Redemption in view from the beginning. It was no afterthought; for God has no afterthoughts.

22. But is not the difficulty greater in regarding the lowest of creatures subservient to man's highest welfare?

Yes, for, to natural reason, some seem absolutely useless, and others harmful. In answer to this, we need only cite a passage from Augustine:

> "If an unskilled person were to enter the shop of a mechanic, he would see many instruments of whose use he would be ignorant, and if very unintelligent they would seem superfluous. Or if an incautious person were to fall into a furnace, or were to wound himself with some steel instrument, he would regard many things harmful, whose use the artisan well knows, and therefore laughs at the folly and unadvised words of the critic. Nevertheless men are so silly, that while they do not venture to blame such a mechanic with respect to tools of which they are ignorant, but when they see them believe them necessary and adapted to some use; nevertheless in this world, whose Maker and Administrator is God, they attempt to criticize many things, the causes for which they do not see, and in regard to the works and tools of the Almighty Workman want to seem to know that of which they are ignorant."

23. For what various uses of man are creatures intended?

Some are for the nourishment of the bodily life.

> Gen. 1:29. "Behold I have given you every herb yielding seed, which is upon the face of all the earth, and every tree in which is the fruit of a tree yielding seed; to you it shall be for food."

> Prov. 27:26. "The lambs are for thy clothing."

Others for man's thankful delight and pleasure.

1 Tim. 6:17. "Who giveth us richly all things to enjoy."

Ps. 145:16. "Thou openest thy hand and satisfieth the desire of every living thing."

1 Tim. 4:4. "Every creature of God is good, and nothing is to be rejected if it be received with thanksgiving."

Some are remedies. e.g. Oil, James 5:17; Oil and wine, Luke 10:34; Figs, 2 Kings 20:7.

Others are preventives of disease, and preservatives of health.

Ps. 103:5. "Who satisfieth thy desire with good things, so that thy youth is renewed like the eagle's."

Some aid man in his life and appointed work on earth. Gen. 1:15. "Lights in the firmament of heaven, to give light upon the earth."

Ps. 78:53. "The sea overwhelmed their enemies."

Acts 14:17. "He gave from heaven rain and fruitful seasons."

Amos 6:12. "Will one plow there with oxen?"

Others are for example and imitation.

Matt. 6:26. "Behold the fouls of the air."

Prov. 6:6. "Go to the ant, thou sluggard."

Is. 40:31. "They shall mount up with wings as eagles."

Matt. 10:27. "My sheep hear my voice and I know them."

1 Cor. 15:41. "One star differeth from another star in glory."

Ps. 125:1, 2. "They that trust in the Lord shall be as Mount Zion. As the mountains are round about Jerusalem."

Ps. 1:3. "Like a tree planted by the streams of water."

24. What proof of this can be found outside of Revelation?

Man's progress in civilization is determined by the progress made in the application of the objects and forces of the natural world to his use. Objects regarded useless for centuries are estimated at a high value when their proper use has been discovered. Illustrations are found in the modern application of steam, light (Photography), electricity, radium and other results of Physics, Chemistry, Astronomy and Meteorology, and in the constant advance of discovery and the cultivation of regions previously unknown, or regarded irreclaimable. The lightning is used to flash man's words around the globe, and even the most irresistible floods of waters are diverted to commercial ends and to carry men from place to place. Niagara is harnessed. All is in virtue of the divine command, "Replenish the earth and subdue it."

End

25. In what did Creation end?

First of all in God's admiring contemplation of the result.

> Gen. 1:31. "And God saw everything that he had made, and behold it was very good."

Nothing that God has created is in itself evil; it can become such only by its use in another sphere than that for which God designed it.

26. What is Optimism?

The theory that the world as it came from God is the very best that was possible.

27. How must this theory be qualified?

By the circumstance that the original creation was only preparatory to still higher stages of perfection attainable only in the New Heavens and the New Earth. The goodness of the creature as it came from God's hands was that of the acorn not of the oak, that of the new-born child, and not that of the fully developed man. So would it have been even if sin had not entered. But through Redemption, as we shall hereafter see, it attains a yet higher grade.

28. What accompanied God's admiring contemplation of Creation?

> Gen. 2:2. "He rested on the seventh day from all his work which he had made."

This is made prominent by the frequent references to it, as in Heb. 4:4; Ex. 20:11; 31:17.

29. Does this mean a cessation of God's activity?

No. For this would be in contradiction to His life, and we read

> 1 John 5:17. "And Jesus answered, My Father worketh even until now, and I work."

The reference is to a change of work. Creation ceases. God's activity is henceforth in the sphere of Providence, and, except where the new Order of Redemption intervenes, through second causes. God's rest is, therefore, only a change in His mode of work. He no longer creates, but sustains and concurs with things created, yet so as not to exclude, when He so wishes, His miraculous activity.

Cautions concerning alleged conflict between Science and Revelation

30. What can be said of an alleged conflict between Science and Revelation on this article?

Between true Science and Revelation, there can be no conflict, for the true in the natural, and the true in the supernatural, cannot be contradictory. But when the facts of the natural world are elevated to the position of a standard by which the supernatural is to be decided, Science passes beyond its own limits, and ceases to be true science (see Chapter 1, 32). When, on the other hand, some theologians push incidental allusions to natural events in the language and according to the popular conceptions of the age in which a book of Holy Scripture is written, to the position of an integral part of Revelation itself, they also sometimes imagine a conflict of Science, with Revelation, where no such conflict exists.

31. Explain this more fully.

Where skeptical scientists and some well-meaning champions of Revelation agree in maintaining that it is an important part of Holy Scripture, that the earth does not move, and hold that the Ptolemaic System of the Universe is essential to belief in Revelation, they should be reminded that the language of every day life that "the sun rises" and "sets," is not an untruth, but only describes a real fact from the standpoint of the ordinary spectator, although not from that of astronomical observation. The most common facts in nature would be unintelligible to all except those technically educated, if they were always described in scientific terminology; and if so stated, would have been without meaning in the age when the Holy Scriptures were written.

32. What other caution must be observed?

The rash acceptance of scientific hypotheses as though they were final. The theories of one generation of learned men in regard to the natural world, are ridiculed by their successors in the next. In the middle of the nineteenth century, the Biblical account of Creation was attacked because it taught the unity of the human race, while only a few decades later, the same account was criticized because of its antagonism to the Darwinian theory of evolution of all forms of life from a common source. One generation attacks the Biblical account of creation because it teaches that light existed before the sun was created; a later generation learnedly treats of the luminous effects produced by electricity generated from the friction of an assumed "star dust."

33. To what should this lead?

To modesty in pressing the claims of "science" as well as to moderation on the part of students of Scripture in regarding any thoroughly established fact as capable of affecting the truth of Revelation.

34. State some of the useless controversies that have been waged?

Such, for instance, as to whether the "day" of the Biblical account of Creation, be the natural day of twenty four hours, as we measure time, or a long period, according to 2 Peter 3:8, "One day is with the Lord as a thousand years." Another is as to whether Gen. 1:7 teaches as an article of faith that there is an immense reservoir somewhere above the clouds. Kindred to this is the question as to whether the world was created in the spring or the autumn. It would be just as pertinent for New Testament students to enter into learned discussions concerning the words that introduce the Sermon on the Mount as given by Luke (Chap. 6:20), "He lifted up his eyes on his disciples," instead of treating of the discourse of the Master. Various theories might be suggested as to how it were possible and how impossible for one "to lift up" his own eyes. Intense literalists could insist that "to lift" must mean to apply one's hands to an object, and that any other conception is heretical; and skeptics might urge the same as an argument for the rejection of the entire record. It is so easy to be diverted by accidentals, and to overlook the essentials of Holy Scripture.

35. What method has been used to explain some apparent difficulties?

The suggestion of Augustine by which the first verse of Genesis refers to an original creation which had fallen into chaos before the events described in the succeeding verses occurred. Then, some urge, the description proceeds as the events would have appeared to one who had been present as day after day recorded something new.

But all this, and all other hypotheses are speculative, and their extended consideration only withdraws attention from what is the actual purport of the account taken as a whole, to which we have referred in Q. 4.

36. Does the occurrence of similar accounts in ancient Oriental literature, deciphered from inscriptions on tablets or otherwise preserved in any way affect the value and force of the Mosaic account?

No. For the Mosaic account gives the history of creation its true religious value, and places it in proper relations to the history of the preparation of Redemption for mankind. The Christian should ever consider it from the standpoint of the fullness of the revelation he has received in Christ.

5. Providence

Definition

1. What is Providence?

God's administration of created things.

Relation to Creation

2. How is it related to Creation?

Since Creation gives being, and Providence preserves and directs it to its end, the latter is only the continuation of the former. Hence Scripture frequently joins them.

> Ps. 121:2, 3, 4. "My help cometh from Jehovah, who made heaven and earth. He will not suffer thy foot to be moved, he that keepeth thee will not slumber. Behold he that keepeth Israel will neither slumber nor sleep." So also Ps. 146:5-10; Acts 17:24-28.

Against what Errorists to be maintained

3. Against what errors must it be constantly maintained?

Those of Epicureans and Deists, who acknowledge a Creator, but teach that all things occur by the operation of forces implanted in Nature from the creation, as though, to use a figure of Augustine, God were a shipbuilder who delivers the vessel, when finished, into other hands, and has for it no further care, or a carpenter who erects a house, and then entirely relinquishes it to its owner.

Proofs

4. What proofs can be given from Scripture for the reality of Providence?

It is found or presupposed on every page. Only a few passages need be cited.

> Matt. 5:45. "Your Father who is in heaven maketh his sun to rise on the evil and the good, and sendeth rain on the just and unjust."
>
> Matt. 6:26. "Your heavenly Father feedeth them."
>
> Matt. 6:30. "If God so clothe the grass of the field which today is, and tomorrow is cast into the oven, shall he not much more clothe you, O ye of little faith?"
>
> 1 Peter 5:7. "Casting all your anxiety upon him; for he careth for you." Acts 17:28. "In him we live and move and have our being."
>
> Heb. 1:3. "Upholding all things by the word of his power."

5. Are there other arguments that might be cited?

A. It is involved in our conception of the Divine Attributes, as the Goodness, Wisdom, Power, and Justice of God. His Goodness implies His constant communication of blessings to those He has created. What sort of Wisdom would it be to create a universe and leave it? Or is it consistent with Omnipotence to limit its sphere to the beginning, instead of deeming it coextensive with the entire sphere of derived being? So also, as supremely just, He can allow no punishment to be inflicted undeservedly, or reward to be given without merit.

B. From the constancy of Nature, and the perpetuity of creatures amidst the changes which centuries bring with them.

C. From the adaptation of creatures to their place, and of parts and functions of creatures to their perpetuity and welfare.

D. From the general purpose of human history, which everywhere shows divine purpose directed towards a given end. The rise and fall of empires, the wonderful preservation of the Christian Church against the plots of enemies and the indifference of its friends, etc.

Its Objects

6. With what objects is Providence occupied?

With all. Nothing is so great as to be beyond it. For angels are beneath its control (Ps. 91:11; Heb. 1:14; 1 Thess. 4:16). Nor is anything so small and unimportant as not to have a place in its plans. For it has to do with young ravens (Ps. 147:9), sparrows (Malt. 10:29), frogs and vermin (Ex. 8:13,18), lilies and grass (Matt. 6:28,30), the hairs of our heads (Matt. 10:30), our tears (Ps. 56:8).

7. What error does this disprove?

The modified casualism of Jerome who taught that it was beneath God's Majesty to regard the humbler creatures. With God the distinction of great and small that obtains among men disappears.

Practical Application of its Universality and Particularity

8. What practical application of this universality and particularity of Providence is made by Holy Scripture?

The doctrine that it is not simply the life of each individual that is regarded, but that, in each individual life, each stage and step are explicitly and separately considered.

9. Cite proofs.

[A.] As to the beginning of man's life, Providence is described, as active in man's conception.

Ps. 139:15, 16. "My frame was not hidden from thee when I was made in secret, and curiously wrought in the lowest parts of the earth. Thine eyes did see my unformed substance, and in thy book they were all written, even the days that were ordained for me." Job 10:8. "Thy hands have framed me and fashioned me." And in his birth.

Ps. 71:6. "By thee have I been holden from the womb; thou art he that took me out of my mother's bowels."

[B.] As to the progress of man's life.

Food.

Ps. 145:15. "The eyes of all wait upon thee,and thou givest them their meat in due season."

Undertakings.

Prov. 20:24. "A man's goings are of Jehovah. How then can man understand his way?"

Calling in life.

Jer. 1:5. "Before thou earnest out of the womb, I sanctified thee: I have appointed thee a prophet unto the nations."

Marriage.

Prov. 19:14. "A prudent wife is from Jehovah."

Children.

Ps. 127:3. "The fruit of the womb is his reward."

Protection from danger.

Ps. 127:1. "Except Jehovah keep the city, the watchman waketh but in vain."

Protection from diseases.

Ps. 91:3. “He will deliver thee from the snare of the fowler, and from the deadly pestilence.”

[C.] As to the end of life.

Job. 14:5. “His days are determined; the number of his months is with thee; and thou hast appointed his bounds, that he cannot pass.”

Ps. 139:16. “The days that were ordained for me when as yet there was none of them.”

10. Does this mean that God has set limits to man’s life and otherwise determined its details irrespective of any agency of man himself?

God’s Providence, comprehending all the circumstances of man’s course and the manner in which in every future contingency man would exercise his freedom, does not absolutely exclude man’s agency. There are limits beyond which man has no freedom. Since the fall no one by any compliance with divinely-appointed conditions can reach the age of a thousand years. Human strength has its utmost limits (Ps. 90:10). But within these limits it is God’s will that man’s free agency be a factor, according to which the period which God would otherwise have appointed may be abbreviated (Ps. 55:23), or lengthened (Eph. 6:3), by His Providential activity. Accordingly, theologians distinguish between “the natural” and “the preternatural limits of life,” and distinguish the latter into “the limit of grace” and “the limit of wrath.” ’The limit of grace," however, does not always indicate a lengthening of life. Sometimes the abbreviation of life is a blessing.

Is. 57:1. “None considering that the righteous is taken away from the evil to come.”

11. Is it, therefore, absolutely necessary that every one die at the particular time and by the particular disease which proves fatal?

No. For such doctrine would deny the efficacy of prayer, and the truth of God’s promises with respect to obedience, and of His threats with respect to disobedience. The preternatural limit of life is always hypothetical, including the condition of godliness or ungodliness, and the use or contempt of means.

12. But if Providence is occupied with all things, does this mean that it has something to do with the wicked deeds of men?

Undoubtedly. For while God gives them no aid, He foreknows them, sustains the nature that sins, permits them, limits them and overrules them for good.

The Three Acts of Providence: 1. Foreknowledge 2. Predetermination 3. Execution by: (a) Preservation (b) Concurrence (c) Government (by Permission, Hindrance, Direction).

13. What acts are comprised in Providence? Three. Of these two are immanent, or occurring

within God, Foreknowledge and Predetermination; and one is transient, viz., the execution of what has been predetermined.

14. But does not this imply succession in God?

No, for the order is anthropological, in order to enable us, by the analogy of what occurs in man, to distinguish what must always be kept separate in our consideration of God.

15. How is the Foreknowledge to be distinguished from the Predetermination?

Foreknowledge comprises all things, bad as well as good. But Predetermination pertains only to what is good.

16. Can anything that God has foreknown occur otherwise than He has foreknown it?

No, for He is omniscient.

17. Must not His foreknowledge, therefore, he the cause of the events foreknown?

By no means. For God foreseeing the end from the beginning is, in those things He has left to human liberty, determined, in His foreknowledge, by the future decision of man. The event does not depend upon God's foreknowledge, but God's foreknowledge depends upon the event. The foreknowledge of God is the record of the result of the exercise of free choice by the creature; for to God the future is ever present. If the free choice of the creature were otherwise than it is, God's foreknowledge of the event would differ. The foreknowledge of God no more brings necessity to things foreknown, than my sight of a house has built it.

18. How is the execution of what has been predetermined effected?

In three ways, viz., by preservation, concurrence and government.

19. What is Preservation?

Since God's presence pervades all things, their existence continues by His omnipresent power. Were He to withdraw His hand, they would return to nothingness. "The continued existence of creatures is more dependent upon God's presence, than rays of light upon the sun" (Calovius).

> Col. 1:17. "By him all things consist."
>
> Heb. 1:3. "Upholding all things by the word of his power."
>
> Acts 17:28. "In him we live and move and have our being."
>
> Ps. 104:29, 30. "Thou hidest thy face, they are troubled; thou takest away their breath, they die, and return to their dust. Thou sendest forth thy spirit, they are created."

This preservation, beyond individuals, belongs also to species. Generation after generation passes away, individuals die, but their places are supplied, and the race remains.

20. What is Concurrence?

Nothing, either great or small occurs, without God's active cooperation (Job 10:8,9; 1 Cor. 12:6; Acts 17:28). Applied to human acts, this implies:

[A.] A certain degree of liberty with respect to man's free will. For otherwise God would not concur or cooperate, but would only operate.

[B.] The activity of God in and through that of the creature. The effect is produced neither by God alone, nor by the creature alone, but, at the same time, by God and the creature. God is the First Cause; creatures are second causes. God acts through second causes, not only by creating and sustaining them, but especially by imparting His energy to all their actions.

21. What qualification must be attached to the explanation of this concurrence?

The abuse of the energy communicated by God, in its application to sinful ends, comes entirely from the creature. This abuse God permits; for otherwise, the freedom of man's will would be denied. God concurs with the effect, not with the defect of an action.

22. What is meant by Government? God's control of all acts of second causes.

23. In what different ways does this occur?

[A.] By permission.

God sometimes places no insuperable barrier in the way of those abusing their free will.

> Ps. 81:12. "I let them go after the stubbornness of their heart, that they might walk in their own counsels."
>
> Acts 14:16. "Who suffered all the nations to walk in their own ways."
>
> Rom. 1:24, 28. God permits even when he does not will what is permitted.

[B.] By hindrance.

God sometimes prevents the actions of creatures from reaching the end they would otherwise attain by the natural exercise of the powers He has allotted them, or by the use of their free wills. ' An illustration is seen, where, in Dan. 3:21, the fire did not harm the three faithful confessors of the only true God, or where, in Num. 22, 11, Balaam's purpose to curse Israel is thwarted, or, in 2 Kings 7:6, where the counsels of the Syrians are thrown into confusion.

[C.] By direction.

All actions of creatures, good and bad, are guided to the ends which He has designed. God has a plan; and every act of man's will is made to contribute to its ultimate result. He brings forth good out of evil, and converts evil into good. Saul went forth to seek asses, and, through God's direction, returned a king. The sons of Jacob sold Joseph into slavery, who, as governor of Egypt, became the means of saving the entire family from famine.

> Gen. 50:20. "Ye meant evil against me; but God meant it for good."

The Jews crucified Christ, and through His death, salvation is prepared for the race, and the highest glory resulted for him whom they hated (Acts 4:27, 28).

[D.] By determination.

God appoints certain limits to the strength and activity of creatures (Job 1:12; 2:6; 1 Chron. 21:27).

Special Providence

24. Is Providence occupied with all things in the same way?

No. God disposes events in one way with respect to the good and in another with respect to the wicked. The former are the objects of His especial care and guidance. Providence considered with respect to them is sometimes called "Special Providence" (Matt. 10:31; Heb. 1:14; Deut. 32:9, 15; Ps 33:18; 37:19, 25; 91:11).

Ordinary and Extraordinary Providence

25. What is meant by the distinction between Ordinary and, Extraordinary Providence?

Ordinary Providence designates God's regular operation through second causes. Extraordinary, refers to His activity either independently of second causes, or through these causes in an unusual way.

"Law of Nature"

26. What other term designates Ordinary Providence?

"Law of Nature." When second causes have been observed to act uniformly under given circumstances and conditions, this uniform method is called "a law." Day has been found to follow night, and summer winter, without exception, in the experience of mankind; and, hence, we deduce the rule or law, according to which all our expectations conform.

27. What caution must be observed in the tracing of "laws"?

The widening of experience often shows that the method accepted as law is not absolutely uniform, but changes under conditions that had not been observed before. The inhabitant of the tropics may know nothing of the solidification of water at a low degree of temperature. An uneducated man would deny the possibility of lighting a candle with a piece of ice; and yet the chemist can do it by attaching to the wick a pellet of sodium. Superficial observation shows that cold contracts objects; but wider observation shows that from 39 degrees Fahrenheit until the freezing point, the law changes. Only a few years ago, the possibility of holding a conversation half way across a continent would have been derided, as would also have been the assertion that the eve could, under certain circumstances, penetrate a human body and see objects on the other side. A so-called "law" is not, therefore, God's ordinary way of working; but it is an inference based upon man's observation. It is the result attained by generalization from the widest sphere of facts that have fallen beneath the experience of the one who undertakes to state the law.

God not bound to His own laws

28. But if human experience were to haze all the details, so far as the past and the present are concerned, could God be bound in the future to the rules underlying such details?

This would make God the creature and subject of law, and would virtually deny that there is a God. For God is nothing, if not supreme and sovereign. He who has fixed the so-called "laws of nature," could just as readily have ordained other laws, varying from them, and, when and where He pleases, He can act through them extraordinarily, or dispense with them altogether.

The doctrine of Miracles: Miracle defined, Ground of its possibility, Ground of its necessity, Proof of its reality, Standpoints of its opponents, counterfeits, evidential value, distinctions, two classes of Miracles: (a) of Nature (b) of Grace Practical Application: the correct estimate of Second Causes

29. What, then, is extraordinary Providence?

A miracle. It may be defined as a suspension of a' law of nature, i.e., an activity that varies from the mode that has heretofore fallen under man's observation. Second causes may be employed in an extraordinary way, so that their activity may be accelerated or retarded; or God may act without them.

30. Upon what then does the possibility of a miracle depend?

Upon the freedom of God. "God works miracles in order to testify that He is omnipotent, and above nature. The ordinary course of things testifies that Nature has an Architect, who is wise, kind, righteous, viz., God. But He acts outside of and beyond this order, as when He raised the dead, or made the sun stand still, or turned it back, in order that we may know that He is Almighty, and stronger than the whole world, and that He can bring aid from outside of the natural order" (Melanchthon).

31. Upon what does the necessity of a miracle depend?

It stands and falls with the necessity of Revelation; for Revelation is a miracle. The order of Nature, violated and disarranged by sin, is restored by God's working over and beyond the sphere of purely natural causes. The two fundamental miracles are Creation and Redemption. The working out of what was introduced by Creation having been interrupted by sin, every miracle, since the fall, points to and centers in Redemption. The necessity for a miracle was introduced by sin. A low view of the extent and significance of sin results in the denial of the necessity of the miraculous. Where human guilt is passed over lightly, the need of a Redeemer is depreciated. The denial of the possibility of the miraculous is grounded, therefore, not so much in intellectual, as in moral difficulties. The strongest arguments are those which appeal more to the conscience than to the understanding.

32. What is the great proof of the reality of miracles?

The Person of Christ, the miracle of miracles (1 Tim. 3:16); and next to this, the regenerate life of the child of God, proceeding from that of Christ (1 Cor. 6:11).

33. From what standpoints is the possibility of miracles attacked?

[A.] From that of Atheism, which in its denial of God, necessarily denies that His Supreme will orders all things, and also makes exception to this order. The most widespread form of Atheism, and the one whose attacks on miracles is most frequently heard, is Materialism, with its assertion that there is neither God, nor mind, nor purpose in the universe.

[B.] From that of Deism, with its conception that when the clock is wound up it henceforth runs forever of itself, and that God acts in nature exclusively through the forces He once placed there. The world, according to it, has been so framed, that there can never be a variation from what ordinarily occurs. What ordinarily occurs must always occur; and what ordinarily does not occur, can never occur. Such are its postulates.

[C.] From that of Pantheism, where God is degraded to a mere personification of the powers of Nature.

34. Does the exposure of pretended miracles in any way affect the argument for the miracles recorded and prophesied in Scripture?

They only point to faith in the miraculous as grounded in the very nature of man's mind. What they abuse and mislead, finds its true end and satisfaction within the limits fixed in Holy Scripture. The detection of counterfeits does. not disprove the value of genuine coins.

35. But have not miracles been wrought by Satan and his adherents?

The magicians in Egypt wrought wonders (Ex. 7:11, 12), and the false prophet in Rev. 19:20. The Israelites, in Deut. 13:1-5, are warned against being misled by errorists notwithstanding their signs and wonders. These may have been nothing more than inexplicable facts transcending the experience of their witnesses, or as supernatural power may be conceded temporarily to the wicked in order that, in the conflict, God may be glorified, by counterbalancing and overcoming their very highest efforts and achievements by the still greater supernatural power with which He interferes for man's deliverance. Every so-called Satanic miracle may be interpreted, however, by a more than usual acquaintance with purely natural resources, as though some one were to appear among uncivilized people and would use wireless telegraphy.

36. Are miracles then evidences of the truth of the cause for which they are wrought?

Not in themselves. A miracle attracts attention, awakens reflection, leads to investigation, and brings the cause proclaimed to the test of Holy Scripture (Gal. 1:8.) "Miracles are seals of doctrine; as, therefore, a seal torn from a letter proves nothing, so miracles, without doctrine, are not valid" (Gerhard). See Chapter 13, 21-23.

37. What distinction was made by the Scholastics?

Into *miracula*, or miracles properly so called, and *mirabilia*, or apparent miracles. The former are deeds utterly surpassing natural powers, and wrought, therefore, only by God (Ps. 136:4). The latter were explained as wrought by the application of natural agents in a mysterious way, so as to excite astonishment, and to be regarded as miraculous.

38. Into what two classes have miracles been divided?

Into Miracles of Nature, and Miracles of Grace. The former were wrought by God in matters subject to sense, as when Christ raised the dead, and stilled the tempest, or when He Himself arose from the tomb. The latter are wrought within men for their salvation, or pertain to man's relation to God. The former are subordinate to the latter.

> John 14:12. "Greater works than these shall he do, because I go unto the Father."

The awakening of one born in sin to spiritual life is more wonderful than the quickening of Lazarus. All external miracles wrought by Christ and His Apostles were for the purpose of bringing men under the influence of spiritual power to justify, regenerate and glorify them.

39. What particular practical application is to be made of the doctrine of Providence?

It leads to a correct estimate of second causes. On the one hand, they are to be diligently used, as the ordinary means through which God communicates His gifts and blessings (i Thess. 4:11; 2 Cor. 3:10, 11; Matt. 4:7). On the other hand, we are not to rest in them; but, in our faithful discharge of the duties of our callings we may be assured that God has ways of caring for us and of rendering our work effective far above all we can ask or think (Ps. 127:1, 2; Matt. 4:4; 6:25-39; Phil. 4:6; 1 Peter 5:7).

6. Of Angels

Place and Estimate of the doctrine

Are we to invoke angels for their aid? This is forbidden by Col. 1:18. "Let no man rob you of your prize by worshiping of the angels." Rev. 19:10. "And I fell down before his feet to worship him. And he saith unto me, See thou do it not: I am a fellow-servant with thee and with thy brethren that hold the testimony of Jesus; worship God." Cf. 22:8, 9. It also conflicts with the sole mediatorship of Christ (Rom. 8:34; 1 Tim. 2:5; 1 John 2:1).

1. Why is the doctrine of Angels treated at this place?

Because after treating of Creation and Providence, we consider the chief creatures of God, Angels and Men, and the chief instruments of God's Providential activity, Angels.

2. Why is so little prominence given it in the Confessions of the Church?

Because with the gift of the Holy Ghost at Pentecost, and His abiding presence with the Church, the consciousness of the favor and nearness of God in Christ, completely subordinates their agency in the heart of the Christian. With the fuller appropriation of assurance of faith and of adoption as children of God, which entered with the study of St. Paul at the Reformation period, the chief allusions in the Confessions are in the cautions given against an abuse of the doctrine.

3. Is the doctrine, therefore, unimportant?

By no means. But the Reformation had to protest against the excessive attention that had been previously accorded it.

Definition

4. What are angels?

Pure and complete spirits, created by God, to be His agents in the administration of creation.

5. Why do we call them "pure" or "complete spirits"?

In distinction from men who need bodies for the completion of their being. Man, between death and the resurrection, exists without body, but it is an incomplete condition endured as a result of sin.

6. Are angels the only pure or complete spirits?

God is such. But angels differ from God in that while He is an infinite, they are finite spirits.

7. But are not angels sometimes described as having bodies?

Yes, but these bodies are assumed temporarily, and cast aside when the purpose for which they have been used has been accomplished. They have no more identity with the personality of angels than the pen has with the writer, or the needle with the seamstress.

Creation Attributes, Number

8. What do we know of their creation?

Nothing more than the fact (Col. 1:16). The entire absence of any allusion to the creation of angels in the Mosaic account shows that the record does not aim to be exhaustive. They are described as being in existence, if not before the creation of the earth, at any rate contemporaneously with it.

> Job 34:4, 7. "Where wast thou when I laid the foundations of the earth, when the morning stars sang together, and all the sons of God shouted for joy?"

That "sons of God" in the Book of Job are angels is proved from Chap. 1:6.

9. What are the attributes common to Good and Bad Angels?

Those belonging to complete finite spirits. They are simple or irresolvable into parts; invisible except through an assumed form; immutable so far as inner physical changes are concerned; immortal, i.e., dependency upon God; and illocal, or independent of ordinary spatial relations. They have extraordinary intelligence, a free will, great power, limitation with respect to presence, but ability to change this presence with extraordinary swiftness.

10. How as to their number?

> Dan. 7:10. "Thousands of thousands ministered unto him, and ten thousand times ten thousand stood before him."

> Matt. 26:53. "He shall even now send me more than twelve legions of angels?"

States

11. How many states of angels are there?

Three. The State of Grace, the State of Glory and the State of Misery. The State of Grace is that in which they were all originally created equally wise and holy, and for eternal happiness (Gen. 1:31; John 8:44).

The State of Glory is that in which the angels who abode in the wisdom and holiness in which they were created, have been admitted to the clear sight of God, and perpetually enjoy His goodness (Matt. 18:10; Ps. 16:11).

The State of Misery is the sad condition of the angels who, of their own accord and by the abuse of their free will, departed from God (2 Peter 2:4; Jude 6).

12. What differences in these three states with respect to the possibility of sinning?

In the State of Grace they were able either to sin or not to sin (*posse peccare aut non peccare*).

In the State of Glory they are not able to sin (*non posse peccare*).

In the State of Misery they cannot refrain from sinning (*non posse non peccare*).

The Good Angels: Impeccability; Ground of Perseverance; Knowledge; Power; Works; Guardian Angels; Their service for the godly; Not to be invoked; Orders; Figurative Names

13. What ground is there for affirming the impeccability of the Good Angels?

The godly, after the resurrection, are said to be immortal, and "equal unto the angels" (Luke 20:36); and the Lord's Prayer refers to the perfection with which God's will is done in heaven (Matt 6:10).

14. But is such impeccability consistent with freedom of the will?

Yes. Not to be able to sin is the highest degree of freedom. Such is the freedom of God. To be raised not only above all imperfection, but especially above all liability to suffer from an imperfection, is the highest perfection. (See Chapter 23:29, 30.)

15. What was the ground for the exaltation of the Good Angels to this higher stage?

No absolute decree of God, for it was based upon the condition of merit. Not .the merit of Christ, for He came to seek that which was lost (Luke 19:10) while the Good Angels were never lost; and He is the "Mediator between God and men" (1 Tim 2:5), not between God and angels. Nor was it any merit of their own; since they were under obligation, in virtue of their creation, to serve God to their utmost power. The sole ground, therefore, is the unmerited goodness of God.

16. What of the knowledge of angels?

When Christ wished to state the impossibility of knowing a certain event, He made it very emphatic by saying that not even the angels in heaven know it (Mark 13:32). Thus He declared both the greatness and the limitations of their knowledge. Only God knows the secrets of men's hearts (1 Kings 8:39). Not only is there much beyond which they have desired to know (1 Peter 1:12), but, in God's own time, this is made known to them by revelation (Eph. 3:10).

17. What of their power?

The destruction of Sennacherib's army of 185,000 men, in one night, by a single angel (2 Kings 19:35), is a sufficient proof. They are said to be "mighty in strength" (Ps. 103:7), "angels of his power" (2 Thess. 1:7).

18. What are the works of Good Angels?

[A.] The adoring worship of God (Dan. 7:10; see Q 10; Is. 6:2; Rev. 4:8; Matt. 6:10) .

[B.] The service of the godly.

> Heb. 1:14. "Are they not all ministering spirits, sent forth to do service for the sake of them that shall inherit salvation?"
>
> Ps. 91:11. "He shall give his angels charge over thee, to keep thee in all thy ways."

19. Has each child of God a guardian angel?

It is going too far to derive such a doctrine from Matt 18:10 and Acts 12:15. The godly are frequently comforted with the assurance that they are protected not by an angel, but by angels. See Ps. 91:11, cited above. A number of angels — sometimes a host — attend one man (Gen. 32:2; 2 Kings 6:16; Luke 16:22), and -rejoice over the repentance of but one sinner (Luke 15:10).

20. Within what sphere do they serve the godly?

Within that of the natural world. They are revealed as active at peculiarly critical epochs in human life (Matt. 1:10; 4:11; Acts 10:3; Luke 16:22). There is no evidence that they work otherwise than through second causes. Their connection with the Kingdom of Grace is only for the disposition of Providential agencies in its service.

The mysteries of incarnation and redemption were beyond their grasp (Eph. 3:9). It is not their office to effect any of those spiritual changes within man, which the Holy Spirit works through the word of the Gospel. Angels bring deliverance from bodily dangers, but they are no way revealed as regenerating or sanctifying.

21. Where is their activity especially prominent?

At every great epoch of God's revelation of Himself in deed. At Creation (Job 38:7); the Giving of the Law (Deut. 33:2; Gal. 3:19); the Incarnation (Luke 1:20; 2:9,13); the Temptation (Matt. 4:11); the Passion (Luke 22:43) 5 the Resurrection (John 20:12); the Ascension (Acts 2:11), and the Final Judgment (Matt. 25:31; Mark 13:27; Matt. 13:41,49; 1 Thess. 4:16; 2 Thess. 1:7).

22. Is this activity confined to individuals?

No. It is extended to nations (Dan. 10), and to the assemblies of Christians (1 Cor. 11:10; 1 Tim. 5:21; Eph. 3:10).

23. Are we to invoke angels for their aid?

This is forbidden by Col. 1:18. "Let no man rob you of your prize by worshiping of the angels."

> Rev. 19:10. "And I fell down before his feet to worship him. And he saith unto me, See thou do it not: I am a fellow-servant with thee and with thy brethren that hold the testimony of Jesus; worship God." Cf. 22:8, 9.

It also conflicts with the sole mediatorship of Christ (Rom. 8:34; 1 Tim. 2:5; 1 John 2:1).

24. But are there not several kinds of worship, one of which belongs to God alone, and another also to angels?

For this argument of the Greek and Roman churches, there is no Scriptural warrant. We indeed should honor and revere them as God's ministers, and thank Him for what He effects for us through their agency; but this is far different from worshiping them or invoking their intercession (1 Cor. 11:10; 1 Tim. 5:21; Luke 15:7, 10).

25. Are there no: instances where worship is actually accorded an angel?

If such passages as Gen. 18:1-3 actually accord such worship, it is because it is given either to the "Angel of the Lord" as the uncreated Angel, who is none less than Jehovah Himself, or to the Angel, as the representative of Jehovah. (The former view is advocated at length by Kurtz, "History of O. T. Covenant" I, Sec. 50.)

26. What different orders of Good Angels are there?

> Col. 1:16. "Things invisible, whether thrones or dominions, or principalities, or powers."
>
> Rom. 8:38. "Nor angels, nor principalities, nor powers."
>
> Eph. 3:10. "The principalities and powers in heavenly places."
>
> 1 Thess. 4:16. "The voice of the archangel."
>
> Jude 9. "Michael the archangel."

27. What higher orders appear in the Old Testament?

Cherubim and Seraphim, distinguished from angels properly so called, in that while angels go forth as messengers, they stand in the presence of God. The Cherubim are described four-winged. Their appearance indicates a special divine presence. They are the attendants of the divine glory as it descends to man (Ps. 18:10; 80:1; 99:1; 2 Sam. 22:11; Is. 37:16). The Seraphim are described six-winged and dwell in the secret glory of God. They do not descend, but are manifested only when man is raised to contemplate the glory of God (Is. 6:2-6; Rev. 4:7 sqq.).

28. By what figure is the brilliancy of their endowments indicated?

They are sometimes called stars (Job 38:7; Ps. 148:3) and compared to lightning (Luke 10:18).

The Bad Angels: Problems concerning their Fall; Its order; Its effect on their endowments; Changed relation towards God; Their future; How now occupied; Demoniacal Possession

29. What problem meets us when we consider the fall of some angels?

That of the origin of evil.

30. Is it explicable?

No. The farthest we can go is to learn that it was God's will that the perfections with which angels were originally endowed should be increased and developed in their struggle against evil. To this end, therefore, they were endowed with a will which was able to sin.

31. Did the sin of the Bad Angels come from any external source?

No, but from the will of beings originally pure and holy spontaneously turning from God.

> John 8:44. "When he speaketh a lie, he speaketh of his own."

32. Did it come from any lack of divine grace which those who did not fall enjoyed?

This would make God the author of their sin.

33. What was the form of the sin whereby they fell?

Because of the motive presented Eve for her sin (Gen. 3:5), and of the finaltemptation addressed our Lord by Satan (Matt. 4:9), many have thought that itwas pride. The root of all pride, however, is unbelief.

34. What was the order of their fall?

First, the fall of a chief, called Satan, "the adversary," or the Devil, "the accuser," or "the Prince of the power of the air" (Eph. 2:2); and through his instrumentality, the fall of the rest. For John 8:44 calls him a "murderer from the beginning," and Luke 11:15, "the prince of the demons," while Matt. 25:41 and Rev. 12:7 refer to the rest as his "angels."

Ecclesiasticus 10:13:

"For pride is the beginning of sin," was cited by the old writers as a proof.

35. What effect had their fall upon their angelic endowments?

A contraction of their knowledge and intellectual penetration; for while an extraordinary knowledge of supernatural things remains, the effort of the devil to lead Christ astray by temptation, and the putting into the heart of Judas the thought of betraying Him, and thereby of preparing Satan's own ruin (1 Cor. 2:7,8), show his ignorance.

A great limitation also of their power. While according to Matt. 12:29; Luke 11:21; Eph. 6:12; 1 Peter 5:8, this power is still such as is not to be overlooked or despised, except by a special permission of God it cannot harm (Job 1:12; 2:6; Matt. 8:31). In Jude 8, this limitation is expressed under the figure of "chains," whereby they are confined until the Day of Judgment. This power God knows how to turn to His own purpose. 1 Tim. 2:25, 26 speaks of those who are taken captive by Satan unto the will of God. Of this the entire drama of the Book of Job is an example.

Their freedom of will was also limited. Henceforth they can will nothing but sin. Their freedom has to do only with a choice between particular evils.

36. What disposition of God have they incurred?

His irreconcilable wrath (2 Peter 2:5; Jude V. 6; Heb. 2:16).

37. What of their disposition towards God and His creatures other than themselves?

Knowing that there is a God (James 2:19), that He is almighty, and that, while infinitely good to the Good Angels and men, He is and will be to eternity severe towards them, not only are they without love, but they fear and hate Him with all the powers of their nature. This hatred extends to all whom He loves and for whom He cares. Like those among men whom they inspire and incite, they "live in malice and envy, hateful and hating one another." Whatever harmony and cooperation exist among them is rooted not in love, but in their desire to harm and overthrow the good.

38. What of their future?

Matt. 25:41. "Eternal fire which is prepared for the devil and his angels."

2 Peter 2:4. "Reserved unto judgment."

Jude 6. "Kept in everlasting bonds under darkness unto the judgment of the great day."

39. Do they know this?

James 2:19. "The demons also believe and shudder."

Matt. 8:29. Art thou come hither to torment us before the time?"

40. Meanwhile how are they occupied?

They are intent upon what may bring ruin upon man, and dishonor God (Luke 22:31; Eph. 6:11, 12; 1 Peter 5:8, 9; Luke 13:16; Job 1:12; 1 Cor. 7:5). Their attacks are directed not only against men individually, but are aimed particularly at the Church and its Means of Grace (Matt. 13:27; 1 Tim. 4:1,2; 1 Thess. 2:18).

41. What was demoniacal possession?

A special temporary bodily possession, permitted by God, in New Testament times, particularly those of the visible ministry of Christ, as a factor in the struggle of the powers of darkness with the Son of God for the control of the human race. After principalities and powers were spoiled in our Lord's resurrection from the dead, we can find no bodily possession like that described in the Gospels.

7. Man As Created

1. How many states of Man are there?

Five: The state of Integrity, the state of Corruption, the state of Grace, the state of Glory, the state of Misery.

2. In which of these was man created?

The state of Integrity.

3. What place does man hold in creation?

According to Gen. 1:26, he is the goal of all the creative acts of God. Cf. Ps. 8:6-8.

4. Of how many parts is man composed? Of two, viz., Body and Soul or Spirit.

5. What is the Body?

The material part of man's nature.

2 Cor. 5:1. "The earthly house of this tabernacle."

6. But does not this imply some amount of impurity?

In no way. On the contrary, even the bodily and material has a spiritual and eternal significance and destiny.

> 1 Cor. 6:19. "Your body is a temple of the Holy Spirit."
>
> Rom. 12:1. "Present your bodies a living sacrifice, which is your spiritual service."
>
> 1 Cor. 15:44. "It is sown a natural body; it is raised a spiritual body."

7. But cannot the soul exist without the body?

Yes, but only as a consequence and punishment of sin. The soul can exist in an abnormal way without body, just as the body also can exist with some of its limbs or organs removed. "We do not long to become bodiless souls. Endowed with bodies here, it is intended we should have them also hereafter" (Luthardt, Glaubenslehre).

8. Is it not often taught, however, that the body is the prison of the soul, or its fetter, by which its heavenward flight is checked?

Such is the teaching of Platonism, and of heathenism generally, which fails to interpret aright the fearful significance of death. Death, or the separation of soul and body, is not of itself a blessing, but a violence done nature, and something which conscience declares ought not to be. The soul was made for the body, as the body was made for the soul, and both together were made for God.

9. Do all theologians agree that mans nature has but two parts?

On this subject, there are two schools, the Dichotomists and the Trichotomists. The former teach as we have said above that man's nature has two parts, body and soul or spirit; the latter that it has three parts, body and soul and spirit. The difference is determined by the question as to whether soul and spirit be the same part of man's nature, designated with reference to different relations, or whether they be different parts.

10. Upon what grounds is the distinction between "soul" and "spirit," as different parts of man's nature based?

The seeming contrast between the terms in such passages as:

> 1 Thess. 5:23. "May your spirit and soul and body be preserved entire."
>
> Heb. 4:12. "Piercing to the dividing of soul and spirit."
>
> 1 Cor. 15:44. "It is sown a psychical body; it is raised a spiritual body."
>
> Luke 1:46, 47. "My soul doth magnify the Lord; and my spirit hath rejoiced in God my Savior."

The soul is regarded, therefore, as the immaterial part of man's nature which he has in common with the lower animals, while the spirit is that which he has in common with God and the angels.

11. By whom was such distinction taught?

The suggestion came from Plato. It was advocated by Justin Martin, Irenaeus, and the Alexandrian school, and became the doctrine of the Greek Church. With various modifications it has been taught in recent times by Olshausen, Neander and Meyer; and elaborated by Delitzsch in his "Biblical Psychology."

12. Why is the theory unsatisfactory?

Because in a number of passages, "soul" and "spirit" are treated as synonyms. If man is described in Matt. 10:28 as "body and soul," he is described in Eccl. 12:7 as "body and spirit." If it is the "spirit" in Matt. 2J:50, it is the "soul" in Matt. 20:28; Acts 20:10.

For this reason, Tertullian, Jerome, Augustine, followed by the theologians of the Western Church, Roman Catholic, Lutheran and Reformed,with only a few exceptions, advocate Dichotomy. It appears prominently in the Small Catechism:

> "I believe that He has given to me my body and soul;"

13. May not the two theories be reconciled?

Yes, by regarding "soul" and "spirit" identical in substance, but diverse in relation. When regarded with respect to earthly relations, I. c, those belonging to the world that now is, it is "soul"; but when referred to the heavenly destiny for which God has created and endowed and redeemed it, it is "spirit." This is not contradicted by the fact that its destiny, even in its earthly environment, does not prevent it from being sometimes called "soul," as in Matt. 10:28. Soul comes from God and goes to God, but its activity is through the body. Where souls of the departed are mentioned, as in Rev. 6:9, their former residence in bodies is implied.

14. What, then, is meant in Heb. 4:12 by "the dividing of soul and spirit"?

Not the separation of the soul from the spirit, but that the all pervasive influence of the Holy Spirit acting through the Word leaves no recess of man's nature, however secret, or by whatever name called, untouched by its operations.

15. What then is the soul or the spirit?

Not an etherealized form of matter or force of the body, as taught by Materialists; for nothing is clearer than the contrast between "soul and body," and "spirit and body" in the passages above cited. But the soul is a living, immaterial, simple substance, inhabiting, sustaining and moving the body.

16. May it not, then, be identical with the Spirit of God?

This is indeed said to dwell in man (Job 32:8; 33:4). But since the two are explicitly distinguished and contrasted in such passages as Rom. 8:16, 26; 1 Cor. 2: it, and man's spirit is sinful and needs the renewing grace of God (2 Cor. 7:1; Eph. 4:23), they cannot be identical, and man's spirit cannot be an emanation of that of God. When God dwells in man, it is by the presence of God's Spirit within man's spirit, as we learn elsewhere occurs in four degrees, viz., the natural life, the Mystical Union, (22), Inspiration (24, 8), Incarnation (21, 21 sqq,), according as it is universal or is more and more restricted, until limited to but one instance.

17. What mode of presence does the soul have in the body?

The answer to this question does not belong properly to Theology. As, however, spirit is a simple substance, i.e., it is indissoluble or indivisible into parts, the soul cannot be conceived of as present in such way that a part of the soul is at one part, and another part of the soul at another part of the body. This presence of a finite spirit in a body has been termed definitive.

18. Do all men come from one ancestor?

Acts 17:26. "He hath made of one every nation of men to dwell on all the face of the earth."

Rom. 5:12. "Through one man, sin entered into the world, and death through sin, and so death passed unto all men, for that all sinned."

19. Has this ever been questioned?

No one seems to seriously dispute this at present. The whole argument of scientists, advocating the Darwinian theory of evolution, is in its favor. But it must not be forgotten that, at the middle of the nineteenth century, theologians and the few scientists in America who maintained the Unity of the Human Race, were ridiculed as singularly unscientific. With great learning, diversity of race peculiarities was urged as an irrefutable argument in favor of diversity of origin. In recent years, the pendulum has swung to the other extreme, and the endeavor been made to find a common source for all animal life, which, then, by the ceaseless struggles of uncounted ages, advanced until man was reached. When the Scriptural account of creation is opposed to this theory, it is summarily discarded as "unscientific," because it has as little support for this "scientific" theory, as it had for its now thoroughly exploded predecessor.

20. But were the old school of nineteenth century scientists the only opponents of the Unity of the Human Race?

No. The Athenians called themselves Autochthones, and boasted of springing from the soil on which they lived. The Preadamites, represented by the French theologian, Peyrere, taught that only Jews had descended from Adam, while the Gentiles had been created in pairs, male and female, in all parts of the earth.

21. Are there not other arguments for the Unity of the Human Race, beyond the Scriptural argument, which are just as strong as those now advanced by comparative zoologists?

Such are:

(1) The Psychological argument, from the identity of the various races of men in processes of thought, and of emotions as love and hatred, fear and hope.
(2) The Linguistic argument, the general laws which govern all languages being the same.
(3) The argument from Comparative Religion. All are responsive to religious appeals, and capable of religious dispositions. There is everywhere the same sense of sin and guilt, and the same recognition, with greater or less degree of intelligence, of a Supreme Being.
(4) The correspondence of the sagas and traditions of races most widely removed from one another.

> "According to science the origin of the human race from one pair is possible, not to say probable. But what Science at least admits, Theology demands upon the ground of the holy record of the fact of universal sinfulness" (Kahnis.)

22. What theories have been advanced to explain how, since Adam, souls enter the world?

There are three theories:

[A.] The Preexistence theory.

Advocated by Plato, Philo, Origen, Kant, Schelling, Coleridge, Wordsworth, Julius Mueller, and, in America, by Edward Beecher. All souls, they teach, have existed before, and have been condemned to have bodies, because, in this ante-temporal state, they have fallen into sin. Occasionally they have vague reminiscences of this former blissful condition, and the desire to return.

This theory directly conflicts with the argument of Romans 5, and the account of Genesis 3, besides being at variance with what has been taught above concerning the body (see 6-8).

[B.] Creationism

Advocated by Aristotle, Ambrose, Jerome, Pelagius, the Greek Church, the Roman Church, most of the theologians of the Reformed Church, there, being, however, some prominent recent exceptions (H. B. Smith, Shedd, Stearns, Strong), and by John Brenz and Calixt among Lutherans. The body alone, they say, is propagated from parent to child. With the coming of every new soul into the world, there is a new creative act of God. A soul is created by God and united with the body, and thus inherits the corruption transmitted by the parents from Adam.

Against this, there are the following objections:

(1) It destroys the unity of human nature, by ascribing parentage alone to the body, and is thus incompatible with the inheritance of intellectual gifts and aptitudes and deformities.

(2) It materializes sin, since the effect of the doctrine is to make sin a subtle physical poison, transmitted through the inherited body, and not from the soul, thus completely reversing the order described by our Lord in Matt. 15:19, 20.

(3) Or if this be denied, it is driven to the alternative of either denying the existence of natural depravity, or of holding that it is created by God with the soul.

[C.] Traducianism

Advocated in a materialistic form by Tertullian, but with more discrimination by Athanasius and Gregory of Nyssa, and held as a probable theory by Augustine and Luther. It is accepted by Lutherans, with a few exceptions. According to this theory, soul as well as body is transmitted from parent to child. This theory is most consistent with the unity of human nature, and with that of the universality of inherited sin. The chief argument urged against it, is that it conflicts with the simplicity of the soul. But one light may enkindle another without diminishing the original flame.

Neither Creationism nor Traducianism exhausts the truth concerning man's origin. Traducianism should be interpreted as Mediate Creationism. God is no less the creator of souls (Is. 57:16; Jer. 1:5; Zech. 12:1), when he uses second causes to bring them into the world. Hence the confessional statement:

> "God not only before the Fall created the body and soul of Eve, but, since the Fall, has created also our bodies and souls" (Formula of Concord, 545).

23. What distinguished the state of Integrity from the state of Corruption which has succeeded?

Man's endowment with the Image of God.

> Gen. 1:27. "God created man in his own image, in the image of God created he him."
>
> Gen. 5:1. "In the day that God created man, in the likeness of God made he him."
>
> Gen. 9:6. "For in the image of God made he man."

24. As God is reported in Gen. 1:26 as saying, "Let us make man in our image, after our likeness," what difference is there between the "image" and the "likeness" of God?

The Greek and Roman Churches make much of a distinction which they here find between qualities essential to the nature and those which perfect it. But "we do not distinguish 'image and likeness,' so as to refer the former to the essence of the soul, and the latter to the holiness, justice and knowledge of God in man, but we teach that the same thing is expressed by both terms, and that 'likeness' is used exegetically" (Gerhard). The proof for this is the promiscuous use of the terms. Scripture sometimes uses -both terms in the same case, sometimes in different cases, and sometimes gives only one term and omits the other. While God uses both terms in the declaration of his purpose (Gen.1:26), when the result is declared the one word "image" is employed. We have no warrant, therefore, to distinguish between these terms.

25. But even though the application of the terms "image" and "likeness" to such distinction cannot be admitted, is not the distinction itself Scriptural?

Yes; for man's spiritual nature was created in the image of God, and is that image in the wide sense of the term; and within that nature as created, certain perfections capable of loss inhered, which constitute "the image" in the special sense of the term. Man's personality, his intellectual and moral nature, constitute the image in the former sense. There are references to the image in this sense in

> James 3:9. "Therewith curse we men who are made after the likeness of God."
>
> Gen. 9:6. "Whoso sheddeth man's blood, by man shall his blood be shed; for in the image of God, made he man."

While Scripture does not refer to this as frequently as to the image in the special sense, it is not because this is excluded, but because the latter is the more important. As Luther has said, "When Moses says that man was made in God's image, he shows thereby that man is not only like God in having reason or understanding and a will, but especially that he is conformed to God, i.e., he has such understanding and will as to understand God, and will what God wills."

26. What then is the image of God In the special sense?

In the Apology of the Augsburg Confession, the Lutheran Church has defined it as Original Righteousness.

27. How is this explained?

"That in man there were embodied such wisdom and righteousness as apprehended God, and in which God was reflected, i.e., to man were given the gifts of the knowledge of God, the fear of God, confidence in God and the like" (Apology, p. 79).

28. Knowledge was, therefore, one, of the constituents cf the image?

Yes, according to Col. 3:10:

> "The new man which is being renewed unto knowledge, after the image of him that created him."

This must not be interpreted, however, as though our first parents had such knowledge as was incapable of being increased, or that it extended to the decrees of God, or that it included all classes of material objects in encyclopedic survey. Contrasts have sometimes been made between the knowledge of Adam and that of Solomon and of Aristotle. Such discussions are scholastic trifles. The knowledge here meant is simply such knowledge of God and of themselves and of the world, as to enable them perfectly to attain the end for which they were destined. Their knowledge is to be estimated not by the number of topics it included, but by its religious value.

29. What other constituent is explicitly mentioned? Righteousness and holiness.

> Eph. 4:24. "Put on the new man, which after God hath been created in righteousness and holiness of truth."

Man had both the strength and the desire to fear, love and serve God above all things. The body was so completely under the control of a holy will that followed in all things the divine Law, as in all its activities and impulses, to be pure, and intent on God's glory.

30. What freedom was implied in this?

Not freedom of independence, since this belongs only to God, but from compulsion, from physical necessity and from servitude. Nevertheless the will was not exempt from mutability. Adam, like the angels at creation, was endowed with the power of sinning and of abstaining from sin. He was sinless, but not impeccable.

31. In what then does the original state of man differ from that which is at last attained by grace?

Augustine answers:

> "The first freedom of the will was to be able not to sin; the final, is not to be able to sin. The first immortality was to be able not to die; the final, is not to be able to die. The first power of perseverance is to be able not to desert the good; the final, is not to be able to desert the good."

32. What external evidences of the presence of this image were there?

[A.] The condition of the body.

Reflecting and expressing outwardly the glory of the soul, and with its various members, eye, ear, heart, etc., used to describe divine attributes. The erect form of man, with his countenance, unlike those of other animals turned towards heaven, reminds man of his origin and the destiny for which he was intended. Besides his body was exempt from all pain and accident and death, as long as this image of God remained unimpaired (Gen. 2:16; Rom. 5:12; 6:23). His immortality was conditional, unlike that of God, which is absolute (1 Tim. 6:16).

[B.] His dominion over all other creatures (Gen. 1:20, 28; 2:16).

This extends not only over brutes and reptiles, but over all the resources and powers of nature, the soil, the mountains, the rivers, the ocean, the winds, the stars and planets, light, heat, electricity, all the various appliances of Physics and Chemistry, Astronomy and Geology to man's interests. Like the knowledge of our first parents, the dominion actually exercised was only such as was then needed in the simplicity of their existence, and was to have been developed in their cultivation of the dominion assigned then. It differed from the more extensive dominion now exercised in the ease with which it was exercised, as contrasted with the painful struggles through which it has developed from age to age in the state which has followed.

[C.] The glory of his home (Gen. 2:8-17).

33. Was the image of God essential or accidental to mans nature?

The answer depends upon what is regarded as the image. If the term be used in the widest sense for man's spiritual nature and personality (see above, 25), then it is essential to man's nature. If, however, it be restricted to the perfections with which this nature was originally endowed in accordance with the New Testament passages which refer to the loss and the restoration of this image, then, of course, it is accidental. The error of Flacius which occasioned a controversy in the Lutheran Church, and reappears in the treatment of Original Sin, was that even in the latter sense, the image of God was essential to human nature.

34. Was it therefore a superadded gift?

It was a gift inhering in and pervading the entire nature, as it came from God's hands, and not something extraneous or mechanically attached thereto. The scholastics distinguished between a so-called "status purorum naturalium' and the image itself; and taught that while the image has been lost, the pura naturalia remains, although corrupted. Apart from the fact that such state never existed, except as a matter of purely abstract speculation, such doctrine represents human nature as created morally indifferent, in opposition to Gen. 1:31."And God saw everything that he had made, and behold it was very good."

The corruption of human nature which has followed does not make that nature as such either sin or morally indifferent. So far as human nature is a creature of God, it is good even when ruined, the ruin coming not from God, but from the abuse of God's creation.

It is incorrect, therefore, to maintain, as Roman Catholic theologians have done, that the image of God had no more to do with man's nature, than a bit has to do with a horse, or a man's clothes with his personality.

35. Would you say, then, that the image was "supernatural"?

Here again, everything depends upon the definition of "supernatural." Many of the discussions of theologians occur from using the same term in two senses. If "supernatural" mean having powers and capacities above the range of human nature, as it is at present, then the image was supernatural; but if the standpoint be that of human nature in man's first state, then it was natural. In a word, it was natural to a normal and incorrupt; it is supernatural, with respect to an enfeebled and corrupt nature.

36. What estimate is to be placed upon the doctrine of mans first state?

Just in the degree that its perfections are denied or diminished, is the significance of sin and its consequences decreased; and just in the degree that sin and its consequences are extenuated, are the necessity and importance of the work of Christ disparaged. If mortality, for instance, were ascribed to man before the Fall, death would not be the wages of sin, and the death of Christ would have to find a different explanation from that of the New Testament.

8. Sin

Definition

1. What is sin?

1 John 3:4. "Sin is lawlessness."

2. What does this mean?

That God has fixed a standard, and that whatever in state or in act, fails to meet its requirements is sin.

Place in Creation

3. What is the standard?

His Law, or the eternal rule of right by which He has prescribed what He wants His creatures to be, to do, or to refrain from doing.

Two parts: Dichotomy vs. Trichotomy

4. Give (3) then, a somewhat fuller definition.

Sin is to be otherwise, and to do otherwise, than God means us to be or do.

Cause and Kinds

5. Who is the cause of sin?

"They teach that although God creates and preserves nature, yet that the cause of sin is the will of the wicked, i.e., of the devil and ungodly men, which will, unaided of God, turned itself away from Him" (Augsburg Confession, Art. Xix).

6. How many kinds of sin are there?

Two: Original and Actual.

Original Sin:: Confessional statement

7. What is Original Sin?

"Since the Fall of Adam, all men begotten according to nature, are born with sin, that is without the fear of God, without trust in God, and with concupiscence; and this disease or vice of origin is truly sin, even now condemning and bringing eternal death upon those not born again through Baptism and the Holy Ghost" (Augsburg Confession, Art. 2).

Beginning

8. Where then does Original Sin begin?

In the Fall of Adam. Rom. 5:12. "Through one man sin entered into the world, and death through sin; and so death passed upon all men, for that all sinned."

Origin and Application of term

9. But is Original Sin a Scriptural term?

No, but a term employed by the Church to express the truth taught in the above passage, as well as frequently elsewhere in Scripture.

10. Does it always refer to the same thing?

Sometimes it designates the act of disobedience to God's prohibition in Paradise ("Original Sin originating"), or the First Sin of our race. Sometimes it refers to the corruption or depravity of human nature in consequence of the First Sin ("Original Sin originated"). Article Second of the Augsburg Confession uses it in the second sense.

The First Sin and its significance

11. What was the significance of the prohibition in Paradise?

It was a test of obedience.

12. What was involved in the disobedience?

Before the external act of reaching forth the hand and taking the forbidden fruit, there was doubt in the intellect (Gen. 3:3), an inordinate desire for greater resemblance or equality with God in the will (Gen. 3:5), and lust for the gratification of sense beyond what God allowed (Gen. 3:16).

13. What commandment was violated?

In breaking one commandment, the whole Law was violated.

Break one link of a chain and the whole chain is broken; cut an ocean cable at one point, and the whole cable is severed.

> James 2:10. "Whosoever shall keep the whole law, and yet stumble in one point, he is guilty of all."

14. Why is the sin known as "the sin of Adam"?

Because while Eve fell and was involved in all the consequences of the Fall, he was the head of the race, and had he proved faithful, God could have provided another mother for his descendants.

Consequences of Fall

15. What were the consequences of the Fall?

[A.] The loss of the divine image, in its strict sense, or the perfections with which human nature was endowed at creation (see above, Chapter VII, 26-30).

[B.] Guilt, or the disgrace and moral taint resulting from sin.

[C.] A state or habit of sin. For the lack of the perfections of the divine image is of itself sin. If the sum of the commandments is love to God, the absence of this love is assuredly sin.

[D.] Punishment, the inseparable attendant of guilt.

Punishments

16. What was the Punishment?

Death.

> Gen. 2:17. "In the day that thou eatest thereof, thou shalt surely die."
>
> Rom. 5:12. "Death passed upon all men, for that all sinned."
>
> Rom. 6:23. "The wages of sin is death."

17. How many forms of this punishment are there?

Three: Death Spiritual, Temporal and Eternal.

[A.] Spiritual death is the separation of the soul from God, or the interruption of the life-communion which the soul had with God.

> Eph. 2:5. "Even when we were dead through our trespasses made he us alive together with Christ."
>
> Col. 2:13. "And you being dead through your trespasses." Cf. Matt. 8:22; Luke 9:60; 15:24; 1 Tim. 5:6.

What the soul is to the body, God was to the soul. With the interruption of this relation, all spiritual life vanished.

[B.] Temporal death, or the separation of the soul from the body.

Eccl. 12:7. "The dust returneth to the earth as it was, and the spirit to God who gave it."

[C.] Eternal death is the eternal state of the soul reunited with the body and separated from God. This is called also "the second death" (Rev. 2:11; 20:14; 21:8; Chapter 39).

Unity of Race

18. How do these three unite?

They are only stages of one and the same death. As in bodily death, one sense, or one portion of the body dies before another, or a twig may blossom even after cut from its stalk, so the separation of the soul from God results in temporal death, and temporal death culminates, if unarrested, in eternal death.

19. How was the warning, "In the day that thou eat est thou shall surely die," fulfilled?

The spiritual death was immediate, and even the processes of temporal death began at once. But the fact that the culmination is reached only by a long process, is doubtless due to the provision which God was making for man's redemption. The shadow of the Cross already fell across the human race, and protected it from the full heat of the divine wrath.

20. You spoke of "the processes of temporal death." Explain this?

By "processes" I mean all infirmities and diseases of body and soul, and the suffering which they bring. The healthiest body has its organs enfeebled or diseased. Since the Fall, health is only a relative term.

Extent of consequences

21. But were this guilt and this punishment limited to our first parents?

Rom. 5:12. "And so death passed upon all men, for that all sinned."

Origin of Soul: Preexistence, Creationism and Traducianism

22. How can we be responsible for the sin of another?

In one sense, Adam's sin was not the sin of another. All humanity was in Adam, and in him lost the endowments that pleased God. Beside, he stood not only as the organic head, but as the federal head of the race.

> 1 Cor. 15:22. "For as in Adam all die, so also in Christ shall all be made alive."

Image of God

23. But have we not an express declaration, "The son shall not bear the iniquity of the father" (Ez. 18:20)?

The prophet is speaking of actual sins, which he enumerates in the context. We do not participate in the guilt of any ancestral sin, since that of Adam. The common nature derived through our parents has been corrupted by Adam's sin; this, with all its sin, we inherit. But the specific sins to which this common corrupt nature led in my ancestors since Adam do not belong to me.

24. How then about Ex. 20:5, "Visiting the iniquity of the fathers upon the children upon the third and upon the fourth generation of them that hate me"?

Here the children share in the guilt of the actual sins of parents by following their example, and committing like sins.

Immediate and Mediate Imputation

25. What two terms have theologians used to explain the relation of Adam's sin to his descendants?

Immediate and Mediate Imputation.

Immediate Imputation is when the first sin in the Garden of Eden is said (as above, 22) to be ours. Mediate Imputation is where the sin of Adam is viewed as the source of the corruption of human nature which has followed, and this corruption is found to merit God's wrath.

The argument of Mediate Imputation is that if the condition of our nature is sinful, and this sinfulness came from Adam, our responsibility for this sinful state means that we partake in his guilt for its existence.

26. Which form of the doctrine is taught by Lutheran Church?

Both; but in accordance with the thoroughly practical character of our Church, chief stress is laid upon the latter, since it is most effective in convincing men of their being by nature beneath God's wrath. Hence the Augsburg Confession in Article 2, defines Original Sin as the corrupt state of our nature, and lays all emphasis upon "Original Sin originated" (see above, 10), which many theologians, particularly in the Reformed Church, regard not as sin itself, but as a punishment of sin.

Negative and Positive Elements

27. Into what elements does the Augsburg Confession resolve Original Sin?

Into a negative, viz., "to be without the fear of God and without trust in God," and a positive element, "to have concupiscence."

Its Constituents

28. How can the former be sin?

By being a violation of the First Commandment, which is the sum of all the commandments. Not to be able to fear and love God is of itself want of conformity with God's Law (see above, 1-4); it is being otherwise than what God wants us to be.

29. What is "concupiscence"?

The temper or attitude or disposition of man's heart and mind in antagonism to all that God wants and is.

> Rom. 8:7. "The carnal mind is enmity against God; for it is not subject to the law of God, neither indeed can be."
>
> 1 Cor. 2:14. "The natural man receiveth not the things of the spirit of God, for they are foolishness unto him."
>
> Matt. 15:19. "For out of the heart come forth evil thoughts, murders, adulteries, fornications, thefts, false witness, railing."
>
> James 1:14. "Each man is tempted, when he is drawn away by his own lust and enticed."
>
> Gal. 5:17. "The flesh lusteth against the Spirit."

This concupiscence is not limited to anyone of the commandments, but is directed against them all. Augustine, and after him, the Medieval Church, was inclined to place its chief sphere in desires contrary to the Sixth Commandment.

Universality of Original Sin

30. How extensive is Original Sin?

With one exception, all are its subjects. The Augsburg Confession uses the words, "All men born according to the common course of nature are born with sin," in order to exempt from its statement the humanity of Christ.

> Heb. 4:15. "In all points, tempted like as we are, yet without sin." Heb. 7:26. "Holy, harmless, undefiled, separate from sinners."

31. Prove this universality.

The entire argument of the fifth chapter of Romans is to the effect that the presence of death is a proof of sin, and that whoever dies must have sinned. The death of Christ we know occurred by His bearing the sins of the human race. "Death reigned," we are told in V. 14, "from Adam to Moses, even over them that had not sinned after the similitude of Adam's transgression," i.e., even where actual sin was wanting.

So in John 3:3, 5, 6, our 'Lord expressly excludes from the kingdom of heaven all who are not regenerate. In the words, "That which is born of the flesh is flesh," He declares that every one who comes into this world is in such condition that for entrance into the new life a great internal change must occur.

In Eph. 2:1-5 St. Paul refers to Christians as having been dead in trespasses and sins, and by their very nature "children of wrath."

External Evidences of Image

32. But it is explicitly declared, "Where there is no law, there is no transgression' (Rom. 4:15). Does not Ms exempt infants who cannot know the law?

The passage must be understood in accordance with the context. The argument of Paul is that death proves sin, and the violation of law, and that even though they be not guilty of actual transgression, in sinning after the similitude of Adam's sin, their death shows that they have transgressed otherwise and are under law. Other passages that might be cited concerning the innocence of little children must also be interpreted with respect to actual sins, and not to Original Sin.

Was it essential or accident

33. Beside infecting all men, what further statement can be made concerning the extent of Original Sin?

It is pervasive. It belongs to all parts and powers of human nature. It is a disease or vicious and depraved habit corrupting the whole man. "It is a deep, wicked, horrible, fathomless, inscrutable, and unspeakable corruption of the entire nature and all its powers, especially of the highest, principal powers of the soul in understanding, heart and will" (Formula of Concord, 592).

Effects on Man's Will

34. What is the consequence of this corruption of the highest powers?

This will be considered hereafter at greater length, under "The Freedom of the Will." But, meanwhile, we may recall what has been cited above in Chapter 1, 32:

"When even the most able and learned men upon earth read or hear the Gospel of the Son of God, and the promise of eternal salvation, they cannot, from their own powers perceive, apprehend, understand or believe and regard it true, but the more diligence and earnestness they employ, in order to comprehend, with their reason, these spiritual things, the less they understand or believe, and before they become enlightened or taught by the Holy Ghost, they regard all this only foolishness or fictions."

Error of Flacius

35. Is this corruption then so great as to justify the assertion that, since the fall, man's nature is sin?

No; for while the word "nature" is sometimes used in a loose sense, not for nature itself, but for a quality or disposition in the nature, as when we say, "It is the nature of the serpent to bite," nevertheless the expression is to be avoided and condemned. Man's nature is not sin, but sinful. Much as one may suffer from diphtheria or typhoid fever, no one can be said to become either of these diseases.

36. Was such error ever taught?

Yes, in the early days of Christianity, by the Manichaeans, and, shortly after the Reformation by Matthias Flacius Illyricus.

37. Repeat the arguments by which his error was refuted.

God created human nature; He cannot be said to create sin.

The Son of God assumed human nature; He did not assume sin.

He redeemed human nature; He does not redeem sin. He justifies and sanctifies human nature; He does neither to sin.

He will at the Last Day raise human nature from the dead; this He will not do with Original Sin.

Original Sin, therefore, is not substantial, but accidental to human nature.

38. How did Flacius come to advocate such a manifestly extreme position?

By his earnestness in refuting the opinion that Original Sin is only a slight corruption of man's powers, and that he still retains some good in him to begin or cowork in things pertaining to God.

Relative Power

39. Has Original Sin equal power in all?

No. In some it reigns and makes them its slaves (Rom. 6:16; Titus 3:3). In others, it is resisted, and its dominion broken (Rom. 8:2,13).

Duration

40. How long does it remain?

Its guilt is removed in justification; its dominion is broken with the beginning of renovation, and gradually and successively disappears as renovation grows. Of this process a vivid picture is found in Rom. VII. Its complete destruction does not occur until in death.

41. What other opinion has been advanced?

That of the Roman Catholic Church, following some scholastics, that, in the baptized, concupiscence is no longer sin.

42. How is this refuted?

The argument of Chemnitz is as follows: Concupiscence in the baptized is one of three things, either a good, or a matter of indifference or an evil. Can it be a good, when Paul says, "In me, that is, in my flesh, dwelleth no good thing" (Rom. 7:18)? Can it be a matter of indifference, when he says again, "The good which I would, I do not; but the evil which I would not that I practice" (Rom. 7:19)? He cannot speak of concupiscence before baptism, but it is the baptized and experienced Christian who makes this confession. In the same chapter this concupiscence is repeatedly called sin, and its conflict with God's law described.

Fruits

43. What are the fruits of Original Sin?

All the wicked deeds forbidden in the Ten Commandments. The moral quality of every deed is determined by the moral quality or character of the doer.

> Matt. 7:17. "Every good tree bringeth forth good fruit; but the corrupt tree bringeth forth evil fruit."
>
> Luke 6:45. "The good man out of the good treasure of his heart bringeth forth that which is good; and the evil man out of the evil treasure, that which is evil; for out of the abundance of the heart, the mouth speaketh."
>
> Matt. 15:19. "For out of the heart, come forth evil thoughts, murders, adulteries, fornications, thefts, false witness, railing."

All the sins of men are, therefore, organically united in the state of sin from which they spring. Original sin is the root; actual sins are the sprouts. Original Sin is the fountain; actual sins are the streams. Original Sin is the ocean; they are the waves that rise and fall upon it. Original Sin is the disease; actual sins are symptoms.

44. Where is this particularly taught?

By David in the Fifty-first Psalm. He traces his great sin which he confesses in verses 2-4, back to the source in Original Sin whence it came, vs. 5, 6, 10. (See Luther's exposition.)

Actual Sins: Definition,

45. When actual sins are spoken of, in what sense must "actual" be regarded?

Not as synonymous with "real," as though Original Sin were not in this sense actual, i.e., a reality; but "actual," because existing in act, as distinguished from Original Sin which refers to state, condition, habit, temper or disposition.

46. Define Actual Sin?

Every action, whether internal or external, that conflicts with God's Law, as well as every omission of an action which the same Law commands.

Causes

47. What are the causes of Actual Sin?

The concupiscence or inner depravity may work in two ways, viz., either spontaneously, or it may be stimulated to activity from without. To the former, James 1:14, 15 is especially applicable:

"Each man is tempted, when he is drawn away by his own lust, and enticed. Then the lust when it hath conceived, beareth sin; and the sin when it is full-grown, bringeth forth death."

When it is stimulated from without, it may be either by the devil or the World.

Temptations

48. How does the devil tempt or stimulate mans inner depravity?

By suggesting the thought, and even the plan for carrying out the thought of sin, as in John 13:2. He has no power to force one to commit the sin which he suggests. The regenerate have greater power to resist him than the unregenerate.

> James 4:7. "Resist the devil, and he will flee from you."

> 1 Cor. 10:13. "God is faithful, who will not suffer you to be tempted above that ye are able, but will, with the temptation, make also the way of escape." Cf. Eph. 6:11-13; 1 Peter 5:9.

49. How does the world stimulate man's inner depravity?

By the teaching, suggestion, advice and example of wicked men and women; as well as by objects that appeal to sense and thus enkindle the desire of sin.

> 1 John 2:14, 15. "Love not the world, neither the things that are in the world. If any man love the world, the love of the Father is not in him. For all that

> is in the world, the lust of the flesh and the lust of the eyes, and the pride of life, is not of the Father', but is of the world."

Inner Actions

50. What is meant by "an inner action"?

A desire or purpose to sin that is called forth or cherished (Matt. 5:27).

Effects

51. What effect has every actual sin?

A disposition of will inclining it to the repetition of similar acts of sin, and ultimately to a particular habit of sin.

Classification

52. How are sins classified?

First, into Voluntary and Involuntary. The former are those deliberately committed, with the knowledge that they are sins; the latter are committed in ignorance, or under the impulse of violent passion, sometimes known as sins of ignorance or infirmity, as contrasted with presumptuous sins.

> Ps. 19:12, 13. "Who can understand his errors? Cleanse thou me from secret sins. Keep back thy servant also from presumptuous sins."

> 1 Tim. 1:13. "I obtained mercy, because I did it ignorantly in unbelief."

53. What is a second mode of classification?

Into sins of commission, or positive acts conflicting with a negative commandment, and sins of omission, consisting in the negation or omission of acts, prescribed by an affirmative commandment.

54. A third?

Into sins directly against God, or those forbidden in the First Table of the Decalogue; against one's neighbor, or those forbidden in the Second Table; and against oneself, as 1 Cor. 6:18, designates fornication, to which may be added drunkenness, suicide, etc.

55. A fourth?

Into sins of heart, mouth and deed. Our Lord treats of these in Matt. 5:21, 22. The first is the most grievous. Habitual hatred toward an innocent neighbor or purpose to injure long cherished in the mind is a more grievous sin than the harsh answer of one to whom injustice has been done.

56. What of the distinction between Venial and Mortal sins?

Of themselves, no sins are venial, but all are mortal. No such scheme of classification, therefore, can be adopted by which particular offenses can be said to be venial and others mortal. Whether a sin be venial or mortal is determined entirely by the relation of the sinner to Christ. The least sin knowingly and deliberately committed is inconsistent with faith, and is mortal. But the regenerate, in their infirmity, and against the most sincere effort of their hearts, are not without sins; these and only these are venial.

Sin against the Holy Ghost

57. Is there any sin irremissible?

Yes. The sin against the Holy Ghost.

> Matt. 12:31, 32. "Every sin and blasphemy shall be forgiven unto men; but the blasphemy against the Spirit shall not be forgiven. And whosoever shall speak a word against the Son of man, it shall be forgiven him; but whosoever shall speak against the Holy Spirit, it shall not be forgiven him, neither in this world, nor in that which is to come."
>
> Mark 3:29. "Whosoever shall blaspheme against the Holy Ghost, hath never forgiveness, but is guilty of an eternal sin."

58. Why is it irremissible?

Not because it exceeds the mercy of God, and the merits of Christ (Is. 1:18), but because the very means by which the grace of God is offered are despised and blasphemed. "It is not as though God were never willing to pity such sinners, for His protestation is universal in which He affirms with an oath (Ez. 18:32), that He does not will the death of him who dies. Neither is it as though Christ had not died and made satisfaction for such sin; for He is the propitiation for the sins of the whole world (1 John 2:2). But it is said to be irremissible by accident; because such sinners are so hardened as to be unwilling to receive Christ, the only remedy for their sins; but persecute Him, and with an inflexible purpose, persist in their fury; and thus cast themselves into eternal destruction... . But if it could so happen that they could be led to a knowledge of this sin, the mercy of God would be accessible even to them" (Baldwin, on 1 Tim. I).

The context in Matthew shows that Christ gave this warning when the Pharisees ascribed His works to the devil (Matt. 12:24). It is not said here that the Pharisees had already incurred such sin, for it seems to be one that belongs peculiarly to the period when the Holy Ghost is fully given, but the warning is that the culmination of such sin as they were committing would be the sin against the Holy Ghost.

59. Is it referred to elsewhere in Holy Scripture?

> Heb. 6:4, 5, 6. "For as touching those who were once enlightened, and tasted of the heavenly gift, and were made partakers of the Holy Spirit, and tasted the good word of God and the powers of the age to come, and then fell away, it is impossible to renew them again unto repentance, seeing they crucify to themselves the Son of God afresh, and put him to an open shame."
>
> Heb. 10:26. "For if we sin willfully after that we have received the knowledge of the truth, there remaineth no more a sacrifice for sins."

60. What is here taught?

That they who commit this sin have been regenerate and godly persons who have deserted the faith, and that it is accompanied by peculiar hostility to the truth and open defiance of the Holy Spirit.

61. Are those who commit this sin ever troubled concerning it?

No. For they are abandoned by the Spirit, from whom all conviction of sin comes.

9. The Grace Of God Towards Fallen Men

The State in which Grace finds man

1. What is the natural fruit of sin?

Eternal death. As seen above (Chapter 8:17, 18), this is simply spiritual death at its maturity, or in its culmination.

2. But is not Eternal Death the result of a new act or volition of God?

No. All man's ruin comes from himself. If anyone be lost, he is lost solely by his own fault. No one is lost by God's will. God permits much that He does not cause (Chapter 5:23).

3. All having sinned, we understand, therefore, that all would have eternally perished, unless God had interrupted the natural order of sin and death?

Such is the clear teaching of Holy Scripture.

Not required by any consideration of Justice

4. God, however, had not interfered, and all had been left to the consequences of their sins, could man have complained?

This would have been nothing less than what is just, and what occurred to the fallen angels.

5. If God had interfered to save one man, or a hundred, or a thousand, and had made no provision for the rest, would there have been any injustice?

Every one who has sinned being justly liable to the full penalty, no one can plead any injustice in case God, out of pure mercy, determines to save others involved in the same guilt.

6. But if He were to save the majority of the race, would the remainder be injured?

The answer is the same, even though justice would exact its extreme penalty in but one case, and all the rest escape.

7. Was such a discrimination shown?

No. But we reach the true doctrine not by arguing concerning the abstract justice of God, but by learning of the universality of the Plan of Redemption as taught in the Gospel.

Motive

8. What moved God to interfere with the natural order of sin, and to provide for man's salvation?

Nothing but His free will (Gal. 1:4; Eph. 1:1, 5, 9, etc.), or "good pleasure" (eudokia) (Eph. 1:5, 9; Phil. 2:13; Luke 2:14). He was not determined by any necessity of His nature or obligation to man.

9. What disposition of God is particularly manifest in this act of His will to save man?

His Grace (see Chapter 2, 73).

> Eph. 1:7. "In whom we have redemption through his blood, the forgiveness of our trespasses according to the riches of his grace." 2:8. "By grace are ye saved through faith; and that not of yourselves, it is the gift of God." Tit. 2:11. "The grace of God hath appeared, bringing salvation unto all men." This implies the absolute absence of any merit in man which could deserve this interference, but that God's love was exercised in spite of that which called for God's wrath.

His Mercy (see Chapter 2); Eph. 2:4; Titus 3:5. This presupposes the foreseen misery of men because of sin and its consequences.

Universality of Grace

10. What do you mean by the universality of Grace?

That it has been extended towards all men. As universal as is sin, so universal is grace. As universal as is misery because of sin, so universal is the mercy for the relief of this misery.

> 1 Tim. 2:4. "God our Savior who would have all men to be saved, and come to the knowledge of the truth."
>
> 2 Peter 3:9. "Not wishing that any should perish, but that all should come to repentance."
>
> John 3:16. "God so loved the world as to give his only begotten Son," etc.

11. But may not the universality of Grace apply simply to the race as a whole?

In its provisions, it is extended to each and every individual alike. No one is excepted or passed by.

> 1 Tim. 1:15. "Faithful is the saying and worthy of all acceptation that Christ Jesus came into the world to save sinners, of whom I am chief."

Rom. 11:32. “God hath shut up all unto disobedience, that he might have mercy upon all.”

12. What is the testimony of the Lutheran Church on this subject?

As the preaching of repentance, so also the promise of the Gospel is universal, i.e., it pertains to all men (Luke 24). Therefore Christ has commanded ‘that repentance and remission of sins should be preached in His name among all nations.’ For God loved the world and gave His Son (John 3:16). Christ bore the sins of the world (John 1:29), gave His flesh for the life of the world (John 6:51), His blood is the propitiation for the sins of the whole world (1 John 1:7; 2:2) (Formula of Concord, 654).

13. Explain somewhat more fully the text “God would have all men to be saved” (1 Tim. 2:4).

“He does not say that it is His will that the godly be saved, but that the world should be saved through Him. For by the expression ‘world,’ He means the whole race of mortals. For although the whole world is not saved through Christ, nevertheless the will of God is commended to us as directed not towards the destruction, but towards the salvation of all” (Wolfgang Musculus quoted by Calovius).

14. Recapitulate the arguments of our theologians in support of this position.

[A.] The universality of Christ’s merits.

1 John 2:2. “He is the propitiation for our sins, and not for ours only, but also for the whole world.”

[B.] The universality of the call.

Matt. 11:28. “Come unto me all ye that labor and are heavy laden, and I will give you rest.”

[C.] The universality of the gift of the Holy Spirit.

Acts 10:17. “I will pour forth of my Spirit upon all flesh.”

[D.] The administration of Word and Sacraments, the purpose of which is the salvation of those to whom they come, even though the results differ with respect to different classes.

[E.] The condemnation of unbelievers for their rejection of the offers of the Gospel.

Contents of God's Will

15. Is it right, then, to say that God willed that all should he saved provided they believe?

No. For it is God's will not only that men be saved, but also that they should believe (see above, 10; 1 Tim. 2:4; 2 Peter 3:9). Just as Christ died even for those who do not or will not believe, so also God's gracious will is independent of man's faith, or any disposition of man towards God. As the call and promise are universal, so also is the will of God of which they are the expression.

Why many are lost

16. If it be God's will that all should believe and be saved, how is it that many are lost?

Because it is not God's will that men be saved against their own wills. Man's will forever retains the freedom to reject what God offers and what God sincerely desires that he accept.

> Matt. 23:37. "O Jerusalem, Jerusalem, that killeth the prophets and stoneth them that are sent unto her! how often would I have gathered thy children together, even as a hen gathereth her chickens under her wings, but ye would not."

Meaning of God's will

17. What is implied in saying that God wills man's salvation?

This is more than a will of complacency (see Chapter 11, 72 c), by which He would be satisfied or gratified with whatever pertains to man's welfare.

18. Why?

Because man being spiritually dead is without any power to will, devise or contribute to his own salvation.

> "In spiritual and divine things, the intellect, heart and will of unregenerate men cannot in any way, by their own natural powers, understand, believe, accept, think, will, begin, effect, do, work or concur in working anything; but they are entirely dead to good and corrupt" (Formula of Concord, 552).

All man's help, therefore, must come alone from God.

19. What then is God's saving will towards man?

It is His purpose to make every provision whereby the salvation of each and every man is rendered possible, all of which is included in the Plan of Redemption that He devised.

Factors of the Plan of Redemption

20. What are included in this plan?

The incarnation and mediatorial work of the Son of God.

The special mission of the Holy Ghost to apply the fruits of this mediatorial office.

The institution of the Means of Grace, through which the various acts of this applying grace are wrought, to the end that men may be called, justified and glorified.

Where Predestination is to be treated

21. What is the proper place for the treatment of Predestination?

After all the details which God's decree and purpose comprised, are learned from the Gospel. For whatever the Gospel contains and proclaims was included in this purpose.

22. What has Luther said on this subject?

> "Follow the order of the Epistle to the Romans, and concern thyself with Christ and the Gospel, that thou mayst recognize thy sins and His grace; then fight with sins as Chapters 1-9 have taught. After that, when thou hast come to the eighth chapter, and art under the cross and suffering, thou wilt learn right well in Chapters 9-11 how comforting predestination is" (Introduction to Romans).

23. What has the Lutheran Church confessed concerning Predestination?

"This is not to be investigated in the secret counsel of God, but to be taught from the Word of God, where it is also revealed. But the Word of God leads us to Christ, who is the Book of Life, in whom all are written and elected that are to be saved, as it is written (Eph. 1:4)"He hath chosen us in him before the foundation of the world." See Chapter 12.

10. The Preparation Of Redemption

When announced

1. When did God first reveal His purpose to redeem man?

As soon as man had fallen. In Gen. 3:15 is a promise, often called the "protevangelium" or "protogospel." "The seed of the woman shall bruise the serpent's head." This refers to the ultimate victory which humanity, "the seed of the woman," is to obtain in the constant struggle which began in Eden. Its still deeper significance gradually became apparent in succeeding prophecies, culminating in One who, while "the seed of the woman" and the true representative of the race, is also true God.

> 1 Cor. 15:22. "For as in Adam all die, even so in Christ shall all be made alive."
>
> 47. "The first man is of the earth, earthy; the second man is of heaven."

Two-fold Preparation

2. What two-fold preparation at once began?

God gradually prepared man for salvation, and prepared salvation for man.

3. How was man prepared for salvation?

Through the education of many centuries, in which his knowledge of sin was deepened, his inability to aid himself was recognized, and his need of redemption from a higher source was acknowledged and devoutly longed for.

4. How was salvation prepared for man?

By the gradual revelation of the Plan of Redemption in type and ceremony and promise, until in the fullness of time (Gal. 4:4) the Son of God became incarnate.

5. State the relation of the two parts of the human race to this two-fold preparation?

The former occurred chiefly in heathenism, exhibiting the efforts of man by the exertion of his own powers to struggle upwards towards God (Acts 17:27). The entire history of the Gentile world is told in the words of Augustine:

> "Thou hast made us for Thyself, and our heart is restless until it rest on Thee."

The latter occurred in Judaism (Rom. 3:1,2). Through the positive revelation, even though incomplete, there was a constant approach of God towards man, through successive stages until Christ came.

Heathenism and Judaism contrasted

6. Are we to understand, then, that the preparation through heathenism was entirely negative, and that through Judaism entirely positive?

No. For in a less degree heathenism afforded some positive elements, in the preparation of the means through which the Gospel was to be diffused. The universal empire of Rome, the universal language, the means of communication between nations, the culture of the race, became important instrumentalities for the progress of the Gospel.

So there was also, a negative element in Judaism. When man attempted to attain righteousness before God by his fulfillment of all the prescriptions of the Law, he learned his helplessness. Rom. 3:20, "Through the law cometh the knowledge of sin." The entire system of rites and ceremonies and sacrifices, declared as the Epistle to the Hebrews shows, the incompleteness and unsatisfactoriness of the then existing order, and pointed to what was higher and better.

Salvability of those who lived before Christ

7. Was there then no salvation for any who lived and died before Christ?

Yes. Where there was faith that received the assurance of God's grace and the promise of salvation hereafter to be provided in a way not understood at the time.

> "Paul cites concerning Abraham (Rom. 4:3), 'He believed God and it was counted unto him for righteousness,' i.e., Abraham knew that God was propitious to him only on account of His promise; he assented to God's promise and did not suffer himself to be withdrawn from it, although he saw that he was impure, and unworthy; he knew that God offers His promise on account of His own truth, and not on account of our works or merits" (Melanchthon).

For further Scriptural proof, see Chapter 11 of the Epistle to the Hebrews.

8. What ground is there for saying that the Old Testament saints had only a general promise concerning a salvation hereafter to be provided?

Eph. 3:5; Luke 10:23, 24; Heb. 11:40; 1 Peter 1:11.

11. The Person Of Christ

Meaning of "Christ"

1. In what relation is the Son of God considered at this place?

Not in His inner Trinitarian relations, but in His Mediatorial Office.

> 1 Tim. 2:5. "There is one God, one mediator between God and man, himself man, Christ Jesus."
>
> Acts 4:12. "In none other is there salvation; neither is there any other name under heaven, that is given among men, whereby we might be saved."

2. What is His name with reference to this office?

Christ.

Jesus was the personal name, which, in common with many others, He bore because of His human nature, even though elevated above the sense in which others possessed it (Matt. 1:21). It designated Him as a man among other men. But Christ, or Messiah, is His official name. We would speak more accurately of "Jesus the Christ," than of Jesus Christ. Christ is the official name of the incarnate Son of God, promised in the Old Testament, and actually sent as taught in the New Testament.

3. What is the meaning of "Christ" or "Messiah"?

The Anointed One.

In the Old Testament, prophets, priests and kings were solemnly set apart by being anointed, as an attestation of official position, and a means of conferring grace for the discharge of official duties. Prophets (1 Kings 19:16; Is. 61:1); Priests (Lev. 4); Kings (1 Sam. 10:1; 16:13; 2 Sam. 2:4). This external anointment with oil was a figure of an inner or spiritual anointing, or designation for office accompanied by the necessary gifts for its exercise, as of all believers in 1 John 2:27, and preeminently Jesus of Nazareth, anointed above all others (Is. 61:1, as interpreted by Luke 4:18; Matt. 12:18), as our Prophet, Priest and King, and, therefore, known as Messiah or Christ.

> John 1:41. "We have found the Messiah, which is, being interpreted, the Christ."

4. What other ideas are included in the name "Christ"?

The unity of the Old and New Testaments, the fulfillment of prophecy, and the historical foundations for Christianity in the religion of Israel.

5. What, therefore, is a prominent subject of argument in the New Testament, and how is it proved?

That Jesus is the Christ. Old Testament prophecies are constantly quoted that are found fulfilled in Jesus of Nazareth.

> Luke 24:27. "Beginning from Moses and from all the prophets, he interpreted to them in all the Scriptures the things concerning himself."
>
> 45, 46. "Then opened he their minds that they might understand the Scriptures; and he said unto them, Thus it is written that the Christ should suffer and rise again from the dead the third day."

Luke 18:31-33; Acts 3:18; 10:43; 26:22, 23; Rom. 1:2.

6. Is this, however, the exclusive line of argument by which the claims of Jesus are enforced?

No. In addressing Gentiles, the argument was from the Ascension and

Resurrection of Jesus to His Lordship over all, and, thence to the truth of the Scriptures to which He appealed and the fulfillment in Him of all their prophecies. This may be seen, e.g., in the sermon of Peter to Cornelius in Acts 10; first, the Lordship of Jesus, as attested by the Resurrection (vs. 35-42); secondly, the fulfillment in Him of prophecy (v. 43), and His Messiahship.

Topics included

7. What topics are included in Christology, or that portion of Theology treating of the Mediatorial Office?

The Person, the States and the Offices of Christ.

Chalcedon Symbol

8. How has the Church summarized its faith on this subject?

Most comprehensively in the symbol of Chalcedon:

> "We, then, following the holy Fathers, all with one consent teach men to confess one and the same Son, our Lord Jesus Christ, the same perfect in Godhead and also perfect in Manhood; truly God and truly Man, of a reasonable soul and body; consubstantial with the Father, according to the Godhead, and consubstantial with us, according to the Manhood; in all things, except sin, like unto us; begotten before all ages of the Father, according to the Godhead, and in these latter days, for us and for our salvation, born of the Virgin Mary, the Mother of God, according to the Manhood; one and the same Christ, Son, Lord, Only-begotten, to be acknowledged in two natures, 'inconfusedly, unchangeably, indivisibly, inseparably'; the distinction of natures being by no means taken away by the union, but rather the property of each nature being preserved and concurring in One Person and One Subsistence, not parted or divided into two persons, but one and the same Son, and only begotten God the Word, the Lord Jesus Christ; as the prophets from the beginning have declared concerning Him, and the Lord Jesus Christ Himself has taught us, and the Creed of the Fathers has handed down to us."

In its simplest form, this truth is stated in the Small Catechism, Creed, Article 11.

The Divinity of Christ

9. What is the first thing to be considered in treating of the Person of Christ?

That He is true God, consubstantial, coequal and coeternal with the Father.

The proof for this is given above, Chap. 3, Sec. 17-23. For "consubstantial," see same chapter, Q. 48.

The divinity of Christ does not consist in divine gifts, but in His entire and complete oneness in all His attributes with God.

The Humanity of Christ

10. What is the second?

That He is true man, consubstantial with us. The proof for this is found in that He has:

[A.] The names of man

Tim. 2:5; John 8:40; Acts 17:31. His favorite designation of Himself is "Son of man." He is called "flesh" (John 1:14), "a child" (Acts 4:27), "Son of Abraham, David," etc., especially in the genealogical tables of Matthew and Luke.

[B.] The parts of a man

Body and soul or spirit, and various parts of His body are mentioned.

[C.] The experiences of men

He was conceived, was born, grew, hungered, thirsted, was fatigued, grieved, wept, exulted, died.

[D.] The acts of men.

He went about, conversed, etc.

Truth of the Humanity

11. Why did the early Church lay such emphasis upon the word "true"?

Particularly against the Docetists who maintained it was not a true body which Christ had, but only the appearance of a body.

12. Upon what arguments did they base this error?

They said that angels repeatedly appeared in human bodies, and yet were not true men; that the Holy Spirit appeared in the form of a dove without being a true dove. They quoted Rom. 8:3, "God sent his Son in the likeness of sinful flesh," laying especial emphasis upon "likeness."

13. How were they answered?

Angels assumed human bodies only temporarily, and for some transient purpose. Christ Himself declares the difference in Luke 24:39.

> "Handle me and see; for a spirit hath not flesh and bones, as ye behold me having."

The union of the Spirit with the dove was symbolical; that of the Son of God with man, personal. The former was temporary; the latter permanent. The emphasis in Rom. 8:3 is not on "likeness," but on "sinful". The meaning is the same as in Phil. 2:7, "He was"found in fashion as a man," i.e., to all outward appearances, He was nothing more than any other man — a child like other children, a Galilean peasant among Galilean peasants. This is not opposed to the truth of His humanity, but is contrasted simply with His State of Glory.

Completeness of the Humanity

14. What is implied in His true manhood?

Its completeness or perfection.

15. Who attacked this?

Apollinaris, in the Fourth Century, who sought to explain the personal union by teaching that the Divine Nature replaced a part of Christ's humanity, viz., the rational soul; and the Monothelites of the Seventh Century, who taught that the Divine Nature took the place of a truly human will.

Unity of Person

16. What is meant by saying that there is but one Person?

That "there is one and the same Christ, Son, Lord, Only-begotten, to be acknowledged in two natures" (Chalcedon). "Who although He be God and man; yet He is not two, but one Christ; one, not by conversion of the Godhead into flesh, but by taking the manhood into God; one altogether, not by confusion of substance, but by Unity of Person" (Athanasian Creed). The difference between "me" and "thee" is never applied to the divine and human natures. There is but one "I" acting and speaking, thinking and feeling and willing through both natures. There is but one "Thou" whom the Father addresses and one "He" to whom the Spirit bears witness.

17. What proof have you of this unity?

In Rom. 1:3, the same person is said to be "made of the seed of David according to the flesh," and declared to be "the Son of God." In Luke 1:3, that which is born of the Virgin Mary is called "the Son of God." In John 1:14, "the Word," who is declared in V. 1, to be God, is said to have become "flesh." In Gal. 2:20, "the Son of God" is said to have given Himself for sinful man.

Relation of Person and Nature

18. Is the person related in the same way to each nature?

The person, with the divine nature, has existed from all eternity. The human nature began in time. The person, therefore, was once without a human nature. But the human nature could not exist without a person. The person of the human nature, therefore, came not from that nature, but from the divine. Since the human nature entered into the world, i.e., was conceived and born and lived by the divine person uniting Himself with our race in the womb of the Virgin Mary, we say that the human nature has no personality of its own, but that the personality of the human nature is that which it has derived from the divine. The Greek theologians called this the doctrine of the anhypostasia of the human nature, which our theologians accept, although stating that enhypostasia is preferable. The unity of the person requires that we must hold to the want of personality on the part of the human nature.

19. If we were to affirm that the human nature had a personality of its own, what would follow?

The doctrine that in Christ, there are two persons, as as well as two natures. Unity of personality could be taught, then, only by finding place for the destruction at some time of the human personality, and its being replaced by the divine.

Double Generation

20. Since there are two natures, can we say there are two Sons, viz., a Son of God and a Son of Man?

No. There is but one Son, at one and the same time Son of God and Son of Man. That through which, He is the Son of God, is His eternal generation of the Father, "true God begotten of the Father from all eternity" (Small Catechism). See Chapter 3, 51-53. That through which He is the Son of Man is His conception by the Holy Ghost and birth of the Virgin Mary (Lukes 1:35; Gal. 4:4). We speak, therefore, of a double generation of Christ: one, eternal; the other, temporal; one, according to the divine; the other, according to the human nature.

Incarnation

21. By what term is the act of the Son of God in assuming human nature known?

Incarnation.

> John 1:14. "And the Word became flesh." Heb. 2:14. "Since the children are partakers of flesh and blood, he also himself in like manner partook of the same." Heb. 2:16; 1 Tim. 3:16; Rom. 9:5; 1:3.

22. Was this peculiar to the Second Person of the Trinity?

Only the Son of God assumed human nature. But the Father who sent the Son into the world, and the Holy Spirit who appears in the conception of Christ (Luke 1:35), just as in creation (Gen. 1:2), were also active. There was a special intervention of God in and beyond the order of nature established at the creation. God, who at creation established an order, in virtue of which men came into the world through certain means, can, at His will, dispense with such means, and provide for a virgin birth. To deny the possibility of this, is to question the existence and almighty power of God. To admit its reality is to admit the possibility of everything else mysterious and supernatural in Christianity.

Consubstantiality of Humanity

23. The conception of Jesus being so unlike that of others, was the human nature that resulted also unlike that of other men?

> "He was consubstantial with us according to the manhood; in all things, except sin, like unto us" (Chalcedon).
>
> Heb. 4:15. "He hath been in all points tempted like as we are, yet without sin."

Christ, therefore, experienced all the infirmities that are common to the race, as hunger, thirst, sleep, fatigue, tears, sorrow, pain; but no individual infirmities are ascribed to Him, as particular diseases which attack some, but do not affect all.

Sinlessness of Humanity

24. How do you prove the sinlessness of Jesus?

[A.] From distinct passages of Scripture
Heb. 4:15, quoted under 23; 2 Cor. 5:21; Heb. 7:26; John 8:46; 1 Peter 1:19; 2:22.
[B.] From His divinity
Sin is a personal matter. It is always a person who sins. But the person of Christ is God.
[C.] From the definition of sin
"Sin is the want of conformity with God's Law." But the Law is the declaration of God's will. God cannot will what is contrary to His will, i.e., Jesus could not sin.

He was, therefore, not only sinless, but impeccable. Admit peccability, and the divinity of Christ is practically denied.

25. But if Christ were impeccable, how do you explain His temptation? Is temptation possible, where a fall is impossible?

Temptation properly is only testing or proving. When gold is brought to the touch-stone or submitted to the blow-pipe or treated with various chemical reagents, there is no possibility of any other result than that it will stand the test and be proved to be gold. We inevitably associate the thought of temptation with that of the possibility of a fall, from the fact that man's nature is corrupt, and that even the regenerate are only partially renewed, and, therefore fallible, and likely, under the test, to show its worst features.

The agony of our Lord's temptation came not from the necessity of a great struggle in order that He might prove Himself victor, but from the fact that it was a part of His passion. That He, the manifestation of the absolute holiness of God, should endure the presence and be subjected to the humiliation of the conversation and suggestions of the lowest and vilest of all creatures, the source and head of all the crime in the universe, was an indignity that called forth all His repugnance to the great enemy.

26. Was there any other particular in which the humanity of Christ was distinguished from that of others?

All the excellences and perfections of human nature He had in the highest degree. These He possessed as the sinless man, and as the one within whose body the Godhead dwelt in a peculiar way. Whatever physical attractiveness He may have had, and for which the old teachers cite Ps. 45:2, came from His holy character as it was expressed in His outward form. While the bodies of others contain the seeds of mortality (Rom. 6:23), that of Christ was by its own nature immortal, His death occurring by an act of His will (John 10:18), and not from inner weakness or external force, and His body, after death, being incorruptible (Acts 2:31).

27. What was the purpose of the Incarnation?

The Redemption of the human race.

> Matt. 20:28. "The Son of man came, to give his life a ransom for many."
>
> Heb. 2:14. "He partook of flesh and blood, that, through death, he might bring to nought him that had the power of death."

28. Would the Son of God not have become incarnate if Adam had not sinned?

The doctrine that He would have come only for the completion of humanity, or to furnish a model of a holy life, or for any other purpose than to rescue men from sin, is without any authority from Scripture. God's will or decree to send His Son into the world everywhere presupposes God's foreknowledge of sin, and His determination to provide a remedy for it.

Personal Union

29. In what two senses is the expression, Personal Union, used?

On the one hand, it designates an act (unüo), and is synonymous with Incarnation.

On the other hand, it refers to a state, resulting from the act (unio). 30. In what does the state of union consist?

In that henceforth both natures have but one person — the personal communion; and, as a result, the intimate and perpetual personal presence of each nature in and with the other.

Attributes of Union

31. How has the Church guarded the statement of this doctrine?

The Chalcedon Symbol (see above, 8) has denied this union negatively as:

[A.] Unconfused

There is no mingling of natures. Although there is a communion, they remain distinct.

[B.] Unchanged

One is not changed into the other.

[C.] Indivisible

i.e., with respect to place. "Nowhere is the human nature unsustained by the Logos, or the Logos not sustaining the human nature. The human nature is not outside of the Logos, nor is the Logos without the human nature."

[D.] Inseparable

i.e., with respect to time. The union is never dissolved, but is perpetual.

Items (a) and (b) are in opposition to the Eutychians; (c) and (d) in opposition to the Nestorians. The Eutychians confused the natures; the Nestorians divided the person.

32. How has the Athanasian Creed defined it?

> "Who although He be God and man: yet He is not two, but one Christ.
> One; not by conversion of the Godhead into flesh; but by taking the manhood into God.
> One altogether; not by confusion of substance, but by Unity of Person.
> For as the reasonable soul and flesh is one man, so God and man is one Christ."

Communion of Natures

33. What follows from this communion of the Person with both natures?

The communion of natures with each other. There is a perichoresis or pervasion or penetration of one nature by the other, or existence of one nature within the other. "The divine nature is said actually to penetrate or perfect the human, and the human to be passively penetrated or perfected by the divine; but not in such way that the divine successively occupies one part of the human after the other, and extensively diffuses itself, through it; but, since it is spiritual and indivisible, it at the same time as a whole perfects and energizes each part of the human nature and that nature as a whole, and remains entire in the entire human nature, and entire in every part" (Baier).

> Col. 2:9. "In him dwelleth all the fullness of the Godhead bodily."

John 1:14; Heb. 2:14.

34. What analogy is there to this communion of natures?

The impartation of the Divine nature by the Mystical Union of Christ with the believer. The Personal Union being closer, more intimate and more exalted implies a more complete communion of natures.

2 Peter 1. "He hath granted unto us his precious and exceeding great promises; that through these ye might become partakers of the divine nature."

Personal Propositions

35. Because of this Personal Union and the Communion of Natures, is it proper to say, "God is man," and "man is God"?

These are known as "Personal Propositions." The person may be designated from either nature; and as there is always only one and the same person, this when designated from the divine nature as God is the same as the person designated from the human nature as man. So also we say, "The Son of man" is "the Son of God."

The doctrine of the Personal Propositions, therefore, is that the concrete of the one nature is rightly predicated of the concrete of the other. An example of this occurs in Jer. 23:6, where the descendant of David is called "The Lord our Righteousness," as also in Matt. 16:16, where Jesus is called "the Son of the Living God."

But the same is not proper with respect to the abstract of the natures. We cannot say, "Divinity is humanity" or the reverse. For the concrete always designates the person, while the abstract refers only to the natures. Neither can we say that the "Divine Nature has become incarnate," or "the human has been deified," for here that which is proper in the concrete is improper in the abstract.

Terms also are found expressing at the same time the concrete of both natures. "Christ" is such a term. We may say, "Christ is God" or "Christ is man," or "Christ is the God-man." So our Catechism, "Jesus Christ, true God begotten of Father, is true man, born of the Virgin Mary."

36. What other result of the Communion of Natures is there?

The impartation of attributes known among theologians as the *Communicatio Idiomatum*. For since the personal union it is impossible to ascribe an attribute to either of the natures which does not belong to the person, designated from either nature; neither can there be an act proceeding from either nature in which the other does not participate. There is a communication from both natures to the person, and of the natures to each other.

Communicatio Idiomatum: Genus Idiomaticum

37. Classify or give the various kinds or genera of the *Communicatio Idiomatum*.

First, from one nature to the person, *Genus Idiomaticum*; secondly, from one nature to the other, *Genus Majestaticum*; thirdly, from both natures to the person, *Genus Apotelesmaticum*.

38. Define more fully the first genus.

The *Genus Idiomaticum* is when the properties of either nature are ascribed to the. concrete of the person. It is a matter of indifference from which nature this concrete be derived. Take for example the human nature, and state one of its properties. Suppose it be "to die." Death then belongs to the person. But since it is a matter of indifference from which nature the name of the person be derived, we can say either "man died" or "God died"; for God and man are one and the same person. Or we may take a property of the divine as "Almighty," and predicating it of the person known from the human nature, may say, "Man is Almighty."

39. What stress has been laid by the Lutheran Church on this point?

The Formula of Concord quotes Luther approvingly:

> "If I believe that only the human nature has suffered for me, I have a Savior of little worth... It is the person that suffers and dies. Now the person is true God; therefore it is rightly said: 'The Son of God suffers.' For although the divinity does not suffer, yet the person which is God suffers in His humanity. For the person, the person, I say, was crucified in His humanity... In His own nature, God cannot die; but now God and man are united in one person, so that the expression 'God's death' is correct, when the man dies who is one thing or one person with God" (pp. 631, 632).

40. Show how this thought of the first genus of the *Commnnicatio Idiomatum* underlies the entire theology of the Church and the religious experience of Christians.

The Augsburg Confession (Art. 3) says:

> "One Christ, true God and true man, was born of the Virgin Mary, truly suffered, was crucified, dead and buried."

Our catechism says:

> "I believe that Jesus Christ, true god begotten of the father from all eternity... has delivered me... with his innocent sufferings and death."

So Passion hymns coming from the pens of those who theoretically may criticize the position above confessionally stated, nevertheless, in the glow of devotion do not hesitate to present it with full force, as e.g., in the words of Isaac Watts:

> "Forbid it, Lord, that I should boast, Save in the death of Christ, my God."

and

> "When Christ, the mighty Maker died, For man the creature's sin."

41. What controversy of the early Church centered about this genus of the Communication

The Nestorian.

The precise point at issue was whether it were correct to call the Virgin Mary, theotokos, i.e., "the mother of God." Nestorius who denied this was condemned, and the formula established that she was "the mother of God, according to His human nature." A mother of nature without personality she could not be, for "mother" and "son" are personal relations. But the person of the human nature she brought forth was none other than the Son of God. Nevertheless we must emphasize "according to His human nature," for she was not mother of God, "according to His divine nature." The Decree of Ephesus says, "She brought forth, according to the flesh, the Word of God made flesh."

42. Upon what Scriptural proofs does this rest?

[A.] Human attributes are ascribed to the concrete of the Divine nature.

Acts 3:15. "Ye killed the Prince of Life."

Acts 20:28. "The Church of the Lord which he purchased with his own blood."

1 Cor. 2:8. "Had they known it, they would not have crucified the Lord of glory."

Gal. 2:20. "The Son of God who loved me and gave himself for me."

Rom. 8:32. "He spared not his own Son, but delivered him up for us all."

[B.] Divine attributes are ascribed to the concrete of the human nature.

John 6:62. "The Son of man ascending where he was before,"

John 8:48. "Before Abraham was born, I am."

[C.] Both divine and human attributes and activities are ascribed to the concrete of the person designated from either or from both natures. 1 Peter 3:18. "Christ was put to death in the flesh, but made alive in the spirit."

Rom. 9:5. "Whose are the fathers, and of whom is Christ as concerning the flesh, who is over all God blessed forever."

Rom. 1:3. "His Son, who was born of the seed of David according to the flesh, and declared to be the Son of God with power."

Genus Majestaticum

43. Define the second genus.

As stated above (37), this has reference to a communication from one nature to the other. Since, however, the human nature can communicate nothing to the divine — for the divine cannot be increased or diminished — the communication is entirely from the divine to the human. The divine is always active, and the human passive. The second genus, therefore, is that according to which the Second Person of the Trinity communicates properties of His divine nature to His human nature for its possession and use.

44. Does this mean that the properties of the divine become those of the human nature?

No. For as seen above (8, 31, 32), the natures remain unchanged, but the properties of the divine nature pervade and exercise themselves in and through the human. The properties of fire never become those of iron, but when a bar is drawn from the furnace, the properties of the fire are active through the iron which it pervades. There cannot be a perichoristic (33) union of one nature with another, without an impartation of qualities. Electricity imparts its properties to the wire which conducts it. The soul acts in and through the body which it animates. The eye sees, the ear hears, because the soul pervades and energizes the body and renders it receptive to external objects in a manner in which they make no impression when the soul has departed. These illustrations are necessarily imperfect and liable to criticism. For as our theologians repeatedly have said:

> "This union is wonderfully unique and uniquely wonderful."

When we rise from the natural to the supernatural, all illustrations offer more points of divergence than of agreement. They prove nothing; but only suggest certain analogies.

45. How has this doctrine been confessionally stated?

> "We hold and teach, with the ancient orthodox church, as it explained this doctrine from the Scriptures, that the human nature in Christ has received this majesty according to the manner of the personal union, viz., because the entire fullness of the divinity dwells in Christ, not as in other holy men and angels, but bodily, as in its own body, so that, with all its majesty, power, glory and efficacy, it shines forth in the assumed human nature of Christ, when and as He wills, and in, with and through it, exerts its divine power, glory and efficacy, as the soul does in the body and fire in glowing iron" (Formula of Concord, 636).

46. Upon what Scriptural grounds does it rest?

> "There is a unanimously received rule of the entire ancient orthodox Church, that whatever Holy Scripture testifies that Christ received in time, He received not according to the divine nature — for, according to this nature, he has everything from eternity — but the person has received it in time, by reason of, and with respect to the assumed human nature" (Formula of Concord, 639).

Such passages are:

> Matt. 11:27. "All things have been delivered unto me of my Father."

> Matt. 28:18. "All authority hath been given unto me in heaven and upon earth."

> John 5:27. "And hath given him authority to execute judgment, because he is a Son of man."

47. Do the Holy Scriptures particularize any divine attributes which are especially conspicuous in and through the assumed humanity?

Yes.

1. Omnipotence, Matt. 28:18; Heb. 2:8;
2. Omniscience, Col. 2:3;
3. Power to quicken, John 6:51; 1 Cor. 15:45;
4. Power to forgive sins, Matt. 9:6;
5. Power to judge, John 5:27;
6. Worship, Phil. 2:9, 10; Heb. 1:8;
7. Omnipresence, Matt. 18:20; 28:20; Eph. 1:23; 4:10.

48. Are all the divine attributes imparted to the human nature of Christ?

Here we must recall the end of the incarnation and of the *Communicatio Idiomatum*, viz., the execution of the Mediatorial Office. There is therefore the complete impartation of all such attributes as are needed for this end. We must also recall the distinction between the Absolute and the Relative Attributes of God (Chap. II, Sec. 23 sqq.). The Relative or Operative Attributes are immediately communicated; but the Absolute, as eternity, infinity, immensity, only mediately, or as they characterize a relative attribute, or belong to the person.

> "The soul perichoristically united with the body, imparts to the body its life and sensitive faculties, so that the body can be said to be living and sentient; but for this reason, the body cannot be said to be spiritual, immortal and invisible as the soul; neither can the calorific and illuminating qualities of fire imparted to iron give to it the lightness and simplicity of fire" (Hollazius).

The relative attributes, however, belong, according to the genus *Idiomaticum*, to the person designated from the human nature, and we can say Jesus is eternal, etc.

49. Were the imparted attributes always used?

As we shall learn under the States of Christ, during the State of Humiliation, Christ refrained from their full use.

Genus Apotelesmaticum

50. What is the third kind or genus of the *Communicatio Idiomatum*?

This is known as the Genus *Apotelesmaticum*, from the Greek *Apotelesma*, an official act. According to it in all the acts of the Mediatorial Office, the person acts not through one nature alone, but through both natures, each contributing that which is peculiar to itself with participation of the other.

51. How has this been confessionally expressed?

> "The distinction of natures being by no means taken way by the union, but rather the property of each being preserved and concurring in One Person and One Subsistence" (Chalcedon Symbol).

52. Are the natures then separate?

No. Never separate, but distinct. Distinct, but always concurring, each nature according to its peculiar endowment. When Christ suffered and died, this was according to the human nature, for the divine could not suffer or die. But the divine sustained the human nature beneath the infinite burden of the world's guilt, and imparted to the human satisfaction infinite divine efficacy and merit. In the prophetical office, it was the mouth and tongue of the human nature that spoke, but the revelation of the mysteries of the Kingdom of God and the speaking with authority came from the divine nature.

53. What Scriptural proofs are there for this Genus?

The work of redemption is referred sometimes to the concrete of the Divine nature.

> 1 John 3:8. "The Son of God was manifested that he might destroy the works of the devil."

Sometimes to the concrete of the human nature.

> Luke 19:10. "The Son of man came to seek and to save that which was lost."

Sometimes to the concrete of both (Heb. 7:21-26; 1 Tim. 2:5; 1 John 1:7).

The argument depends, however, not upon individual passages, but upon the entire tenor of Scripture. The entire end of the incarnation was the accomplishment of that which is attained through the work wrought and the sacrifice offered by the one person in and through the concurrence of the two natures.

Estimate of doctrine

54. How in general is the doctrine of the *Communicatio Idiomatum* to be estimated?

> "Whoever has the patience to think out what the Apostle's words: 'The Word was made flesh' mean, cannot regard the doctrine of the *Communicatio Idiomatum* an extravagant fancy of orthodox scholasticism. It follows necessarily from the Personal Union. Every Christian who prays to Him who is exalted to the Right Hand of God, looks with the eyes of his faith upon a glorified man, in whom what is human is thoroughly pervaded by what is divine. Even Calvin cannot think of the glorified body otherwise than as filled with the powers of the divine nature. But it is just this participation of Christ's human nature in the attributes of the divine, that constitutes the *Communicatio Idiomatum*" (Kahnis).

> "Mutual communication of properties is the essence of every alliance, of all loving communion. Only selfishness which would keep all to itself that is its own, resists it; for it desires to part everything and to impart nothing" (Sartorius, Divine Love, Eng. Tr., 146).

55. Is this doctrine of the *Communicatio Idiomatum* offered as a sufficient explanation of the mode in which the divine is related to the human in Christ?

By no means.

> "Why do we not give God glory, by believing, with the simple obedience of faith what Scripture teaches, even though we cannot understand or grasp the mode, as to how this could occur without equalizing or confusing the natures? For who can sufficiently explain or understand the mode of the union, from which this communication arises and upon which it depends? The angel answered both Sarah and Mary who asked concerning the mode:

'Is anything too hard for Jehovah?' 'No word of God shall be void of power' (Gen. 18; Luke 1)... The ancients say correctly that if we cannot say what God is, we should beware of thinking or saying of Him as He is not. So in this article" (Chemnitz, De Duabus Naturis, in sq.).

12. The States of Christ

Basis of Distinction

1. Upon what is the distinction in the States of Christ based?

Although the communication of divine attributes began with the personal union, i.e., with the very conception of the human nature, nevertheless they were not only not immediately exercised, but two periods are to be clearly distinguished, one in which their activity through the human nature was, to a great extent, repressed, and another in which it is fully exercised. The former is called the State of Humiliation; the latter, the State of Exaltation.

2. What is the origin of the terms?

> Phil. 2:8, 9. "He humbled himself." "God also highly exalted him."

The contrast of the ecclesiastical Latin Status Exinanitionis and Status Exaltationis, is based upon verses 7 and 9. In verse 7, the Vulgate translates the Greek... by semet ipsum exinanivit, i.e., "made himself empty" or "made himself of none effect." The former state is, therefore, literally one "of emptying," or "self-renunciation."

Humiliation: Pertaining to which nature

3. Of what is the humiliation or emptying predicated, the divine or the human nature?

Neither without the person. The divine person was humbled, but not according to or in the divine nature, but according to and in the human nature.

Not synonymous with Incarnation

4. But is not the humiliation synonymous with the incarnation?

By no means. For the Son of God remained incarnate, after the humiliation was over.

5. Did they not coincide in their origin?

Yes, but the incarnation was permanent; while the humiliation was temporary. The incarnation itself implies condescension indeed, but no humiliation; although the mode of incarnation chosen by the Son of God involved humiliation. Hence we teach that humiliation presupposes incarnation, and that it is a state of the incarnate Word, the Logos (...) not the Logos (...).

6. Why do we deny that the humiliation was of the divine nature?

Because God cannot be humbled in His own nature. He assumed human nature for the very end that in that nature He might experience all that humiliation implied.

Not a hiding

7. But might not the humiliation, or emptying, be a mere hiding (xputhis) of communicated power?

God's hiding Himself in clouds and darkness or in inaccessible light, is nowhere called an emptying or humiliation of Himself.

The sedes doctrinae

8. What passage of Scripture is the sedes doctrinae concerning the States of Christ?

Phil. 2:5-11.

Explanation, clause by clause of Phil. 2:5-11

9. Explain the first part of this passage.

This profound theological paragraph occurs, we may say, almost incidentally, in a most direct practical exhortation. The Philippians are urged in verse 3 to do nothing from motives that would advance the glory of either self or any party or faction with which anyone might be identified. Instead of this, "in lowliness of mind, each should esteem other better than himself." To enforce this, the example of Christ is cited, who instead of claiming for Himself the full honor that was His due, kept it entirely in the background. His highest motive was the salvation and elevation of fallen men. The description given is that of Jesus in His humanity, as He lived among His fellowmen, in seeming forgetfulness of self (for this is the meaning of Kenosis), intent upon the good of others. "Have, then, this mind in you which was in Christ Jesus, who existing in the form of God, counted not the being on an equality with God a thing to be grasped at" (vs. 5, 6).

10. What then is the meaning of "form of God"?

It does not point to a condition prior to the incarnation, but to one that according to what we have learned (Chap. XI, 43-49) continued to exist throughout the entire period in which He had also "the form of a servant" (v. 7). It was the incarnate Christ who had existed and continued to exist in the form of God.

> "Many presumptuously assume 'the form of God' without 'existing in' it. Such are the devil, Antichrist and the sons of Adam. This is regarded by God and all angels and saints and even by their own consciences as robbery. But Christ existed therein, and had it from His very nature. For Him to

> assert it was not robbery, for He regarded it His own natural property" (Luther).

The contrast is between actually possessing the divine majesty and glory, and grasping after it by those to whom it does not belong.

11. What is the meaning of "emptied himself?

It means that He did not assert Himself, or make a display of this majesty and glory. The contrast is between others who from "vain glory" constantly boast of what they do not possess, and Jesus who, like a ruler moving incognito among his subjects, refrains from exercising what He actually possesses.

12. Explain "form of a servant."

Certainly not the human nature; for this has been exalted to the Right Hand of God, since the form of a servant has been laid aside. But it means that "He sought not His own honor and good, but our profit and salvation. It was a willing service, spontaneously undertaken, for the good of others. Such service is indescribable, because the servant and slave is none other than the indescribable person who is the eternal God, whom all angels and all creatures serve" (Luther Erlangen Ed. 8:160.).

> Matt. 20:28. "The Son of man came not to be ministered unto, but to minister."

> Luke 22:27. "I am in the midst of you as he that serveth."

13. "Being made in the likeness of man."

Like other men, He was conceived and born, was a child and grew in wisdom and stature, was an Israelite among other Israelites, a Galilean among other Galileans, a poor peasant among other poor peasants, with no external mark distinguishing him among the rest.

14. "And being found in fashion as a man."

This refers to the continuance of the state introduced by the preceding clause.

> "His experience was that of every other man, eating, drinking, sleeping, waking, walking, standing, hungering, thirsting, shivering, sweating,

fatigued, working, clothing Himself, sheltered in a house, praying — all things just as others" (Luther).

15. "Humbled himself."

That is, He did and suffered what would have been a humiliation, if He had been nothing more than a man.

> "He did still more and became less than all men, stooped beneath them, and served them with the highest service by giving His body and life for us" (Luther).

16. "Becoming obedient unto death, even the death of the cross."

The humiliation deepens. It descends step by step. The Lord of the Law becomes subject to its most minute and extreme requirements. The Prince of Life dies; and His death is no ordinary one, but the shameful death of the cross (Gal. 3:13).

Definition

17. How, then, is the State of Humiliation defined?

It is that in which the Divine Person, according to His assumed human nature, abstains from the full use of the divine attributes communicated in the personal union.

18. Why is this qualified by "according to His assumed human nature"?

Because it is only through this nature that He can be humbled and exalted. The Son of God might have come to earth as man, with His humanity glorified, as it will appear on the Day of Judgment, but the humiliation consists in the holding of such communicated glory in reserve.

19. Why is it limited by the word "full"?

Because He occasionally asserted Himself, as in the working of miracles, and at

His triumphal entry into Jerusalem.

What attributes conspicuously involved

20. What especially prominent divine attributes are not fully exercised?

Omnipotence.

For if exercised, His sufferings for our sins would not have been rendered. With a glance He asserted His power, and the band of soldiers sent to arrest Him were prostrated. But at once withholding its exercise, He submitted Himself, and laid down His life, which none could take from Him (John 10:18).

Omniscience.

He was ignorant of when the Day of Judgment would occur (Matt. 24:36).

Omnipresence.

> John 11:15. "I am glad for your sakes, that I was not there."

His possession of all things.

> 2 Cor. 8:9. "Though he was rich, yet for your sakes he became poor, that ye through his poverty, might become rich."

> Matt. 8:20. "The Son of man hath not where to lay his head."

Duration

21. How long did the State of Humiliation last?

From the first moment of the conception to the last moment in the grave. Phil. 2:8, "Even the death of the cross" is the extreme limit, including of course not simply the act, but the state which followed.

Stages, or grades, viz., conception and birth, circumcision, childhood, visible life among men, passion, death, burial.

22. What various stages or grades are enumerated?

Conception and birth, circumcision, childhood, visible life among men, passion, death and burial.

23. How is the humiliation manifest in the conception and birth?

The former is expressed in the Te Deum:

> "When thou tookest upon thee, to deliver man, thou didst not abhor the womb of the Virgin."

The latter, in the poverty of His mother and of His birthplace.

24. What is involved in the controversy concerning the article of the Creed, "Conceived by the Holy Ghost, born of the Virgin Mary"?

> "They who deny the birth of the God-man of the Virgin Mary, will always question also the preexistence and deity of Christ in general; and therefore also the union and reconciliation of God and man in Him. They who will not leave unchallenged the new birth through creative interposition of a second original man into the old human nature, regard Christianity in general as only the perfecting and not the renovation of humanity. They know only of a gradual improvement of man, but nothing at all of the new creature in Christ Jesus" (Sartorius, Divine Love, p. 138 sq.).

25. How is the humiliation manifest in the circumcision?

It was the solemn act by which Christ formally declared and assumed the obligation to fulfill the entire law on man's behalf, and

> "...by which God the Father removed the intolerable yoke of the Law from the human race and placed it upon His incarnate Son."

"For with respect to His own person, He was not under the Law; but by circumcision He was made under the Law for us" (Gerhard).

Gal. 5:3. "I testify again to every man that receiveth circumcision, that he is a debtor to do the whole law."

Rom. 2:25. "For circumcision indeed profiteth, if them be a doer of the Law."

26a. How in His childhood?

He lived in a despised village among rough neighbors, and amidst narrow and contracted surroundings; was contemptuously called "a Nazarene," by the more cultivated of His race and nation; was subject to Mary and Joseph, although their Lord (Luke 2:51); learned the trade of Joseph and worked with His own hands for a livelihood (Mark 6:3), and submitted even to unjust and harsh rebukes (Luke 2:48).

26b. How in His visible life among men?

Answered above, 15.

27. How in His passion?

In its widest sense, this embraces all the afflictions and sorrows He endured, His temptation in the wilderness (Matt. 4; see Chap. 11:25), the slanders, reproaches and plots of adversaries (Matt. 12:24; John 7:1; 8:6; 9:16, 12), hunger, thirst, fatigue, poverty, etc., beginning with the massacre of the infants at Bethlehem and the flight into Egypt. In its narrower sense, it is the extremity of suffering which He experienced at the very close of His life (Matt. 20:18, 19).

28. Were His sufferings only bodily?

They pertained to both soul and body. He suffered as He foresaw them in the future (Matt. 12:50) and particularly as the crisis approached (Luke 22:44; Matt. 26:38; Mark 14:33). The ingratitude of the Jews, the treachery of Judas, the cowardice of the disciples, the denial of Peter, the false accusations, the ridicule and insults of the soldiers and of the rabble, all inflicted deep wounds.

29. What was the culmination of these sufferings?

The sense of God's wrath which found expression in the complaint that He was forsaken.

> Matt. 27:46. "My God, my God, why hast thou forsaken me?"

Nevertheless this was tempered by the word "my," declaring an inner consciousness, beneath the seeming separation, of His union and communion with God. This word, was "a witness of His triumphant faith, standing the test of the extreme death-struggle" (Van Oettingen).

30. How did this suffering differ from that endured by others, so as to add to its intensity?

He bore the sins of the world (John 1:29). Others are sustained and consoled by the assurance of the sympathy and vicarious sufferings of Christ. He faced the storm in all its fury alone, except so far as His union with the Father and the Spirit afforded Him comfort.

31. What of His bodily sufferings?

No part of His body escaped. Gerhard's hymn, "O Sacred Head now wounded," and Bernard's "*Salve caput cruentatum*" dwell on this. 'Thorns pierce the divine head; paleness, saliva and blood mar His countenance; His eyes are almost ruptured by the fists of His enemies; blows descend repeatedly on His cheeks; His ears are tortured by horrid blasphemies and reproaches; a kiss is imprinted on His mouth as a sign of betrayal; chains bind His hands, and nails pierce them as well as His feet; His shoulders are burdened with the cross; His back and breast and arms are torn by the scOurge; His tongue is tortured by thirst and the bitterness of the myrrh; His side is pierced by a spear; His whole body already a mass of wounds is stretched and tortured on the cross" (Quenstedt).

32. What must be particularly observed in connection with these sufferings?

They were not merely such as seemed to be endured, but were true and real (Is. 53:4). They were borne voluntarily, not by constraint or force (Heb. 10:7). They occurred not accidentally, but in accordance with a divine plan (Acts 2:23; 4:28) .

33. What was involved in the death of Christ?

The dissolution of the natural union between His soul and body, but not of the union between the divine and human natures.

34. What is the meaning of Christ's dying words, "It is finished"? (John 19:30.)

That, with His death, all prophecy is fulfilled, the types and shadows of the ceremonial law have reached their end, the work for which He had been sent to earth in accordance with God's eternal decree is at last completed, all the penalties allotted to sin and sinners have been endured, the rage of His enemies against Him and His people has found its limit, and, above all, redemption is now perfected. "Hence the propitiatory sacrifice which Christ made for us on the altar of the cross is not imperfect, or insufficient or only half obtained, but is perfect, complete and absolute" (Gerhard, in "Harmony").

> Heb. 10:14. "By one offering he hath perfected for ever them that are sanctified."

(See also Chapter 14, 14-16.)

35. What place had the burial of Christ?

It attested the truth of His death, and consecrated the grave as the resting place of believers.

Exaltation: Definition

36. Define the State of Exaltation.

It is that in which Christ, according to His human nature, fully exercises the communicated attributes of the divine nature.

37. Has it its stages or degrees?

Yes. In this respect, it is like the State of Exaltation. The definition, strictly taken, belongs only to its culmination (1 Cor. 15:27, 28), although relatively true at the very first stage or grade.

When did it begin

38. When did the State of Exaltation begin?

With the quickening or union of soul and body in the grave.

39. What confessional difference is there on this point?

The Reformed Church regards "the descent into hell" as a part of the humiliation; the Lutheran Church, as we shall see, regards it the first grade of the State of Exaltation.

The sedes doctrinae

40. What determines this difference?

The fact that the Lutheran Church regards 1 Peter 3:18, 19 as the sedes doctrinae, and the Reformed Church Acts 2:27.

41. Why do we not regard the latter passage as referring to the descent?

Because the true meaning of the passage is, as A. R. V. translates:

> "Thou wilt not leave my soul unto Hades,"

not "in Hades," as it has been misinterpreted, but "unto Hades." The thought is:

> "My soul shall not be delivered over to the power of death." There is no reference here to any "descent."

42. What appears prominently in 1 Peter 3:18, 19? The fact that the descent occurred after the "quickening," or reunion of soul and body.

"Being put to death in the flesh, but made alive in the spirit, in which also he went and preached unto the spirits in prison."

Confessional statement

43. What is the confessional definition of this article? It is guarded with the greatest caution and earnestly warns against laying importance upon speculations as to details.

> "We simply believe that the entire person, God and man, after the burial descended into hell, conquered the devil, destroyed the power of hell, and took from the devil all his might. We should not, however, trouble ourselves with sublime and acute thoughts, as to how this occurred" (Formula of Concord, 643).
>
> "How this occurred we should reserve until the other world, where not only this point, but also still others will be removed, which we here simply believe, and cannot comprehend with our blind reason" (p. 522).

Christ preaching to the spirits, not a preaching of the Gospel

44. Could the preaching to the spirits in prison have been a preaching of the Gospel?

No. The word in the Greek is not the word for "preaching the Gospel," *euaggelizo*, but *kerusso*, which means simply "to publish" or "proclaim." Undoubtedly, this might mean to "proclaim the Gospel," if the thought were expressed in other parts of Holy Scripture. There is no warrant, however, for believing that any opportunity for hearing the Gospel will be given after death. If it were so, then, since the Gospel would be preached to the large majority after death, and under circumstances rendering the appeal even more forcible than in this world, where the veil of sense conceals the realities of the world to come, this life could not be called the "accepted time," "the day of salvation," the period of grace (2 Cor. 6:2), when all men everywhere are commanded to repent (Acts 17:30). It would be only a preparatory dispensation, the portal or vestibule to that which is to come. (See Chapter XXXV, 17.)

45. But is there not a reference to a preaching of the Gospel to the dead in the immediate context to 1 Peter 3:18, 19, viz., in 1 Peter 4:6, "For to this end was the Gospel preached even to the dead"?

This does not mean that the Gospel was preached to them since they have died, but that those now dead once heard the Gospel just as those to whom the Apostle was writing. In verse 5, there is a reference to the day of judgment, when "the living and the dead" are to be judged. As this refers to a judgment of those now dead after they have been quickened, so in verse 6, "dead" means those now dead, while they lived on earth. They who had heard and believed the Gospel are chiefly in mind. The day of their deliverance is here foretold.

Why to antediluvians

46. Why is there a special allusion to the antediluvians as those to whom Christ preached?

Their open defiance and ridicule of Noah as a preacher of righteousness was typical of those who, in Peter's days, "mocked" preachers of the Gospel (2 Peter 3:3, 4). The discomfiture of the antediluvian mockers when Christ proclaimed His victory in the spirit world, was typical of the fate of all who similarly array themselves against His cause.

Was there a preaching to Old Testament saints

47. Did this proclamation of Christ's victory extend also to the saints of the Old Testament, who died in faith of the promises fulfilled by His death and resurrection?

The Roman Catholic Church teaches that by this preaching, they were released from the so-called *limbus pairum* and transferred to heaven. Of this, however, Scripture says nothing. As a matter of speculation, we may regard it probable that the proclamation of victory announced to one class to their terror was made to another class, to their joy and triumph. We dare not think of those who departed in faith as until then "in prison."

48. According to which nature did Christ make the descensus?

The Divine Person descended into hell, according to the human nature.

49. What, then, are the grades of the State of Exaltation?

The Descent into Hell, Resurrection, Ascension and Session at the Right Hand of God.

Resurrection

50. What is the Resurrection?

The act by which Christ brought forth from the sepulchre His body, and by various tests and at various times showed Himself alive to His disciples, as a proof of His divine authority, an evidence of the completion of His work of Redemption, and a confirmation of faith in the future resurrection of the dead. 51. Was the resurrection an act peculiar to the Son? All three persons of the Trinity were active, as in all external acts of God. Eph. 1:20 declares that the Father raised Christ from the dead (cf. Rom. 6:4; Col. 2:12). John 10:17, Christ says that He takes up His life of Himself. In Rom. 8:11 it is said that the Spirit raised up Jesus from the dead.

52. When did Christ rise from the dead?

On the third day, as Scripture repeatedly declares and the Church confesses. Jewish computation counts each day during which He was dead as one, whether it be the whole or only a part. There was one day, and parts of two others, the Jews reckoning their time from sunset to sunset.

Characteristics of Christ's resurrected body

53. What were the characteristics of His resurrection body?

[A.] It was a true body.

> Luke 24:39. "Handle me and see; for a spirit hath not flesh and blood as ye see me having."

To prove this "He ate before them" (v. 43).

[B.] It was the same body which He had before, with the print of the nails, and the scar of the spear (John 20:25, 27).

[C.] It was a glorified body.

> Phil. 3:21. "Who shall fashion anew the body of our humiliation, that it may be conformed to the body of his glory."

54. What is meant by "a glorified body"?

Since in the passage just quoted, it is declared that the resurrection body of believers is to be fashioned after that of Christ, and in 1 Cor. 15:42-44, there is a description of the resurrection body of believers, it follows that that of Christ possesses in the highest degree what is there described. All is summed up in the expression a "spiritual body." "A spiritual body," however, is not a body which is transformed into spirit. For there is a contrast between the body in the present life, as a "psychical" or soul body, and in the resurrection as a "spiritual" body. But since the "psychical body" is not body that is "soul," but one that has the properties of the soul (cf. above, Chap. VII, 13), the spiritual body is one that has the properties of the spirit. The reference is to a higher grade of endowments than those which we know now. In virtue of this, even before His death and resurrection, Christ walked upon the waves of the Sea of Galilee (Matt. 14:25), and after the resurrection, entered a room, even though the doors were closed (John 20:19), and vanished at will (Luke 24:31, or suddenly made His presence known (Mark 16:12). (See Chap. 36, 12-16.)

55. How do you explain the possession of these endowments as in Matt. 14:25, even before the resurrection?

In virtue of the personal union, they were possessed throughout the entire State of Humiliation, although not ordinarily exercised. But with the State of Exaltation, they are freely exercised.

56. Docs this same principle obtain in applying the terms "glorify" and "glorified"?

Yes. During the State of Humiliation, in one sense, Jesus, according to His human nature, was "not yet glorified" (John 7:39; 17:2, 5), i.e., He did not exercise the honor and power that were His. But, in another sense, He was glorified, whenever He permitted them to shine forth, as in His miracles (John 2:11). Because in His body dwelt all the fullness of the Godhead (Col. 2:9), it had these spiritual properties from the beginning, but their use was kept in abeyance and reserved for the State of Exaltation.

57. Why was the stone rolled away from the door of the sepulchre?

Not because its presence prevented the coming forth of Christ, for, as He penetrated walls with His resurrection body, He could with equal ease have penetrated the sealed rock, but in order to afford His disciples and the faithful women a sure proof that the tomb was empty. There is nothing in the record to show that the resurrection was subsequent to the rolling away of the stone.

Place of doctrine of Resurrection in preaching of the Apostles

58. Why has the resurrection of Christ such prominence in the preaching and teaching of the Apostles?

[A.] Because our Lord appealed to it as the test of the truth of His claims (Matt. 16:21; 17:9; John 2:19), and to the early Christians it was the greatest of all proofs of His divine authority, and especially of His Godhead (Rom. 1:4; 1 Cor. 15:14-19; Acts 2:32; 3:15; 4 ’-33, etc.).

[B.] Because it attested the perfection of the righteousness acquired by Christ's mediation. He was man's substitute.

As such He bore man's sins and died, the just for the unjust. If death had held Him fast, it would have bound us. But as death cannot hold Him, we are free; He has satisfied the law; and His righteousness procured for us surpasses all the powers of death.

> Rom. 4:25. "Who was delivered up for our trespasses, and raised again for our justification."

i.e., just as our sins caused His death, so our potential justification, or the full provision He has made for our justification, caused His resurrection.

[C.] Because it is the pledge of our own resurrection.

> 1 Cor. 15:20. "But now hath Christ been raised from the dead, the first-fruits of them that are asleep." 2 Cor. 4:14.

[D.] Because from it flows the applying grace of the Holy Spirit.

> Rom. 6:4. "That like as Christ was raised from the dead through the glory of the Father, so we also might walk in newness of life."

Its place in Apologetics

59. What place does the resurrection of Christ have in Apologetics?

> "The resurrection of Christ is a fact. It is the fixed point to which the threads of all Apologetics will ever be attached. Apologetics will always have to start from the resurrection of Christ. He is historically proved by it to be the personal miracle. The awakening of Jesus from the dead is the great miracle which contains and carries those mighty deeds performed by Him and recorded in the Gospels, as also those which were done in His name. In short by His resurrection, He is declared to be the Son of God with power according to the spirit of holiness; in Him the world is fully overcome, and God is glorified. From this, too, the existence of a living and life-giving God is proved. From ignorance of the power of God, Paul and Jesus in common, explain the denial of a resurrection (1 Cor. 15:39; Matt. 22:29)" (Auberlen).

A Church historian whose free criticism of Christianity has deservedly been subjected to the criticism of scholars who have followed him, viz., F. C. Baur, correctly affirmed that the energy and enthusiasm which imparted to the early Church its aggressive force and made it victorious was "the conviction that the resurrection of Jesus was the most fixed and incontrovertible certainty."

The Ascension

60. What is the Ascension of Christ?

> "The visible and glorious triumph of Christ as victor, raising His body above the clouds, and then, in an invisible way, extending it above all heavens, so as to occupy His Kingdom unto the end of the world, and everywhere, in a heavenly manner, afford us aid" (Calovius).

61. May it not have been a mere disappearance as, in Gen. 17:22, God is said to have gone up from Abraham?

No, for the disciples saw him depart by a visible and local motion (Luke 24:51; Acts 1:9), in virtue of the endowments of a glorified and supernatural body, as He entered upon a higher degree of the use of His Majesty than He had exercised during the period between the Resurrection and Ascension.

> "It was a true and real ascension, the body being raised above the earth. See Acts 1:9. Nevertheless it is not to be excessively scrutinized or defined according to the natural mode, so that the presence upon earth of the body which was raised to heaven is denied. For it is not only in heaven, but we read in Eph. 4:10, that 'He ascended far above all the heavens that He might fill all things'" (Baier).

62. What is the heaven which Christ entered?

Not the visible, astronomical heaven, which is its symbol, but the state or condition within which the glory of God is most fully displayed.

> John 17:5. "And now, Father, glorify thou me with thine own self with the glory which I had with thee before the world was."

63. What was the end of the Ascension?

First of all, His glorious triumph (Eph. 2:15). Then although, according to his promise, never absent on earth until the end of the world (Matt. 28:20), nevertheless He withdrew His visible presence, that He might send the Holy Spirit (John 16:7), prepare abodes in heaven for believers (John 14:2), and train them to believe in Him as though absent.

John 20:29. "Blessed are they that have not seen and yet have believed."

I Peter 1:8. "Whom not having seen ye love; on whom though now ye see him not, yet believed, ye rejoice greatly with joy unspeakable and full of glory."

64. What exhortation and consolation are given by the Ascension?

The exhortation.

Col. 3:1, 2. "If then ye were raised together with Christ, seek the things that are above, where Christ is, seated on the right hand of God," etc.

The consolation.

John 17:24. "Father, I desire that they also whom thou hast given me, be with me where I am, that they may behold my glory."

The Session at the Right Hand of God.

65. What is the Session at the Right Hand of God?

It is manifest that neither "Right Hand," nor "sitting" can be taken literally. To localize the "Right Hand" is in conflict with God's spirituality. The Right Hand of God is declared to be omnipresent.

Ps. 139:7-10. "Whither shall I go from thy Spirit? or whither shall I flee from thy presence? If I ascend up into heaven, thou art there; if I make my bed in Sheol, behold thou art there. If I take the wings of the morning and dwell in the uttermost parts of the sea, even there shall thy hand lead me and thy right hand shall hold me."

66. What is meant by referring various organs and parts of the human body to God?

The eye and ear symbolize His knowledge and care.

Ps. 34:15. "The eyes of Jehovah are toward the righteous, and his ears are open unto their cry."

The finger symbolizes the union of power and wisdom.

> Luke 11:20. "If I by the finger of God cast out demons, then is the kingdom of God come upon you."

The arm, His omnipotent power.

> Luke 1:51. "He hath shewed strength with his arm."

The feet, His absolute dominion and sovereignty.

> Ps. 8:6. "Thou hast put all things under feet."

The arm and right hand are frequently united to indicate power in various manifestations.

> Deut. 5:15. "Jehovah thy God brought thee out thence by a mighty hand and by an outstretched arm."

> Ps. 89:13. "Thou hast a mighty arm. Strong is thy hand, and high is thy right hand."

The Right Hand denotes, therefore, the power and majesty of God in the very highest degree.

> Ex. 15:6. "Thy right hand, O Jehovah, is glorious in power. Thy right hand, O Jehovah, dashes in pieces the enemy."

> Ps. 18:35. "Thy right hand hath holden me up." 21:8. "Thy right hand will find out those that hate thee."

Hence it is called "the Right Hand of Power" (Matt. 26:64), "the Right Hand of Majesty" (Heb. I 13), "the Right Hand of the throne of Majesty" (Heb. 8:1), "the Right Hand of the throne of God" (Heb. 12:2).

67. Coming back to question 64, what, then, is meant by Christ's sitting at the Right Hand of God?

It is the full participation of the human nature of Christ in God's reign over all things in heaven and earth. Christ, the divine person, according to His human nature, exercises fully the sway over all things which belonged to Him in the human nature, as well as the divine, from the first moment of the personal union.[1]

1 As contrasted with other statements in which the Reformed seem to antagonize Lutheran teachers on this subject, reference may be made to the admirable explanation of Calvin on Eph.

68. Is it synonymous with "reigning"?

Not exactly. It is reigning with a certain end in view. For this, be it noted, is a stage in His Mediatorial Office, and is directed towards the salvation of men. It is the administration by Christ, according to His human nature, of the three-fold Kingdom, of Power, Grace and Glory, the application of redemption.

69. How is this declared in our Confessions?

"He ascended into heaven, that He might it on the Right Hand of the Father, and forever reign, and have dominion over all creatures, and sanctify them that believe in Him, by sending the Holy Ghost into their hearts, to rule, comfort and quicken them, and to defend them against the devil and the power of sin" (Augsburg Confession, Art. III).

1:20.

"This passage clearly shows what the Right Hand of God means, viz., not any locality, but the power which the Father conferred upon Christ, in order that, in his name, the latter should administer the government of heaven and earth. God is said to have raised Christ to his Right Hand, because he made him associate in the government, and through him he exercises all his power. Inasmuch as the Right Hand of God fills heaven and earth, it follows that the Kingdom, as well as the power of Christ is universally diffused. Hence they are in error, who, from Christ's sitting at the Right Hand of God, endeavor to prove that Christ is only in heaven."

13. The Offices Of Christ, Christ As Prophet

Relation to what precedes

1. What relation has the contents of the two preceding chapters to what is now to be treated?

The Personal Union and the two States of Christ are means; the Offices of Christ are the end, i.e., the Son of God became incarnate and humbled Himself and was exalted in order to be our Prophet, Priest and King.

Three functions of Mediatorial Office

2. What three things belong to the Mediatorial Office?

[A.] The Revelation of God's Will.
[B.] The Preparation of Redemption.
[C.] The Application of Redemption.

The first is comprised in His office of Prophet, the second, in that of Priest; and the third, in that of King.

3. What Scriptural ground is there for this distinction?

He is called Prophet.

Acts 3:32. "Moses indeed said, A prophet shall the Lord God raise up unto you from among your brethren like unto me."

Matt. 11:9. "A prophet? Yea, and I say unto you, much more than a prophet."

Priest.

Heb. 4:14. "Having then a great high priest who hath passed through the heavens, Jesus the Son of God." 7:17. "For it is witnessed of him, Thou art a priest forever after the order of Melchizedek."

King.

Matt. 21:5. "Tell ye the daughter of Zion, Behold thy King cometh unto thee." Rev. 17:14. "The Lamb shall overcome them, for he is Lord of lords and Kings of kings."

Meaning of "Prophet"

4. What is the meaning of "prophet"?

Not simply, or chiefly one who predicts, but the interpreter or spokesman of God. The word "pro" means "forth" rather than "before" in a temporal sense. "Elijah and Paul were prophets, not because they foretold the future, but because they enlightened the present"" (Stanley, as quoted by Century Dictionary). Daniel was as truly a prophet when he interpreted the dream of Nebuchadnezzar as when he foretold future events.

Prophetic Office defined and explained

5. What, then, is the Prophetic Office?

It is that by which Christ declares to men, for all time, and for all places, the nature and will of God.

> John 1:18. "No man hath seen God at any time; the only-begotten Son, who is in the bosom of the Father, he hath revealed him."
>
> Heb. 1:2. "God hath, at the end of these days, spoken unto us in his Son."
>
> Mark 9:7. "This is my beloved Son; hear ye him."

The word of the Father, spoken at the Transfiguration, means, "There is no reason why you should lament the departure of Moses and Elias. Here is my Son who will teach you, as well as all who follow you until the end of time, fully and plainly, all that you need to know concerning me and my will and the world to come. Hear ye Him."

6. What does this imply?

That "all who would think or speculate in a saving manner concerning God must make all things subordinate to the humanity of Christ" (Luther, de Wette I, 226). "For this end, God had His Son to become incarnate, in order to withdraw us from the contemplation of His majesty, to that of His flesh" (Melanchthon, "Loci Communes," I ed.). Christ is thus the great and only Revealer of God to man. A great American preacher, of another Church, has expressed this with great force:

> "Why do I believe in God? If some man asked me, when on the street, I think, I should have an answer to give him. I could give one great reason — two great reasons which are really one great reason — why I believe in God. I believe in God, my friends, I believe in God with all my soul, because this world is inexplicable without Him and explicable with Him, and because Jesus Christ believed in Him; and it was Jesus Christ that showed me that this world demanded God and was inexplicable without Him, and that made certain every suspicion and dream that I had had before" (Phillips Brooks, "Addresses," p. 56).

In revealing God to man, Christ also revealed man to himself:

> "Not only do we know God only through Jesus Christ, but we know ourselves only through Jesus Christ. We know life and death only by Him. Except by Jesus Christ, we know not what life is, nor what death is, nor what God is, nor what we ourselves are" (Pascal, "Thoughts").

Revelations before the Incarnation

7. But was there no revelation of God to men prior to the incarnation?

Yes. But this revelation was partial, incomplete and preparatory.

> Heb. 1:1, 2. "God, having of old time spoken unto the fathers in the prophets by divers portions and in divers manners, hath at the end of these days spoken unto us in his Son."

Beside this, whatever revelations they made came to them through the Son, as the Word, or Revealer of God. They were the reflection of the light which was approaching in the advent of the Son.

> 1 Peter 1:10, 11. "The prophets sought and searched diligently who prophesied of the grace that should come unto you, searching what time or what manner of time the Spirit of Christ, which was in them did point unto."

8. Who is by preeminence the great prophet of the Old Testament, and how is the Old Testament prophetic office contrasted with that of Christ?

Moses; between whom as the prophet of the Old Testament, and Christ as the prophet of the New Testament, the contrast is frequently drawn (Deut. 18:15-18; John 1:21, 25; Acts 3:22; 7:37). The former received that which he taught externally by revelation of God in the Mount (Heb. 8:7); the latter by His anointing, i.e., a peculiar gift of the Holy Spirit with His human nature, as the temple of the Godhead bodily, and the incarnate Word of God (Is. 61:1; John 1:14). It was the duty of the Old Testament prophets and Moses as the greatest to declare: "Thus saith the Lord." It was the prerogative of Christ to proclaim: "Verily, verily, I say unto you." It was for them to declare the authority of God's word. But none but Christ could say:

"Heaven and earth shall pass away; but my words shall not pass away" (Matt. 24:35).

Christ's Preaching of the Law

9. What was the subject of Christ's teaching?

Both Law and Gospel.

10. How did He teach the Law?

[A.] By republishing it, without the Rabbinical additions by which it had been overlaid and obscured, and without the ceremonial and forensic elements, which belonged only to the Old Testament,

[B.] By indicating its spiritual character and application.

11. Where was this especially done?

In the Sermon on the Mount, which is a restatement of the Law, with a presentation of its spiritual application, introductory to the declaration of the Gospel.

12. In what words does Christ make most clear his relation to the Law?

> Matt. 5:17, 18. "Think not that I came to destroy the law or the prophets; I came not to destroy, but to fulfill. For verily I say unto you, Till heaven and earth pass away, one jot or one tittle shall in no wise pass away from the law, till all things be accomplished."

13. How was this further enforced?

By His holy example, in complying with all the precepts of the Law, both in letter and in spirit. His life was a model and standard as to how the two tables of the Law are to be fulfilled. There is no object lesson so complete in all its details and so impressive in its effects, as that presented in the record of His visible intercourse among men.

> Matt. 22:42. "Not my will, but thine be done."

Phil. 2:5. "Have this mind in you which was in Christ Jesus."

Rom. 15:2, 3. "Let each one of us please his neighbor for that which is good unto edifying. For Christ also pleased not himself."

1 Peter 2:21. "Christ also suffered for you, leaving you an example, that ye should follow his steps."

Luke 16:24. "If any man would come after me, let him deny himself, and take up his cross, and follow me."

14. Was the preaching of the Law by Christ merely a reaffirmation of its principles, or was it accompanied also by a reaffirmation of the authority of the Old Testament Scriptures?

We need only refer to His frequent appeals to the authority of Scripture:

Matt. 21:42. "Did ye never read in the Scriptures?"

Matt. 22:22. "Ye do err, not knowing the Scriptures."

Matt. 26:52. "That the Scriptures of the prophets might be fulfilled."

Luke 24:45. "Then opened he their minds that they might understand the Scriptures."

As well as to His customary formula, "It is written" (Matt. 4:4, 6, 7, 10; 11:10; 21:13; 26:24, 31; Mark 7:6; 9:12; 11:17; 14:21, 27, etc.).

According to the teaching of Jesus, it was sufficient that a passage appealed to was in the canon of the Old Testament as received by the Jewish Church of His period, to make it authoritative (John 10:34).

15. But did not His leaching contain a criticism of the Law?

Undoubtedly, as in passages where He leads His hearers from the treatment of the merely external side of the Law to its deeper meaning, i.e., from the shell to the kernel, as in Matt. 5:21-48, or where He exacts more than its merely provisional prescriptions allowed, as in Matt. 19:7-12. His criticism has to do not with the books or the text of the Old Testament, but entirely with its material, which, while of equal obligation for those upon whom it was enjoined, must be divided, in the light of the coming of*Christ, into that which belongs to the forensic and ceremonial laws, and is, therefore, of only temporary value, and that which belongs to the Moral Law, and, therefore, permanent. (Chapter XXV, 16, 27-33.)

> John 1:17. "For the law was given through Moses; grace and truth came through Jesus Christ."

16. Was the preaching of the Law the main object of this office?

No.

The Law He preached, because men had forgotten and perverted what Moses had taught them. He showed how the most searching spiritual requirements were taught even by Moses (Matt. 22:36-40).

The Formula of Concord (508), therefore, calls "the preaching of Moses and the Law" "a strange work of Christ" (see Is. 28:21), subordinate "to His proper office, to preach grace, console and quicken, which is properly the preaching of the Gospel."

Christ's Preaching of the Gospel

17. What is included in the Gospel?

All things pertaining to His person and work announced in order to call forth and sustain faith (Chapter 25, 34-39). The teaching of doctrine is subordinate to the bringing of men to a knowledge of the Son Himself, and through the Son to a knowledge of the Father.

> Matt. 11:27. "Neither knoweth any man the Father save the Son, and he to whomsoever the Son will reveal him."

> 1 John 4:9. "Herein was the love of God manifested in us, that God hath sent his only begotten Son into the world."

How Prophetic Office is continued; its two stages

18. The Prophetic Office embraces, then, more than the function of teaching?

It includes also the impartation of spiritual power whereby through the Holy Spirit He moves men's hearts to embrace the doctrine of the Gospel (John 6:45).

19. What two stages of this office are there?

The Immediate and the Mediate. The former was when Christ, in His own person instructed men. The latter He exercised through the Apostles, and through all who preach the Word and by their lives bear witness to the faith, until the end of time.

> John 20:21. "As the Father hath sent me, even so send I you."

> Luke 10:16. "He that heareth you, heareth me." Eph. 4:11-13.

Progress in Christ's teaching

20. Was there progress in Christ's teaching?

The contents of the Gospel were not announced in all their fullness at once. Christ adapted His teaching to the capacity of those whom He taught.

> John 16:12. "I have yet many things to say unto you, but ye cannot bear them now."

> Mark 4:34. "And without a parable, spake he not unto them; but privately to his own disciples, he expounded all things."

His sufferings and death He did not announce until they were immediately impending. Neither was their significance realized until after His ascension and the gift of the Holy Spirit at Pentecost. Even after Pentecost, the universality of redemption and the complete freedom of the Christian from the Mosaic ritual were only gradually apprehended, and amid considerable controversy in the Apostolic Church, as the Book of Acts clearly shows. The gift of the Holy Spirit as the Great Teacher was to be apprehended and utilized through the struggles of believers towards the light.

> John 16:26. "But the Comforter, even the Holy Spirit, whom the Father shall send in my name, he shall teach you all things, and bring to your remembrance all that I said unto you."

Miracles as seals of the Prophetic Office

21. What were the seals of His Prophetic office? His miracles (John 3:2; Luke 24:19).

22. What was their special function?

> John 20:30, 31. "Many other signs therefore did Jesus in the presence of the disciples, which are not written in this book; but these are written that ye may believe that Jesus is the Christ, the Son of God."

On this, Gerhard ("Harmony of Gospels") says:[2]

> "We see in this passage that this purpose is assigned miracles, viz., of being aids and supports of faith, by exciting and preparing the minds of men to believe God's Word and promises, which are worthy of belief even without miracles, or, as the Apostle says (1 Tim. 1:15), 'worthy of all acceptation.' Miracles, however, only confirm, they do not impart faith. They who believe not from the Word, but from miracles, in the time of temptation do not remain steadfast."

23. What is meant by the promise (John 14:12) that greater miracles will be wrought by those who follow Him as preachers of the Gospel?

The reference is to inner spiritual miracles in the conversion of men. The number brought to the knowledge of salvation by the immediate exercise of His office was very small when compared with the thousands whom He converted mediately at Pentecost through the sermon of Peter. The changed lives of converts to Christianity is an ever repeated miracle. So also is the spread of Christianity and

2 My esteemed colleague, Prof. Dr. Spaeth, in a sermon to the students of our Seminary, 1905, on the Gospel Lesson for Epiphany, illustrated this in one very condensed sentence: "From the star to the Word; from the Word to Christ."

its perpetuity through ages of incessant conflict.

14. Christ As Priest

Defined

1. What is the Priestly Office of Christ?

That according to which, as our only Priest, He offered Himself as the all-sufficient and only sacrifice for our sins and intercedes with God, that we may be reconciled to Him and enjoy all the blessings of everlasting life.

According to which nature

2. According to which nature is Christ our Priest?

In all the functions of His Mediatorial Office, He always acts according to both natures (see above, Chapter 11, 50-53).

> "Christ is our righteousness, neither according to the divine nature alone, nor according to the human nature alone, but the entire Christ according to both natures, alone in His obedience, which, as God and man, He rendered the Father even to death" (Formula of Concord, 501).

Old Testament types

3. What Old Testament types were there of Christ's priesthood?

Two: the Levitical priesthood, and that of Melchizedek. The main argument of the Epistle to the Hebrews is to show the inferiority of the Levitical priesthood to that of Christ. The Levitical priests were of the tribe of Levi; Christ was of Judah. The former were mere men; the latter, was also God. The former were sinners, who had to make satisfaction for themselves; the latter was holy and spotless, whose offering is entirely for us. The former differed from the victims they offered; with the latter, priest and victim were one. The former were numerous, because each one could not fulfill all parts of his office; the latter needed no assistant or substitute. The sacrifices of the former were unable to expiate sin, and, therefore, had to be frequently repeated; that of the latter was offered once for all. The priesthood of Melchizedek is shown to surpass that of the Levitical order, and to be a better type of that of Christ for the following reasons: The name means "King of righteousness," and he was "King of Salem," i.e., of peace, both of which are united in Christ. His genealogy was not known, thus typifying the eternity of Christ's person. He united, like Christ, kingship and priesthood in the same person. As a superior, he blessed Abraham, the ancestor of Aaron and the Levitical priests. He broke through the line of the regular, external succession, having neither predecessors nor followers in his office.

The two functions of the Priesthood: 1. Meaning of Satisfaction;

To whom made; Vicarious Satisfaction no injustice; Attributes of God vindicated; Personal Objects of the Satisfaction; Extent of the Atonement; Real Objects; from what has the Satisfaction redeemed; by what means was it afforded; the Active and the Passive Obedience; difference between the sacrifice of Christ and Old Testament sacrifices; when made; does the Resurrection belong to the Satisfaction

4. What are the two functions of this priesthood?

The sacrificial offering and the sacerdotal intercession; or satisfaction and intercession.

5. Is the term "satisfaction' found in Holy Scripture?

No. It is used to express the thought variously stated in different passages.

> Is. 53:4-6. "He hath borne our griefs and carried our sorrows He was wounded for our transgressions, he was bruised for our iniquities; the chastisement of our peace was upon him Jehovah hath laid on him the iniquities of us all."
>
> Matt. 20:28. "To give his life a ransom for many." 1 Tim. 2:6. "Who gave himself a ransom for all."
>
> 1 John 2:2. "He is the propitiation for our sins."
>
> 1 John 4:10. "He sent his Son, to be the propitiation for our sins."
>
> Rom. 4:25. "Whom God hath set forth to be a propitiation through faith in his blood."
>
> Rom. 5:11. "While we were enemies we were reconciled to God through the death of his Son."
>
> Eph. 1:7. "In whom we have redemption through his blood."
>
> 2 Cor. 5:21. "Him who knew no sin he made to be sin on our behalf, that we might become the righteousness of God in him."
>
> Gal. 3:13. "Christ hath redeemed us from the curse of the law, having become a curse for us."
>
> 1 Pet. 1:18, 19. "Knowing that ye were redeemed not with corruptible things, with silver or gold, from your vain manner of life, handed down from your fathers, but with precious blood as of a lamb without blemish and without spot, even the blood of Christ."

These passages concur in teaching that penalties due men on account of their sins have been endured by Christ; that, as a result, God is reconciled with those who had been beneath His wrath; that, they are delivered from all liability to punishment, and instead thereof, receive the rewards of Christ's perfect obedience to the law. That is, Christ had met all the demands of the Law for man; He has satisfied it.

6. What other term is synonymous?

Redemption presents one side of satisfaction, viz., the payment of the price by which man is freed from the consequences of sin. The word is used in two senses. Sometimes it means deliverance or liberation itself, as in Luke 21:28; Rom. 8:23; Eph. 4:30, but generally as in passages above given "the payment of the price of redemption."

7. Whom did Christ satisfy?

> 2 Cor. 5:19, "God was in Christ reconciling the world unto himself,"

Shows that it was not only the Father, but the entire Trinity that was offended because of sin, and was reconciled; as well as that it was not merely the Son, but the entire Trinity in and through the Son that made the offering for sin.

8. In what relation did God receive satisfaction?

Not as a mere private creditor, ready at will to exact or relieve from an obligation, but as a most just judge maintaining the absolute inviolability of His law.

9. But is not the rendering of satisfaction by one from whom it was not demanded a violation of law?

In human courts the bondsman is accountable for the payment of a debt for which he is surety.

> "In this sense, it is said by theologians, that punishment must necessarily be inflicted impersonally for every sin, but not at once personally upon every sinner, since by peculiar grace God can exempt some from this penalty, when a bondsman is substituted in his place" (Turretin).

10. Is it not an act of injustice to allow an innocent one to suffer for the guilt of another?

Not when the innocent one, by his own free will, assumes the burden (Heb. 10:7), and retains the power, at will, to relinquish it.

John 10:18. "No one taketh my life away from me, but I lay it down of myself. I have power to lay it down, and I have power to take it up again."

Nor when he has the power to bear the penalties to the utmost, and, after exhausting them, to be both free himself and to bring deliverance to others.

11. What attributes of God are especially prominent in this provision for a satisfaction for sin?

His justice in vindicating the Law, and inexorably demanding punishment even when His Son occupied the place of the sinner. His holiness in tolerating the sinner only upon the condition of the payment of his debt and the removal of his guilt. Above all His love in providing such a satisfaction for such enemies.

Rom. 5:7, 8. "For scarcely for a righteous man will one die; for peradventure for the good man, some would even dare to die. But God commendeth his own love towards us, in that while we were yet sinners Christ died for us."

12. For whom was this satisfaction rendered?

For all men. This is proved by:
[A.] Express declarations that Christ's work was for all.

2 Cor. 5:14, 15. "One died for all." "He died for all."

Heb. 2:9. "That, by the grace of God, he should taste of death for every man."

Rom. 8:32. "He delivered him up for us all."

[B.] Statements ascribing it to the world.

John 1:29. "Behold the Lamb of God that taketh away the sin of the world."

John 3:16. "God so loved the world that he gave his only begotten Son that whosoever believeth in him should not perish."

1 John 2:2. "He is the propitiation for the whole world."

[C.] Declarations that it included even those who ultimately perish.

> Rom. 14:15. "Destroy not with thy meat him for whom Christ died."
>
> Heb. 10:29. "Counted the blood of the covenant wherewith he was sacrificed an unholy thing."

1 Cor. 8:11.

13. May not these passages be explained by the saying of Peter Lombard: Christ died sufficiently, but not efficiently for all"?

This would not be consistent with the argument in the context of the passages above cited. Besides no lack of efficacy in the satisfaction can be proved from the fact that this efficacy is not appropriated by all. We can not ascribe a patient's serious illness to a lack of efficacy in the medicine when he fails to take it.

14. For what sins was this satisfaction rendered?

For all sins, and all their guilt and punishment.

> "That He might be a sacrifice not only for original guilt, but for all actual sins of men" (Augsburg Confession, Art. 3).
>
> 1 John 1:7. "The blood of Jesus Christ, his Son, cleanseth us from all sin."
>
> Gal. 3:13. "Christ redeemed us from the curse of the law, having become a curse for us." [3]

3 Thus, in our stead, Luther says in a famous passage, Christ is no longer "an innocent and sinless person, the Son of God born of the virgin, but a sinner, who has and bears the sin of Saul, the blasphemer and persecutor, and of Peter, the denier of his Master, and of David, the adulterer and murderer; in a word, He bears and has all the sins of all men in His body. Not that He has committed these sins, but that being committed by us, He assumed them and transferred them to His own body, in order to render satisfaction for them with His own blood. The general law of Moses, therefore, lays hold of Him, although innocent in His person, because it finds Him among sinners and robbers, just as a magistrate holds and punishes as guilty one whom he finds among robbers even though he had never committed anything wrong or worthy of death. Christ, however, was not only found among sinners, but even of His own accord and by the will of the Father wished to be the associate of sinners by assuming the flesh and blood of those who, as sinners and robbers, were sunk into all sins. When the Law, therefore, found Him among robbers, it condemned and killed him as a robber. But some one may say: 'It is blasphemous to call the Son of God a sinner and a curse.' I answer: If you want to deny this, deny also that He suffered, was crucified arid died.' It is no less absurd to say that the Son of God was crucified, than that He was a sinner. But it it is not absurd to confess and believe that Christ was crucified between thieves, it is not absurd to say the other. Certainly there is something in the words of Paul: 'Christ became a curse for us.' 'He made Him to be sin for us, in order that we might be

(See also Chapter 12, 34.)

15. Has any other doctrine ever been widely taught?

Yes, the prevalent view of the scholastics, which has pervaded the teaching and life of Roman Catholics, that the satisfaction of Christ availed for sins which men have committed before baptism, and that for those committed since then, it avails only so as to compensate for guilt, but not for punishment, except by commuting it, through the administration of the Power of the Keys, from that which is infinite and eternal, to that which the believing can offset, partly in this world and partly in the world to come, in Purgatory, by their own satisfactions. It was on this point that the Protestant Reformation of the Sixteenth Century began.

16. What is the consequence of the doctrine that the satisfaction of Christ is complete only with the respect to sins committed before baptism?

Only one part of the work of redemption is ascribed to Christ, while another, which may readily be interpreted as the greater part, is left to men. According to this theory, what Christ has begun, man has to complete.

17. What are the various punishments of sins, and How has Christ redeemed from each?

The curse of the law (Gal. 3:13).

(See above, 14.) The dominion of Satan.

> Heb. 2:14. "Since the children are sharers in flesh and blood, he also himself in like manner partook of the same; that through death he might bring to naught him that had the power of death, that is, the devil."

---

made the righteousness of God in Him.' So John the Baptist calls Him the Lamb of God, bearing the sins of the world, John 1:29. He Himself is innocent, because the Lamb of God without spot or blemish, but since He bears the sins of the world, His innocency is weighed down by the sins and guilt of the whole world. Whatever sins I and you have done have become the sins of Christ, as though He Himself had committed them. Isa. 53:6 says: 'The Lord hath laid upon Him the iniquity of us all.' These words we ought not to extenuate, but to give them their proper force." On Gal. 3:13.

The wrath of God.

1 Thess. 1:10. "Jesus who delivereth us from the wrath to come."

Death.

Heb. 2:14. (See above).

1 Cor. 15:55. "O death, where is thy victory? O death where is thy sting?"

Eternal condemnation.

Rom. 8:1. "There is, therefore, now no condemnation to them that are in Christ Jesus."

18. By what means was the satisfaction of Christ rendered?

By His obedience to the law.

> Rom. 5:19. "For as through the one man's disobedience, the many were made sinners, so through the obedience of the one shall the many be made righteous."

19. How has this been confessionally stated?

> "His obedience, not only in suffering and dying, but also that he in our stead was voluntarily subject to the Law, and fulfilled it by His obedience, is imputed to us for righteousness, so that, on account of this complete obedience, which, by deed and by suffering, in life and in death, He rendered His heavenly Father for us, God forgives our sins, regards us godly and righteous, and eternally saves us" (Formula of Concord, 572).

20. What two factors are comprised in this obedience?

It has been divided into the Active and the Passive Obedience.

21. What is the Active Obedience?

Christ's perfect compliance with all the requirements of the Law, Moral, Ceremonial and Forensic, prescribed as the condition of eternal life and its rewards.

> Matt. 5:17. "I came not to destroy, but to fulfill."
>
> Gal. 4:4, 5. "Born under the law, that he might redeem them that were under the law."
>
> Rom. 10:4. "Christ is the end of the law unto righteousness to every one that believeth."

This can be illustrated by a careful study of the history of His life in the Gospels, in which He will be seen to have done fully all that the law demanded, and to have abstained entirely from all that it prohibited.

22. What is the result of such complete conformity to the law?

The acquiring of the merit and rewards promised obedience.

> Matt. 3:15. "It becometh us to fulfill all righteousness."
>
> Rom. 10:4. "Christ is the end of the law for righteousness."
>
> 1 Cor. 1:30. "Christ Jesus who was made unto us wisdom from God and righteousness."

23. Was this subjection to the Law rendered in order that He might Himself win the rewards?

No. For personally He not only was Lord of the Law, but already possessed all things. Personally He could not acquire righteousness for Himself; as He already had it. All the merit and reward belongs, therefore, to those, for whom He was vicariously under the law.

> Phil. 3:9. "And he found in him, not having a righteousness of mine own, even that which is of the law, but that which is through faith in Christ."

> Rom. 1:17. "For therein is revealed a righteousness of God, from faith unto faith."

24. What is the Passive Obedience?

The bearing of the guilt and the payment of the penalties due the violated law because of men's sin. For proofs, see above under 12, 14, 17, and 1 Peter 1:18, 19; 2:24; Heb. 9:28; Is. 53; 2 Cor. 5:21.

25. Can the Active and Passive Obedience be separated?

Only in thought. They are the positive and negative sides of the same thing. Man could have no righteousness with the guilt of sin reckoned to him and its penalties impending. By His passive obedience Christ transfers all the penalties to Himself and endures them; by His active obedience, a righteousness is provided in which the guilt of sin disappears as night flees before the rising of the sun, or man's shame and nakedness are covered by a spotless robe.

26. Does righteousness, however, consist in deeds and sufferings?

As righteous deeds and sufferings are the revelation and proofs of an inner righteousness which has preceded, so the Active and Passive Obediences testify to what the Son of God, in His incarnate person, is for those for whom He lived and labored and toiled and cared. What Christ did and suffered is the revelation of what Christ was, and is, and forever will be.

> Rom. 5:8. "God commendeth his own love towards us, that, while we were yet sinners, Christ died for us."

> John 15:13. "Greater love hath no man than this, that a man lay down his life for his friends."

As the life and death of Christ were the revelation of God's gracious will towards man, the resurrection and ascension were the pledges of the power at the service of this love (Phil. 3:9), and the unassailable character of the righteousness provided through His satisfaction. His satisfaction, however, culminates, centers, is concentrated in his self-surrender to all our conditions and sufferings.

27. How then did Christ's sacrifice differ from that of the Old Testament sacrifices?

They were not true and real, but only figurative sacrifices; as the essence of the sacrifice lies in the cheerful self-surrender of the victim. Paul has laid down the principle underlying reward when he says (1 Cor. 9:17), "If I do this of mine own will" (or "willingly," A. V.), "I have a reward." The sacrifice of Christ, therefore, was the entire state or condition of obedience, to the law, in which He voluntarily surrendered Himself for man's sin, and for the purchase of life and salvation.

28. When was the satisfaction rendered?

It comprised the entire State of Humiliation, in all its acts and sufferings. For all were part or expressions of His meritorious obedience.

29. Does the resurrection belong to His satisfaction?

It was not part of the satisfaction, because the law imposed no obligation upon man to rise from the dead, as both godly and wicked will do, at Christ's call, at the last day. But it is the most powerful proof that Christ completed the work which he undertook, and that full satisfaction has been afforded. Beyond this, it declares that all the power through which Christ rose from the dead is at the service of those to whom this satisfaction is applied.

2. The Intercession; its stages and objects; its modes; its ground; its reality; its duration

30. What is the second function of the Priesthood of Christ?

The Intercession, or that by which, as High Priest, He prays to God for those whom He has redeemed.

31. How is this Intercession to be distinguished as to its stages and its objects?

[A.] As to stages, into Preparatory and Glorious.

The former occurred during the State of Humiliation, viz., in His Sacerdotal Prayer (John 17), in His prayer for Peter (Luke 22:32), for His murderers (Luke 23:34), and the promise of the Comforter (John 14:16). The latter occurs in the State of Exaltation.

> Rom. 8:34. "Who is at the right hand of God, who also maketh intercession for us."
>
> Heb. 4:14-16. "Having then a great high priest, who hath passed through the heavens, Jesus the Son of God, let us hold fast our confession. For we have not an priest that cannot be touched with the feeling of our infirmities; but one that hath been in all points tempted like as we are, yet without sin. Let us, therefore, draw near with boldness to the throne of grace, that we may receive mercy, and find grace to help us in time of need."
>
> Heb. 7:25. "Wherefore he is able to save unto the uttermost them that draw near unto God through him, seeing he ever liveth to make intercession for them."
>
> Heb. 9:24. "For Christ entered into heaven itself, now to appear before the face of God for us."
>
> 1 John 2:2. "If any man sin, we have an Advocate with the Father, Jesus Christ, the righteous."

[B.] As to objects, it is distinguished into General and Special.

The General is for all men, even while they care nothing for His grace, as He prayed for his crucifiers (Luke 23:34). The Special is for believers. In this sense, He says (John 17:9), "I pray not for the world, but for those whom thou hast given me."

32. But does He pray for the two classes of objects in the same way?

For the former, He prays that they may be brought to repentance and faith (Luke 13:8; 23:34). For the latter, that they may be kept firm in faith (John 17:11) and in union with one another (John 17:21), be sanctified (John 17:17), and enjoy His eternal glory (John 17:24) The Intercessory Prayer of John 17 was doubtless spoken by Jesus in the hearing of His disciples, in order that the general subjects of His intercession for His people might be known to the Church on earth.

33. What is the ground of His intercession?

Not simply His personal relation with the Father, but that which He bears because of the completion of His mediatorial work. The intercession presupposes the satisfaction or propitiation and its merits.

> John 17:4. "I have finished the work which thou gavest me to do."

See especially Heb. 5:25-27, where the ground of the intercession is stated as the offering which he made "once for all, when he offered up himself."

Also 1 John 2:2, where the fact that "he is the propitiation for our sins" is the ground for his being "Advocate with the Father," V. 1. Cf. Heb. 5:12.

34. What is the mode?

Real, not figurative. It is more, therefore, than the efficacy of the satisfaction as this continues to be operative. But as to how the Ascended Son addresses the Father, we need not inquire. It is another mystery, like that referred to above (Chapter 12:43). This much only can we affirm, viz., that it is in a manner corresponding to the Right Hand of God, and not, as in Heb. 5:7, "in the form of a servant," which has been laid aside (Phil. 2:7-10).

35. How long does the Intercession continue?

Throughout eternity.

> Heb. 7:25. "He ever liveth to make intercession for them."

In Heb. 9:24-27, Christ is referred to as continuing in the holy place where he has once entered, unlike other priests who entered thither once every year. In Heb. 5:6; 7:17, he is called "a priest forever," in Heb. 3:3, "a priest continually," and in 7:24, as having "an unchangeable priesthood."

36. But How can this Intercession profit those who are beyond the possibility of a fall, and partake of completed salvation?

All their security and bliss in the world to come are inseparable from their relation to Christ. It is His eternal intercession that sustains them.

37. But is not this explanation contrary to John 16:26, 27?

The passage referred to is:

> "I say not unto you that I will pray the Father for you; for the Father himself loveth you."

It does not mean that Christ will ever cease to pray for His people, but that He will no longer pray for them alone, for they also, because of their access to the Father, who is now reconciled and loves them through Christ, will pray with Him. The intercession is not removed by the love of the Father, but the true mode of prayer in the name of Christ is here taught the disciples.

Moral Theories of Atonement criticized

38. What explanation can be given of the various Moral Theories of the Atonement, i.e., those which find the efficacy of Christ's work solely in the appeal which they make to us?

They spring from a very superficial view of the guilt of sin and all that this implies.

The more sin is minimized the less need is felt of any satisfaction. The result at last is that, with the native goodness of human nature exalted, nothing is left for which a satisfaction is deemed necessary, and the entire life of Christ on earth, ending with His heroic death is made simply an incentive to evoke virtue in men, and especially to enkindle love to God and all that is godlike. Such theories perish, as straw at the touch of the flame, before such arraignments of this much vaunted human nature, as are found in Holy Scripture, particularly in the opening chapters of the Epistle to the Romans. "It will not be possible to recognize the benefits of Christ, unless we understand our evils" (Apology, 83). Hence the Law must be first taught in all its rigor and depth, before the Gospel can be properly applied.

39. But are such theories entirely without foundation?

They are, as a rule, partial and one-sided statements of truth. While there is no appeal made to the consciences of men so forcible and impressive as that which comes from the holy life and the self-sacrificing love of Christ, it is doing violence to scripture to regard these the only ends of Christ's mission, and, on this basis to pass by all the declarations concerning the need of a ransom, and His vicarious satisfaction.

Refutation of the use of chief proof texts appealed to

40. But why, then, is reconciliation said to be, as in 2 Cor. 5:18-20, a reconciliation of men to God instead of God to men?

The passage referred to is not a full treatment of the entire doctrine of the provisions of divine grace, but only a practical exhortation to men to appropriate and use that reconciliation which in verses 14, 15, God has provided for men in Christ. The doctrine clearly taught in many Scripture passages underlies this statement also, that God's love for sinful man always precedes man's feeblest desire for a return to God. Man is potentially justified in the satisfaction made through Christ, but this potentiality is actualized only when by faith he makes it his. God, in other words, has done everything on his part that reconciliation be effected; it is for man to avail himself of such reconciliation, upon the terms under which it is now offered.

15. Christ As King

Definition

1. In what relation is the Kingship of Christ considered here?

Not with reference to his rule in His divine nature, from all eternity ("the essential Kingship"') but as a part of the Mediatorial Office ("the personal Kingship") exercised according to both natures (Chapter 11, 50), and beginning, therefore, with His conception.

2. Define it?

It is His dominion over all things for the application of Redemption.

Stages

3. What stages belong to this Kingship?

In the State of Humiliation, Christ ordinarily refrained not only from the assertion of His claims as King, but also according to His human nature, from the use of its prerogatives. Like Ulysses in Ithaca, "he came unto his own, and they that were his own received him not" (John 1:11). He had not where to lay His head (Matt. 8:20) His majesty was not displayed, because His kingdom was not of this world (John 19:36) and did not come "with observation" (Matt. 17:20). It was only through his passion and death that He entered into glory (Luke 24:26), and into the exercise of all power in heaven and earth (Matt. 28:18). Nor was there any resort to earthly pomp and glory in the collection and government of His Church; this was accomplished solely by His call to enjoy spiritual blessings, the forgiveness of sins, sonship with God, peace of conscience, etc. Even after he had asserted His majesty by rising from the dead, and was about to ascend to heaven, he recalled His disciples from their thought concerning any kingdom characterized by earthly dignities (Acts 1:6, 8, 9), to the duties of humble and painful service, just as he had previously warned the mother of James and John (Matt. 20:23). But the final goal of the kingdom both for the King and His obedient subjects, is a most prominent subject of revelation, prophecy and promise.

Spheres

4. Within what spheres is this Kingship exercised?

The Kingdom of Power, the Kingdom of Grace and the Kingdom of Glory. The distinction corresponds to the diverse modes in which Christ regards His subjects and governs them.

Kingdom of Power

5. What is the Kingdom of Power?

That by which Christ, according to both natures, rules and disposes all things in heaven and earth, for the collection, preservation and salvation of His people.

> Heb. 2:8. "Thou hast put all things under his feet."
>
> Phil. 2:10. "That at the name of Jesus every knee should bow of things in heaven and things on earth and things under the earth."
>
> Eph. 1:21, 22. "Far above all principality, and power, and might, and dominion, and every name that is named, not only in this world, but also in that which is to come: And hath put all things under his feet, and gave him to be the head over all things to the church."

6. How was this Kingship occasionally asserted even during His State of Humiliation?

By His miracles, in which He showed that He was master of the powers of Nature, and of demons.

> Matt. 8:27. "What manner of man is this, that even the winds and the sea obey him?"
>
> Matt. 14:26. "And the disciples saw him walking on the sea."
>
> Matt. 8:16. "He cast out the spirits with his word and healed all that were sick."
>
> Luke 7:14, 15. "And he said, Young man, I say unto thee arise; and he that was dead sat up and began to speak."

7. Where does it culminate?

In the State of Exaltation. (See above, Chapter 12:67 sqq.). Here belongs the application to Christ also in His human nature, of all that belongs to Him in His divine, in the treatment of Providence (see above, Chapter 5).

8. If the Kingdom of Power is Christ's dominion over all things, how can there be also a Kingdom of Grace and a Kingdom of Glory?

In one sense, the Kingdom of Power comprehends the Kingdoms of Grace and of Glory. But in use, it is restricted to that sphere in which Christ displays nothing but power.

Kingdom of Grace

9. What then is the Kingdom of Grace?

It is that through which He bestows spiritual blessings in this life; or that "in which, through the Word and Sacraments, He collects and preserves the Church Militant and abundantly furnishes it with spiritual blessings." The full treatment of this subject belongs to the chapters concerning the Applying Grace of the Holy

Spirit, or Soteriology that are immediately to follow.

10. Who are the subjects?

All believers of all nations and peoples, all ranks and classes.

Matt. 28:18-20.

Gal. 3:28. "There can be neither Jew nor Greek, there can be neither bond nor free, there can be no male and female: for ye are all one man in Christ Jesus."

11. What is its peculiar sphere?

The inner life.

Matt. 17:20, 21. "The kingdom of God cometh not with observation; neither shall they say, Lo here! or, There! for lo, the kingdom of God is within you."

Rom. 14:17. "The kingdom of God is not eating and drinking, but righteousness and peace and joy in the Holy Ghost."

12. What are its characteristics?

[A.] In the world, but not of the world (John 17:9-11)

[B.] Here (as in passages under 11), and yet in the future, as in the petition of the Lord's Prayer; the reference being to successive stages, in its diffusion among men, in its crises and periods of development, and in the appropriation of its blessings by individuals.

13. How is it ruled?

By the Holy Spirit exerting His efficacy through Word and Sacraments, and thereby impressing His law upon men's hearts (Heb. 8:10).

14. To what privilege are its subjects admitted? They share in the rule.

1 Pet. 2:9. "Ye are an elect race, a royal priesthood, a holy nation, a people for God's own possession."

1 Cor. 3:21. "For all things are yours."

Kingdom of Glory

15. What is the Kingdom of Glory?

The rule of the exalted Savior over the Triumphant Church, i.e., saints and angels in Heaven.

1 John 17:24. "I desire that they also whom thou hast given me, be with me where I am, that they may behold my glory."

1 Pet. 2:22. "Who is on the right hand of God, having gone into heaven; angels and authorities and powers being made subject to him."

Heb. 12:22, 23; Matt. 25:34; Luke 22:29, 30.

16. What different stages of this kingdom are there?

It began with the Ascension, but will not reach its consummation until the Final Judgment.

17. Is it eternal?

Rev. 11:15. "The kingdom of the world is become the kingdom of our Lord and his Christ; and he shall reign forever and ever."

18. But is not this inconsistent with 1 Cor. 15:24-28?

"Then cometh the end when he shall deliver the kingdom to God, even the Father," etc. "Kingdom" may refer here materially to all who constitute the kingdom, i.e., the Church or mystical body of Christ; and the passage would then mean that Christ will present to the Father all His people whose salvation is now perfected. Or, as it is more frequently explained by our theologians, the reference is only to the mode of administration, as the Kingdom of Grace, with its means, Word and Sacraments, passes entirely into the Kingdom of Glory, where we shall see and know Him without means. There is no deposition or abdication, but only the presentation of all that has been accomplished to God. Verse 28, referring to the subjection of the Son to the Father must be understood of the divine person of the Son according to the human nature. The whole history of redemption, from its beginning to its consummation will then be understood, and the mystery explained of the Son's voluntary subjection for its accomplishment, and of all that was effected by this subjection.

16. The Mission Of The Holy Ghost

Place of doctrine

1. What is the second item in the Plan of Redemption?

As stated above (Chapter 9, 20), the first item was the incarnation and mediatorial work of the Son of God. This has been considered. The second item, to which we now come is the special mission of the Holy Ghost to apply the fruits of this mediatorial office.

2. Repeat a few passages of Scripture in which this is taught.

> John 7:39. "The Spirit was not yet given, because that Jesus was not yet glorified."
>
> John 14:16. "I will pray the Father and he shall give you another Comforter, that he may be with you forever, even the Spirit of truth."
>
> John 16:7. "If I go not away, the Comforter will not come; but if I go, I will send him unto you," etc.
>
> Acts 1:8. "Ye shall receive power, when the Holy Spirit is come upon you."

Different Modes and Degrees of Presence

3. How are these passages to be explained?

Not as though the Holy Ghost had not always been omnipresent. But just as God has different modes of presence and the Son of God, notwithstanding His omnipresence came into the world in a peculiar way when He became incarnate, so the coming of the Holy Ghost refers to a higher stage of His gracious efficacy.

4. But was He not present with the godly of the Old Testament, and was He not active also daring the ministry of Jesus?

Undoubtedly. The Psalmist (Ps. 51:11) prays that the Holy Spirit be not taken from him. In 2 Sam. 23:2, David declares that the Spirit spoke through him, as also 2 Peter 1:21 teaches when it says that "holy men of God spake as they were moved by the Holy Ghost." So the Spirit descended upon Christ at His baptism (John 1:32), and Christ had preached to Nicodemus the necessity of the new birth of the Spirit (John 3:5). But the reference here is to the presence of the Spirit with His gifts in highest measure. Before Pentecost, His gracious presence had been sporadic and occasional; then He came to abide with believers forever (John 14:16), and to enter into a closer and more inner relation with them (Heb. 8:10), through a clearer, wider and more forcible presentation of the Gospel.

Foundation of Mission

5. Upon what did this mission depend?

Upon the ascension of Christ to the Right Hand of God.

> Acts 2:33. "Being therefore by the right hand of God exalted and having received of the Father the gift of the Holy Spirit, he hath poured forth this."

Relation to Pentecostal Miracle

6. Does not this refer, however, to the miracle of Pentecost?

The miraculous signs of His coming and presence at Pentecost were one thing; the coming and presence themselves were another. The peculiar presence in which He came was permanent and never withdrawn.

> John 14:16. "That he may be with you forever."

Meaning of "Not yet given" (John 7:39)

7. How was this stated in the Reformation period?

Luther:

> "'Not yet given' means not that He did not then exert in His nature, or in heaven, but that He was not present then in His revelation or His works. For it is the peculiar office and work of the Holy Ghost to reveal and glorify Christ, and to testify concerning Him. But this office was still in the future, viz., the preaching of forgiveness of sins, and how we are redeemed from death, and have comfort and joy in Christ. All this that now belongs to us was unheard of at that time. That salvation, righteousness, joy and life are ours through Christ, no one knew... It was the old preaching, viz., that of the Law, that was heard, concerning which we have often declared that the preaching of Law and Gospel must be distinguished. For if the Law is preached it causes sin; it is sorry and dry preaching, and makes hearts and consciences hungry, terrified, troubled, and athirst so that they sigh for God's grace. Such preaching continues until Christ rises from the dead and is glorified" (Luther, on John 7:39).

Calvin:

> "He speaks comparatively, just as when the New is opposed to the Old Testament. God promises His Spirit to the believing, as though this had never been given the fathers. Undoubtedly the disciples had received already the first-fruits of the Spirit. Whence their faith save from the Spirit? Therefore, the Evangelist does not absolutely deny that the grace of the Spirit had been offered before Christ's death, but that it was not so clear

and conspicuous as it would be afterward. For it is the chief adornment of Christ's Kingdom, that, by His Spirit, He governs the Church. But when He ascended to the Right Hand of the Father, He assumed the righteous and as it were formal possession of His kingdom. It is no wonder, then, that He deferred the full offer of the Spirit, until this time. Nevertheless one question remains to be considered, viz., as to whether He means here the| visible graces of the Spirit, or regeneration, the fruit of adoption. My answer is: In these visible gifts, as in a mirror, the Spirit appeared, who had been promised by the coming of Christ; nevertheless the proper subject here treated is the virtue of the Spirit, whereby we are regenerated and made new creatures in Christ" (Calvin, on same passage).

Confessional statement

8. What is the Confessional declaration on this subject?

"Afterward He ascended into heaven, that He might sit at the right hand of the Father, and forever reign and have dominion over all creatures, and sanctify them that believe in Him, by sending the Holy Ghost into their hearts, to rule, comfort and quicken them, and to defend them against the devil and the power of sin" (Augsburg Confession, Art. III).

17. Faith in Christ

Instrument by which Christ's work is applied

1. How are the fruits of the Mediatorial Office applied by the Holy Ghost?

Through faith in Christ.

> Eph. 2:8. "For by grace have ye been saved through faith; and that not of yourselves, it is the gift of God."
>
> Rom. 3:25. "Whom God set forth to be a propitiation through faith in his blood."

Confessional statement

2. How has the doctrine of Holy Scripture on this subject been summarized in the Augsburg Confession?

> "Men cannot be justified before God by their own strength, merits or works, but are freely justified for Christ's sake through faith, when they believe that they are received into favor and that their sins are forgiven for Christ's sake, who, by His death hath made satisfaction for our sins. This

> faith God imputes for righteousness in His sight (Rom. 3 and 4)." (Article 4.)

Distinctions between: (a) Subjective and Objective (b) Human and Divine (c) Direct and Discursive (d) As an act and as a habit (e) Explicit and Implicit (f) Crude and Energized

3. What distinctions have been made by theologians with respect to faith?

They distinguish between:

[A.] Subjective and Objective; [B.] Human and Divine; [C.] Direct and Discursive; [D.] Faith as an act, and faith as a habit; [E.] Explicit and Implicit; [F.] Crude faith (*tides informis*) and Faith energized by love (*tides formata caritate*).

4. How do they distinguish between Subjective and Objective Faith?

The former is believing; the second is what is believed. The former is faith in the proper sense of the term, and is its usual meaning in Scripture; the second is faith by metonomy, according to which an object is named for its contents. As it is said that Jerusalem went out to hear John the Baptist (Matt. 3:5), when the meaning is that its inhabitants went out, so "faith" in a very few passages of Scripture, but very frequently in the usage of the Church stands for what is believed.

> Jude 3. "Contend earnestly for the faith."

> Gal. 1:23. "Preacheth the faith."

5. What is Human Faith?

It may be mere opinion. Hence in popular usage "believe" often means no more than "suppose"; or "be of the opinion." "Are you sure of this?" we ask of one who has reported something to us; and are apt to hear the answer, "Well, I believe it," meaning no more than, "I have sufficient evidence to warrant the opinion." Referring to this in his Introduction to the Epistle to the Romans, Luther says:

> "Faith is not man's opinion and dream, which some take to be faith… . When they hear the Gospel, they immediately devise from their own powers the imagination in their hearts, to which they give expression in the words 'I believe.' This they regard the right faith. Nevertheless it is nothing but man's thought and imagination."

Or it may be Historical Faith, i.e., a persuasion of the truth of facts, outside of the range of one's experience, upon the ground of clear testimony.

> "Faith doth not signify merely the knowledge of the history" (Augsburg Confession, Art. XX).

Such also is the mere intellectual apprehension of the dogmas of the Church, as when it amounts to no more than the recitation by rote of the Catechism, or the mastering of a system of Dogmatics.

> "Very many other passages they corrupt in the schools, because they do not teach the righteousness of faith, and because they understand by faith merely a knowledge of history and dogmas, and do not understand by it that virtue which apprehends the promise of grace and of righteousness" (Apology, 158).

6. What is Divine Faith?

Let Luther answer:

> "Faith is a divine work in us, which transforms us, and begets us anew of God. It makes us entirely different men in heart, mind, sense and all powers, and brings with it the Holy Spirit… . Faith is a living, wide-awake confidence in God's grace, that is so certain that one who has it is ready to die a thousand times for it… . Pray God to work faith in thee; otherwise thou shalt remain eternally without faith, though thou thinkest and doest whatever thou wilt or canst" (Introduction to Romans).

> "Faith is that my whole heart takes to itself this treasure. It is not my doing, not my presenting or giving, not my work or preparation" (Apology, 91).

> "Faith is when my heart and the Holy Ghost in the heart says, The promise of God is true and certain" (Apology, 103).

7. What is the distinction between Direct and Discursive Faith?

This distinction does not respect faith itself, for what is called "direct" and what is called "discursive," are essentially the same; but it has respect to difference of ability for examining self and recognizing faith when present. "Discursive faith" is that which is a subject of reflection and analysis by a mature Christian, as distinguished from the faith of a child who believes without thinking of the faith itself, but simply of the object which faith apprehends. Direct faith is occupied with the object of faith, viz., Christ, while discursive faith is occupied with the direct faith.

8. What is the distinction between faith as a habit and faith as an act?

The one is a state or a condition or fixed relation towards Christ; the other is an act prompted by the state, and emerging from it. The confidence which we have in a fellowman, the love which a husband has for his wife, or a parent for his child, lies deeper than the conscious acts which give it expression. The child of God has faith in Christ when asleep as well as when awake; when his mind is concentrated on business, or on intricate mathematical calculations, just as truly as when reading the Holy Scriptures, receiving the Lord's Supper, in prayer, or driven to the divine promises for comfort under the stress of some overwhelming affliction.

9. What is the distinction between Explicit and Implicit Faith?

Explicit Faith is where what is believed is known; Implicit, where the acceptance of what is known carries with it the acceptance of particulars that are unknown. Thus the Old Testament saints believed many things implicitly, which we believe explicitly. The scholastics have abused this principle in teaching that one who accepts the authority of the Church, accepts thereby all that the Church teaches or has taught or will teach. According to this a servant girl or hostler who cannot read, if he be in subjection to the Roman Catholic Church, holds implicitly to all the Decrees and. Canons of Trent, even though he have never seen or heard of them, or thought on most of the subjects they discuss.

10. What is the distinction between "Crude Faith" and "Faith energized by Love"?

This distinction Protestants repudiate; but it is necessary to know it in order to understand the discussions of the Reformation. It is based upon the scholastic definition of "faith," as mere assent to what the Church teaches. As such faith manifestly could not justify, they found the justifying virtue of faith in the love by which it might be pervaded (Gal. 5:6). The Reformers held that men are justified, neither on account of their love nor their faith, but that when justified on account of Christ through faith, love inevitably followed. Love, therefore, instead of being the condition of the efficacy of faith, is the fruit of the justification received through faith.

> "Faith alone receives remission of sins, justifies and regenerates. Then love and other good works follow" (Apology, 139).

Distinction of prepositions "propter" and "per"

11. When you say that the fruits of the Mediatorial Office are applied through faith, what do you mean?

That faith is never the ground of salvation, but only the organ through which the salvation provided by God is applied. The Augsburg Confession very clearly draws this distinction when it says that "men are justified for Christ's sake through faith," "*propter Christum per fidem*" not "*propter Udem per Christum*".

In what does the value of faith lie

12. In what then does the value of faith lie?

Entirely in its object, as the value of a ring is that of the gem which it contains, or that of a vessel is often no more than that of the precious substance which it encloses.

Various objects of faith enumerated, as distinguished from the proper object here required

13. What then is the proper object of the faith through which the Holy Ghost brings salvation?

Before answering this, it would be well to consider the various objects with which faith may be occupied.

14. State some of these objects.

> "In the eleventh chapter of Hebrews, various and diverse objects of faith are described, as the article of Creation, the prediction of the coming flood, the hiding of Moses, the institution of the Passover, the passage of the Red Sea, the fall of the walls of Jericho, etc. In the Gospels, where faith is commended, very frequently its objects are described, as the cure of diseases or certain bodily deliverances. The example of the faith of Abraham which Paul cites (Rom. 4:3), is seen by a reference to Gen. 17:5 to be the promise concerning the fruitfulness of his body and the external bodily seed. Now, we do not deny that there are various objects with respect to even earthly things, with which faith is occupied. But the question here is, What is the object, with respect to which faith justifies? Sometimes Scripture speaks of the object of faith in general; at other times, it defines the object by the apprehension of which faith justifies. The question is different when we afterwards treat of the exercises of faith, under the cross, in obedience, in prayer, and in expectation of bodily and spiritual things, after the person has been already reconciled by faith. There is a difference between faith apprehending Christ, who is the end of the Law for righteousness to every one that believeth, and the exercises of faith which are directed towards other objects, nevertheless these exercises always presuppose, as their foundation, that God has been reconciled by faith" (Chemnitz, Loci).

15. Now we are ready to learn the proper object which faith apprehends, so as to obtain the fruits of Christ's Mediatorial Office?

> "When we speak of Justifying Faith, we must keep in mind that these three things concur: the promise, and that gratuitous, and the merits of Christ, as the price or propitiation" (Apology).

In other words: "Promise, grace and Christ's merit." All are summarized in the words: "The grace of God promised because of the merits of Christ," or "The merits of Christ gratuitously offered in the promise of the Gospel." (See Augsburg Confession, Art. IV, above, under 2.) Our faith rests entirely upon God's promise and that promise has been made because of nothing within us that deserves it, but solely because of Christ's merits. All these objects are combined in justifying faith.

16. Cite a few of the many statements of our Confessions on this subject.

> "The Law requires of us our works and our perfection. But the Gospel freely offers, for Christ's sake, to us who have been vanquished by sin and death, reconciliation, which is received not by works but by faith alone. This faith brings to God not confidence in our own merits, but only confidence in the promise, or the mercy promised in Christ."

> "As often as we speak of faith we wish an object understood, viz., the promised mercy. For faith justifies and saves only because it receives the promised mercy."

> "The Propitiator profits us, when by faith we apprehend the mercy promised in Him, and present it against the wrath and judgment of God" (Apology, 91, 92, 101).

> "Faith alone is the means or instrument whereby we lay hold of Christ, and thus in Christ of that righteousness which avails before of God, for the sake of which this faith is imputed to us for righteousness (Rom. 4:5)."

> "Faith justifies because in the promise of the Gospel, it lays hold of and accepts the merit of Christ; for if we are to be justified thereby, this must be applied and appropriated by faith" (Formula of Concord, 501, 572).

17. What Scriptural proofs of this can be given?

> Rom. 3:22. "The righteousness of God through faith in Jesus Christ."
>
> Rom. 3:26. "The justifier of him that hath faith in Jesus."
>
> Phil. 3:9. "And"be found in him having the righteousness which is from God by faith."
>
> Acts 16:31. "And they said, Believe on the Lord Jesus Christ, and thou shalt be saved, and thy house."
>
> Rom. 3:24. "Being justified freely by his grace through the redemption that is in Christ Jesus."
>
> Rom. 4:16. "It is of faith that it might be by grace, to the end that the promise may be sure to all the seed."

The argument may also be stated thus: The Word of God is divided into Law and Gospel. But the Law cannot be an object of justifying faith (Gal. 3:22; Rom. 3:21-27; 10:5, 6). There remains then only the Gospel, or the gratuitous promise of the forgiveness of sins and righteousness before God for Christ's sake.

18. Is it not an arbitrary matter, however, to restrict the faith, which receives the forgiveness of sins to the one article concerning the merits of Christ gratuitously given, and to ignore other articles of faith?

The other articles are not ignored or disparaged. Faith accepts every word of God that is offered it. It is an attitude of heart and mind that believes everything that it learns comes from God. But the question here is concerning the particular object which gives to faith all its justifying power. "As the sum, scope and goal of all Scripture is Christ, in His Mediatorial Office (Luke 24:27-44; Rom. 10:4; John 5:39, 46; Heb. 10:7), so faith, in assenting to all the Word of God, regards the scope of all Scripture, and refers all other articles to the promised grace because of Christ as Mediator. In vain is faith occupied with other articles of Scripture, if it do not hold Christ, the Head (Col. 2:19). To this effect, this item is added in the definition of faith. For the article of Redemption cannot be thoroughly understood, unless we be acquainted with the other parts of God's Word that precede; and yet we must firmly hold that faith justifies only with respect to the one object, viz., Christ" (Chemnitz), and this one object in a particular relation, i.e., the promise of gratuitous reconciliation for the sake of Christ as Mediator.

General and special faith contrasted

19. Are the acts of Justifying Faith, with respect to its object, of one kind?

> "Some are common and general; others special. The general are directed towards the object considered in itself, without application to the believer; as when; with respect to the merit of Christ, one believes that Christ suffered, died, rose again; or, with respect to the grace of God, that God, from pure grace and mercy, wishes to forgive sins. The special are such as are directed to their object with an application to the believer. Such act of faith, with respect to the merit of Christ, is when one believes that Christ has suffered and died for him; or, with respect to the grace of God,' that he will receive grace and forgiveness of sins." "The general are common to true believers and hypocrites, and necessary for justification; for no one can believe that Christ died for him, without believing that Christ died" (Bechmann).

The elements of faith: Knowledge, Assent, Confidence

20. Analyze faith into its elements.

While faith, properly speaking, is nothing but confidence, theologians generally enumerate three elements: Knowledge, Assent and Confidence.

21. What of the first?

An explicit acquaintance with the objects of faith is presupposed. The fact of redemption as taught in Holy Scripture must be known in order that there should be acts of faith.

> Rom. 10:14. "How shall they believe in him whom they have not heard."

> Heb. 11:6. "He that cometh to God must believe that he is and that he is; a rewarder of them that seek after him."

Luke 1:77; Eph. 1:17; Is. 53:11.

22. What of the second?

Assent is a judgment of the intellect by which what is taught in Holy Scripture concerning the Mediatorship of: Christ and the grace of God is approved as true. By a general assent, the universal promises concerning the grace of God and merit of Christ are judged to be true. By a special assent, man is led by the workings of the Holy Spirit, to apply the general propositions concerning the Mediatorship of Christ and the grace of God to himself, and thus to believe that Christ actually died for him (See above, under 20.)

> 1 Tim. 1:15. "Faithful is the saying and worthy of all acceptation that Christ Jesus came into the world to save sinners" (General Assent)
>
> "of whom I am chief" (Special Assent).
>
> Gal. 2:20. "Who loved me and gave himself for me" (Special Assent).

Illustrate further from explanation of the Creed in our Catechism.

23. What of the third?

Confidence is an act or attitude of the will produced by the work of the Holy Ghost, whereby man relies upon the merits of Christ offered in the gratuitous promise of the Gospel, and commits himself with security to the provisions which God has therein made for his salvation.

> "Confidence involves the reliance of the entire heart and will upon the merit of Christ" (Koenig).

24. What does this confidence imply?

A sincere and earnest desire for the mercy of God acquired by Christ's merits. The confidence of hypocrites is vain, because they do not really desire the grace of God and forgiveness. The promise is, "Blessed are they that hunger and thirst after righteousness; for they shall be filled." (Matt. 5:6).

Characteristics of Confidence — refers to a present good, a personal good, and that good as a means to an end

25. What are some of the characteristics of confidence with respect to its object?

[A.] It has as its object a present good.

The ungodly confide in their riches, which they esteem a present good; the godly, in an Omnipresent and everlasting God. This good, our theologians have noted, while present sometimes really and physically, is at other times present only morally, as by promise and efficacy, or is apprehended as though present. Thus the godly in the Old Testament trusted in a Messiah that was to come.

> Heb. 11:13. "Not having received the promises, but having seen and greeted them from afar."

We trust in redemption, which two thousand years ago was purchased; but its merit and efficacy extend to the present (Heb. 13:8).

[B.] This object is also a personal good.

Or one pertaining to the person who exercises the confidence. For this reason, it has been called "appropriative," since it takes the object to itself, as its own. Thus we take the merit of Christ and His offering for sin.

[C.] It is a good which is received in order to obtain some other good.

And that, too, one which can be secured only with great difficulty. A general has confidence in his army, for his success in a campaign. A patient has confidence in a physician for bringing him possible relief from a disease. A student relies upon his scholarship, for enabling him to pass tests and gain standing. Thus men put their confidence in the mediation of Christ, as a means of obtaining from God grace, the forgiveness of sins and eternal life.

All these elements are comprehended in the definition,

> "Confidence is an act whereby the will rests in Christ as Mediator, not only as a present good, but as our own, and the cause of another good, viz., the obtaining of remission of sins and life everlasting" (Baier).

How distinguished from Hope

26. How is confidence distinguished from Hope?

Confidence refers to a present; hope to a future good. Confidence relies on it as something that now is; hope, as something that is to come. Confidence is directed towards a means; hope towards the end itself.

> "Hope expects future blessings and deliverance from trouble; faith receives the present reconciliation and concludes in the heart that God has forgiven my sins, that He is now gracious to me" (Apology, 144).

Scriptural argument for Confidence as belonging to Faith

27. Scriptural proofs that faith includes confidence?

[A.] The frequent use of the Greek preposition cis with the accusative after the verb pisteuein, which very literally rendered into English is "to believe into," i.e., "to believe into him" or "believe into his name."

> John 3:16. "Whosoever believeth into him."

> John 1:12. "Them that believe into his name."

> Acts 10:43. "Every one that believeth into him shall receive remission of sins."

This cannot mean simple intellectual assent but an act of the will directed towards an object. Here an examination of the force of the prepositions used with the verb pisteuein and noun pistis would be profitable.

[B.] From the names applied to faith.

It is called:

Hypostasis.

> Heb. 11:1, "assurance of things hoped for" (R. V., A. R. V.);

> "giving substance to things hoped for" (Marginal Reading, R. V., A. R. V.). See Thayer's Lexicon.

Plerophoria.

> Rom. 4:21. "Being fully assured that what he had promised."

> Col. 2:2. "The full assurance of the understanding."

Pepoithesis.

> Rom. 8:38. "I am persuaded that neither death, nor life," etc.

> 2 Tim. 1:12. "I am persuaded that he is able to guard that which I have committed unto him."

Parrhesia.

> Heb. 4:16. "Let us draw near with boldness."

The word means literally "freedom of speech." Our Catechism paraphrases the passage,

> "That we call upon him with all cheerfulness and confidence, even as beloved children entreat their affectionate parent."

To these Scriptural proofs, to which a number of others were added by the Reformers, we may add the every day usage of our language in which every one understands the expression, "I do not believe in such a man," or "in a particular school of medicine as Allopathy or Homoeopathy," as meaning, "I have no confidence in it."

The Augustinian formula: Credere Deum, Deo, in Deum

28. How have the three elements of faith been sometimes distinguished?

By an Augustinian formula, that "*Credere Deum*" "*Credere Deo*," and "*Credere in Deum*," are three distinct things. The former means "to believe that there is a God"; the second, "to believe what God says"; the third, "to commit oneself to God, or have confidence in God." In all our dealing with fellow-men, we learn, first of all, to know, then to approve, and then to rely upon or entrust oneself to. The relations between bride and groom, patient and physician, capitalist and confidential clerk, furnish illustrations from every day life as to how faith is at length attained.

Sometimes, however, knowledge is regarded as presupposed, but not as an element of faith. Then the definition becomes:

"Faith is assent joined with confidence, or confidence joined with assent, and, consisting of these acts united, is called by the name now of the former, and again of the latter, the other always being connotated" (Baier).

Degrees of faith, and relation to efficacy

29. Are there degrees of faith?

Luke 17:5. "Lord, increase our faith."

Mark 9:24. "I believe; help thou mine unbelief."

2 Thess. t:3. "Your faith groweth exceedingly."

Our Lord rebukes his disciples as "of little faith," Matt. 6:30; 8:26 and Matt. 15:28, commends the Syrophenician woman, as "of great faith."

30. Is the efficacy of faith in proportion to its degree?

Not with respect to justification, since all the efficacy of faith comes from the object which it apprehends, viz., the righteousness of Christ. The weakest faith and the strongest partake of all that Christ is, and thus equally justify. But when the question is concerning the comfort which faith receives and concerning its efficiency as an instrument for advancing the Kingdom of God, the rule obtains:

"According to your faith, be it done unto you," Matt. 9:29.

Double office of faith

31. Has faith, then, more than one office?

It has two, one receptive or apprehensive, by which man takes to himself the righteousness of Christ, and the other operative, by which the justified man is active in works of love.

Relation to the New Life

32. How does the Augsburg Confession treat of the operative office or energy of faith?

> "Also they teach that this faith is bound to bring forth good fruits, and that it is necessary to do good works commanded by God, because of God's will, but not that we should rely on those works to merit justification before God" (Art. VI). "Because through faith the Holy Ghost is received, hearts are renewed and endowed with new affections, so as to be able to bring forth good works" (Art. XX).

33. What classical passage from Luther's Introduction to the Epistle to the Romans should be kept in memory?

> "Oh, it is a living, active, busy thing that we have in faith. It is impossible for one who has faith to do otherwise than incessantly to do good. He asks not whether good works are to be done, but before the question can be asked, he has already done them, and is always busy... Faith is a living, wide-awake confidence in God's grace, that is so certain, that one who has it, is ready to die a thousand times for it... It is as impossible, therefore, to separate works from faith, as it is to separate heat and light from fire."

To this may be added a paraphrase of Luther by Tyndale ("Introduction to Romans"),

> "Where the Spirit is, there it is always summer, and there are always good fruits."

> "Faith keepeth not holiday, neither suffereth any man to be idle, wheresoever she is."

34. What is the meaning of Gal 5:6, "In Christ Jesus, neither circumcision availeth anything, nor uncircumcision but faith working through love"?

The reference is not to faith as an object that is to justify, but to faith regarded as having justified. The thought is: Wherever there is faith, there is Justification, and wherever there is justification there is love, and wherever there is love, it inevitably expresses itself in works. Faith works through love, because through faith man being brought into right relations with God, the love of God is shed abroad in his heart, and sets in motion all his powers.

35. Where do we learn concerning the means employed by the Holy Ghost to work faith?

Under Regeneration (Chapters 21; 24, 1).

Faith may be lost; and if so, may be again recovered

36. Can faith be lost?

[A.] There are passages of Scripture that directly affirm this:

> Gal. 5:4. "Ye are severed from Christ, ye that would be justified by the law; ye are fallen away from grace."
>
> 1 Tim. 1:18. "Some made shipwreck concerning the faith."
>
> Rev. 2:5. "Remember, therefore, whence thou hast fallen, and repent."
>
> Luke 8:13. "These have no root who for a while believe, and in time of temptation fall away."

[B.] There are examples of those who fell:

David, Solomon, Peter, Alexander, Hymenseus, Philetus, Demas, as well as of those who committed the sin against the Holy Ghost (see Chapter 8:57-60).

[C.] Numerous parables and figures are employed to enforce this truth.

There are the allegories concerning the degenerate vineyard (Is. 5:1-4), the fruitless tree (Matt. 3:10), the dead branch of the vine (John 15:6), the broken shoots of the olive (Rom. 11:17-21), the barren fig tree (Luke 13:6-9), the salt which has lost its savor (Matt. 5:13), the bad leaven (Matt. 16:6; f Cor. 5:6, 7), adulterated silver (Is. 1:21; Ez. 22:18), water that has become lukewarm (Rev. 3:16); the parables of the house where the unclean spirit had been expelled (Luke 11:24); the lost sheep and lost coin (Luke 15); the figures of the race (1 Cor. 9:24, 26; Gal. 5:7); the struggle between the flesh and spirit (Gal. 5:16, 17).

[D.] There are most direct and explicit warnings.

The entire section, 1 Cor. 9:27. 10:12, is an argument in which the Apostle first states how deeply he realizes the possibility of his own fall, and ends, "Let him that thinketh he standeth, take heed lest he fall."

So also Heb. 4:11.

> "Let us, therefore, give diligence to enter into that rest, that no man fall after the same example of disobedience."

Cf. in O. T. Ex. 18:24.

37. Can faith, if lost, be restored?

That it is sometimes never restored is clear from Heb. 6:4-6. This, however, does not occur from God's will (Ez. 18:32; 33:11; 2 Peter 3:9). (See above, Chapter 8:58.) That it is sometimes restored is clear from the cases of David and Peter, the constant admonitions given the fallen to repent, and the example of other returns commended by our Lord (Matt. 18:21, 22; cf. John 6:37). The perpetual intercession of Christ (1 John 2:1) is another proof.

Assurance of Faith

38. Can one know whether he have faith?

There are circumstances when it may and frequently does happen that amidst severe temptations, true children of God doubt concerning the presence of a faith which they, nevertheless, truly have. If Christ on the cross felt that He was abandoned (Matt. 27:46), doubt and uncertainty can be expected in those within whom the remnants of sin remain, whose experience is that of Paul as described in Romans 7, and whose prayer must always be that of Mark 9:24 (see above, 29).

> "Concerning the presence, operation and gifts of the Holy Ghost, we should not and cannot always judge from sense, i.e., as to how and when they are experienced in the heart, but because they are often covered and occur in great weakness, we should be certain from and according to the promise that preaching and hearing the Word of God is an office and work of the Holy Ghost, whereby he is certainly efficacious" (Formula of Concord, 583).

Cf. Chapter 21, 37.

39. Faith, then, must be more than mere probability?

Faith in itself, that is, in its ideal and normal condition, is certainty. This is involved in what has been said above concerning confidence (see above, 25-27).

40. Upon what does this certainty depend?

Not upon man's ability to read the secret will of God, or upon any new personal revelation, but upon what God has already revealed in the Gospel.

> Rom. 10:6-9. "The righteousness which is of faith saith thus, Say not in thy heart, Who shall ascend into heaven? (that is, to bring Christ down), or who shall descend into the abyss (that is, to bring Christ up from the dead). But what saith it? The word is nigh thee, in thy mouth and in thy heart: that is, the word of faith which we preach, that, if thou shalt confess with thy mouth Jesus as Lord, and believe in thy heart, that God raised him from the dead, thou shalt be saved."
>
> Rom. 4:16. "It is of faith, that it may be according to grace; to the end, that the promise may be sure to all the seed."
>
> Heb. 6:18; 1 John 5:13.

Assurance dependent upon clearness of apprehension of the Gospel

41. In what respect does the Gospel bring a certainty that cannot be found in the Law?

> "If eternal life could be apprehended by doubt, no promise would be more fitting than that of the Law; for, on account of the condition of perfect obedience annexed to it, it leaves consciences in perpetual doubt. But as it is not doubt, but faith which justifies, God has offered the gratuitous promise of the Gospel, which relies not upon our works, but upon the mercy of God because of the obedience of His Son as Mediator" (Chemnitz).

42. How do the Sacraments afford an argument for the certainty of faith?

Because, as we shall see later, it is their office to offer and apply to the individual the gratuitous promise of the Gospel which is offered in general in the. read and preached Word.

Scriptural examples

43. What examples of certainty of faith are recorded in Holy Scripture?

Abraham (Rom. 4:18-21), David (Ps. 23:4; 27:1; 31:5), Paul (Rom. 8:37-39; 2 Tim. 2:7, 8).

The Witness of the Spirit

44. All this shows that one can and should have certainty of faith, but how is this obtained?

> Rom. 8:17. "The Spirit himself beareth witness with our spirit that we are children of God."
>
> 1 John 5:19. "He that believeth on the Son of God hath the witness in him."
>
> Gal. 4:6. "Because ye are sons, God sent forth the spirit of his Son into our hearts, crying Abba Father."

This is no new and peculiar revelation, but the answer of the Holy Spirit working within man's heart, through the Word and Sacraments, to the individual assurance of God's grace tendered through these means.

45. Explain this more fully.

The testimony of the Holy Spirit through the Word is: "That whosoever believeth in him should not perish but have everlasting life." "God will have all men to be saved." "Come unto me, all ye that labor." Through the Sacraments:

"He that believeth and is baptized shall be saved."

"Given and shed for thee for the remission of sins."

The answer of man's heart, "Jesus is Lord," and still more so that of Thomas, "My Lord and my God," can come only from the Holy Ghost (i Cor. 12:3). When man from his heart exclaims, "Lord, I believe," or "I know whom I have believed," or "I am persuaded that nothing can separate me from the love of God," it is the confession of a testimony which the Holy Spirit has given within. There is thus, first, the external assurance of Word and Sacraments; secondly, the presence and efficacy of the Spirit always attending them; thirdly, the effect of this efficacy in the faith of the heart that is wrought; fourthly, the consciousness of this faith resulting from the same working; and fifthly, its expression or confession.

46. By what term is this witness of the Spirit sometimes designated?

Sealing.

Eph. 1:13. "In whom, having also believed, ye were sealed with the Holy Spirit of promise, which is an earnest of our inheritance."

1 Cor. 1:22. "God who also sealed us and gave us the earnest of the Spirit in our hearts."

Eph. 4:30. "And grieve not the Holy Spirit of God, in whom ye were sealed unto the day of redemption."

As a seal is affixed to an important document as a mark of authenticity, so the testimony of the Spirit is referred to as sure evidence of the certainty of faith.

Faith and self-examination

47. Can the presence of faith be decided by self-examination?

2 Cor. 13:5. "Try your own selves, whether ye are in the faith; prove your own selves. Or know ye not as to your own selves, that Jesus Christ is in you, except ye be reprobates?"

Such examination includes reflection on one's attitude towards sin and the law, on one's special assent and confidence in the Gospel, and on the question as to whether the fruits of faith be present.

48. But what if such examination result in the revelation only of one's spiritual poverty, and faith itself be hidden?

If there be hungering and thirst after righteousness and the desire for grace and faith, that of itself is faith, even though weak and struggling with doubt.

> 1 John 3:20. "If our heart condemn us, God is greater than our heart, and knoweth all things."

> 2 Tim. 2:13. "If we are faithless, yet he abideth faithful; he cannot deny himself."

The very longing for such righteousness is a proof of the presence of the Holy Spirit.

49. Against what must we guard in every such self-examination, whether daily or before partaking of the Lord's Supper?

Against putting the assurance of faith in place of faith itself and its contents. Man is not justified by faith in his faith, but by faith in the promise of God gratuitously given through the merits of Christ as Mediator. Men must constantly be warned that justification comes not "on account of" or "because of" our faith, but solely "through faith on account of Christ."

50. What was Luther's advice to Brenz when troubled by doubts concerning the assurance of faith?

> "I am accustomed, for the better understanding of this point, to conceive this idea, that there is no quality in my heart at all, call it either faith or charity; but instead of these I set Christ Himself, and I say, 'There is my righteousness"

The highest achievement of faith is to be so absorbed in looking to Christ as to forget itself. The children of Israel, who were bitten by serpents in the wilderness (Num. 21:6-9), were healed upon the condition of looking upon the brazen serpent. Their attention was occupied, not with an analysis of the act of looking, but with the object of their gaze itself. So, important as self-examination is, Luther warns against its abuse, and seeks to turn morbid habits of introspection away from their ordinary channel to the righteousness outside of and above man in the merits of his Redeemer (Chapter 21:37).

Is salvation ever possible without faith

51. Is there salvation without faith?

> "The answer is given in Mark 16:16; Heb. 11:6; John 3:6; 5:18. If God then were to save one without faith, He would act contrary to His own word, and would deny Himself, which is impossible. For Paul writes (2 Tim. 2:13), 'He cannot deny himself.' Just as impossible, therefore, as it is for divine truth to lie, so impossible is it for one to be saved without faith. This is entirely different, however, from the question as to whether in death or after death, God could give faith, and he could then be saved by faith. Who will doubt that He could so do? But that He actually so does, no one can prove" (Luther to von Rechenberg, De Wette's Luther's Briefe, 2, 455).

18. Justification

Various meanings

1. In what senses is the word "justify" used in Holy Scripture?

Nowhere, in either the Old or New Testament, does it mean, in any passage or reference, the infusion of a new quality; but it has various other meanings, as in Ps. 51:4, the recognition and celebration of God's righteousness; in James 2:21, the proof or declaration of the justification that had been received; in Ez. 16:51, the manifestation of relative righteousness when contrasted with the greater guilt of others sinning more grievously; in Luke 10:29, the Pharisaic ambition for reputation for righteousness, etc. A well-established meaning is the forensic sense, viz., that by which a judge officially declares one to have a righteous claim, and therefore acquits a defendant of the charges brought against him.

> Deut. 25:1. "If there be a controversy between men, and they come unto judgment, and the judges judge them; then they shall justify the righteous and condemn the wicked."
>
> Prov. 17:15. "He that justifieth the wicked and he that condemneth the righteous, both of them alike are an abomination to Jehovah."
>
> Is. 5:23. "Woe unto them that justify the wicked for a bribe." 2 Sam. 15:41.

Proofs of Forensic sense at this place

2. In what sense is it used in the treatment of the justification of man, the sinner, before God?

In the forensic sense. For this, the proofs are:

[A.] The contrast made between "justify" and "condemn," showing that they are contradictories.

> Rom. 8:33, 34. "Who shall lay anything to the charge of God's elect? It is God that justifieth. Who is he that condemneth?"
>
> 1:16. "The judgment came of one to condemnation; but the free gift came of many trespasses unto justification."
>
> Matt. 12:37. "For by thy words shalt thou be justified and by thy words shalt thou be condemned."

[B.] The use of synonymous forensic phrases.

In Ps. 143:2 it is synonymous with "enter not into judgment"; in John 3:18, with "not judged"; in John 5:24, with "not come into judgment."

[C.] The entire argument of the third and fourth chapters of Romans.

We need cite but one verse:

> Rom. 4:5. "To him that worketh not, but believeth on him that justifieth the ungodly, his faith is reckoned for righteousness."

[D.] All the factors of a court of justice are given in passages referring to justification.

The Judge.

> Rom. 8:33. "It is God that justifieth."

A Defendant.

> Rom. 3:19. "That every mouth may be stopped, and all the world may be brought under judgment of God."

A Plaintiff or Accuser.

> John 5:45. "There is one that accuseth you, even Moses."

A Witness.

Rom. 2:15. "Their conscience bearing witness."

An Indictment.

Col. 2:14. "The bond written in ordinances that was against us."

A Sentence.

Deut. 27:26. "Cursed is every one that continueth not in all things written in the book of the law to do them."

A Code of Laws.

Deut. 27:26. "The book of the law."

An Advocate.

1 John 2:2. "If any man sin we have an advocate with the Father."

A Satisfaction.

Rom. 8:19. "Through the obedience of the one shall the many be made righteous."

An Acquittal.

Rom. 8:1. "There is, therefore, no condemnation to them that are in Christ Jesus." Ps. 32:1.

Definition

3. Justification being used, therefore, in a forensic sense, how is it defined?

It is non-imputation or forgiveness of sins and the imputation of the righteousness of Christ. They are actually two sides of one and the same act. For there can be no forgiveness of sins without righteousness; and wherever the righteousness of Christ is interposed there is forgiveness of sins.

4. What Scriptural proofs are there for this?

[A.] The non-imputation of sins.

Ps. 32:1, 2. "Blessed is he whose transgression is forgiven, whose sin is covered. Blessed is the man unto whom Jehovah imputeth not iniquity." 2 Cor. 5:19. "God was in Christ, reconciling the world unto himself, not reckoning unto them their trespasses."

[B.] The imputation of Christ's righteousness.

Rom. 5:19. "For as through the one man's disobedience, the many were made sinners, even so through the obedience of the one, shall the many be made righteous." 2 Cor. 5:21. "That we might become the righteousness of God in him." Phil. 3:9. "And he found in him, not having a righteousness of mine own, even that which is of the law, but that which is through faith in Christ, the righteousness which is from God by faith."

What sins not imputed

5. Of what sins is there a non-imputation?

Since the satisfaction of Christ was made for all sins (Chapter 14, 14), there is a non-imputation or forgiveness of all the sins of the justified.

What righteousness of Christ imputed

6. What righteousness of Christ is imputed?

"We unanimously believe, teach and confess that Christ is our righteousness, neither according to the divine nature alone nor according to the human nature alone, but the entire Christ according to both natures, in His obedience, which as God and man He rendered the Father even to death" (Formula of Concord, 501). The foundation for this is Rom. 5:19, above cited. It is not the righteousness, therefore, which the unincarnate Son of God had from all eternity, or the righteousness of Christ at the Right Hand of God, mystically united with the believer, but the righteousness alone acquired by the subjection of the God-man to the law (Gal. 4:4, 5).

Meaning of "impute"

7. What is the meaning of the word "impute" or "reckon"?

This can be best learned by the study of the fourth chapter of Romans, in which it occurs eleven times, viz., in verses 2, 4, 5, 6, 8, 9, 10, 11, 22, 23, 24. It will be seen, from these passages that, in them, it very clearly means, "to put to the account of." This, when applied to sins, means "to charge against," but when applied to Christ's righteousness, "to credit with."

8. Where is such distinction drawn?

> Rom. 4:4, 5. "Now to him that worketh, the reward is not reckoned as of grace, but as of debt. But to him that worketh not but believeth on him that justifieth the ungodly, his faith is reckoned for righteousness."

The act of imputation is the same in both cases; but the distinction in its ground, results in two species of imputation:

[A.] Imputation of debt

When the effect of an action is accounted to the person acting, or, in other words, when the imputation is based upon something in the person to whom the effect or fruit of an action is reckoned.

[B.] Imputation of grace

When the effect is accounted as belonging not to the person acting, but to the one for whose advantages the work was undertaken. It is expressly declared to be "of grace," i.e., gratis or "for nothing," not that it is without a foundation absolutely, but because it is without foundation in the person receiving the benefit. When Paul declares (v. 5), that it is the ungodly who are justified "of grace," he shows that the personal foundation within them, is directly the contrary to the reward which they receive. If a friend were to do the work of another friend, in order that the wages might be given not to the laborer, but to the one in whose stead the labor was done, it would be imputation of grace, or vicarious imputation.

9. Apply this to the article of Justification.

"The imputation of righteousness consists in the grace and mercy of God, which, on account of a foundation inhering in Christ, covers sin, so that it is not imputed, and so that the foundation which does not inhere in the believer, is imputed to him out of grace, as though it inhered in him with the perfection that is due" (Chemnitz).

Ground of imputation

10. But is there need of any foundation? Could not God have justified man without any ground whatever?

> "God has revealed His will in the Law and this cannot be broken. One jot or one tittle shall in no wise pass away from the Law till all be fulfilled (Matt. 5:18). God, therefore, according to His revealed will, will not justify anyone without righteousness, i.e., unless satisfaction be made, according to the law for sin, and perfect obedience be rendered. But in Rom. 3:31, Paul declares that, when faith is imputed for righteousness, the Law is not destroyed, but established, i.e., righteousness is imputed not without a foundation. This, however, as has been shown, is not in believers; but God has set forth His Son, as Mediator, made under the Law, which He has satisfied by bearing sins, and by His perfect obedience (1 Cor. 1:30; 2 Cor. 5:21; Rom. 5:19; Rom. 8:4)" (Chemnitz).

In what sense is faith imputed (Rom 4:5)

11. What is meant by the expression, "Faith is imputed" (Rom. 4:5)?

Faith receiving the righteousness of Christ, or the righteousness of Christ received by faith. All the value of faith lies in the object which it apprehends. (See Chapter 17, 12, 15-19.)

> "Faith is not imputed: for righteousness, in so far as it is our act; but only as it receives the righteousness of Christ" (Koenig).

> "Faith justifies, not because it is so good a work and so fair a virtue, but because, in the promise of the Gospel, it lays hold of and accepts the merits of Christ" (Formula of Concord, 572).

12. What is meant by the expression, "Faith justifies"?

Not that faith of itself justifies; but that God justifies with respect to faith embracing the merits of Christ, or with respect to the merits of Christ which man by faith embraces.'

Denial of man's agency

13. Has man then no part in his own justification?

None whatever. It is the work of God alone, the Father (Rom. 8:33, the Son (Matt. 9:6), the Holy Ghost (1 Cor. 6:11).

Justification not an internal work

14. Is it a work of God within man?

Inseparable as it is from Regeneration, a work of God within man, Justification itself is entirely external. It is a work of God by which man is placed in right relations to the Law.

15. Why cannot love justify or contribute towards justification?

Because it is not by love, but by faith, that man receives the promise of the Gospel and the merits of Christ. Neither can man have love towards God until he is justified.

> "How can the human heart love God, while it 'knows that He is terribly angry?" (Apology, 104).

Faith does not justify as a root

16. May we not say that faith justifies because it is the root of good works?

This would be to change the ground of justification from the merits of Christ, to something within man. Man would be justified not through faith for Christ's sake, but only through Christ for the sake of the new life of obedience that was to follow. While good works and a godly life are the inevitable fruit of faith, they are no condition of Justification, before, in or after regeneration.

Importance of the Exclusive Particles

17. In what formulas has this doctrine been expressed?

In the so-called Exclusive Particles:

"Without works," "without law," "freely," "not of works."

18. What is their force?

"These exclusive particles are all comprised in the expression: 'By faith alone in Christ we are justified before God and saved.' For thereby works are excluded, not in the sense that a true faith can exist without contrition, or that good works must not follow faith as sure fruits... but that they are excluded in the article of Justification before God.... Their true sense is:

"(1) That all confidence in our works in the article of Justification be entirely excluded, so that our works be regarded neither entirely, nor in half, nor in the least part the cause or merit of Justification.

(2) That this office abide with faith alone, that it alone and nothing else whatever is the means or instrument by and through which, God's grace and the merit of Christ are appropriated in the promise of the Gospel; and that from this office, love and all the fruits of the Spirit are excluded.

(3) That neither renewal, sanctification, virtues nor good works be constituted a form or part or cause of our Justification" (Formula of Concord, 576).

19. What then is the meaning of the formula:

"We are justified by 'faith alone, without works"?

Not that faith can ever be alone, or ever be without good works, but that it is only the faith apprehending Christ that receives justification, and that the works inseparably belonging to faith, have nothing whatever to do with faith's appropriation of God's promise and Christ's merit. The words "without works" became necessary, when "by faith alone" was regarded as so ambiguous as to admit of the conception of faith as nothing more than potential good works.

20. What four reasons did Melanchthon urge for keeping these "exclusives" always in view?

1. The glory of Christ.

By seeking some ground of Justification within self, men extenuate the wrath of God, minimize the significance of sin, and deprive Christ of some of the credit for their salvation. As Luther has somewhere said, they make of Christ only a patch on the garment of their own righteousness.

2. The comfort of distressed consciences.

If man has to contribute the smallest part towards his own justification he will always be in anxiety to know whether this part have actually been rendered with the perfection demanded by the Law, and will never be relieved of his doubts. There can never be assurance of faith. Hence the entire Roman Catholic system is "a theology of doubt," and repudiates the doctrine of the certainty of faith.[4]

3. The offering of true prayer.

For this is impossible until one actually knows that God is reconciled to him.

4. The difference between the Law and the Gospel.

It is the particle "gratis" that marks the distinction ("Loci," third edition, Corpus Reformatorum, 21, 753-5).

James 2:24

21. How is James 2:21-24 to be understood?

> James 2:24. "Ye see that by works a man is justified, and not only by his faith."

4 "*Cum nullus scire valeat eertitudine fidei, cui non potest subesse falsum, se gratiam Dei esse consecutum.*" Decree of Trent "On Justification," Cap. IX. It is such doctrine that Luther criticizes on Genesis XLI:

"I ought to be certain concerning what I ought to think of God, or rather concerning what God thinks of me. It was a horrible error of the Pontifical doctrine that it led men to doubt concerning the forgiveness of sins and grace. 'Acknowledge,' they said, 'that thou art a sinner, and that, too, such a sinner, as not to be able to be sure of thy salvation.' Thus the whole world was sunk in doubt and erroneous opinions concerning God."

Our answer is:

1. We lay down the general principle that those passages of Scripture which treat of a subject professedly and in extended argument are to be taken as the norms whereby to judge mere incidental allusions in other passages. Applying this principle to the case before us, its result is that the Epistles of St. Paul to the Romans and Galatians are to be taken as the true sedes doctrinae with respect to justification. If a conflict between Paul and James on this subject could be established, the former's statement would have the preponderance.
2. But that such conflict cannot be proved we maintain upon the ground: That Paul treats of Justification before God, while James treats of the manner in which Justification may be recognized by men. Before men one is justified, i.e., declared to be righteous, by works as the inevitable fruits of faith. "Paul is treating of those who are to be justified before God, in whose case faith alone, appropriating the grace of God and merit of Christ, can avail; but James treats of men who have already been justified through faith, but who are to be recognized in this world by means of their good works" (Hutter). See Apology, pp. 125-128.

No degrees of Justification

22. Is Justification gradual?

No. It is not a process, but an act of God, and, as such, is instantaneous, perfect and uniform. Faith has degrees. Sanctification has degrees. But Justification is always the same, whether the faith be weak or strong. That which gives faith all its worth being the merit of Christ, this merit is just as effective where the faith is weak as where it is strong, at the very first moment when the least spark of faith appears, as when it has reached the highest grade attainable.

23. May not some sins be forgiven, while others remain unforgiven?

If the least sin be forgiven, all sins are forgiven; if the least sin remain unforgiven, not a single sin is actually forgiven. The entire righteousness of Christ is perfectly and completely ours, or we are without any righteousness, or shelter from God's wrath. The righteousness of Christ avails no more for the redeemed in heaven, than it does on earth for the humblest Christian, who with stammering tongue addresses God as his reconciled Father, and whose faith is clouded by many infirmities.

1 John 1:7. "The blood of Jesus Christ, his Son, cleanseth us from all sin."

Rom. 8:1. "There is, therefore, now no condemnation to them that are in Christ Jesus."

24. But is not the righteousness of some believers much greater than that of others? For instance, is not that of Mary the mother of Jesus, the Apostle John, the Apostle Paul, etc., greater than that of the penitent thief?

There are great differences with respect to inherent righteousness attained through sanctification; but with respect to imputed righteousness which alone is the ground of the forgiveness of sins and the favor of God, all are alike. No righteousness of Christ is attainable, either in this world or the next, which the humblest child of God does not already have.

Rom. 3:22. "Even the righteousness of God, through faith in Jesus Christ unto all them that believe; for there is no distinction."

19. The Gospel Call

The order of Salvation

1. What is meant by the Order of Salvation?

The process of the Holy Spirit in conferring faith and working through its activity; or the series of acts, whereby the Holy Spirit confers, sustains and works through, faith.

2. Where do we find a popular summary of this Order?

In the Catechism, Creed, Part 3:

> "The Holy Ghost hath called me by the Gospel, enlightened me by His gifts, and sanctified and preserved me in the true faith, in like manner as He calls, gathers, enlightens and sanctifies the whole Christian Church on earth, and preserves it in union with Jesus Christ in the true faith."

3. What are the acts belonging to this Order?

The Call, Illumination, Regeneration and Conversion, Mystical Union, and Sanctification.

4. What difficulty is experienced in their treatment?

The line between them is not always sharply drawn.

They overlap one another. So close, too. is their connection that one act in its wider sense sometimes stands by synecdoche for what in the strictest sense is designated by another term.

Definition

5. What is the Call?

The announcement to men of God's gracious will and the provision He has made for their salvation through the mediatorial work of Christ, accompanied by the invitation to accept these blessings through faith (Matt. 22:3-9, 14).

Two elements

6. What two things concur in the call?

The presentation through the preaching of the Word of the great truths of the Gospel, as intended for each individual; and the impressing of these truths inwardly upon the heart and conscience, so as to influence a decision of man's will.

> John 6:44. "No man can come unto me except the Father that sent me draw him."
>
> 1 Cor. 12:3. "No man can say Jesus is Lord but in the Holy Spirit."

Is there a double word

7. Is it true, then, that there is a double Word of God, and that besides the outward Word which is offered to all, there is an inner Word which is offered to only a few?

> "That many are called and few are chosen is not owing to the fact that the meaning of the call, made through the Word, is as though God were to say: 'Outwardly, through the Word, I indeed call to my Kingdom all of you, to whom I give my Word, yet, in my heart, I intend it not for all, but only for a few; for it is my will that the greater part of those whom I call through the Word should not be enlightened or converted, but be and remain lost, although, through the Word, I declare myself to them otherwise.' For this

> would be to assign to God contradictory wills. That is, it would thus be taught that God, who is eternal truth, would be contrary to Himself; and yet God punishes the fault when one thing is declared and another is thought and meant in the heart (Ps. 5:9; 12:2 sq.)" (Formula of Concord, 655).

Cf. Chapter 24,22

Explanation of difference in results

8. Is there, therefore, an inner presence of the Holy Spirit with the Word wherever preached?

Always. The differences in results in the call do not depend upon differences in God's will, or upon the call having an irresistible efficacy attached to it in one case, and having no efficacy attached to it in the other. The efficacy of the Word and call is constant; the difference in results is determined by a difference in man's attitude towards the call.

9. How has this been confessionally stated?

The reason why "few receive the Word and follow it, and the greater number despise the Word and will not come to the wedding" is "the perverse will of man, who rejects or perverts the means and instrument of the Holy Ghost, which God offers him through the call, and resists the Holy Ghost who wishes to be efficacious, and works through the Word, as Christ says (Matt. 23:37), 'How often would I have gathered thee together, and ye would not.'"

Rom 8:28

10. But does not Rom. 8:28, "Whom he predestinated them he also called," restrict the call to a class, viz., to those predestinated from all eternity, and ultimately "glorified"?

No. Paul does not say that none were called except the predestinated, or none were called except the justified; but he exhibits the succession of acts through which those at last glorified are brought to salvation. These are in the order mentioned,

Predestination, Vocation, Justification, Glorification.[5]

Attributes of Call

11. What attributes belong, therefore, to the call?

It is earnest, serious, sufficient and efficacious. Matt. 23:37, cited under Q. 9, furnishes the proof, even though there were none other from the universality of grace (Chapter 9, 10).

Subjects, Objects

12. To whom is the call addressed?

To those who in this world are not by faith partakers of Christ.

> Col. 2:12. "Ye were at that time separate from Christ, alienated from the commonwealth of Israel, and strangers from the covenants of the promise, having no hope, and without God in the world."
>
> Luke 1:79. "To shine upon them that sit in darkness and in the shadow of, death, to guide our feet into the way of peace."
>
> Matt. 11:28. "Come unto me all ye that labor and are heavy laden, and I will give you rest."

13. To what does it urge?

> Acts 26:17, 18. "Unto whom I send thee, to open their eyes, that they may turn from darkness to light, and from the power of Satan unto God, that they may receive remission of sins and an inheritance among them that are sanctified by faith in me."
>
> 1 Pet. 2:9. "Who called you out of darkness into his marvelous light."

5 See my Commentary on Romans, p. 172.

Relation of Law and Gospel to Call

14. By what means does the call come?

By the external Word as the ever efficacious instrument through which the Holy Spirit works.

> Rom. 10:14, 17. "How shall they believe in him of whom they have not heard, and how shall they hear without a preacher? So belief cometh of hearing, and hearing by the Word of Christ."

The office of the Law, as we shall learn, at the proper place, is to prepare the way for the preaching of the Gospel (Gal. 3:24). It is not Law, but Gospel which is the proper means of the call.

> Rom. 1:16. "The Gospel is the power of God unto salvation to every one that believeth." Matt. 16:15. "Preach the Gospel to the whole creation."

The announcement of the grace of God in Christ is Gospel, and not Law.

Nor does the Word come only in its general form, but as applied to individuals in the Sacraments.

> "Christ causes the promise of the Gospel to be offered not only in general, but through the Sacraments, which He attaches as seals of the promise, He seals and confirms it to every believer."

Inequalities

15. But does the Gospel come to all in the same form or degree?

It is not only God's will that all should be saved, (1 Tim. 2:4), but Christ has commanded that the Gospel should be proclaimed everywhere and to all men (Matt. 28:19; Mark 16:15). But that the Gospel is preached at all times and in all lands and to an equal degree cannot be affirmed. Paul says that it is the power of God unto salvation "to the Jew first and also to the Greek." It was a dispensation hid in God for ages, and only made known in a late period (Eph. 3:5, 9, 10). Even believers of the Old Testament dispensation received it in a very vague and indefinite form (Matt. 13:17). The call of individuals of different nationalities proceeds successively. The history of the entire missionary activity of the Church is outlined in Acts 1:8.

> "Ye shall be my witnesses both in Jerusalem and in all Judea and Samaria and unto the uttermost part of the earth."

It is only as the end of the world approaches that the will and command of Christ are absolutely fulfilled.

> Matt. 24:14. "And this gospel of the kingdom shall be preached in the whole world for a testimony unto all the nations: and then shall the end come."

16. What results from the consideration of this inequality?

Difficulties are suggested which we should candidly acknowledge we cannot explain. Theology deals with revealed facts, not with suppositions.

> "When we see that God gives His Word at one place, but not at another; removes it from one place, and allows it to remain at another... in these and similar questions, Paul fixes a limit as to how far we should go" (Formula of Concord, 659).

> Rom. 11:22. "Behold the goodness and severity of God: toward them that fell, severity; but toward thee, God's goodness, if thou continue in his goodness; otherwise thou shalt also be cut off."

The doctrine of the call comes as a practical matter to those who have heard the Gospel. It is not for them to speculate concerning those who have not heard it, or who have not heard it to the same degree, or under similar favorable circumstances.

> Deut. 29:29. "The secret things belong unto Jehovah our God; but the things that are revealed belong unto us and to our children forever."

17. Does this mean that we are not to be concerned about the fact that there are many millions who have not heard the call?

By no means. But since the call does not come except through the preaching of the Word, and in order that this Word be preached, men must be sent (Rom. 10:14 sqq.), and as, further, it is Christ's command that the call be addressed all men, this becomes the great motive for missionary activity. His will that the call be made universal lays an inevitable duty upon those whom He has called and commissioned as His ambassadors (2 Cor. 5:20; Matt. 28:18, 19).

Preparatory invitations

18. Is there not a preparatory work of the Holy Spirit even prior to and without the Gospel, which is sometimes termed a call or calling?

There are "invitations and incentives to inquire after the worship and people of God," sometimes termed "the indirect call," but not a call in the proper sense. "For they do not have as their immediate end the giving of eternal salvation to man or the knowledge of Christ as Redeemer, but only the bringing of men to the gate of the true church" (Quenstedt). Such are the traces of God's Providential government of the universe, and the voice of conscience.

> Rom. 1:20. "The invisible things of him since the creation of the world are clearly seen, being perceived through the things that are made, even his everlasting power and divinity; that they may be without excuse."
>
> Rom 2:15. "They show the work of the law written in their hearts, their conscience bearing witness therewith, and their thoughts one with another accusing or else excusing them."
>
> Acts 17:23. "What, therefore, ye worship in ignorance, him declare I unto you," etc.
>
> Acts 17:27. "That they should seek God if haply they might find him."
>
> Rom. 10:18. "Their sound went out into all the earth, and their words unto the ends of the world."

The early apologists of Christianity, following St. Paul on the Areopagus, appealed to these convictions and incentives, as in the words of Tertullian, "*O testimonium animae naturaliter Christianae!*" and in what Justin Martyr and others wrote concerning the Logos *spermatikos*. Another form of indirect influence is through the reports concerning Christianity diffused among the heathen.

> 1 Thess. 1:8. "In every place your faith to Godward is gone forth."

Call under the Old Testament

19. Was the Gospel call addressed those who lived under the Old Testament?

Yes, from Gen. 3:15 on. The fourth chapter of Romans shows the identity of the mode of salvation under the Old and New Testament. Abraham was justified by faith in the promise (Rom. 4:3). That promise given him, before circumcision, was the basis of the call, trusting which he went forth "not knowing whither" (Heb. 11:8). There was a difference in degree of explicitness; but call and promise were otherwise the same. (See Chapter 16, 4.) The Gospel in the Old Testament offered God's grace in and through the promise of a mediation and Mediator whom God would, in due time, provide (Chapter 17, 14). This promise being accepted so far as then revealed, was the ground of the righteousness of the Old Testament saints.

> Acts 10:43. "To him bear all the prophets witness, that through his name every one that believeth on him shall receive remission of sins."

20. Was there not a difference between the scope of the call in the Old Testament and the New Testament?

Yes. For while under the Old Testament it was particularistic and addressed only to those who belonged to the chosen people, under the New Testament, it is universal.

> Eph. 3 14-6. "The mystery of Christ, which in other generations was not made known unto the sons of men as it hath now been revealed unto his holy apostles and prophets in the Spirit, that the Gentiles are fellow-heirs and fellow-members of the body and fellow-partakers of the promise in Christ Jesus through the Gospel."

> Acts 10:45. "They of the circumcision that believed were amazed, because that on the Gentiles also was poured out the gift of the Holy Spirit."

20. Illumination

Condition of Man to whom the Call comes

1. In what state does the Gospel call find man?

He is of himself able neither to respond to it, nor even to understand what it means.

2. How is this taught in our Confessions?

> "Although man's reason or natural understanding has still indeed a dim spark of the knowledge that there is a God, as also (Rom.s1:19 sqq.) of the doctrine of the Law; yet it is so ignorant, blind and perverted, that when even the most able and learned men on earth read or hear the Gospel of the Son of God and the promise of eternal salvation, they cannot, from their own powers, perceive, apprehend, understand or believe and regard it true, but the more diligence and earnestness they employ in order to comprehend, with their reason, those spiritual things, the less they understand or believe, and before they become enlightened or taught of the Holy Ghost, they regard all this as only foolishness or fictions" (Formula of Concord).

3. Is this statement Scriptural?

1 Cor. 2:14. "The natural man receiveth not the things of the Spirit of God: for they are foolishness unto him, neither can he know them, because they are spiritually judged."

1:21. "Seeing that, in the wisdom of God, the world, through its wisdom, knew not God."

Eph. 4:17, 18. "The Gentiles walk in the vanity of their mind, being darkened in their understanding, alienated from the life of God, because of the ignorance that is in them, because of the hardening of their heart."

Matt. 13:13. "Seeing they see not, and hearing they hear not, neither do they understand."

Rom. 3:11. "There is none that understandeth."

Hence man, in his natural state is called darkness, and is said to dwell in darkness.

Eph. 5:8. "Ye were once darkness, but are now light in the Lord."

Acts 26:18. "To open their eyes, that they may turn from darkness to light."

John 1:5. "The light shineth in the darkness and the darkness apprehended it not."

Luke 1:79. "To shine upon them that sit in darkness and in the shadow of death."

4. What illustration of this can be cited?

"The prayers of saints, in which they pray that they may be taught, enlightened and sanctified of God. Thus they declare that those things which they ask of God they cannot have from their own natural powers; as in Ps. 119 alone, David prays more than ten times that God may impart to him understanding. For similar prayers in the writings of Paul, see Eph. 1:17; Col. 1:19; Phil. 1:9" (Formula of Concord, 554).

Luther, in Preface to First German edition of his Works (Walch XIV, 424), calls attention to the prayers of David in Ps. 119 for enlightenment and instruction, as made by one who had the Books of Moses in his hands, but who needed "a true Master"' to interpret their meaning.

5. Is man's natural condition simply one of ignorance?

No. It is more. It is not simply one of the lack of knowledge, but one of perversion, corruption and hostility to the truth.

> "God's Word testifies that the understanding, heart and will of the natural unregenerate man in divine things are not only turned entirely from God, but also turned and perverted against God to every evil; also that he is not only weak, feeble, impotent and dead to good, but also through Original Sin, he is so lamentably perverted, infected and corrupted that, by his disposition and nature, he is entirely evil, perverse and hostile to God" (Formula of Concord, 555).

6. Scriptural proofs?

> Rom. 8:7. "The mind of the flesh" (i.e. of the natural man, John 3:6) "is enmity against God; for it is not subject to the law of God, neither indeed can be."
>
> Gal. 5:17. "For the flesh lusteth against the Spirit for these are contrary the one to the other."
>
> Jer. 17:9. "The heart is deceitful above all things, and it is exceedingly corrupt: who can know it?"
>
> 1 Cor. 1:18. "The word of the cross is to them that are perishing foolishness.

7. What, therefore is necessary, in order that the Gospel call may reach the end for which it has been intended?

Unless there be with it a peculiar activity of the Holy Spirit rendering man receptive and docile with respect to its message, it is fruitless (Is. 28:11, 12; John 1:5).

Definition

8. What is this activity?

Illumination, a process whereby there is communicated not only new truths but the power to apprehend and appreciate them, and the desire to learn their real significance. It removes prejudices, disarms hostility, properly interprets the facts taught in the Gospel message, shows what they are in their relations, and makes of them a personal application. It imparts, maintains and cultivates a habit or frame of mind which regards divine truths in a light, not only unknown but contrary to that of Nature.

> 1 Cor. 2:14, 15. "The natural man receiveth not the things of the Spirit of God: for they are foolishness unto him; and he cannot know them, because they are spiritually judged."

Confessional statements

9. How is this stated in our Confessions?

"The Holy Ghost opens the understanding and heart to understand the. Scriptures, and to give heed to the Word, as it is written (Luke 24:45), 'Then opened he their mind, that they might understand the scriptures';[6] also (Acts 16:14) 'Lydia heard us, whose heart the Lord opened'" (Formula of Concord, 557).

Scripture Proofs

10. Give a few more Scripture texts referring to Illumination.

> 2 Cor. 4:6. "God hath shined into our hearts, to give the light of the knowledge of the glory of God in the face of Jesus Christ."

> Eph. 1:18, 19. "Having the eyes of your understanding enlightened, that ye may know what is the hope of his calling, what the riches of the glory of his

6 "Gerhard on"Harmony of the Gospels": *Non solum exteriori vaticiniorum explicatione, sed etiam interna mentis illuminatione.*

inheritance in the saints, and what the exceeding greatness of his power toward us who believe."

John 8:12. "I am the Light of the world: he that followeth me shall not walk in darkness, but shall have the light of life."

Means

11. What are the Means of Illumination?

The Word of God.

Ps. 119:105. "Thy word is a lamp unto my feet, and a light unto my path."

Ps. 119:130. "The opening of thy words giveth light."

2 Pet. 1:19. "The word of prophecy, whereunto ye do well that ye take heed as unto a light shining in a dark place, until the day dawn and the day-star arise in your hearts."

Rom. 14:17.

Both Law,

Rom. 3:20. "Through the law cometh the knowledge of sin."

And Gospel,

2 Cor. 4:4. "Lest the light of the Gospel of the glory of Christ should dawn upon them."

Is there ever Immediate Illumination

12. Is there no immediate Illumination?

No instance can be found in Holy Scripture. Even where the miraculous element enters, as in the conversion of Paul and the conversion of the thousands at Pentecost, it is the Word through which the Spirit works; to Paul, the words from the open heavens, "Why persecutest thou me"; to the multitude, the sermon of Peter.

13. But is not Illumination to be sought in the abstraction of the mind from earthly things, and in awaiting silently a supernatural divine light?

There is no benefit to be derived from turning from other objects except to fix the attention upon some word of God or its application in our experience; nor is there any supernatural divine light to be expected except that for which we have the promise in the ordinary use of Holy Scripture. Meditation and Prayer are to be constantly employed, as exercises whereby we resort to the Word. (See Chapter 1, 40.) Here the words of one of the collects belong:

> "Blessed Lord, Who hast caused all Holy Scripture to be written for our learning: Grant that we may in such wise hear them, read, mark, learn and inwardly digest them, that by patience and comfort of Thy holy Word, we may embrace and ever hold fast the blessed hope of everlasting life" (General Collect 49, "Common Service").

Forms

14. Is the illuminating power of the Word restricted to the acts of hearing, reading and meditating?

No. The word that has been heard and laid to heart is assimilated into the life of the one who has received it by faith, and becomes an abiding source of light and comfort. "It is called 'the engrafted word' (James 1:21). If united with the hearts of hearers and readers, like food with the body, leaven with the mass, seed with the field, the graft with the tree, as an ordinary means of the Holy Spirit, it can illumine no less than save souls" (Hollaz). (2 Cor. 3:2, 3.)

Legal and evangelical

15. What two kinds of illumination are there?

They correspond to the diverse offices of Law and Gospel. The effect of illumination by the Law is to convict of sin (Rom. 3:20 [see above, 11], 7:7). This it does not simply by revealing external violations of God's commands, but especially by discerning "the thoughts and intents of the heart" (Heb. 4:12). Illumination by the Gospel leads to faith, and renders "wise unto salvation" (2 Tim. 3:14). The two forms of illumination are contrasted in 2 Cor. 3:6-9.

16. What are the gifts communicated by this illumination, as referred to in our Catechism, "enlightened me with his gifts"?

> Is. 11:2. "And the Spirit of God shall rest upon him, the spirit of wisdom and understanding, the spirit of counsel and might, the spirit of knowledge and the fear of Jehovah"

"the seven-fold gift of the Spirit."

17. Is Illumination limited to the intellect?

It belongs to it primarily, but through the intellect influences also the will. As the will can arrest the process of illumination by its resistance when a knowledge of sin unavoidably makes itself felt, the gracious working of the Spirit enters to overcome this resistance and communicate more knowledge. Legal illumination may be arrested at any point, unless the will partake of the movement. The highest degree is attained only subsequently to the entrance of faith. When through faith we have been led to love God we learn to know Him as He is.

> "If any man willeth to do his will, he shall know of the teaching whether it is of God" (John 7:17).
>
> "In thy light shall we see light" (Ps. 36:9).

Gradual

18. Illumination, then, is gradual?

Undoubtedly. The natural knowledge precedes the supernatural. There is even a natural and external knowledge of what has been supernaturally revealed. The supernatural knowledge begins with legal illumination, or "awakening," which has various degrees, and is followed by evangelical illumination which also has its successive parts, before, contemporaneous with and after faith, or, as Paul says, "from faith to faith" (Rom. 1:17). There is no irresistible grace. The process may be arrested at any time, during this life, by the array of man's will against that of God.

19. But was not the illumination of Paul on the way to Damascus sudden and complete?

In the first place, we must distinguish between the extraordinary circumstances attending Paul's conversion, pertaining rather to his preparation for the Apostolate, with his call, as he says to the Galatians, "not from men, neither through man, but through Jesus Christ and God the Father" (Gal 1:1), and the various acts which led to the conversion itself. Secondly, we note that the vision of the Risen Jesus convinced Paul of the truth of the claims of Him he had been persecuting. Nevertheless there had been years of preparation for the critical hour, and the sermon of Stephen had impressed truths, with which Paul was struggling inwardly, while he tried to escape their force by his outward violence. With the occurrence on his journey, his illumination simply passed from one stage to another, which also gradually progressed as the record in Acts and in the Epistle to the Galatians shows. Moments there are seemingly decisive, in the lives of nations and churches as well as of individuals, which are only the culmination of long processes, that are hidden from view.

20. What illustrations have been given?

Chemnitz says that "these matters are best learned not from idle disputations, or from the examples of others, but from the serious exercises of one's own repentance. But since most live without any exercise of faith and prayer, they accumulate many inextricable things concerning things of which they have no knowledge."[7]

7 With this introduction he enters into a minute examination of the various stages which Augustine has recorded in his "Confessions" concerning his conversion. (Loci Theologici 1:185.) Hollazius has quoted from Calixt the account which a Jew, Gerson, had given concerning his

21. What caution must be employed in the study of all such examples?

Not to make any particular case the standard according to which all others are judged (1 Cor. 12:4-6). Our faith must be tested according to the standards laid down in Holy Scripture. (See Chapter 17, 44, 45, 47, 48, 49.)

Different senses of the Term

22. Is the term Illumination always restricted to the particular stage of grace just explained?

It is sometimes used ecclesiastically in a wide sense for the entire work of grace as deliverance from the darkness. Thus Chemnitz, in his "Harmony," on John 1:9, says:

"(1) In contrast with the darkness of ignorance He illumines us by the revelation of His Word and the enlightening of His Spirit, unto true knowledge.

"(2) In contrast with the darkness of sins, He illumines us by the imputation of righteousness, the forgiveness of sins and the renewal begun in this life.

"(3) In contrast with the darkness of God's wrath, He causes the face of God to shine upon us by reconciliation and adoption.

"(4) In contrast with the darkness of miseries, he beams upon us with consolation, relief and deliverance.

"(5) In contrast with the external darkness of death and damnation, He illumines us with eternal life and salvation (2 Tim. 1:10; Col. 1:12)."

Here illumination becomes synonymous with salvation. It was also used by the early Greek writers of the Church for Baptism.

---

experience. He was a pawnbroker and had loaned a Christian woman eight shillings for which she pledged a German New Testament. Finding it in his possession, he undertook to read it, "not that I had any doubt concerning the truth of the Jewish religion, or because I believed any article of the Christian faith, but to learn to know what the influential error could be which had misled and ruined so many thousands. In the presence of two of my relatives I read it through, not without blasphemies. But meanwhile my heart was touched, and when I noticed that the Evangelists and Apostles and Christ himself appealed so often to the Old Testament, and continually cited passage after passage from it, I was induced to read it the second time and secretly, without the knowledge of any one, not even of my wife, and to compare the passages cited with the text of the Old Testament. When I did this, such light shone upon me that for it I give God everlasting thanks." "Here," adds Hollazius, "who does not not see that there was illumination which for a time was without regeneration and sanctification"?

21. Regeneration

Definition

1. What is Regeneration?

The act of the Holy Spirit by which new and spiritual life is imparted to man who is dead in sins.

John 3:3. "Except one be born anew, he cannot see the kingdom of God."

2. How is it related to Illumination?

By illumination man is brought to see his lost condition and to learn of the provision made in Christ for his salvation. This act, as it progresses, includes a certain disposition of the will towards the offered grace. Regeneration occurs when the act of self-surrender to God's will and promise is accomplished by the inner workings of the Holy Spirit in Word or Sacrament. Illumination influences the will, but it belongs to regeneration to determine the decision.

3. What brief definition, then, can be given?

"Regeneration is the act whereby one is made believing"; or "the act by which faith is given," or "the act by which faith is conferred." (See Chapter 17, 6.)

Confessional statement

4. How is this taught in our Confessions?

> "That we may obtain this faith, the office of teaching the Gospel and administering the Sacraments was instituted. For through the Word and Sacraments, as through instruments, the Holy Ghost is given who worketh faith where and when it pleases God in them that hear the Gospel" (Augsburg Confession, Art. V).

> "Man is and remains an enemy of God, until by the power of the Holy Ghost, through the preached and heard Word, out of pure grace, without any cooperation of his own, he is converted, made believing, regenerated and renewed" (Formula of Concord, 552, cf. 563).

"How is this effected?" asks our Catechism, and then answers:

> "When our heavenly Father gives us His Holy Spirit, so that by His grace we believe His holy Word and live a godly life here on earth, and in heaven forever" (On Second Petition of Lord's Prayer).

Scripture Proofs of Man's Inability

5. But is it not an extreme statement to maintain, that, even after man has been brought to see his sins, and to learn of the offered grace, he cannot, of his own powers, believe?

The answer may be learned by considering the following texts:

> Phil. 2:13. "For it is God who worketh in you both to will and to work, for his good pleasure." Here the will to do God's will is ascribed to a work of God in man.

> 2 Cor. 3:5. "Our sufficiency is from God."

> Phil. 1:6. "He who began a good work in you, will perfect it."

John 15:5. "Apart from me, ye can do nothing." Here Augustine notes that our Lord does not say:

"Apart from me, ye can act only with difficulty," or "Apart from me, ye can do nothing great," but absolutely "nothing," i.e. "nothing whatever."

John 6:44. "No man can come to me, except the Father that sent me draw me."

1 Cor. 12:3. "No one can say, Jesus is Lord, but in the Holy Spirit."

Eph. 2:8. "By grace have ye been saved through faith; and that not of yourselves, it is the gift of God."

John 6:29. "This is the work of God that ye believe on him whom he hath sent."

Phil. 1:29. "To you, it hath been granted, in the behalf of Christ, not only to believe on him, but also to suffer on his behalf."

1 Cor. 4:7. "What hast thou which thou dist not receive?"

Illustrations given in the Confessions

6. What figures with respect to men's inability are employed by our Confessions?

"The Scriptures teach that man is not only weak and sick, but also entirely dead (Eph. 2:1, 5; Col. 2:13) As now a man who is physically dead cannot, of his own powers prepare or adapt himself to recover temporal life, so man who is spiritually dead in sins cannot, of his own strength, adapt or apply himself to the acquisition of spiritual and heavenly righteousness and life, unless he be delivered and quickened by the Son of God from the death of sin" (Formula of Concord, 553).

"Of his own natural powers, he can begin, work or cooperate in spiritual things, and in his own conversion and regeneration, as little as a stone or a block or clay" (ibid. 556).

The question of Responsibility

7. But does not this practically deny man's responsibility?

No.

> "For in another respect, man is not a stone or block. For a stone or block does not resist that which moves it, and does not understand and is not sensible of what is being done with it, as a man, as long as he is not converted, with his will resists God the Lord. And it is nevertheless true that a man before his conversion is still a rational creature, having an understanding and will, yet not an understanding with respect to divine things, or a will to will something good and salutary. Yet he can do nothing for his conversion, and is, in this respect, much worse than a stone and block; for he resists the Word and will of God, until God awakens him from the death of sin, enlightens and renews him. And although God does not force man to become godly (for those who always resist the Holy Ghost and persistently oppose the known truth, as Stephen says of the hardened Jews (Acts 7:51) will not be converted), yet God the Lord draws the man whom He wishes to convert, and draws him too in such a way that his understanding, in place of 'darkened' becomes enlightened, and his will, in place of perverse, becomes obedient. The Scriptures call this 'creating a new heart' (Ps. 51:10)."

In what respect is man's will free

8. From this I understand that man's will has a certain freedom?

It is always free to resist and reject the offered grace. (See Chapter 19, 9.) While regeneration comes altogether and alone of God's free gift, the absence of regeneration is due to man's repulse of what God has offered.

9. But does the resistance of the will to the grace of God ever entirely cease?

Never in this life.

> Rom. 7:23. "I see a law in my members warring against the law of my mind."

> Gal. 5:17. "For the flesh lusteth against the Spirit."

But in the regenerate, this resistance is constantly lamented, and is contrary to the main purpose of the life.

> Rom. 7:25. "I of myself with the mind, indeed, serve the law of God."

> Rom 7:22. "I delight in the law of God after the inward man."

On the other hand, one not regenerate wholly resists God and is altogether a servant of sin (John 8:34; Rom. 6:16).

How is Regeneration wrought

10. How is Regeneration wrought?

Through the Word and Sacraments (see above, 4); also,

> "By this means, and in no other way, namely through His holy Word, when it is heard as preached or is read, and the holy Sacraments when they are used according to the Word, God desires to call men to eternal salvation, to draw them to Himself, and to convert, regenerate and sanctify them" (Formula of Concord, 562)

Rom. 10:17; 1 Cor. 1:21; James 1:18; 1 Peter 1:23

Law, Gospel and Sacraments, in their relation to Regeneration

11. Is Regeneration wrought by all parts of God's Word?

Only by the Gospel. For that the Law does not regenerate is manifest from

> 2 Cor. 3:6. "The letter killeth, but the Spirit giveth life."

> Rom. 3:20. "Through the law, cometh the knowledge of sin."

For the regenerating efficacy of the Gospel:

> 1 Cor. 4:15. "In Christ Jesus I begot you through the Gospel."
>
> John 6:63. "The words which I have spoken unto you are spirit and are life."

Hence the Augsburg Confession (Art. V), declares

> "...the Holy Ghost who worketh faith in them that hear the Gospel, to wit, that God, not for our own merits but for Christ's sake, justifieth those who believe."

12. How do the Sacraments regenerate?

Not apart or as separate instrumentalities from the Gospel, but only as means by which the word of the Gospel is applied to the individual. Baptism is by preeminence "the Sacrament of regeneration."

> John 3:5. "Except one be born of water and the Spirit, he cannot enter the kingdom of God."
>
> Tit. 3:5. "According to his mercy he saved us, through the washing of regeneration and renewing of the Holy Spirit."
>
> Gal. 3:26, 27. "Ye are all sons of God through faith in Christ Jesus; for as many of you as were baptized unto Christ, have put on Christ."

Substantial or Accidental; Instantaneous or Gradual

13. Is Regeneration a "substantial ' or an"accidental" change, as was discussed in the Flacian controversy?

There is no destruction of personality in regeneration; but only the endowment of the hitherto unregenerate person with a new life. (See Chapter VII, 33; 8:35-38.) The "stony heart" and "the heart of flesh" (Ez. 11:19), the "old man" and the "new" are the same, but their properties have changed.

14. Is Regeneration instantaneous or gradual?

The answer depends upon the precise meaning of Regeneration. If it comprehend the entire activity of the Holy Spirit whereby faith is given and nurtured (for faith grows, see Chapter 17, 29), it is gradual. But if restricted to the beginning of spiritual life, "the enkindling of a spark of faith," it is instantaneous, like justification, its inseparable result.

Subjects — Infant Faith

15. Who are subjects of Regeneration?

The question back of this is whether infants as well as adults are capable of faith, and therefore, subjects of regeneration. Here, in the absence of express statements of Scripture, we must beware, on the one hand, of setting limits to what God can or may do, and, on the other, of prescribing what He must do.

> John 3:8. "The wind bloweth where it will, and thou hearest the voice thereof, but knowest not whence it cometh and whither it goeth: so is every one that is born of the Spirit."

It almost seems as though the words of our Lord to Nicodemus concerning the new birth have in view the declaration as to the mysteriousness of God's work in Eccl. 11:5.

> "As thou knowest not what is the way of the wind nor how the bones do grow in the womb of her that is with child, even so thou knowest not the work of God who doeth all."

16. What cautions, therefore, are to be observed?

[A.] That the details concerning the regeneration of adults stated in connection with directions concerning the missionary preaching of the Apostolic Church, or in letters to New Testament congregations, be not made the absolute standards whereby to decide the question of the possibility of infant regeneration.

When, for example, in the tenth chapter of Romans, Paul is making his most urgent appeal for sending missionaries to the heathen, he declares that, in order that they be brought to faith, they must hear the Gospel. Such declaration cannot be construed, however, so as to deny that God may have other modes of working with infants.

[B.] That we ever keep in mind that the efficacy of faith for justification depends not upon its perfection or stage of development, but solely upon its contents.

The question is one simply of the possibility for receptive capacity wrought by the Holy Spirit (Chapter 17, 29, 30). Faith, as we have learned (Chapter 17, 11), is never a ground, but only an organ for receiving God's grace.

[C.] That the distinctions between "Direct" and "Discursive," "Habitual" and "Active," "Implicit" and "Explicit Faith" (Chapter 17, 7, 8, 9) be also taken into account.

[D.] That, in our estimate, we include also the fact that, apart from and before all intelligence and ability to communicate with the outward world and self-consciousness, children have sin, and that this is not a physical, but a moral and spiritual defect.

(See Augsburg Confession, Art. II; see above, Chapter 8:7.) What reason for denying the possibility of infant faith can 'they allege who acknowledge the fact of innate depravity, and the innate' knowledge of God?

[E.] That as the object of faith (see Chapter 17, 15) is simply the promise of God, we dare not deny the possibility of faith where the apprehension of what is embraced in the promise does not rise above the standard of the saints in the earlier period of the Old Testament: Faith in its ultimate essence is such reliance upon God that it is ready to accept anything that He teaches or to do anything that He directs.

Its objects grow in number and clearness with the growth of revelation. The test of its reality is not the extent of its range, but its inner disposition towards God. So whatever faith can be claimed for infants may be nothing more than an attitude of heart and mind towards God which, with growing intelligence, is to grasp one promise and revealed fact after another.

17. What proofs are there of the possibility of infant faith and regeneration?

[A.] The influence of the Holy Spirit in an extraordinary way upon certain infants before birth, and shortly after.

> Jer. 1:5. "Before thou earnest out of the womb I sanctified thee."
>
> Luke 1:41. "When Elizabeth heard the salutation of Mary, the babe leaped in her womb; and Elizabeth was filled with the Holy Spirit."
>
> Ps. 22:9. "Thou didst make me trust when I was upon my mother's breasts."

[B.] The express ascription of faith to little children.

> Matt. 18:6. "Whoso shall cause one of these little ones who believe on me to stumble."

That this passage refers to "little children" literally, and not to believers in general, as in I John 2:18, is manifest from the context (v. 3). Mark 10:13-16 shows that the children were such as were carried in arms. "They were indeed"called"' (Matt. 18:2), and may have been four or five years old, nevertheless even, in such, faith could not have arisen from human instruction, but must be ascribed to an inner divine working" (Spener). We are inclined to ascribe the faith of these children to the attractive personality of Christ. The Word came to them in His look and manner and the gentle but authoritative tones of His voice, which called forth their confidence, and prepared them for the loving reception of all that He would say and do.

[C.] From their right to entrance into the kingdom of heaven, and the fact that such entrance is through regeneration.

> John 3:3. "Except one be born anew, he cannot see the kingdom of God."

> John 3:5. "Except one be born of water and the Spirit, he cannot enter into the kingdom of God."

18. How has the doctrine of infant faith or regeneration been guarded?

> "The Holy Ghost is efficacious in them according to their measure." "Although, therefore, we do not understand of what nature that action of God in infants is, nevertheless it is certain that in them new and holy movements are wrought, just as in John, when, in the womb, new movements occurred. For although we must not imagine that infants understand, nevertheless these movements and inclinations to believe Christ and to love God, are, in a measure, like the movements of faith and love. This is what we say when we say that infants have faith" (Wittenberg Concord (1536), signed by Luther, Melanchthon, Bugenhagen, Jonas, Bucer and others).

> "There is no doubt that infants, members of the Church of Christ do not have such faith, i.e., so explicit, and, so to say, so perceptible to sense, as adults, in whom the Holy Spirit is efficacious through the external hearing of the Gospel" (Brentz, "Apology of Wittenberg Confession").

> "When we say that infants believe, it must not be imagined that they know or perceive the movements of faith."
>
> "Since it is certain that baptized infants are members of the Church, and please God, it is certain also that the Holy Spirit is efficacious in them, and, indeed, so efficacious that they can receive the grace of God and the forgiveness of sins."
>
> "And although we can neither understand nor explain in words what that action and operation of the Spirit in baptized infants is, nevertheless from the Word of God, it is certain. But this action or operation of the Holy Spirit in infants we call faith, and say that little children believe" (Chemnitz). See Chapter 27.

18. Can Regeneration be lost?

This is equivalent to the question whether faith may be lost. The answer is Yes. (See Chapter 17, 36, 37.)

19. Is not Regeneration as a theological term sometimes used in a wider sense than that which has thus far been considered?

In Matt. 19:28, "In the regeneration when the Son of man shall sit on the throne of his glory," the reference is to the renewal and restitution of all things at the Second Coming of Christ, according to the promise.

> Rev. 21:5, "And he that sitteth on the throne, said, Behold, I make all things new."
>
> 2 Pet. 3:13. "According to his promise, we look for new heavens and a new earth, wherein dwelleth righteousness."

Entrance into the full enjoyment of the culmination of the kingdom of glory, is regeneration; just as entrance into the kingdom of grace or its portal, is also called regeneration.

But beside this Biblical usage, its ecclesiastical meaning has had a considerable latitude, which occasioned confusion and rendered a more precise definition and consistent employment of the term necessary. Of this the Formula of Concord says:

"Because the word 'regeneration' is sometimes employed for the word 'justification,' it is necessary that this word be properly explained, in order that the renewal which follows the justification of faith may not be confounded therewith, but that they may properly distinguished from one another… . Again it is taken for sanctification and renewal" (572-3). (See the entire passage for fuller statement.)

Distinctions and Synonyms

20. How would you distinguish it from Justification and Sanctification?

Regeneration and Justification are both acts of God alone; Sanctification is an act in which man cooperates. Regeneration is an act within man; Justification, an act outside of man; Sanctification begins with an inward act and works into the outward life. Regeneration, gives faith; through faith man is justified; the inevitable result of Justification is the beginning of Sanctification.

21. What synonyms has it? The nearest equivalents are:

[A.] Quickening.

Eph. 2:4, 5. "God, being rich in mercy, for his great love wherewith he loved us, even when we were dead through our trespasses, made us alive together with Christ."

[B.] Creating anew.

2 Cor. 5:17. "If any man be in Christ, he is a new creation."

Gal. 6:15. "Neither is circumcision anything, nor uncircumcision, but a new creature."

Ps. 51:10.

22. Are there any other terms that cover to a considerable extent the same ground?

The terms Repentance and Conversion are generically the same with specific differences. By this we refer, of course, to the Biblical terms whose meaning must be decided by a reference to the original Greek of the New Testament.

23. What is the meaning of Repentance?

The English word has acquired the meaning of "sorrow or contrition for what one has done or left undone," and like "penitence" is etymologically from the same root as "pain." But the Greek noun *metanoia*, used twenty-four times, and the verb *metanoein*, used thirty-one times in the New Testament, refer to "a change of mind," and are almost equivalent to "conversion," which means simply "a radical change," beginning of course in the mind or heart. With this agrees the definition, "A change of mental and spiritual habit" (Century Dictionary).

Repentance

24. What important result followed a revision of the definition?

The Reformation. Luther wrote in the spring of 1518 both to his spiritual father, Staupitz, and to Pope Leo X, ascribing his course of protest to the new meaning the word had received by his study of the New Testament. The cry of John the Baptist, *metanoeite* (Matt. 3:2), the Vulgate had translated: *Poenitentiam agite*. This came to mean "Do penance," or, even when not so superficially interpreted, was regarded as equivalent to "Be contrite" or "Experience a certain degree of sorrow." But its true sense, Luther found, was:

> "Assume another mind and disposition," "Make a change of mind and a passover of spirit, so as to be wise now in heavenly as you were formerly in earthly things, as Paul says (Rom. 12:2), 'Be ye transformed by the renewing of your mind.'"

25. How did this discovery influence Luther?

> "While previously there was scarcely a word in all Scripture more bitter to me, than the word 'repentance,' now there is none that sounds sweeter or more grateful."

The explanation is that if the pain or sorrow which one experiences on account of sin be the condition of forgiveness or justification, one will always be uncertain as to whether he have the required amount of sorrow. But with the wider meaning of repentance, just as of conversion, a two-fold relation is taught. There is something from which one turns or changes, viz., sin; and something towards which this act is directed, viz., God, or what is the same, God's promise in Christ.

26. In what, then, does Repentance coincide with Regeneration?

A change of mind or attitude towards sin and God, is attended by a change of life, or the impartation of new life. The command to repent, was not only the announcement of a requirement, but also the declaration of the Gospel and of the presence of divine grace rendering repentance possible (Titus 2:11-14).

27. What are the two parts of Repentance?

> "Now Repentance consists properly of these two parts: One is contrition, that is, terrors smiting the conscience through the knowledge of sin; the other is faith, which, born of the promise or absolution, believes that, for Christ's sake, sins are forgiven, comforts the conscience and delivers it from terrors" (Augsburg Confession, Art. XII).

28. What inferences may be derived from this?

1. No true repentance without faith.

2. Wherever there is faith, there is repentance.

3. Contrition and faith act reciprocally upon each other.

With faith, sorrow for sin constantly grows and deepens. "Terrors smiting the conscience through the knowledge of sin" may not be as poignant or be attended with such emotion as on the first discovery of guilt, but the hatred of sin becomes a principle that is ever more pervasive and determined.

29. What was the first of Luther's 95 Theses?

> "Our Lord and Master Jesus Christ in saying 'Repent ye,' etc., intended that the whole life of believers should be penitence."

30. How is this expressed in our Catechism?

> "Baptism signifies that the old Adam is to be drowned by daily sorrow and repentance, together with all sins and evil lusts; and that again the new man should daily come forth, and rise, that shall live in the presence of God in righteousness and purity for ever."

31. In what, however does Repentance differ from Regeneration?

[A.] Regeneration is an act of God.

Repentance is a state of man, resulting from Regeneration. God gives Repentance (Acts 5:31; 11:18; 2 Tim. 2:25), just as in Regeneration He gives faith. As Regeneration is not faith, but the act by which faith is wrought, and as faith is an essential part of Repentance, it is through Regeneration that God effects Repentance. When man is urged to repent, he can obey only by the exercise of new powers given him in Regeneration.

[B.] Regeneration is more prospective in its look, and has reference to the new life.

Repentance is more retrospective, and suggests more the state of sin which is being forsaken. Or to speak in scholastic terms, the former emphasizes the terminus ad quern; the latter, the terminus a quo.

Conversion: Distinguished from Regeneration; can man cooperate; is the will passive; no encouragement of security. Errors of Pelagianism, Semi-Pelagianism, Synergism, Enthusiasm

32. How does Conversion differ from Repentance?

Conversion, like Regeneration, refers properly to the activity of God in effecting Repentance.

33. How does Conversion differ from Regeneration?

In the wide sense of the term, it includes Regeneration, being the activity of God through which the entire change with respect to man, both inwardly and outwardly, is accomplished. Illumination, Regeneration and Sanctification, as well as Justification, are thus comprised in one term. In a more restricted sense, it is used to describe the process whereby Repentance is effected. A man partially illumined, and not regenerated could not be said to be converted. Regeneration, therefore, when regarded as the culmination of the call and Illumination, is Conversion in the most ordinary sense of the term. If infant regeneration be admitted, Conversion becomes the bringing into activity of the new powers given in Regeneration, so that the child, with its progressive illumination, is led by the Holy Spirit to exercise these new powers in acts of faith.

34. Can man in any way cooperate in his Conversion?

Here everything depends upon the definition of Conversion. If it be so wide as to embrace Renovation, and refer to man's exercise of the powers given him in the new birth man can cooperate; but if it refer to the exercise of purely natural powers, see above, 3; also the following:

> "In spiritual and divine things, the intellect, heart and will of the unregenerate man cannot, in any way, by their own natural powers, understand, believe, accept, think, will, begin, effect, do, work or concur in working anything ... so that, in man's nature, since the Fall, there is before Regeneration, not the least spark of spiritual power present" (Formula of Concord, 552).

35. Is it right to say that in Conversion the will is purely passive?

> "When Luther says that with respect to his conversion, man is purely passive, i.e., does nothing whatever thereto, but only suffers what God wills in him, his meaning is not that conversion occurs without the preaching and hearing of God's Word; his meaning also is not that in conversion no new emotion is awakened in us by the Holy Ghost, and no spiritual operation begun; but he means that man of himself, or from his natural powers, cannot contribute anything or help to his conversion, and that conversion is not only in part, but altogether an operation, gift and present and work of the Holy Ghost alone, who accomplishes and effects it, by his virtue and power, through the Word, in the understanding, heart and will of man" (Formula of Concord, 569).

36. Does this encourage men to be idle and secure with respect to their Conversion?

> "The mathematical point, in which the liberated will begins to act cannot be determined. But when prevenient grace, i.e., the first beginnings of faith and conversion are given man, immediately a struggle between the flesh and the Spirit begins; and it is manifest that this struggle cannot occur without a movement of our will. In the beginning, the desire is very obscure, the assent languid, the obedience weak; and these gifts ought to grow. But they grow in us, not as a log is drawn by violent impulse, or as lilies grow without laboring or caring; but by endeavoring, by struggling, by asking, by seeking, by beating, and that not of ourselves" (Chemnitz, Loci I, 185).

Of this Paul uses a brilliant illustration in 2 Tim. 1:6. "Stir into flame the gift of God that is in thee."

37. But suppose some one would object:

> "As I cannot perceive the presence of the Holy Spirit, and, without this presence, all my efforts are useless, therefore I will make no effort to do God's will" what answer could be given?

> "Sometimes, indeed, the heart perceives that which it apprehends in the promise; but frequently, yea even more frequently it experiences that the Holy Ghost hides his aid in groanings which cannot be uttered (Rom. 8:26). There one must not inquire as to whether he perceive, for strength is made perfect in weakness; but by faith he must rest on God, according to the promise, even though he feel nothing; yea, even though he feel the contrary. To this effect, Augustine says: 'If you be not drawn, pray that you be drawn' (Chemnitz, ibid., 186). See also Chapter 17, 38 sqq.

Note: "The object of the Spirit's work is not to produce in us certain feelings, the consciousness of which will make us think better of ourselves, and give us confidence towards God. That which He shows us of ourselves is only evil; that which He shows us of God is only good. He does not enable us to feel or to believe in order that we may be comforted by our feeling or faith. Even when working mo.t powerfully in us, he turns our eye away from His own work in us, to fix it on God and his love, in Christ Jesus our Lord" (Bonar, "God's Way of Peace," 1-39).

38. Against what errors has the Lutheran Church particularly guarded in the treatment of this article?

[A.] Pelagianism which concedes that man by his own powers can turn to God and believe the Gospel.

[B.] Semi-Pelagianism which teaches that while man is unable without divine aid to attain salvation, yet he can make a beginning, and prepare himself for grace which completes the work.

[C.] Synergism which acknowledges that man, of his own powers, is too feeble by nature to move towards God, nevertheless, when the Holy Spirit makes the beginning, "the will of man, from its own natural powers, can, to a certain extent, although feebly, cooperate."

Hence Melanchthon erred in the last edition of his Loci, in enumerating three causes of conversion, viz., the Holy Spirit, the Word and the will of man.

[D.] "Enthusiasm," which teaches "that God, without means, without the hearing of God's Word or the use of the holy Sacraments, draws men to Himself and enlightens, justifies and saves them" (Formula of Concord, 499).

See also Augsburg Confession, Art. V; Apology, 215; Schmalkald Articles, 332. This will be more amply treated under "Means of Grace," Chapter 24.

22. The Mystical Union

Defined

1. Besides the righteousness of Christ and the gifts which it has purchased what else does faith receive?

Christ Himself who dwells in a peculiar way in every regenerate and justified soul.

> Gal. 2:20. "It is no longer I that live, but Christ liveth in me."
>
> John 15:5. "I am the vine, ye are the branches; he that abideth in me and I in him, the same beareth much fruit."
>
> John 14:23. "My Father will love him and we, will come unto him, and make our abode with him."
>
> Eph. 3:17. "That Christ may dwell in your hearts through faith."
>
> 1 Cor. 6:17. "He that is joined unto the Lord is one spirit."

What it means

2. Does this mean no more than that the influence or the power or the gifts of Christ live in the believer, as a parent lives in a child, or a great teacher in his followers?

No fair interpretation of the passages above given could lead to such doctrine. The power and gifts are there, because of the presence of Christ Himself, pervading the entire life of the believer.

> "It is a state of most immediate personal contact, such as is possible only within a religious relation" (Kahler).

Confessional treatment

3. Is this doctrine treated explicitly in the Church's Confessions?

No; except in the allusion, among false doctrines concerning the Righteousness of Christ which are repudiated:

> "We reject and condemn all the following errors: ...That not God Himself, but only the gifts of God dwell in the believer" (Formula of Concord, 503).

The fuller treatment of the subject in the later Lutheran theologians of the orthodox period (not until after the middle of the XVII Century) was to meet the various extravagant opinions of a false mysticism which was widely prevalent at the time in Germany.

Luther's explanation

4. How does Luther treat it?

> "Christ thus inhering and bound up with me" (literally, "glued to me," conglutinatus mihi), "and abiding in me, lives in me the life which I am living; yea, the life by which I thus live, is Christ Himself... This inherence frees me from the terrors of the law and sin, takes me out of my own skin, and transfers me into Christ and His Kingdom, which is a kingdom of

> grace, righteousness, peace, joy, life, salvation and eternal glory... . Because He lives in me, whatever grace, righteousness, life, peace, salvation is in me is that of Christ Himself, and, nevertheless, it is mine through that union (conglutinationem) and inherence which is by faith, and whereby Christ and I are made as it were one body in spirit." . . . "You are. so bound up with Christ, that from you and Him there is made but one person, which cannot be separated, but so perpetually adheres to Him, that you can say with confidence: 'I am Christ,' i.e., Christ's righteousness, victory, life, etc., are mine; and Christ, in turn, says, 'I am that sinner," i.e., his sins, death, etc., are mine, because he adheres to me, and I to him; for by faith we are joined into one body and one bone (Eph. 5:30). This faith joins Christ and me more closely than the husband is joined to the wife" (On Gal. 2:20).

Treatment by Apostles

5. Who gives the most prominence to this doctrine?

> "Paul lays the greatest stress on Justification; John, on the Mystical Union; Peter, on Sanctification, as a preparation for eternal life" (Kahnis).

Practical Application

6. What practical application has been made of this doctrine?

"Think of the majesty of these guests" (the Father and the Son, John 14:23), "and you will better understand the kindness of this coming" ("We will come unto him"). "Since in this life, we cannot ascend to God, so as to be present with Him (2 Cor. 5:8), but as long as this life lasts, 'we are absent from the Lord' (v. 6), God, of His immense kindness, descends to us, and comes to us, i.e., the highest majesty comes to the most abject vileness, heaven to earth, the Creator to the creature, the Lord to the servant. What love for man! 'Lord, what is man that thou art mindful of him, or the son of man that thou visitest him?' (Ps. 8:4). How men are pleased when earthly kings and princes turn aside to visit them! But what is this, compared with the coming of God! Earthly kings become a burden to those whom they visit, because of the expense attending their entertainment; but these heavenly guests come, not with empty hands, but with a store of priceless gifts" (Gerhard, on John 14:23).

Caution

7. Is the term "Mystical Union' and its separate treatment in Lutheran Dogmatics entirely satisfactory?

No. For as above stated (under 3), a polemical motive or necessity determined the attention which it received, as a distinct article. Where the historical treatment is not considered, it may properly find a place under Sanctification. Thus Schaeffer (Ms. Lectures on Dogmatics), "The state denoted by this expression (which is liable to abuse and not to be unconditionally commended) can only be the highest point of Sanctification or identical with it. It must be considered as none other than the presence of the Holy Spirit abiding in the heart of the regenerate through the word of the Gospel, such presence being inseparable from a peculiar, gracious presence of the entire Trinity."

23. Renovation Or Sanctification

Definition

1. What is Renovation or Renewal in its widest sense?

Any change whereby what has deteriorated is restored to its original strength and vigor.

2. How is the term applied to spiritual things?

It is often used in a wider sense so as to embrace also Regeneration and Justification.

> 2 Cor. 5:17. "If any man is in Christ, he is a new creature; the old things are passed away; behold, they are become new."

Or it may include Regeneration, but not Justification. Illustrations of this wider sense of the term may be found also in the Symbolical Books of the Lutheran Church. Wherever the word occurs, it becomes an important matter to decide whether it be used in the wider or the stricter sense.

3. What does it mean in the stricter sense?

The renewal of character and life, wrought by the Holy Spirit. As such, it is synonymous with Sanctification, which has been well defined, as "the work of the Holy Trinity, by which He consecrates us in soul and body, filling us with virtues of every kind, and expelling vices of every kind, and brings to us the grace of God and kingdom of heaven" (Calovius).

> Eph. 4:23. "That ye be renewed in the spirit of your mind, and put on the new man that after God hath been created in righteousness and holiness of truth."
>
> Col. 3:10. Eph. 3:16-19. 1 Thess. 5:23. "And the God of peace himself sanctify you wholly; and may your spirit and soul and body, be preserved entire, without blame, at the coming of the Lord Jesus."
>
> 1 Cor. 3:16, 17 "Know ye not that ye are a temple of God, and that the Spirit of God dwelleth in you?" "For the temple of God is holy and such are ye."

Distinctions

4. How is Renovation distinguished from Regeneration and Justification?

Regeneration and Justification are acts of God alone; Renovation, an act of God in which the regenerate concur, through powers given in the new birth. Regeneration presupposes that its subject has been, up to the act, entirely dead in sin; Justification, that he is guilty, and needs forgiveness and believes in Christ; Renewal, that he has been already regenerated and justified. Regeneration is directed alone to the gift of faith; Justification, to the gift of imputed, and Sanctification, to that of inherent righteousness. Regeneration consists in the granting of a new life principle; Justification, in the forgiveness of sins, and the bestowal of Christ's righteousness; Renovation, in the restoration of the image of God, begun in this life, and completed in the life to come. Regeneration and Justification are instantaneous; Renovation gradual.

The distinction is carefully drawn by Paul in Titus 3:5, "the washing of regeneration and renewing of the Holy Spirit"

Two sides

5. What are the two sides of Renewal?

Both are comprised in Eph. 4:22, 23, 24.

> "That ye put away as concerning your former manner of life, the old man, that waxeth corrupt after the lusts of deceit, and that ye be renewed in the spirit of your mind, and put on the new man, that after God hath been created in righteousness and holiness of truth." The "old man" refers to the remnants of the corrupt nature in all parts and powers of the regenerate man, darkness and perversity of intellect, disordered affections, emotions, appetites, the self-centered disposition of man; the new man is the restored image of God. (See Chapter VII, 26 sqq.)

Condition of "the Old Man"

6. What is the condition of the old man?

He has lost the sovereignty and has received his deathblow (Rom. 6:6) but dies slowly, and with powerful struggles in which he endeavors to regain the ascendancy. A detailed description of this conflict is given in Rom. 7.

7. Give a few Confessional statements?

> "But what is the old man? It is that which is born in us from Adam, malicious, hateful, envious, lascivious, avaricious, indolent, haughty, yea unbelieving, infected with all vices and having by nature nothing good in it. Whenever we are received into the kingdom of Christ, these things must daily decrease, that we daily become more gentle, more patient, more meek, and ever withdrawn more and more from unbelief, avarice, hatred, envy, haughtiness" (Large Catechism, 474).

> "They maintain a constant struggle against the old Adam; for like an intractable, pugnacious, obstinate animal, he is still a part of them, and must be coerced to the obedience of Christ, not only by the doctrine and threats of the Law, but also oftentimes by the club of punishments and troubles until the sinful flesh is entirely put off, and man is perfectly renewed in the resurrection, where he needs no longer either the preaching of the Law, or its threats and reproofs, as also no longer the Gospel; as these belong to this mortal, imperfect life" (Formula of Concord, 599).

As related to various parts of our nature

8. How does Renewal affect the various parts of our nature?

The intellect (Col. 3:10) "Renewed unto knowledge"; the will, which is liberated (Rom. 8:2; Gal. 4:7; 2 Cor. 3:17; Rom. 6:17), and seeks God's will as its supreme object (1 John 5:2; Gal. 5:24); the desires and affections (Col. 3:2); all powers of body and soul (Rom. 12:1; 6:12, 13; 1 Cor. 6:20); life in all its relations (1 Cor. 10:31; Col. 3:17).

Its Active Principle

9. What is the active principle of Renovation?

Love. 1 Tim. 1:5 and the entire 13th chapter of First Corinthians, i.e., love towards God (1 John 4:19 sq.), exercising itself in love to our fellow-men (1 John 4:1116; John 13:14), and thus fulfilling the Law (Matt. 22:37-40; Rom. 13:10). A very ample discussion of this subject is found in the "Apology," Chapter 3, "Love and the Fulfilling of the Law," pp. 104-161.

The Divine Side

10. Under Question 4 it was stated that Renovation is a work of God and man cooperating. State this more fully.

God not only begins but completes the work of grace in man (Phil. 1:6; 1 Thess. 5:23; John 17:17; 15:4; Eph. 5:25, 26). While in the passages just cited, the work of sanctification is referred to Father and Son, it is referred in a peculiar sense to the Holy Spirit (2 Thess. 2:13; 1 Peter 1:2; Rom. 15:16; Titus 3:5, etc.).

The Means: Word and Sacraments according, each, to its peculiar sphere; Modes in which the Means are applied

11. Through what means is Renewal or Sanctification wrought?

Through the Word and Sacraments. The Word of the Law reveals the remnants of sin still inhering in the regenerate (Rom. 7'.y Gal. 5:17), and declares the way in which God would have them walk (Ps. 119:105; 1:2; Heb. 8:10). The Word of the Gospel stimulates to the practice of particular virtues (1 Peter 4:1; 2:21; Phil. 2:4, 5; 2 Cor. 5:14; 1 Cor. 15:58; 1 John 4:10, 1 1; 3:3). The Gospel nourishes love through which the renewal progresses.

The Sacraments are means of sealing and-individualizing the general promise of the Gospel. Thus Baptism becomes a washing of renewal, as well as of regeneration (Titus 3:5), and the Lord's Supper a bond of union not only with Christ (John 15:1,5), but also with our fellow Christians (1 Cor. 10:17). The same is taught of Baptism in 1 Cor. 12:12, 13; Eph. 4:3-6. The remembrance of Baptism is an incentive to holy living (Rom. 6:4; Gal. 3:2,7; Col. 2:11, 12; 1 Peter 3:21).

12. How are these means applied?

By His Providential dealings, God continually reminds us of these means, or leads us to seek in them sources of divine strength. The trials and afflictions of life, of themselves consequences of sin, are employed to reveal to us our helplessness and to drive us to God for strength and comfort and direction. Through these experiences, long known and familiar truths acquire new meanings. Under their discipline, Christian character is deepened, or, to use Scripture language for the same thought, the fruits of the Spirit are borne (Gal. 5:22; 2 Cor. 12:7-9; Heb. 12: it; 1 Peter 1:6, 7). Hence "suffering for Christ" is called a "gift of God" (Phil. 1:29), and the Apology says:

> "Afflictions are signs to which God has added promises." The limitations, however, must be made that they profit only as they lead to the Word. To the unregenerate, they are punishment and signs of God's anger; to the regenerate, they are chastisements inflicted in love (Rom. 8:1; Heb. 12:11).

13. What follows the appropriation of the Word?

The Holy Spirit incites to prayer, and prays in and through the prayer of the child of God (Rom. 8:26) whether the prayer be expressed in words, or be only the earnest desire awakened by some divine promise, and directed towards God in humble submission to His will. Thus there is no wish or purpose of the regenerate that is independent of the promptings of the Holy Spirit within them (Gal. 5:22, 25; 2 Cor. 10:5; John 15:4; Gal. 2:20).

The Human Side

14. Has man no part to perform in Renovation?

Yes.

He cooperates through the new powers given in regeneration. Yet these new powers are not left to their independent exercise. They are stimulated and pervaded by the divine energy and presence. The Holy Spirit acts in man by influencing his will, and making man willing to do God's will, even filling him with delight in doing God's commands. Thus all man's energies respond to God's will, and he "works out his own salvation," while "God works in him to will to do" (Phil. 2:12, 13). "By the grace of God" ("yet not I, but the grace of God in me," 1 Cor. 15:10), men become "zealous of good works" (Titus 2:14), "purify themselves" (1 Peter 1:22), and "perfect holiness" (2 Cor. 7:1).

Prayer and Renovation

15. In what act of man does this appear?

In prayer, which is the beginning, middle and end of all man's appropriation of God's word and of the activities that follow (Phil. 4:6). Prayer is the voice of faith, taking to one's self a promise of God, and claiming that, for Christ's sake, it be fulfilled. It pervades the entire Christian life.

> 1 Thess. 5:17. "Pray without ceasing."
>
> Rom. 12:12. "Continuing steadfastly in prayer."
>
> Matt. 7:7. "Ask, seek, knock."

It affords the energy for all the duties of that life from the word which it appropriates and pleads (James 5:13, 16; 4:2, last clause).

All its efficacy is in the faith which it expresses (James 1:6; 5:15; Heb. 11:6), but all the efficacy of faith is that of the word of promise which God has offered, and it has apprehended, and for whose fulfillment it asks.

> 1 John 5:15. "If we know that he heareth us whatsoever we ask, we know that we 1 have the petitions which we have asked of him."

> John 14:13. "Whatsoever ye shall ask in my name, that will I do." 16:23. Requests to God for objects not included directly or indirectly in His promises are not prayers.

16. What, therefore, are the elements of Prayer?

[A.] The consciousness of reconciliation with God.

How can one call upon God in faith "while one knows that He is terribly angry, and is oppressing us with temporal and perpetual calamities?" (Apology, 104.)

[B.] The founding of all requests upon the name of Christ, i.e., when we look to Christ as the only Mediator, through whose intercession we approach the Throne of Grace with confidence. (See above, 15.)

[C.] A sure word of promise.

[D.] Unhesitating confidence that such promise will be fulfilled.

> James 1:6, 7. "Let him ask in faith nothing doubting; for he that doubteth is like the surge of the sea driven by the wind and tossed; for let not that man think that he shall receive anything of the Lord."

[E.] Unreserved submission to the will of God, as to how the prayer be answered.

[F.] The pleading of the promise with God.

It is also to be remembered that "prayer is much more than petition, which is only one department of it; it is nothing less than the whole spiritual action of the soul turned towards God as its true and adequate object." It "is man's inmost movement towards a Higher Power." "Prayer is emphatically religion in action" (Liddon).

17. Is prayer always an act?

Like faith and love, it is also a habit, which produces acts.

> 1 Thess. 5:17. "Pray without ceasing."

Gradual

18. Is Renewal or Sanctification instantaneous?

The struggle as described in Rom. 7 very clearly points to a gradual process. In Col. 1:9-11, an increase of spiritual gifts is prayed for those who had already experienced a renewal (3:9, 10). So on the positive side. 2 Cor. 4:16. "Our inward man is renewed day by day." 3:18. "Beholding, as in a mirror the glory of the Lord, we are transformed into the same image from glory to glory."

Perfection and Perfectionism

19. Does it ever reach perfection in this life?

No one, in this life, can reach a standard which is beyond that of those who are to use the Lord's Prayer; and in it, with the petition for "daily bread," we also ask for "the forgiveness of sins."

> 1 John 1:8. "If we say that we have no sin, we deceive ourselves and the truth is not in us."
>
> James 3:2. "For in many things we all stumble."
>
> Ps. 19:12. "Who can discern his errors; cleanse thou me from hidden faults."

20. To what passages of Scripture do the advocates of Perfectionism appeal, and how are they answered?

They cite:

[a.] 1 John 2:5. "Whoso keepeth his Word, in him verily hath the love of God been perfected."

Our answer is that this means that the love of God is perfected in the degree that the Word is kept. This is the high ideal after which every Christian must aim, although it is unattainable in this world.

[b.] 1 John 4:17. "Herein is love made perfect with us."

This is again a statement of the goal towards which love is directed. This goal the succeeding clause finds attained "in the day of judgment." The words & tout& reTsXeiwrat, mean literally:

"In this has it reached its goal."

[c.] 1 John 3:9. "Whoso is born of God doeth no sin, because his seed abideth in him, and he cannot sin, because he is begotten of God."

Here we distinguish between the "doing" of sin consciously and deliberately, and 'the "having" of sin in the remnants of the old nature, and the actual sins resulting, over which one constantly mourns and against which he struggles. "So long as regeneration and the seed of God remain, he cannot sin. He may lose his regeneration and sin; but as long as the seed of God remain in us, it does not admit sin. This seed is in the heart, and it keeps Christ in your heart, so that you do not desire to sin. If you see an outward object that suggests the thought, it says: 'Brother, brother, dismiss that thought; for you are born of God.' Sin allures, it grumbles, it would like to be master; but your will shall not be brought into subjection. Christ is not asleep, but is stronger than the strong man." (Luther), who has been quoted also as saying:

> "A child of God in this conflict receives wounds daily, but never throws away his arms or makes peace with his deadly foe. Sin is ever active, but no longer dominant; the normal direction of life's energies is against sin, is an absence of sin, a no-will-to-sin, a no-power-to-sin."

These passages must all be interpreted so as to harmonize with the most clear and explicit statement of I John 1:8:

"If we say that we have no sin, we deceive ourselves, and the truth is not in us."

21. Is there any disparagement by this of perfection itself?

No. It is the standard towards which the Christian must constantly strive (Matt. 5:18). All that falls short of it, is sin.

22. How do the advocates of Perfectionism sometimes define their position?

By lowering the standard of the divine law, so as to regard it as demanding only the highest degree possible; for, they urge, God does not demand impossibilities. An act, they concede, falls short of God's strict commands; but they apologize for it upon the ground that the standard is lowered to the level of human weakness. The spirituality of the law is overlooked, and the comprehensiveness of the obedience (Gal. 3:10) it requires is forgotten. Man's righteousness is made to consist in a fulfillment of Law which an indulgent God is imagined to accommodate to man's weakness.

Office of Good Works

23. What is the Relation of Good Works to Renovation?

They are both instrumentalities and fruits of Renovation.[8]

24. What do you mean by calling them "instrumentalities"?

That the new spiritual life given in regeneration develops as it is exercised. Christian character is matured and strengthened as man becomes an organ through which the Holy Spirit works. It is a law of our nature that the repetition of acts which at first require much effort, results in a habit in which the consciousness of effort vanishes. They are thus said to become "a second nature." So with the various virtues and duties of the Christian life. Through the new powers given in regeneration, the Holy Spirit cooperating, man is enabled more and more to bring himself under control, and devote all his energies to God's service. Each act of the new obedience not only influences his future ability to bring forth similar fruits, but, taken together they act upon his entire spiritual condition.

How Good Works are produced

25. How, then, does the Holy Spirit renew men?

Not simply by the infusion of spiritual qualities, while they are passive, but by dwelling within them, and, as a life-force, stimulating the regenerate to the exercise of all the gifts given them.[9]

> Luke 19:13. "He gave them ten pounds and said unto them, Trade ye herewith till I come."

Unemployed talents, unexercised gifts and graces are taken away; talents employed and exercised are multiplied (Matt. 25:28, 29). The possession of a truth which is not confessed or of endowments that are not used for the profit of our fellow-men, or the withholding of our activities from objects to which the Holy

8 Partim ut finis et effectus ad renovationem se habent, partim ad rationem formalem ejus spectant. — (Baier.)

9 Per quae ad incrementum spiritualium virium tenditur. — (Baier.)

Spirit prompts, leads to their removal, just as in the body there is an atrophy of the muscles, when members are long disused.

26. What warning does Scripture give?

Passages concerning "hardening of the heart," of which Heb. 3:7-12 is a type, refer not simply to the formal rejection of the claims and comfort of the Gospel, but rather to the neglect of manifest duties, and the contentment with lower planes of Christian living, when higher ideals are clearly in sight. Of this, we are warned in 1 Thess. 5:19. "Quench not the Spirit."

27. How are Good Works fruits of Renovation?

No better explanation can be given than that of the Apology (104 sqq.):

> "Because faith brings the Holy Ghost and produces in our hearts a new life, it must produce spiritual movements in hearts. This is shown in Jer. 31:33, I will put my law in their inward parts, and in their heart will I write it.' ... The law cannot be kept without Christ; neither can it be kept without the Holy Ghost; and the Holy Ghost is received only by faith." "God is not loved, until we apprehend His mercy in Christ," and without love there are no good works, for they spring, as Gal. 5:6 declares, from "faith working through love" (1 Tim. 1:5). (See also Chapter 17. 31-34)

Good Works defined, and the definition explained clause by clause:

> "Acts," "Free," "the Law, the standard," "the light in which Law is seen" "the motive"

28. Give a definition of Good Works.

The definition of Good Works, at the time of the Reformation, ranked next only to that of "Justification" and "Faith."

Every word in the following definition is significant:

> "Good Works are the free acts of justified persons, rendered according to the standard of the divine law, and with the light afforded by true faith in Christ, to the glory of God and the edification of man" (Hollaz).

29. Explain the term "free acts."

"Acts" denote not only external works ("actions") but also internal movements of the heart and will, the exercise of the affections, the purposes and designs of the mind.

They are "free acts," because wrought by man's free or liberated will. Man's heart is in their production; so that, just to the extent that renovation has progressed, he is unconscious of the effort involved. It has become as natural for him to do good works, as it is to breathe—an act of which he is rarely conscious unless something be wrong.

> "He does everything, so far as he is born anew, out of a free and cheerful spirit; and this is called not properly 'a work of the law,' but 'a fruit of the Spirit or, as Paul names it, 'the law of the mind' and 'the law of Christ" (Formula of Concord, 598).

> "If the believing children of God would be completely renewed, they would, of themselves, do what they are in duty bound to do; just as sun, moon and all the constellations of heaven have their regular course according to the arrangement which God once gave them, or just as the holy angels render an entirely voluntary obedience" (ibid., 596).

In the General Collect of the "Common Service," we pray, "O God, whose service is perfect freedom," and at the close of Vespers "that our hearts may be set to obey Thy commandments." Good Works, therefore, are free, not because it is a matter of indifference whether they be done, or because there is any absence of obligation to do them, but because they are free from external constraint. All the constraint comes from within. The new nature cannot do otherwise than express itself thus. (See Chapter 17, 33.) They are necessary "because of God's command and our debt." See also Augsburg Confession, Arts. VI, XX.

30. How has the principle here stated been paradoxically expressed?

By Luther, in one of the simplest, but yet, next to the Small Catechism, the greatest of his books, his "Liberty of a Christian Man," which is devoted to the discussion of two theses:

> "I. A Christian man is the most free lord of all and subject to none.

> "II. A Christian man is the most dutiful servant of all, and subject to every one."
>
> "By faith, he rises above himself to God; by love, he sinks below himself to his neighbor."

A distinguished American preacher (Phillips Brooks) has phrased the same thought thus:

> "The purpose and result of freedom is service. It sounds to us at first like a contradiction, a paradox. God frees our souls not from service, not from duty, but into service and duty.... The freedom of a man consists in the larger opportunity to be and to do all that God makes him capable of being and doing" (Address, "Beauty of a Life of Service").

31. But are there no Good Works before justification?

> "Civil works, i.e., the outward works of the Law can be done in a measure, without Christ and without the Holy Ghost, nevertheless those things which belong peculiarly to the divine Law, i.e., the affections of the heart toward God which are commanded in the First Table cannot be rendered without the Holy Ghost" (Apology, 105).
>
> "Man's will has some liberty for the attainment of civil righteousness, and for the choice of things subject to reason. Nevertheless it has no power without the Holy Ghost, to work the righteousness of God... Although nature is able in some sort to do the outward work (for it is able to keep the hands from theft and murder) yet it cannot work the inward motions, such as the fear of God, trust in God, chastity, patience, etc." (Augsburg Confession, Art. XVIII).
>
> "Good works do not make a good man, but a good man does good works. Bad works do not make a bad man, but a bad man does bad works. As trees exist before their fruit, and as the fruit does not make a tree either good or bad, but, on the contrary, a tree of either kind produces fruit of the same kind; so the person of the man must be good or bad before he can do either a good or a bad work. A bad or a good house does not make a bad or a good carpenter, but a good or a bad carpenter makes a bad or a good house" (Luther, on "Liberty of a Christian Man").

32. In saying that "Good Works are wrought according to the standard of the divine Law," what errors are rejected?

[A.] That conscience is the standard. Conscience, our theologians say, is not a *norma normans*, but a *norma normata.*

It is like a watch which must itself be set according to the sun. Conscience must constantly be brought to the standard of the Law, in order that its errors be corrected (1 Cor. 4:4).

[B.] That the Gospel is the standard.

For it is the office of the Gospel to declare the promise of free grace. Incidentally it cooperates with the Law by affording the power to do good works (1 Tim. 1:5), i.e., with the promise the Holy Spirit is given, through whom good works are wrought. But even to the regenerate, the Law alone remains the standard. This will be treated under "The Third Use of the Law" (Chapter 25, 25).

[C.] That there is any standard beyond or in addition to the Law.

Rome teaches that beside the Law, there are so-called "evangelical counsels." The Law, it is taught, prescribes only what one is in duty bound to do; but that man can earn merit by complying with certain rules which, nevertheless, may be omitted without sin. Works done according to such counsels (particularly, according to the vows of poverty, celibacy and obedience) are called "works of supererogation." Through them, a treasury or fund of superabundant merits is formed, from which the Church can draw, in order to abbreviate the required satisfaction in Purgatory. But against this is

> Luke 17:10. "When ye shall have done all the things that are commanded you, say, We are unprofitable servants; we have done that which it was our duty to do."

Mark 7:9-13 shows that this was the fundamental error of Pharisaism. Manifest duties prescribed in the Ten Commandments were neglected, in order to attain an imaginary higher holiness taught by traditions.

Against this, the Reformers maintained that any requirement not directly or indirectly taught in the Ten Commandments could not be the standard of any good work.

> "Outside of the Ten Commandments, no work or thing can be pleasing to God, however great or precious it be in the eyes of the world" (Large Catechism, 435).

33. What favorite illustration was used by the Reformers?

Luther on Genesis (Erlangen ed., Latin, 6, 132), as well as Melanchthon in the Apology (288), tells a story of St. Anthony, the Eastern monk. He dreamed of a shoemaker of Alexandria who was to have in the next world a degree of glory equal to that to be allotted him. With much concern, he went to Alexandria, to learn what remarkable life this eminent saint could be living. To his surprise, he found him earning a livelihood for himself and family by the work of his hands. Anthony found him, and asked:

> "Some things about you I want to know. What are you doing? What are you eating and drinking? How do you pray? When do you pray? Do you keep awake whole nights and devote them to prayer?" The answer was:
>
> "Nothing at all like this. Every morning and night I thank God for His faithful care and protection; I pray for the forgiveness of all my sins through Christ, and earnestly beseech Him to govern me by His Spirit, and not permit me to fall into temptation. Then, I devote myself to my trade, and work for my family and myself. There is nothing more, except that I strive daily to do nothing contrary to conscience."
>
> "When Anthony heard this," continues Luther, "he was surprised and learned that self-chosen rites are no worship. No mean garments, no coarse fare, no fasts, no long prayers, no vigils, nor any other works can profit with respect to everlasting life."

34. Why does the definition add, "with the light afforded by true faith in Christ"?

Because of the need of spiritual illumination. (See Chapter 20.) The veil which obscures the full force of the Law must be removed. (See Formula of Concord, 507. 591.)

35. Why does it conclude with the words "to the glory of God and the edification of men"?

Because all free acts of justified persons, rendered according to the standard of the Divine Law, and with the light afforded by faith in Christ, have this end. "His works are to be done freely with the sole object of pleasing God" (Luther). (Matt. 5:16; 1 Cor. 10:31; 14:12; Rom. 1:14.)

In what sense any works are good

36. But can any works meet this standard?

No works can be done with the perfection which the Law demands.

> Deut. 6:5. "Thou shalt love Jehovah thy God, with all thy heart, and with all thy soul, and with all thy mind."
>
> Gal. 5:17. "For the flesh lusteth against the Spirit, and the Spirit against the flesh, so that ye may not do the things that ye would."
>
> Is. 64:6. "All our righteousnesses are as a polluted garment."
>
> "Neither are they rendered with the promptness and alacrity that is due, but we work very sluggishly, or we defile them by the intervention or attendance of inordinate self-consciousness" (Baier).

37. How then can they be called "Good Works"?

Only relatively; and yet they are really good, because they are wrought by those with whom God in Christ is reconciled, and are the fruits of the Holy Spirit working in regenerate hearts.

38. How is this confessionally expressed?

> "They are holy, divine works, sacrifices and acts, pertaining to the government of Christ, who thus displays His kingdom to the world... . The dangers, labors and sufferings of the Apostle Paul, of Athanasius, Augustine, etc, are holy works, are true sacrifices acceptable to God, are contests of Christ, through which He repressed the devil. David's labors in waging wars and in the administration of the State, are holy works, are true sacrifices, are contests of God, defending the people who have the Word of God, in order that His knowledge may not be entirely extinguished on earth. We think this also concerning every good work in the humblest callings and in private persons. Through these works, Christ celebrates His victory over the devil" (Apology, 115 sqq.).

> "The commandments of God according to each one's calling, viz., that the father brought up his family, that the mother bore children, that the Prince governed the commonwealth" (Augsburg Confession, Art. XXVI).

The question of Rewards

39. Are Good Works rewards?

Forgiveness of sins, salvation and eternal life are given gratuitously through faith on account of Christ. They are entirely and exclusively the rewards of Christ's fulfillment of the Law, and never, nor in any way, of Good Works. But to those who, on account of Christ, receive forgiveness of sins, life and salvation, rewards are offered, not of merit, but from God's free grace, to the awarding of which He is bound only by His promise.

40. How has this been explained?

> "Forgiveness of sins, reconciliation with God, salvation and eternal life do not depend upon our merits; but they are given gratuitously, because of the merit and obedience of the Son of God, and are received by faith. But in those who have been reconciled, rewards, spiritual and bodily, in this life and after this life are ascribed to Good Works, inasmuch as by faith on account of the Mediator they please God; and that from the gratuitous divine promise, not that God is debtor, because of the perfection and worth of our works, but, because of His paternal liberality and mercy for Christ's sake, He has promised that the obedience of His children in this life, however rudimentary, languid, imperfect and impure, He will reward" (Chemnitz).

41. Do the Lutheran Confessions teach such doctrine?

Yes.

> "If the adversaries will concede that we are accounted righteous by faith because of Christ, and that Good Works please because of Christ, we will not contend much concerning the term, 'reward.' ...We confess what we have often testified that although justification and eternal life pertain to faith, nevertheless Good Works merit other bodily and spiritual rewards, and degrees of rewards, according to 1 Cor. 3:8, 'Every man shall receive his

> own reward according to his own labor.' ...Because men are accepted on account of faith, for this very reason, the inchoate fulfilling of the law pleases, and has a reward in this world and the next" (Apology, X 53 sqq.).

42. But does not the Apology go too far in saying that they "merit" these rewards?

The connection shows the sense in which it is used, and that it is not "a reward of debt," but "of grace" (Rom. 4:4), that is meant. To avoid all misunderstanding, it is better to say as above (Q. 37), that "rewards are offered, not of merit, but of God's free grace."

43. Give some Scripture proofs.

We may begin with the Fourth Commandment; then also

> 1 Tim. 4:8. "Godliness is profitable for all things, having promise of the life which now is and that which is to come."
>
> Luke 14:14. "Thou shalt be recompensed in the resurrection of the just."
>
> Gal. 6:9. "In due season, we shall reap, if we faint not." Deut. 28:1-14.

Scripture is full of such promises.

44. But is there not a difference of rewards?

> "There will be different rewards, according to different labors. But the remission of sins is equal and alike to all" (Apology, 116).

The rewards of the justified are *secundum opera*, not *propter opera*.

24. The Word As The Means Of Grace

Reference to previous statements

1. In the treatment of the various acts of the Applying Grace of the Holy Spirit, what has been a most prominent feature of them all?

The fact that they are wrought through means. (See Chapter 19, The Call, 2, 6, 7, 8, 14; Chapter 20, Illumination, 11, 12, 14; Chapter 21, Regeneration, 10-12, 38; Chapter XXII, Renewal, 11-14.) The confessional statements are found in Augsburg Confession, Art. 5:28:10; Apology, 170:36; 215:13; Schmalkald Articles, 33 2:3; 333: Io; Large Catechism, 444:42; Formula of Concord, 497:4; 552:4; 555:16; 561:48; 562:50; 662:76; 669:30.

Is the doctrine of Means a limitation of God's sovereignty

2. Is it not a limitation of God's sovereignty and power to affirm that these acts are accomplished only through means?

Theology does not deal with divine possibilities, but with what God has revealed concerning Himself and His various forms of activity. Not only have we no promise of His intervention otherwise, but He constantly turns us away from any expectation of such aid to the simple means, in' and through which He promises to be always found with His entire efficacy.

Are Means ever dispensed with

3. But in extraordinary cases, does He not dispense with means?

Even there, means are employed; but in an extraordinary way. At Pentecost the multitudes were converted through the Word, although this Word was given under extraordinary conditions and circumstances, just as the multitudes in the wilderness were sustained not without bread, but with bread furnished in an extraordinary manner.

Relative position of the Word and the Sacraments

4. Are not these means variously designated?

Sometimes Word and Sacraments are said to be these means; as in Augsburg Confession, Art. V:

> "Through the Word and Sacraments, as through instruments, the Holy Ghost is given." At other times, the Word alone is mentioned, as in the Schmalkald Articles, 332:3:
>
> "God grants His Spirit and grace to no one, except through or with the preceding outward Word' At still other times, it is"the preaching of the Word" (Formula of Concord, 566:71), or "the daily reading of the Word" (ibid. 555:16), that is mentioned. This diversity appears equally in Holy Scripture. Thus in 1 Peter 1:23, the new birth is ascribed to the Holy Spirit working through the Word, while in John 3:5 it is referred to His work through baptism.

5. How are these statements harmonized?

By regarding the Word as the only proper Means of Grace, and recognizing it as coming to men in two different forms. Sometimes it reaches us, without any external rite or ceremony, as when preached or read (Rom. 10:8); sometimes, accompanied by a divinely ordained ceremony, in the Sacraments (Eph. 5:26). This determines the distinction between the Audible and the Visible Word.

What is the Word

6. But what is the Word?

In its widest sense, it is the entire revelation which God has made of Himself for man's salvation. In its stricter sense, it is the assurance of the grace of God in Christ, preceded by the assertion of God's claims and the revelation of man's sin and need, and followed by knowledge imparted for the support, comfort, defense and growth of faith unto life everlasting.

> Rom. 10:8, 9. "The word is nigh thee, in thy mouth and in thy heart; that is the word of faith which we preach, that it thou shalt confess with thy mouth, Jesus as Lord, and shall believe in thy heart that God raised him from the dead, thou shalt be saved.

'The soul can do without everything except the Word of God... . But you will ask: 'What is this Word, and by what means is it to be used, since there are so many words of God?' I answer that the Apostle Paul explains what it is, namely the Gospel of God concerning His Son, incarnate, suffering, risen, glorified" (Luther, Liberty of a Christian Man).

The Holy Scriptures as the Record

7. Where is it to be found?

In the Holy Scriptures, as an inspired and inerrant record of revelation, and in all preaching and teaching, that accords with them as a standard (see Chapter 1, 35).

In what senses are they inspired (a) Through activity of the Holy Spirit, in and through the writers; (b) through His activity in preserving and gathering them into one volume so that one organism is the result; (c) through the presence and activity of the Holy Spirit in the communion of believers in its relation to Holy Scripture; (d) through His presence and activity in the truth which they contain even when its form is changed; (e) through the Personality of Christ in the Word; (f) through the presence and activity of the Holy Spirit whenever and wherever the Word is now used.

8. In what senses are the Holy Scriptures inspired?

[A.] Through the activity of the Holy Spirit in and through the writers, when they were written. Scripture "is inspired for it comes from God; it is human for it comes through man. But remember we do not say that the human is without the divine. The Spirit is incarnate in the Word, as the Son was incarnate in Christ. There is deep significance in the fact that the title of 'the Word' is given both to Christ, the Revealer, and to the Bible, the revelation of God, so that in some passages great critics differ as to which is meant. As Christ without confusion of natures, is truly human as well as divine, so is this Word. As the human in Christ though distinct from the divine was never separate from it, and His human acts were never those of a merely human being, His toils, His merits and His blood were those of God, so is the written Word, though most human of books, as Christ, the Son of Man, was most human of men, truly divine. Its humanities are no accidents; they are divinely planned. It is essential to God's conception of this Book that it shall be written by these men and in this way. He created, reared, made and chose these men and inspired them to do this thing in their way, because their way was His way" (Krauth, "The Bible a Perfect Book"). The form of each particular book and statement was determined in part by the freedom and the circumstances of each writer; but back of the human composers was the divine Author who knows how to turn every element of the writer's freedom and limitations into account for his purposes, just as in Providence, not a sparrow falls without its significance in God's world-plan. "They were moved not by being deprived of their own mind (like the 'enthusiasm' the heathen imagined in their prophets), but because they attempted nothing of themselves, but only followed the Spirit obediently as their guide" (Calvin, on 1 Peter 1:20).

[B.] Through the activity of the Holy Spirit in preserving and gathering the Scriptures into one volume, in which one part is adjusted to another, so that the contribution of each writer finds its place in one organism. They are no mere library of books that have been accidentally collected, but they form one inwardly united whole, in which they mutually interpret each other. "How marvelous is the harmony between the beginning and the end of Holy Scripture, from the creation of the heavens and the earth, to the new heaven and the new earth of the world to come! And the entire course from that beginning to that end is a great, progressive and connected whole. Notwithstanding the different ages in which they were written, the diverse relations and circumstances, the varieties in station and culture of their writers, one thought pervades all, from beginning to end there is but one purpose" (Luthardt, "Glaubenslehre"). Tota Scriptara sacra, units liber dicitur, quia uno Spirita scripta est (Jerome, on Is. 29). 'They who wrote the several parts often knew nothing of each other; they knew nothing of that whole for which they were laboring. Neither accident nor human intention brought this to pass, but a higher Spirit. Scripture is a wonderful structure — a structure for which there must have been an architect. It is the ruling mind that knows how to utilize and combine individual efforts" (Luthardt, "Saving Truths of Christianity," 211 sqq.). "Not only are the various writings, when considered separately worthy of God, but they together exhibit one complete and harmonious body, unimpaired by excess or defects" (Bengel). "Why take many lutes and pipes, unless revelation were designed to be symphony as well as melody, whose unity should not be that of the simple strain, but that by which the Great Composer pours His own divine spirit of music into many parts, whilst wind and touch on instruments faithful to their own nature, unite in 'Creation' or 'Messiah,' to form what is at once truly theirs, and, because such, truly His?" (Krauth).

If, then, no part or passage of Holy Scripture can be properly understood, except when examined in the light shed upon it by all other parts, and regarded in its peculiar place in the entire canon, and if the collection of this canon was a gradual process continuing throughout centuries, the activity of the Holy Spirit which we call "inspiration" was not confined to the mere act of the composition of each book separately.

[C.] This leads us to a further statement as to this process. The result attained was through the presence of the Holy Spirit in the communion of believers or Christian Church in its proper sense. The promise is:

> "The Word of the Lord abideth forever" (1 Peter 1:25). But the way in which God accomplishes this, is by the establishment of an organism, which accepts and perpetuates this word, and works through it. It is in this sense that the Church is called "the pillar and ground of the truth" (1 Tim. 3:15). Here we must constantly turn from the superficial view of the Church as an external body, with legislative functions and traditional authority, to the Church as the united number of those who, being true believers, constitute the one body of Christ, "the circle of humanity within which God inwardly dwells," and "the true beginning of the Kingdom of God on earth" (Kahler).

Its members, individually and collectively have the promise that Christ will ever be with them (Matt. 18:20; 28:20), and that the Holy Spirit will also abide with them, and lead them into all truth (John 14:26; 15:26, 27; 16:13). This presence of the Holy Spirit imparts a new faculty to every one who receives Him (1 Cor. 2:14, 15). The Spirit in the heart of each believer and the Spirit in Holy Scripture correspond and harmonize (Rom. 8:16). Endowed with this new spiritual sense, they accurately discriminate between that which comes and does not come from God, for Christ says (John 10:4, 5), 'The sheep follow him; for they know his voice; and a stranger will they not follow, for they know not the voice of strangers." As Luther says on John 7:14, "A Christian soon scents out from afar where God's Word is or where human doctrine, which one speaks of himself, is" (Erlangen ed., 48:144).

The Divine Architect, therefore, of the wonderful structure of Holy Scripture, described under (b), has brought it together, part by part, and maintained it, not by the decree of any councils, whether of Laodicea or any other, or the resolution of any synods or the decisions of any theologians, or even by a long line of external witnesses, but by His work, as "Author and Architect in the hearts of the godly," as Flacius* terms it. He "turns man's heart whithersoever he will" (Prov. 21:1).

The gradual formation of the canon of Scripture and its separation as something distinct from other books is, thus, the product of a true inspiration pervading the community of believers as a whole unto the end of time.

Such inspiration is not the enthusiasm of ultra Mysticism, condemned in Art. V of the Augsburg Confession, but is the result of the work of the Holy Spirit through the Word, previously received and laid to heart and assimilated and acting within individual men. Spirit and Word, or Word and Spirit are never separated. But the elementary stages in their joint work are the basis for their gifts in ampler measure. Through the impulse, therefore, of the Holy Spirit, working by the Word, first in the individual believer, and then uniting all in manifold testimonies conspiring to one end, there is a concurrence of numberless factors to results far above the intentional effort of anyone when he wrote. In time, false and spurious books are lost or lose their assumed authority, because the religious life of believers has no use for them, while others, from generation to generation, stand the test, not of mere scholarly research — a subordinate factor — but of religious value to souls illumined by God's Spirit, viz., of the true Church. This has been well stated by Claus Harms in the fifth of his "Sermons on the Bible" (Kiel, 1842):

> "Believing men endowed with the spirit of investigation and discrimination, and externally as well as internally called to the work have made their decision; they have rejected and they have accepted. What they have recognized and received as the pure Word of God, they have brought together and transmitted to the congregation of believers for reading. Thus both the Old and the New Testament, each, became a book, not blown together by the wind, but constructed by the Spirit, who, being f Tractatus vii:6s8; 1:63. invoked, and acting upon believing men, has made out of no less than eighty separate writings one writing. It is in this sense, we say that the Bible has been brought us by the Church."

[D.] Through the activity of the Holy Spirit in the divine truth which they contain, or which has been drawn directly or indirectly from these "pure fountains of Israel." For this truth is so independent of the precise form in which it was first presented, that, when expressed in other words, it is no less inspired than before. The manner in which Old Testament passages are quoted in the New will illustrate this. The New Testament writers, under the guidance of inspiration often rise above the letter of an Old Testament text, so as to penetrate its very heart and catch its spirit, rather than to be bound to a merely mechanical repetition of its very words. For although every word be prized, yet after all, as Flacius remarks, words are, "signa tantum et umbrae" and valuable only as they stand for "res," i.e., realities (Tractatus 5:480).

[E.] Through the personality of Christ, in the Word, as this is brought into closest contact with the reader. The heart of Holy Scripture is revealed truth, i.e., those truths which man cannot learn by his natural powers, and the heart of all revealed truth is Jesus Christ.

> John 20:31. "These are written, that ye may believe that Jesus is the Christ, the Son of God, and that believing, ye may have life in his name." — Cf. John 5:39.

Luther paraphrases John 5:39:

> "See that ye so study the Scriptures as to seek and find me in them. He who reads them so as to find me in them is the true master of Scripture, the dust is away from his eyes, and he will certainly find in them eternal life. But whosoever does not find me there, he has not studied or understood them aright, and does not have eternal life. Even though he were to read them a thousand times, and were to continually turn their pages, all would be to no purpose" (Erlangen ed., 19:92). So also in the well-known comment on the Epistle of James:
>
> "The true touchstone by which to test all books is to notice whether or not they are occupied with Christ, since all Scripture testifies of Christ (Rom. 3:21), and St. Paul wants to know of nothing but Christ (1 Cor. 2:2). What does not teach Christ is not apostolical, even though St. Peter or Paul teach it. On the other hand, whatever preaches Christ is truly apostolical, even though this be done by Judas, Annas, Pilate or Herod" (ibid. 63:157).
>
> "The Christian does not have faith in Christ because he believes that Scripture is divinely inspired, but he believes that Scripture is divinely inspired, because through the truth revealed in it, he has attained to faith in Christ" (Th. Harnack, "Canon and Inspiration," p. 351).

It is according to this standard that the Protestant Churches reject the Apocrypha; for these books bear no testimony concerning Christ, and Christ bears no testimony concerning them.

[F.] Through the activity of the Holy Spirit with and in all who read or hear the Word today. It is a never failing fountain of divine life and energy (Heb. 4:12). Viva dei voluntas Spiritus Sanctus est (Melanchthon, "Loci Communes"). Life means activity (see Chapter ii, 46). "Scripture was divinely inspired not only while it was being written, God breathing through the writers, but also while it is being read, God breathing through the Scriptures, and the Scriptures breathing Him" (Bengel). It is not simply a store-house of information concerning God; it is the revelation of God Himself. It is not simply a series of declarations as to how God spoke of old; in it God still speaks. We read not simply of the way, but we find there the very life of God Himself. The great Author of Holy Scripture remained in and with it, when the writers through whom He wrote laid down their pens and departed from this world, some of them not understanding as well as others who were to follow them (i Peter 1:11), the subjects which they treated and, therefore, their own statements. He whose real message it is, sees that it reaches the end for which He prepared it, and attends it with His illuminating and regenerating power. It is inspired because through it there is the direct touch of God upon man's soul.

The Supreme Test of Holy Scripture

9. What, then, is the supreme test of the claims of Scripture, or of any portion or book of Scripture?

Not literary-historical criticism, but the religious use of Scripture, i.e., its office and fruits as a Means of Grace. For if literary-historical criticism were the supreme test, then only the limited few who would have access to historical sources and would have the requisite literary training, could be judges. In view of constant progress in the collection of new sources of information and the adoption of improved scientific methods, each generation successively would discredit the results of those before it. The criticism of the beginning of the Twentieth Century will be an anachronism before the next century opens. But the test is to be made by the humblest of men. The Word of God and its inerrant record are not simply for the aristocracy of science but are intended for all. "Erudition has never had the key to the Kingdom of Heaven" (Tischendorf). Scholar and peasant, the most cultivated and the most illiterate, meet here on an even footing. It is a radical error to elevate men who have no higher than linguistic attainments to the chair of judges in regard to the real meaning and purpose of Scripture. As unquestioned attainments in the study of the English language and literature do not qualify one to be a critic and interpreter of Blackstone's Commentaries or of a treatise on physics or mathematics, or scientific music written in English; as even more than ability to read and write English with facility is necessary in order to interpret the masterpieces of English prose and poetry; so one may know Hebrew like the

Rabbis of old, or Greek like the philosophers who heard Paul on the Areopagus, without being a competent judge concerning the Old or the New Testament. Three qualifications are required of every competent translator, viz., knowledge of the language from which he translates, knowledge of the language into which he translates, and familiarity with the subject that is treated. The most advanced authority in Semitic or Aryan philology can not assume to be a very successful interpreter of such treatises, deciphered from those languages as are of a technical character. The jurist will have to aid him in regard to legal transactions, and modern medical science in regard to the primitive beginnings of its branches found in the documents which he indeed must translate. As soon as he passes beyond the limits of his own calling as a philologist, he loses his standing as a scholar. Nowhere is the classical rule, Ne sutor supra crepidam more pertinent than in Biblical Criticism.

10. But how is this religious test effective?

By the presence of the Holy Spirit, Scripture is self-evidencing.

"No human reason, no illumination beyond and above the Word, no Council, no Pope, but only the Word is the legitimate interpreter of the Word itself. If you ask the proof, the question must be declined; for the truth, sufficiency and clearness of God's Word need no proof. This is an axiom, a fundamental principle. The truth of every statement must be proved from the Word, but the Word itself derives its truth from no higher principle. That this assertion as an axiom needs no further proof comes from the fact that the Word of God is no mere Word, but because it is spirit and life... . That the Word is selfevidencing is equivalent to saying that the Spirit of God, of Whom the Word is the bearer, shows the truth of the Word to man's spirit. No one, therefore, is a competent judge of the divine origin, truth, clearness and sufficiency of the Word, unless he have experienced its enlightening and quickening power" (*Philippi*, "Symbolics," p. 327). "Scripture is its own light" (Luther, Er. ed., 15:422).

The testimony of the Spirit is superior to all reason. For as God alone is a sufficient witness in His own Word, so also the Word will never gain credit in the hearts of men, until it be confirmed by the internal testimony of the Spirit. It is necessary, therefore, that the same Spirit, who spake by the mouths of the prophets, should penetrate into our hearts, to convince us that they faithfully delivered the oracles which were committed to them... . It is an undeniable truth, that they who have been inwardly taught by the Spirit, are in entire acquiescence with Scripture, and that it is self-authenticated, carrying with it its own evidence, and ought not to be made the subject of demonstration and arguments from reason... . For the truth is vindicated from every doubt, when unassisted by foreign aid, it is sufficient for its own support. But that this is the peculiar property of

Scripture, appears from the insufficiency of any human compositions to make an equal impression on our hearts" (Calvin, "Institutes," I, Chapters VII, Viii).

To those who ask for the proof of its source, its one answer, therefore, is:

> "Come and read," and as they read, with minds intent on the truth, the Holy Spirit interprets "Every theoretical proof which may be attempted, every logical demonstration of truth, yea even the practical appeal to experience is vain, without the presupposition of a receptive organ, of a developed sensorium for the particular sphere of life that is concerned. Who can explain to the blind or even to the aesthetically unreceptive the true beauty of a painting, or bring to scientific understanding the aesthetical principles which here prevail? Who can disclose to the deaf or even to those without musical talent the deep mysteries of the great musical master-pieces? Who is in a condition to convince materialistic stupidity which regards only that which is comprehensible and sensually perceptible as true, of the overwhelming power of the, architecture of the world? The worlds of Nature and of Spirit, their reciprocally conditioning and connecting laws remain dead and unintelligible, where our sense is dead." Van Oettingens1:8. and confirms Scripture as Christ to the disciples at Emmans (Luke 24:27). It is not pure literature like the poems of Homer or history of Thucydides. It makes a personal appeal to the heart of every reader. It deals not with absolute issues, but with those of each generation, that successively comes under its influence, and of everv order of men, from the slave to the monarch. Its scope is not only as universal as human history, but it enters into every imaginable form and relation of man's experience.
>
> Heb. 4:12. "For the word of God is living and active and sharper than any two-edged sword, and piercing even to the dividing of soul and spirit, of both joints and marrow, and quick to discern the thoughts and intents of the heart."

11. Illustrate this.

The pastor of Zion's and St. Michael's congregation, Philadelphia (1779-1822) was an accomplished Hebrew scholar and Professor in the University of Pennsylvania. But when in 1793, within a few weeks he lost over six hundred of his people from yellow fever, when whole days were spent in the graveyard with one funeral crowding upon another, and while he hastened hither and thither to prepare the dying for death and to console the afflicted, and, like Moses in Num. 16:48, daily conducted a brief service in his church for those still well, but among whom the destroying angel from night to night was to find more victims, he learned more of the reality and efficacy of God's Word, than a hundred life-times of scholarly research could have ever afforded. It is in the close practical application of the Gospel to the deepest wants of men, and particularly in hours of greatest trial, that such evidence is afforded as sweeps away all doubts.* *Only two days before his death, Luther wrote at Eisleben:

"1. Virgilium in Bucolicis nemo potest intelligere, nisi fuerit quinque annis pastor. Virgilium in Georgicis nemo potest intelligere, nisi fuerit quinque annis agricola.

"2. Ciceronem in epistolis (sic praecipio) nemo integre intelligit, nisi viginti annis sit versatus in republica aliqua insigni.

"3. Scripturas sacras sciat se nemo degustasse satis, nisi centum annis cum Prophetis, ut Elia et Elisaeo, Joanne Baptista, Christo et Apostolis ecclesias gubernarit."

The Book of Psalms, for example, exists not simply as a collection of hymns for the worship of Jews in olden times, but each psalm, and even each verse, has a wonderful history under the Christian dispensation, entering into the deepest experiences and the most hidden struggles and victories of the godly in all ages of the Church. What a history of the Twenty-third Psalm, for example, could be compiled from God's Book of Remembrance, if He were to place what it contains on this subject within man's reach! What an experience in Christian life and thought would the Gospel of John afford, to one who would be permitted to read the record of only a small portion of its use in the centuries that have followed its composition! How can the Fourth Gospel be separated from Christianity, or Christianity be separated from the Fourth Gospel, as some modern advocates of a reconstruction of Christianity propose? If but one verse, John 3:16, were to be torn from us, it would be as though one of the brightest planets had disappeared from our heaven.

12. But is it possible for this test to be applied by any individual or by any age of the Church to all the details or even all the books of Holy Scripture?

No. But just as we confide in one whom we have repeatedly found faithful, and implicitly believe that his words are true and his character spotless, because of what he has shown himself to be in cases where the test has been before our eyes, so our experience with the Word of God and with its record in many places, is the ground of confidence of its truth and power in all places. The most advanced student of the Scriptures has grasped, after all, only a small portion of its contents. The Church, like the individual Christian progresses, from age to age, in its apprehension and confession of what they contain, but never will exhaust their resources. "For such is the depth of the Christian Scriptures, that even if I were to attempt to study them and nothing else from early boyhood to decrepit old age, with the utmost leisure, the most unwearied zeal, and talents greater than I have, I would be still daily making progress in discovering their treasures; not that there is so great difficulty in coming through them to know the things necessary for salvation, but when anyone has accepted these truths, with the faith that is indispensable for a life of piety and uprightness, so many things which are veiled under manifold shadows of mystery remain to be inquired into by those who are advancing in the study, and so great is the depth of wisdom not only in the words in which these have been expressed, but also in the things themselves, that the experience of the oldest, the ablest and the most zealous students of Scriptures, illustrates what Scripture itself has said: 'When a mafi hath done, then hath he just begun' (Augustine, Letter Cxxxvii,"Nicene and Post-Nicene Fathers," I, 474). 'The painter, by the most delicate stroke of his brush; the musician, by the swiftest touch of fleeting notes, exercises the highest skill of his art. In everything that is highly finished, it is the most minute details that escape rude ears and eyes, which yet bestow the most exquisite and profound delight. Such is the case with Holy Scripture" (Bengel).

"Whilst everything in the Scriptures is for man, it does not follow that every part is equally valuable to every man. The Bible is framed with reference to the average want of a whole race. Everything in it is there for somebody, although it may not be specially meant for you. And yet the parts, which seem to the individual, least adapted to his wants, may have even for him a priceless value; they may inspire him with a sense of new necessities, may enlarge his mind and heart, and lead him out of himself into a wider sphere" (Krauth, lit supra).

Proper Place of Literary-historical criticism

13. Is no weight whatever, therefore, to be attached to literary-historical criticism?

It has a very important place, when subordinated to the religious use of Scripture. The former deals exclusively with the merely human; the latter, chiefly, although not exclusively, with the divine side of Scripture. The former may serve, at times and within certain limits, as a corrective of wrong inferences of the religious use of Scripture and what it implies. The main function of such criticism is to show the progressive character of revelation, and to mark the different stages through which the faithful passed until they received the full revelation of God in Christ, and the complete record of that revelation in the New Testament

Scriptures.

14. Distinguish further between the religions use of literary-historical criticism and literary-historical criticism separated from religious criticism.

This is well stated by Auberlen:

> "Such criticism is possible only when one, by the operation of the Spirit, has been brought into inward unison with the mind and essence of revelation — with the mind of Christ (1 Cor. 2:15, 16). From such a position the single books of Scripture are estimated, and a different value ascribed to them acording as they are occupied with Christ, i.e., as they stand in closer or remoter connection with the central point of the Gospel. Thus the Old Testament is less central than the New, the Book of Esther than Genesis, Ecclesiastes than Isaiah, the Epistle of James than that of Romans, though to all of these is given their essential place and signification in the entire Bible. It is quite common for the devout mind, in the practical use of the Scriptures, for edification, to make such distinctions, though it is often done unconsciously; and no one has been bolder in this respect than he to whom we are ac*As an illustration, reference may be made to the constant demands for "The New Testament and Psalms" in a separate volume. The soul in its deepest sorrows seeks consolation not from Chronicles or Proverbs, but from the Gospels or the Epistles. customed to look as one of the most spiritual men since the days of the apostles, Luther. His well-known opinions concerning the Epistle of James and other biblical books are not indeed to be followed, and they admonish us to care and humility in this matter. But if Scripture is now so often and so rightly called an organism, it must also have its more and less honorable members." Thus "a principal point of view is furnished for the unbiased historical study of the Bible; and this by no means tends to lower the Word of God, but rather serves to open up and unfold its manifold wealth, and to reveal the wisdom of God in educating men by providing for their most varied wants and for the different stages of their progress. The clearest example of this is the Gospels, rising up in an ascending line from Mark to John. This kind of dogmatic criticism, viz., the spiritual, is wide as the heavens from the unspiritual criticism of a rationalistic dogmatism" ("Divine Revelation," Engl. Transl., 269 sq.),

15. Is there such criticism in the New Testament Scriptures themselves?

Yes. The Epistle to the Hebrews combines literary-historical with religious criticism; and by its reverent treatment of the Old Testament, furnishes a model for critics of all succeeding ages.

16. What principle should always be remembered in such studies?

That of the powerlessness and perversity of all scholarly attainments when not thoroughly pervaded by the illumining influences of the Holy Spirit. Recall what the Formula of Concord has declared concerning "even the most able and learned men on earth" (Chapter 20, 2).

Estimate of the human factor

17. But are not some of the most conservative defenders of traditional theories of inspiration also open to criticism?

Yes, when they ignore or endeavor to conceal the human element in Scripture (see above, 8 a) or, what is the same, raise the human factor to an equality with the divine, as when it is claimed that the Hebrew vowel points are inspired, or, to quote again Dr. Krauth, when "it was thought to border on the sin against the Holy Ghost to intimate that the Greek, in which He inspired Matthew to write was not as pure at that of Plato. These were monstrous suppositions, at war with facts, totally uncalled for by any interest of the cause, they were destined to sustain, and rejected, even when they were most prevalent, by many of the profoundest minds and most pious hearts in all ages of the Church. Such a view contradicts every page of the Bible, a day's perusal of which suggests more difficulties against the theory than any ingenuity would be able to solve in a thousand years. This view, however, mars the Bible and stultifies its very plan. It makes a question of life and death out of matters, that have no more connection with the life of revelation, than has the spelling of a word, with the grandeur of 'Paradise Lost'" (ut supra).

18. Would you say then that some things in Scripture are unimportant, and may be readily surrendered?

By no means. Even the accidents of Scripture, if we may so speak, are important in their own place. In sacris Scripturis nil est supervacuum (Chrysostom). But "the mind of the Spirit" can be learned no more from detached and isolated passages, than a house can be judged from a single slate or shingle, or a flower from one petal or stamen, or an opera from a single bar of music. Detach a few letters from a sentence, and what is their value? That Erastus was treasurer of Corinth, that Paul left his cloak at Troas, that Manasseh was twelve years old when he began to reign, that Ehud begat Eleazar, are incidents that have no meaning whatever, except as details helping to make up the background, in the light of which the historical events pertaining to the center of the Gospel are unfolded. To raise them to a central place is not to honor, but to dishonor and misinterpret Holy Scripture. Luthardt, in his "Glaubenslehre," goes so far as to show that even the silence of Scripture is inspired. For it is just this silence of the Old Testament concerning Melchizedek, that is used in the Epistle to the Hebrews in showing how he is a type of Christ.

The very variations and divergences in narrating the same event only show how the Holy Spirit, through no want of foresight, preserved the truly human framework of the record with all its limitations, while filling it with His own divine power as to the central facts presented. Augustine was right when he found a design in even the obscurities of Holy Scripture. "This obscurity is beneficial, whether the sense of the author is at last reached after the discussion of many other interpretations, or whether though that sense remain concealed, other truths are brought out by the discussion of the obscurity" (*De Civitate Dei*, 20, 19).

Organic relation of parts

19. Upon what principle of interpretation has the Lutheran Church, therefore, always insisted?

That no passage dare be regarded by itself, and that, as Scripture forms a consistent whole, there is "an analogy of faith," which is the center and rule of the rest. Each verse and each word has its place; but what this is the "analogy of faith" must decide. See Chapter 1, 22-26.

20. In view of all that has been thus far presented in this chapter, would you say "The Bible is the Word of God," or "The Bible contains the Word of God"?

This question is already answered in 8 b. and 18. The various records of the various revelations of God (Heb. 1:1) are combined in one record and one revelation. The whole must be interpreted in the light of each part, and each part must be interpreted in the light of the whole. In this sense we can say: 'The Bible is the Word of God."

The expression, "The Bible contains the Word of God" is capable of a true, and of some very erroneous interpretations. It may mean that with much chaff there is some wheat, and with much dross there is some gold, and that when the human element is carefully separated from the divine, we have at last the pure Word of God. In this sense, it is clear that it cannot be accepted. Every note of the sublime strain, every stroke of the painter's brush, is needed for the full effect. Even the delicate touch in the description in Mark 6:39, that the grass on which the multitude received their meal was "green" is not needless. The divine element is active in and through everything in Scripture that is human.

It may be interpreted also as meaning that the Bible is a vessel full of the water of life, and that every drop that is drawn from it is equally valuable. Some good people open their Bibles at random, and hope to find divine guidance in the first text on which their eyes light, without considering the place the text has in the entire argument of divine revelation. Some preachers, in the selection and treatment of a text, pay no regard to the context or argument in which it stands, or its relations to the central doctrine of the Gospel. The letters in a word, the words in a sentence, the sentences in a paragraph, the paragraph or Chapter in a book, the book in a "testament," and even the testament as a whole needs the whole Bible to interpret it.

But there is a true sense in which we say not only that "the Bible is," but that "the Bible contains the Word of God." This occurs when each part, even the most insignificant and seemingly trifling, even the discrepancies between various human inspired writers, and all that pertains to the limitations of their nature and environment and age and language, are regarded as bearing on the one great end and one great theme of revelation and its clear and inerrant record.

It occurs also where God speaks in Scripture not only in an entire argument, or in recounting human history, but in clear and direct briefer statements, as in the Ten Commandments, the Lord's Prayer, the Sermon on the Mount, the institution of the Sacraments, the parting discourse to the disciples, the Sacerdotal Prayer, the Gospel history in general and in detail, the sermons of the Apostles in Acts, the treatment of the great theme of faith in the Epistles of Paul, and of love in those of

John, and of hope in those of Peter. Here we find the very center and key by which all else is explained. To speak with greatest accuracy, we may say: The Holy Scriptures are a highly organized and divinely prepared instrumentality for communicating the Word of God to men. As the body, the organ of the soul, has its heart and lungs and head, so Holy Scripture, as the organ of the Holy Spirit, for conveying God's Word, has an order in its various parts. As Melanchthon says in the first edition of his Loci Communes, with Luther's endorsement, "The Epistle to the Romans is the index and canon of all Scripture."

21. Why was such peculiar position ascribed to one book of the Bible, and one author?

Because it undertakes, upon the basis of a most thorough survey of all that the Old Testament taught, to interpret the real significance of the incarnation of the Son of God, and of the life and death and resurrection and ascension of Jesus. It rests not simply upon the external authority of the Apostle, but upon the internal authority of the Word which it contains, bringing to a focus the whole argument of the Old Testament, and then adding to this the Word of the New Testament declared by Christ, and enforced by His sitting at the Right Hand of God, and the gift of the Holy Spirit. Here again we recur to a brilliant exposition of the significance of Paul, written, with the glow of one who has made a new discovery, in the opening years of the Reformation:

> "In the number of the divine volumes, some record laws, other examples of life and character, some obscure prophecies concerning Christ, and still others what Christ did. But who has explained more thoroughly, more accurately, and at greater length than Paul, the gifts which Christ acquired by His blood for the entire human race? It is something to repeat the laws of life, in order that one may know what he should and what he should not do; it is something to present before the eyes examples of life as a stimulus to virtues; it is something to recount what Christ did as a model of absolute virtue; but it is by far most important to know what is Christ's true glory, why He descended to earth, and of what profit to the world is the incarnation of the Eternal Word; for it is in this that the sum of our salvation consists. Laws prescribe the form of what is honorable, and afford us examples; and Christ, above all others, is the archetype. But what the kindness of Christ obtained for the human race was declared to the whole world by the Gospel of Paul. Laws and models of virtues foreshadow, but the kindness of Christ proclaimed by Paul completes and fulfills... It is from Paul that we learn peculiarly what is the meaning and what the value of the benefits obtained by Christ... . Inasmuch as to know Christ is not

only to know His deeds, but with a thankful heart to embrace the benefits, which through Him the Heavenly Father has shed abroad throughout the whole world, and which alone distinguish those who are truly Christian from the godless heathen... . Other sacred writers, indeed, have mentioned these benefits here and there; but more obscurely, and so as not to have been readily understood, unless Paul, in his numerous epistles and discussions, had made the entire argument clear"* (Melanchthon, January 25th, 1520). "Neither the predictions of the Prophets, nor the histories of the Gospel can be understood unless you follow his commentaries like a river to the sea. For since the sum and substance of Theology consists in the treatment of human nature, the tyranny of sin, the reign of law and the origin and propagation of absolute virtue, the Sacraments, only Paul has displayed these topics to the eyes of mortals. In short, we would be ignorant of the grace of our redemption, and, therefore, of Christ Himself, if God had withheld Paul from the world. For to know Christ is not to know the history of His deeds, but to recognize the great benefits which through Him God diffused throughout the world... In vain you study the Gospel history, unless, under Paul's guidance, you observe the scope and use of that history" (Melanchthon, same year).

No distinction between Inner and Outward Word

22. Is a distinction between an Inner and an Outward Word to be admitted?

There are not two words, of which one is and the other is not a Means of Grace, but the Holy Spirit acts through the outward word and through this alone. (See Chapter 19, 7.)

> "The Spirit is nowhere to be sought save in and with the Word" (Luther, Erl. ed., 48:73).

[A.] From the Psalms. 119:92:

> "Unless thy law had been my delight, I should have perished." 105:

> "Thy word is a lamp unto my feet, and a light unto my path." 19:7:

> "The law of Jehovah is perfect, restoring the soul."

God teaches, converts, illumines as the principal; the word as the instrumental cause or the means.

[B.] From the Prophets, Is. 55:10, 11:

> "My word shall not return unto me void, but it shall accomplish that which I please, and it shall prosper in the thing whereto I sent it."

[C.] From the words of Christ

Especially the Parable of the Sower, Matt. 13:23; Mark 4:20; Luke 8:20.

[D.] From the testimony of the Apostles

> Rom. 1:16: "The gospel is the power of God unto salvation."
>
> Rom. 10:17: "Faith cometh of hearing, and hearing by the word of Christ."
>
> Rom. 15:4: "That we through patience and confidence of the Scriptures might have hope."
>
> Eph. 1:13; Col. 1:6; 2 Tim. 3:15, 16; Heb. 4:12; James 1:18, 21; 1 Peter 1:23.

[E.] From passages declaring that through the preaching and teaching of ministers it is God who speaks and acts

Matt. 10:20; Rom. 15:18; 2 Cor. 13:3; Acts 11:14; 9:15; 2:40, 41.

To this, we may add all passages which turn men from imaginary or desired supplementary revelations to the testimony of Scripture.

> Is. 8:19. "When they shall say unto you, Seek unto them that have familiar spirits and unto wizards that chirp and that mutter... To the law and to the testimony! if they speak not according to this word, surely there is no morning for them."
>
> Luke 16:29. "They have Moses and the prophets, let them hear them."

Even the Apostolic preaching had to be verified by the testimony of the Scriptures, Acts 17:11.

23. What proofs for this can be given?

> "God binds us to His oral word, since He says in Luke 10:16, 'He that heareth you, heareth me.' Here He speaks of the oral word proceeding out of the mouth of a man, and sounding in the ears of other men, not of a spiritual word from heaven, but of that which sounds through men's mouths" (Luther, Erl. ed., 57:63.)

Scripture more than a "directory"

24. Is it the office of the Word simply to afford directions that are to be followed in order to obtain salvation?

It is more than a directory and guide to Christ. It does more than "give directions how to live." It brings and communicates the grace concerning which it instructs. It has an inherent and objective efficacy, derived from its divine institution and promise, and explained by the constant presence and activity of the Holy Spirit in and with it.

> Rom. 1:16. "The gospel is the power of God unto salvation."
>
> John 6:63. "The words that I have spoken unto you, are spirit and are life."
>
> 1 Pet. 1.22. "Begotten again, not of corruptible seed, but of incorruptible, through the word of God."
>
> Matt. 4:4. "Man shall not live by bread alone, but by every word that proceedeth out of the mouth of God."
>
> Eph. 6:17, Heb. 4:12, Rom. 10:5-10, Is. 55:10.

Spirit and Word inseparable

25. What testimony is given to the presence of the Holy Spirit in and with the Word?

The words of Scripture are repeatedly cited as the words of the Holy Spirit.

> Acts 1:16. "It was needful that the Scripture be fulfilled, which the Holy Spirit spake before by the mouth of David."
>
> Acts 28:25. "Well spake the Holy Spirit through Isaiah the prophet."
>
> Heb. 3:7. "The Holy Spirit saith," introducing a quotation from a Psalm. 10:15. "The Holy Spirit also beareth witness," introducing a quotation from Jeremiah.

Spirit and Word are declared to be inseparable for all time.

> Is. 59:21. "My Spirit that is upon thee, and my words which I have put in thy mouth, shall not depart out of thy mouth, nor out of the mouth oi thy seed, nor out of the mouth of thy seeds' seed, saith Jehovah, from henceforth and for ever."

Efficacy of Word

26. Is the Word, then, always efficacious?

To reach its end, the Word must be accepted by the person to whom it comes. But its rejection is no more indication of any lack of efficacy in the Word itself, than the refusal to take a prescribed remedy would demonstrate that it is worthless. When our theologians say that the Word has efficacy, even without regard to its being used, they mean that wherever found, the Holy Spirit is present with his illuminating and regenerating influences. That some believe and others believe not, that some are converted and others remain impenitent, is not attributable to different degrees of presence and efficacy (see Chapter 19, 8), but to the resistance or non-resistance of the Holy Spirit as He comes to us in and through the Word (see Chapter 19, 9; Chapter 21, 7, 8).

Explanation of Prayer for the Spirit as interpreter

27. But if the Holy Spirit is always in and with the Word, why do we constantly pray for the coming and presence of the Spirit?

Precisely as we pray for the coming of the Kingdom of God. Of this, our Catechism teaches:

> "The Kingdom of God comes indeed of itself, without our prayer; but we pray in this petition that it may come unto us also."

So when we pray God to give us His Holy Spirit, we ask that we may ever remember and grasp by faith the presence of the Spirit, and be ever receptive to His influences.

Rom. 8:26. "In like manner the Spirit also helpeth our infirmity; for we know not how to pray as we ought; but the Spirit himself maketh intercession for us with groanings that cannot be uttered."

The prayer for the gift of the Spirit, has been preceded by the presence of the Spirit in the heart of him who prays. It is like the coming of Christ, celebrated in the Advent Season, who came indeed in answer to prophecy, nearly 2000 years ago; but whose advent is repeated in every heart, as it yearns for a higher realization of all that which His coming means for it.

The Church as the instrumentality for communicating the Word

28. How does the Word reach men?

Through the instrumentality of the Church and its ministry.

Rom. 10:14, 15. "How then shall they call on him whom they have not believed? and how shall they believe in him of whom they have not heard? and how shall they hear without a preacher? and how shall they preach except they be sent?"

"The Holy Ghost has a peculiar congregation in the world, which is the mother that bears every Christian, through the Word of God, which He reveals and preaches and through which He illumines and enkindles hearts" (Luther, Large Catechism, 444:42).

29. But how is it apprehended?

Either as preached or read, or as sealed with an element in the Sacraments.

The Preached Word

30. What is the special function of the preached and of the read Word?

The preached Word, with the concurrent testimony of the preacher and congregation which it presupposes, is used more as a means of awakening, encouraging, stimulating, and producing conviction and decision.

> "When the Word is read at home it is not as fruitful or as forcible as in public preaching and through the mouth of the preacher whom God has called for this purpose" (Luther, Erl. ed., 3:401).

> 1 Cor. 1:21. "It was God's good pleasure, through the foolishness of the preaching, to save them that believe."

Cf. above Rom. 10:14, 15; also Rom. 10:8. "The word of faith which we preach." Rom. 10:17. "Faith cometh by hearing."

The voice of the Holy Spirit is heard through the voice of the preacher or the voices of the united congregation in confession, prayer and hymn (which are also different forms of preaching, see Chapter 29, 27). The conversions recorded in the New Testament were through the preached word. Although the preparatory use of the read word appears in some instances, it was the voice of the living preacher speaking as the result of deep conviction that brought such influences to ultimate fruition.

> "Because the word of preaching is pervaded by the Spirits i.e., because the personal Spirit of God is efficaciously present in, with and under the voice of man, preaching comes from the Word of God like sunbeams from the beaming sun" (Besser, on Rom. 10:17).

> "For the hearing and preaching of God's Word are instruments of the Holy Ghost, by, with and through which He desires to work efficaciously, and to convert men to God and to work in them both to will and to do" (Formula of Concord, 562).

Nevertheless, "it is not from the inspired personality of the preacher, but from the inspired Word itself, that the efficacy proceeds."

> "Although undoubtedly one who, in word and deed, clearly shows the subjective effect of the Word in his own life, moves many to open their ears to the preaching of the Gospel, who would have closed them, if there had been a glaring contrast between the personality of the preacher, and his message; yet, this personal factor is only paedagogical or propaedeutical. It is analogous to the objective miracles of Revelation, whose office is to lead to the Word. The Word is in itself the living seed of regeneration; the hand which does the sowing can add to it no further efficacy" (*Philippi*, 5:2:15)

The Read Word

31. How does the read Word differ?

It is "by means of the daily exercise of reading and applying to practice God's Word," that we are "preserved in faith and his heavenly gifts, strengthened from day to day, and supported unto the end" (Formula of Concord, 555). It is thus preparatory or supplementary to the preached word. It is necessarily more restricted in scope than the preached word; for printed Bibles in wide circulation date only from the Reformation. Even with the wide diffusion of intelligence and education today, there are millions of Christians still who are dependent upon the voice of the living preacher for all their religious knowledge. But the written word remains the rule and guide for all time according to which the preached word must be judged; as well as the source whence the preacher derives the material and inspiration for his sermons. The preached word can never dispense with the read word; nor the read word with the preached word. Bible and preacher belong together. "What God hath joined together, let not man put asunder." Cargoes of Bibles without missionaries will never convert the heathen. Armies of preachers, without the Holy Scriptures in their hands and on their lips and in their hearts, would only lead us back to the heathenism of our forefathers.

32. How is this "daily exercise of reading" to be observed so as to derive from it the benefits for which the Scriptures have been given?

[A.] By constantly remembering the purpose of Scripture.

Not as a model of literature, or an aggregate of historical documents, or a storehouse of secular learning, but as a Means of Grace.

[B.] By ever fixing our eyes on the center of Scripture, Christ.

And judging all books and all passages with respect to their relation to Him, and His interpretation of them.

[C.] By learning more and more of the scope and purport of particular books and paragraphs, and in order to grasp their unity

Undertaking the reading of large portions at one time, as, in current literature, we read an address or lecture or even long argument at a single sitting. It is the general temper and disposition that we gain by protracted contact with the life-giving Spirit of God, speaking through the Word, that is to be prized even more than any facts or detached texts with which we may store the memory. God did not give the Bible as a repository of texts, but as one complete revelation of Himself to sinful man.

[D.] By prizing single words and passages of Scripture only with reference to the whole of which they are a part.

The microscopic examination of Scripture has its place, where particular words focus or bring to a head an entire argument.

[E.] By comparing Scripture with Scripture.

The tables of parallel passages in some of our Bibles are important aids, but, as one advances, it is chiefly his own knowledge of Scripture, upon which he must draw.

[F.] By living in Scripture, making it the key to decipher one's own life, and finding every hour in such a life, illustrations of its power and truth.

> "As thou readest, think that every syllable pertaineth to thine one self, and suck out the pith of the Scripture, and arm thyself against all assaults" (Tyndale).
>
> "What are all the Psalms of David but definitions and descriptions of faith, of love and of hope?" 'The Psalter is nothing but a school, and series of exercises of faith."
>
> "He who reads it without faith, finds nothing there but darkness and cold; he remains without light and without warmth" (Luther).

Preaching as a Means of Grace

33. Is the success of preaching as a means of grace conditioned by the observance of similar principles by the preacher?

Undoubtedly. For it is not preaching itself, but the Word as preached which is a means of grace. This demands not only that nothing be preached but what comes directly or indirectly from Holy Scripture, but also that the contents of Holy Scripture be preached in due proportion and in the proper order. Nothing that God has revealed is without its appropriate use and application; but it is all important that the center of what is scriptural hold the chief place, and that all else be urged only with reference towards such center. Everything that concerns man as a moral and religious being should be treated in the light of Law and Gospel. Not only is Christ the center of all true preaching of the Word, but we must learn to grasp and inculcate what is central in the doctrine concerning Christ. True preaching in fact is not so much a preaching about Christ, as it is preaching Christ Himself, and that the crucified Christ.

> 1 Cor. 1:23, 24. "But we preach Christ crucified, unto Jews a stumblingblock, and unto Gentiles foolishness; but unto them that are called, both Jews and Greeks, Christ the power of God and the wisdom of God."

> 1 Cor. 2:2. "I determined not to know anything among you, save Jesus Christ, and him crucified."

The proper theme of the pulpit is not philosophy, not literature, not ethical or economical or sociological theories, even for audiences of highly educated people, but the cross in its manifold relations and with its many lessons. He who abides close to the cross, will be sure to find hearers to whom his words will be like cold water to the parched tongue. All preaching that has been of permanent influence has been a preaching of the crucified. Jesus, which, as will be seen below, is a preaching of Law (Chapter 25, 24). as well as Gospel. The chief stress in the Sacrament of the Lord's Supper lies upon this central fact of Christianity, which recalls the Church, as often as it is administered, to what must be at once the standard, and the beginning and end of all its preaching. Even the crucifix, under the Papacy, had its use, as Luther thought (Walch ed. 21:441), in attracting the mind of the dying from their own merits and works to the suffering Savior as their only hope.

34. What keeps preaching close to this center?

[A.] The proper understanding of Scripture.

He who reads the Scriptures in order to find Christ at every point, cannot but make Christ the beginning, middle and end of every sermon.

[B.] The testimony of the lives of those who have preceded us.

In whom "Jesus Christ, the same yesterday, today and forever" was manifested and glorified (Heb. 12:8).

[C.] A proper appreciation of the spiritual life as it is struggling in much weakness in the hearts of even the humblest of our hearers.

Shall they whose hearts are hungering for the Gospel be put off with mere husks?

[D.] Close contact, therefore, with the common life of Christ as it pervades the entire "communion of saints," from those saints who speak or are spoken of in Scripture (e.g., Heb. 11) to those who are with us today in our congregations as well as elsewhere.

35. What especial provision has been an important aid in preserving the true proportion in preaching the Word?

The Church Year with its lessons. It has retained its hold, not because of any Church authority which has determined it, but because it has met an important demand of the religious life of the communion of saints, with what has been found after centuries of trial to be most edifying. With all the stress the Lutheran Church lays upon sound doctrine and scientific theology, and the prominence of Dogmatics in its history, its preaching has been preserved from being dogmatical by its devotion to the annual cycle of Gospel Lessons. In them Christ appears not as an abstraction, but, in all His relations, as a concrete reality, progressively unfolding His revelation of the Kingdom of God.

A well known theologian of the Reformed Church, in advocating the Church Year to those with whom it is not, as with us, an inheritance, writes:

> "Thus does the Church Year call forth the whole Order of Salvation before our eyes, and its different Sundays are as so many pearls, strung in regular order upon one string. For the congregation, the preaching of the historic Christ in all His fullness is in this way promoted and rendered fruitful. He is thus depicted before their eyes in the various stadia of His life of humiliation and exaltation, and the great facts of salvation are in this way constantly anew brought to light in their natural order. The preacher has in connection with this method, no chain attached to his foot, but rather a clue placed in his hands, which of itself decides his choice of texts, saves him perplexity and loss of time, and quickens his homiletic power of discovery by directing his eye now and then to texts which lie outside of the beaten paths of the most familiar ones. The communion of saints, finally is fostered and preserved, where the choice of the material for preaching is no longer dependent upon absolute caprice, but the eye of the Church, even in different lands and communities, is methodically directed to the same or similar facts, and thus God's saving revelation in Christ is, from year to year, constantly to a greater extent inwardly lived through" (Van Oosterzee, "Practical Theology," 228 sqq.).

36. How may this system be abused?

By resting in it, instead of simply making it the outline around which to cluster the entire contents of Holy Scripture. No prescribed course of lessons can ever be a substitute for the entire canon of revelation. The best system only offers suggestions which not only cannot be universally binding, but in which the peculiar demands of time, place and circumstances always will advise changes. Wherever there is true life, there is adaptation to change and ever changing relations.

Antithesis of the Roman Catholic Church

37. How does the teaching of the Roman Catholic Church concerning the Word as a Means of Grace differ from that of the Lutheran Church?

According to Rome, the only proper Means of Grace are the Sacraments; and it is the office of the Word, either in the form of tradition promulgated by Papal authority, or of Holy Scripture in the Latin Vulgate, to lead to the Sacraments.

Difference of the Reformed view

38. How does the teaching of the Reformed Church or Churches differ from the Lutheran in this respect?

While there is often an approach to the Lutheran view, nevertheless there is a lack of clearness in declaring that the external Word is actually a means through which the Holy Spirit imparts His grace. Zwingli objected to the idea of "means of grace."

> "A channel or vehicle," (he says)("*Ratio Fidei*") "is not necessary for the Spirit, since He Himself is the virtue or energy, by which all things are borne, and has no need of being borne."

The "Means of Grace," with the Reformed are, therefore, ordinances by which man approaches God, rather than instrumentalities by which God approaches man. According to Calvin, the office of the Word is simply to declare to us God's will, a thought which is true as far as it goes. The Word is regarded, therefore, as like the Sacraments in their system, a sign, a pledge, a seal, of that which only becomes ours by the inner illumination of the Spirit. We hold, however, in accordance with the Scriptural passages already cited, that the Word is more than a sign or seal or pledge or guide or directory, but, in addition to teaching the way of life, that, by the agency of the Holy Spirit, it actually confers upon the believing that whereof it speaks; it not only offers blessings to faith, but also through the Holy Spirit who is with it, produces the faith which receives these blessings; it not only renders us receptive to the Holy Spirit, but is the means through which the Spirit works. With the Reformed, the Holy Scriptures are regarded chiefly as a storehouse of divine truths, a digest of doctrines that are to be received: with the Lutheran Church they are chiefly a Means of Grace, charged with divine life, energy and salvation, which is communicated to all using them aright, the dwelling-place of the Holy Spirit with all His gifts. With the Reformed, the Holy Scriptures are regarded more in the light of a code of laws; with Lutherans, more as a divine seed that, by the presence of the Spirit, is to bring forth a bountiful harvest.

25. The Law And The Gospel

Division of the Word

1. How is the Word of God divided?

Into Law and Gospel, or Command and Promise.

Distinction explained

2. Does this distinction coincide with that between the Old and the New Testaments?

No. There is Gospel in the Old Testament, as the promise concerning Christ was made from man's fall (Gen. 3:15), and became fuller and clearer as the time of its fulfillment approached (see Chapter 10, 1, 5). There is also Law in the New Testament, of which the Sermon on the Mount is a summary (see Chapter 13, 9-12). But in the Old Testament, Law; in the New Testament, Gospel preponderates.

3. Where is this distinction briefly stated?

> John 1:17. "The law was given through Moses; grace and truth came through Jesus Christ."

> 2 Cor. 3:6. "Who also made us sufficient as ministers of a new covenant; not of the letter, but of the spirit; for the letter killeth, but the spirit giveth life."

In the former passage, the grace of the Gospel is contrasted with the inflexible rigor of the Law; and the fulfillment of the promise and the presence of the substance under the Gospel, with the types and shadows of the Law.

In the second passage, the points of contrast are:

a. Between the Law, or letter

As prescribing a course of conduct and making demands, but giving no power to obey; and the Gospel as bringing the Holy Spirit with His regenerating and renewing powers.

b. Between the Law as leading to despair

When the impossibility of meeting its demands is learned; and the Gospel as encouraging and cheering with its offer of Christ's righteousness as our own.

c. Between the Law, as except through Christ nothing but a letter, and the Gospel

As being the fulfillment of the Law in us by the enkindling of love,

d. Between the Law as containing much that is typical and unintelligible until its true interpretation is found in the Gospel, and the Gospel as the goal of all that towards which the Law is directed.

4. What importance is attached to the distinction between Law and Gospel?

> "This distinction between Law and Gospel is the highest art in Christianity, which all who boast or accept the Christian name, can or should know. For where there is a defect on this point, a Christian cannot be distinguished from a heathen or a Jew; for it is just here that the difference lies" (Luther).

The greatest care must be taken:

> "...lest these two doctrines be mingled with one another, or out of the Gospel a law be made, whereby the merit of Christ is obscured and troubled consciences robbed of the comfort they would otherwise have" (Formula of Concord, 589).

5. What, then, is the main point of difference?

Everything in Holy Scripture that commands us to do or to give or to be something, or that forbids us to do or give, or be, is Law. Everything that asks us to receive something is Gospel.

> "By the Law, nothing else is meant than God's Word and command, wherein He enjoins what we should do and leave undone, and demands our obedience. But the Gospel is that doctrine or Word of God that neither requires works of us, nor enjoins the doing of anything, but announces only the offered grace of the forgiveness of sins and eternal life. The Gospel offers God's gifts and bids us only open the sack to receive them, while the Law gives nothing, but only takes and demands of us" (Luther).

Everything that reproves sin and threatens is Law; everything that encourages and comforts and offers the grace of God is Gospel (see Formula of Concord, 593).

> "The Law shows sin; the Gospel, grace. The Law indicates the disease; the Gospel, the remedy. The Law, to use the words of Paul, is a minister of death; the Gospel, of life and peace" (Melanchthon).

> Rom. 3:20. "Through the law cometh the knowledge of sin.;"

> Rom. 7:7. "I had not known sin except through the law."

> Gal. 3:12. "The law is not of faith; but he that doeth them, shall live in them."

Different senses of both terms

6. Are the words "Law" and "Gospel" used in Holy Scripture in but one sense?

Each has various meanings. In its widest sense, Law includes all that God has revealed (Ps. 1:2). In a narrower sense, it refers to the Old Testament (John 10:34), and particularly, the Pentateuch (Luke 24:44). In its strictest sense, as used here, it is God's revelation of His will concerning man's character and acts. So "Gospel," in the widest sense, means all the doctrine taught by Christ and His Apostles (Mark 1:1-14; 16:15). But as contradistinguished from Law it designates the promise of grace through Christ, whether before His coming, or since He has come (Is. 41:27; 52:7; Rom. 10:16; 1:2).

Divisions of the Law

7. How has the Law been divided?

Into universal and particular. The former has been declared from the beginning, and pertains to all times and places. The latter was prescribed for temporary purposes to a particular nation. The former we know as the Moral Law; the latter is divided, according to its diverse purposes, into the Forensic and the Ceremonial.

The Moral Law: Defined, distinguished, Office of the Natural Law, the Revealed Moral Law, where found, where repeated, test as to whether a precept belong to Moral Law, an organic whole, its sphere, nature of the obedience it demands, result of its preaching, because it cannot justify is it useless, the three uses of the Law, how should it be preached

8. What is the Moral Law?

God's declaration concerning what He would have man be, do or omit to do.

> "Divine doctrine, wherein the true and unmistakable will of God is revealed, as to how man ought to be, in his nature, thoughts, words and works, in order to be pleasing and acceptable to God."
>
> "Divine doctrine teaching what is right and pleasing to God, and reproving everything that is sin and contrary to God's will" (see Chapter 8:2-4).

9. How has the Moral Law been distinguished?

Into Natural and Revealed. The former designates the original knowledge of

God's will impressed upon man's nature when created, and constituting one of the features of the Image of God (Eph. 4:24; Col. 3:10). (See Chapter VII, 27, 28.) While, by the Fall, this knowledge was largely lost and greatly corrupted and perverted, some traces of it still remain. Conscience, or the power to discriminate between right and wrong belongs to some extent to all men. "Human reason naturally understands in some way the law" (Apology, 85).

> Rom. 2:14, 15. "For when the Gentiles that have not the law do by nature the things of the law, these not having the law, are the law unto themselves, in that they show the work of the law written in their hearts, their conscience bearing witness therewith, and their thoughts one with another accusing or else excusing them."

10. What is the office of the Natural Law?

To stimulate men to seek after God (Acts 17:27), and when they fail to respond to convict them of sin (Rom. 1:20).

11. What shows its feebleness in man's fallen estate?

Its merely superficial effects. The knowledge of the extent of the inner corruption of the heart is learned only from the revealed law.

> Rom. 7:7, 8. "I have not known sin except through the law" (i.e. the revealed Moral Law); "for I had not known coveting except the law had said, Thou shalt not covet." "For apart from the law sin is dead."

The connection shows that the meaning is, that unless the Revealed Moral Law be known, the knowledge of sin is so weak that it may be accounted dead.

12. What is the Revealed Moral Law?

The declarations of God's will repeatedly given to man since the Fall, and formally promulgated through Moses on Mt. Sinai, concerning matters of universal and permanent obligation.

13. Where is it summarized?

In general, in the Ten Commandments, and still further by Christ in Matt. 22:37-40:

"Thou shalt love the Lord thy God with all thy heart, and with all thy soul, and with all thy mind. This is the first and great commandment. And a second like unto it, is this, Thou shalt love thy neighbor as thyself. On these two commandments the whole law hangeth and the prophets."

14. Where are the Ten Commandments repeated?

In Matt. 19:18, 19; Mark 10:19; Luke 18:20; Rom. 13:9

15. Where is their meaning fully explained and applied?

In the Sermon on the Mount.

16. How can the perpetual obligation of particular precepts be determined, and their place in the Moral Law established?

Any precept of the Old Testament sanctioned by the express words of Christ or any of the inspired writers of the New Testament, belongs most clearly to the Moral Law.

17. Can we say that everything in the Ten Commandments as reported in Ex. 20 belongs to the Moral Law?

In the promise of the Fourth Commandment, the particular blessing was local and national. St. Paul, accordingly, shows in Eph. 6:3, that there was a generic blessing, which lifted the promise to a higher level and gave it a vaster range. So the Third Commandment, concerning the Sabbath, contains a ceremonial element, which our Catechism, following St. Paul in Col. 2:16, traces to a generic command of universal obligation concerning the preaching and hearing of God's Word, and of a cessation of labor for that purpose.

18. Is the Moral Law a code of coordinate and parallel precepts?

It is an organic whole, reducible first to two, and at last to one commandment, that of supreme love to God (Matt. 22:37-40; Luke 10:2j) .

19. What is its sphere?

It includes all the acts and states and relations of men. But it lays chief stress upon the inner life, the thoughts and intents of the heart (Matt. 5:22, 28), and summarizes all its demands in the one word "love."

20. What obedience does the Moral Law demand? That which is the most perfect and complete:

[A.] As to the source of the acts.

As above seen they must proceed from entire and completely self-surrendering and self-forgetting love, and be wrought by man's undivided powers.

[B.] As to the details of the acts.

The failure of the least particular vitiates the whole. A chain is no stronger than its weakest link.

> Deut. 27:26. "Cursed be he that confirmeth not the words of this law, to do them."

> Gal. 3:10. "Cursed is he that continueth not in all things written in the book of the law, to do them."

> James 2:10. "For whosoever shall keep the whole law, and yet shall stumble in one point, he is guilty of all."

[C.] As to perseverance.

Even if perfection were attainable for a time, it is valueless unless maintained to the end.

> Ez. 18:24. "When the righteous turneth away from his righteousness, and committeth iniquity, and doeth according to all the abominations that the wicked man doeth, shall he live? None of his righteous deeds that he hath done shall be remembered; in his trespass that he hath trespassed, and in his sin that he hath sinned, in them shall he die."

21. What is the result?

Man, because of his depraved and enfeebled nature, being unable to meet these demands, the Law which has been given for eternal life, becomes accidentally the occasion for eternal death.

> Rom. 7:10, 12 "The commandment which was unto lite, this I found to be unto death... So that the law is holy and righteous and good... but sin, that it might be shown to be sin, by working death to me through that which is good."

The Epistle to the Romans opens with a long argument, showing the inability both of the Gentiles by the Natural, and of the Jews by the Revealed Law to attain justification before God.

> Rom. 3:20, 22. "By the works of the law, shall no flesh be justified; for by the law is the knowledge of sin... If the Law, therefore, cannot justify, is it not useless?

> "As the argument is invalid, 'Money does not justify, therefore it is useless'; 'the eyes do not justify, therefore they should be torn out'; 'the hands do not justify, therefore they must be amputated'; so, too, the argument is equally fallacious that the Law is useless, because it does not justify. We should ascribe to everything its proper office and use. In denying that it justifies, we do not destroy or condemn the Law" (Luther).

Another illustration of Luther is that the Law is food which the organs of the invalid, enfeebled by sin cannot digest.

23. What, then, is the use of the Law? It has a three-fold use:

[A.] Political.
By its threats of punishment, it checks the violence of godless men, and protects society against external acts of crime. It is of this use that 1 Tim. 1:9 sq. speaks:

> "The law is not made for a righteous man, but for the lawless and unruly, for the ungodly and sinners, for the unholy and profane, for murderers of fathers and murderers of mothers, for fornicators," etc.

[B.] Elenchtical.
As it convicts or convinces of sin.

> Rom. 3:20. "Through the law, cometh the knowledge of sin."

This it does by bringing evidence not attainable by the light of nature, and by showing that what is chiefly significant is that, beneath the act, there is. such a desperate state of sin. The Law is not only the standard, by which sins are discerned, but the light which displays them in all their heinousness and enormity.

It does more than instruct concerning sin; the Holy Spirit uses it as a means to condemn and terrify on account of sin.

> Rom. 4:15. "For the law worketh wrath."

> John 16:8. "He will convict the world of sin, and of righteousness and of judgment."

Thus the law indirectly leads or forces men to Christ (Gal. 3:24). This indirect office has been separated from the elenchtical use by our later Lutheran theologians and called the pedagogical.

24. Do not the sufferings of Christ belong to the elenchtical use of the law?

Before proceeding to the third or didactic use, state whether the consideration of the sufferings of Christ, as an exhibition of God's anger against sin, does not belong to the elenchtical use of the law, rather than to the Gospel.

The consideration of the sufferings of Christ has a double effect. They reveal, as nowhere else, the guilt of sin, and they testify to the love of God for sinners. The former belongs to the elenchtical use of the law; the latter to the Gospel. See Formula of Concord, 591:

> "What more forcible declaration of God's wrath against sin is there, than the suffering and death of Christ His Son? But as long as this all preaches God's wrath and terrifies men, it is still properly the preaching neither of the Gospel, nor of Christ, but of Moses and the Law against the impenitent. For the Gospel and Christ were never provided in order to terrify and condemn, but in order to comfort and cheer those who are terrified and timid."

25. What, then, is the didactic or third use?

As a guide and standard for the regenerate.

> "The Holy Ghost teaches the regenerate, in the Ten Commandments, in what good works 'God hath before ordained that they should walk' (Eph. 2:10)" (Formula of Concord, 597).

26. But why is this necessary, when the regenerate have the Holy Spirit who constantly impels them to do God's will?

Because of their corrupt nature which is only partially renewed, they can never trust their own impulses, but must constantly test them by God's law, in order to determine what is of God and what is of the flesh.

27. What is necessary for fulfilling the duty of a true Christian pastor in preaching the Law?

That all of these uses of the Law be constantly urged, and that none of their requirements be abated. The hearts of men are receptive to the Gospel only to the extent that they have been enlightened by the Law.

> Matt. 5:6. "Blessed are they that hunger and thirst alter righteousness; for they shall be filled."

Great danger is always imminent lest the demands of the Law be relaxed in accommodation to the weaknesses of men, and lest, in commending purely external morality and urging its demands, its insufficiency for justification, and the deeper righteousness of the heart be overlooked.

Relation of Forensic and Ceremonial Laws to the Moral

28. What were the Forensic and the Ceremonial Law?

The Forensic Law was the code of the Israelitic State; the Ceremonial, the ritual of the Israelitic Church.

29. How were they related to the Moral Law?

They are applications of the Moral Law to the temporary circumstances and conditions of the Jewish people. The Ceremonial Law provided for a series of exercises of the First Table of the Law, by defining the rites of worship and its circumstances. The Forensic Law provided for a series of exercises of the Second Table, by prescribing rules of conduct in respect to man's social and civil relations. In the theocracy, everything was determined by direct and minute prescription. In the educational process, whereby God was training for Himself a people, at first nothing whatever was left to human freedom or man's enlightened conscience. The period was one which had not received the endowment of the Spirit in His fullness. (See Chapter 16, 4.)

30. How did the Forensic and Ceremonial Laws differ from the Moral?

[A.] In mode of revelation.

The Moral was implanted in man's nature, at his creation; and on Sinai was only republished, whereas the Forensic and Ceremonial were given only through Moses.

[B.] In obligation.

The Moral Law is universal; the Forensic and Ceremonial Laws were obligatory only as long as the Israelitic State stood, and even then only upon Jews.

[C.] In duration.

The Moral Law is perpetual; since it is the declaration of God's eternal will. But, as the Epistle to the Hebrews shows in a long argument, the Forensic and Ceremonial are limited in duration.

[D.] In purpose.

The object of the Forensic and Ceremonial Laws was to keep Israel separate from other nations, that through it God's purposes for the race might be prepared. The Moral Law was to direct the experience and destiny of people of all nations and times, not only within, but beyond and above the limits of Israel.

31. How do you prove the abrogation of the Forensic Law?

The destruction of the Jewish State renders its administration an impossibility. Obedience to the rulers of other governments is commanded (Rom. 13:1, 5; 1 Peter 2:13 sq.). Citizenship in other States is approved (Acts 22:25; 25:10).

The Ceremonial Law: its contents, object, abrogation

32. What were the contents of the Ceremonial Law?

Regulations concerning:

[A.] Sacred persons.

The high priest, the priests, Levites, Nazarites, etc., and prescriptions concerning personal matters, as food and drink, clothing and other matters pertaining to the individual or domestic life.

[B.] Sacred things

The furniture, vessels and utensils for public worship, and the sacrifices and sacraments of the Old Testament.

A sacrifice is a sacred action, in which an object is offered to God through a prescribed ceremony, as an acknowledgment of the guilt of sin (Heb. 10:3), and a testimony to the complete and perfect sacrifice which God was hereafter to provide.

[C.] Sacred times

The Sabbath, the Feast of Trumpets, the Day of Atonement, the Feast of Tabernacles, the Feast of Pentecost, the Sabbatical Year, the Feast of Jubilee.

[D.] Sacred places

The Holy City, the Tabernacle, the Temple. In these buildings, each of its three divisions, the Court, the Holy Place and the Holy of Holies, had its peculiar significance.

33. What was the chief object of the Ceremonial Law?

To foreshadow the blessings to be procured and offered through Christ.

> Col. 2:16, 17. "Let no man therefore judge you in meat, or in drink, or in respect of a feast day, or of a new moon, or a sabbath day: which are a shadow of the things to come; but the body is Christ's."

34. How is the abrogation of the Ceremonial Law proved?

[A.] From the argument of the Epistle to the Hebrews concerning Melchisedek.

> Heb. 7:12. "For the priesthood being changed, there is made of necessity a change also of the law."

[B.] From its argument concerning the temporary character of the first tabernacle.

> Heb. 9:9, 12 "Which is a figure for the time present... But Christ having come through the greater and more perfect tabernacle."

[C.] From the proceedings of the council at Jerusalem, the first synod of the Christian Church. (Acts 15:1 sqq.).

[D.] From Peter's vision (Acts 10:11).

[E.] From Paul's rebuke of Peter (Gal. 2:14-16), and of the Galatians, who insisted on the permanence of ceremonial ordinances.

> Gal. 4:10, 11. "Ye observe days and months and seasons and years. I am afraid of you, lest by any means 1 have bestowed labor upon you in vain."

> Gal. 5:2. "If ye receive circumcision, Christ shall profit you nothing."

[F.] When the body comes, its shadow disappears; the type yields to the antitype (Heb. 10, 11; Col. 2:17).

Definition of Gospel

35. How is "Gospel" to be defined when contrasted with "Law"?

The promise of the gratuitous forgiveness of sins for Christ's sake. (See (above, 6.)

In the New Testament the verb "euaggelizein" occurs fifty-six, and the noun "euaggelion," seventy-two times, In the Gospels and Acts, the reference is simply to "good tidings." In Luke 16:16, the contrast with "Law" first appears. In the Epistles the restriction to the specific good tidings brought by Christ becomes very marked, as in Gal. 1:8; Rom. 1:16. A study of the passages in the Gospels, in the light of the use of the word in the Epistles, shows that the same specific meaning belongs also there.

> "It is the complex of the promises which are grateful, joyful and salutary to sinful men, a summary of which is found in John 3:16" (Baier).

36. How does the Gospel regard Christ?

Solely in His Mediatorial Office, with its Priestly functions as the very center.

37. Can any doctrine concerning the goodness or the Fatherhood of God, which is not based upon a clear confession of the divinity and priestly work of Christ be termed "Gospel"?

In answer to some modern theologians who have bad a wide hearing and who claim that the Gospel is not doctrine concerning Jesus Christ, but only concerning God the Father, we turn to Paul.

> Rom. 1:1-4. "The Gospel of God, concerning his Son, Jesus Christ our Lord," etc.

The Gospel not a New Law

38. May it not be regarded a new law, offering salvation upon easier terms than were given by the former law?

Law and Gospel differ not in degree, but in kind. The Gospel offers an entirely different righteousness from that which is attainable by the Law (Rom. 1:17; 3:21).

In what Law and Gospel differ and in what they coincide

39. How do they differ?

[A.] In revelation.

The Law partially by Nature (Rom. 2:15); the Gospel only through Christ (John 1:18; Rom. 16:26; Col. 1:26; Eph. 3:9; Matt. 1 1:25-27) .

[B.] In subject matter.

The Law is doctrine concerning works, prescribing what we ought to be, to do, or to omit to do (Ex. 20); the Gospel is doctrine concerning faith (Rom. 1:17) offering Christ and bringing the Holy Spirit.

[C.] In form.

The promises of the Law are conditional, requiring perfect obedience (Lev. 18:5); those of the Gospel are gratuitous (Rom. 3:23-25; 4:4, 5).

[D.] In effect.

The Law accuses, terrifies, works wrath (Rom. 3:20; 4:20); the Gospel consoles. The Law makes known the disease; the Gospel brings the physician and the remedy (Rom. 1:16). (See also above, 3, 5.)

40. In what do they coincide?

Both are heavenly doctrine divinely revealed. Of both God is author. Of both the purpose is salvation, the inadequacy of the law being attributable to no inherent weakness, but to man's inability, in his enfeebled state, to fulfill its requirements (Rom. 8:3; 7:12, 13). Both are universal; the Law announces a universal obligation; the other tenders a universal promise. Both are of perpetual validity; .the Law (Matt. 5:18); the Gospel (Matt. 28:19 sq.; Rev. 14:6).

They harmoniously unite and cooperate, when the Law demands complete obedience, and the Gospel declares that this complete obedience has been rendered for us by Christ.

> Rom. 3:31. "Do we then make the law of none effect through faith? nay, we establish the law."

In Illumination, the Law shows the need of faith; in Regeneration, the Gospel brings faith. In the Renewal, the Law indicates the works that please God; while the Gospel brings the true motives and the strength to do these works (2 Cor. 5:14, 15).

26. The Sacraments

Two modes of applying the Gospel

1. In what two ways is the Gospel applied as a Means of Grace?

Either to a congregation, i.e., a number of persons at the same time; or to an individual, separate and apart from all others. The former occurs in preaching; the latter in the pastoral care of souls, in the absolution, and in the Sacraments.

2. What distinguishes the Sacraments from other means of individualizing the general word, of the Gospel?

That the word is accompanied by a divinely appointed action and the use of an external object or element, through which the promise is sealed.

Definition of Sacrament

3. Define a Sacrament?

It is an action appointed by Christ, in which the general promise of the Gospel concerning the forgiveness of sins for Christ's sake is applied and sealed to an individual in the use of an external element.

4. Why do you call it an action?

Because the institution prescribes an action, without which there is no Sacrament. The command is "baptize," "this do ye," "take this and divide it." In the administration of the Sacraments, all else is simply preparatory or supplementary to the action.

Origin and history of term

5. Is the term "Sacrament" biblical?

No. It is an ecclesiastical term used to express the features which the two divinely-prescribed actions of the New Testament, Baptism and the Lord's Supper have in common, as contradistinguished from all other rites.

6. Whence was it derived?

In classical Latin, it designated the money deposited as a pledge by each party to a law suit. Transferred to military language, it soon meant the soldier's oath. In the Vulgate, it was the equivalent of the Greek "musterion both of the Lxx of Dan. 2:18; 4:6, and of the New Testament in Eph. 3:3; 5:32; 1 Tim. 3:16. Tertullian applied it to Baptism, as an application of the military oath to the Christian warfare. Augustine defines it in general as"a visible form of invisible grace." There was much variation in its use up to the time of the Reformation.

7. How was it employed by the Reformers?

In Luther's earlier reformatory writings, he suggests that, because of the abuse of the term, it be entirely abolished. He declares that there is but one Sacrament, referring to the Incarnation, according to the Vulgate of 1 Tim. 3:16, and suggests further that the term "sacramental sign" be substituted. Gradually, however, he recurred to the current term, although, like Melanchthon, wavering in its application, so as sometimes to include "Absolution," as a third sacrament. This is the classification in the Apology, 214.

8. How could Absolution be regarded as a Sacrament?

Because, like Baptism and the Lord's Supper, it applies the general promise of the Gospel to an individual. Unlike Baptism and the Lord's Supper, there is in Absolution no divinely prescribed action in which this is done; hence it soon ceased to be reckoned among the Sacraments.

Peculiar office of a Sacrament

9. What, therefore, is the peculiar office of a Sacrament?

To apply to an individual the general promise of the Gospel concerning the forgiveness t of sins, in connection with an external divinely appointed rite offering through earthly elements a pledge of the grace which is present.

10. How do our Confessions describe them?

> "They are rites which have the command of God and to which the promise of grace has been added" (Apology, 213).
>
> "Christ causes the promise of the Gospel to be offered not only in general, but, through the Sacraments, which He attaches as seals of the promise, He seals and thereby confirms the certainty of the promise of the Gospel to every believer" (Formula of Concord, 656).

11. How is this thought amplified by our theologians?

Melanchthon has more fully stated this in his Loci Communes (first edition):

> "Signs do not justify. The Apostle says: 'Circumcision is nothing.' So Baptism is nothing and the partaking of the Lord's Supper is nothing, but only witnesses and seals of God's will towards thee, whereby thy conscience may be assured, if it doubt concerning grace and the benevolence of God towards itself As Hezekiah could not doubt that he would recover when he heard the promise)and saw this promise confirmed by a sign; as Gideon could not doubt that he would conquer, when he was confirmed by so many signs, so thou oughtest not to doubt that thou hast obtained mercy when thou hast heard the Gospel, and hast received the seal of the Gospel, baptism and the body and blood of the Lord. Hezekiah could have recovered, even without a sign, if he had been willing to believe the bare promise, or Gideon would have conquered without a sign, if he had believed. So, provided only thou believest, thou canst, even without a sign, be justified. Signs, then, do not justify, but by such signs the faith of Hezekiah and of Gideon was aided and confirmed. Thus, too, lest amidst the constant attacks of sin, we may despair of God's mercy, our weakness is

> encouraged by signs. If God Himself were to converse with thee face to face, if He would offer thee some peculiar pledge of His mercy, as a miracle of any kind whatever, then thou wouldst consider this as nothing else than a sign of the divine favor. As to these signs, therefore, thou shouldst think so as to believe as certainly, when thou receivest Baptism and partakest of the Lord's Supper, that God pities thee, as thou wouldst believe, if God were to converse with thee, or to perform any other miracle, which would pertain peculiarly to thee. Signs have been instituted for the purpose of exciting faith."

> "As the sight of Christ did not justify Stephen when he was about to be murdered, but confirmed the faith by which he was justified, so partaking of the Holy Supper does not justify, but confirms faith."

Luther, in the "Babylonian Captivity," says:

> "In every promise, God is accustomed to add a sign, as a monument or memorial of His promise, whereby it may be the more faithfully preserved and may admonish more forcibly. Thus in connection with the promise to Noah concerning not again destroying the world by flood, God gave His bow in the clouds, by which He said He would be mindful of His covenant. To Abraham, after the promise of the inheritance of his seed, He gave circumcision as a seal of the righteousness of faith. So to Gideon, He gave the sign of the dry and the wet fleece... . Likewise in the Mass, in this chief promise of all, He added as a memorial sign, His own body and His own blood, in the bread and wine, as He says: 'Do this in remembrance of me.' So in Baptism He adds to the words of the promise the sign of the application of water" (Weimar ed., 6:547 sq.).

Whose act is the Sacrament

12. Whose action is that of the Sacraments?

God's and particularly Christ's, who has instituted and commanded their observance, and has promised to work through them.

> "Only He who is the author of grace can define the means through which He is willing to confer the grace which He freely confers; for He alone can communicate that infinite power to them, through which they are qualified to confer grace."

How a Sacrament differs from a sacrifice

13. How does a Sacrament differ from a sacrifice?

In a Sacrament God offers something to man; in a sacrifice, man offers something to God.

> "A Sacrament is a ceremony or work, in which God presents to us that which the promise annexed to the ceremony offers, as baptism is a work, not which we offer to God, but in which God baptizes us, i.e., a minister in the place of God; and God here offers and presents the remission of sins, according to the promise, Mark 16:16. A sacrifice, on the contrary, is a ceremony or work, which we render God in order to afford Him honor" (Apology, 262).

The three essentials of a Sacrament

14. What are the three essentials of a Sacrament?

[A.] A divine institution.

There must be an express and direct command of Christ, directing that it be observed for all time. No institution prescribed merely by the Church, is a Sacrament. Even Apostolic precedent for a practice, does not raise it to the rank of Sacraments. Appeal must be made to the example and appointment of the Lord Jesus.

[B.] An earthly element.

The term "element" when used in treating of the Sacraments always refers to something visible, tangible, corporeal, material. Inaccurate writers refer to "the heavenly and earthly elements." But there are no "heavenly elements." A Sacrament has a visible, material object, prescribed by Christ at its institution, which is used as a medium for conveying and applying the word of the Sacrament.

[C.] A special heavenly gift, also defined at the institution.

In both New Testament Sacraments, the forgiveness of sins is promised, offered and communicated with the sacramental act. In the Lord's Supper, the Body and Blood of Christ are with the elements, as pledges of this gift of the forgiveness of sins; and in both Baptism and the Lord's Supper, the word of promise both makes the Sacrament and applies its efficacy. *Accedit verbum ad clementum, et fit Sacramentum*. Neither the element without the Word, nor the Word without the element, but Word and element united, or rather the element as pervaded and energized by the express word of divine appointment, constitutes the Sacrament. There is no magical power inherent in the elements, even when consecrated. Their office is simply that of an instrument through which the divine promise is impressed upon the heart and mind of the recipient.

Importance of the Sacramental "word"

15. Is this last point so explained in the Confessions?

The Small Catechism teaches that "the water without the Word is simply water, and no baptism," and that "remission of sins, life and salvation," are imparted in the Lord's Supper, not "through the bodily eating and drinking," but through the words, "Given and shed for you for the remission of sins." The Large Catechism says of Baptism that "if the Word be taken away, the water is the same as that with which the servant cooks" (468).[10] So of the Lord's Supper, p. 477. The Schmalkald Articles define Baptism as "nothing else than the Word of God in the water commanded at its institution."

16. How may this be summed up?

> "There is not one grace in the word of promise, and another which is tendered in the Sacraments; neither is there one promise in the Gospel, and another in the Sacraments. But the grace is the same, and the word is one and the same, except that in the Sacraments, the Word, by means of the signs divinely instituted is, because of our infirmity, rendered visible, as Augustine says" (Chemnitz, Examen, 243).

Confirmation and Ordination not Sacraments

17. Why is Confirmation not reckoned among the Sacraments?

It is without the authority of any command of Christ. As an ecclesiastical rite, it has been used with profit; but this is all that can be claimed for it. See Apology, 214:6: (Compare Chapter 27, 34.)

---

10 Here Calvin agrees with Luther: "Verbo sublato perit tota vis sacramentorum. Quid enim aliud sunt sacramenta quam Verbi sigilla? . . Porro Verbum promissionem hie significat." On Eph. 5 -.26.

18. But has not Ordination sacramental validity?

No. Christ did not command that His ministers be set apart by the laying on of hands, neither did He institute such rite by His example. There is, indeed, Apostolic precedent for the formal commissioning of missionaries and pastors in this way (Acts 13:3; 1 Tim. 4:14; 2 Tim. 1:6); but no command that this must always occur. It is the call, and not the laying on of hands that makes one a minister. Besides this rite has no earthly element. The scholastics and Roman teachers are divided as to whether it be the hands of the officiating bishop or the chrism, or be found in the Sacrament of the eucharist which is partaken of in both kinds by the person ordained. As to the gift referred to in 1 Tim. 4:14 and 2 Tim. 16, this is not the forgiveness of sins, but the gifts needed for efficiency as a minister of the Gospel.

Not everything that God has instituted and commanded, a Sacrament

19. Does the rank of Sacraments belong to all objects having God's command?

> "If among the Sacraments, all things ought to be numbered which have God's command, and to which promises have been added, why do we not add prayer, which most truly can be called a Sacrament? For it has both God's command and very many promises. Alms could also be reckoned here" (Apology, 215).

When does the Sacrament exist

20. When does the Sacrament actually exist?

Only in the sacramental action accompanying the prescribed word; for that alone is the Sacrament. In Baptism all that precedes the administration of water in the name of the Father and of the Son and of the Holy Ghost, is only preparatory, and for the purpose of awakening and encouraging faith in the word of divine promise which is to be thus applied. In the Lord's Supper, the consecration effects no change in the elements, but prepares the hearts and minds of the communicants for the reception of what is to be offered them in the Sacrament which follows.

Where does the right to administer the Sacraments belong

21. To whom does the right to administer the Sacraments belong?

The Power of the Keys, i.e., of administering both Word and Sacraments belongs to the Church or congregation of believers.

> "For wherever the Church is, there is authority to administer the Gospel... . Here belong the words of Christ which testify that the Keys have been given to the Church, and not merely to certain persons (Matt. 18:20), 'Where two or three are gathered together in my name,' etc." (Schmalkald Articles, 350).

But in order that this right be exercised by the Church, the office of the ministry of the Word and Sacraments has been instituted. "Where there is therefore a true Church, the right to elect and ordain ministers necessarily exists" (ibid.).

The Sacraments, therefore, are administered by ministers, not as individuals directly commissioned by divine authority, nor as a self-perpetuating order, but as the executives of the congregation of believers, who have been called and duly recognized as such in whatever way it sees fit. As the administration of the Sacraments belongs not to believers as individuals, there is no transfer to ministers of individual rights, but there is simply the designation of those who are to fill an office which belongs to a congregation collectively.

> "Of Ecclesiastical Order they teach that no one should publicly teach in the Church or administer the Sacraments unless he be regularly called" (Augsburg Confession, XIV, 345)

22. Are there no exceptions?

It has been the practice of the Lutheran Church to allow Lay Baptism in case of extreme necessity, but not to allow under any circumstances an exception in regard to the Lord's Supper. The reason for this will be given under the treatment of each of the Sacraments.

Upon what does their efficacy depend

23. Upon what does the efficacy of the Sacraments depend?

Not upon the character of the minister, as the Donatists taught (1 Cor. 3:7; Rom. 3:3; Matt. 23:2, 3). Nor upon his intention, as Rome teaches. For then, just as with respect to the character, no one could be sure that he had received a Sacrament except by reading the heart of ia minister. Nor upon the regularity of his call, however important this may be (Heb. 5:4; Rom. 10:15); otherwise no one, without examining the credentials of the minister, could be sure that he had received a Sacrament. This would soon involve an entanglement in "endless genealogies." Nor upon the work that is wrought, the opus operatum. For it is not the sacramental action, but the Word that accompanies the action, which communicates saving grace; and this Word received, not by the body, but by the heart and mind, so as to awaken faith. Without faith, "sine bono motn utentis' no benefit is received from the Sacraments.

24. How do our Confessions stale this last point?

> "They condemn those who teach that the Sacraments justify by the outward act, and do not teach that, in the use of the Sacraments, faith which believes that sins are forgiven, is required" (Augsburg Confession, Art. XII).
>
> "What need will there be of faith, if the Sacraments justify by the outward act (*ex opere operato*), without a good disposition on the part of the one using them?" (Apology, 166).
>
> "We condemn the whole crowd of scholastic doctors, who teach that the Sacraments confer grace *ex opere operato*, without a good disposition on the part of the one using them, provided he do not place a hindrance in the way. This is absolutely a Jewish opinion, to hold that we are justified by a ceremony, without a good disposition of heart."
>
> "The promise is useless unless it be received by faith. But the Sacraments are the signs of the promises" (Apology, 2:6).

25. Is, therefore, their efficacy depended upon the faith of the recipient?

Be very careful here to distinguish the saving reception of their efficacy, from the efficacy itself. The efficacy of a medicine is one thing; the use of the medicine so as to be benefited by the efficacy is another. As the efficacy of the Sacraments is nothing more than that of the Word connected with the Sacraments, all that has been said concerning the relation of faith to the Word belongs here (see Chapters 19,8; 24, 26). When the efficacy of Word and Sacraments encounters man's unbelief and persistent resistance, their efficacy is not destroyed; but it is transformed from an efficacy of grace to one of judgment (2 Cor. 2:16; 1 Cor. 11:29).

26. We repeat the question: Upon what does the efficacy depend?

Upon God's appointment and promise.

> "The Word by which it was instituted and became a Sacrament, does not become false, because of the person and his unbelief. For he does not say, 'If you believe or if you are worthy, you receive my body and blood,' but, 'Take, eat and drink, this is my body and blood." No matter whether you be worthy or unworthy, you have here His body and blood, by virtue of these words which are added to the bread and wine. Upon these words rest all our foundation."
>
> "We approach the Sacrament, in order to receive there a treasure. Why so? Because the words stand here and give us the same" (Large Catechism, 478). (See also above, 14.)

In what sense are they necessary

27. Are the Sacraments necessary for salvation?

Everything that God enjoins, demands recognition and fulfillment. Of nothing that God has instituted and asked us to observe, dare we say that it is unnecessary. Its necessity is that of God's command (*Necessitas praecepti*) and our obligations to comply (*Necessitas debiti*). But while God binds us, He does not bind Himself to these means. According to Mark 16:16, only he that believeth not shall be condemned. Here belongs the saying of Bernard: *Non defectus, sed contemptus sacramenti damnat.*

What is their chief purpose

28. What is the chief purpose of the Sacraments?

Here we distinguish between the Sacraments as actions of God, and the use of the Sacraments by men; between the divine institution and man's response to and compliance with, its provision; between the sacramental and the sacrificial side of that which occurs wherever the Sacraments are administered. The question before us is, what is that which God confers or means to confer by His own act.

The Sacraments, therefore, cannot be acts of worship, or means of confessing Christ before men, or of declaring the unity that subsists or ought to subsist among Christians, or of typifying other Christian virtues. For all these pertain to man's reception of the Sacraments, or to the sacrificial, instead of the sacramental side of the ceremony. Their chief purpose is well summarized in the Augsburg Confession:

> "The Sacraments were ordained, not only to be marks of profession, among men, but rather to be signs and testimonies of the will of God toward us, instituted to awaken and confirm faith in them that use them" (Art. XIII).

> "Through the Word and Sacraments, as through instruments, the Holy Ghost is given, who worketh faith, where and when it pleaseth God, in them that hear the Gospel" (Art. V).

29. In saying that they 'are signs and testimonies of the will of God toward us' is it meant that these signs are the elements of the Sacraments?

It is the entire Sacrament that constitutes "the sign." It is not the water of Baptism that is the sign, but the water when taken in connection with the Word. In the Lord's Supper, the bread and wine are signs, only in connection with the Gospel that accompanies them.

30. Is their influence, then, merely of a didactic character?

They are no merely pictorial or emblematic representation of the mode in which God imparts His grace; but they actually "awaken and confirm faith," since the Holy Spirit works through the Gospel of which they give assurance.

> "God at the same time by the Word and by the rite, moves hearts to believe (Rom. 10:17). But just as the Word enters ears, in order to strike hearts, so the rite meets the eyes in order to move the hearts" (Apology. 2:4).

What are their secondary ends

31. Such being the primary, what are the secondary ends of the sacraments?

[A.] They are marks of the Church distinguishing it from other assemblies.

As Christ instituted the Sacraments, and commended them to the Church, with the injunction to perpetually observe them until His return, the Church is to be found only where this divine institution is observed.

[B.] They are perpetual memorials of God's intervention on behalf of His people, and, particularly, of the blessings of Redemption.

As the Passover was a memorial to the Israelites (Ex. 12:4), so, in the Lord's Supper, Christ has left a perpetual memorial of the salvation procured through His death (Luke 22:19; 1 Cor. 11:24-26). Baptism is a remembrance of deliverance from the ocean of sin in which our race was lost (1 Peter 3:20, 21). Not only to the believer, but to the world they are constant witnesses of the great facts of Redemption.

[C.] They are indications of the new life expected of those who have experienced such deliverance.

(Rom. 5:4; 1 Cor. 10:21).

[D.] They are means whereby the mutual love of Christians is promoted in the common use of the same ordinances.

(1 Cor. 1:17).

The question as to Old Testament Sacraments

32. Were there Sacraments under the Old Testament?

The way of salvation under the Old Testament was the same as under the New, "the same substance of the promise, the same faith, the same grace, the same righteousness, the same salvation and eternal life, in and on account of Christ, who was promised in the Old Testament as to come, (and was announced in the New

Testament as having come." The question to be determined is as to whether the promise of grace under the Old Testament was made exclusively through the audible Word, or whether there were not also rites in which it assumed a visible form, as in the New Testament Sacraments. The answer is that Circumcision and the Passover were such rites applying the word of promise individually, and sealing it by an external action, with a visible element.

The differences between Baptism and the Lord's Supper

33. Were there not other Old Testament acts that had a sacramental character?

The passage of the Israelites through the Red Sea and the eating of the manna in the wilderness are referred to in 1 Cor. 9:1-4, as having sacramental significance, and as figures of the New Testament Sacraments. The cloud and the miraculous passage through the sea testified to God's love and care for every Israelite journeying towards the land of promise. Every drop of spray that touched him as he walked between the walls of waters assured .him of the divine favor. So the manna was also a pledge of God's grace and mercy, and a declaration of the supernatural agencies at the service of those who were content to trust in God's promises. Every grain of manna eaten brought the certainty of God's promise forcibly to each individual. But, unlike Circumcision and the Passover, they were only temporary, and were not institutions to be observed by the Israelitic Church. They were acts of God, but not rites.

34. But in what do the so-called Sacraments of the Old Testament differ from those of the New Testament?

The former were to be abrogated in course of time; the latter are to be used until the end of the world. The former were for Israelites; the latter are for all nations. The former foreshadowed the blessings of the Gospel; the latter proclaimed their presence. The former were prenunciative; the latter annunciative of Christ, as Augustine declares. The New Testament ordinances only are Sacraments in the fullest and clearest sense.

35. How do the two Sacraments of the New Testament differ?

Baptism is the Sacrament of initiation; the Lord's Supper the Sacrament for the confirmation of faith. Baptism is for the beginning of new spiritual life; the Lord's Supper is for its nourishment. Baptism is administered but once to an individual (Eph. 4:5); the Lord's Supper, according to 1 Cor. 11:20, is to be frequently repeated. Baptism is retrospective in its emphasis referring particularly to deliverance from the former life of sin and death; the Lord's Supper is prospective, being a preparation for our last hour. Baptism is recognized, upon the basis of John 3:5; Titus 3:5:1 Peter 3:21, as of higher necessity than the Lord's Supper.

27. Of Holy Baptism

Definition

1. Define Baptism.

A divinely instituted action, enjoined upon the Church until the end of time, in which, with the application of water, in the name of the Father and of the Son and of the Holy Ghost, the Gospel promise of the forgiveness of sins is offered to every one baptized, and is most certainly imparted to every one who believes.

2. How does Baptism meet the three requirements of a Sacrament above given (Chapter 26, 14)?

It has a divine institution, an earthly element and a heavenly gift.

Institution

3. When was it instituted?

By our Lord Jesus Christ, when His sacrificial offering for sin had been completed, and, having risen from the dead, He assumed the full exercise of His Kingly Office. The institution looked forward to the gift of the Holy Spirit on the Day of Pentecost, through which its administration by the Church was to be rendered efficacious.

4. Where is the institution recorded?

> Matt. 28:18-20. "And Jesus came to them and spake unto them, saying, All authority hath been given unto me in heaven and on earth. Go ye, therefore, and make disciples of all the nations, baptizing them into the name of the Father, and of the Son, and of the Holy Spirit, teaching them to observe all things whatsoever I have commanded you; and lo, I am with you always, even unto the end of the world."

> Mark 16:15, 16. "And he said unto them, Go ye into all the world and preach the gospel to the whole creation. He that believeth and is baptized shall be saved; and he that believeth not shall be condemned.' V. 20."And they went forth and preached everywhere, the Lord working with them and confirming the word with signs following."

5. But John certainly baptized before this?

Luther calls John's baptism "the vestibule to Christian Baptism." It was a sacred action individually sealing the word of promise with an earthly element, but without the certification of a divine institution and serving only a provisional purpose. It has some sacramental features, being "a baptism of repentance for the remission of sins." But John's preaching was not concerning the Christ who had come and fulfilled the law for man, but concerning the Christ who was to come (John 1:30). He himself contrasted his baptism with that of Christ (Matt. 3:11; John 1:33). The Holy Spirit had not vet been given in New Testament fullness (John 7:39), (see Chapter 16, 3-5), and Acts 19:2-6 is irreconcilable with the theory that the two rites are identical.

> "Both baptisms signified the same thing, but with this distinction that John's was a testimony of grace that was yet to be preached, while Christ's baptism was a testimony of grace that had already been conferred" (Melanchthon, "Loci Communes").

John, however, was the greatest of the Old Testament prophets, and even more than a prophet, because he could point to the Lamb of God, as he walked before those to whom he preached (John 1:29). Chemnitz terms John's baptism, therefore, "a transient sacrament."

Our authority, however, for the baptism which the Church employs rests not upon John's example and preaching, nor upon that of the disciples of Jesus who continued for a time the same rite (John 4:12), but solely upon Christ's parting command. By it He raised a rite which thus far was of only temporary significance, to the rank of a Sacrament, and in so doing made of it a new institution.

Meaning of formula

6. What is Baptism according to the words of institution?

An introduction into the new life that comes from the revelation of God, as Father, Son and Holy Ghost.

7. How is this established?

By the fact that, according to Matt. 28:19; Acts 8:16; 19:5; Rom. 6:3; 1 Cor. 1:13; 10:2; Gal. 3:27, Baptism is "into the name." It is an action directed towards a certain goal, i.e., to self-surrender, ownership, obedience, communion with the name of Father, Son and Holy Ghost (see Chapter 2, 13:15). Elsewhere, as Acts 2:38; 10:48, it is "in the name," i.e., "by authority of." It is Baptism into the One Name, which all three share. Baptism is said, in some passages, to be "in the name" or "into the name of the Lord Jesus," or "into Christ Jesus," or "into Christ" (Acts 2:38; 8:16; 19:5; 10:48; Rom. 6:3; Gal. 3:27). This means, through Baptism to enter into life-communion with all that Jesus is and has done and to surrender oneself, with implicit faith and obedience, to the revelation of God that has been made in and through Jesus Christ, as the Israelites were "baptized into Moses" (1 Cor. 10:2).

> "He is baptized into a whole Christ, and so also into His death. It is just as if, at that moment, Christ suffered, died, and were buried for such a man, and such a man suffered, died, were buried with Christ" (Bengel).

Who baptizes

8. Who is it that baptizes?

The opinion is readily entertained that the external act is that simply of the minister, while it is only the inner act which attends the external and that imparts grace, which is of God. Of this Luther says:

> "Be on your guard against making such distinction as to ascribe the external work to man, and the internal to God, but ascribe both to God alone, and regard the person of the one ministering as nothing more than a vicarious instrument of God, through which God in heaven applies the

water with His own hands, and promises forgiveness of sins, speaking to thee, with man's voice, through the mouth of the minister" ("Babylonian Captivity," Erl. ed., 5:60 sq.).

The Element

9. What is the earthly element?

The most common and readily accessible material object in the world. Neither the sand of the desert, nor the soil of the earth, nor the dust of the street, nor the leaves of the trees, nor the grass of the meadows, is as common or as universally procurable as water. More than two thirds of the surface of the globe is covered by it, while the remaining third is honeycombed by subterranean streams and pierced everywhere by springs and currents, large and small, that carry it into the remotest regions. The atmosphere holds it in a rarefied form, and periodically precipitates it in abundant measure. In Baptism, God makes the most common thing the vehicle of His richest grace.

10. Is there no prescription as to the quality?

None whatever. All that is required is that it be water. But whether this water be clear or clouded, pure or impure, cold or warm, filtered or distilled, running or stagnant, from the Jordan or the Mississippi, caught from the clouds or taken from the ocean, is a matter of absolute indifference. But there must be water (John 3:5; Acts 8:38; Eph. 5:26).

11. Is there no prescription as to the quantity?

None whatever. The attention is withdrawn from anxiety concerning such externalities to the word of promise, which is the chief thing in the Sacrament. If the validity of the rite depended upon the amount of water, conscience might readily be distressed if there were doubt as to whether the person were completely covered by the stream, or whether by accident some portion of the body had been left exposed. If insistence is placed upon such external circumstance, then others could readily be suggested as necessary to make the correspondence with New Testament precedents complete.

12. Is Immersion a valid method of baptism?

Not all the arguments urged by immersionists can be admitted as proving in particular instances that this was the method practiced, as e.g., when the baptized were said to have "gone into," or to have "come out of the water". For how does this prove the total submergence of the body in the water? Nevertheless there are passages, as Rom. 6:4; Col. 2:12, which seem to refer to immersion. The practice of the early Church clearly testifies to going into the water and to running water, by preference, as a common mode, falling in as it did with Oriental usages, as to bathing. It is impossible, however, to prove that it was complete submersion.

13. But does this prove that it was the only mode?

No. The term baptism is used in Mark 7:3, 4, of the washing of cups and vessels and tables; in Luke 11:38, of washing before taking meals, which could not have been immersion; and of the sprinkling of the Israelites as they passed through the way opened in the Red Sea, by the cloud from above and the spray from the walls of water on either side (1 Cor. 10:2). Neither can the baptism of the Holy Spirit be conceived of as an immersion into the Spirit; but, on the contrary, must be referred to His being poured forth upon the disciples from above.

14. How early do we find the justification of Sprinkling or Pouring, as a mode of Baptism?

In the earliest of the uninspired writings of the Christian Church, 'The Teaching of the Twelve Apostles." The words are:

> "Pour water upon the head thrice, in the name of the Father and Son and Holy Spirit" (Chapter 7).

The Heavenly Gift

15. What is the heavenly gift?

[A.] The Triune God; for we are baptized into the name of the Father and of the Son and of the Holy Ghost (see above, 6, 7).

[B.] The Word of God.

> Eph. 5:26. "Having cleansed it with the washing of water with the word."

[C.] The Holy Spirit.

> John 3:5. "Except one be born of water and of the Spirit, he cannot enter into the kingdom of God." (d) The Forgiveness of Sins.

Acts 2:38. "Repent and be baptized every one of you in the name of Jesus Christ unto the remission of your sins; and ye shall receive the gift of the Holy Ghost." Cf. Chapter XXVI 9 and 14.

All these concur and are combined hi the statement, that the heavenly gift is the Word of God as the organ, through which the Holy Spirit applies the merits of Christ, on account of which we have forgiveness of sins, and thus introduces one into communion with the Triune God.[11]

The Minister

16. By whom is Baptism administered?

This question has been answered in general under Chapter 26, 21. The words of institution of Baptism were spoken to the eleven Apostles (Matt. 28:16); but that the administration was not restricted to them, is clear from the fact that it is an ordinance that is to be observed until the end of time (v. 20). Paul seems to have been baptized by Ananias (Acts 9:18, cf. Gal. 1:17). Like the Power of the Keys it belongs to the entire Church (Matt. 18:17-20), and is administered by those who have been called as the Church's official executives (1 Cor. 4:1).

17. Does the validity of Baptism depend upon the regularity of the administrator's call?

No; for then the attention would be withdrawn from the word to matters that are purely external, and conscience could never be satisfied, until it could prove by the surest vouchers, the regularity of the external succession of those from whom they received baptism. While men are responsible to God for having acted without a regular call, God uses their ministry to bring His Word to men. The only test, therefore, of the validity of Baptism, is that which can always be made, viz., as to whether the essentials of the Sacrament have been observed, i.e., the use of the element and the words of institution.

18. Why did not our Lord administer Baptism?

The usual answer is, because a difference would thus have been made between those, whom He would have baptized by His own hands and those whom He

11 Some Lutheran theologians press the analogy between the two Sacraments to such extent, as to insist that there must be in Baptism that which corresponds to the 'Body and Blood' of Christ in the Holy Supper. The most convenient summary of the discussion is in Baier, pp. 526-538.

would have baptized through the hands of His ministers. But beside this, it must not be forgotten, that the period for Christian Baptism did not come until after our Lord's ascension, and the gift of the Holy Spirit at Pentecost.

19. How do we explain Paul's declaration that he was sent to preach and not to baptize (1 Cor.1:17)?

Paul was both an apostle and a minister like other ministers. As a minister, he baptized (1 Cor. 1:14-16). But his chief work was that of the apostolate, to give forth his apostolic witness for all times and places. No peculiar spiritual endowment was needed to baptize; but such endowment was needful for preaching. The relation of baptism to preaching was that of the seal to the letter.

20. Can no one baptize except a regularly called minister?

In case of imminent peril of death the Lutheran Church allows lay baptism. The usual argument is that if God approved the act of circumcision by Zipporah, although done in wrath, so that the life of her child was spared (Ex. 4:25), He may be presumed under the New Testament much more to favor an exception to the regular rule concerning baptism, when it cannot be had elsewhere, and its necessity is so urgent (John 3:5).

> "In case of necessity, even a layman absolves and becomes the pastor of another; as Augustine narrates the story of two Christians in a ship, one of whom baptized the catechumen, who, after baptism, then absolved the baptizer" (Schmalkald Articles, 350).

21. How is the necessity of such departure from the rule safeguarded?

The Churches in which it is authorized prescribe for its public announcement and ratification, not that this is necessary for its validity, but to protect against its unrestricted use. Lay Baptism, without urgent necessity, is still Baptism, however culpable the administrator may be for disturbing the regular order of the Church.

Subjects

22. Who are to be baptized?

Not inanimate objects, as bells or ships, but only sinful men, who having been born in sin, are capable of regeneration (John 3:5, 6). All such, without distinction of race, station, sex or age, are proper subjects of Baptism, provided they comply with the prescribed conditions. Matt. 28:19, as shown, under 4; also Gal. 3:27, 28.

> "For as many of you as were baptized into Christ, have put on Christ. There can be neither Jew nor Greek, there can be neither bond nor tree, there can be no male and female; for ye are all one man in Christ Jesus."

The condition has its explanation in the fact that God's richest blessings ought not to be offered where they will surely be abused, and increase the guilt and condemnation of the recipient.

23. The only persons concerning whose right to Baptism there seems to be any difference of opinion, are little children. Give, therefore, a somewhat fuller argument on this subject.

[A.] Infants need baptism. They are born in a state of sin, and cannot enter the Kingdom of God unless they be regenerated.

> John 3:6. "That which is born of the flesh, is flesh."

> Rom. 5:12. "Death passed unto all men, for that all sinned."

> Eph. 2:1, 3 "Ye were dead through your trespasses and sins... And were by nature children of wrath."

The Greek pronoun "Us" of John 3:5 is very emphatic and exclusive:

> "Except one be born of water and the Spirit, he cannot enter into the kingdom of God."

But as we learn from Matt. 18:14, "It is not the will of your Father who is in heaven, that one of these little ones perish," it must be God's will that they meet the conditions through which they are delivered from their sinful state; and this is through baptism.

[B.] Christ Himself asserts their rights.

> Matt. 19:14. "For to such belongeth the kingdom of heaven."

They have, therefore, admittance to the portal of the Kingdom of Heaven, which, (according to John 3:5, is Baptism.

[C.] The promise of the forgiveness of sins and of the gift of the Holy Ghost is theirs.

> Acts 2:38, 39. "Repent ye, and be baptized every one of you in the name of Jesus Christ unto the remission of your sins; and ye shall receive the gift of the Holy Ghost. For to you is the promise and to your children."

[D.] From the capacity of infants for faith and its fruits.

Matt. 18:2, 3, 6; Is. 8:2; cf. Matt. 21:15; Luke 1:15, 41, 44.

(Concerning Infant Faith, see above, Chapter 21, 15-18.)

[E.] From the universal command for baptism.

(See above, under 4.) With this command, unless children be excluded by some other command, the duty of baptizing them is clear. If children are to be excluded from baptism, because they are not mentioned explicitly, then women, on the same ground, must be excluded from the Lord's Supper.

[F.] From the relation of baptism to circumcision.

Rendering it unnecessary that, where this was understood, they should be mentioned. When God made His covenant with Abraham, He expressly commanded that children should be admitted into His Church. For this, circumcision was the initiatory rite (Gen. 17:12). But circumcision, as such initiatory rite, has been superseded by baptism (Col. r:11, 12).

[G.] From the apostolic practice of the baptism of entire families.

As that of Lydia (Acts 16:15), of the Philippian jailer (Acts 16:33), of Stephanas (1 Cor. 1:16). It is improbable that these households were composed entirely of adults.

24. Is this attested also by the practice of the Church in the earliest period after the Apostles?

Among the Fathers, there is not a single voice against the validity and apostolic origin of infant baptism. Origen, born in A. D. 185, calls it "an apostolic tradition." When in the Pelagian controversy, Augustine urged the usage of Infant Baptism as an argument for Original Sin, Pelagius, instead of assailing it, answered that children were baptized, not for what they then needed, but for what they would need hereafter. The opponents of Infant Baptism are unable, therefore, to find any period in the history of the Church, in which they can prove that it did not exist.

25. But are not the children of Christian parents already in covenant relations to God, in virtue of their birth?

We who have been born Israelites, says Paul in Eph. 2:1, were dead through trespasses and sins, even as others. Nevertheless it is true, as a recent theologian has put it, that:

> "...children whose parents are Christian have the preparatory consecration of a Christian family spirit, and are from the beginning under the influence of the Holy Spirit" (Rohnert).

They are children of devout and constant prayer. Hence the statement of 1 Cor. 7:14.

> "For the unbelieving husband is sanctified in the wife, and the unbelieving wife is sanctified in the brother; else were your children unclean, but now are they holy."

This, however, is an external holiness. They are brought within the sphere, in which the Means of Grace are administered, and through them, the Holy Spirit given. But that the reference is not yet to regeneration, may be inferred from the fact that the holiness of the children is of the same kind as the "sanctification" of the unbelieving husband or wife. Their covenant privilege, prior to baptism and faith, is found in access to the Means of Grace. The covenant is not actually concluded until then, although commenced.

Effect

26. What is the effect of Baptism?

Its immediate effect is Regeneration and Renovation, as is clearly taught in Titus 3:5; John 3:5. (See above, Chapter 21, 12; 23, 11.) The ultimate end is salvation and eternal life, as is taught in Mark 16:16; 1 Peter 3:21.

27. Are all the baptized saved?

No more than all hearers of the Word. The objective efficacy of word and Sacrament, when not appropriated by faith confers no benefit. (See Chapter 26, 25.) Faith also which has been both the effect of baptism and has received its blessings, may be cast aside. (See Chapter 17, 36.) The doctrines of baptismal grace, on the one hand, and of the inamissibility and the irresistibility of grace, on the other hand, are absolutely irreconcilable.

Relation to Faith

28. Has Baptism the same relation to faith in all its subjects?

To infants it comes, prior to faith, to bring them the assurance of God's grace and apply the Gospel. (See Chapter 21, 15-18).

> "We bring the child in the purpose and hope, that it may believe, and we pray that God may grant it faith; but we do not baptize it upon that, but solely upon the command of God" (Large Catechism, 473).

In adults, it is a means of confirming and strengthening faith which has been received previously through the hearing of the Gospel.

> Acts 2:41. "They then that received his word, were baptized.

> Acts 8:12. "When they believed Philip preaching good tidings concerning the kingdom of God and the name of Jesus Christ, they were baptized." (See also Chapter 21, 10, 11.)

29. But how are the difficulties concerning the possibility of infant regeneration and infant faith met?

Lest the argument of Lutheran theologians may be regarded as prejudiced, we refer to Calvin:

'How,' it is inquired, 'are infants regenerated, who have no knowledge either of good or evil?'

We reply, that the work of God is not yet without existence, because it is not observed or understood by us. Now it is certain that some infants are saved; and that they are previously regenerated by the Lord, is beyond all doubt. For if they are born in a state of corruption, it is necessary for them to be purified before they be admitted into the Kingdom of God... What do we require more when the Judge Himself declareth that there is no entrance into the heavenly life, except for those who are born again? And, to silence all objectors, by sanctifying John the Baptist in his mother's womb, he exhibited an example of what he was able to do for others." "But our opponents say, 'Faith cometh by hearing,' of which they have not yet acquired the use, and cannot be capable of knowing God. But they do not consider that when the apostle makes hearing the source of faith, he only describes the ordinary economy and dispensation of God, which He generally observes in the calling of His people; but does, not prescribe a perpetual rule for Him, precluding His employment of any other method; which He has certainly employed in the calling of many, to whom He has given the knowledge of Himself in an internal manner, by the illumination of His Spirit, without the intervention of any preaching. But, as they think, it would be so great absurdity for any knowledge of God to be given infants, to whom Moses denies the knowledge of good and evil, I would beg them to inform me, what danger can result from our affirming that they already receive some portion of that grace, of which they will ere long enjoy the full abundance? For if the plenitude of life consists in the perfect knowledge of God — when some of them whom death removes from the present state in their earliest infancy, pass into eternal life, they are certainly admitted to the immediate contemplation of the presence of God.

As the Lord, therefore, will illumine them with the full splendor of His countenance in heaven, why may He not also, if such be His pleasure, irradiate them with some faint rays of it already in the present life; especially if He does not deliver them from all ignorance before He liberates them from the prison of the body? Not that I would hastily affirm them to be endued with the same faith which we experience in ourselves, or at all to possess a similar knowledge of faith, which I would prefer leaving in suspense" (Institutes, Book IV, Chapter 16, 17-19).

30. But cannot this doctrine be greatly abased?

Undoubtedly; particularly if more stress is laid upon the inner change effected in infant baptism than upon the external word and promise of God which makes the baptism "a gracious water of life' There is a tendency to regard the grace of God as given"because of" the inner change (i.e., *propter fidem*) rather than because of the merits of Christ gratuitously offered through the Word and Sacraments. Here the various points involved in the full treatment of Justification by Faith must be kept in mind, and its distinctions between the meritorious and the instrumental causes be accurately observed. As in regard to Justification in general, so also here, we must look away from our faith and from all that is in us, even though it be the blessed work of the Holy Spirit, as our Regeneration and our Renewal, solely and entirely to the objective work of Christ for us and His objective word and promise to us. This, after all, is the principal thing in our baptism. The all important matter is not that in infancy our hearts by God's grace were endowed with a faint spark of spiritual life, but that the word and promise brought us then are offered us anew every day of our lives through the covenant which God then made with us. With all confidence, we can leave to Him the manner in which He applied and fulfilled the promise then made, as well as the manner in which this works in us today and will work until it reaches its complete fruition in another world. Nowhere more than in Baptism is man taught to realize his own helplessness in spiritual things, and the sole efficacy of divine grace.

Perpetuity

31. Is the importation of the efficacy of Baptism confined to the moment of its administration?

The efficacy of Baptism consisting in the word of promise which it communicates, is reapplied with every remembrance of one's baptism. The assurance of what was brought one in his baptism is a never-failing fountain of encouragement, consolation and spiritual strength. It is the seal of the covenant of grace which God made with us once and forever, and which thus is always in force upon the condition then unalterably fixed.

> Is. 54:10. "For the mountains may depart and the hills be removed: but my lovingkindness shall not depart from thee, neither shall my covenant of peace be removed."

> 2 Tim. 2:13. "It we are faithless, he abideth faithful; for he cannot deny himself."

32. But what comfort does this afford, if we have broken its conditions?

Here let Luther answer:

> "Our baptism abides forever; and even though some one should fall from it and sin, we nevertheless always have access thereto... Repentance is nothing else than a return to baptism... Our baptism is not something past, which we can no longer use after we have fallen into sin."

Referring to the error of Jerome that after the ship of baptism has foundered and gone down in the sea of sin, penance is provided as a plank on which we may again be delivered, he continues:

> "The ship never breaks, for it is an institution of God... It happens indeed that we slip and fall out of the ship. Yet if anyone fall out, let him see to it that he return" (Large Catechism, 475).

> "The people should be admonished to reflect upon their baptism, and be instructed that it means that God takes them into His favor not only in childhood, but also throughout their entire lives. Baptism is, therefore, not only a sign for children, but it urges and admonishes adults also to repent" (Melanchthon in German Visitation Articles of 1527).

> "Let the pastors teach that the effect of baptism ought to last throughout the entire life, i.e., that we ought always to repent and, at the same time, to believe that God wishes to forgive us" (Latin copy of same document).

So in that edition of the Loci Communes, which Luther said, with complimentary extravagance, was worthy of being regarded canonical, Melanchthon says:

> "I venture to say that no more efficacious consolation can be offered the dying than the mention of this sacrament, viz., if they be admonished of baptism, and be assured that in it they received a seal of the divine promise, that they may certainly know that God will lead them through death to life. Suppose Moses had baptized the Israelites before they entered the waters. Ought he not then to have admonished them, while they were passing through the midst of the sea, concerning the sign which they had received as to the issue of what was transpiring, and to have urged them to remember that this sign was given them for the very purpose of protecting against any doubt that they would be saved? Baptism has the same use in the mortifying of our sinful flesh. It admonishes the terrified conscience concerning the remission of sins, and assures it of God's grace, so as to dispel all temptations to despair. Just as long as this struggle lasts, is there need of this sign. But since the former is not completed until the old man entirely perishes, there is perpetual need of this sign throughout our entire life, that it may console conscience in this constant mortification. Hence it is apparent that these signs are nothing but memorials, whereby faith may be exercised."

Repetition

33. Can Baptism be repeated?

No. For there is but one baptism (Eph. 4:5). God's covenant once made remains God's covenant forever. "Though we were a hundred times put under water, it would, nevertheless, be but one baptism" (ibid.).

Relation of Confirmation

34. Is there not a renewal of the covenant in Confirmation?

Baptism is God's act. Confirmation is on the one hand, man's formal public recognition of the significance of his baptism, and, on the other, the Church's attestation that, since this significance is recognized, the person should be admitted to the Lord's Supper.

Necessity

35. In what sense is Baptism necessary?

This question and its answer have already been anticipated (see Chapter 26, 27). Nothing that God has enjoined can be a matter of indifference.

36. What does the Augsburg Confession mean when it condemns the Anabaptists for teaching that children are saved without baptism?

It must be interpreted historically. The statement is directed against the depreciation of Infant Baptism by the Anabaptists who denied its validity and efficacy, and, therefore, that it is in any sense a means of saving grace. It does not deal with the possibilities of salvation where baptism is not accessible or attainable. We dare not limit God's power and mercy by the boundaries of what He has imposed upon us.

37. Has God anywhere promised His saving grace except in the observance of the provisions of the Order of Salvation which He has revealed to us?

Nowhere. But the universality of redemption (Chapter 14, 12) and of His will for the salvation of all (Chapter 9, 10), especially of little children (Matt. 18:14), warrants us in entertaining the hope that God has His own way of communicating His regenerating grace to those from whom it is denied by the unbelief of parents and the indifference of the Church.

38. What has been the prevalent opinion of Lutheran theologians on this point?

> "The children of believing parents, accidentally deprived of baptism, we believe are regenerated and saved by the extraordinary grace of God" (Baier). "For the necessity of baptism is not absolute. On our"part, we are under obligations to receive baptism. Nevertheless an extraordinary action of God is not to be denied in infants offered in prayer to Christ by godly parents and the Church, and who die before there can be opportunity for Baptism; since God does not bind His grace and efficacy to Baptism in such a way as not to be able and willing, in case of necessity to act extraordinarily" (Gerhard).

39. Is the same affirmed of the children of unbelieving parents?

Above, under Question 25, the peculiar relation of the children of believing parents to God's grace and promise, has already been treated. This, in connection with the promises made to prayer, afford the presumption of a special intervention of God on their behalf. But since there are no such promises concerning the children of unbelieving parents, we are not authorized to entertain the hope of their salvation, except with considerable qualification.

> "The unbaptized infants of unbelievers we commit to the divine judgment" (Baier).

See 1 Cor. 5:12. This, however, does not exclude the hope that God may also impart to them His grace; although, in the lack of revelation on the subject, this cannot be accepted as an article of faith.

Accidentals

40. In its administration, what are the essentials of Baptism?

Only the words of institution and the application of the water in the name of the Father and of the Son and of the Holy Ghost. All else is only preparatory and supplementary to what is properly speaking the baptism, and has the authority only of Church rites, which, while they are not to be arbitrarily changed, are not to be used except as they promote edification.

28. Of The Holy Supper

Definition and sedes doctrinae

1. What is the Lord's Supper?

The second Sacrament of the New Testament in which in connection with bread and wine, the true body and blood of Christ are offered and received by all communicants; to the comfort and salvation of those who accept in faith the promise of the Gospel attending it, and to the condemnation of all unbelieving communicants.

2. From what passages of Scripture is the doctrine of the Lord's Supper to be learned?

Matt. 26:26-28; Mark 14:22-25; Luke 22:19, 20; 1 Cor. 11:23-29. These are the *sedes doctrinae*, i.e., the passages in which the doctrine is explicitly and directly treated. John 6:53-58 does not refer to the Lord's Supper, but to the spiritual appropriation of Christ by faith. If it would apply to the Lord's Supper, we would have to dispense entirely with bread and wine, as it contains no allusion to any earthly elements; and we would be forced to deny the possibility of the salvation of any, except through the use of this Sacrament, and, with others, all baptized children, who had not been admitted to the Holy Supper would be lost.[12]

12 See Luther Erlangen Ed. (second edition) 15:368 or First hd. 12:368; Chemnitz, "Fundamenta Sacrae Coenae," 80-84.

Elements

3. What are the elements?

[A.] Bread.

One of the most widely used and generally obtainable kinds of food. There is no need for a scrupulous regard to the particular kind of bread. It may be wheaten, or rye or rice; it may be leavened or unleavened; kneaded or unkneaded; salted or sweetened or neither; cut or broken; administered in crumbs or in wafers. All this is of no more importance than the color or temperature of the water of baptism. The general use of wafers by the Lutheran Church has been determined more by convenience and readiness of disposing of those that remain after a communion, than by any other reason. The breaking of the bread does not belong, as has been taught in the Reformed Church, to the sacramental action. The use of several kinds or forms of bread at the same time, brings to the Lord's Table the reminiscences of former controversies, and should not occur.

[B.] Wine, or the fermented juice of the grape. In a vine-growing country, this was a common drink, readily obtained, and nevertheless highly esteemed. Our Lord had no intention, in the institution of this ordinance, to torment the consciences of His followers with legal prescriptions concerning an exact conformity in all respects with the minute details of the externals in the first Supper. As in baptism, so also here, the chief thing in the Sacrament is the word of the Gospel which it applies; so that neither the quantity nor the quality nor the color of the wine is in any way significant. It is important, however, that in the choice of the wine, there be no reflection cast upon that which was used by Christ in the original institution.

Heavenly Gift

4. What is the heavenly gift?

The Body and Blood of Christ, as the words of institution declare.

Literal interpretation of Words

5. But are these words to be interpreted literally?

Our first argument for a literal interpretation rests upon the hermeneutical principle that the burden of proof rests upon the advocates of a figurative interpretation. A declaration is presumed to be intended for literal application unless sufficient reasons are alleged to the contrary. Those parts of Scripture containing divine commands, promises, warnings, threats, and articles of faith, must be guarded with the utmost care from all suggestions, which, under the pretext of a figure, would deprive them of their real force. Here we must remember this important fact: There is no divine command, promise or article of faith that is not expressed somewhere in Holy Scripture in clear, distinct and proper, as distinguished from figurative terms. Every figurative passage must have the key of its interpretation in one that is literal.

But if these words be interpreted figuratively, the doctrine of the Lord's Supper is without a single support in any literal declaration of Holy Scripture. The explanation comes entirely from man's ingenuity outside of the Scriptures, and not from them.

6. What warning does Scripture give concerning the effort to explain away what God has declared?

The fall of our first parents who were induced to believe that God could not mean that which His words said (Gen. 3:1-5).

7. What example is commended for the opposite of this?

That of Abraham (Rom. 4:18-20), who had many motives to tempt him to explain away the force of God's command.

> "As when Abraham heard God's word concerning offering his son, although indeed he had cause enough for disputing as to whether the words should be understood according to the letter or with a moderate or mild interpretation, since they conflicted not only with all reason, and with divine and natural law, but also with the chief article of faith concerning the promised seed, Christ, who was to be born of Isaac; yet, as before, when the promise of the blessed seed from Isaac was given him (although it appeared to his reason impossible), he gave God the honor of truth, and most confidently believed that God could do what He promised; so he also here understands and believes God's word and command plainly and simply, as they sound, according to the letter, and resigns the entire matter to the divine omnipotence and wisdom, which he knows has many more modes and ways to fulfill the promise of the seed from Isaac, then he, with his blind reason, can comprehend" (Formula of Concord, 609).

8. What would follow from our rejection of a literal interpretation because of our inability to understand how this could be possible?

Our Lord referred Nicodemus to the mystery of the wind as one his reason could not explain (John 3:8). So Job was overwhelmed with a catalogue of mysteries filling four chapters (Job 38-42), when he yielded to a similar skepticism. What will become of the doctrine of the Trinity, of the Incarnation, of the Resurrection from the dead, if we start out with the assumption that we will accept nothing except what we can understand and explain? Would there be any faith whatever if such a standard were exacted?

9. Are there no other arguments for the literal meaning of these words?

In the Lord's Supper a new and hitherto unknown ordinance was introduced. The use of figurative language under such circumstances, would be highly improbable. Add to this the fact that as a Sacrament of the New Testament, it replaces a rite or so-called Sacrament of the Old Testament, which is related to it as shadow to substance (Col. 2:17; Heb. 10:1). But if we interpret the words figuratively, we have nothing more than one shadow succeeding another; and, what is still more remarkable, a less clear figure of the suffering Redeemer replacing a far more striking one, for the Paschal Lamb represents the suffering Lamb of God far more aptly than does the sacramental bread.

10. What is the argument from the testamentary character of the Holy Supper?

Nowhere as in a last will and testament, are clearness and plainness and simplicity, so carefully studied, or are mere rhetorical expressions so rigidly excluded. In drawing up wills, every effort is used to avoid ambiguities which might leave room for future misunderstandings. Hence the style is intensely literal. In answer to this, the last words of Jacob, Moses and David are cited as being decidedly rhetorical and abounding in figures. But this is explained by the fact that these figurative passages are not testamentary, but prophetical. Prophecy deals largely in figures.

11. Is there any variation in which the words are reported?

This can best be answered thus:

> Matt. 26:26. "Take, eat; this is my body."
>
> Mark 14:22. "Take ye; this is my body."
>
> Luke 22:19. "This is my body which is given for you; this do in remembrance of me."
>
> 1 Cor. 11:24. "This is my body which is for you; this do in remembrance of me."
>
> Matt. 26:27, 28. "Drink ye all of it; for this is my blood of the covenant, which is poured out for many unto remission of sins."
>
> Mark 14:24. "This is my blood of the covenant, which is poured out for many."
>
> Luke 22:20. "This cup is the new covenant in my blood, even that which is poured out for you."
>
> 1 Cor. 11:25. "This cup is the new covenant in my blood; this do as oft as ye drink it in remembrance of me."

The substantial harmony is remarkable. There are just such variations in minor matters as might be expected of independent and truthful reporters whose individuality is not suppressed by inspiration. But in that which defines the Sacrament, there is no variation whatever as to the presence of the body of Christ, while the variation in the references to the blood involves no contradiction. "This is my body," say all four witnesses. "This is my blood of the covenant," say two, while the other two say, "This cup is the new covenant in my blood."

If all this were meant to be figurative, what an opportunity there would have been to have declared it! But of this, there is not the faintest trace.

12. What evidence is there corroborative of the literal interpretation?

> 1 Cor. 11:27. "Whosoever shall eat the bread or drink the cup of the Lord in an unworthy manner, shall be guilty of the body and blood of the Lord."

> 1 Cor. 11:29. "For he that eateth and drinketh, eateth and drinketh judgment unto himself, it he discern not the body."

The unworthy are guilty of having dishonored the body and blood of the Lord, by not receiving it reverently and in faith. They do not discern the Lord's body, when they make no difference between a meal in which there is a communion of the body, and one in which there is none.

> 1 Cor. 10:16. "The cup of blessing which we bless, is it not a communion of the blood of Christ? The bread which we break is it not a communion of the body of Christ?"

The cup of blessing is not the emblem, the sign, the seal, but the real means of imparting or receiving the blood, as the bread is the means of receiving the body of Christ. This passage Luther calls:

> "The living remedy of my heart against all temptations concerning this Sacrament" (Erl. ed., 29, 244).

Opposing arguments answered

13. What are the chief arguments on the other side?

The first is:

> "A true body cannot be in more than one place at the same time."

This is based upon the assumption that the body can acquire no new properties in virtue of its union with a divine nature. Nevertheless even in man's body, matter attains a new range of properties from its union with the soul, so that it is said to be "animated." If this be the case in the natural or physical, how much more so, in the spiritual body? Such "spiritual body" does not mean a body transformed into spirit, but simply endowed with new properties pertaining to spirit. What thus occurs in the bodies of believers should not be denied to occur in a still higher degree in the body of Christ. If the body, by union with a finite spirit, acquire finite spiritual endowments, so when united with the Infinite Spirit, it may attain infinite spiritual endowments.

14. How many modes of the presence of the body of Christ are there?

"The one body of Christ," says Luther, "has a threefold mode of being anywhere.

> "First, the comprehensible, bodily mode, as He went about in the body on earth...
>
> "Secondly, the incomprehensible, spiritual, according to which He neither occupies nor makes room, but penetrates all creatures according to His will... This mode He used when He rose from the closed sepulchre and passed through the closed doors, and in the bread and wine of the Holy Supper.
>
> "Thirdly, the divine, heavenly mode, since He is one person with God, according to which all creatures must be far more penetrable and present to Him than they are according to the second mode... Where God is, there also must He be. But who will say or think how this occurs? ...Because, therefore, it is unknown to us, and yet is true, we should not deny His words before we know how to prove to a certainty that the body of Christ cannot be where God is' (Formula of Concord, 619). See also above, Chapter 11, 48.

15. What is the second chief argument?

That the doctrine of the Real Presence in the Lord's Supper conflicts with the article concerning the Ascension of Christ to heaven. This, however, is a misconception of the Ascension. It did not localize the body of Christ at the Right Hand of God; for this is an erroneous conception of the Right Hand (see Chapter 12, 65-67). But it was the entrance into the full use of the communicated divine power and presence (see Chapter 12, 60).

> Eph. 4:10. "He ascended far above the heavens, that he might till all things."

Phil. 3:21. All declarations of our Lord concerning absence from His disciples, as Luke 24:27, and leaving the world (John 13:1), refer to different modes of His presence, and not to any real withdrawal (Matt. 28:20; Mark 16:19, 20). As His coming into the world implied no local change; for even during His State of Humiliation the Son of Man was in heaven (John 3:13), so His going forth from the world was no absolute separation. The Ascension instead of forming an adverse argument only confirms that derived from the liberal interpretation of the words of institution.

Sacramental Presence

16. How is the presence of the Body and Blood of Christ in the Lord's Supper defined?

As real, substantial and sacramental. By "real" we mean the reverse of figurative or emblematic. By "substantial," the reverse of potential, i.e., it is not only the effect of the sacrifice of His body and blood that is present and efficacious, but they are themselves there. By "sacramental" we distinguish it from every other form of presence that is conceivable. It is a presence found in the Lord's Supper, and nowhere else.

Sacramental Union

17. You have shown thus far that in this Sacrament the heavenly gift is the Body and Blood of Christ. State now the relation which they have to the bread and wine.

It is not that of Transubstantiation. There is no change of the substance of the bread and wine into the substance of body and blood of Christ, so that only the accidents of bread and wine remain. Such a doctrine is without the very least support from Holy Scripture. On the contrary, Scripture speaks of the bread as existing after the consecration (1 Cor. 10:16; 11:26 sq.), and Christ calls it, after consecration, "the fruit of the vine" (Matt. 26:29; Mark 14:29). Bread and wine are called the "communion of the body and blood," i.e., the medium through which they are communicated. A communion requires the union of two objects; if the one be changed into the other, the communion is destroyed.

18. This doctrine seems to me to remove from the Lord's Supper one of the essentials of a Sacrament. (See Chapter 26, 14.)

You are correct. According to it, the earthly element is annihilated.

19. What kindred doctrine is rejected?

The Lutheran Church and its theologians, with one consent, repudiate Consubstantiation, although many writers and books of reference prepared by those outside of her communion, insist upon ascribing it to her, and even show irritation when we protest against the misrepresentation which has been often corrected. It is a term invented to stigmatize a doctrine which is rejected by those who use it, and must be classed with the opprobrious terms or nicknames not uncommon where there is an excess of polemical zeal. Murray's "Dictionary of the English Language" correctly says of Consubstantiation:

> "A term used controversially to designate the Lutheran doctrine of the Savior's presence 'in, with and under the substance-unchanged bread and wine'; but not used by the Lutheran Church, nor accepted by Lutherans as a correct expression of their view."

It is difficult in all Church History to find a well established example of Consubstantiation taught anywhere. The term "consubstantial' is familiar from the doctrines of the Trinity (Chapter 3, 48), and the Person of Christ (Chapter 11, 8). It is a technical theological term, equivalent to the Greek"homoousios," and meaning "of one substance." Applied here, it would mean that the bread and body of Christ, and the wine and His blood become one substance. But as the bread remains bread and has all its properties, the body of Christ would be with it a merely natural substance and partake of these properties. So Hooker, in his classical "Ecclesiastical Polity," states his conception of Consubstantiation to be "the kneading up of both substances as it were into one lump" (Book V, LXVII, 510).

One form of consubstantiation is that of an acid and an alkali, uniting in a salt, and forming a new substance.

From all such attempts to explain the presence, etc., our Church has abstained. It teaches no "Impanation" or inclusion of the body of Christ in the bread, or "Subpanation," or presence beneath the bread, or any other such "figments."

20. How then is the doctrine of the Sacramental Union stated?

According to 1 Cor. 10:16, we simply affirm that the bread and wine are the means for conveying the real and substantial (see above, 16), yet spiritual and glorified body of Christ (see Chapters 12, 53-55; 11, 45). The union is such that the heavenly and the earthly object, each retains its own substance, and is truly received by one and the same act on the part of the one using it.

21. Is the expression that the body and blood of Christ are "in, with and under" the bread and wine, an adequate statement of the doctrine?

It is intended simply to affirm the doctrine of the Real Presence, and to guard it against the abuses of Transubstantiation, Consubstantiation, Impanation, Subpanation, etc., but after all fails to define it adequately, since we deal with a mystery where faith must be content with knowing more clearly what the sacramental union is not, than with describing fully what it is. Where the Word of God declares no more than "This is my body" and "the bread is the communion of the body," a cautious reserve is more commendable than an ambitious attempt exhaustively to state in scientific formula what we are asked simply to believe.

> "Thus with all humility and obedience, we should simply believe the plain, firm, clear and solemn word of our Creator and Redeemer, without any doubt or disputation as to how it may agree with our reason, or be possible. For these words the Lord, who is infinite wisdom, and truth itself, has spoken, and everything which He promises, He also can execute and accomplish" (Formula of Concord, 609).
>
> *Mysteria divinitatis recthis adoraverimus, quam vestigaverimus* (Melanchthon).

22. What is meant by the expression, "This cup is the new covenant in my blood"?

"This cup is in virtue of my blood the new covenant." A fuller statement would be, that it is through the blood of Christ, that the new covenant has been made, and that to attest and seal the certainty of its establishment, the very blood through which this has been accomplished is here offered to the communicants.

Sacramental Eating

23. In what manner are the Body and Blood of Christ received?

While in the Lord's Supper the bread and wine are received and appropriated in a natural manner, just as any other food, the Body and Blood of Christ are received and appropriated in a supernatural and inexplicable way.

24. May this not be simply by faith?

How then could the unbelieving receive them to their condemnation, as is clearly taught in 1 Cor. 11:27, 29? The eating and drinking of the heavenly object must be one that can be affirmed of both believers and unbelievers. Through the medium of the bread and wine, the Body and Blood are communicated in a supernatural way to the body of the communicant. This is what is meant by the oral reception and mianducation of which the Formula of Concord says:

> "We believe, teach and confess that the Body and Blood of Christ are received with the bread and wine, not only spiritually by faith, but also orally; yet not in a Capernaitic, but in a supernatural, heavenly mode, because of the sacramental union" (512).

25. What is meant by the "Capernaitic mode"?

The false interpretation of the spiritual eating by the people of Capernaum, as related in John 6:52. "How can this man give us his flesh to eat?" Unlike the bread and wine, the Body and Blood of Christ are not subject to the processes of mastication, swallowing, digestion, etc. All our knowledge of the presence and reception of Christ ends with the fact that, with the bread, the Body, and, with the wine, the Blood is received and appropriated. We have no assurance of the presence of either, a second before or after the eating of the bread and the drinking of the wine.

26. Discriminate the modes of "eating," and state their relation to the Lord's Supper.

There are three, viz., the Natural, the Spiritual and the Sacramental. The Natural is that, by which food is ordinarily taken, and the bread is eaten in the

Lord's Supper. The Spiritual, is the appropriation of Christ and His benefits by faith, as expounded in the sixth chapter of John (see above, 2). The Sacramental occurs nowhere except in the Lord's Supper, as above explained.

The Natural and Sacramental always concur in the Lord's Supper. The Spiritual occurs also outside of and without the Lord's Supper. In the Lord's Supper, it may be present or not. As the Natural eating is subordinate and a means for the Sacramental, so the Sacramental has been instituted by God to be a means for the Spiritual, although by man's abuse of God's gifts this end is often not attained. As in every Sacrament there are three things, an element, a heavenly gift and a divine promise, the Natural eating appropriates the first; the Sacramental, the second; and the Spiritual, the third.

> "You have no need to teach us that the mere bodily eating is of no profit. We say more, viz., that the mere bodily eating is poisonous and deadly, as Paul says in 1 Cor. 11:29. But this is no proof that the body of Christ is not present. It proves only the contrary. For if it were not there, the mere bodily eating would be harmless and profitable... For although, in the Holy Supper, the godless divide and separate the two to their own condemnation, and eat the body of Christ without the Word, and only with the mouth and without the heart, i.e, in an entirely bodily and not a spiritual way, nevertheless this is not according to Christ's institution, in which He combined the two, the receiving of His Word and the receiving of His body, eating spiritually with the heart and bodily with the mouth. The abuse of the godless cannot set aside or change God's institution and order" (Luther, Erlangen ed., 30:86 sq.).

Sacramental Promise

27. Having considered the element, and the heavenly gift, the third factor of the Sacrament remains.

This is the divine promise given at its institution:

"Given for you" (Luke 22:19). "For you" (1 Cor. 11:28). "Poured out for you" (Luke 22:20). "Poured out for many unto remission of sins" (Matt. 26:28). "Poured out for many" (Mark 14:26).

28. How does the Catechism estimate the force of these words?

It regards them the most important part of the entire Sacrament. "How can bodily eating and drinking do such great things?" it asks, and then answers:

> "It is not the eating and drinking indeed that does it, but the words that stand here, 'Given and shed for you for the remission of sins.' These words which accompany the bodily eating and drinking, are the chief things in the Sacrament, and he that believes these words has what they declare and mean, namely the forgiveness of sins."

The only true preparation for receiving the communion, it continues, is to "have faith in these words, 'Given and shed for you for the remission of sins.' But he who believes not these words or doubts, is unworthy and unprepared; for the words, for you, require truly believing hearts." So the Large Catechism says:

> "Bring thyself into this you, that His speaking with thee be not in vain. For in this, He offers to us the entire treasure which He has brought for us from heaven" (483).

This is in harmony with what Luther says concerning Baptism in his Babylonian Captivity:

> "Look more to the Word, than to the sign; more to faith, than to the work or use of the sign.

29. But how can the assurance and promise of God's grace to us individually be the chief thing in the Sacrament, when the Body and Blood of Christ are also there?

Because the Son of God has flesh and blood for no other purpose than that His promise of forgiveness of sins, life and salvation, may be offered and fulfilled to us. Unless that promise be appropriated by faith, the Body and Blood of Christ are abused, and bring condemnation instead of blessing. As the Natural eating, therefore, is subordinate to the Sacramental, so the Sacramental is subordinate to the Spiritual. On God's part, the most important gift is the promise; on our part, the most important act is faith in the promise.

30. Since, however, the promise is given also outside of the Sacrament, does not this involve a depreciation of the Lord's Supper?

By no means. For when faith accepts all that Christ has spoken concerning this ordinance, and prompts to the careful observance of all that He has commanded, it gains especial assurance and comfort from the promise as herein communicated. Even although the same promise has been heard a thousand times outside of the Sacrament, it acquires a new force when it has as its pledge and seal the very Body and Blood that were the price of our redemption.

Sacrament as a Memorial

31. In what sense is the Lord's Supper a memorial service?

That it is such is clearly taught.

> Luke 22:19. "This do in remembrance of me."
>
> 1 Cor. 11:25, 26. "This do, as oft as ye drink it, in remembrance of me. For as often as ye eat this bread and drink this cup, ye proclaim the Lord's death till he come."

But the particular truth commemorated is not the mode of His death, but the great fact of His death and the significance of all that is comprised in Redemption.

32. Explain this more fully.

Assuming the doctrine of the Real Presence and the Sacramental Union and Eating, the entire Plan of Salvation and much that it presupposes are most forcibly set forth in the Holy Supper.

The proclamation of death and the presence of blood that has been shed, preach the Law as well as the Gospel, by arraigning all who partake of the Holy Supper, of a guilt that called for the death of the Son of God. But with this announcement of guilt, there is also the proclamation of the remedy which has been provided. While "without the shedding of blood, there is no remission" (Heb. 9:22), here we are assured that this requirement has been met, and that blood has actually been shed for us; and, as a pledge of this, it is actually offered to and applied to each communicant. The days of Old Testament waiting are over; the promise has been fulfilled; the sacrifice so long expected is actually here. It is not the body that is to be given, but that has been given. It is not the blood that is to be shed, but that has been shed, of which the cup is a communion. Nor can there be any doubt concerning the persons for whom it is intended. We need not search for any secret counsel of God concerning our salvation. For here is the surest evidence of His gracious will toward us. What is it that He will not grant, when He gives us His Son, and, when as a pledge, that His Son has actually been given, offers us nothing less than His very body and His very blood! How forcibly this is impressed, when each one, by himself, is made to realize that redemption has been provided for him, and the Son of God belongs individually to him! For this reason, the main stress rests upon those very small monosyllables, "For you."

> "All the good things that God the Lord has, belong to Christ, and here become entirely mine. But that I may have a sign and assurance that such inexpressibly great blessings are mine, I take to myself the body and blood of Jesus Christ." "If I believe that His body and blood are mine, I have the Lord Jesus entirely and completely and all that He can do is mine, so that my heart is joyful and full of courage; for I am not left to my own piety, but to His innocent blood and pure body which I receive" (Luther, Walch's ed., XI, 842 sq.).

33. What is the main difficulty concerning the acceptance of the Real Presence?

Not its mysteriousness; for it presents no greater difficulties than the Trinity or the Incarnation, but the difficulty lies in the words "For you"; since no pastor who believes in a limited atonement, and holds that Christ died only for the elect, can say to each communicant:

> "This is the Body of Christ given for thee." "This is the blood of the New Testament shed for thy sins."

For to do this, he must, according to his doctrine, be able to know what God has reserved for His own knowledge, viz., who are included in the number of His elect. Starting, therefore, with this practical difficulty, the next step is to find arguments by which to explain the Real Presence away.

34. Has the chief effect of the Lord's Supper throughout the nearly two thousand years of its use, been to proclaim Law and Gospel, as suggested under 31?

Undoubtedly. While the greater number of communicants may not be able to express fully what it is to them, nevertheless these are the facts particularly impressed upon the hearts of Christian people, as they receive the communion. They are also the great truths which the constant use of this ordinance proclaims, from generation to generation, to the world which surrounds the Church.

Not a sacrifice

35. Is the Holy Supper in any sense a sacrifice?

A Sacrament is an institution and action of God; a sacrifice is an action of man (Chapter 26, 13). In a Sacrament, God offers man something; in a sacrifice, man offers God something. It is God who offers to man bread and wine, with the assurance that the Body and Blood of Christ accompany them as the pledge of His forgiveness, love and favor. There is an entire perversion of the Holy Supper, where man is regarded as, through an officiating priest, offering to God the Body and Blood of Christ, in order to propitiate Him for our sins. The Lord's Supper does not presuppose an angry God who is to be reconciled by an offering to be made on our behalf; but it most forcibly declares that the sacrifice for our sins was made once for all by the death of Christ upon the cross, and in order to call forth our faith and increase our love brings to us the Body and Blood of the covenant offered for us. It presupposes God's love, and declares that forgiveness of sins and every blessing are present, and have only to be appropriated by faith. The Holy Supper is not, therefore, a sacrifice.

Sacrificial side

36. But is not the use of the Holy Supper sacrificial?

Every act of man called forth by a command and promise of God is sacrificial. Our coming to the Lord's Supper and taking, eating and drinking are sacrifices. They are not propitiatory, in order to purchase reconciliation; for this has been done by Christ. But they are eucharistic sacrifices, or offerings of gratitude and praise for what He has done for us.

> "There is but one propitiatory sacrifice in the world, viz., the death of Christ. The rest are eucharistic sacrifices, which are called sacrifices of praise" (Apology, 263).

Ministers

37. Through whom is the Lord's Supper administered?

Through those whom the Church has regularly called and appointed as its ministers (Chapter 26, 21).

38. But is there no necessity that justifies the administration by a layman?

The unanimous judgment of our Church teaches and the practice of the Church is against it. The necessity cannot be as urgent as that of Baptism (John 3:5).

Administration in both kinds

39. In the administration is it essential that both the bread and the wine be given to all communicants?

We have no right to depart from the original institution, enforced, as it is, by the words of Christ, "This do ye." The advocates of "communion in one form" (the Roman Catholic Church) acknowledge that at the institution all received both bread and wine. Our Lord, with the greatest explicitness commands the use of the wine by all communicants.

> "Drink ye all of it" (Matt. 26:27);

> "And they all drank of it" (Mark 14:23);

> "And he received a cup, and when he had given thanks, he said, Take this and divide it among yourselves" (Luke 22:17).

The irregularities in the Corinthian Church show that laymen as well as ministers partook of the wine (1 Cor. 11:21). The practice of the Church for many centuries was in accord with this usage.

40. Upon what grounds, therefore, has the withdrawal of the cup been defended?

The advocates of the withdrawal of the cup argue, first, that the Church has the right to change the original institution, and, secondly, have invented the doctrine of "sacramental concomitance," according to which, since, in receiving the body, the blood of Christ is regarded as included, it is deemed unnecessary to administer the other, as it seems a needless repetition. The effect of this is to place the word of the Church above that of Christ. The real explanation is that it draws a sharp line between clergy and laity, and relieves the administration of difficulties suggested by the doctrine of Transubstantiation. For if the wine be changed, as this doctrine teaches, into the blood of Christ, the spilling of the least drop is fraught with the most serious consequences.

To whom to be administered

41. To whom is the Holy Supper to be administered?

The Lord's Supper was not instituted until at the very close of Christ's ministry, when His disciples had been under His instruction for several years. It is the Sacrament of mature Christianity. It was not offered to the multitudes that thronged to hear Him preach, or to the children who cried "Hosanna!" but to the inner circle of those who had entered and were still to enter most fully and deeply into His experience. The First Epistle to the Corinthians (11:20-34) treats particularly of the preparation required for its profitable use.

> 1 Cor. 11:28. "But let a man prove himself and so let him eat of the bread and drink of the cup"

It is manifest, therefore, that it should be administered to none who are incapable of such self-examination (see Chapter 27, 7). It is, therefore, not a Sacrament for little children or for those of feeble or disordered mind. The Church also, according to circumstances of time and place, has to make regulations to guard the Sacrament from abuse, and to serve the highest interests of the greatest number of communicants. "None are admitted except they be first proved" (Augsburg Confession, Art. XXIV). Hence it is entirely within its province to interpose even a human ordinance, as Confirmation, as requirement for the admission to the Holy Supper of those who have been baptized in infancy. Nor can any Church be satisfied with regarding the regulations made by any other Church sufficient for its own guidance in the use of the Power of the Keys, connected with this Sacrament. Each Church must be responsible for the enforcement of its own standard.

42. Are no doctrinal tests necessary?

Paul clearly shows that it is a dishonor to Christ to make no difference between a meal through which the Body of Christ is communicated and ordinary meals.

> 1 Cor. 11:29. "For he that eateth and drinketh, eateth and drinketh judgment unto himself, if he discern not the body."

The Church, therefore, must make such tests as may deter those from partaking who would eat and drink judgment to themselves or would encourage others in such guilt.

43. Is the faith which is required for the profitable use of the Lord's Supper merely doctrinal correctness concerning this article?

We must always revert to what our Catechism calls "the chief thing in the Sacrament" (see above, 26-31).

> "He is truly worthy and well prepared, who has faith in these words, 'Given and shed for you for the remission of sins.' But he who believes not these words or doubts, is unworthy and unprepared; for the words 'for you' require truly believing hearts" (Small Catechism).

44. Does the Sacrament bring condemnation where there is weak faith?

Not if it be true faith in Christ, and in His words, "For you."

> Rom. 8:1. "There is therefore now no condemnation to them that are in Christ Jesus."

The Lord's Supper was instituted not to condemn, but to comfort and strengthen the weak faith of Christians (see Chapter 17, 29, 30). What may seem the strongest faith, is after all weak, when regarded according to the divine standard.

> "For Christians of weak faith, diffident and troubled, who, because of the greatness and number of their sins, £re terrified, and think, that, in this

> their great impurity, they are not worthy of this precious treasure and the benefits of Christ, and who feel and lament their weakness of faith, and from their hearts desire to serve God with stronger and more joyful faith and pure obedience, are truly worthy guests, for whom this Sacrament has been especially instituted, as Christ says (Matt. 11:28), 'Come unto me all ye that labor and are heavy laden: and I will give you rest'" (Formula of Concord, 614).

45. Does the Catechism mean that doubts should deter one from receiving the Sacrament?

No. They should only impel us all the more to turn away from them to the sacramental promise itself (Chapter 17, 48-51).

46. Should a pastor administer the communion to himself?

When the Schmalkald Articles (314:8, 9) condemn "self-communion," they refer to private, not to public communion, and denounce any use of the Sacrament by a minister "for his own private devotion," apart from other communicants. The Lutheran Orders of the Sixteenth Century which allow or prescribe the self-administration, do so upon the presupposition of Private Confession and Absolution by another pastor. Others directly forbid it. The following is the judgment of some of our theologians concerning it: The general principle is laid down that:

> "...it is nowhere commanded that different persons always perform the part of ministrant and recipient, nor is it anywhere forbidden a pastor, in time of necessity, to administer the communion to himself. It is, therefore, an adiaphoron" (Hollazius).

Nevertheless:

> "...the nearer the administration of the Sacrament approaches the first institution, the better and safer is it. But in the first institution, the person administering, viz., Christ, and the persons receiving, viz., the disciples, were different. As no one ordinarily absolves himself from sins, so no one gives the Sacrament to himself" (Hollazius).

Gerhard quotes Pelargus approvingly concerning our Lord's going to John the Baptist for Baptism, and the fuller confirmation of faith to be obtained when one can hear the promise of the Gospel pronounced by the voice of another. Bechmann puts the question: "Can a minister administer the Holy Supper to himself?" and answers it:

> "He can, if another orthodox minister cannot be had. But if one can be had, it is better to use his ministry, to avoid the suspicion of contempt for the ministry."

With this Gerhard and Hollazius agree. If the Lord's Supper were chiefly sacrificial (see above, 35, 36), whether propitiatory as in the Roman, or eucharistic as in the Reformed, there would be no reason why any pastor should give this question any consideration. The difficulty arises in attempting to reconcile the sacramental function of the pastor, with his simultaneous sacrificial attitude.[13]

Sacrament as a communion

47. Has the Lord's Supper any other purpose than that of individualizing the general promise of the Gospel?

Emphasizing, first of all, the importance of the individual in his relation to Christ, through this individual union with Christ, it is a Sacrament also of the union of individual Christians with each other.

> 1 Cor. 10:17. "Seeing we who are many are one bread, one body; for we all partake of the one bread."

The bread being "the communion of the body of Christ" (v. 16), all who partake of the bread receive the one body of Christ, and are thus united into one body. This design of the Lord's Supper is of course defeated, as to themselves, by unbelieving communicants. But this does not prevent it from being to believers an institution, which makes visible and strengthens the inner bond of union with one another. It is a cord or tendon binding together the members of congregations, and uniting congregations, and communions, and the Church of all ages, as in the same elements, through the same words, the same Christ, with all His blessings, is offered and received, so that the same experience of the love and mercy of God becomes the common property of all who use the Sacrament aright.

13 "It is placed in the liberty of the minister, I think, as to whether, when he has consecrated, he always himself should commune or not. Meanwhile attention should be paid to what has been, without superstition, the prevailing custom in any church. If the custom so hold, I never would advise the consecrating minister vastly to change it, not that it (i.e. consistency with the past) is absolutely necessary, but so that the more infirm may not be offended, and unnecessary disturbances be agitated in a peaceful and tranquil Church."— (Hutter, Loci, 727.)

48. What follows from this?

The Lord's Supper declares not only the union of Christians with one another by becoming "one bread in Christ," but also their life of service for one another. If they are one bread with Christ, and Christ is imparted for the life of others, they share also in this, as in all else that Christ is and does. The one bread that is eaten by believers, is Christ and all believers united with him. Luther says with customary force:

> "How is it that we are all one bread and eat one another? It is in this way: When I eat the Sacrament, I eat it externally; but internally I partake of all the blessings of Christ, and of Christ Himself, just as though I were eating bodily bread, which strengthens me inwardly... So also among us, it comes to pass that we all become one cake and eat one another. You know that when bread is made, all the grains of wheat are ground together and pulverized, so that in a bag of flour all the grains are thoroughly mingled, so that the flour of each becomes that of another, and none retains its own form, but loses its own body. So also when wine is made, each little grape mingles its juice with that of others, and loses its own form. So with us. If I make myself common property, and serve you so that I am used as you have need of me, I am your food. As when hungry, you use bread so that it helps your body and gives you strength; so also, when I serve you in any necessity, I am also your bread. If then you are a Christian, you so act that you and all you have is for my service, and I partake of it, just as I do of food or drink... Is it not, then, a great matter that the Supreme Majesty comes to me and imparts Himself to me as my own! and then, that all the saints come to me, and accept me as theirs, and care for me, and serve me and help me!" (Luther, Erlangen ed., XI, 189 sq.)

He treats of the same subject at great length in a sermon on the Holy Sacrament of the True Body of Christ (1519), from which we quote only a few sentences:

> "The reception of this Sacrament is nothing else than the reception of a sure sign, of this communion or incorporation with Christ and all saints; just as if a citizen were furnished with a testimonial or certificate of his citizenship... All the spiritual blessings of Christ and His saints are received by one who receives this Sacrament, as well as all their sorrows and sins, so that love enkindles love and unites. He who will share in what is enjoyed must also help pay, and return love for love. He who injures a single citizen, injures the whole city and all the citizens; he who benefits one, deserves the favor and thanks of all" (Erlangen ed., 27:28-30).

Prophetical side

49. Is there not also a prophetic element in the Lord's Supper?

It is a formal announcement and declaration not only of the death and resurrection, but also of the second coming and complete triumph of Christ, and in this triumph of the Lord, that of all who believe unto the end, whatever be the infirmities of this mortal life. In an Easter sermon, Harless speaks of the celebration of the Lord's Supper as:

> "...the Church's confession of the world-conquering power of the death of Christ, since it points forward to the Lord's return (1 Cor. 11:26)."

He compares such constant celebration in all Christian congregations at all times throughout the whole world to "the sound of chimes, 1 Cor. 11:26."Ye proclaim the Lord's death, till he come." Luke 22:18. "I shall not drink from henceforth of the fruit of the vine, until the kingdom of God shall come." Matt. 26:29.

> "The Jewish passover was succeeded by the Lord's Supper; this will be further succeeded by something heavenly" (Bengel).

> "As the Old Testament passover was a promise and earnest of the Holy Supper, so the Holy Supper is a promise and earnest of the Supper of the Lamb in the kingdom of glory (Rev. 19:9)" (Besser).

> "If, therefore, by the gift of the body and blood of Christ in the Holy Supper, we are assured of the forgiveness of sins, we have at the same time a pledge, thereby, of everlasting life and the future resurrection. In this sense, our Catechism says very aptly that 'through these words, the remission of sins, life and salvation are granted unto us in the sacrament; for where forgiveness of sins is, there are also life and salvation" (*Philippi*, "Kirchliche Glaubenslehre," 5:2:476).

Sacrament as an epitome of doctrine

50. What important practical result follows from these uses of the Lord's Supper?

It constantly recalls the minds of those who use it aright to the most central facts and truths of Christianity. In the light of this Holy Sacrament, the proper relation between the various doctrines and duties of our religion, is set forth and maintained. The words of the Gospel which it brings and seals to the individual, every time he communes, condense all that is taught in both Old and New Testament. It is an impressive summary of God's entire revelation of Himself to man. It fixes the lines along which faith moves and according to which it works, in proclaiming in loud tones and without interruption the great day of Christ's coming, and the dawn of the kingdom of undisturbed peace to all the ends of the earth. The Lord's Supper is the morning bell for the approaching day. This is the glorious meaning of the words: 'This do, as oft as ye drink it in remembrance of me.' It is the congregation's loud confession of the kingdom of peace, founded here upon earth by Christ's death, but to be completed with the appearing of the Lord at the time when there will be a new heaven and a new earth." its further study of God's Word and in the practice of the duties and the bearing of the trials of the Christian life. Nor is its testimony confined to communicants. It shows forth the Lord's death and all that it means to those as yet outside the Church. Without interruption, it has come down from a period before men could read the message of the Gospel in the canon of the New Testament, and even before its very first book was written, and through all these ages, it gave the very same testimony as it is giving today.

51. What three parts belong to the sacramental action?

> "The consecration, the distribution and the reception" (Formula of Concord, 617).

Consecration

52. What is the consecration?

It is described in the original institution as follows:

> Matt. 26:26, 27. "Jesus took bread and blessed it... And he took a cup and gave thanks."

It may be defined as the setting apart of the elements for sacramental use by the repetition of the words of institution and prayer (Formula of Concord, 512). "Whatever is sanctified, is sanctified by the Word of God and prayer (1 Tim. 4:5)" (Hollaz). The form of the prayer being left to the judgment of the Church, the Lord's Prayer is not absolutely necessary, but is employed because nothing better can be found. "The words of institution should in no way be omitted, but should be publicly recited." (Formula of Concord, 512). Nevertheless the presence of the Body and Blood of Christ is not dependent upon the declaration of the minister, but upon the original institution (ibid. 512, 615). There is no promise of any presence where there is a mere consecration and no further use of the Sacrament. *Extra usum, nullum sacramentum.*

Distribution

53. What is the distribution?

The act by which the consecrated elements are offered to the communicants, with the words, declaring in Christ's name, what he said and tendering what he gave at the first distribution. Whether the elements be given into the band or directly applied to the lips of the communicant is of itself a matter of indifference, but in practice should be regulated with a view to good order and with regard to what the experience of the Church has found to be preferable for the avoidance of abuses, and most impressive for serving the ends of the Sacrament.

Reception

54. What is the reception?

The taking and eating, and the taking and drinking. Christ gives no assurance of any special presence of His Body and Blood with the consecrated except in the eating and drinking. It is only in the culmination of this sacramental action, that the Sacrament actually occurs.

How often

55. How often should the Lord's Supper be received?

Here regard must be had to the two-fold purpose of the Lord's Supper.

[A.] The confirmation and strengthening of faith by the assurance given the individual of the forgiveness of his sins and of the favor of God, through the pledge of the body and blood of Christ offered all who commune.

[B.] The confession of our faith, the recognition of others as Christian brethren, and the uniting of Christian people as one congregation, and of Christian congregations as one body in Christ.

Accordingly as individual Christians, there are times when we especially need the Lord's Supper, and when our hearts are more open than at other times for its consolation. But as members of congregations and of synods, it is sometimes a privilege, as well as a duty, to commune even where no such exceptional need be felt. Where a weekly communion is administered or advocated, it is never the intention that all members of the congregation should commune, but only to provide for the individual need, to which allusion has been made above.

> "We hold one communion every holy day, and also other days, when any desire the Sacrament, it is given to such as ask for it" (Augsburg Confession, Art. XXIV).

But where, as generally among us today, it is administered only occasionally, the purpose is to provide by a general or congregational communion for the second, as well as for the first of the ends mentioned.

56. What admonition concerning this does our Catechism give?

The Introduction to the Catechism says:

> "You are to be guided by the following principles: That we are to compel no one to believe or to receive the Lord's Supper; that we are not to establish any laws on this point, or appoint the time and place; but that we should so preach as to influence the people, without any law adopted by us, to urge and as it were compel us who are pastors to administer the Lord's Supper to them. Now this object may be attained if we address them in the following manner: It is to be feared that he who does not desire to receive the Lord's Supper, at least three or four times during the year, despises the Sacrament and is no Christian. So, too, he is no Christian, who neither

believes nor obeys the Gospel; for Christ did not say: 'Omit or despise this but 'This do ye, as oft as ye drink it.'"

29. The Church

Relation to what precedes

1. Recapitulate the several stages in the Plan of Salvation already noted.

(1) The Incarnation of the Son of God and His Mediatorial Work.
(2) The Gift of the Holy Spirit to apply the fruits of Christ's Mediatorial Office.
(3) The Activity of the Holy Spirit in this work through the Means of Grace.

2. What remains to be treated?

The Organism through which God provides for the administration of the Means of Grace.

3. What is this Organism?

The Holy Christian Church.

Origin

4. When did the Church begin?

In one sense of the term, with the very first promise of Redemption and its acceptance by believing men. In the eleventh chapter of Hebrews, there is a long catalogue of those who, under the Old Testament, lived and died in faith of the coming revelation of God in Jesus Christ. So in Acts 7:38, Stephen speaks of "the church in the wilderness." But in its proper sense, it began only with the special gift of the Holy Spirit at Pentecost, when the full revelation of God in Christ had been made, the Holy Sacraments had been instituted, and God's people were furnished with the endowments through which their work was to be accomplished. It is a term which belongs particularly to the Pentecostal period of Christianity. Of the one hundred and fourteen times in which it is mentioned, in the New Testament, we find it in only two passages in the Gospels, Matt. 16:18; 18:17. In the former of these, it is most distinctly referred to as something in the future.

"Upon this rock, I will build my Church."

Definition

5. How is the Church defined?

> "The Church is the congregation of saints, in which the Gospel is rightly taught and the Sacraments are rightly administered" (Augsburg Confession, Art. VII).

It is:

> "...the congregation of saints who have with each other the fellowship of the same gospel or doctrine, and of the same Holy Spirit who renews, sanctifies and governs their hearts" (Apology, 163).

> "Men scattered throughout the whole world, who agree concerning the Gospel, and have the same Christ, the same Holy Ghost and the same Sacraments" (ibid.).

> "The Church is a spiritual people, the true people of God, regenerated by the Holy Ghost."

> "Only they are the people, according to the Gospel, who receive the promise of the Spirit" (ibid., 164).

> "This Church exists, viz., the truly believing and righteous men scattered throughout the whole world" (ibid., 165).

> "Thank God, today a child seven years old knows what the Church is, viz., saints, believers and lambs who hear the voice of their Shepherd" (Schmalkald Articles, 335).
>
> "The Church, which is the company of God's people" (Scotch Confession, XVI).
>
> The community or whole body of Christ's faithful people collectively" (Murray's Dictionary).[14]

6. How can it be proved that only regenerate and believing persons constitute the Church?

In the first place, the New Testament word for Church, *ecclesia*, does not denote all men, but, as the etymology shows, "some called out of the promiscuous multitude." It is described in Eph. 4:11-16, as a spiritual body, depending entirely upon Christ with all its joints and parts "fitly framed and knit together," and with Him as its Head. It is inconceivable how they could be members of Christ without partaking of His spiritual life.

> Rom. 8:9. "If any man hath not the Spirit of Christ, he is none of his."

It is described also in 1 Peter 2:4-9, as "a spiritual house," composed of "living stones," resting on Christ, the chief corner stone, and then, abandoning the figure, its members are exhorted:

> 1 Pet. 2:9. "Ye are an elect race, a royal priesthood, a holy nation, a people for God's own possession, that ye may show forth the excellences of him who called you out of darkness into his marvelous light."

When Christ, therefore, in Matt. 16:18 sq., refers to "my church," and its foundation, the allusion to the same object as is described in the above passage, is manifest.

Under another figure it is "the Bride of Christ," "sanctified by the washing of water with the word" (Eph. 5:26). It is only, however, of the community of believers that this can be affirmed.

In the Greek of 1 Cor. 1:2, the definition of the Church we have above given, is very clear. We translate literally:

---

14 One of the most recent definitions is that of Kahler: "The Church is the personal communion of those who have communion with the living Christ." (Wissenschatt der Chr. Lehre, 1893, P385.)

> 1 Cor. 1:2. "To the church of God, which is at Corinth, the sanctified in Christ Jesus."

7. But is the term always restricted to the regenerate and believing?

By the very common figure of speech, synechdoche, a part is put for the whole, or the whole for a part. Men speak of a bundle of wheat, although straw and chaff compose the greater part; and of so many tons of copper and iron, meaning the ore with all the impurities which are run off in the slag; or of a cup of coffee when only a small portion of the decoction comes from the berry. Even a gold ring is an alloy. In the same way, while the word "church," in the strict sense, comprises none but believing and regenerate children of God, in a wider sense it includes those who are associated with them in a visible organization. It is thus:

> "...the external, visible society which is held together by the bond of the same profession of the true doctrine and the communion of the Sacraments" (Quenstedt).
>
> "We grant that in this life, hypocrites and wicked men have been mingled with the Church and that they are members of the Church according to the outward fellowship of the signs of the Church, i.e., of Word, profession and Sacraments" (Apology, 162).
>
> "Although, therefore, hypocrites and wicked men are members of the true Church according to outward rites, yet when the Church is defined, it is necessary to define that which is the living body of Christ" (Apology, 163).

Unbelievers and hypocrites do not actually belong to the Church, but are only externally attached to it, like dead branches to a living vine, or a parasite to an animal, or a fungus to a tree.

Organic structure

8. How is the Church properly so called divided? Into the Church Militant and the Church Triumphant.

The former is composed of the regenerate, who, in this world, are in constant conflict with Satan (Eph. 6:10; 1 Peter 5:8, 9), the world (1 John 5:4) and the flesh

Rom. 7:23; Gal. 5:17). The latter, of those who, as victors have passed beyond these scenes of earthly warfare.

> Rev. 2:10. "Be thou faithful unto death, and I will give thee the crown of life."

> Rev. 7:9. "A great multitude, which no man could number, out of every nation and of all tribes and peoples and tongues, standing before the throne and before the Lamb, arrayed in white robes and palms in their hands."

Sometimes the word "Church" designates both the Militant and Triumphant, as in Heb. 12:23.

> "To the general assembly and church of the firstborn who are enrolled in Heaven."

9. How is this assembly of believers united?

In Christ their spiritual Head. The Mystical Union of Christ with each believer (see Chapter 22) produces a mystical union of all believers in Him into a spiritual organism.

> Eph. 1:22, 23. "He put all things in subjection under his feet, and gave him to be head over all things to his church, which is his body, the fullness of him that filleth all in all."

> Eph. 4:15. "Grown up in all things into him, who is the head, even Christ, from whom all the body fitly framed and knit together through that which every joint supplieth." etc.

> Eph. 5:23. "Christ also is head of the church."

> Col. 1:18. "And he is the head of the body, the church."

> Col. 2:19. "The head, from whom all the body, being supplied and knit together through the joints and bands, increaseth with the increase of God."

10. In what sense is Christ called "Head of the Church"?

No figure is applicable in all its relations. The head is only one member of the body, and is dependent upon the body for life and efficiency. Not so with Christ's headship of His Church. He is called "the Head of the Church" to indicate His supremacy, and its dependence upon Him for direction and influence. It is not simply a moral power that He exercises, but by His presence and union with its members and through the Word and Sacraments, He carries to completion all His plans for its advancement.

Attributes

11. What are the Attributes of the Church?

They are comprehended in the declaration of the Nicene Creed:

> "I believe that there is One, Holy, Catholic and Apostolic Church."

And in that of the Augsburg Confession, Art. VII:

> "They teach that One Holy Church is to continue forever."

12. What is meant by the Unity of the Church?

Two things: First, that all the regenerate children of God have an inner union and communion with one another through their common faith in Christ, a common love enkindled by this faith, and a presence of Christ and the Holy Spirit in their hearts, uniting them into one Mystical Body (see above, 9).

> Eph. 4:4-6. "There is one body and one Spirit, even as also ye were called in one hope of your calling, one Lord, one faith, one baptism, one God and Father of all."

> "It is called one, because, brought by one Lord, through one baptism, into one Mystical Body, under one Head, it is ruled by one Spirit, is bound together by the unity of faith, hope and love, professes one faith and is called by one calling to one heavenly inheritance" (Gerhard).

Secondly, that there is no plurality of Churches. For the Church being the congregation of all the regenerate and believing in all ages of the world, it can have no predecessor or successor, nor any rival or ally existing contemporaneously. For, however diverse their lot in life, or separated by time, place, race, language, nationality, church organization, outward rites, or ecclesiastical names, all who really are Christ's constitute the One Church.

13. In what definition of the Church is this unity made prominent?

When it is called "the communion of saints." 'This," says Luther, "is the meaning of this addition" (communion of saints):

> "I believe that there is upon earth a holy assembly and congregation composed entirely of saints, under one Head, even Christ, called together by the Holy Ghost in one faith, one mind and understanding, with manifold gifts, yet one in love, without sects or schisms. And I also am a part and member of the same, a participant and joint owner of all the good it possesses, brought to it and incorporated into it by the Holy Ghost... By means of this congregation. He brings us to Christ, and teaches and preaches to us the Word, whereby He promotes sanctification" (Large Catechism).

> "The Creed does not ask us to 'believe in the Church.' For this belongs to God alone: and the Church is not God, but an assembly congregated by God. Neither do we confess, 'We believe the Church: In this respect, the Church's authority is beneath that of Prophets and Apostles, speaking or writing, and that too, not of a faith made elsewhere under a condition, but with absolute assent, as to ambassadors of the Lord, through whom the Holy Spirit spake (2 Tim. 3:16; 2 Pet. 1:21). The Church, however, we never believe with such absolute assent, but only with conditionate assent, in so far, viz., as its words and decrees exactly agree with the oracles of the Apostles and Prophets... But we profess that we bell-eve that there Is a Church. This means that the entire human race has not been rejected by God, but that there is a perpetual Church, which, as it began in Paradise, and has been preserved to the present, will last until the end of the world... Thus, therefore, the word, 'to believe' refers to no external condition of the Church. For since faith will not cease until this visible world will have attained its end, the Church can be abolished or interrupted no more than faith itself. But if any time could occur in which the duration or continuance of the Church, could be broken or interrupted in this world, not only the certainty of the faith and truth of the divine Word would be imperiled, but Christ would desert a part of His office, for He would cease to be the Head of His Church (Eph. 5:22; 5:23)" (Hutter, Loci, 521).

14. What is meant by the Holiness of the Church?

That all believing and regenerate persons constituting the Church are subjects of the sanctifying influences of the Holy Spirit, and taken together constitute a holy or sanctified organism.

> 1 Cor. 3:17. "For the temple of God is holy; and such are ye."
>
> 1 Peter 2:9. "Ye are an elect race, a royal priesthood, a holy nation, a people for God's own possession."
>
> Eph. 5:25, 26. "Christ loved the church and gave himself for it, that he might sanctity it."
>
> "This holiness consists not in an alb, a tonsure, a long gown, and other of their ceremonies, devised by them beyond Holy Scripture, but in the Word of God and true faith" (Schmalkald Articles, 335).

15. What is meant by the Catholicity of the Church?

That it is raised above the limitations of time and place.

It is not restricted, like the Israelitic church to a race or nationality. The term "Roman Catholic" is a contradiction; for if the Church be "catholic," it cannot be Roman, and if it be Roman it cannot be catholic. We might as well speak of "frozen fire." Hence the contradiction of the opening words of Chapter 1 of the Decrees of the Vatican Council: "The Holy Catholic Apostolic Roman Church believes and confesses."

> Matt. 28:19. "Make disciples of all nations."
>
> Luke 24:47. Acts 1:8. "Ye shall be my witnesses, both in Jerusalem, and in all Judea and Samaria, and unto the uttermost part of the earth."
>
> Rev. 7:9. "And behold, a great multitude, which no man could number, out of every nation, and of all tribes and peoples and tongues, standing before the throne and before the Lamb, arrayed in white robes and with palms in their hands."

The term "catholic" also distinguishes the one universal Church from particular churches, or assemblies of believers in particular times, places or countries. Thus certain of the Epistles were written to particular churches, while others, because directed to Christians everywhere, are called "catholic epistles."

"Catholic" also designates the doctrine as that which is absolutely essential to Christianity.

> "It is manifest that the Church of Christ is bound to no particular abode or place on earth, but to the Gospel and doctrine of Christ" (Chemnitz, Loci Theologici, III, 17).

16. What is meant by the Apostolicity of the Church?

This does not designate, as Rome maintains, any Apostolic succession of bishops or hierarchical government of the Church. Nor does it mean merely that it was founded through the instrumentality of the Apostles (Rev. 21:14). But it affirms that it rests upon the revelation of God in Christ made once for all in the fullness of time, and transmitted, as the one, complete Gospel, admitting of no change, alteration, modification, evolution or addition, to all ages through the Apostles as chosen witnesses. It faithfully holds, confesses and propagates the same old doctrines which the Apostles taught, and represents all that for which the Apostles stood.

> Gal. 1:8. "Though we or an angel from heaven, should preach unto you any gospel but that which we have preached unto you, let him be accursed."

> Eph. 2:20. "Being built upon the foundation of the Apostles and Prophets, Christ Jesus, himself being the corner stone."

17. What is meant by the Perpetuity of the Church?

That until the end of time, Christ will have faithful witnesses upon earth. Particular churches have perished and may perish, but not to such extent that the line of confessors entirely vanishes, and while some disappear, others are found to take their place.

> Matt. 16:18. "Upon this rock will I build my church, and the gates of Hades shall not prevail against it."

> 1 Cor. 11:26. "Ye proclaim the Lord's death till he come."

> Matt. 28:20. "Lo, I am with you always, even unto the end of the world."

Holy Scripture, on the contrary, abounds in assurances of the discomfiture of its enemies and of the success of its efforts to fulfill the Lord's commission.

18. Is the lot of the Church one of uninterrupted progress?

By no means. It bears the cross of Christ. But as night follows day, and day night; as winter succeeds autumn, and autumn summer; so its path through the ages, is in alternate light and shade. It has been compared to a boat, now in the deepest trough of the sea and apparently on the point of being completely overwhelmed; and then again, riding in triumph upon the crest of the waves. Or again, to the moon in the heavens, now totally obscured by black clouds, then covered only by a very thin veil, and then bursting forth in unobstructed splendor.

> "A thousand times has this religion been on the point of universal destruction, and every time that it has been in this condition, God has raised it up by some extraordinary stroke of His power" (Pascal).

Every victory is only the prophecy of a new conflict that immediately impends; every seeming defeat only the preparation for a surely approaching victory.

19. What index is there of its real prosperity or adversity?

> "Scripture is the life of the Church; the Church is the guardian of Scripture. When the Church is strong, Scripture shines forth; when the Church is sick, Scripture is imprisoned. Thus Scripture and the Church exhibit together the appearance of health or else of sickness; so that this treatment of Scripture corresponds with the state of the Church" (Bengel).
>
> "The Bible and the Church stand and fall together" (Claus Harms). (See above, Chapter 24, 8 c.)

Intermingling with others

20. What scriptural foundation is there for the doctrine that hypocrites and wicked men are mingled with the true Church in the same outward assembly?

Matt. 13:24-43. The Parable of the Tares and the Wheat. They grow together until the end of time. Premature attempts to separate them are perilous to the wheat (v. 30). This however is not intended to discourage Church discipline for notorious offenses (Matt. 18:17; 1 Cor. 5:5).

Matt. 13:47-50, the Parable of the Net. It enclosed fish of every kind. The separation occurs in the end of the world.

Matt. 3:12, the figure of the threshing-floor, where the separation of the chaff from the wheat also awaits the Day of Judgment. Judas was enrolled among the Apostles, and from Acts, the Epistles and Revelation, we learn that there were unbelievers and hypocrites in the Apostolic churches.

21. Are such persons to be regarded Members of the Church?

Only God can tell with certainty who they are who truly believe, and, therefore, are true members of the Church.

> 2 Tim. 2:19. "The Lord knoweth them that are his."

Others are members of the Church solely by outward profession and the common use of Word and Sacraments. The Church has both body and soul. They are members of its body, but not of its soul. True members of the Church belong both to its body and its soul. As an institution for administering the Means of Grace, it is the Church, on its external side, that meets us. Men, therefore, have to be classified according to their profession, not according to what they are at heart, for this is impossible to man's eye.

Visible and Invisible

22. Is the distinction between a Visible and an Invisible church correct?

This distinction is not found in our Lutheran Confessions, nor is it used by Luther, but was adopted from Zwingli by Melanchthon in the later editions of his Loci. It is so thoroughly current in Protestant Theology, that it would be very difficult to dispense with it. But it should always be used with much discrimination. The very same distinction is meant by it, as has been drawn above (7) between the Church properly so called and the Church by synechdoche. The expression "Invisible," is intended to declare that man cannot see the line which divides all true believers from the unbelievers who are mingled with them in the profession of the same faith; while "Visible" refers to the congregation or assembly of those who profess the faith, who are heard in the preaching of the Word, and who are seen in the administration of the Sacraments.

This distinction is open to criticism, since, in one sense, the Church is always visible; for we can always know where it is to be found. We can tell where there is wheat, even though there be many tares with it. Hence it has been said paradoxically:

> "The Church is a visible-invisible body," i.e., visible, according to outward marks whose presence indicates the existence there of true believers; and invisible, because the precise line which separates the two classes within the assembly of those who profess faith in Christ cannot be accurately traced by man's eye.

> "The Church properly so called, is not distinctly, but only confusedly visible. But the particular Church which is so called by synechdoche is so visible, that, as to its members, it can be distinctly recognized as true, and distinguished from false or corrupt churches"[15] (Baier).

15 The following quoted by V. Oettingen from Hackenschmidt (Der Christliche Glaube, 1901, p. 306 sq.) is very suggestive: "It is with the Church as it is with the Lord of the Church. This Jesus, this man of flesh and blood is the Savior, but not as this man, but as faith regards in him the glory of God. The Church which we see, this Christendom, these bodies of men whom we can reckon in statistics, divided into so many denominations, is the Church; but not as we see it, but as we believe it to be. Well do I know how sad is the external condition of the Church; but, as a believing Christian, I do not take into account its faults, its divisions, its errors, nor the thousands whose knowledge is so imperfect, and whose lives are so censurable. I look to Christ who has redeemed all these millions with His blood, and who has named them all with His .Name. I hear the Word of God which is nowhere without efficacy. I trust the Holy Ghost who nowhere allows Himself to be without a witness. I, therefore, confess: 'I believe that there is one holy Church; one, in spite of all temporal divisions; holy, in spite of all improprieties that cry to

Marks

23. How can the true Church be distinguished?

> "The Church is the congregation of saints, in which the Gospel is rightly taught and the Sacraments rightly administered" (Aug. Conf., Art. VII).

> "We say and know certainly that this Church wherein saints live, is and abides truly on earth, namely that some of God's children are here and there, in all the world, in various kingdoms, islands, lands and cities, from the rising of the sun to its setting, who have truly learned to know Christ and His Gospel. And we add the marks 'the pure doctrine of the Gospel,' and the Sacraments" (Apology).

It has been alleged that in the above definition of the Church, Melanchthon has confounded two things. 'The congregation of saints" refers to the Church properly so called, or as some term it, the "Invisible Church"; while the marks enumerated belong to the assembly of those professing the faith, within which the real Church is, viz., the Church by synechdoche or "Visible Church." But there is no such error. Every word was chosen advisedly. The Augsburg Confession means that in every assembly, within which the Word of God is purely preached and the Sacraments are properly administered, there are some truly believing and spiritually minded children of God. The marks mentioned refer to the Church in both senses. Wherever a true visible Church exists, there also is an invisible Church. The visible Church is a mark of the invisible.

> "In this mixed crowd, there are always some elect, i.e., some who accept God's Word with true faith and receive the Holy Ghost. For the ministry of

---

heaven; just as a believing Christian, I do not regard my faults and sins, but look to Christ, who is my righteousness, and as I entertain the assurance that I also belong to the Church of God and am a member of the Body of Christ. The true Church of Christ is made manifest in the Word and Sacraments, and in the walk and conversation of its living members. But what is externally perceptible is its clothing, the form of a servant, its beggar's dress, its cross. Nevertheless even in spite of these imperfections, faith recognizes here God's Church, and, in patience and hope, bears with that in it which is displeasing.'" So also *Philippi* (Symbolik 352): "The Church is not only visible, but invisible. There are not two churches, but one and the same Church, regarded on different sides. Body and soul do not constitute two men, but they form one and the same man, one and the same corporeal-spiritual personality. The body has not the precedence, nor is the soul merely a casual supplementary accident; but the body is rather the organ and vehicle by which the soul expresses itself. This is our Church's living, real, ideal idea of the Church. The one true Church, the congregation of believers, is at the same time visible and invisible; according to its faith, invisible; but according to the various forms of manifesting this faith, visible."

the Word can never be without fruit. It is just this true, pure little flock that the Scriptures call 'the Church'" (Luther, Walch's ed., VI, 2398).

24. Show that the Preaching of the Word is a mark of the Church.

[A.] "God's people have God's Word."

> Eph. 2:20. "Being built upon the foundation of the apostles and prophets, Christ Jesus himself being the chief corner stone."
>
> John 10:27. "My sheep hear my voice and they follow me."

[B.] "God's Word has always its fruit."

> Is. 55:11. "My word shall not return unto me void, but it shall accomplish that which I please, and it shall prosper in the thing whereto I sent it."

See also Matt. 18:20:

> "Where two or three are gathered together in my name, there am I in the midst of them."

In the Parable of the Sower (Matt. 13, Mark 4, Luke 8), while most of the seed is lost, a portion of it reaches perfection. Upon the assurance of such passages, Luther concludes:

> "God's people cannot be without God's Word, nor can God's Word be without a people."

25. What proof is there that the Sacraments are marks of the Church?

> Eph. 5:26. "Having cleansed the Church by the washing of water with the word."
>
> 1 Cor. 12:13. "For in one Spirit were we all baptized into one body."
>
> Luke 22:19. "This do in remembrance of me."

26. Are then all marks of the Church of the same importance?

No. The Word is the one indispensable mark. "The Church is nowhere except where the Word is and they who believe the Word." The administration of the Sacraments being commanded by the Word, belongs to the Word. Beside this, the essential factor in the Sacraments is the Word that accompanies them (see Chapter 26, 14-16). As the Israelites were for forty years without circumcision while they wandered through the wilderness, so there may be peculiar circumstances when the Church, without a ministry, may temporarily be without Sacraments.

27. What is meant by "the pure Preaching of the Word"?

Preaching is not limited to the sermons of pastors, but denotes:

> "...the entire public teaching of the faith revealed in God's Word. This is determined ordinarily by the Symbols or Confessions of Faith published in the name of the entire Church or approved by the Church. Regard is not to be had to the mind or private opinion of particular teachers; nor if any such cherish a heterodox opinion, is the entire Church, on that account, to be accused of impurity" (Bechmann). See Chapter 24, 30.

But this statement must be qualified by the exception that, whatever be the official utterances of an ecclesiastical body, its failure to hold representative teachers to the standard which it has set in its Confessions, may largely counteract the force of its professed faith.

28. When it is said that the "pure preaching" is a mark, how is this to be interpreted?

Not in the most rigid sense, as though the presence of the least error would deprive an assembly of the name of "church." The term may be used in a relative as well as an absolute sense.

> "The more purely the Word of God is preached in a Church, and the nearer the preaching and doctrine comes to the norm of Holy Scripture, the purer will be the Church; the further it recedes from the rule of the Word, the more impure and corrupt will be the Church. Nevertheless it does not cease to be a Church because of some corruption, since God always begets and preserves for Himself a holy seed and spiritual sons, even when the public ministry of the visible Church has been corrupted... Definitions, rides and

canons ought to be given with respect to the ideal; and corrupt churches ought to be reformed, restored and purified according to the norm and form of the purer doctrine" (Gerhard)

"Into the churches of the Corinthians and Galatians some errors had crept, but they still retained the name of 'church.'

(a) Since not all embraced their errors (1 Cor. 15:12; Gal. 4:21);
(b) they still retained some heads of doctrine (Gal. 3:28; 5:1);
(c) they did not obstinately defend these errors, and hope of their conversion and reformation still remained" (ibid.).

29. What errors are here guarded against?

"They are of two classes. Some leave the foundation of the faith unimpaired, such as occur in very many churches. Others overthrow the foundation of faith; some directly, as that of the Photinians, when they deny the divinity and satisfaction of Christ; others indirectly, when an article of faith is not formally denied, nevertheless an inference is made from it which conflicts with an article of faith, as that of the Flacians" (see above, Chapter 8, 35-38).

"When the pure preaching of the Word is said to be a mark of the Church, that is meant which is opposed to corruptions subverting the foundations of the faith. That is said to be a 'pure preaching of the word' which contains no errors or corruptions subverting the foundations of the faith" (Bechmann).

30. What is meant by "the right administration of the Sacraments"?

This has reference to the essentials, and not to the rites and ceremonies that accompany it. Whether the bread be fermented or unfermented, the wafer be given into the hands or the mouth of the communicated, whether the prayer in the consecration precede the words of institution or follow them, whether the communicants stand or kneel or sit in their pews, whether the sexes commune together or separately, etc., have nothing to do with the essentials. But essentials are affected when the elements are administered in but one form, when the Lord's Supper is changed into a sacrifice, or when the words of institution are not used, or are changed so as not to teach what in their form as given by the Lord they actually declare.

> "Although such corruptions may not absolutely remove the Church — for some can be regenerated in such assembly by the Word and, as members, can constitute the Church, nevertheless they render the Church impure, so that no one, who is rightly informed in the doctrine of the Sacraments can join it" (Bechmann).

Relation of Attributes and Marks

31. Do the Attributes of the Church belong to it also as an external body?

They do. As the Unity of the Church properly so called consists in its faith in Christ, so the Unity of the Church as an external visible assembly consists in its common possession of the Marks of the Church above enumerated.

> "Unto the true unity of the Church, it is sufficient to agree concerning the doctrine of the Gospel and the administration of the Sacraments" (Augsburg Confession, Art. VII).

> John 10:16. "And they shall hear my voice, and they shall become one flesh, one shepherd."

So the Holiness of the Church is to be determined by the question whether it has and teaches the Holy Word which alone sanctifies or makes holy (John 17:17).

> "God's Word is the treasury that sanctifies everything, whereby all the saints were sanctified. Whatever be the hour when God's Word is taught, preached, heard, read or meditated upon, person, day and work are then sanctified, not because of the external work, but because of the Word, which makes saints of us all" (Large Catechism, 403).

Its Apostolicity and Catholicity are designations of the doctrine the Church has received, and its Perpetuity depends upon the promise:

> 1 Pet. 1:24, 25. "All flesh is as grass, and all the glory thereof as the flower of grass. The grass withereth, and the flower falleth: but the word of the Lord abideth forever, and this is the word of good tidings which was preached unto you."

Other Marks rejected

32. Have not other marks been proposed besides those above given?

Rome claims that there are fifteen:

1. The name Catholic;
2. Antiquity;
3. Long Continued and Uninterrupted Duration;
4. Geographical Extent and Numerical Strength;
5. The Succession of Bishops;
6. Doctrinal Agreement with the Ancient Church;
7. Union of Members under one Visible Head;
8. Efficacy of Doctrine;
9. Holiness of Doctrine;
10. Holiness of the Life of its Teachers;
11. Glory of Miracles;
12. Temporal Prosperity;
13. Prophetic Sight;
14. Confession of Adversaries;
15. Unhappy End of the Church's Enemies.

Without examining them in detail, they all are subordinate to the one test of conformity with Holy Scripture.

> Isa. 8:20. "To the law and to the testimony; if they speak not according to this word, surely there is no morning for them."
>
> Gal.1:8. "But though we or an angel from heaven, should preach unto you any gospel other than that which we preached unto you, let him be anathema.'
>
> Ps. 119:105.

33. To dwell upon but one of these marks, why cannot the succession of Bishops be admitted as a mark of the Church?

The New Testament knows nothing of diocesan bishops. The New Testament bishops are identical with presbyters, elders or pastors. (See Chapter 30, 7-9.) If it be claimed that the bishops of today are the direct successors of the apostles, we answer that if a mere external succession be considered as determining claims, then the priesthood of Caiaphas is to be preferred to that of Jesus. For Caiaphas was in the direct line, while Jesus was of the order of Melchisedek, that is out of the ordinary line of succession (Heb. 7:3). Paul discriminates often between the external and internal succession, particularly in Rom. 4, where he shows how grace rendered believers spiritual children of Abraham. His argument is that under the New Testament, it is only a spiritual succession that is to be regarded.

> Rom. 4:11. "That he might be the father of all them that believe, though they be in uncircumcision."
>
> Matt. 3:8. "Say not within yourselves, We have Abraham to our father; for I say unto you, that God is able of these stones, to raise up children unto Abraham."

The sermon of Stephen in Acts 7, was a defense of Christianity against the advocates of a local, personal succession, in which he triumphantly maintains the Christian Church's true doctrinal succession of patriarchs and prophets.

Moreover, that the local and personal, apart from the doctrinal succession is invalid, is manifest from the Apostolic predictions concerning the departure from the faith of those in the line of regular succession, and the consequent duty of avoiding them (Acts 20:30; 2 Peter 2:1; 2 Thess. 2:4).

Membership

34. Who are the members of the Church?

As above noted, all regenerate and believing children of God, including adults not yet baptized who believe in Christ, and true believers in Christ who have been unjustly excommunicated from some particular church. Others are "in the Church" but not "of the Church" (i.e., the opposite of John 17:11, 14).

> "It is one thing to be a part, but quite another to be a member of the Church" (Hutter, 519).

No salvation except through Church

35. Is the declaration, "*Extra ecclesiam nulla salus est*," "Outside of the Church there is no salvation," correct?

Yes, but not in the sense in which it is ordinarily used. It is correct because all who believe are members of the Church through their faith in Christ. The expression is, therefore, equivalent to: 'There is no salvation without faith." But if it be interpreted as meaning that none are saved unless they be recognized as externally connected with some visible and particular church, it can be accepted only with some qualifications. While baptism is ordinarily necessary to salvation, and such baptism can come only through the Church, and so as to connect the person baptized with the Church, there may be extraordinary cases where persons are brought to faith in Christ through the reading of Holy Scripture and devout books, or the memory of religious instruction received in childhood, without any direct connection with a particular church.

36. But would this justify one in saying that any are saved without the instrumentality of the Church?

No. The Communion of Saints or congregation of believers directly or indirectly is instrumental in the salvation of all who attain faith in Christ. Even in such extraordinary cases, as those above mentioned, there is no real independence of the Church and its agencies. What is extraordinary, is that the influence of the Church reaches the individual in a different mode from that which is usual. When some of the mutineers of the ship "Bounty" on Pitcairn's Island, in their isolation for many years from the civilized world, came to repentance and faith, and even are said to have established a Christian congregation, it must not be thought, that the Church or "communion of saints" had nothing to do with it. For it was under these circumstances, that the preaching of the Word through the Church heard many years before, asserted its power.

Hence the Large Catechism says:

> "Outside of this Christian Church, there is no forgiveness, as also there can be no sanctification" (446).
>
> "The Holy Ghost has appointed a congregation upon earth by which He speaks and does everything... We believe in Him, who, through the Word, daily brings us into the fellowship of this Christian people" (447).

So, as in many other places, Luther says in his "Commentary to the Galatians" (Erlangen ed., Latin, 2:257):

> "The allegory teaches that the Church ought to do nothing but teach the Gospel rightly and purely, and thus beget children. Thus we are all in turn fathers and children, for we are begotten one of the other. I have been begotten through the Gospel of others; and they in turn beget others, and thus this generation will continue until the end of the world... For she (viz., Sarah, as a figure of the true Church) teaches, nurses and bears us in her womb, and on her breast and arms, and fashions and perfects us according to the form of Christ, until we grow into a perfect man. Thus all things are done through the administration of the Word."

To the same purport a recent theologian has said:

> "Except through this communion, no one has ever become a child of God, either in the first years of Christianity or today. Even the disciples of Jesus could follow the call of the Lord only in the fellowship (Acts 2:42, 46; 4:29 sqq.), which the Holy Ghost created, that they might attain full assurance of faith. This occurred particularly in the case of even the miraculously called Apostle Paul, who became a joyful witness of the Gospel only through the address of Ananias (Acts 9:17 sqq.), and the baptism which he received (Acts 22:16)... The Holy Spirit works indeed where and as He wills (John 3:8 sqq.), but according to the Lord's order, He has bound Himself to the Word and Sacraments, in order that within the communion of the Means of Grace, and through them, He may lead individual souls to Christ, as to their only Mediator and Savior. Only in such communion do they attain the full, and joyful certainty of their being in a state of grace and children of God. No child is born without a mother" (Van Oettingen, "Dogmatik," II, 2:480).

No Platonic State

37. What inference do we derive from this?

That it is not simply the Means of Grace that are efficacious to bring salvation and to nurture the divine life in men; but that for the application of these means, so as to reach the end designed of God, truly believing children of God are necessary, in whose hands and on whose tongues and through whose lives, the Holy Spirit works, in and by the Word which they have taken to heart.

> Matt. 18:19. "If two of you shall agree on earth touching anything, that they shall ask, it shall be done for them of my Father who is in heaven. For where two or three are gathered together in my name, there am I in the midst of them."

In accord with this principle, Chemnitz in his Examen (I, 65, 66), shows that the gift or charism of interpreting Scripture, in its more difficult passages belongs to the Church.

> "God willed that the gift of interpretation should exist in the Church... This gift God did not want to be either despised or rejected, but to be reverently employed, as an organ and means for discovering and understanding the true and sound sense of Scripture... But this gift of interpretation is not outside of the Church in the unregenerate; it is the light of the Holy Spirit enkindled in the heart of the godly."

This, however, must be carefully guarded against the Donatistic error that the Means of Grace, as administered by the unregenerate, are inefficacious. For, in preaching the Word and administering the Sacraments, the godless, in their official position, are only channels, through which the spiritual force of the true "communion of saints," i.e., of the Holy Spirit acting in this communion is exerted. They owe their position and influence to the fact that they are regarded as and in a certain sense actually are representatives of God and His people. As the senseless type and pages become the means of transmitting intellectual and moral forces, so whatever be the organ that brings to men the Word of God, it is always more nearly or more remotely mediated by the communion of saints. Directly or indirectly, the gifts of the Holy Spirit are imparted through the fellowship of believers.

Thus, whenever any important advance is made within the Church, it is traceable to some sanctified personality, through whom a force previously long and widely diffused throughout the Christian communion is at last concentrated in a representative. Paul's life cannot be understood simply by the sudden crisis on the road to Damascus, but must be studied as it emerges from the spiritual life which underlay the historical and external course of Judaism, as this, again, was stimulated and directed by unanswerable evidence that Jesus of Nazareth was not only the promised Messiah, but, by His resurrection from the dead, had proved that He is God over all, and on the throne of heaven.

Nor was Luther an isolated phenomenon in Church History. That he was a true growth out of the spiritual life of his predecessors, in no way contradicts the fact that God raised him up for a special mission. Beneath the surface of a corrupt Church, the life of the true Church existed, like a stream forced for a time through an underground passage. In him this life was concentrated from various directions.

It is not so much this or that teacher who determined his career, as it was the common religious life which came to him through family influences before the schools of the Church could reach him. This life was indeed sustained and developed by a course, which led through Staupitz to Tauler, and through Tauler to Augustine, and through Augustine to Paul, and through Paul to Christ. It gained force and intensity through every soul whom he heard in the confessional, or with whom he corresponded or conversed concerning religious topics. The congregations to which he preached and the attentive students to whom he lectured, and the tens of thousands whom he reached through his pen, acted and reacted upon him as well as he upon them. If Luther lived in Melanchthon, Melanchthon also lived in Luther. What the former taught the latter put into admirable form, upon which the former again built. If Luther actually furnished the material for the "Loci Communes," Melanchthon was not without his influence also on even the Small Catechism. Thus "the communion of saints," through the ever active Spirit of God impelling it, constantly leads to the Holy Scriptures and applies their material for spiritual growth to the mind and heart of the individual.

38. What estimate, therefore, should be placed upon the significance of the individual in the service and progress of the Kingdom of God?

As in secular history, the individual is, under God, largely the product of the various elements that have preceded and now surround him, so in the experience of the Church, there is a common religious spirit as the educative force whereby all Christians are influenced and men are trained for their responsibilities and opportunities. No one within the Church can be properly estimated, except by the study of the common religious life, that has entered into his being from without, and molded him as a member of "the communion of saints." He is to be considered not simply as an isolated unit, with respect to the rest of humanity, but is indebted to the faith both of predecessors and contemporaries, through whom God has awakened and sustained his faith. There is:

> "...a spirit of life born of God's Spirit which like a vivifying breath pervades all history, sometimes clearly expressed and testifying to the truth in thoughts and words, and at other times hidden in a different form, and sometimes forced into the background and traceable only where the soul of the Christian converses with God in prayer" (Thomasius, "Dogmengeschichte," I, 19).

By such spirit, pervading the Church as a community, all Christians are born, trained and molded.

39. Why does the Apology of the Augsburg Confession indignantly repudiate the charge that the Lutheran conception of the Church mas that of "a Platonic State"?

Because the ideal state described by Plato in which all things were to be in common was a pure fiction. But that upon which the Reformers insisted, with its community not of bodily, but of spiritual things, is a reality, although an object not of sight, but of faith. There is a spiritual house which God is building on earth, composed of living stones. Each stone rests on other stones, and supports still others, all being cemented together into one spiritual structure. It is not only a building but a living organism, with head and eyes and ears and brain and heart and feet and hands and lungs and arteries and veins, each minute part supplying the want of some other part. As a spiritual organism, its influences are spiritual, its power is spiritual, its means are spiritual. All its life and efficiency come from the omnipresent and ever living Holy Spirit dwelling in the heart of each believer, and directing the testimony of his life and his prayers towards the edification of all the children of God on earth.

The Communion of Saints

40. But how does this agree with the doctrine that the Gospel deals with us not as a community but with individuals?

True, indeed, it is that, "in matters of faith, every man shall give an account of himself to God," and that, as every one is born by himself, and must die by himself, so also he is regenerated and justified as an individual — a doctrine which the Sacraments especially teach. But this is not separatism. In the preaching of the Gospel, the individual and the community act and react upon one another. The individual is for the community, and the community is for the individual. The progress of the individual is dependent upon the common life of the Church which he receives, while the progress of the Church is dependent upon the constant deepening of the spirituality of the individual. Christianity elevates man, first by seeking him out as an individual, and then by giving him a name and place among "the people of God" (1 Peter 2:10).

41. But is not Religion purely a matter between God and the individual?

No. It makes one "a member of the Church," i.e., he, thereby, finds a place' in which he is utilized for the common good (Rom. 12:4-8, etc.). The heroes of the faith are those in whom this thought has become intensified. With them, self and party constantly yield before the common good. Pastors and congregations languish as they are self-centered. As in secular life, the condition of progress is "public spirit," and intelligent "public opinion" is a far more potent factor than the tyranny of political parties or even the influence of legislation; so, for a healthful religious life, the wide outlook of the Gospel and the community of interests which this establishes and develops, accomplish more than all external efforts at ecclesiastical organization. The strength of an outward organization depends upon whether or not it be a true expression of inner oneness. First unity, then union.

42. Where in the Holy Scriptures do we find the most extended argument to this effect?

In the Epistle to the Romans, which is properly a discussion of the world-embracing mission of Christianity, in the light of which all extended distinctions as those of Jew and Gentile, Greek and Barbarian, are unworthy of notice. It strikes at the root of all dissensions among those who apprehend the great facts of the common lot of all men under the same law and the same condemnation, and of their common interest in the same Christ and the same grace and the same redemption and the same Holy Spirit and the same glorious destiny in eternity; and, on this ground, treats of duties to the Church, and the government and society, and of the true motives of the Christian life.

43. What daily reminds us of the same principle of the Church as a community?

The Lord's Prayer. For in it each child of God prays not simply for himself, but also for all other children of God. In the "our" and "us" of the Lord's Prayer, all Christians on earth pray with one another and for one another. I ask nothing for myself except by including in the petition all others who are in Christ. It is the prayer of the one Christian family on earth around the one family altar.

44. How is this common or community spirit of the Church maintained?

The public services of each particular congregation have as their end not only instruction in God's Word and the cultivation of inward godliness in the use of the Means of Grace, but also the support and development of the common life that exists about that center.

To estimate the importance of presence at the assemblies of believers, solely by the standard of one's own personal edification derived from what he hears, is an indication of a very narrow form of Christianity.

The association of Christian people and of congregations, upon the basis of the same faith, for united Christian effort, has an influence more far-reaching than the goal which is directly in view. Much as may be directly accomplished in missionary and evangelistic and eleemosynary work, the greatest gain after all is in the contact of Christians, otherwise separated, with each other, and the reactive force of their fellowship. Even the greatest of inspired men confesses to unknown and obscure Christians at Rome:

> Rom. 1:11, 12. "For I long to see you, that I may impart unto you some spiritual gift, to the end ye may be established; that is, that I with you may be comforted, each of us by the other's faith."

That is, Paul could derive from their fellowship what his call to the Apostolate and his admission, in ecstatic rapture, to the third heaven could not give. 1 Cor. 7:14 also teaches that, through the believing wife, the common spirit of life in the Christian community reaches the unbelieving husband with its influences directed to make of him an entirely different man, and, as has happened in numberless instances, to bring him to repentance and faith.

The value of a Christian education, and of liberal training under Church influences, lies not merely in the learning of doctrine and the criticism of secular topics from a Christian standpoint, but to a great degree, in the concentration upon the individual, at a formative period, of the common Christian spirit of the Church's life.

45. How do the Sacraments declare the importance of the community thought in the Church?

One Baptism unites all the regenerate.

> 1 Cor. 12:12 sq. "For as the body is one and hath many members, and all the members of the body being many, are one body; so also is Christ. For in

> one Spirit we were all baptized unto one body, and were all made to drink of one Spirit."

The Holy Supper is not only the communion of Christians with their Savior. but also that of Christians with one another (see Chapter 28, 47, 48). For this reason, private communion, except for the sick, is not encouraged by our Church.

> 1 Cor. 10:17. "Seeing that we who are many, are one Bread, one Body: for we all partake of the one bread."

Hence in the earliest Communion Prayer of the Christian Church, of which we have knowledge, this apposite thought occurs:

> "Just as this broken bread was scattered over the hills, and having been gathered together became one, so let Thy Church be gathered together from the ends of the earth into Thy kingdom" (Teaching of the Twelve Apostles, IX; cf. also close of Exhortation to Communion in "Common Service").

46. What two spheres, then, does this communion comprise?

There is an inner communion of faith, hope, love, prayer and all the gifts and graces of the Holy Spirit which unites all Christians, however widely separated externally, or unknown to one another. There is an external communion in the common use of the Word and Sacraments. Both have their degrees. The closest external communion is where believers recognize each other as brethren in a common confession of the same faith, and by unitedly partaking of the Lord's Supper. But such communion exists also in a lower degree, where the testimony to the truth, the sermons, the edifying books, the hymns, the prayers, the holy lives and triumphant deaths of believers encourage and strengthen those whom they have not met personally, as the writings of Augustine and the hymns of Bernard, and the witnesses to Christ in every age and every land appeal to us. How far, such communion may extend, the great variety of sources from which our hymn books and manuals of devotion are compiled, suggests.[16] The external communion is the

16 Lowell, "Godminster Chimes.":
"Moravian hymn and Roman chant
 In one devotion blend,
 To speak the soul's eternal want
 Of Him, the inmost friend;
 One prayer soars cleansed with martyrs' fire,
 One choked with sinners' tears.
 In Heaven both meet in one desire,

starting point through which these influences extend in numberless directions, so that the prayer made in the closet encircles the earth with its results, and the unpretending but sincere word spoken or written in obscurity, ends its mission for Christ only at the consummation of all things. There is no denomination or circle of Christians, however rigorous and isolated it may be, that is not influenced by every testimony for Christ, and every administration of grace prompted by the Holy Ghost among other Christians. Rome may continue to anathematize Luther, but the effect of Luther's testimony will constantly work even within its walls, through which some struggling rays of light still penetrate.

The Lutheran, as a true Church

47. Is the Lutheran Church true and catholic?

"True" it is, in so far as and because in it, the Word is preached purely and the Sacraments are administered according to their institution. "Catholic" it is, in so far as and because it holds the catholic doctrine delivered by Christ and His apostles for all times and for all places.

48. But how can it be a true Church when it has so many divisions?

The unity of the Church, as an external body, lies in its faith and confession (32). Divergencies in organization or in practice growing out of historical antecedents, differences of nationality or language, or the convenience of its members do not affect this unity.

> "Just as dissimilar spaces of day and night do not injure the unity of the Church, so we believe that the true unity of the Church is not injured by dissimilar rites instituted by men" (Apology, 169).

49. But how is Rome's objection concerning the recent origin of our Church to be met?

We answer:

"We have no new Bible, but the old Bible, which the Church Universal, of all times, has acknowledged as canonical. We have no new Baptism, or one diverse from that which was instituted by Christ. We have no new Lord's Supper; neither

---

And God one music hears."

do we mutilate it, nor celebrate it otherwise than Christ administered it, nor apply it to idolatrous, superstitious and unscriptural uses. We have no new form of absolution other than that which we read was used by Christ and His Apostles, and of which we have a summary in the words: 'Son, be of good cheer; thy sins are forgiven thee.' We firmly embrace the ancient symbols, the Apostles', the Nicene and the Athanasian, and prefer them far above all other Confessions or Symbolical Books. Nor, in the worship of God, can anything new be detected in our churches. We abhor all rites and ceremonies to which the idea either of merit or of absolute necessity is attached. But, in the exercise of Christian liberty, we freely observe whatever promotes good order and propriety."' Then, on the other hand, we arraign Rome for the following novelties:

> "It is new, that man can be justified before God not only in the name and by the merit of Christ, but by his own works."
>
> "It is new and contrary to the Apostolic canon in the Synod at Jerusalem, that man, by his own strength can bear the yoke of the Law, and make satisfaction thereto."
>
> "It is new that the authority of the Church exceeds that of Holy Scripture."
>
> "It is new that the Pope of Rome is Head of the Universal Church, as the Vicar of Christ."
>
> "It is new that baptism is to be administered to bells, that they may thereby have power to scatter lightning and thunder and tempests."
>
> "It is new that laymen are allowed the use of the Sacrament of the Eucharist only in one form, that Sacraments confer grace ex opere operato, that the Sacrament of the Lord's Supper is a propitiatory sacrifice, that the body of Christ ought daily to be offered to God the Father in a bloodless manner for the sins, punishments and guilt of the living and the dead."
>
> "It is new that every sin, in whatever way committed in thought, word and deed, must be confessed individually to the priest, with enumeration of all circumstances, that could change the form of the deed."
>
> "It is new that the value of the Absolution depends on the worthiness and intention of the priest."

> "It is new that man can satisfy God for the punishments of sins, both eternal and temporal."
>
> "It is new that indulgences can be purchased for a certain price."
>
> "It is new that priests are to be bound to perpetual celibacy."
>
> "It is new that the Virgin Mary and Saints are to be invoked, and that their merits profit those invoking under everlasting life" (Hutter, L. T., 525, sq.).

50. Is the Lutheran the true and catholic Church?

It is one thing to say that it is "true and catholic," and quite another to declare that it is "the true catholic Church."

> "By reason of quantity, or extent, it is not catholic, i.e., universal, but particular; since it does not embrace in its limits all the regenerate and elect of all times and places. While, therefore, it is an orthodox, it is a particular Church" (Hollaz).
>
> "Notwithstanding the importance which belongs to ecclesiastical distinctions, no particular Church can claim to be the only Church absolutely, and, therefore, to be the only body that imparts salvation, but the Church exists and has its. place in earth, in so far as Jesus Christ is believed and confessed. The one Church of Christ, therefore, extends through all these particular churches, and baptism, provided only it be Christian baptism, confers membership therein. Every other claim, as, e.g., that too readily advanced by Rome, is fanaticism" (Luthardt, "Kirchliche Glaubenlehre," 512).[17]
>
> The Lutheran Church, as the true Church, is not absolutely the Church of the Lord, viz., the spiritual body of Christ. For not all its members belong to this Body; since many are nothing more than those who make confession only by mouth, and are not true believers. Then, too, there are such members in other churches."

17 *Philippi* (Symbolik, 356): "It" (i.e. the Lutheran Ch.) "numbers among its members not only those within its walls, but some in the Catholic Church itself. For all those belong to it who, even without withdrawing from Catholic Church connections, have been raised above Catholic externalism and Catholic work-righteousness. Of such, there have been not a few at all times... According to the view of our Church, therefore, the way of salvation within the Catholic Church is of course rendered difficult, but is not made impossible."

> "The One, Holy, Catholic, Apostolic, or the True Church, which is also the Spiritual Body of Jesus Christ, pervades all church communions. It is the one fold of the One Shepherd, which is not simply to be expected in the future, but is present from the beginning through all periods of time and in spite of the prevalent ecclesiastical divisions, and which, therefore, need not and cannot and dare not be attained by false unions. But, the fact that salvation is to be found in all does riot render it a matter of indifference to what Church communion one belongs. For it is not a matter of indifference whether a Church communion, by its pure and uncorrupted preaching of the Gospel, render the way of salvation plain and readily accessible, or, by its mingling of truth and error, obscure and makes it difficult" (*Philippi*, "Glaubenslehre," IV, 19).

The two extremes of Unionism and of Ecclesiasticism, whether in its Roman or in any other so-called High Church form, both fail by attempting to comprise within external lines of fellowship all whom they claim to be true children of God. Lutheranism, while most clear and decided in its warnings against error wherever found, and earnest in avoiding all alliances which may in any way compromise the clearness of its testimony to all that it learns from God's Word, or which may prevent it from uttering its protests, nevertheless, has in its Confessions formally stated what has been taught by the three theologians above cited.

51. Where is this stated in our Confessions?

> "Neither are we dreaming of a Platonic State, but we say that this Church exists, viz., the truly believing and righteous men, scattered throughout the whole world" (Apology, Latin, 165).

> "Some of God's children are here and there, in all the world, in various kingdoms, islands, lands and cities, from the rising of the sun to its setting" (Apology, German, 165).

> "It is not our purpose to condemn men who err from a certain simplicity of mind, much less entire Churches."

> "We have no doubt whatever that in those Churches which have hitherto not agreed with us in all things, many godly men are found" (Book of Concord, Introduction, pp. 16, 17).

The authors of the Formula of Concord, in the same introduction, refer to the persecutions of the French and Dutch Reformed with their atrocities in the

Massacre of St. Bartholomew and the horrors wrought by the Duke of Alva in the Netherlands, and protest:

> "It has never been our purpose to occasion trouble or danger to the godly who today are suffering persecution."

They declare further, that "for the shedding of that innocent blood, reckoning will be demanded at the awful judgment of the Lord, and before the tribunal of Christ," and affirm the "fellowship of grief," they have with these martyrs.

Luther went so far as to say:

> "I believe and am sure that even under the Papacy the true Church remains... Some among the mass are true Christians; for although they are misled, nevertheless, by God's grace, they are wonderfully preserved" (Erlangen ed., 18:9).

52. How is this consistent with the severe criticism and condemnation declared in portions of our Confessions against those who dissent from our doctrine?

The Church, as such, is not responsible for the statements of individual writers, or for the spirit in which such statements may be uttered. But so far as the Confessions of the Church are concerned, such severity is found only where their authors have believed the Lutheran doctrine to have been willfully misrepresented and even persecuted, notwithstanding ample opportunity to learn the truth. The historical relations of the time and place of a controversy must always be studied, in order to appreciate the precise force and value of a condemnation, in a document which the controversy has occasioned.

Function and Authority

53. What is the special office and calling of the Church?

To administer the Word and Sacraments. The Church saves only by bringing the saving Word.

54. Whence has it this authority and commission?

From the Lord Jesus Christ, the Head of the Church, who has entrusted it with the Power of the Keys.

> Matt. 16:19. "I will give unto thee the keys of the kingdom of heaven; and whatsoever thou shalt loose on earth shall be loosed in heaven."
>
> Matt. 18:18. "What things soever ye shall bind on earth shall be bound in heaven; and what things soever ye shall loose on earth, shall be loosed in heaven."
>
> John 20:23. "Whosesoever sins ye forgive, they are forgiven unto them; whosesoever sins ye retain, they are retained."
>
> "This is a power or commandment from God of preaching the Gospel, of remitting and retaining sins, and of administering the Sacraments" (Augsburg Confession, Art. XXVIII).

55. Does not this power belong, however, to a class or order within the Church?

As will be seen later, there are no classes or orders within the Church. The Christian Ministry is not an order but an office. It is an instrumentality whereby the Church acts. In other words, it is the executive of the Church in performing this work. This is proved as follows:

In Matt. 18:18-20, the Power of the Keys is said to exist wherever "two or three are gathered together in my name." Wherever, then, there is a Christian congregation, there is authority to communicate to penitent and believing individuals the Gospel promise of the gratuitous forgiveness of sins for Christ's sake.

> "Just as the promise of the Gospel belongs certainly and immediately to the entire Church, so the Keys belong immediately to the entire Church, because the Keys are nothing else than the office whereby this promise is communicated to every one who desires it" (Schmalkald Articles, 343).

56. Can the Church, at its will, dispense with the ministerial office?

By no means. But it is for the Church to call, appoint and ordain those who are to exercise the functions of this office.

57. Explain the call or appointment by the Church?

The authority delegated by Christ rests ultimately in any congregation of two or three believers. Such assembly, as the spirit of Christ influences it, will act with reference to the interests of the entire Church, and according to a fixed order. But it is never to be forgotten, that all the power of the Church exists in its smallest congregation, and is not derived by the local assemblies, through large Particular Churches, and by Particular Churches from the Church Universal, and by the Church Universal from Christ. The New Testament conception of Christ, dwelling in the heart of the believer, and making him a king and priest unto God, does not provide for a long and complicated series of agencies whereby we may reach Christ and Christ may reach us.

External Organization

58. What inevitably results?

The gathering of believers into local congregations and their further organization into congregational unions or Particular Churches, according to the necessities or the peculiar circumstances of the time or place. As the Church assumes a more settled form in the lands in which it is planted, and extends its missionary, benevolent and educational operations, a form of external organization, known as "the Representative Church" inevitably follows. United activity always means attention to details of organization, which, however, according to the New Testament conception, must be in accord with the principle of Christian Liberty.

59. How is the organization effected?

Generally in accordance with what has been gradually developed in the experience of the Church. The Acts of the Apostles and the Epistles show the first beginnings of this process in response to needs that were then felt. But not even the practice of the Apostolic Church is a rule which is absolutely obligatory on the Church of succeeding periods.

> "The Apostles commanded to abstain from blood (Acts 15:29). Who observeth that nowadays? And yet they do not sin who observe it not" (Augsburg Confession, Article XXVIII).

Nevertheless the highest respect is paid to what has been found serviceable in the past, and no break with historical antecedents is justifiable, unless a rule or practice is clearly recognized as having survived its usefulness.

> "We cheerfully maintain the old traditions made in the Church for the sake of usefulness and tranquility; and we interpret them in a more moderate way to the exclusion of the opinion which holds that they justify" (Apology, 224).

Church Traditions

60. What matters may be particularly classed under the head of Church Traditions?

All regulations for its government, the constitutions of congregations and Church Bodies, the mode of calling and inducting its ministry, the times and forms of public service, the lessons, the hymns, the prayers, the ceremonies connected with the administration of the Sacraments and other ministerial acts, etc.

61. What general principles must guide their use?

[A.] Consciences Not To Be Burdened.

> "Consciences are not to be burdened as if such service were necessary to salvation" (Augsburg Confession, Art. XV).

[B.] May Be Changed.

> "The Church of God of every place and every time has, according to its circumstances, the authority, power and right, to change, to diminish and to increase them, without thoughtlessness and offense, in an orderly and becoming way, as at any time may be regarded best for good order, Christian discipline and the edification of the Church" (Formula of Concord, 645).

[C.] "No Church should condemn another, because one has less or more external ceremonies not commanded by God than the other, if otherwise there is agreement among them in doctrine and all its articles, as also in the right use of the Holy Sacraments" (ibid., 524).

Hutter ("Loci," 518) declares that uniformity:

> "...is neither possible, nor useful, nor necessary. It is impossible because of the great diversity of causes that determine the introduction of such ceremonies... It is useless, not only on account of the danger of a new

> Jewish bondage (Gal. 5:1), but on account of the fear of offense that might be occasioned because of the omission of this or that very unimportant ceremony... It is unnecessary, for human traditions do not promote salvation, and hence, in accordance with human liberty, can be observed or omitted."

62. But may not a rite or ceremony become the badge of a confession?

Yes; and under such circumstances, it is no longer a matter of indifference. A blue ribbon on the breast is of itself an adiaphoron; but when it is recognized as a mark of those who hold a certain doctrine or who adhere to a certain party, it would be a falsehood for one not belonging to the number of those using it, to adopt it as his own, in order to derive advantages which otherwise he could not claim.

> "At a time when a confession of the heavenly truth is required, when the enemies of Gods Word desire to suppress the pure doctrine of the Holy Gospel, the entire Church of God, yea every Christian, but especially the ministers of the Word are bound, according to God's Word, to confess the godly doctrine... and, even in such things that are truly and of themselves adiaphora, they must not yield to the adversaries or permit these adiaphora to be forced upon them" (Formula of Concord, 645).

63. What notable illustration of this principle is found in Holy Scripture?

The effort of certain Judaizing partisans in the Apostolic churches to enforce the continuance of circumcision as necessary to salvation. When no such claim was made, Paul did not object to its retention, as Acts" 16:3 shows. But when the attempt was made to force all Gentile converts to accept it, he maintained that the time had come for its absolute repudiation. It had become a badge of Judaistic narrowness and exclusiveness, unworthy of those who had been called to the freedom of the Gospel.

> Gal. 5:2. "Behold I Paul say unto you, that, it ye receive circumcision, Christ will profit you nothing."

A similar decision is called for when the demand is made for the abolition of an adiaphoron upon the ground that its retention jeopardizes or even excludes salvation.

64. Is then one at entire liberty, according to his own judgment, to comply or not with the regulations concerning adiaphora which the Church, from time to time, may make?

"Such ordinances it behooveth the churches to keep for charity and quietness' sake, so that one offend not another, that all things may be done in order and without tumult in the Church (1 Cor. 14:40; Phil. 2:14)" (Augsburg Confession, Article XXVIII).

"For the sake of avoiding scandal, we should observe them in proper place" (Apology, 298). The duty of obedience, when they are not urged as necessary for salvation is based upon the Fourth Commandment.

1 Pet. 2:13. "Be subject to every ordinance of man for the Lord's sake.'"

65. What doctrinal principle should decide all liturgical regulations and practices?

"The chief service of God is to teach the Gospel" (Apology, 225).

"The children sing psalms, in order that they may become familiar with passages of Scripture; the people also sing, in order that they may either learn or pray" (ibid.).

"Ceremonies ought to be observed, to teach Scripture, and that those admonished by the Word may derive from it faith and the fear of God, and, thus may pray... Nowhere has it been written that the act of learning lessons not understood, is of any profit, or that ceremonies profit, not because they teach or admonish, but *ex opere operato*, because they are thus performed or witnessed" (Apology, 259).[18]

18 Here also belongs the solution of the Language Question. The Gospel being for all languages and peoples, a faith that cannot be successfully taught and preached except in some one particular language, cannot be Gospel.

"I have no regard for those who are so devoted to one language and despise all others; for I would like to educate youth and men, who might serve Christ and converse with men also in foreign lands, that it might not be with us as with the Waldenses and Bohemians, who have so confined their faith to their own language, that they cannot speak intelligently and clearly with any one,

"There should be no theatrical pomp, no courtly splendor, but a propriety that would declare by external rites the place we give to the Word and Sacraments, and the other exercises of the Church, and that would lead outsiders to respect the Word and Sacraments, and the meetings held by Christian congregations" (Chemnitz, "Examen").

66. What gives a Confession of Faith or a doctrinal decision of a synod its validity?

Nothing but the scriptural truth which it contains. The decrees of the Synod of Nice have stood the test of time, not through the labors of ecclesiastical politicians and diplomatists who may have had much to do with the precise form in which they were phrased, nor through the vote of the synod and the approval of the Emperor. The resolution of an ecclesiastical council only proposes to Christian hearts and consciences, i.e., to the jury of the Christian community, for generations to come, a declaration that must stand or fall on its own intrinsic merits. It stands before the Christian community of all ages only like a resolution that has been moved and seconded in parliamentary bodies. The Augsburg Confession is approved not because of the names of the princes who signed it. All the representations of certain writers who have tried to trace the political and other unworthy motives that determined the composition of other of our Confessions, might be conceded, and yet not affect their force. That which gives them their influence is their fidelity to God's Word. The hold which even systems of error may have for ages, is traceable to a certain amount of truth which underlies them, and is the salt which may long delay their total dissolution. No weight of numbers or authority of organization determines the decision. It must be that of the truth apprehended and recognized by the body of believers that constitutes the heart and kernel of the external Church.

2 Cor. 4:2. "By the manifestation of the truth commending ourselves to every man's conscience in the sight of God."

The Church is called upon not to enforce blind submission to what it has already attained, but to use the clear truth as an instrument of appeal to consciences, and to maintain its authority by persuasion, and not by external force of any kind.

until he first learn their language. But the Holy Ghost did not so in the beginning. He did not wait until the whole world came to Jerusalem and learned Hebrew, but gave various tongues for the Apostles to speak wherever they went." — (Luther, "German Mass.")

"The Word which has created the heavens and the earth must do the work, or nothing in the universe can do it. I will preach, I will talk, I will write; but never will I force anyone by violence" (Luther, Er. ed., 28:219).

"This is the difference between the two forms of government: The godly win men by means of the Word; the wicked force to a prescribed course by means of the sword" (ibid., 12:383).

"Unser Herr Gott thut nicht Grosses mit Gewalt" (ibid., 57:32).

Open Questions

67. Are there then Open Questions?

Such there were undoubtedly in the Apostolic Church. The significance of the great facts of Christianity and of their relations were apprehended with different degrees of clearness. Even after the gift of the Holy Ghost at Pentecost, the Apostles, the intimate companions and immediate disciples of Christ were led by a gradual process and through many conflicts to a full conception of the universal scope of Christianity, and of the freedom which the Gospel brought. It was the especial mission of Paul to be the expounder and champion of these principles. The narrow prejudices of Judaism were much more deeply rooted and extensively ramified in all their ideas than those who had been converted to Christianity themselves knew. With gentleness and tenderness, but at the same time with a firmness, that could not be turned from its course, those thus erring were dealt with. Rom. 14:1-6; 1 Cor. 8:9-14; Acts 15:1-29, declare the principle, and, at the same time, show the limits of Christian toleration.

Such was also the case at the Reformation. The decision with which Luther spoke and the rigor with which he acted against opponents are to be explained, not so much from the failure of these antagonists to reach a standard of faith that was a law to his own conscience, as from the fact that persistent and hostile attacks, and not unfrequently the arts of intrigue and diplomacy had been directed against what he prized more dearly than life itself. He esteemed them, as Paul did the Judaizing teachers, against whom the Epistle to the Galatians was written. But that, when such spirit was laid aside, patience was exercised even where complete doctrinal agreement was not reached on absolutely all points, is shown by the Wittenberg Concord of 1536, where a satisfactory basis for church fellowship was found, even when there was a difference upon a minor point, viz., the communion of the unworthy.[19]

Errors conflicting with doctrine of the Church — Heresy, Schism, Sectarianism, Syncretism, Secularism, etc

68. What forms of error are in conflict with the true doctrine and the practical efficiency of the Church?

Heresy, Schism, Sectarianism, Syncretism and Secularism.

69. What is Heresy?

The obstinate advocacy and propagation of error directly attacking the foundations of the faith. The etymology suggests an arbitrary or self-determined choice separating one from the unity of the Church.

70. What is Schism?

A violent rupture of the external organization of the Church destroying its peace and interrupting the mutual love that should prevail among Christian brethren. A schism is not necessarily accompanied with doctrinal unsoundness.

71. What is Sectarianism?

An unjustifiable emphasis upon distinctive characteristics externally separating those who profess to be Christians. When a particular form of Church organization, among a number that are equally valid; or a particular mode of administering a Sacrament; or a particular form of Christian experience; or connection with some particular ecclesiastical body, is made a test of Christian fellowship, independently of any regard to conformity to the marks of the Church, or as supplementing them, we find Sectarianism. It makes central what, in reality, belongs only to the circumference of Christianity, and forces to the circumference what is central. It makes, for instance, ordination by a bishop in the line of what is affirmed to be "Apostolic Succession," the test of a true minister of the Gospel, and is willing to extend such ecclesiastical fellowship even to those holding errors on what is fundamental to Christianity. Or in its most extravagant forms, it requires a

19 For a most discriminating and earnest treatment of Church Toleration, and an eloquent appeal for its exercise, see Luther s "Light Sermons" preached at Wittenberg in 1523, on his return from the Wartburg. Erlangen Edition 28:202-284.

style of clothing, or mode of wearing the hair, or absence of buttons or of other trifles, as tests of a Christian profession. Among Lutherans in America, the sectarian spirit is apt to enter when a particular synod or group of synods united in a general organization so esteems and extols itself as to ignore the rest of Christendom and represents God's promises to the universal Church as applicable in all their extent only to some particular circle (*ecclesiola in ecclesia*). Sectarianism is characterized by the violation of the Confessional principles that have been stated under 23 sqq.

72. What is Syncretism?

The ignoring of doctrines essential to the clear and full confession of Christianity, in the effort to establish a basis of union in externals. Sectarianism and Syncretism often coincide. The Syncretism may be exercised only with respect to those ready to support some particular form of Church government or practice, or to unite in some organization, as when, e.g., the "Historic Episcopate" is proposed as a basis, and all the results of the struggles of the Reformation are surrendered; or it may be universalistic in its scope and endeavor so as to make the basis of external union and fellowship absolutely co-extensive with that of the existence of some degree of Christian life, as when nothing more is demanded than the "Articles" of the Evangelical Alliance, or Melanchthon's dream of "a consensus of good men."

73. Why is Syncretism to be condemned?

Because the commission to the Church is explicitly "to observe all things whatsoever I have commanded you" (Matt. 28:20). A true servant of Jesus Christ cannot allow any restriction upon his proclaiming what he believes to be God's Word.

> Acts 20:27. "I shrank not from declaring unto you all the counsel of God."

This is "the good deposit" which he is to keep without impairment (2 Tim. 1:14). Any Church alliance, therefore, which impairs the clearness or force of his testimony in regard to any doctrine or any practice involving doctrine is to be avoided.

74. Docs the rejection of Syncretism mean, therefore, that all Church fellowship with those who have not attained the same degree of light and knowledge with one's self is to be renounced and condemned?

One has no right to separate himself from those whose attitude is not that of actual and uncompromising opponents of the truth, until after the most patient efforts to remove their prejudices have failed, and ample time has been afforded for them to see their error. On the contrary, it is one's duty, wherever placed by God's call, like the prophets of the Old Testament or like our Lord and His Apostles, in the synagogues, to bear unremitting testimony to his confession, until such opponents themselves break off the relation.

> Acts 13:46. "It was necessary that the word of God should first be spoken to you. Seeing ye thrust it from you, and judge yourselves unworthy of eternal life, lo, we turn to the Gentiles."

The teacher is not to withdraw himself from his ignorant pupils in order to seek association with cultivated scholars, nor the pastor from his unappreciative people in order to find a select circle of more saintly souls, nor the "See Chapter 32:8. physician to abandon his hospital for a health resort where only sound applicants are admitted. It is a wise provision of Providence that not all the truly godly people on earth are gathered into one corner by themselves, but that they are scattered throughout all lands and all denominations of professed Christians. Thus the real Church, or"communion of saints," penetrates everywhere with its influences, as a tree which sends its roots and tenderest and most minute fibers through a greater space beneath the soil, than is covered by the trunk and branches that bask in the sunlight. The aim of the Christian life is not to cultivate spirituality by avoiding conflicts, but, ever through the contrasts and frictions, to bring the truth to clearer testimony and to deepen the convictions of those thus exercised.

It is quite a different matter, however, to seek associations with errorists who are in open and avowed antagonism to the faith of the Church, or to any of its articles. Where Providence has fixed our lot, we are to abide and testify, as long as our protests will be heard; but where such is not the case, we cannot, without a very clear call, put ourselves in such relations that the clearness of our testimony, may be misunderstood.

75. Is this the principle and spirit of the Confessions?

> "Just as in all families and in all states, concord should be maintained by mutual offices, and tranquility cannot be retained, unless men keep secret and forgive certain mistakes, so Paul commands that love exist in order that it may preserve concord in the Church, bear with the harsher manners of brethren, keep secret less serious mistakes, prevent the Church from flying apart into various schisms, and enmities and factions and heresies arising from the schisms. For concord must necessarily be rent asunder wherever either the bishops impose upon the people heavier burdens, or have no respect to weakness in the people" (Apology. 123-4).

The great moderation of the Formula of Concord concerning the article of the Descent of Christ to Hell, is a model for theologians of later times.

> "It is our unanimous advice that there should be no disputation concerning it, but that it should be believed and taught only in the simplest manner... It is sufficient to know that Christ descended to hell... but how this occurred we should reserve until the other world, where not only this point, but also still others will be revealed, which we here simply believe and cannot comprehend with our blind reason" (p. 522).

A similar moderation characterizes Article XI of the same document concerning Predestination and Election where the Formula declares all that the Gospel states concerning this mystery, and warns against the manifold speculations concerning it, in which reason is only too fond of indulging.

> "For curiosity has always much more pleasure therewith, than with what God has revealed to us in His Word" (ibid., 658).

To these statements may be added the words of Melanchthon in his Loci (3rd edition):

> "Let us not praise those tramps who wander around and unite with no church, because they nowhere find their ideals realized; something is always lacking in the life or the discipline. But let us seek the Church, in which the articles of faith are correctly taught and defended; let us unite with it, and heed and love it as it teaches, and join our prayers and confession with those of its members."

76. How then is the line to be drawn, within which such charity is to be exercised?

A distinction is made, on the one hand, between the hearers of the Word, i.e., the private members of churches and those who are commissioned as the public teachers of the churches, i.e., pastors and teachers of theology, who represent and shape the public teaching of doctrine. The tests required of the latter are much greater than those exacted of the former.

A distinction is made also between questions that have never entered into discussion and been settled by a confessional utterance of the Church, and those which have been thus settled. It is a wrong to the Church to allow it to be again confused on a subject over which it has already struggled, and, as a result attained entire clearness of conviction. What is an open question, at one time, may cease to be such under different circumstances, and particularly with a greater degree of light and knowledge. A distinction is also to be made between purely incidental allusions, illustrations, quotations and arguments in our Confessions, and those statements which are the professed topics of discussion and decide the controversies that have occasioned the preparation of a particular article.

77. What is Secularism?

The turning aside of the Church from its office of preaching the Word and administering the Sacraments, into extensive business operations more or less immediately or remotely connected with the preservation and extension of the Church as an outward organization. As the Church has a body as well as a soul, and that body has secular relations, some activity within this sphere cannot be avoided, but it is possible for a communion by such entanglements to lose much of its spiritual influence. Let it never be forgotten that the abuses which called forth the Reformation culminated in zeal for the worldly display of the Church, and precipitated a conflict by unevangelical efforts made in collecting the needed funds. It was the secular side of the Church's administration which did violence to its proper and most sacred functions, as the administrator of Word and Sacrament to the hearts and consciences of sinful men as individuals. It was the exaltation of external organization above the spiritual body, the communion of saints. In proportion as the attention and activities of the Church are absorbed in its external relations, the great principle is in danger of being overlooked, that "the Church is principally a fellowship of faith and the Holy Ghost in hearts" (Apology, 162).

78. In what does Secularism culminate?

In Anti-Christ, the incarnation and embodiment of the principle which transforms the Church into a worldly government with political machinery and perpetuates or repristinates the false conceptions of religion maintained in Apostolic times by a worldly and anti-Christian Judaism (Chapter 37, 13 sqq.).

79. Against what other tendencies must especial care be taken?

[A.] That which so emphasizes correctness of teaching, as to make the special object of justifying faith (see Chapter XVIII, 15-18), not the merits of Christ, but the dogmas of the Church as true statements of scriptural doctrine; or which instead of regarding the Holy Scriptures as an instrumental cause, elevates them to the place of the meritorious cause of our justification before God.

[B.] That which so emphasizes the importance of the spirituality and inwardness of Christianity, as to be intent chiefly on spiritual exercises and the emotional elements of the Christian life, rather than on Christ and the great objective facts of His salvation and the truths that are taught in Holy Scripture.

[C.] That which makes one particular type or variety of Christian experience, the standard according to which all must conform, or elevates the privileges enjoyed by some few into rules to be followed by all, or which insures scriptural truth as important or unimportant according to its assumed value for edification.

Leading types of doctrine and life

80. What are the three leading types of ecclesiastical doctrine and life?

> "The character of Catholicism consists in externalism, spiritless corporeity, realism degenerating into coarse empiricism and materialism. On the other hand, in extreme antagonism to Catholicism, that of the Reformed Church consists in bodiless intellectualism and idealism degenerating finally into complete subjectivism and spiritualism. The Lutheran conception of doctrine is the true original mean between the two extremes. It presents the unity and interpenetrating pervasion of the inward and outward, the bodily and the spiritual, the real and the ideal. We have a God who is true man; Spirit who is true Word; an invisible Church which is at the same time visible; the earthly element as the actual vehicle of the heavenly, etc. (a

> divine purpose evoking, sustaining, controlling and directing the free acts of men). The Lutheran Church, therefore, does not enter into union with either of these extremes, but is itself their actual union. In the cause of external union, it cannot surrender its complete for a half truth. It can only invite to its full truth such as are absolutely in error, or who stand half in truth and half in error" (*Philippi*, "Symbolik," 372 sq.).

Note: The writer quoted does not mean by "half truth" to say that to the Lutheran Church the departures of the Reformed from its standard of a pure faith are as important as those at the other extreme.

The Roman Catholic Church begins its entire system with its doctrine of the Church. Every other doctrine is a logical deduction from the pure externalism that there prevails. "Faith is assent to that which the Church teaches," and "the Church is as readily comprehensible to the senses as the Kingdom of France or the Republic of Venice." It culminates and centers in the Priesthood, the Priesthood in the Episcopate, the Episcopate in the Pope, whose definitions and interpretations of doctrine are final. Theology is thus restricted to the ecclesiastical pronouncement of Councils and Popes. The Reformed Church starts with the attempt to derive a conception of God from the Holy Scriptures, and to frame its statement of all other doctrines of revelation by logical deduction from this premise. Its fundamental doctrine is that of Predestination.

The Lutheran Church starts with the revelation of God in Jesus Christ upon the background of the universal sinfulness and helplessness of man. Justification by Faith alone is the center towards which all rays of its teaching converge, and whence again they proceed.

81. How is this distinction modified?

According as men or particular Church bodies are better or worse than the general type which they represent. Rome changes chiefly by developing its type to a greater extreme. But the various Protestant bodies act and react upon each other, dividing Churches and theologians into various schools or tendencies, as the Reformed may be influenced by either Roman or Lutheran elements, or as Lutherans may be influenced by either Roman or Reformed principles.

30. The Ministry

Definition

1. Through what instrumentality does the Church chiefly administer the Means of Grace?

Through the Christian Ministry.

2. What is the Ministry?

An office entrusted to certain persons, specially prepared and set apart for its duties. In the wide sense, every office in the Church, is a ministry, and the distinction between ministers and 'laymen is one between the office-bearers and the non-official members of the Church. In a narrower sense, the term belongs only to those commissioned by the Church to preach the Gospel and administer the Sacraments.

Permanent and Temporary Elements

3. Is the designation of a special class of men to till this office simply a matter of convenience?

It is not within the liberty of the Church to dispense with the office. For it rests upon a divine institution.

> 1 Cor. 12:28. "God hath set some in the church, first apostles, secondly prophets, thirdly teachers, then miracles, then divers kinds of healings, helps, governments," etc.

> Eph. 4:11. "And he gave some to be apostles, and some prophets, and some evangelists, and some pastors and teachers, for the perfecting of the saints, unto the work of ministering."

The form and mode of office may vary. Some of these forms are but temporary and belong only to the period of the founding of Christianity; but the permanency of organization under bearers of an office pervades all that has been written concerning the Apostolic Church. A ministry is indispensable to the establishment, growth and proper administration of the Church.

4. Is this classification of offices absolute for the Church of later times?

No; for the Acts and the Epistles show that the organization of the Church gradually progressed, according to its needs, and had no divinely formulated Constitution, transmitted by inspiration, to be inflexibly adhered to for all time. Modifications and combinations of offices, on the one hand, and, on the other, a separation of duties and offices arose, as the Church passed from its missionary to its settled form, and as provisional plans were succeeded by more permanent adjustments. As. Dr. H. M. Muhlenberg constantly realized in laying the foundations of the Lutheran Church in America, the Ecclesia Plantanda is one thing; the Ecclesia Plantata, another.

5. What was the ultimate result?

The Apostles as such had no successors; for they were for all lands and ages. When the period of extraordinary was succeeded by that of only ordinary gifts of the Spirit, there was a merging of a number of these offices into one, that of the local pastor, teacher, preacher and chief presbyter or president of the congregation. The Church, in its freedom, from time to time instituted other offices, to administer the duties connected with its common and united interests.

All pastors bishops

6. Is there no distinction in the New Testament between Presbyters and Bishops?

None whatever. Paul sends for the presbyters of Ephesus (Acts 20:17), and speaks of them as "bishops" (v. 28). According to Phil. 1:1, there were a number of bishops in the church at Philippi. 1 Tim. 3 and Titus 1, in enumerating the duties of church officers, know only bishops and deacons. Nowhere is there any coordination of bishops, presbyters and deacons. The testimony of Titus 1:5, 7 is very clear. After declaring the necessity to "appoint elders in every city," and enumerating the qualifications of the bearers of the office, Paul continues, "For a bishop must be blameless." The allusion would be without any meaning if the presbyterate were regarded a different office from the episcopate.

7. Is there any Confessional declaration on this subject?

> "By the confession of all, even of the adversaries, it is clear that this power by divine right is common to all who preside over churches, whether they be called pastors or elders or bishops. Accordingly Jerome openly teaches that all who preside over churches are both bishops and elders... Jerome teaches that it is by human authority, the grades of bishop and of elder or pastor are distinct... By divine authority, the grades of bishop and pastor are not diverse."

8. Is there any serious dissent from this even among scholarly advocates of diocesan episcopacy?

None whatever. "It is a fact," says Bishop Lightfoot, probably the most scholarly representative of the Church of England in the Nineteenth Century:

> "...now generally recognized by theologians of all shades of opinion, that in the language of the New Testament, the same officer in the Church is called indifferently 'bishop' (*episkopos*) and"elder' or 'presbyter' (*presbyteros*)' (On Philippians, p. 95).

Even Thomas Aquinas, the scholastic whose writings have been officially endorsed by the Papal Chair, declares:

> "...as to name, bishops and presbyters formerly were not distinguished. The Apostle applies the name 'bishop' to both."

High churchmen endeavor to establish the divine right of diocesan bishops by claiming that they are the successors of the New Testament Apostles, while priests are the successors of the New Testament bishops. A complete refutation of this theory has been made by Bishop Lightfoot in his excursus on "The Christian Ministry," in volume above mentioned.

9. If the distinction between bishops and presbyters be not made by divine right, is it admissible?

Not when urged as a matter of necessity, or insisted upon as a condition of fellowship. But Diocesan Episcopacy is a perfectly legitimate form of Church government, when adopted upon principles of expediency, and in the spirit of Christian freedom. The general principle that has been followed in our Church is to accept whatever form of organization has been prevalent, unless it be urged from wrong foundations, or be connected with doctrinal errors. Hence, at the Reformation, there would have been no break with the organization then existing, if the bishops had kept within the limits allowed by the Gospel. "The bishops might easily retain lawful obedience, if they would not urge men to observe such traditions as cannot be kept with a good conscience" (Augsburg Confession, Art. XXVIII).

The Ministry and the Priesthood

10. Is it proper to call Ministers "priests"?

While etymologically the word "priest' corresponds to"presbyter," it is always used and understood in the sense of a member of an order, set apart to offer sacrifices. The New Testament knows of but two priesthoods, one is that of our Lord Jesus Christ, "the great High Priest" of the Christian faith (Heb. 4:14), and the other that of the spiritual priesthood of believers (1 Peter 2:5, 9; Rev. 1:6), comprising all true children of God by faith in Jesus Christ. The offering of the former was His life, as an expiatory sacrifice for the sins of the world; that of the latter is the eucharistic sacrifice of prayer, praise and thanksgiving, the cheerful self-surrender of body and soul to the service of God. Beyond these, there neither is nor can be any priesthood. Every minister of the Word should be, like all the regenerate and believing in his congregation, a spiritual priest, but he is such, in virtue of his personal and individual relation to God, and not in any official capacity, or as a minister.

Neither in his official acts, is his representative capacity chiefly that of the priesthood, comprising all the believing, in his congregation. A minister of the Gospel is, first of all, a representative of God to men, one divinely called to preach the Gospel, in God's name, and to apply its promises to individuals in the Sacraments. He can offer nothing to God in man's behalf, but offers to man that which God has provided (see Chapter 28, 35). In offering to God the prayers and thanksgivings of the congregations, he is only one of their number, acting as the spokesman or voice of the whole body. In so doing, he does not intercede or pray to God for them; but it is his office to pray with them and lead the oral declarations of the prayers of their hearts.

11. But is not the office of teaching and preaching and administering the Sacraments a prerogative of the spiritual priesthood?

The spiritual priesthood and the ministry are entirely distinct institutions. The former has reference to the personal relation of the individual towards God, and his direct and immediate access, through Christ, to the Throne of Grace. The latter has reference to the public performance of duties that are to be discharged, according to direct instructions in God's name. The spiritual priesthood is the prerogative of the individual; the ministry is found only where there is a congregation, i.e., two or three gathered together in Christ's name (Matt. 18:17, 20). There is no scriptural foundation for the idea that, simply for the sake of good order, there is a transfer to one individual of rights that belong to each individual in a congregation. The functions of the ministry belong not to the uncalled, but the called members of the Church, i.e., those called to this particular office. To use an illustration, the Presidency of the United States is not an office whose duties abstractly speaking inhere in every one of the many millions of its citizens, but which, to avoid a conflict of authority, they transfer to one man. It is an office to which no citizen has the right, unless he be duly elected and inaugurated; since it belongs to the whole nation and not to the individual. This distinction which is true of an earthly government, applies with even greater force to that which is of divine appointment. A man's call as a Christian is one thing; his call as a minister is another.

12. Give the statement of our Confessions on this subject.

> "No one should in the Church publicly teach or administer the Sacraments without a regular call" (Augsburg Confession, Art. XIV).

13. Scripture proofs?

> Rom. 10:15. "How shall they preach, except they be sent?"
>
> Tit. 1:5. "Appoint elders in every city."
>
> Heb. 5:4. "No man taketh the honor unto himself, but when he is called of God, even as was Aaron."

As "ambassadors of God" (2 Cor. 5:20), as "stewards of the mysteries o£ God" (1 Cor. 4:1), they must have credentials of their appointment subject to the tests of their brethren in Christ, and their fellowmen. As the Power of the Keys, or authority to administer the Word and Sacrament belongs to the congregation as a unit and not individually (Matt. 18:20; see Augsburg Confession, Art. XXVIII), it is for the congregation as a unit, to decide who they are to be, that, in this particular, are to act as its executives.

The Call to the Ministry. Immediate and Mediate Call distinguished; Mode of Mediate Call; Preparatory factors; "Call" in special sense; Part of the Ministry and Laity in giving Call; Lay preaching; Limits of Ministry as determined by Call.

14. Has the form of the Call to the ministry been uniform in all ages?

A distinction is made between the immediate call, such as Moses received by the voice of God from the burning bush (Ex. 3:10), and by which the Prophets of the Old, and the Apostles of the New Testament were designated, or whereby one expressly mentioned by God was called through some one else, whom God had directed to act for Him, as was Aaron, through Moses (Ex. 4:14; 28:1); and the mediate call, through the Church acting in God's name.

15. Is there any divinely-prescribed order according to which the Church proceeds in giving the Call?

No one can be a minister without a call; but the precise mode has been left to the liberty of the Church, guided by the ordinary operation of the Holy Spirit through the Means of Grace. Here, as elsewhere, the experience of the Church has resulted in the prescription of certain principles of procedure, which, for good order's sake, are to be faithfully observed.

16. What is the order as we now find it?

It comprises some matters that are actually preparatory to the call; others belonging to it in the most special sense; and still others, which, while most closely connected with it, simply confirm, declare, ratify and attest it.

17. What prepares for the Call?

The series of agencies whereby one is led to enter upon a course of theological training and to be approved as a candidate for the ministry. In a settled condition of the Church, men are no longer called directly into the office. But, just as the apostles accompanied their Master for three years, and a considerable period intervened between the immediate call of Paul and his entrance upon his office, so years are required before one can attain that knowledge and maturity of conviction and judgment needful for the duties of the ministry. In every case there have been influences, emanating from the communion of believers that have led to the resolution to seek the ministry.

> 1 Tim. 3:1. "If a man seeketh the office of a bishop, he desireth a good work."

18. Is the Call to the ministry cm inner conviction of duty wrought by the Holy Spirit upon man's heart?

> "We answer: We grant that God, by an inner impulse, inspires the purpose to assume the office of the ministry, without regard to its perils and difficulties. To this belongs the secret impulse which leads some to study theology. We grant also that in accepting the holy office, no one should be influenced by avarice or ambition or any vicious desire, but by the sincere love of God and the desire of edifying the Church. If anyone be disposed to call these two praiseworthy dispositions a secret call in the sound sense, we do not greatly object. Meanwhile we warn, first, that, on account of such inner or secret call, no one ought to assume the duties of the ministry, unless an external and regular call of the Church be added, lest the doors, be opened for Anabaptistic confusions and enthusiastic revelations... We

warn also, in the second place, that the call of that person does not immediately cease to be a call, whose mind, in undertaking the ministerial office, was perhaps contaminated in the beginning by the taint of ambition or avarice or any other impure motive" (Gerhard, VI, 48; see also above, Chapter 26, 23).

19. What other agencies may be mentioned as preparing the way for the Call?

The expressed desire of parents; the suggestion of a pastor or teacher or friend, particularly at some critical point in life as confirmation, or at an illness, or under severe affliction or bereavement; the general opinion of some circle of Christian friends determined by the interest and efficiency of the person concerned in Sunday-school or other congregational work, or other forms of Christian labor. The general acquaintance of pastors' sons with the lives and works of their fathers, often occasions the desire to follow them in the holy office.

20. What is the next stage in preparing the way?

The Church's approval of the person as one deemed worthy of becoming a candidate for the office, and entering upon a course of preparation. This has to do not only with the beginning of his course, but proceeds throughout its various stages, constituting a continuous examination, not only bringing the candidate under the eyes of representatives of the Church, but also continually revealing him more and more to himself. It culminates when he obtains the final official approval of the Church in his recommendation for ordination.

21. What is the Call in the most special sense?

The election and designation of a person for the work of the ministry.

22. By whom is the Call given?

The right to call is not limited to any class within the Church. It belongs neither to the ministry alone, nor to the laity alone; but to both in due order. That the ministry is not a self-perpetuating order, but that the voice of the laity is also to be heard in the choice of pastors, is manifest (a) from the gift of the Power of the Keys to the whole Church, as is taught in Matt. 16 and 18; (b) the testing of teachers required of the people (Matt. 7:15; John 10:27; 1 Thess. 5:19, 20, 21; 1 John 4:1); and (c) especially from the practice of the Apostolic Church (Acts 1:23; 6:3; 14:23).

If, however, the ministry be without a voice in determining who are to be ministers, and this be limited to the votes of the laity in local congregations, those very persons are excluded whose training and experience best fits them for judging the qualifications of candidates.

23. Is there, then, no true ministry except where the Call comes from both portions of the Church?

We may adapt here the words of Gerhard concerning the giving of absolution, which, while belonging to the whole Church is exercised only through ministers:

> "We distinguish between the power and the exercise of the power. The power is and remains with the Church; but the execution of the power is through the presbyters of the Church, i.e., the ministry and those who represent the rest of the Church. The power is and remains his, in whose name and by whose authority it is exercised. But the exercise of ecclesiastical power, in calling and electing ministers, in loosing and binding sins, is in the name and by the authority of the entire Church" (VI, 57).

Since, also, the Church is "wherever two or three are gathered together in Christ's name" (Matt. 18:17, 20), it is not a matter of absolute necessity that both or all classes of the Church be represented. Because, however, of manifest abuses that have entered and are apt to enter when both are not guaranteed their rights, that mode of extending the call is best where provision is made for the participation of both ministers and laymen.

24. How is this accomplished?

When the examination and the approval of the examination are allotted to the ministers, and the voice of the laity is heard, either in the local congregation, or representatively in Synods in calling a candidate to a definite field of labor.

25. But are all laymen, or all communicant members of churches competent to give a discriminating judgment as to the qualifications of a candidate?

The exercise of the right should be guarded by such constitutional provisions, limiting the electors and otherwise qualifying it, as to prevent abuses as far as possible.

26. When is a modification of this principle justifiable?

In a formative condition of the Church, whether occasioned by a confused condition as the result of deterioration of doctrine and life, or connected with missionary activity. Thus when the peasants in their XII Articles of 1525 claimed the right of each congregation to elect its own pastor, Luther answered that as long as the people did not furnish the support, they could not claim that one whom they elected should be supported by the magistrates. The designation of the rulers as bishops *pro tempore* and the entire Episcopal system of Church government which was adopted as the first form for our Lutheran Churches in Germany, originally as a purely temporary expedient, are to be explained upon this ground.

27. Where a regularly called pastor cannot be had, is it never proper for a layman to preach or teach publicly in the Church?

> "When a Christian is among heathen ignorant of the Christian faith, then, according to his ability, he can teach others and propagate Christian doctrine at the promptings of love and necessity. But where a church has been established, let no one, without an ordinary call, undertake the holy office" (Hollaz).

Similar occasions may occur temporarily in communities in a Christian land, not adequately provided with a ministry, or churches. Lay activity may very properly supply the deficiency, but not as a permanent matter. Where a congregation results and the provision has its sanction, the ministry springs up in virtue of the call that is given.

28. How about the preaching of theological students?

> "There is a distinction between preaching exercises and the regular office of preaching. The sermons of students are exercises in which they modestly offer to the Church services that are hereafter to be rendered, but do not claim for themselves the regular office of preaching" (Hollaz).

This is not, however, a completely satisfactory statement. The preaching of students is justifiable only upon the ground that it is in response to a regular call of the congregation or its representatives for a temporary service. The distinction is between a call for a more permanent and one for a merely temporary discharge of ministerial functions.

29. Is the Call which constitutes the ministry limited to the pastorate of a local congregation?

Many so maintain. But even in Apostolic times, the ministry of preaching the Word and administering the Sacraments was not confined to a form so restrictedly local. Wherever there are general interests of the Church that are served by preachers and teachers filling such offices as are needed and in accordance with clear calls, there are also true ministers of the Church. What a congregation of Christian people can do in the call of a pastor, a congregation of congregations in the representative Church can also effect. This limitation, however, must be made; Such call must always carry with it the appointment to distinct work. For the ministry is an office, not an order.

30. If one called to the ministry ceases to discharge its duties is he any longer a minister?

There is no ministry where there is no ministering. He who does not minister is no minister. This ministry must always be one of the Word and Sacraments. There are no ministerial duties that authorize the demitting of this function. The Roman Catholic doctrine of a character *indelibilis* imparted by ordination cannot be admitted, and yet it underlies the claim which men make to be regarded ministers, when they neither teach the Word nor administer the Sacraments, and who refer to their ordination as permanently investing them with the office.

> "The duty of a priest is to preach, and unless he does so, he is just as much a priest, as the picture of a man is a man. It is the ministry of the Word that makes a priest or bishop" (Luther, "Babylonian Captivity").

Ordination: Definition; Not absolutely necessary; Ordinary form; Lutheran estimate of; Who is to ordain; Congregational or Synodical Ordination; Reordination; Ordination sine titulo.

31. What is Ordination?

The formal induction into his office of one who has been called to the ministry. It is the solemn, public ratification and attestation of the Call.

32. Does Ordination make one a minister?

The Call is all that is essential. Ordination is important but not essential. One called but not ordained is in reality a minister; only, for the sake of good order, he should hold his rights in abeyance until ordained, or the Call may be conditioned in explicit terms upon his ordination. As it is not the inauguration of the President of the United States but the votes of the people, that gives him the title to his office, so it is not ordination, but the being *rite locatus*, i.e., the Call in due form and order, that decides one's claims as a minister.

33. Is not Ordination a divinely prescribed ceremony?

No. See Chapter 26, 18.

34. What is the ordinary form of Ordination?

Prayer with the laying on of hands (1 Tim. 4:14; 5:22; 2 Tim. 1:6).

35. What is the chief thing in Ordination?

Not the laying on of hands, but the prayer which accompanies it, or, rather, the word of God which the prayer appropriates and pleads with God. This is the "prophecy" of 1 Tim. 4:14. In 2 Tim. 1; 6, the words "laying on of hands" are used by synechdoche for the entire ceremony including the prayer and prophecy. Hands are laid on the person ordained, simply to designate the individual to whom the promises of the Gospel concerning the ministry are applied, and to whom the office is entrusted.

36. What is the exact estimate of such ceremony in the Lutheran Church?

> "We declare that the rite of Ordination ought by no means to be omitted, but that except in case of necessity, it should always be employed in constituting the ministry of the Church, both on account of the ancient custom of the Apostolic Church and that nearest the times of the Apostles, in which, by prayers and the laying on of hands, the presbytery ordained ministers elected by the Church, and as it were consecrated them to God, and on account of certain salutary ends. Although Paul was immediately called, nevertheless he is sent to Ananias, who imposes his hands, that his call may be manifest to the Church (Acts 9:17), and, afterwards (Acts 13:3),

> when he is to be sent to the heathen, he is again appointed a teacher of the Gentiles by the laying on of hands; this rite being employed in order that his call might be declared publicly to be legitimate, and others might not boast in like manner of it. But if this was done in one who had been immediately called, how much more appropriate in those whose call is mediate" (Gerhard, VI, 97, largely from Chemnitz).

37. By whom is Ordination administered?

The laying on of hands recorded in Scripture was by the presbytery (1 Tim. 4:14), i.e., the entire body of the presbyters or elders or pastors, through their representatives. When Paul speaks in 2 Tim. 1:6 of the laying on of his hands, it indicates that he was one of the presbytery. Paul himself had received the laying on of hands from Ananias, a layman (Acts 9:17). The contention of those who urge that only a diocesan bishop in the line of an external succession, either from Apostolic times, or traceable to a period of practically universal recognition in Christendom can ordain, is inadmissible, both for the reason above cited and because of what has been said above concerning the identity of presbyter and bishop in the New Testament (see above, 7-9).

The object of Ordination being to afford the widest and fullest recognition of the persons ordained is among us generally administered, under synodical authority, by its President, assisted by its other officers. This corresponds both with the New Testament conception of laying on of hands by the presbytery, and with what has force in the claim for episcopal ordination, since a synodical President is, in his supervisory capacity, a temporary diocesan bishop.

38. Can Ordination be administered by the authority simply of a congregation?

> "Wherever there is a true Church, the right to elect and ordain ministers necessarily exists" (Schmalkald Articles, 350).

> "The Church which has the spiritual priesthood, certainly has the right to elect and ordain ministers" (ibid.).

> "Formerly the people elected pastors and bishops. Then a bishop was added, either of that or a neighboring church, who confirmed the one elected by the laying on of hands; neither was ordination anything else than such ratification" (ibid.).

Nevertheless the right is one that except for most weighty cause should not be exercised, as confusion results if arbitrarily employed, and much of the impressiveness of the ceremony is lost, when the Church in general is not heard through its official representatives. But:

> "...if the bishops are heretics or will not ordain suitable persons, the churches are in duty bound before God, according to divine law, to ordain for themselves pastors and ministers. Even though this be now called an irregularity or schism, it should be known that the godless doctrine and tyranny of the bishops are responsible for it" (ibid.).

39. Should ministers who have been ordained in other communions be reordained on entering the Lutheran ministry?

The answer to this question is determined by the consideration as to the extent to which the recognition of previous ordination would be regarded as the endorsement of the tests for the ministry in use in another communion. Where fundamental doctrines of Christianity, such as the Divinity of Christ are publicly repudiated, or where the entire teaching of the Gospel has been perverted and attacked, as by Rome, such public recognition of the change of attitude on the part of one who would enter the Lutheran ministry, would seem to be especially important. Where the change has occurred from inner conviction as the result of deep inner conflict, such attestation, instead of being a humiliation, would be a relief and confirmation of the person ordained.

40. Should one be ordained "*sine titulo*"?

That is. without respect to some field of labor. On general principles, No: for ordination is the recognition of the call, and the call is to specific ministerial work. Our writers declare that ordination "*sine titulo*" amounts to ordination to the apostolate, which is without authority. On the other hand, the practice in the older portion of the Lutheran Church in America, where followed, has its historical explanation in the peculiar organization of the Church in its earliest years, according to which the "United Pastors" were regarded as all belonging to the "United Congregations," and dividing the labor among each other from time to time. A field of labor was, therefore, always assured in every ordination, viz., within the "collegiate parish" of the "United Congregations," although the specific district was undetermined. Where this rule is not enforced, the ministry assumes the character of an order, instead of an office.

Are there grades

41. Are there different grades of ministers of the Word?

It has been shown above (7-9) that the New Testament does not recognize any distinction between bishops and presbyters.

> "In 1 Cor. 3:6, Paul makes ministers equal and teaches that the Church is above the ministers. Hence superiority or lordship over the Church is not ascribed to Peter" (Schmalkald Articles, 340).

There is no divine law designating a certain number of grades and perpetually imposing them upon the Church. Nevertheless the importance of order and organization is clearly taught, and this necessitates the subordination of equals to each other for the welfare of the entire spiritual body of believers. Some become primi inter pares.

> "1. Although in the ministry, there are diverse orders, nevertheless the power of the ministry in preaching the Word and administering the Sacraments, and the power of jurisdiction consisting in the use of the Keys, belongs equally to all ministers; and, therefore, the Word preached, the Sacraments administered and the absolution announced by one lawfully called to the ministry. even though he be of the lowest grade of the ministry, are just as valid and efficacious, as though preached, administered and announced by the highest bishop, prophet or apostle. For as the diversity of gifts, so also that of grades does not change the force or efficacy of the doctrine and Sacraments (1 Cor. 3:5, 7; 2 Cor. 12:9; Gal. 2:8)."

> "2. The diversity of grades depends indeed upon divine law, both 'by reason of genus,' so far as a distinction of grades is necessary for good order and tranquility in the Church; and 'by reason of gifts,' so far as by the variety and diversity of gifts, God declares that He wishes that there should be distinct grades among the ministers; and 'by reason of certain grades in particular,' in so far as He Himself distinguished and preferred the office of prophets and apostles to that of others. Nevertheless it cannot be said absolutely and generally concerning all grades of the ministry, that their institution and distinction depend upon divine institution, inasmuch as these grades, in a fixed and necessary number, have neither been prescribed by God, nor used by the apostles, in like manner as the Sacraments have been restricted to the number two by divine institution and Apostolic practice; but liberty has been left to the Church, with respect to

> circumstances, viz., of time and place, in any Church organization, to establish either more or fewer grades among ministers" (Gerhard, VI, 137, 138).

For these reasons, the practice of licensing candidates for the ministry for several years prior to their ordination, which was long the custom in the Lutheran Church of America, was entirely legitimate and valid.

Power of Ministers

42. What Power or Authority have ministers?

> "The power of the bishops, by the rule of the Gospel, is a power or commandment from God, of preaching the Gospel of remitting or retaining sins, and of administering the Sacraments." "Bishops, as bishops, i.e., those who have the administration of the Word and Sacraments committed to them, have no other jurisdiction at all, but only to remit sin, also to take cognizance of doctrine, and to reject doctrine inconsistent with the Gospel, and to exclude from the communion of the Church, without human force, but by the word, those whose wickedness is known" (Augsburg Confession, Art. XXVIII).

43. These seem to be functions whose exercise dare not be declined by ministers. Are there any, besides these, that are permitted them?

> "It is lawful for bishops or pastors to make ordinances whereby things may be done in order in the Church; not that by them, we may merit grace, or satisfy for sins, or that men's consciences should be bound to esteem them as necessary services, and think that they sin when they violate them without offense of others" (ibid.).

44. How are these two different spheres classified?

The former is designated as "Inner," and the latter, as "External" Power; The former deals directly with spiritual things; the latter, with the secular side of the Church, as an external, visible organization. The old distinction derived from the Mediaeval Church, between "Power of Order," and "Power of Jurisdiction," although retained by some of our writers, is not used with uniform consistency, even where most current, and besides has to be considerably modified in accordance with our different conception of the Church.

45. In what sense is "preaching" a prerogative of the ministry?

As a public and official act on the part of a representative of the Church. In a more private way, the instruction of Apollos by Aquila and Priscilla (Acts 18:26), and the command that parents instruct their children (Eph. 6:14), and that believers should teach and admonish each other (Col. 3:16), show that there is a duty in this respect incumbent also upon laymen. (Concerning the question as to whether there be exceptional cases in which laymen may preach, see above, 28, 29.)

46. Are laymen absolutely forbidden to administer the Sacraments?

With but one exception, viz., where there is imminent danger of death of an unbaptized person before a pastor can be secured to administer baptism (see Chapter 27, 18).

47. Has an ordained minister the right to preach and administer the Sacraments everywhere?

His authority is limited by the terms of his call. He cannot exercise ministerial authority within the parish of another pastor, except by the consent of the latter, and at the call of the Church, through its proper officials.

Preaching as a function of the Ministry

48. What subjects are to be treated in the preaching of the Word?

The entire contents of Revelation, viz., Law and Gospel in their proper proportion, and in their application to all the wants of the hearers as moral and religious beings.

> Matt. 28:20. "Teaching them to observe all things whatsoever I commanded you."

Acts 20:27. "I shrank not from declaring unto you all the counsel of God."

Nothing is to be preached but what God has revealed, or what is connected with the application of such revealed Word. Nor is anything that God has revealed to be withheld or ignored. There must be the clear, positive, distinct presentation of doctrine, and the earnest warning against all current errors that may endanger the spiritual life of those who hear. Nor is the preaching to be exclusively doctrinal, but it is to comprise all the duties of the Christian life, in every calling and relation in which God has placed the members of the congregation as individuals. Fearlessly and searchingly, but with humility and love and judgment, sins are to be exposed and censured. The consolations and encouragements of the Gospel are to be administered to all the penitent and believing. The Pastoral Epistles of Paul afford full directions as to all this.

> "In our churches, all the sermons are occupied with such topics as these: repentance, the fear of God, faith in Christ, the righteousness of faith, the consolation of consciences, the exercises of faith, prayer, the cross, the authority of magistrates, the distinction between the Kingdom of Christ and civil affairs, marriage, the education of children," etc. (Apology, 225).

> "It is not sufficient to preach the work, life and sufferings of Christ in an historic manner... Preaching should have as its object the promoting of faith in Christ, so that he may not only be Christ, but a Christ for you and for me. This is accomplished by preaching why Christ came and what He has brought, and by showing how all we Christians are kings and priests, and lords of all things" (Luther, on "Christian Liberty").

49. Has the congregation the right to prescribe the subjects that are to be included or excluded in the preaching of the Word?

The right of election belongs to the congregation; but when a pastor accepts the call, he is not responsible to the congregation, but alone to God for the faithful discharge of the duties of his office. Otherwise his ministerial acts would not be performed in the name of God.

Gal. 1:10. "If I were still pleasing men, I should not be a servant of Christ."

> "What would be our judgment of a physician who made the choice of his medicines dependent upon the taste of the sick?" (Van Oosterzee).

Administration of Sacraments of the Ministry

50. What is required in the administration of the Sacraments?

That all the essentials of the original institution be observed, and nothing be added or omitted that would impair or obscure their force. As in the preaching of the Word, so in the administration of the Sacraments, the demands and preferences of the congregation dare not determine the course of the pastor, except in things that are clearly matters of indifference. The will of the congregation cannot relieve him of his personal responsibility for all who are admitted or refused.

Administration of Power of Keys: Confession and Absolution, private and public, Part of Ministry in Discipline.

51. What is the office of remitting and retaining sins?

> "The remission of sins is to be announced not only universally and indeterminatively to all the penitent and believing in Christ, but also determinatively and individually to those who, confession being made, give probable signs of repentance and faith, and ask to be absolved of their sins. Nor is this a mere declaration, but it is efficacious in confirming the forgiveness of sins made by God' (Baier). (See Chapter 26, 8.)

So the retention of sins is the announcement to a notorious and obstinate offender that God will not forgive his sins, as long as he remains in his impenitence, and his exclusion, for this reason, from the Lord's Supper and the fellowship of the Church.

> "This likewise is not merely declaratory, but is efficacious."

52. By what terms is this individual dealing between a pastor and a parishioner known?

As "Private Confession" and "Private Absolution." This does not mean "secret"; but, just as in 2 Peter 1:20, it is said that "no prophecy is of any private interpretation," where the merely arbitrary judgment of the individual is excluded, so also here. The first meaning of "private" in the "Century Dictionary" is:

> "Peculiar to, belonging to, or concerning an individual only: respecting particular individuals; personal." A "private corporation" is not a "secret corporation," "private law" is not "secret law," "private property" is not "secret property," "private judgment" is not "secret judgment."

The Latin word "*privatiis*" was opposed to "*publicus*"; the latter meaning "what belongs to the state," the former "what belongs to the individual." It is in this sense, therefore, that the word is to be understood in our Confessions, as in Augsburg Confession, Art. XI, where it is said: 'They teach that Private Absolution ought to be retained in all the churches," i.e., the assurance given the individual penitent that he has been redeemed by Christ, that forgiveness of sins is offered not simply to the world in general but to him in particular, that it is God's will that he should be forgiven, and that, if this treasure be not his, it will be only because he will reject it. Private Absolution is nothing but the personal application of the Gospel message (Chapter 26, 1, 8). So Private Confession is individual or personal confession, even though made in the presence of an entire congregation or in the presence of the pastor alone. It may be made also through an approved formula or confessional prayer, in the first person, singular number, as in the words:

> "I, a poor sinful man, confess unto Thee, my Creator and Redeemer."

53. What various forms of confession are there?

[A.] Confession of our sins to God alone.

Of the necessity and profitableness of such confession, the people should be diligently admonished. Examples of it are found in Ps. 32:3-5; 1 John 1:9. This may be a confession not only of individual sins (Ps. 51:2, 3), but also of general sinfulness, as in Luke 18:13; Ps. 51:5, 10.

[B.] Confession to one's neighbor, when we see that we have done him a wrong. (Luke 17:4; James 5:16; Matt. 5:23).

[C.] General confession to a minister, where one declares his sinfulness, or where some particular sins have burdened the conscience.

(2 Sam. 12:13; Matt. 3:5).

[D.] Public confession of sins which have given public offense.

For this ecclesiastical practice, precedents are found in the narrative of the woman who was a sinner in Luke 7, and the case of discipline in the church at Corinth (1 Cor. 5; 2 Cor. 2:7).

[E.] To these Chemnitz (Examen) adds a history of the process which resulted at last in the Auricular Confession of the Papists.

As the confession of notorious sins often led into the publishing of details which should not be mentioned in the congregation, it was preceded by confidential interviews with the priest, in which what should be made public and what should be kept secret, was determined. The next stage was the requirement of the secret confession of each sin, as the condition of its forgiveness.

54. How does Lutheran Private Confession differ from that of the Roman confessional?

[A.] It is not exacted as necessary.

The personal confession of sins is recommended as an aid for receiving absolution. "Confession" (i.e., such personal confession to a pastor):

> "...is of human right only. Nevertheless, on account of the very great benefit of absolution, and because it is otherwise useful to the conscience, confession is retained among us" (Augsburg Confession, Article XXV).

> "We retain Confession, especially on account of the absolution which is the Word of God, that the Power of the Keys proclaims concerning individuals" (Apology, 196).

It is intended particularly:

> "...for timid consciences and inexperienced youth, in order that they may be instructed in Christian doctrine" (Schmalkald Articles).

[B.] The enumeration of details is not urged.

> "In confession an enumeration of all sins is not necessary" (Augsburg Confession, XI).

> "They teach that an enumeration of sins is not necessary, and that consciences be not burdened with anxiety to enumerate all sins" (ibid., XXV).

> "Ministers have the command to remit sins; they have not the command to investigate secret sins" (Apology, 196).

> "Although it is of advantage to accustom inexperienced men to enumerate some things, in order that they may be the more readily taught" (ibid., 176).

> "The enumeration of sins ought to be free to every one, as to what he wishes to enumerate or not" (Schmalkald Articles, 331).

[C.] The chief purpose of reflection.

The chief purpose of reflection concerning individual sins is to lead to the deeper conviction of the state of sin, and the entire corruption of man's nature, whence particular acts of sin have proceeded; so that a general confession of sinfulness may follow.

55. How are some of the advantages of such Confession and Absolution obtained?

By the general public Confession and Declaration of Grace that precedes the Holy Communion. The chief design of this service is to cultivate and deepen the sense of individual sin, and to prepare for the absolution communicated in the words of distribution.

56. Can Church Discipline be exercised by a congregation independently of the ministry?

No. For while the Keys belong to the entire Church, it employs them only by providing for a ministry, through which this is done. In 1 Cor. 5:3-5, we learn that, in order that discipline could be exercised in the Corinthian church, the presence of Paul, and in his absence, his written approval, was necessary. (See Chapter 32.)

External duties of Ministry

57. Mention some of the matters comprised within the sphere of External Power.

All the provisions included in the Constitutions of congregations, Synods, General Bodies, the educational and benevolent institutions of the Church, Missionary Boards and Societies, and all other agencies for the dissemination of God's Word, the supply and training of ministers, the regulations for worship and the preaching of the Gospel, the settlement of disputes and controversies, the publication and circulation of Church literature, the support of the destitute, the administration of Church funds and the making of collections for these objects. While the ministry shares this power with the laity, it is in general their judgment, experience and training which determine its direction. Such power is exercised not by the rigid enforcement of laws, but by the appeal which the presentation of the causes above mentioned makes upon the hearts and consciences of individuals. The external is entirely subordinate to the inner power. The ministry of preaching the

Word and administering the Sacraments is above that which is occupied with the details of Church government and external administration.

Deacons and Deaconesses

58. What other ministers are there beside the ministers of the Word?

Deacons, or the executive aids of pastors, chiefly in the external administration of the Church. While the question as to whether "the seven" of Acts 6:3 are the same as the deacons elsewhere mentioned in the New Testament, is one on which there is not unanimity among Bible students, nevertheless, the general principle of the more thorough organization and division of labor is the same in both classes of passages. Acts 7 and 8 clearly show that "the seven" preached as well as attended to the secular responsibilities of the infant Church. The qualifications of deacons required by 1 Tim. 3:8-13, show that their duties were not purely secular.

59. What were the Deaconesses of the early Church?

Women officially commissioned for congregational service. They were nothing more than female deacons.

> Rom. 16:1. "Phoebe, our sister, who is a deaconess of the church that is at Cenchreae."

In 1 Tim. 3:8-10, there is a statement concerning the qualifications in general for "deacons." Then, in V. 11, it is the female deacons, who are meant by the designation "women"; after which V. 12 refers to the male deacons. It would be a strange break to understand V. 11 as meaning women in general, or the wives of deacons.

The End of the Ministry

60. What is the end of the Ministry?

Its ultimate end is the salvation of men.

> 1 Tim. 4:16. "Take heed to thyself and to thy teaching. Continue in these things; for in doing this, thou shalt save both thyself and them that hear thee."

Its intermediate end is the reconciliation of men with God.

> 2 Cor. 5:18, 20. "God gave unto us the ministry of reconciliation... We are ambassadors on behalf of Christ, as though God were entreating by us; we beseech you, on behalf of Christ, be ye reconciled to God."

As well as the edification of believers in faith and other Christian virtues.

> Eph. 4:12, 13. "For the perfecting of the saints, unto the work of ministering, unto the building up of the body of Christ, till we all attain unto the unity of the faith, and of the knowledge of the Son of God, unto a full grown man, unto the measure of the stature of the fullness of Christ."

The end of the ministry, therefore, is not simply to increase, from year to year, the roll of communicants, but to deepen each member of the Church in all the gifts and graces of Christian character. The outward extension of the Church and all about it that meets men's eyes are subordinate to its inner growth, i.e., to the bringing to men "righteousness, peace and joy in the Holy Ghost" (Rom. 14:17). Such is the only test of a successful pastorate.

Comfort with respect to its duties

61. What special comfort have ministers of the Word who recognize their office as coming to them from a clearly divine call?

> "God's call carries with it God's aid. An earthly ruler who sends a servant on an embassy protects him with a large squadron of cavalry. So whenever God calls one to dangers, He promises him His aid and protection. When He called Moses to lead Israel, He said: 'I will be with thee.' When He called the Israelites to the desert, what withstood them, or what did they lack, as they obeyed? The sea saw them and fled, Jordan turned backwards, the heaven rained manna, the earth gave water, their clothing did not wear out, their feet were not bruised, their enemies were stricken with fear. When Jeremiah was called and realized how inadequate he was for so great a work, he heard the words: T am with thee-, to deliver thee.' When the Apostles went forth without silver or gold, without purse or staff, what did they lack? What perils overcame them? Let us, therefore, take heed to walk obediently as God calls us, however dangerous be the way. For it is not by

disobedience, but by obedience, that, through faith, we are accustomed to avoid the perils that threaten us" (Brentz, on Acts 1).

31. The Church's Confessions

Necessity

1. Why are Confessions of Faith necessary?

In order to distinguish Church organizations which have reached certain conclusions from Holy Scripture, and embodied them in formal definitions from other organizations or other modes of teaching which also appeal to Scripture as their authority. A Confession of Faith is as necessary for a Church organization as a Constitution is for a society.

2. But is not the Bible a sufficient confession?

The Bible can never be made a Confession of Faith. It is the absolute rule and source of faith. But when its truth is received, man's answer is his confession.

> Rom. 10:10. "With the heart, man believeth unto righteousness and with the mouth confession is made unto salvation.

In Mark 9:23, the Word of God is:

> "All things are possible to him that believeth."

The human answer to this, i.e., the confession of faith which it evokes is:

> Mark 9:24. "Lord, I believe; help thou mine unbelief."

In order that a number of persons may join in a confession, there is need of a prearranged form. Such in a general sense are the hymns of the Church. But in a narrower sense, the term "Confession" refers to those documents which have originated from some crisis in the Church's history, when a necessity has arisen of carefully discriminating what is regarded the truth from what is regarded error with reference to the teachings of Scripture.

3. Within what spheres are such Confessions necessary?

[A.] They are bonds of union between the members of the Church, by which they recognize each other as holding to the same interpretation of God's Word.

[B.] They are marks by which those outside the communion may distinguish it from other assemblies. [C.] They are solemn contracts by which those entrusted with official positions as representatives of the Church, especially pastors and public teachers, are to be regulated in the administration of their office.

4. Why should such confessional obligation be exacted especially of a pastor?

Because the Church, by its ordination, endorses the candidate as its representative. It commits the teaching and preaching and the administration of the Sacraments into his hands, not so as to be determined by his own judgment, but to be administered in accordance with what the Church believes and confesses to be the pure Word of God, and what in her long experience she has found to be the most efficient mode of administering the Word. Ministers are representatives of God only as executives of what God has entrusted to the Church.

Precise Function

5. But does not this assume that the conscience of the pastor must be determined by the judgment of the Church rather than by Holy Scripture?

He is expected to have been a faithful student of Holy Scripture, and to have tested the statements of the Confessions according to this standard.

> "We confessionally accept the first unaltered Augsburg Confession, not because it was composed by our theologians, but because it has been derived from God's Word" (Formula of Concord, 536).

Confessions of Faith, our theologians have repeatedly said, are not a "*norma credendorum*," for this pertains only to the Scriptures, but they are a "*norma docendorum*." (See Chapter 1, 35.)

6. If, however, the judgment of the pastor or candidate should differ from that of the Church?

As a Christian teacher and a professed representative of God to men, if thoroughly candid and true to his call, he would not consent to be known before men by a name which stands for doctrines which he repudiates.

Nature of Test

7. What should be the nature of the confessional test?

Clear, definite, explicit, and avoiding all ambiguous phrases which may be a pretext for a union upon words among those who are at controversy concerning that for which these words stand. If, for example, at the Reformation period, the formula: "We hold that man is justified before God by faith alone," had been accepted by the Roman Catholics, in the sense that justification comes through faith alone, because faith is "the mother of good works," and without faith there can be no such works, or because faith is the foundation of love, and the justifying value of faith is the love which energizes it, our Lutheran forefathers could not have subscribed with them any such statements. In all Confessions of Faith, as in all articles of agreement in civil life, such as are interpreted by our courts of justice, there can be no real and lasting understanding, unless the two parties to the contract, employ its terms in the same sense. No one understanding the situation, would buy or sell a farm or rent a house upon terms susceptible of diverse interpretations. If, then, in our business transactions, we demand agreements "in black and and white," how much more important is this necessary in the Church, whose entire strength consists in the clearness of its testimony!

Confessional obligation analyzed

8. What two things are involved in a confessional obligation?

First of all, and chiefly, loyalty to the faith of the Confession. That faith is capable of expression in various forms and ways. But whatever be the mode in which it appears, and however manifold its applications, it is always the same faith and, as coming from God, demands the same recognition. Because of this, it includes, in the second place, loyalty also to the particular Confession, as one of the many forms in which this faith is expressed Where the faith has been thoroughly appropriated and has really entered into the life, it unconsciously combines fidelity to an historical Confession which is found to be scriptural, with the greatest freedom of adaptation and adjustment to variations of time and place, and to the ever shifting movements of thought and discussion. The results of the Reformation are the basis, but not the limit of the thought and life of the Church of later centuries. It is for us to recognize and highly prize and jealously guard whatever has been wrought by the Holy Spirit at every important epoch of the Church; but we cannot rest in this. New issues will constantly demand new expressions of the same precious faith. All progress is by the combination of two forces, fidelity to the past and fidelity to the present. Neither the Augsburg Confession nor the Schmalkald Articles, nor the Formula of Concord can be the ultimate definition of the Church's faith. Whenever some widespread error or gross abuse requires some emphatic repudiation on the part of the Church of a later age, the embodiment of such conviction in synodical action gives it the rank of a confessional position.

Precautions to be observed

9. Are there no precautions, however, to be observed in subscribing to the Confessions?

> "They are not to be received other or further than as witnesses, in what manner, since the time of the Apostles, the doctrine of the Apostles and prophets has been preserved... They are only a witness and declaration of the faith, as to how the Holy Scriptures have been understood and explained in the articles in controversy, and by what arguments the dogmas conflicting with the Holy Scripture were rejected and condemned" (Formula of Concord, 491-2).

Their authority rests entirely upon their agreement with Scripture, and not upon the decision of the Church.

> "Whoever regards doctrines of the Lutheran Church as true on the ground that they are Lutheran, is no Lutheran" (Kahnis, I, 5).

10. May we not then subscribe to them, "in so far as" they agree with Holy Scripture?

No; for this would not tell what the person making the subscription accepted or rejected. We could subscribe with such a formula equally well to the Decrees of Trent or of Dort, the Westminster Confession or the Heidelberg Catechism, the Book of Mormon or the Koran, as to the Augsburg Confession. We could stand in a large theological library, and pointing to the alcoves say:

> "All religious truth within these books, that is in harmony with Holy Scripture, I accept. In so far as they are in conformity with God's Word, I accept them all!"

The next question inevitably must be, as to what the doctrines are that are confessed, or as to what the statements are which are acknowledged and approved. If this is evaded, there is no confession. Hence we repudiate the so-called "quatenus subscription," as an evasion, and ask for a "quia subscription," as alone fulfilling the scriptural requirement:

> 1 Pet. 3:15. "Be ready always to give answer to every man that asketh you a reason concerning the hope that is in you, yet with meekness and fear."

The Lutheran Confessions classified

11. How may the Confessions of the Lutheran Church be grouped?

Into two classes:

I. Practical handbooks for popular instruction

The Small Catechism, and the Large Catechism.

II. Theological Confessions

[A.] The Symbols of Lutheran Catholicity:

1. The Augsburg Confession.

It exhibits the faith confessed by the Lutheran Church as the basis of all true Christianity. Although the Articles concerning abuses, and the close of nearly all the doctrinal articles are negative, it is preponderantly positive. Its tone is throughout irenic.

2. *The Apology.*

The Apology is an official interpretation of the articles of the Augsburg Confession that were misrepresented.

[B.] The Symbol of Lutheran Determination and Particularity

The Schmalkald Articles.

After years of protest have failed to make an impression upon those who in the Roman Church have perverted the Gospel, this Confession dissolves forever all communion with this corrupt organization, and leaves it to its just fate. It makes few additions to positive doctrine. It is preponderantly negative. Polemical in tone, it is, from beginning to end, a call to arms against deadly errors and obstinate errorists.

[C.] The Symbol of Lutheran Reflection upon the contents of its faith and doctrine.

The Formula of Concord.

Here the Church, in the maturity of its powers, examines and judges itself. It subjects its conceptions of the faith to rigid analysis and discriminating criticism, and frames and fixes the terminology of theological definitions, which under its decisions lose the ambiguity that at many points had caused confusion and controversy. In it, the positive and negative elements are most carefully balanced. The predominant characteristics of the Formula are its scientific exactness and the judicial poise with which it keeps the golden mean between the extremes on both sides, which it states at the beginning of the discussion of every topic.

The Confessions may be classified and designated otherwise as follows:

I. The Catechisms are symbols pertaining to the religious life of the individual Christian.

II. The other Confessions are symbols pertaining to the ecclesiastical organization and define the principles that are to govern the Church in preaching the Word and administering the Sacraments.

1. The Augsburg Confession (1530), with its supplement, the Apology (1531) represents the opening youth of the Lutheran Church. In it the Church has the outlook and temper of an earnest and godly child thirteen years old, who has attained a knowledge of the treasures of the Gospel, and who, in the spirit of true devotion, is making his confirmation vow. There is here the simplicity, ingenuousness, amiability and sanguine expectations concerning an untried future that characterize this particular stage of life.
2. The Schmalkald Articles (1537) represents the Lutheran Church on the very verge of its majority. Twenty years had passed since the XCV Theses, when this later document was drawn up by the same hand. Cast out of the old home, and thrown on his own resources, the adult is now able to assert his complete independence. With youthful impetuosity he takes up the sword and makes aggressive warfare against the enemy who spurns all attempts at peace.
3. The Formula of Concord (1577) comes forty years later. The Church has passed the period of youth and looks back upon the varied experiences that have, in unexpected ways, put faith to the trial, and thoroughly tested the earlier declarations. With powers matured but not enfeebled by age, the results of the intervening period are reviewed with the calmness and thoroughness of a discriminating judge.

Abuse of Confessions

12. How may Confessions be abused?

[A.] By resting in them.

This happens when we are satisfied with them as the irrefutable productions of our fathers, and a precious legacy of the Lutheran Church, instead of making them simply the starting point of our own thought and growth. They are really appreciated and assimilated only in the degree that, as individuals, we pass through conflicts, similar to those which called them forth.

[B.] By neglecting the fresh and independent study of Holy Scripture.

...in the light of all increased facilities which later ages may have brought. Theological students and pastors, intent chiefly on statements of dogmas, to the neglect of the devout religious use and thorough exegetical study of the Bible, especially of the New Testament, are false to the Confessional principle with which the Formula of Concord opens.

[C.] By using them in a legalistic and mechanical way.

Just as the Holy Scriptures are abused by neglecting to treat them as an organism, and treating them as though they are simply a treasury of proof texts of equal force and value in whatever relation they may be placed, so also the Confessions must always be interpreted upon their historical background, and their statements should be applied in the sense in which they were intended by their authors. Incidental illustrations, citations and even arguments do not have the authority that belongs to the form in which the doctrine itself is stated.

[D.] By putting the Confession in place of the doctrines which it confesses.

It is not the formal subscription to the Confessions, but it is the sincere acceptance of the doctrines they state and defend, that determines the real ecclesiastical standing of a pastor. This, however, does not render it unnecessary, for the proper order and organization of the Church, that pastors who have learned to know and accept the doctrines of the Confessions be required to give them their formal subscription.

Objections answered

13. But does subscription to Confessions produce absolute harmony among all who comply with this requirement?

No more than there is absolute unity among all who profess to cherish the Holy Scriptures as the Word of God, or to worship Jesus Christ as their Savior. In this world, the Church will always be under the cross, and dissensions will occur whatever be the means adopted to avoid them. There is at least one thing, however, that is more to be valued than even peace and harmony, and that is faithful testimony to the entire truth of God's Word.

14. Are not the controversies settled in our Confessions merely such as belonged to the Church in Germany over three hundred years ago, and, therefore, of no very great importance to us in America?

The errors controverted reappear wherever the Gospel is preached. The questions of the XVI Century are just as living and important today, as they were then. A Church which assumes to be independent of the labors and testimony of its fathers, in so far as they are true, will ultimately be called upon to pass through the same experience, and to return to their testimony which it had deemed unnecessary.

Rules for controversies

15. How are doctrinal controversies to be conducted? By carefully keeping in mind two scriptural principles:

[A.] Contend For The Faith.

Jude 3. "Contend earnestly for the faith which was once for all delivered to the saints."

Tit. 1:13. "Reprove them sharply, that they may be sound in the faith."

[B.] With Humility.

2 Tim. 2:24, 25. "And the Lord's servant must not strive, but be gentle towards all, apt to teach, forbearing, in meekness correcting them that oppose themselves; if peradventure God may give them repentance unto the knowledge of the truth."

1 Tim. 3:3. "The bishop must be no brawler, no striker; but gentle, not contentious."

Tit. 1:7. "Not self-willed, not soon angry, no brawler, no striker."

Jude 9. "But Michael the archangel, when contending with the devil he disputed about the body of Moses, durst not bring against him a railing judgment, but said, The Lord rebuke thee."

Fidelity in the proclamation of the truth, and the exposure of error, is perfectly consistent with the *upaxos* (non-controversial 1 Tim. 3:3; Titus 3:2) temper or spirit, of which no better example can be given than that of "the faithful witness" (Rev. 1:5) our Lord Jesus Christ. No love of ease or peace suppresses His testimony, as we read in the Gospels, neither do the errors of His opponents provoke Him to harsh denunciations, except when, as a last resort, in the spirit of love, He seeks by the most forcible words to arouse them from the stupor into which they had been beguiled. The silence of Jesus, after His words are rejected, is more significant than any utterance could have been.

16. Has any statement on this subject been made by our theologians?

Yes. Luther has somewhere said:

> "Non docendo, sed disputando, Veritas antittititr" i.e., "It is not by teaching, but by wrangling, that the truth is lost."

Nor can a better interpretation of this be found than the words of Chemnitz:

> "We must always keep it in mind that the purpose of the Son of God, in coining forth from the secret abode of the Eternal Father, and revealing heavenly doctrine, was not to found here and there seminaries for disputations, in which theologians might make a display of their intellectual acumen, but, on the contrary, that humanity might be instructed concerning the true knowledge of God and all things necessary for attaining eternal salvation. For this reason, in respect to every article of faith, our chief care should be as to how and in what manner the doctrine which is taught be applied to practice in the earnest exercises of repentance, faith, obedience and prayer. For thus minds will advance at the same time both in learning and in godliness. For it has been truly said that Theology consists more in disposition than in knowledge" (Loci Theologici, p. 17).

17. What does this last statement mean?

It refers to the doctrine that all agree upon theoretically, but are apt to forget in the heat of controversy, that it is not the elaboration of argument, or the profundity of learning, or the sharpness in drawing distinctions, or fluency in debate, or height of eloquence, that produces conviction, but the illuminating influences of the Holy Spirit, imparted through "the still, small voice" of the Word, when it is treated in a reverent and prayerful spirit. Men reach deeply settled convictions not amidst the heat of personal or partisan discussion, but in the silence of the study and the closet.

18. What model of controversial composition may be mentioned?

The "*Examen Concilii Tridentini*," by Dr. Martin Chemnitz, in which the controversy affords only the starting point for a most exhaustive and dispassionate discussion of the principles that underly it. Thus the negative element forms a small part of the treatment, and the opponents and their attacks are obscured by the material of permanent value that prevails.

32. Church Discipline

The two spheres

1. What two spheres are there for the exercise of Church discipline?

The discipline of members of the Church as individual Christians, and the discipline of ministers.

2. Have those who occupy the ministerial office any prerogative exempting them from the same discipline as other members of the Church?

By no means. But as the bearers of an office, they have responsibilities not incumbent upon private members, and, hence, are subjects of discipline, from which otherwise they would be free.

The Object

3. What is the main object of the discipline of a member of the Church?

The reformation of the one who has sinned, and the salvation of his soul.

> 1 Cor. 5:5. "To deliver such an one unto Satan for the destruction of the flesh, that the spirit may be saved in the day of the Lord Jesus."

> Matt. 18:15. "If he hear thee, thou hast gained thy brother."

> Gal. 6:1. "If a man be overtaken in a fault, ye which are spiritual restore such an one in the spirit of gentleness."

4. But is this the only object?

No. A second object is that the sin of which he is guilty may not contaminate and ruin others.

> 1 Cor. 5:6, 7. "Know ye not that a little leaven leaveneth the whole lump? Purge out the old leaven, that ye may be a new lump."

A third object is that the order of the Church may be preserved.

> 1 Thess. 3:6. "Now we command you, brethren, in the name of our Lord Jesus Christ, that ye withdraw yourselves from every brother that walketh disorderly."

> 1 Thess. 3:14, 15. "If any man obeyeth not our word by this epistle, note that man, that ye may have no company with him, to the end that he may be ashamed. And yet count him not as an enemy, but admonish him as a brother."

A fourth object is that the confession and testimony of the Church to the truth, and against every form of sin and error may be clear and unequivocal.

> Rev. 2:2. "I know thy works and thy toil and thy patience, and that thou canst not bear evil men, and didst try them that call themselves apostles, and they are not, and didst rind them false."

> Rev. 2:14. "I have a few things against thee, because thou hast there some that hold the teaching of Balaam who taught Balak to cast a stumbling-block before the children of Israel."

> Eph. 5:11. "Have no fellowship with the unfruitful works of darkness, but rather even reprove them."

Indispensable

5 Has the Church, therefore, any authority to dispense with Church Discipline?

> 1 Cor. 5:11. "I wrote unto you not to keep company, it any man that is named a brother be a fornicator, or covetous, or an idolater, or a reviler, or a drunkard, or an extortioner, with such an one, no not to eat."

6. What do our Confessions declare on this subject?

In Augsburg Confession, Art. XXVIII, among the just rights of "bishops," is "to exclude from the communion of the Church, wicked men whose wickedness is known, and this without human force, simply by the Word."

The Apology (German ed.), Art. XI, "On Confession," declares:

> "Besides it has always been announced by our preachers that they should be excommunicate. d and excluded who live in public crimes, fornication, adultery, etc.; likewise they who despise the Holy Sacraments."

So also the Schmalkald Articles (Part III, Art. IX):

> "The 'Greater Excommunication,' as the Pope calls it, we regard only as a civil penalty, and not pertaining to us ministers of the Church. But the 'Less' is true Christian excommunication, which prohibits manifest and obstinate sinners from the Sacrament and other communion of the Church until they are reformed and avoid sin."

7. What have our theologians to say on the subject?

Chemnitz, in the "*Kirchen-Ordnung*" of Lower Saxony (A. D. 1585), states the necessity of discipline for earthly governments, families and schools, and adds;

> "Much more in the holy house of God, without necessary, wholesome discipline, instituted and administered according to God's Word, nothing can be done in an orderly, right, Christian and proper way."

Fecht, quoted by Dr. Walther (*Pastorale*, 318), declares that:

> "...the entire building of the Church rests upon two pillars, the teaching of sound doctrine and the administration of discipline"; (and that) "the lack

of discipline is the chief cause of the decline of our Church... Orthodox theologians have constantly complained of this laxity, and have urged the restoration of stricter discipline."

Offenses noticed

8. With what offenses is this discipline occupied?

"They are of two classes: Those pertaining to doctrine, and those pertaining to the life. A doctrinal error either arises from simple ignorance and has no obstinacy conjoined with it or, it has its origin in malice and lack of honesty, and is obstinately defended against the judgment of the Church derived from Holy Scripture. A fall in life and character is an offense committed either in words or deeds, and is either public or private. A public offense is one that has been openly done or is widely known and entails scandal; a private, is one secretly committed of which only a single person, or at most a very few have knowledge, and is without public and notorious scandal" (Gerhard, VI, 192).

Grades

9. What grades of Church Discipline are there?

Our theologians generally give three:

1. Admonition and Reproof;
2. The "Minor Excommunication," or suspension, for a time, from the Lord's Supper; and
3. The "Greater Excommunication," or total expulsion from the Church, which is rarely employed and only in the most flagrant cases.

Divinely-prescribed order

10. Is there a divinely prescribed order for the process?

Yes; and especially for private offenses.

Matt. 18:15-17. "If thy brother sin against thee, go, show him his fault between thee and him alone; it he hear thee, thou hast gained thy brother.

> But if he hear thee not, take with thee one or two more, that at the mouth of two witnesses or three, every word may be established. And if he refuse to hear them, tell it unto the church; and it he refuse to hear the church also, let him be unto thee as the Gentile and the publican."

11. Is this limited to acts which are personally injurious or hostile to the person reproving?

"The Greek phrase *eis se* can be rendered in Latin *apud te* or *coram te*, that is, 'in your knowledge'" (Gerhard). This interpretation of "*eis*" seems to be overdrawn. Calvin's interpretation is better:

> "There are very many who allow no public censures, until the sinner has been admonished privately. But the restriction in the words of Christ is manifest. For He does not absolutely and without exception command that whoever sin be admonished or reproved secretly and without any witness, but He wants this way to be tried by us when we have been offended privately, not indeed in our own interests, but because it is fitting that we be grieved, whenever God is offended. For Christ is not treating here concerning the patient endurance of injuries, but teaches that mildness should be cultivated by us generally, lest, by treating the weak too harshly, we destroy those who should be saved. Therefore, the particle 'against thee,' does not designate an injury offered some one, but distinguishes between secret and manifest sins. For if anyone sin against the whole Church, Paul wants him to be publicly rebuked, so that not even elders are to be spared. And certainly it is ridiculous to require that one who has sinned with public offense, commonly known as *flagitium*, be admonished by each one individually; for if there were a thousand witnesses, he would have to be admonished a thousand times. The distinction, therefore, which Christ expressly makes, must be retained, lest some one by publishing secret sins rashly and unnecessarily malign his brother."

Note also should be taken of the fact that this direction of our Lord is not permissive, but mandatory. It declares not a privilege which the believer may exercise at his discretion, but a duty.

12. What caution, however, is to be employed with reference to this private interview?

> "Prudence must be exercised; for when one has sinned from ignorance or infirmity, a kind admonition, with an exhortation to avoid future lapses is enough; but when one has sinned from malice a more severe reproof should be administered. 'Friendly reproof,' says Ambrose, 'accomplishes more than violent charges; the former inspires shame, the latter excites indignation.' Neither in such administration of reproof should we indulge our personal feelings or private resentment (1 Tim. 5:21) but every effort should be made to bring about the conversion and salvation of the one who has fallen" (Gerhard).

Dannhauer lays down the following requisites for such admonition, viz., (a) Truth, the person must be sure of the charge; (b) Prudence, at the right time; (c) Friendliness, i.e., with tenderness and sympathy (Ps. 141. 5); (d) Sincerity; (e) Moderation and considerateness.

13. How in regard to public offenses?

Such previous private process is not necessary (1 Tim. 5:20). So Paul rebuked Peter promptly and openly (Gal. 2:11). Nevertheless even here, a private interview may often remove misunderstandings and prevent much further trouble.

Excommunication

14. When must resort be had to excommunication?

Only when all other measures have failed to bring the offender to repentance; and then, too, only because of sins of peculiar enormity, and which occasion scandal.

15. To whom does the decision as to excommunication belong?

First of all to the Church, i.e., the congregation.

> Matt. 18:17. "Tell it unto the church."

> 1 Cor. 5:13. "Put away the wicked man from among yourselves."

As the Key of binding it belongs not simply to the ministry, but to the whole Church (Matt. 18:17, 18, 20). (Chapter 29, 54; 30, 56.) But just as the preaching of the Word, the administration of the Sacraments and the exercise of the Key of loosing require the ministerial office, so here. In 1 Cor. 5:3, 4, the Apostle gives the Corinthian congregation a written authorization to proceed in a disciplinary case, "as though I were present."

Hence the Schmalkald Articles declare:

> "The common jurisdiction of excommunicating those guilty of manifest crimes belongs to all pastors."

A congregation cannot excommunicate without a pastor, neither can a pastor excommunicate simply according to his own judgment and without the authorization of the congregation, in accordance with the mode of procedure which its Constitution may define. It would be entirely within the authority of the Church for it to make a constitutional provision requiring, for final decision, the endorsement of a representative of the Church outside of the congregation, as often in Germany the approval of the Consistory has been prescribed, in order to remove such disciplinary action as far as possible from a sphere in which personal and partisan influence may be dominant.

16. Why is the presence and concurrence of the ministry so important?

[A.] Because in the trial of such cases, the congregation needs to be guided by the teaching office of the Church, that it may adhere closely to what is taught in the Holy Scriptures, and not take the power into its own hand.

[B.] Because the personal dealing with souls belongs first of all to the pastoral office, and such procedure should not proceed without the faithful discharge of pastoral duty with respect to the accused.

[C.] Because the execution of the decision is incumbent on the pastor.

17. What penalties are imposed by such discipline?

The Church has no other power but that of the Word; it can therefore impose no other than spiritual penalties. They are in reality only the external testimony to those which it believes God has already imposed. They are nothing more than exclusion from the rights and privileges of full membership, combined with the emphatic condemnation of the conduct of the one convicted.

18. But what if the Excommunication be unjust?

It is not valid before God, although it may be the duty of the one wronged to submit to it, under protest, until his innocence can be established.

Secret sins

19. Does not the Key of binding, as well as that of loosing refer to secret as well as to public offenses?

> "The Keys are an office and power given by Christ to the Church for binding and loosing sins, not only such as are gross and well known, but also such as are subtle, hidden and known only to God" (Schmalkald Articles, III, VII).

This refers, however, to the private dealing of the pastor with his people; and to the sins also of which even the pastor is ignorant, when he in general gives the assurance of forgiveness or of retention.

20. How is the discipline of pastors distinguished from that of other members of the Church?

It has reference to the continuance or the non-continuance of the official endorsement given at their ordination that they are proper persons to be entrusted with the care of souls, and the office of the Word and Sacraments. A responsibility for the career of the minister is not only assumed at his ordination, but remains until the endorsement be withdrawn.

> 1 Tim. 5:22. "Lay hands suddenly upon no man, neither be partaker of other men's sins."

Discipline of Pastors

21. What special provision does the New Testament make with respect to the discipline of pastors?

> 1 Tim. 5:19. "Against an elder, receive not an accusation except at the mouth of two or three witnesses."

33. The Christian Family

Place of Family

1. What other institutions besides the ministry are there through which the spiritual welfare of man is promoted?

The Family and the State.

2. What is the office of the Family?

Not only to be the birth-place and nursery of members and ministers of the Church, but a school for the training of husband and wife, parents and children in Christian character, for the strengthening of their faith, the growth of Christian love, the exercise of patience and self-denial and self-sacrificing devotion, and the cultivation and nurture of all influences that are made effective in the service of God. According to the scriptural ideal, the Church is composed of families, i.e., miniature churches, the only true "*ecclesiolae in ecclesiis.*" What the pastor is to the congregation, the father is to his household. Each of the parts of Luther's Catechism begins with the words:

> "In the plain form in which the father of the household is to teach his family."

He is not only to teach, but daily to pray with his wife and children. The mutual love of husband and wife is to be the outgrowth of their common faith in Christ, their common love and sympathy for all included in Christ's love, their common possession of the hopes of the Gospel, and their common interest in what is spiritual and eternal and of what is temporal only as subordinated to these higher objects.

3. How does the Church exert its most effective influence?

By directing, stimulating and impelling the Christian life within families. What is heard in the Church is carried into the family circle, and affords material for instruction and practice during the rest of the week. While family life even among church members is very largely far beneath this ideal, and while also there are many godly persons outside of families, or in families where there is little sympathy with what is Christian, nevertheless, as a rule, the leaders of God's people in all ages of the Church have been trained under such conditions. It is the office of the Church and the ministry, not only to deal with men as individuals, but also to create, protect and promote the family as the chief center of religious life and activity.

4. What is a Christian Family?

A number of Christian people forming one household as the result of the marriage of a Christian man with a Christian woman.

> *Summus amicitiae gradus est foedus conjugale* (Melanchthon).

Marriage with unbelievers

5. Is it wrong for one in the communion of the Church to marry an unbeliever?

Two distinctions must be made here: (a) A marriage may be lawful, but not advisable, (b) One baptized and a child himself of a Christian family, and showing an outward respect for Christianity, must not be accounted at once an unbeliever simply because of not being in the communion of some particular congregation. The question, as we must answer it, is where there is an avowed antagonism to Christianity, or such an outward deportment as to show clearly the absence of all religious principle. To this apply:

> 2 Cor. 6:14. "Be ye not unequally yoked with unbelievers; for what fellowship hath righteousness and iniquity? or what communion hath light with darkness?"

1 Cor. 7:39. "She is free to be married to whom she will; only in the Lord."

6. May there not be a Christian home even with such defect?

There may be, where the Christian husband or wife, with positiveness and patience, always lets the Christian confession be known, and is not rendered indifferent by the worldliness of the other.

> 1 Cor. 7:14, 16. "For the unbelieving husband is sanctified in the wife, and the unbelieving wife is sanctified in the brother... or how knowest thou, O wife, whether thou wilt save thy husband? and how knoweth thou, O husband, whether thou wilt save thy wife."

> 1 Pet. 3:1. "that even if any obey not the word, they may, without the word, be gained by the behavior of their wives, beholding your chaste behavior coupled with fear."

See Chapter 27, 25.

Meaning of Marriage Ceremony

7. What is the significance of the ecclesiastical marriage ceremony?

To testify that a Christian minister has sufficient knowledge of the parties entering into the relation, to declare that it is a union upon which God's blessing can be asked. It is an endorsement of the claim that, according to divine law, there is no barrier to the marriage then contracted.

Marriage indissoluble

8. Is marriage under any circumstances dissoluble?

Not according to divine law (Matt. 19:6). A legitimate divorce, *apud forum divinum*, does not properly separate husband and wife, and dissolve the contract. Its office is only to formally declare the contract to have been already broken by the crime of one of the parties, and to relieve the party sinned against of obligations that were contingent upon the fidelity of the one who has been found to be faithless. Only God's law can annul or revoke what God's law has sanctioned. Man's law cannot touch it.

> "Marriage is the legitimate and indissoluble union of one man and one woman" (Melanchthon, who also maintained that where an offense was so clear as to justify a divorce, the guilty party should be punished, like any other criminal, by the civil authorities, i.e., divorce and the penitentiary should go together).

When is Divorce permissible

9. What are the offenses that completely break the marriage covenant, and justify divorce?

Only two: Adultery (Matt. 19:9; 5:32), and Malicious Desertion (1 Cor. 7:15).

> "The separation of persons illegitimately united is properly not divorce, but a declaration that there had been no marriage union" (Baier).

Precautions to be observed in admitting persons to ceremony

10. What care is to be taken in regard to marriages?

That those entering into this estate are not previously related in the prohibited degrees of consanguinity and affinity defined in Leviticus 18.

11. But if it should be objected that these prohibitions belong to the Ceremonial Law, and have been abrogated since the coming of Christ, what answer shall be given?

The first answer is that, in the very same chapter, it is expressly said that it was because of their violation of these prescriptions, that the Gentiles were punished by God's judgments — a statement that could not be applied to violations only of the Ceremonial Law.

Another answer is that Paul's reproof of the church at Corinth (1 Cor. 5), is because of its passing over a violation of this law, without imposing church discipline, and that he expressly declares in V. 1, that it is of universal application.

To this may be added the charge of John the Baptist against Philip and Herodias (Matt. 14:3, 4), where their crime is not simply adultery, but incest.

12. What other precaution is to be taken?

That neither has been the guilty party in a proceeding for divorce (Matt. 5:32; 19:9; Mark 10:11, 12; Luke 16:18), unless the one wronged have meanwhile died. In the face of the clear words of prohibition in this case, as well as that mentioned under 10, no Christian pastor with a good conscience can pronounce over such marriage the words: "What God hath joined together," for no word of man can make God do what He has declared to be sin.

13. Can a pastor perform the ceremony for those who are avowed atheists or otherwise defiant opponents of the Christian religion, or when one party professes to be such while the other claims to be a Christian?

This also would involve a lack of pastoral fidelity.

> Num. 24:13. "If Balak would give me his house full of silver and gold, I cannot go beyond the word of Jehovah, to do either good or bad of mine own mind; what Jehovah speaketh, that will I speak."

14. Should the Church or pastors have anything to do with marriages that have been contracted in violation of God's law?

A marriage in clear violation of God's law is a sin not only in its beginning, but in its continuance, and subjects the persons concerned to Church discipline. Pastoral prudence however must be exercised in regard to those who have erred in ignorance and who, after a long period has elapsed, with possibly the responsibilities of a family added, come to repentance.

Relation of Family to other institutions

15. How does the Family, as a divine institution, enable us to estimate other institutions?

Any alliance or organization, whether of a religious or a social nature; any engagements or occupations, except from urgent necessity, that interfere with the cultivation of home life, and the fulfillment by husband and wife of duties due each other and their children, is a violation of the divine order. Even ecclesiastical activities that lead to the renunciation of family responsibilities, fall under the class condemned in Mark 7:11-13. No Christian man or woman, however peculiar the opportunities for doing good that invite him from his home, is justified in secluding himself from the closest association and the most intimate companionship with his family, and particularly from exerting within it his most immediate religious influence. Something is wrong, when he is known and appreciated more by strangers than by his own household, or when his interests and enjoyments are largely separated from theirs.

> "Marriage, according to God's Word, is not only placed on an equality with other conditions of life, but it transcends them all, whether they be that of emperor, prince, bishop, or whatever they will" (Large Catechism, 420).

No higher dignity could be accorded it, than to be made a symbol of the union between Christ and the Church (Eph. 5:25).

Celibacy

16. But is not Celibacy especially commended by Paul in 1 Cor. 7?

The language is most explicit in assigning as a reason the peculiar circumstances of Christians at Corinth. While extolling marriage and in very plain terms showing the perils which would come by its disparagement, he advises only "by reason of the distress that is upon us" (1 Cor. 7:26), and as a matter of Christian expediency, that, for the time being, no new responsibilities be assumed, but that the Corinthian Christians remain precisely as they were.

17. What is meant by Luke 18:29?

The passage reads:

> "There is no man that hath left house or wife or brethren or parents or children, for the kingdom of God's sake, who shall not receive manifold more in this time, and in the world to come eternal lite."

In other passages, as e.g., Matt. 10:39, similar consolation is afforded those who for Christ's sake, lose their own lives. "Here it would be ridiculous," says the Apology (289), "to hold that it would be a service to God to kill ourself. So, too, would be the thought that it is a service to God, without His command, to forsake possessions, friends, wife and children." The reference is to cases where fidelity to the confession of Christ's name has resulted or will result in such loss.

> "Take they then our life,
> Goods, fame, child and wife,
> When their worst is done.
> They yet have nothing won,
> The Kingdom ours remaineth."

There is no reference to a voluntary abandonment of them, as though in this way a higher grade of holiness were attainable.

Family as a Religious Center

18. What of the Christian Family as a center of religions influence?

It is not enough that as individuals we should confess Christ's name and live in a manner worthy of His calling, but that as members of families we should contribute to the formation of centers of influence that should diffuse its light and life near and far. Where husband and wife have separate interests and provide for children only from the instincts of natural affection, or so as to keep within the limits of respectability, the family soon disintegrates and leaves no impression upon the world or society. Permanency of family life is rooted in religious principle.

> "As experience teaches, that where there are honorable old families who stand well and have many children, they have their origin in the fact that some of them were well brought up and were mindful of their parents. On the contrary, it is written of the wicked, 'Let his posterity be cut off; and in

the generation following, let his name be blotted out' (Ps. 109:13)" (Large Catechism, 410).

19. Is family religious instruction sufficient?

No. The children are to be brought to the public services of the Church. In some parts of the country, the practice of supporting a church by renting its sittings, has largely excluded the children from its services; and it is little wonder that, as they grow up, the habit of church attendance is never formed.

> "Let the young people attend the preaching, especially during the time when it is devoted to the Catechism, that they may hear it explained, and may learn to understand what every part contains, and be able to explain what they have heard, and when asked may give a correct answer, so that the preaching may not be without profit"' (Large Catechism, 390).

Education and Schools

20. What admonition does the Large Catechism give concerning Christian education?

> "If we want to have proper persons both for civil and ecclesiastical government, we must spare no diligence, time or cost in teaching and educating our children, that they may serve God and the world, and we must not think only how we may amass money and possessions for them... Let every one know, therefore, that above all things it is his duty, or otherwise he will lose the divine favor, to bring up his children in the fear and knowledge of God; and, if they have talents, to have them instructed and trained in a liberal education, that men may be able to have their aid in government and in whatever is necessary" (p. 415).

21. How has Luther elsewhere discussed this?

> "In schools of all kinds, the chief and most common lesson should be the Scriptures, and for young boys the Gospels. Would to God, each town had also a girls' school, in which girls might be taught the Gospel for an hour daily, either in German or Latin! ...Should not every Christian be expected, by his ninth or tenth year, to know all the holy Gospels, containing as they

do his very name and life? ...But where the Holy Scriptures are not the rule, I advise no one to send his child. Everything must perish where God's Word is not studied unceasingly" (Address to the German Nobility).

22. Should the school be expected to afford all the religious instruction?

The family must, after all, be the center and chief nursery of religious life, not only by direct instruction in Holy Scripture and the Catechism, and by daily family prayer, but especially by the Christian temper and spirit which pervade it throughout. No school can take its place, or exert the same amount of influence. All reforms in regard to the Christian education of the young should begin with the family.

Summary

23. What is the sum and substance of the doctrine concerning marriage?

That it has as its chief end, the administration of the Word, and the advancement of the kingdom of God. If it be sometimes commended as a protection against certain temptations, as in Augsburg Confession, Art. XXIII, upon the basis of 1 Cor. 7:2, this must be understood as referring to cases where the higher motive could not be appreciated. To marry for this as the chief end, would be like being industrious for no other motive than to avoid the temptation of stealing. Where marriage is depreciated and its cares and responsibilities are avoided except for such reasons as Paul could plead, or where it is prohibited by Church or State, a fearful penalty is often paid in the corruption of life and morals that follow. It is against this that not only the Augsburg Confession, but the Apology (247-58, 291) warns,

> "God avenges the contempt of His own gift and ordinance" (Apology, 255).

34. The State

Place of State

1. What has the State to do with spiritual things?

It is not a human, but a divine institution (Rom. 13:1-4; 1 Peter 2:13, 14), for the regulation of the external life, defining the various earthly callings and their duties and prescribing the conduct of men in their manifold relations to each other. It restrains the violence of the ungodly, and to the godly it affords not only salutary discipline, but also important aid in the discharge of their obligations towards both God and men. While often abused as an instrument of unrighteousness, nevertheless, in its ideal form, as well as in its general effect, it gives the Church protection and a place for the latter's administration of spiritual interests.

2. Does the Heavenly Citizenship of the Christian (Phil. 3:20) justify him in indifference to the prerogatives cf earthly citizenship?

Paul did not hesitate to avail himself of the privileges belonging to him as a Roman citizen (Acts 16:37; 22:25). To neglect them is to fail to use talents which God has given, and to forsake at least part of one's earthly calling. It is God's order to develop our spiritual capacities through our use of that which is bodily; the heavenly, through the earthly; the eternal, through the temporal.

3. What is the teaching of our Confession on this subject?

> "Of civil affairs, they teach that lawful civil ordinances are good works of God, and that it is right for Christians to bear civil office, to sit as judges, to determine matters by the Imperial and other existing laws, to award just punishments, to engage in just wars, to serve as soldiers, to make legal contracts, to hold property, to make oath when required by the magistrates, to marry, to be given in marriage." "Therefore, Christians are necessarily bound to obey their own magistrates and laws, save only when commanded to sin, for then they ought to obey God rather than men (Acts 5:29)" (Augsburg Confession, Article XVI).

War

4. Passing by other acts that are here justified, we ask concerning going to war and serving as soldiers.

War is a great evil; but it is inevitable in a world of sin. Violence is an evil, but must be resorted to when other methods are exhausted. A nation without an army and navy is like a city without a police force, viz., at the mercy of the lawless. The failure of those charged with their protection to strike a blow for the rescue of the innocent from oppression is not an example of Christian love, but an outrage upon divine justice. Peace with flagrant violators of law is treachery to God. Hence the Gospel brings not only peace, but war — "peace to men of good will" (Luke 2:14), but war with those who array themselves against God's law (Matt. 10:34). Hence there will be no ceasing of wars until Christ's return, and the reign of sin on earth closes (Matt. 24:6, 7). When the soldiers, therefore, came to the preacher of repentance in the wilderness (Luke 3:24) for spiritual instruction, they were not advised to abandon their calling; neither was the centurion repelled by our Lord, as one whose occupation was unlawful, but, on the contrary, he received the highest commendation (Matt. 8:10), just as at a later time Cornelius (Acts 10:22). The words: "He beareth not the sword in vain" (Rom. 13:4), completely vindicate war for just grounds, as a last resort. For this reason, the Augsburg Confession (Art. XVI), says:

> "It is right for Christians to engage in just wars and serve as soldiers." (Art. XX):

> "The Emperor may follow David's example in making wars to drive away the Turk from his country."

Wars become less numerous and their horrors are mitigated as the principles of Christianity pervade the world. Resort to arbitration, instead of the sword, is a result of the progress of the Gospel. But terrible as war is, it is not the worst evil in the universe. This is found in the sin, i.e., the disregard of the rights of God and man, which, on the part of the one side or the other (and frequently of both), occasions war.

Oaths

5. Give a summary of the doctrine of the Oath.

[A.] Definition

> "An oath is an invocation of the name of God, in which we ask God to be witness of our heart, viz., that we do not wish to deceive men in regard to that whereof we testify, and, at the same time, ask God to punish us if we should deceive."

Since an oath is so serious a matter, and it may easily happen that even in lawful cases the name of God may be taken in vain, Augustine says that Christ censured the custom of taking oath lightly, inconsiderately and without necessity."

[B.] When Are They Lawful.

> "Since useless and rash oaths are forbidden, the question is, under what circumstances they are lawful. The answer is: Either when the magistrate prescribes or our calling requires it. This rule can be clearly drawn from examples in Scripture, where the godly are said to have used oaths, as Gen. 21:23; 31:53 (cf. Deut. 10:20; Is. 45:23 sqq.)."

Under such circumstances, the oath becomes a religious act, "a confession that he by whom we swear is the true God," and "a testimony that His name is highly esteemed by us."

> "Oaths, therefore, ought to be required and taken, when every human proof ceases; when otherwise controversies cannot be settled; when the welfare of our neighbor is imperiled; in short, when the glory of God's name is especially concerned in that concerning which the oath is taken" (Chemnitz, Loci, I, 47 sqq.).

Church and State

6. What errors have been prevalent concerning the relation of Church and State?

On the one hand, the Church has assumed authority over the State. Against this our fathers protested in the Augsburg Confession that this involved an entire perversion of the power granted in the Gospel. This power is concerned entirely with spiritual things, the administration of the Word and the Sacraments, and the making of regulations for this end.

> "Therefore, since the power of the Church grants eternal things, and is exercised only by the ministry of the Word, it does not interfere with civil government; no more than the. art of singing interferes with civil government. For civil government deals with other things than does the Gospel; the civil rulers defend not souls, but bodies and bodily things against manifest injuries, and restrain men with the sword, and with bodily punishments, in order to preserve civil justice and peace. Therefore, the power of the Church and the civil power must not be confounded" (Art. XXVIII).

7. But has not the State also assumed authority over the Church?

This form of usurpation is sometimes called Caesaropapacy, i.e., where, instead of the Pope, a civil ruler undertakes to exercise power in regard to spiritual things. The Civil Ruler has no power to preach the Word, to administer the Sacraments, to absolve the penitent or to punish for any other offenses than those which are outwardly committed. It is a usurpation of power, when the State prescribes that which it is the prerogative of a Christian congregation to determine, as when it appoints pastors, superintendents, bishops, and transfers them from place to place; when it interferes with the exercise of such Church discipline as is clearly within the power of the congregation or pastor; when it ordains or regulates the Constitution of a Church Body with respect to spiritual functions; when it appoints or forbids the subject of the preaching or of the public prayers; when it requires a pastor to testify in court concerning matters of which he has knowledge only from the confidence reposed in him as a spiritual adviser; when by law it attempts to enforce the union or the separation of churches one from one another, or to discriminate in favor of or against those so uniting or separating.

8. Does not the reorganization of the Church at the time of the Reformation afford the precedent for such usurpation of power on the part of the State?

The problem before the Reformers was simply this: The break with the traditional Church Government had come without their seeking and against their will, when they had protested against abuses which were so manifest that, in their simplicity, they supposed it was only necessary to declare what they were in order that they might be corrected. To appeal to the people constituting the congregations for a reformation of the Church Government was impossible in the condition in which the Reformation found them. The Preface to the Small Catechism shows the condition in which Luther found the churches during the Saxon Church Visitation in 1528. He says:

> "The people, especially those who live in the villages, seem to have no knowledge whatever of Christian doctrine, and many of the pastors are ignorant and incompetent teachers. Nevertheless, they all maintain that they are Christians, that they have been baptized, and that they have received the Lord's Supper. Yet they cannot recite the Lord's Prayer, the Creed or the Ten Commandments; they live as if they were irrational creatures, and now that the Gospel has come to them, they grossly abuse their liberty."

Neither the people themselves, nor even the ministry was in a condition to undertake so great a responsibility. As it was difficult to surrender the hope that the bishops might still be won over to the Evangelical cause, and the frame work of the old government be then retained under their administration, a temporary plan was devised, according to which the chief magistrate of each German principality which embraced the Reformation, not as ruler, but as the best representative of the laity, assumed episcopal functions, administering ecclesiastical power through entirely different agents and advisers from those employed in the administration of his civil duties. It was entirely a provisional expedient for a peculiar emergency. Nevertheless, not only did it gain permanence with years, but gradually the power was claimed as belonging to the sovereign as a part of his civil duties. The "Episcopal" passed over into the "Territorial form" of Church government, in clear violation of the principles which the Church at the Reformation had determined.

9. May we not derive the inference hence, that the precedents of Church government in Europe cannot be applied to the circumstances of the Church in America, except with great discrimination?

The Lutheran Church has never had the opportunity until in America, to apply her principles without interference from the State. In every regulation and precedent transplanted from Europe, the influence of the State Church is to be considered, and adjustment to be made to the diverse circumstances of a free and self-governing Church.

Limitations of power of the people and majorities

10. Has any particular form of government higher authority than another?

With constant recognition of the defect of all earthly ordinances, the existing form is generally commended as the best for the circumstances and degree of cultivation of the people who are addressed in Holy Scripture. The desire for radical change is discouraged, except where consistency with the past cannot be maintained without doing violence to conscience. The course of history, the rise and fall of nations, and the modifications in governments are regulated by Providential forces over which even the most influential leaders have but little direct control. Even where their power has been most effective, it has generally been so unconsciously and without any purpose on their part. The Patriarchal, the Theocratic, the Monarchical, the Democratic or Republican forms of government, when established, have all alike divine sanction.

11. Is the declaration: "Government of the people, by the people, for the people," strictly correct?

Theologically, it is not. It seems to ignore the supreme authority and paramount claims of God. But this, doubtless, was not so meant. Such ideal, however, can be realized only when, by the new birth, men enter into the enjoyment of the Kingship which Christ has provided for them (see Chapter 15, 14). We would prefer:

> "Government of God through the people, by God through the people, for God through the people."

The secular power is strong and efficient only when firmly laid upon foundations prepared by God. Its most powerful equipment is the love and confidence of its subjects, springing from their fear and love of God, and their appreciation of all in the character of a ruler and the manifold laws of the State that proceed from the same source. But the arbitrary judgment of the people has no more authority than the arbitrary judgment of a despot. Before "the voice of the people" can be accepted as "the voice of God," it must be tested by the Divine Word.

12. Upon what principle of the Reformation is a government of God through the people and by God through the people founded?

Upon the statement of the Protest made at Spires in 1529 that "in matters pertaining to God's honor and to our souls' salvation, every one must stand and give an account of himself before God." The principle which was defined for the very center of man's being, his spiritual life, was sure to work its way out to the circumference; for to the Christian, all things have religious significance. It is the principle of the independence of the Christian conscience because of its complete subjection alone to God, and of individual responsibility to God for the exercise of all the trusts and the use of all the opportunities of life.

13. Is it consistent with the Christian calling for one as a member of a nation of free rulers to cast his ballot and give his support in accord simply with the demands of conventions and caucuses, trusts or unions, employers or parties?

No. A Christian man cannot vote by order. By so doing he denies his Christian faith, in virtue of which he is no man's bondsman, but a king and priest unto God. It is also a violation of the oath of office, if such have been made; for the oath is the solemn recognition of individual responsibility, and assertion of the individual's freedom of men, in his supreme obligation to God. The conscience of no leader in Church or in State, of no political party or "ring" within a party, of no caucus or corporation, or institution, of no public opinion dare be adopted as one's own. The judgment of the Christian is always discriminating, and can never be confined by purely worldly trammels, without involving a denial of Christ He who under circumstances suppressing individual convictions of duty promises loyalty to any authority outside of God's Word, renounces Christ.

> 1 Thess. 5:21. "Prove all things; hold fast that which is good."
>
> Matt. 23:9, 10. "Call no man your father on the earth; for one is your Father, even he who is in heaven. Neither be ye called masters; for one is your master even Christ."
>
> 1 Cor. 7:23. "Ye were bought with a price; become not bond servants of men."
>
> Eph. 3:22. "Not with eye service as menpleasers, but in singleness of heart, fearing the Lord."
>
> Rom. 14:12. "Each one of us shall give account of himself to God."

The Church and the ministry, therefore, do not depart from their proper calling, and obtrude into politics, by branding all party domination that attempts to suppress the conscience of the individual, as essentially and thoroughly immoral, and the prolific root of every other form of dishonesty and immorality.

The Christian and Political Wrongs

14. Is the Christian to seek no remedy for manifest abuses in the State?

In an absolute monarchy, and without a Providential call, he often can do nothing else than passively submit, but in a government in which he is one of the electors, i.e., of the rulers, he shares in the responsibility for the continuance of a wrong, where his voice and vote may contribute something, even though very feebly, towards a testimony against it. The strongest influence, however, is that which diffuses and deeply implants the principles which lie at the foundation of all effective measures to bring about a change. Thus our Lord, during His ministry, undermined a number of the deeply entrenched and widely extended abuses in the Roman Empire, by insisting upon and inspiring that love of man to his fellow man, with which they could not exist.

The Church and Political Wrongs

15. What responsibility has the Church in regard to laws enacted or crimes tolerated under the sanction of laws, that are clearly contrary to the Holy Scriptures?

We may take as an illustration the laxity of the laws in many States concerning Marriage and Divorce. It is unquestionably the duty of the Church to clearly present the teaching of God's Word on the subject, and to condemn all practice in violation of this teaching whether permitted by the laws or not; and to do so, not only by synodical action, but in the instruction of catechumens, and in preaching from the pulpit, and to enforce discipline against members who offend and pastors who place their official endorsement upon such irregularities by performing the marriage ceremony where the laws of God do not allow. But the organization of the Church cannot be legitimately used as political machinery to effect a change. In efforts to correct abuses in the State, Christians must act not as members of a Church, but as citizens with consciences enlightened and stimulated by all the influences derived from the Church's instruction. The two spheres must be carefully distinguished. Fidelity to God may require duties just as clearly in the one sphere as in the other. But ecclesiastical must no more mingle with political duties, than political domination over the Church be tolerated. What we condemn in the Pope when he undertakes to exercise temporal power, and in an absolute monarch when he encroaches upon the functions of the Church, is no less to be condemned when, instead of the Pope we have an organized Church, or instead of the monarch, "the sovereign people."

Responsibility of one State for the wrongs of another

16. Has one State no responsibility with respect to wrongs that outrage humanity continued for years by another State, and in the face of repeated protests?

There are extraordinary circumstances when the common brotherhood of man, exclusive of all suggestions of self-interest, asserts itself. An overwhelming calamity impoverishing a State, as an inroad of famine or pestilence, justifies measures of relief. So atrocities such as those under Turkish rule, with which Christendom is periodically startled and shocked, may well suggest the thought as to whether the commonwealth of nations should tolerate a government, whose rule is stained by such succession of crimes, and which seems to be founded throughout upon violence and oppression. Such was Luther's judgment concerning the Turk. The question is as to whether the same extraordinary circumstances which justify the interference of an individual in the family of his neighbor, as when he rescues a wife from the murderous blows of her husband, are not also to be considered with respect to nations.

The Sphere of Religious Liberty

17. Is it within the power of the State to punish heresy?

No, so far as it concerns only the private opinions of individuals; or even their public confession, provided this involve no immoral practice. It is the office of the Church to take cognizance of spiritual things, as they belong both to the inner and the outer life. It is the office of the State to deal only with the external life.

18. But cannot the State make religions tests?

Only when they are directly connected with the external life, as when e.g., a Mormon would not be admitted to hold office, where the ground of exclusion would be, not his adherence to the Book of Mormon, but his justification of polygamy as practiced contrary to the laws of the State and in violation of sound morality; or where an Atheist would not be permitted to testify in court, upon the ground that his denial of God and a future world destroyed all guarantee of his respect for truth. But even such exclusion is something very different from death, fine or imprisonment. The State has the right, from motives of public policy, to make whatever provisions it sees fit to limit the exercise of privileges or the holding of offices to certain classes of the community, or to discriminate against others; and religious lines may sometimes determine such policy, as where the accession to a throne may be conditional upon adherence to a particular Confession, or as ministers of all churches are by law excluded from the precincts of Girard College.

19. Did Luther never advocate the punishment of heresy by death?

Never. When he demanded the punishment of Anabaptists by the State, it was not because of their doctrine; but because they incited insurrections and sought to overthrow the magistracy. Under the guise of religion, they plotted against the State, and, wherever the opportunity came, usurped its power.

20. Is the State, therefore, without jurisdiction in regard to ecclesiastical affairs?

The external affairs of the Church enter within a sphere where they cannot be ignored by the State. The Church has a body as well as a soul; and this body, like all other corporations, falls under the control of the civil government. If it is to have a fixed place of worship, it will not be long before it must acquire property by a legal title, and must be able to enforce its right to that property before the courts. If its various congregations are to have any permanency, it must have officers whose time and labor must be secured by the collection of funds; and these funds must be regulated by law. If it is to distribute alms, and to accumulate means by receiving bequests and donations, it will need at every step the aid of legal provisions. As a promoter of public morality, and the greatest prop whereby to support, by moral sentiment, the authority of the government, it can justly ask certain favors and exemptions. As Marriage has both its religious and its civil side, the State often provides for what is practically a combination of the two offices and constitutes ministers officers of the courts for this purpose, under the strict guardianship and supervision of law. It is the duty of the State also to clearly define the limits of the ecclesiastical sphere, and to keep it rigorously within its own bounds, in order that the authority of religion may not be invoked, as has often been done, for what is clearly an infringement of civil law. It may appoint days of fasting, of prayer and of thanksgiving; and under special stress of circumstances ask that the attention of Christian congregations be called to certain subjects closely connected with its supervision. It is also within its power to adapt its ecclesiastical requirements to the distinctive features of the various Confessions represented among its subjects.

National Life in the service of the Kingdom of God

21. What can be said concerning the varied lots of Earthly Governments?

Earthly States, like men, are born, grow, flourish, decline and die. Each kingdom and empire and republic is a part of a great world-plan, of which its founders know nothing, and which no contemporary generation can interpret for itself. Each nationality has its peculiar type of character and its especial mission with reference to the Kingdom of God. The Philosophy of History is outlined in Nebuchadnezzar's vision with its earthly empires succeeding one another, until displaced by the stone cut out of the mountain without hands (Dan. 2:35).

35. Life After Death

The Goal of Revelation

1. Towards what end are the entire Revelation of God in Christ and all the details of the Plan of Redemption which it announces, directed?

Towards a world to come. There is a concurrence of all things towards results not attainable in this life, but in one that is to follow. The consequences of sin in their full measure, the deliverance from sin in its full extent, the positive blessings of divine grace in their complete significance, and the glory of the Kingdom of God, except in its feeblest beginnings, await a consummation that comes only after this world has passed away.

> Rom. 8:18. "The sufferings of this present time are not worthy to be compared with the glory which shall be revealed in us."
>
> Gal. 1:14. "That he might deliver us out of this present evil world."
>
> 1 Tim. 4:8. "Having promise of the life which now is and of that which is to come."
>
> Matt. 12:32. "Whosoever shall speak against the Holy Spirit, it shall be forgiven him neither in this world, nor in that which is to come."

> 2 Pet. 3:13. "According to his promise, we look for new heavens and a new earth, wherein dwelleth righteousness."

Definition of Death

2. What is Death?

In its most usual sense, it denotes bodily or temporal death, i.e., the separation of the immortal soul from the body. As has been shown before (Chapter 8, 17, 18), there are three forms or rather stages of death, viz., spiritual, temporal and eternal. It is the office of divine grace to interfere with and remove spiritual death in this world, so that, while temporal death still remains, it is transformed into an instrument of blessing, and eternal death is supplanted by eternal life.

What is peculiar to man's State

3. What is peculiar about man's death?

It is contrary to the order of Creation. Unlike other creatures, man was endowed with the Image of God, one of the features of which was Immortality (see Chapter 7, 23-33). Soul and body were created to be forever united, and the separation is a violent interruption of God's order. It results in a condition that God never intended. While a body is not essential for the soul, since the soul can exist without it; nevertheless soul without body is in an incomplete and abnormal condition. Man, without body, is deformed, and mutilated by his deprival of an important constituent of his nature (Chapter 7, 6-8), The highest goal of man, in his present state, is not incorporeity; but beyond this, the final restoration of body to soul, after the period of separation has been completed (2 Cor. 5:4).

4. What is the relation of death to the two parts of mans being that are thereby separated?

Death not only separates body from soul, but it resolves the body into its constituent elements.

> Ecc. 12:7. "The dust returneth to the earth as it was, and the spirit returneth unto God who gave it."

The soul, however, as the center of man's personality, is itself unaffected by death, except as it suffers by the loss of a body. The continuity of personal existence is clearly taught in such passages as Luke 23:43; 16:19 sqq.; 2 Cor. 5:1; Rev. 14:13, among many others.

Estimate of arguments for the Immortality of the Soul

5. Is the doctrine of the Immortality of the Soul peculiar to Christianity?

With exceptions that often require only closer investigation to remove them, this doctrine underlies all the religions of the world, and has been maintained by the deepest thinkers even where Christianity was unknown. It has been supported by a series of arguments closely resembling those adduced by Natural Theology for the Existence of God. Such are:

[A.] The Metaphysical Proof.

From the simplicity and immateriality of the soul.

[B.] The Teleological Proof.

From the inadequacy of this life to satisfy the aspirations of man's heart, or to fully exercise his higher capacities.

> "Without immortality, life is a beginning without an end, a question without an answer, the merest outline, a torso, a fragment, a race without a goal, a battle without a victory" (Kahnis).

[C.] The Analogical.

No absolute annihilation in Nature. One life is developed out of another — the plant out of the seed, the butterfly out of the caterpillar, etc.

[D.] The Moral.

In this life, virtues do not receive the rewards, and vices the punishments that are their due. Hence there must be a future in which all these inequalities will be adjusted.

[E.] The Theological.

The communion of man with God in this life must be the foretaste of a higher communion hereafter.

[F.] The Historical.

From the universality of its acceptance (*ex consensu gentium et sapientum*).

6. What estimate is to be placed upon these proofs?

Like the arguments for the existence of God, they are not properly proofs, but are efforts of man, as he reflects upon himself to explain and adjust what he finds to be an inevitable inference from his deepest thought, intensest convictions and predominant motives. The thought of immortality seems inseparable from the consciousness of personality. Like all other doctrines of Natural Religion, it exists only as an hypothesis, until established upon the firm foundation of Divine Revelation. What Natural Theology only suggests becomes a certainty through the Gospel.

> 2 Tim. 1:10. "Who hath brought life and immortality to light through the gospel."

7. How may this be illustrated?

Let us consider the first argument above adduced, the Metaphysical Proof, which endeavors to establish immortality upon the very nature of the soul. But immortality in the absolute sense belongs only to God (1 Tim. 6:16), and, therefore, belongs *per se* only to the Divine Nature.

> 'The *non posse mori* of man is not based necessarily upon the nature of the soul. If men — all men, not merely the godly, but the godless, not merely the spiritual, but the unspiritual — are preserved eternally beyond bodily death, the reason for this is found not in the nature of the soul itself, but in the will of God who sustains them; and that God so wills, can be known only from His Word. What we need to investigate is not the nature of the soul, but the Word of God" (Kliefoth).

> "The Christian has no need of the philosophical proofs for the immortality of the soul. He acknowledges but one proof for immortality, the biblical, and that is enough for him" (Rohnert).

Old Testament doctrine concerning it

8. Has there been no progress in the revelation of this doctrine?

The Old Testament only incidentally alludes to the future life, but in terms certainly implying the continuity of existence after death and life beyond the grave. The departed are said to be gathered to their fathers (Gen. 2 5:8; 35:29, etc). The translation of Enoch (Gen. 5:24), and Elijah (2 Kings 2:11), points to another state of existence. So also such passages as

> Ps. 16:10, 11. "For thou wilt not leave my soul to Sheol; neither wilt thou suffer thy holy one to see corruption."

Our Lord expounds the Old Testament doctrine of Immortality in Luke 20:37, 38, where, in His argument for the Resurrection, from the expression "the God of Abraham and the God of Isaac and the God of Jacob" (Ex. 3:6), He declares:

> "Now he is not the God of the dead, but of the living; for all live unto him."

But while the doctrine is contained in the Old Testament, it is only in the New Testament that it appears in its complete form. (See 2 Tim. 6:10; above, under 6.) Even in the New Testament, there is progress in its revelation; since it was not until Christ arose from the dead, that this doctrine in its final form became manifest.

Causes, Extent and Offices of death

9. What causes of this separation are enumerated in Scripture?

Three are mentioned:
[A.] The devil.

> John 8:44. "He is a murderer from the beginning."

[B.] Man's sin.

> James 1:15. "Sin when it is full grown, bringeth forth death."

[C.] The judgment of God.

> Rom. 6:23. "The wages of sin is death."

As to the first, sin entered the world through the temptation addressed our first parents by Satan, from hatred of God and envy of their happy estate, as the account of Gen. 3 shows.

As to the second, nothing can be more explicit than the statement of Rom. 5:12, "As through one man sin entered into the world, and death through sin, and so death passed unto all men, for that all sinned."

As to the third, while God has no pleasure in the death of him that dieth (Ez. 18:23), yet as a most just judge He has to pronounce sentence upon the guilty.

> Ps. 90:3, 7. "Thou turnest man to destruction, and sayest, Return, ye children of men... For we are consumed in thine anger and by thy wrath are we troubled."

10. Is bodily or temporal death limited to the moment of separation of soul from the body and the state which succeeds?

It includes all the sorrows, pains and diseases which finally culminate in this event.

11. What two-fold office does death serve?

[A.] It is a punishment, as has already been shown.

[B.] But according to the Order of Redemption, it is also an instrumentality for imparting blessing.

The beginnings of death, in this world, its sorrows, labors and pains, as well as the prospect of death which awaits every one, awaken the longing for redemption and lead to an appreciation of the salvation which God has prepared and offers. Thus in Ps. 90, the consideration of mortality and its evils, leads to the prayer in vs. 15-17. So the Church has adopted, in the same spirit, the sequence of Notker of the Tenth Century, for the burial service:

> "In the midst of life, we are in death. Of whom may we seek for succor, but, of Thee, O Lord, who for our sins art justly displeased?"

12. Is this the only way in which the curse is changed into a blessing?

To the regenerate, it is no longer a punishment, but a chastisement. "To them that are in Christ Jesus," there is no wrath and no condemnation (Rom. 8:1). Toward them God has no other thoughts but those of love. Death, therefore, is said to be "abolished" with respect to them (2 Tim. 1:10), i.e., it is of none effect, it has lost its power. Instead of being an enemy, it is used by God to transfer the believer from the vale of tears to the abodes of happiness.

> 2 Cor. 5:8. "We are willing rather to be absent from the body, and to be at home with the Lord."

> Phil. 1:23. “Having the desire to depart and be with Christ which is very far better.”
>
> Rev. 14:13. “Blessed are the dead who die in the Lord from henceforth; yea, saith the Spirit, that they may rest from their labors; for their works follow with them.”

Instead of being victor, it has become a slave to bring about his highest blessedness.

> 1 Cor. 1:22. “All things are yours, whether Paul, or Apollos, or Cephas, or the world, or life, or death.”
>
> 1 Cor. 15:54. “Death is swallowed up in victory.”
>
> Is. 57:1, 2. “The righteous is taken away from the evil to come; he entereth into peace.”
>
> “Death itself serves this purpose, viz., to abolish this flesh of sin, that we may rise absolutely new. Neither is there now in the death of the believer, since by faith he has overcome the terrors of death, that sting and sense of wrath of, which Paul speaks in 1 Cor. 15:56. This strength of sin, this sense of wrath is truly a punishment as long as it is present; without this sense of wrath, death is not properly a punishment” (Apology, 208).
>
> “If you hear the Law, it will say in the language of the ancient chant: ‘In the midst of life, we are in death.’ But the Gospel and faith invert this, and sing: ‘In the midst of death, we are in life.’ The Gospel teaches in death itself there is life — a thought unknown and impossible to reason” (Luther, on Genesis, VI, 206. Erl. ed., Latin).

State of Souls after death. What they carry with them; A Provisional State; No Purgatory, neither Repentance nor Unconsciousness after Death taught in Holy Scripture, Distinction between State after Death, and that which follows the General Judgment; Temporal Standards inadmissible.

13. Do the dead carry nothing with them?

Their personality continues with all its past experiences and memories (Luke 16:24, 27)

14. Have they any knowledge of what is occurring on earth?

No direct knowledge, except by a miracle, can be inferred from any Scripture testimony. The prayer of the souls under the altar in Rev. 6:9-11 may have been prompted, by information concerning the condition of the Church on earth communicated to them in their heavenly abode.

15. What is the general condition of souls after death?

> "A provisional one between this life of beginning and the future life of completion" (Kliefoth).

The condition prior to the resurrection and the general judgment must be regarded so as to give these critical events the importance with which the Holy Scriptures invest them. It is not the hour of death towards which the child of God is to look for the realization of his hopes, or against which the wicked are warned as the culmination of their doom.

16. Is the state one, then, in which the souls of believers are subjected to a process of purification and preparation for heaven?

There is not the least foundation in Holy Scripture for such doctrine. The doctrine of Purgatory, according to which those who depart in Christ suffer for a long period for venial sins for which they had made no satisfaction in this life, is in conflict with almost every article of the Christian faith. It declares that God inflicts punishment where guilt has been forgiven; that the merits of Christ must be supplemented by satisfactions of our own; that the Gospel, instead of providing the free forgiveness of sins, only commutes eternal into temporal punishment; that some sins are retained when others are forgiven; that there is condemnation even for those who are in Christ.

17. Is there any possibility of saving repentance after death?

There is as little foundation for this as for the doctrine of Purgatory. Scripture constantly insists upon the fact that all the issues of the future world depend upon one's attitude towards Christ in this life.

> 2 Cor. 6:2. "Behold, now is the acceptable time; behold now is the day of salvation."

If such repentance could occur in the future life, this would only be extending the present world into that which follows. Or if the offers of salvation were to be made still more extensively than here, this would not be "the day of salvation," but only its portal or vestibule. It has been shown before that no support for such doctrine can be derived from the preaching by Christ to the spirits in prison (Chapter 12, 44).

18. May not the state between Death and Resurrection be one of unconsciousness?

In support of this, the frequent references in Holy Scripture to death as "a sleep" are cited. The figure is one which evidently arises from the resemblance of one who is bodily asleep to one who is dead. But as sleep is only a suspension of activity, while he enjoys needed rest, so the death of the believer is a removal from the cares and struggles and activities of this world, in expectation of the resurrection which will restore him in body and soul to the sphere whence he is taken. That it cannot mean a complete suspension of consciousness, and even of communications with others is shown from the Parable of the Rich Alan and Lazarus (Luke 16:23-31), the words of Christ to the penitent thief (Luke 23:43), and the blessedness of believers said to begin immediately after their departure (Rev. 14:13).

19. State briefly what is meant by "Life after Death."

That the godly enter into bliss, and the ungodly into misery, at death. The state between Death and the Resurrection differs from that which follows the Resurrection and General Judgment only in degree. The line dividing the two sections of humanity is fixed at death. The happiness of the one and the misery of 'the other are both inexpressible.

> 2 Cor. 5:1, 8 "For we know that if the earthly house of our tabernacle be dissolved, we have a building from God, a house not made with hands, eternal in the heavens... Willing to be absent from the body, and to be at home with the Lord."
>
> Luke 16:26. "Between us and your, there is a great gulf fixed."

20. Is the period between Death and Resurrection one that is to be reckoned according to the standard by which time is measured in this life?

Luther repeatedly warns us that the Eternal World is above and beyond the limitations of time. "Before God a thousand years are scarcely a day; and when the Resurrection comes, it will seem to Adam and the old fathers, as though they had been alive only a half hour before" (Erl ed., 18:267). He compares it to our experience in sleeping and waking.

> "Often have I tried to observe the moment in which I fell asleep and awoke; but before I could notice that I was asleep, I was again awake'" (On Genesis XXV, Erl., Latin, VI, 330).

21. What may be said concerning the very limited amount of details which Holy Scripture gives on the whole subject of Life after Death?

That there is nothing more that it is profitable for us to know; and, therefore, that additional speculation is worse than useless.

36. The Resurrection Of The Body

Definition and Scriptural Grounds

1. What is the Resurrection of the Dead?

The restoration to the immortal soul of the body with which it was endowed in this world.

> "I believe the resurrection of the body" (*carnis resurrectionem*, Apostles Creed).
>
> "I look for the resurrection of the dead" (Nicene Creed).
>
> "At whose coming all men shall rise again with their bodies" (Athanasian Creed).
>
> "At the consummation of the world, Christ shall appear for judgment, and shall raise up all the dead" (Augsburg Confession, Art. XVII).
>
> "And shall raise up me and all the dead at the last day" (Small Catechism).
>
> "Scripture testifies that it is precisely the substance of this our flesh, but without sin, which will rise again" (Formula of Concord, 548).

2. What scriptural grounds are there for this doctrine?

First of all, our Lord has declared that they who deny or misinterpret this doctrine have no knowledge of Scripture (Matt. 22:19). The reference here is of course to the Scriptures then in the hands of His hearers, viz., of the Old Testament. A few out of many other passages may be cited:

> John 5:28, 29. "The hour cometh in which all that are in the tombs shall hear his voice, and shall come forth; they that have done good, unto the resurrection of life; and they that have done evil, unto the resurrection of judgment."
>
> John 6:39. "This is the will of Him that sent me, that of all that which he hath given me, I should lose nothing, but should raise it up at the last day."
>
> 1 Cor. 15:12-14. "Now if Christ hath been preached unto you that he hath been raised from the dead, how say some among you that there is no resurrection of the dead? But if there is no resurrection of the dead, neither hath Christ been raised; and it Christ hath not been raised, then is our preaching vain, your faith also is vain."
>
> 1 Thess. 4:16. "And the dead in Christ shall rise first."

Holy Scripture charges it as the characteristic error of the Sadducees, that they denied the doctrine of the resurrection (Mark 12:18-23; Luke 20:27-33; Acts 4:2; 23:6-8).

3. Is the New Testament content with declaring the Resurrection as an irrefutable fact?

No. It enters into arguments, some of them of considerable length, to establish it. Those directly given and those which may be drawn by just inference from other passages are;

1. The resurrection of Christ (1 Cor. 15);
2. The Justice of God (2 Cor. 5:10). As men have sinned in the body they are also judged in the body.
3. The salvation which redemption brings for the body as well as the soul (1 Cor. 6:15; Rom. 6:12, 13).
4. The refashioning of the body after the model of the risen body of Christ (Phil. 3:20, 21; 1 Cor. 15:49);

5. Incorporation with Christ and participation in His resurrection-power through baptism (Rom. 6:3; Col. 2:12).
6. The translation of Enoch, Moses and Elijah.
7. The figure of the first fruits (1 Cor. 15:20).
8. Examples afforded of those who have arisen from the dead: the daughter of Jairus (Matt. 9:25), Lazarus (John 11:43), Tabitha (Acts 9:41), the widow's son (Luke 7:15), those who arose at the burial of Christ (Matt. 27:52), as well as Old Testament examples (1 Kings 17:22; 2 Kings 4:35).

Old Testament Testimony estimated

4. What is the value of the Old Testament prophecies concerning the Resurrection?

Their full force can be appreciated and their true meaning interpreted only in the light of the New Testament. Such passages are:

> Is. 26:19. "Thy dead shall live; my dead bodies shall arise."
>
> Dan. 12:2. "And many of them that sleep in the dust of the earth shall awake, some to everlasting life, and some to shame and everlasting contempt."
>
> Ez. 36:1-14. The vision of the dead bones.
>
> Hos. 12:14. "I will ransom them from the power of Sheol; I will redeem them from death; O death where are thy plagues; O Sheol where is thy destruction."
>
> Ps. 17:15; 49:15; Job 14:12-15. They were sufficient to cherish the popular belief and expectation of the Resurrection before that of Christ had completely established it. It is only in the New Testament that we read of the universality of the Resurrection.

Arguments from Nature estimated

5. Is this article known by the Light of Nature?

The Existence of God; the Justice of God; the Immortality of the Soul, are sometimes called "Mixed Articles of faith," because they are suggested by Nature, although fully established only by revelation. But in the Resurrection of the Dead, we have a "Pure Article," i.e., one that is unknown except by revelation, 'and which never can be demonstrated or supported by philosophical argumentation. When Paul preached the doctrine to the Greek philosophers at Athens, the report is:

> Acts 17:32. "Now when they heard of the resurrection of the dead, some mocked, but others said, We will hear thee again of this matter."

When he argued it before the Roman governor (Acts 26:8), the result was that he was pronounced insane (Acts 26:24). Even the disciples, who not only had back of them the Old Testament prophecies, and the general belief of the Jewish people, but, most of all, had been for years pupils in the school of Christ, were persuaded with the utmost difficulty to admit the possibility of their Lord's resurrection (Luke 24:11; John 20:25; Matt. 28:17).

It is, however, not an unusual argument in Holy Scripture to show the absurdities into which persons must fall who are unwilling to accept anything as true except when they can understand the reason for its existence (1 Cor. 15:36-38; John 3:7, 8; Job 38.41). (See Chapter 1,27, 32).

Misinterpretation of

6. What has been a frequent method of explaining away the Resurrection?

By interpreting it as a graphic mode of stating the Immortality of the Soul, or by referring it to spiritual quickening from the death of sin. Concerning such errors, it is said:

> 2 Tim. 2:16, 17. "Their word will eat as doth a gangrene; of whom is Hymenaeus and Philetus, men who concerning the truth have erred, saying that the resurrection is past already, and overthrow the faith of some."

Source of

7. Whence does the Resurrection come?

By no power inhering in the body which gradually matures, nor by any influence exerted upon it from the soul; not even by a new power introduced through regeneration or by a peculiar immanence of the Holy Spirit in the bodies of believers, or by the effects produced by sacramental grace — since like death, the Resurrection is common to regenerate and unregenerate; but by a new and direct act of God operating outside of and beyond human nature. The same Omnipotence that originally called the world out of nothing intervenes to restore to the soul its body that has moldered to dust.

Agents, Means, Subjects

8. Who will raise the dead?

The act is referred sometimes simply to God as in 2 Cor. 1:9; 1 Cor. 15:38, and to each of the persons of the Trinity, the Father (John 5:21; 2 Cor. 4:14, compared with Acts 3:26), the Son (John 5:25), the Holy Spirit (Rom. 8:11). (See Chapter 3, 62, 63.)

It is referred, however, repeatedly to the Son in a peculiar way.

> John 6:40. "I will raise him up at the last day."

> 1 Thess. 4:14. "Them that are asleep in Jesus will God bring with him."

> John 11:25. "I am the resurrection and the life." 5:28, 29. "All that are in their tombs shall hear his voice and shall come forth."

It is an act not simply of His divine nature, but of the person also through the human nature. As the power to judge is given him, "because he is the Son of man," so also the power to raise again the dead.

> 1 Cor. 15:21. "For since by man came death, by man came also the resurrection from the dead."

In raising the dead, He exercises one of the functions of His Mediatorial Office as King (Chapter 15).

> Rom. 14:9. "For to this end, Christ died and lived again, that he might be Lord of both the dead and the living."

9. By what means will they be raised?

Not by the mere will and silent energy of the Son of God, but by His "voice"' (John 5:28). As He spake, *Talitha cumi* (Mark 5:41), "Young man, I say unto thee, Arise" (Luke 7:14), "Lazarus, come forth" (John 11:43), so the word is the efficacious means here. Attending or preparatory to this will be "the voice of the archangel and the trump of God" (1 Thess. 4:16), "His angels with a great sound of a trumpet" (Matt. 24:31).

> 1 Cor. 15:52. "For the trumpet shall sound."
>
> "What or of what nature this trumpet will be we think that no one can exactly know, and, for this reason, its explanation is most properly deferred until the event occurs. This, however, is certain, that it will serve to assemble men to the judgment seat of Christ" (Gerhard, "Harmony," p. 753).

10. Who will be raised?

All who shall have died. "All who are in the tombs shall hear his voice" (John 5:28). Not merely the righteous, but also the wicked; "they that have done good unto the resurrection of life, and they that have done evil, to the resurrection of Judgment" (John 5:29). "All the nations" (Matt. 25:32), "the small," i.e., children, as well as "the great," i.e., adults (Rev. 20:12). Enoch and Elijah who were translated without seeing death are of course excepted, as well as those who arose at Christ's death and who may have been similarly translated (Matt. 52).

The Resurrection of the Ungodly

11. Will the ungodly be raised again because of the merits of Christ?

No. The ungodly will rise, not in virtue of Christ's merits, but because of God's immutable decree, by which it was appointed unto man once to die, but after that the judgment (Heb. 9:27). The justice of God demands that the body which has sinned share in the punishments of sin. Nowhere are any other than salutary effects ascribed to the resurrection of Christ. 1 Cor. 1:22, "In Christ, shall all be made alive," must, therefore, be understood, not absolutely and universally, but in accordance with the argument which is directed to exhibiting the blessings brought by Christ's resurrection, and the immediate context which shows how Christ is the first fruits of the harvest that follows.

Nature of the Resurrection Body

12. Will the Resurrection Body be a material body? It will be of the same nature as that which Christ had after His resurrection.

> Phil. 3:21. "Who shall fashion anew the body of our humiliation, that it may be conformed to the body of his glory."

Since Christ, however, offered His resurrection body to the test of the senses,

> Luke 24:39. "See my hands and my feet. Handle me and see; for a spirit hath not flesh and bones, as ye behold me having?"

And as further He showed to Thomas the very wounds of the crucifixion (John 20:27), it is a real and material body that is assumed, and the very same body, although with new attributes, that the person had during his residence on earth.

The literal Resurrection of the Body, established by the texts of Scripture above given is confirmed further:

[A.] From the article of Creation.

For man was created both with soul and body. If the literal body were not to share in the salvation brought the soul, the evil wrought by sin would not be entirely repaired, and man's being would be incomplete to all eternity as one consequence of sin.

[B.] From the article of Redemption.

For Christ redeemed the body as well as the soul. Very significant are the words of 1 Cor. 6:13, "The body is for the Lord; and the Lord for the body." Of this the greatest pledge is His Incarnation, in which He assumed not only a human soul, but also a human body. In the Lord's Supper He reminds us of the important place in redemption which His body bore, and, thereby, suggests the destiny of the bodies of those who have been thus redeemed.

[C.] From the article of Sanctification.

> Rom. 12:1. "Present your bodies a living sacrifice." 1 Cor. 6:15. "Know ye not that your bodies are members of Christ."

The various bodily organs are specified as partakers of this sanctification, viz., the mouth (Eph. 4:29), the tongue (1 Peter 3:15), the hands (Eph. 4:28), the feet (Rom. 10:15; Matt. 25:36), the eyes (Ps. 119:37, 18), the ears (James 1:19), the members in general (Rom. 6:13).

13. Do you hold that there is necessarily an atomistic identity between the body that is buried and the one that is raised?

Such identity does not continue even in this life. The atoms of matter that constitute our bodies are constantly changing. The adult body is one that has been repeatedly changed in all its constituents since infancy. Nevertheless the features are the same, and the scars of wounds remain.

Of the Resurrection Body we are justified in affirming no other identity with that which is buried, than that which belongs to the body at two periods in the present world. Or to use the figure of the Resurrection proposed by Paul in 1 Cor. 15:37, 38, there is no atomistic identity of the grain of wheat sown this fall with the harvest which is gathered next summer.

14. Do we know anything as to the stature of the Resurrection Body?

There have been three theories:

[A.] The view given by Lombardus that the bodies of believers will conform to the stature of Christ.

In favor of this Eph. 4:13; Rom. 8:29 are cited. The misapplication is manifest. Some, upon the same basis, have argued that in the resurrection women will become men, so as to be conformed to the image of Christ.

[B.] That of Augustine, according to which every one will have the form he had or would have in the maturity of his youth.

Here again Eph. 4:13 is misapplied.

[C.] That of Gerhard which teaches that every one will rise at the age and with the stature he had at death.

This is maintained on the basis of the distinction between the dead "great and small" that is taught in Rev. 11:18; 20:12.

15. What are the Attributes of the Resurrection Body?

While the body is the same, it has certain new qualities. Scripture is very explicit in the enumeration of the attributes of the resurrection bodies of the godly; those of the ungodly can be known only by inference.

First of all, it teaches that the resurrection body will be much more than a restoral of that which believers have in this life, much more even than the sinless body of Adam, prior to the Fall, and without the weaknesses and diseases that then entered. It will be fashioned not after the image of the First, but of the Second Adam.

> 1 Cor. 15:49. "As we have borne the image of the earthly, we shall also bear the image of the heavenly."

> Phil. 3:21. "That it may be conformed to the body of his glory."

What was observed, therefore, concerning the body of Christ during the period between His resurrection and ascension, aids in the interpretation of the discussion of these attributes in 1 Cor. 15:39-50, 53-55.

16. Enumerate, therefore, these Attributes.

They are:
1. Immortality and Incorruptibility;
2. Glory and Brilliancy;
3. Perfection of Powers;
4. Spirituality.

Noticed and refuted by Augustine (*De Civitate Dei*, XXII, 17).

17. Explain them in detail.

1. Immortality.

> Luke 20:36. "For neither can they die any more."

> 1 Cor. 15:42. "It is sown in corruption; it is raised in incorruption."

This includes immunity from all sufferings, from hunger and thirst, from disease and pain, as well as from the possibility of death.

> Rev. 7:16. "They shall hunger no more, neither thirst anymore; neither shall the sun strike upon them, nor any heat."

2. Glory and Brilliancy.

> 1 Cor. 15:43. "It is sown in dishonor; it is raised in glory."

> Matt. 13:43. "Then shall the righteous shine forth as the sun in the kingdom of their father." Dan. 12:3; 2 Cor. 3:18.

Everything that defiled and rendered the body unsightly will disappear. All the lines of care and anxiety, all the traces of disease will vanish. The whole body and especially the countenance will reflect the glory of God, as Moses on descending from the Mount (Ex. 34:25), and our Lord at the Transfiguration (Matt. 17:2). But this glory will not be equal; it will have its degrees.

> 1 Cor. 15:41. "One star differeth from another star in glory."

3. Perfection of Powers.

> 1 Cor. 15:43. "It is sown in weakness; it is raised in power."

Instead of inability to meet the demands of the present life, it will be endowed with all the capacities needed for the service of God in the higher life. While a true body, like that of our Lord in His post-resurrection appearances, it, nevertheless, can be at will superior to the attraction of gravitation, just as He could appear in closed rooms or could walk on the waves or ascend into heaven. The sight of God promised the godly may be through the eyes of the resurrection body (1 John 3:2; 1 Cor. 13:12).

> "The body will have sharp eyes, so as to be able to see through a mountain, and quick ears, so as to be able to hear from one end of the earth to the other" (Luther).

4. Spirituality.

> 1 Cor. 15:44. "It is sown a natural body; it is raised a spiritual body. If there is a natural body, there is also a spiritual body."

This cannot mean that the body is to be etherialized, or transformed into spirit; but the reference is to the new spiritual properties with which it is endowed, and that from the basis of the three preceding attributes. The original reads:

> "It is sown a psychical body; it is raised a spiritual body."

As, therefore, in this world, "the psychical body" cannot mean body that is soul, so, in the world to come, "the spiritual body" cannot mean body that is spirit. The distinction between "soul" and "spirit" (see Chapter 7, 13) must be observed in correctly estimating this passage. "A spiritual body" is one having the properties needed for the higher stage of being to which the body is now elevated. The attribute "heavenly" which is also applied to the resurrection body is nothing more than a synonym of "spiritual."

18. What of the resurrection bodies of the godless?

They will also be adapted to the condition of their souls in the future world. They will be immortal and indestructible, but in other respects be the very reverse of the bodies of the godly.

19. What can be said of the last generation of believers on earth, who do not die, but are alive at the general resurrection?

Their bodies will be changed, so as to receive the properties given those that arise from the dead.

> 1 Cor. 15:51. "We shall not all sleep, but we shall all be changed."
>
> 1 Thess. 4:15. "We that are alive, that are left unto the coming of the Lord, shall in no wise precede them that are fallen asleep."
>
> V. 16, 17. "The dead in Christ shall rise first; then we that are alive, that are left, shall together with them be caught up in the clouds to meet the Lord in the air; and so shall we ever be with the Lord."

The Resurrection not a Process

20. Will the Resurrection be a process continuing through a considerable period?

> 1 Cor. 15:51, 52. "We shall all be changed in a moment, in the twinkling of an eye, at the last trump."

How to treat difficulties concerning it

21. If difficulties concerning the Resurrection occur, how are they to be regarded?

> "If you want to be Christians, you must believe that there will be a Resurrection of the Dead in the flesh, when Christ shall come to judge the

quick and the dead. But our faith concerning this is not vain, if we be not able to perfectly comprehend how this will be" (Augustine, De Civitate Dei, XX, 20).

37. The Return Of Christ

Relation to the Resurrection

1. When will the Resurrection occur?

At the Second Coming of Christ.

2. Is the Second Coming promised only with respect to its relations to the individual?

It has reference also to the future of the Church. For while its individual members constantly come and go, and a few decades, at most, measure the career of its most influential leaders, the Church has a life of its own and continues unaffected by the removal of generation after generation that it trains for heaven. But just as the life of the individual, so also the life of the Church has a goal; and that goal is the Second Coming of Christ.

> Eph. 5:27. "That he might present the church to himself, a glorious church, not having spot or wrinkle or any such thing, but that it should be holy and without blemish."

What the Resurrection is to the body, this glorification will be to the Church.

The Two States of the Church

3. What resemblance is there between the condition of the Church in this life and that of the individual believer?

The Head of the Church is in heaven, while the Church itself is on earth. It is like a colony of citizens in a strange land, on a remote continent.

> Phil. 3:20. "For our citizenship is in heaven, whence also we wait for a Savior. the Lord Jesus Christ."

None of the attributes of the Church (Chapter 29, 12-16) are fully realized here. The external does not correspond to the internal Church. The Unity of the Church is impaired by the separations into various confessions and parties. Its Holiness, by the sins which are in its members, and which often disgrace its outward form. Its Apostolicity, by variations from apostolic purity of teaching. Its Catholicity, by the fact that it is not universally diffused throughout the world.

Besides this, it is in incessant conflict with the world, which, according to the divine ideal, should only serve to promote its progress (1 Cor. 3:22). Although it is its office, according to the divine commission, to fill the earth with the message of the Gospel (Matt. 28:20; Mark 16:15; Rom. 10:18), it meets with most formidable obstacles at every step forward. The power of the Prince of this world (John 16:11; 14:30) continues, until the end of this order of things comes.

4. But is not the power of evil gradually broken by the preaching of the Gospel and the wide diffusion of the principles of Christianity?

Until "the end of the world" (Matt. 13:40), wheat and tares grow together (v. 30), good and evil both advancing, the good becoming better and the evil worse. Every now and then, throughout the Church's history, there is a crisis, when there is an open conflict, as when two poles of an electric battery meet and are discharged. This is followed by a period of silent recuperation of force on the part of both elements. But, as night follows day, and winter summer, so every period of the Church's peace and prosperity, is followed by one of sorrow and tribulation, until, in the very darkest hour of human history, its course is forever changed by the return of the Lord Jesus.

5. What estimate is placed, therefore, upon the Return of the Lord?

All the hopes of believers center upon it, as affording them final and complete deliverance; and the fruition and consummation of God's promises of love.

> John 14:3. "If I go and prepare a place for you, I come again, and will receive you unto myself; that where I am, there ye may be also."
>
> Luke 21:28. "When these things begin to come to pass, look up and lift up your heads, because your redemption draweth nigh."
>
> Tit. 1:13. "Looking for the blessed hope and appearing of the great God and our Savior Jesus Christ."
>
> 2 Thess. 1:10. "When he shall come to the glorified in his saints, and to be marveled at in all them that believe in that day."
>
> 2 Tim. 4:8. "The crown which the Lord, the righteous judge shall give to me at that day; and not to me only, but to all that have loved his appearing."

Hence the significant expressions "that day" (Matt, 7:22; 2 Thess. 1:10; 2 Tim. 1:12, 18, etc.); "the day of the Lord" (2 Peter 1:10; 1 Thess. 5:2); "the day of the Lord Jesus" (1 Cor. 5:5; 2 Cor. 1:14); "the day of Christ" (Phil. 1:10; 2 Thess. 2:2); "the day of our Lord" (1 Cor. 1:8); "the day" (1 Cor. 3:13); "the great day" (Jude 6); "the last day" (John 6:39); "the day of redemption" (Eph. 4:30). It has been termed "the day for which all other days were made."

The Two States of Creation

6. Is there not even a wider scope for its decision?

All creation is represented as awaiting it. Rom. 8:19, "For the earnest expectation of the creation waiteth for the revealing of the sons of God." V. 21, "The creation itself shall be delivered from the bondage of corruption into the liberty of the glory of the children of God."

All this is connected with the resurrection, as V. 23 continues:

> "We ourselves groan within ourselves, waiting for our adoption, to wit, the redemption of our body."

The Time

7. When will this event, toward which all things tend, occur?

Christ always discouraged and even reproved the asking of this question. It was His constant teaching that men should be ready for it whenever it would come, whether this should be in the immediate future, or should be long delayed. Awaiting it in faith, they were to be satisfied with whatever time God would appoint for its appearance.

> Acts 1:7. "It is not for you to know times or seasons which the Father hath set within his own authority."

Even He Himself abstained, in His assumed human nature, from its knowledge.

> Matt. 24:36. "But of that day and hour, knoweth no one, not even the angels of heaven, neither the Son, but the Father only."

But while this is a rebuke to all curious speculations which can readily prefer eschatological problems to the nearest duties of the Christian life, the Holy Scriptures give certain signs by which its approach may be known.

8. What may be said of such signs in general?

The fullest statement of them is found in Matt. 24, Mark 13 and Luke 21. In the examination of these passages, considerable difficulty results from the fact that the Destruction of Jerusalem and the End of the World are considered together. The former being a type of the latter, there is a correspondence of signs; just as history is said to repeat itself, or to move in cycles.

These signs have been grouped into two classes. Some are found at all periods of the world's history; and point forward to Christ's return, just as the bow in the cloud points backward to the deliverance effected by the Flood. Others are deferred until the event is imminent, and of these some indicate a more remote and others a nearer approach. The thought underlying this distinction may be stated otherwise by saying that signs appearing at the very beginning of Christianity and recurring frequently, reappear with greater frequency and intensity as the end approaches.

The Signs: 1. Universal Preaching of the Gospel; 2. Conversion of Israel; Decline and Oppression of Church, including the career of Antichrist; 4. Extraordinary Historical Events; 5. Supernatural Material Phenomena.

9. What are these signs?

1. The Universal Preaching of the Gospel;
2. The No more satisfactory discussion in a brief form, of the relation of the two events, can be readily found than that of Schaeffer, on Matt. 24, in Vol. II of "The Lutheran Commentary," New York, 1895. Conversion of Jews in large numbers;
3. The Decline and Oppression of the Church;
4. Extraordinary Historical Events;
5. Extraordinary occurrences in the physical world.

10. What of the first?

The Universal Preaching of the Gospel. This we learn from:

> Matt. 24:14. "This gospel of the kingdom shall be preached in the whole world for a testimony unto all the nations; and then shall the end come."
>
> Acts 1:8. "Ye shall be witnesses in Jerusalem and in all Judea and in Samaria, and unto the uttermost part of the earth."

This means that no power or violence shall be able to withstand the progress of the Gospel, that no difficulties will prevent it from being brought to the knowledge of all peoples, that even though many centuries intervene and though at times the area of those beneath its influence is contracted instead of extended, nevertheless it has a world-wide destiny even before the Lord returns to assert His authority. Not until the Means of Grace are within reach of every human being will the end come. The statement is not that Christianity in some form or other, but that the simple Gospel, i.e., the gratuitous promise of forgiveness of sins (Chapter 25, 35) in all its clearness and fullness is to be made known everywhere.

> Mark 13:10. "The gospel must first be preached unto all the nations."

We cannot infer that the meaning of these passages is that the end will come as soon as missionary preaching will reach all nations. In order that the force of "the testimony" may reach them it may be allowed to develop its powers in the Christian lives which it will mold, the Christian activities it will call into being, and the settled churches it will found, during a long period. This would be "a time of visitation" for the nations, such as Jerusalem once had (Luke 19:42, 44).

11. What of the second, the Conversion of the Jews?

> Rom. 11:25, 26. "A hardening in part hath befallen Israel, until the fullness of the Gentiles be come in; and so all Israel shall be saved."
>
> "In saying 'all Israel' the universal must be restricted, according to the custom of Scripture, to a great number of the Jews. As 'the fullness of the Gentiles' does not mean each and every nation, for such conversion of the Gentiles to the Church is not to be expected, but only a large number of Gentiles, so the salvation and conversion of the Jews one and all, is not to be hoped for. It is apparent, therefore, that Paul is prophesying concerning a remarkable conversion of Jews, a large portion of whom, before the Last Day, will acknowledge the Messiah and be brought to the faith of Christians" (Baldwin).
>
> "These words are not received in a uniform sense by expositors. Some understood, by the name of Israel, not the Jewish people, but all believers without distinction. There are others who think that, by this mystery, the Apostle wants to indicate that, before the Day of Judgment, a great multitude of Jews will be converted to the Christian faith. While neither interpretation is impious, yet when the entire context is more carefully examined, the latter explanation, I think, is more in harmony with the words and present purpose of Paul" (Hunnius).

Note: For discussion of the various interpretations of this passage, see my "Annotations on Romans," Lutheran Commentary, Vol. VII, 238,246.

The meaning is that the hostility of the Jewish race as such to Christ will cease. It will be a Christian nation or race, like some of the Gentile nations before it, i.e., one within which there will be large numbers of truly believing spiritually-minded Christian people.

12. What of the third, the Decline and Oppression of the Church?

> 1 Thess. 2:3. The day of the Lord will not come, "except the falling away come first."

As the preaching of the Gospel extends to nation after nation, and wins more and more outward adherents, the number of those who are Christians only by profession increases, and the continuance, under the Christian name, of heathen theories and practices results. As the Church directly after the Apostles had to contend against the introduction into Christianity of ideas and principles from the heathen cults of the East, so the converts to Christianity from every heathen people carry with them into their new religious life much of their former heathenism, which disappears only after generations have come and gone, and that, too, often only after the most severe conflicts. Accompanying this, are the corrupting tendencies of the secularizing process in the Church, with its exaggeration of the organization and external name and machinery above the spiritual conception of the Kingdom of God within the hearts of men. With the preaching of Law and Gospel obscured, spiritual motives lose their power; and even those who profess the name of Christ become more and more absorbed in purely worldly interests. A flood of false prophets arises within the Church (Matt. 24:11). They not only err themselves, but seek to make their error the standard of the Church's doctrine and practice; and every protest on the part of those who are really spiritually minded excites first their ridicule and contempt, and, then, their persecution. This process constantly recurring in the history of the Church, will reach its most aggravated form, as the end approaches. This will be "the great apostasy," which will assume to reconstruct Christianity according to the standards of a revived heathenism, and produce a religion Christian in name, but heathen in spirit and in teaching. One of its characteristics will be the security with which it will disregard and criticize the promises and warnings of Holy Scripture.

> 2 Pet. 3:3, 4. "In the last days, mockers shall come with mockery, walking after their lusts, and saying: Where is the promise of his coming? for from the day that the fathers tell asleep, all things continue as they were from the beginning of the creation."

Hence both from outside the Church and from the ranks of its professed members, successive waves of persecution shall spend their fury upon those who faithfully confess Christ's name. The early days of Christianity will be repeated on a vaster scale:

> Mark 13:9. "They shall deliver you up to councils; and in synagogues shall ye be beaten; and before governors and kings shall ye stand, for my sake, for a testimony unto them."

> 2 Tim. 3:1. "Know this that in the last days, grievous times shall come."

13. In what will this spurious Christianity and its persecuting spirit be concentrated?

In Antichrist (Chapter 29, 78). First, in a number of antichrists:

> 1 John 2:18. "Little children, it is the last hour; and as ye have hear"' that antichrist cometh, even now have there arisen many antichrists; whereby we know that it is the last hour."

Thus already in the days of the Apostles, the antichristic principle is present and active in prominent representatives who have been members of the Christian Church externally, as V. 19 declares: "They went out from us." The antichristic principle and elements pervade the entire history of the Church, just as the tares grow in the wheat fields (Matt. 13:24 sqq). At various crises, the power of these antichrists is peculiarly active and threatening. But they come and go, like the flowers of the field, that bloom and then die or are forgotten, while Christianity survives, to witness the rise and fall of their successors. Wave after wave rushes upon this rock only to be dashed to pieces (2 Tim. 3:9). But this force rallies after every onset. It reaches its culmination at last in one who is to be above all others "the Antichrist."

> 2 Thess. 2:3, 4. "It will not be, except the falling away come first, and the man of sin be revealed, the son of perdition, he that opposeth and exalteth himself against all that is called God or is worshipped; so that he sitteth in the temple of God, setting himself forth as God. vs. 8-10."The lawless one whom the Lord Jesus shall slay with the breath of his mouth and bring to naught by the manifestation of his coming; even he whose coming is according to the working of Satan with all power and signs and lying wonders, and with all deceit of unrighteousness for them that perish."

> 1 John 4:3. "This is the spirit of the antichrist whereof ye have heard that it cometh." See also Rev. 11-15.

14. When can Christians know for a certainty as to who Antichrist is?

The details of prophecy can be read only in their fulfillment (1 Peter 1). While the coming of Christ was clearly predicted, who and what He was to be was not clearly known until He actually appeared, although the scribes with the Old Testament in their hands assumed to be true interpreters of its details (John 7:41, 42). So concerning Antichrist. The antichristic principles were recognizable from the moment of their origination, and as they embodied themselves in parties and individuals, "the little antichrists," or heresiarchs of Church History. These sane principles are working still and should be guarded against.

> 1 John 4:1. "Beloved, believe not every spirit, but prove the spirits whether they are of God."

But it becomes Christians to be reserved in their judgment as to who precisely will be "the personal concentration of sin, the God of this world and the organ of Satan," whose sway will be broken and power destroyed by the second coming of Christ.

15. What warning concerning a premature decision concerning the fulfillment of the prophecy concerning Antichrist does Church History give?

In periods of great persecution or strenuous opposition to the Church, there has always been a disposition to find in the particular persecutor or antagonist of the time or place, the Antichrist of Scripture.[20]

> "When Judaism persecuted the first Church, Antichrist was said to be a Jew, who was to arise from the tribe of Dan. When the Roman Empire attacked Christianity, the Emperors Nero and Valerian were regarded as fulfilling this prophecy. The African Church saw Antichrist in Genseric the king of the Vandals. Mohammed received this title, when his conquests threatened Christendom. The sects of the Middle Ages, the Cathari, the Abbott Joachim of Floris, the Albigenses, the Hussites referred it to the Papacy" (Kliefoth).

20 Dr. Julius F. Sachse in "The German Sectarians of Pennsylvania," Vol. I (Philadelphia, 1899), 343, gives a translation of the pamphlet of the Germantown Dunker, Christopher Saur, published in 1739, against Conrad Beissel, founder of the cloister at Ephrata, in which he demonstrates that the latter is none else than the 666 of the Apocalypse! The horizon of sectarianism is very contracted, and it constantly magnifies what is nearest its vision.

In this, they were followed by the Reformers, both Lutheran and Reformed.

16. Are there not antichristic principles in the Papacy?

Melanchthon has enumerated them in the appendix to the Schmalkald Articles (345):

> "The marks of Antichrist plainly agree with the kingdom of the Pope and his adherents. For Paul (2 Thess. 2:3) in describing Antichrist, calls him an enemy of Christ, 'who opposeth and exalteth himself above all that is called God, or is worshiped, so that he as God sitteth in the temple of God.' He speaks, therefore, of one ruling in the Church, not of heathen kings, and he calls this one the adversary of Christ, because he will devise doctrine conflicting with the Gospel, and will assume to himself divine authority.
>
> "Now it is manifest:
>
> "I. The Pope rules in the Church.
>
> "II. His doctrine conflicts in many ways with the Gospel and he assumes to himself divine authority in a threefold manner:
>
> "1. By assuming the right to change the doctrine of Christ and services instituted by God, and wanting his own doctrine and services to be observed as divine.
>
> "2. By assuming the power not only of binding and loosing in this life, but also authority over souls after this life.
>
> "3. By not wanting to be judged by the Church or by any one, and preferring his own authority to the decision of councils and of the entire Church. But to be unwilling to be judged by the Church or by any one, is to make oneself God.
>
> "III. These horrible errors and this impiety he defends with the greatest cruelty, and puts to death those dissenting."

17. Is not this enough to show that the Pope is Antichrist?

The dogma of the Immaculate Conception of Mary and that of the Infallibility of the Pope, both sanctioned and proclaimed in the second half of the Nineteenth

Century are additional items in the evidence beyond what the Reformers had before them; since the former is intended to give to His mother a place that belongs only to her Lord and Savior, and the latter officially and formally declares what had long been the claim before, that the voice of the Pope must be received as the voice of God.

Notwithstanding all this, it cannot be shown that everything is to be found in the Pope that is contained in the warnings against Antichrist. There is no open hostility or formal denial of Christ, and these are given as marks of Antichrist (1 John 2:22; 4:3; 2 John 7). Neither does the Papacy which is an institution or corporation correspond to the Scriptural description of the Pope as an individual. Nor can we resort to the expedient of some theologians who find the one Antichrist in the succession of occupants of the Papal see. ("Antichrist is a man, successively one, raised up by Satan," Quenstedt). Antichrist may yet arise out of the Papacy, when all these premises are carried to their conclusions, and embodied in some monster of wickedness, of Titanic mold, who is yet to arise, or the same elements may be asserted from some other source.

For us, the duty is not to speculate concerning a future Antichrist, but to be on our guard against all antichristic principles, in whatever form or from whatever source they come.

18. What of the fourth sign of the Second Coming, viz., the Extraordinary Historical Events?

This refers to the prevalence of wars and rumors of wars, pestilences, famines, etc. While they occur through all time and point forward towards the end, they increase in extent and degree, as this approaches.

19. What of the fifth?

Earthquakes, eclipses, the falling of stars, and other phenomena, transcending the natural order of such events. As the period for the efficacy of the Holy Spirit through the Word and Sacraments closes, the miraculous element again appears.

The Chiliastic Interpretation examined

20. Will there be a two-fold coming or manifestation of Christ?

This is held by those who teach that Christ will come first to raise the godly, and that they will reign with him on earth for a thousand years, after which the wicked will be raised, and the General Judgment occur.

Concerning this the Augsburg Confession, Art. 17, declares:

> "They teach that in the consummation of the world, Christ shall appear to judge, and shall raise up all the dead, and shall give unto the godly and elect eternal life and everlasting joys; but ungodly men and the devils shall He condemn unto endless torments... They condemn others also who now scatter Jewish opinions that, before the resurrection of the dead, the godly shall occupy the kingdom of the world, the wicked being everywhere suppressed."

While it is true that this article was directed against the gross Chiliasm of the Anabaptists of the Reformation period, it clearly disclaims all responsibility for any teaching that separates between a resurrection for the godly and a resurrection for the ungodly by any long period of time, and which affirms that there are two comings of Christ in the future.

21. Why is such opinion rejected?

Holy Scripture nowhere teaches it. Christ's coming and His rewards to the godly and His condemnation of the godless are always closely connected in the Scriptural accounts of the Judgment. Our Lord expressly says that it is "at the last day" that He will raise and give eternal life to the believing (John 6:39, 40). When it is affirmed that it has sufficient scriptural basis in Rev. 20:1-6, the answer is that it is not proper to construct a dogma alone from a book concerning whose canonicity there has been such extended dissent, and to make it the standard whereby to interpret the plain language of books whose authority is most thoroughly established; particularly when it is a book which, from beginning to end, deals in figurative statements. Beside this,

> "...the simple fact that Chiliasm has almost as many forms as it has advocates, proves how insecure is the scriptural foundation of this doctrine" (Kahnis).

While there is much prophecy that still awaits fulfillment, we can in faith confidently expect that God, in his own time, will give the interpretation.

Characteristics of the Second Coming

22. What will be the characteristics of Christ's Second Coming?

[A.] It will be visible.

The first coining of Christ, by which He became incarnate, was invisible. Of the second, it is said:

> Matt. 24:30. "They shall see the Son of Man coming on the clouds of heaven."
>
> Acts 1:11. "This Jesus shall so come again, in like manner as ye have seen him going into heaven."

[B.] It will be glorious.

The first coming was in humility and weakness. The second will be "with power and great glory."

> "If at the Transfiguration, 'his face did shine as the sun, and his garments became white as the light' (Matt. 17:2), what will this brightness be at the highest grade of the State of Exaltation? Such will be the glory, that no one could endure it, unless divinely sustained" (Gerhard).

In His divinely-human person, He will be made manifest as "King of kings and Lord of lords" (Rev. 19:16). The "throne of his glory"' has been defined as "the manifestation of the hitherto invisible Right Hand of God."

[C.] It will be public.

Unlike the vision on the road to Damascus, unlike the glorious appearance at the Transfiguration, unlike even the Ascension, which was witnessed by only a few, "all the tribes of the earth" shall see Him coming (Matt. 24:30).

[D.] It will be local.

In this it corresponds to the Ascension (Chapter 12, 60).

[E.] It will be sudden and unexpected.

Even though preceded by signs, none of them will be so clearly interpreted or interpretable as to prevent it from being a surprise even to those earnestly expecting it. The hour comes with the silent approach of a thief (Matt. 24:43), and at last bursts upon the world with the suddenness of lightning (Matt. 24:27).

> Matt. 24:42. "Watch, therefore, for ye know not on what day your Lord cometh."

38. The General Judgment

Scriptural and Confessional Declarations

1. What will follow the Second Coming of Christ?

> Matt. 25:31, 32. "When the Son of Man shall come in his glory, and all the angels with him, then shall he sit on the throne of his glory, and before him shall be gathered all the nations, and he shall separate them one from another, as the shepherd separateth the sheep from the goats."

Hence the Church confesses:

> "From thence, he shall come to judge the quick and the dead" (Apostles' Creed).
>
> "And he shall come again with glory to judge both the quick and the dead" (Nicene Creed).
>
> "At whose coming all men shall rise again with their bodies, and shall give account for their own works" (Athanasian Creed).
>
> "At the consummation of the world, Christ shall appear for judgment" (Augsburg Confession).

Christ as Judge

2. Is judgment to be ascribed exclusively to the Son?

As we have previously learned (Chapter 3, 63), in all external acts, there is a concurrence of all persons of the Trinity. Beside this, in some passages judgment is ascribed simply to God (Heb. 12:23; Rom. 2:5; Deut. 32:36; Ps. 98:9); in others to the Father (John 8:50; Acts 17:31; 1 Peter 2:23); and in still others, as John 16:8, to the Holy Spirit.

3. But does not Christ say that "the Father judgeth no man" (John 5:22)?

This means that the Father does not judge alone or apart from the Son, but only in and through the Son; just as he loves the world and redeems it and offers it salvation only in and through Christ. The Father has given to the Son the prerogative of exercising judgment visibly.

> John 5:22. "For neither doth the Father judge any man, but he hath given all judgment unto the Son; that all may honor the Son even as they honor the Father."

4. Is it not said also that it is not the office of Christ to judge?

Yes.

> John 12:47. "I came not to judge the world, but to save the world."

The meaning is not to deny that He exercised judgment even during the State of Humiliation; but as the next verse ("He that rejecteth me hath one that judgeth him; the word that I spake the same shall judge him in the last day") and John 3:18, show, that the. guilty can blame no one but themselves for their condemnation. The great end of Christ's incarnation and mediatorial work, which includes His return to judge the world, is the salvation of men. The Plan of Redemption comprises within its compass even those who will be finally lost (Chapter 9, 16-19). But while God wills the salvation of all. He does not will that they be saved outside of the order which He has provided.

John 3:19. "This is the judgment that light is come into the world, and men loved the darkness rather than the light; for their works were evil."

The office of Judge, therefore, so far as the wicked are concerned is only incidental to the chief object of the Mediatorial office; just as the punishment of criminals is only a secondary end of the office of a magistrate, and the punishment and expulsion of unruly scholars not the main duty of a schoolmaster.

"Christ's office is not directed chiefly to judging, hut to helping. This is Christ's principal office, for which He was sent into the world. But when one will not accept His aid, and entrust himself to Him, who wants to help him, what else can occur than that he who will not have life, should have death? He says: 'Whoever will not follow me, must feel that he remains a sinner': and then strict judgment is passed on him. so that he remains in his sins, since he will not have righteousness. He who will not have help and blessing, must have the curse. He who will not accept health, must remain sick. He who declines to go to heaven, must go to hell. For while it is not Christ's office to cast into hell, and to curse or to judge, but He wants to help and to rescue: nevertheless, it is also true, that he who will not accept such help, must remain in his sins... A physician says to a sick man: 'I want you to get well. I cannot save your life: but I want to help to do it.' But if the sufferer will not allow this, or accept his services as doctor, the latter says: 'Now I will not talk to you as your doctor, but, because you compel me. I must be your judge, and say: You are going to die.'" (Luther, Erl. ed., 48:294 sq.).

5. Are Love and Justice mutually exclusive?

The love of God for those whom through Christ He saves is one of the grounds for the exercise of His justice. A difference must be made between those who are within the Order which He has provided, and those who, by the persistent opposition of their will to that of God, are outside of it. Hence Christ says:

John 9:39. "For judgment came I into this world."

It is only through this final intervention of Christ as Judge, that complete deliverance for His people comes.

2 Thess. 1:7. 8. "To you that are afflicted, rest with us, at the revelation of the Lord Jesus from heaven with the angels of his power in flaming fire rendering vengeance to them that know not God."

6. According to what nature will Christ be our judge?

According to both natures (Chapter 11, 16, 31, 50).

Holy Scripture is very explicit in its statements that judgment will be exercised in and through the assumed human nature. The Judge is repeatedly called "the Son of Man" (Matt. 16:27; 19:28; 24:30), "Jesus Christ" (Rom. 2:16). (Chapter 11, 2.)

> Acts 17:31. "He will judge the world in righteousness by the man whom he hath ordained."
>
> John 5:27. "He gave him authority to execute judgment because he is a Son of Man." (Cf. Chapter 36, 8.)

The accounts of the judgment, as e.g., that of Matt. 24, declare that He will be visible to all in His human form, as He appears to judge the world (Chapter 37, 22 a).

Concerning this Augustine has said that, since the sight of God belongs only to "the pure in heart" (Matt. 5:8), and "seeing face to face" is promised only to the believing (1 Cor. 13:12), it will be only through the human nature that He will be universally visible at the Day of Judgment, i.e., that it will be the glorified form of a servant" that will then be made manifest ("On the Trinity," Migne ed., 8:840 sq.).

Christ will sit in judgment according to that nature, according to which He stood in judgment before man's tribunal. He will be judge in the nature in which He was judged.

In what sense Christians will be judges

7. Are not the faithful followers of Christ also to be judges?

> 1 Cor. 6:2, 3. "Know ye not that the saints shall judge the world? ...Know ye not that we shall judge angels?"
>
> Matt. 19:28. "When the Son of Man shall sit upon the throne of his glory, ye also shall sit upon twelve thrones, judging the twelve tribes of Israel."

We cannot infer from these passages that it will be the office of the saints to give sentence, but the meaning probably is that they will be assigned places of high dignity, as those who, according to Rev. 3:21, are to share the throne of Christ and will approve each sentence. Nevertheless the judgment of the world by Apostles and other believers is not restricted to the Last Day. As it is the spoken word of Christ that is to be the means of judging (John 12:48), they who become the organs through which this word is published, judge the world not only by their preaching, but by the testimony of the "living epistles known and read of men," given in their lives. It is in connection with the preaching of the Seventy, that Christ says that He beheld Satan fall as lightning. It was by the holy life of John the Baptist, as well as by his words, that Herod felt himself condemned (Mark 6:20). So the act of faith, on the part of Noah, in building the ark, "condemned the world" (Heb. 11:7). All this we may regard as anticipatory of the Judgment Day, when it is the Gospel as proclaimed by the Apostles that is the standard of the judgment.

> Rom. 2:16. "The day when God shall judge the secrets of men, according to my gospel, by Jesus Christ."

Office of angels in the Judgment

8. What will be the office of angels at the judgment?

[A.] As at the nativity, temptation, passion, resurrection and ascension, they attended Christ, so also will they be with Him as He returns to judge the world (Matt. 25:31; 1 Thess. 4:16; 2 Thess. 1:7; Jude 14).

[B.] They will assemble those who are to* be judged (Matt. 24:31).

[C.] They will separate the two classes (Matt. 13:49).

[D.] They will execute the sentence of the Judge, both by committing the wicked to their eternal prison (Matt. 13:41, 42), and conducting those whom the Judge will approve to eternal bliss (1 Thess. 4:17).

Who are to be judged

9. Who are to be judged?

All men.

> 2 Cor. 5:10. "For we must all be made manifest before the judgment seat of Christ; that each one may receive the things done in the body, according to what he hath done, whether it be good or bad."

> Rom. 14:10. "For we shall all stand before the judgment-seat of God."

The righteous (1 Cor. 4:4, 5; 2 Tim. 4:8, etc.). The ungodly (Rom. 2:5; Jude 15;

Matt. 11:22, etc.).

They are sometimes classified, as in the Apostles' Creed, as "the quick and the dead" (Acts 10:42; 2 Tim. 4:1; 1 Peter 4:5). At any time one may take his stand on earth, and to him the sum of all men will be those then living, and those who have died. At the Last Day, it will be those to whom the return of Christ anticipates death, together with those then in their graves. The expression does not mean that those who have preceded us have been judged or will be judged since their death. It looks forward to the resurrection day with the bringing of all at that time before the judgment seat of Christ.

10. But will the righteous both judge (7) and be judged?

So it is declared. As their resurrection will precede that of the ungodly (1 Thess. 4:16), so we may infer the same of their public recognition as those who, for Christ's sake, are justified, and, therefore, to be raised to the position of partakers in Christ's Judgment of the world, as they had been in His sufferings and resurrection.

What will be judged

11. What will be judged?

Not only all men, but all that they have been and are. A merely human judge must regard particular deeds, and determine as to how they correspond with the letter of the statutes which he is sworn to administer. But the Judge at the Last Day is one, who, "with eyes as a flame of fire" (Rev. 1:14), "searches the reins and the heart" (Rev. 2:23). "All things are naked and laid open before the eyes to him, with whom we have to do" (Heb. 4:14). There is no need, therefore, for Him to balance individual virtues with individual sins. His gaze penetrates the innermost personality of every individual. Each one is judged by that which determines and controls his whole life.

> "To every individual, the first and last question of the Eternal Judge will be as to whether he have received or rejected the grace of God in Christ, whether he believe or not in the Son of God" (Kliefoth).
>
> John 5:24. "He that believeth him that sent me, hath eternal lite, and cometh not into judgment, but hath passed out of death into Hie."
>
> John 3:18. "He that believeth on him, is not judged; he that believeth not, hath been judged already, because he hath not believed on the name of the only-begotten Son of God."

There is not a wicked deed that does not have its root and source in unbelief; there is not a good deed that is not the fruit of faith. The crucial question, therefore, will be that of faith or unbelief.

> "That I may be found in him, not having a righteousness of mine own, even that which is of the law, but that which is through faith in Christ, the righteousness which is from God by faith" (Phil. 3:9).

> *Non propter, sed secundum opera*

12. Are we, then, to infer that in the Final Judgment, no account is to be taken of works?

Undoubtedly men will be judged according to their works, as these are the fruits and testimonies of faith or of unbelief (Chapter 23, 37-40). The words "according to their works" constitute a formula that is often repeated in Holy Scripture, and must be carefully distinguished from that by which it has often been misinterpreted, viz., "on account of their works." The wicked indeed, will be judged "on account of their works," and "on account of their unbelief" as well as "according to their works"; but the righteous, not "on account of," but "according to their works." *Non propter, sed secundum opera.*

> Ps. 62:12. "Thou renderest to every man according to his work."

> Prov. 24:12. "Shall not he render to every man according to his work?"

> Jer. 25:14. "I will recompense them according to their deeds."

> Jer. 32:19. "To give every one according to his ways, and according to the fruit of his doing."

> Matt. 16:27. "Then shall he render to every man according to his deeds."

> Rom. 2:6. "Who will render to every man according to his works."

> 1 Cor. 3:8. "Each shall receive his own reward according to his own labor."

> 2 Cor. 5:10. "We must all be made manifest before the judgment-seat of Christ; that each one may receive the things done in the body, according to that; he hath done, whether it be good or bad."

> 1 Pet. 1:17. "Who, without respect of persons, judgeth according to each man's work."
>
> Rev. 22:12. "My reward is with me to render to each man, according as his work is?"

13. Will account be taken only of works in general?

No; but in all their details. Especial prominence will be given the inquiry as to how faith shall have expressed itself in deeds of merciful love. Beneath external compliance with the demands of morality, the external manifestation of the Spirit of Christ will be read in the record of activity for the relief of suffering humanity, in liberality towards the poor, in forgiveness of enemies and meekness under false charges and undeserved punishments, in scrupulous avoidance of all causes of offense, in sympathy towards all representatives of Christ, in efforts for advancing the Kingdom of God (Matt. 25:35-40; Luke 6:35; Luke 14:13 sq.; Mark 9:42; 1 Thess. 4:6; 1 Cor. 3:8). The words of our mouths and the secret thoughts and purposes of the heart, good and evil, will appear in judgment (Matt. 12:36 sq.; Rom. 2:16; 1 Cor. 4:5; Matt. 6:4, 6; Eph. 5:11-13; 1 Tim. 5:24, 25).

The Sins of the Godly at the Judgment

14. Does this necessarily mean that every sin of the righteous will be examined and published on the Day of Judgment?

The majority of our Lutheran theologians say that it does not. The reasons for this opinion are enumerated as follows by Gerhard:

> "1. From the description of the judicial process in Matt. 25. For in it the godly, who are placed at the right hand of Christ as Judge, hear not the publication of their sins, but the enumeration of their good works.
>
> "2. From the gratuitous promise and mercy of God. For He declares that He does not remember our sins" (Is. 43:25; Jer. 31:34; Ez. 18:22), that He "casts our sins behind our backs" (Is. 38:17); that He "casts our sins into the depths of the sea" (Micah 7:19); that He "blots out, as a thick cloud, our sins."

"3. From the immutability of God. What God has forgiven in this life, He will not demand an account of in the life to come.

"4. From the disposition of the Judge towards the godly. He will come as Redeemer (Luke 21:28; Rom. 8:23), as Savior (Matt. 25:35; John 14:3), as Advocate (Rom. 8:34; 1 John 2:1), as the awarder of the crown (2 Tim. 4:8; Rev. 2:10).

"He will not, therefore, come as a severe Judge, producing the sins of the godly to the public gaze of all, and calling them to a rigid examination. For it is the part of an advocate not to publish, but to cover; not to accuse, but to excuse; not to convict, but to favor.

"5. From the office of Christ. For as the only Mediator between God and man, He took our sins upon Himself, and afforded a perfect satisfaction for them, which believers apply to themselves by true faith (Is. 53:5; John 1:29; Rom. 4:25; 2 Cor. 5:19, 21; 1 Peter 2:24). But if He were to reveal the sins of the godly in judgment, He would act contrary to His own office, since He would reveal the sins which He suffered to be placed upon Him, in order that He might afford a most sufficient ransom whereby they might be abolished and removed.

"6. From the example of those who have been converted. He has not reproached those for their sins, who in this life have been converted to God by true repentance, but, according to his promise, has not remembered their sins, and has treated such persons as a most indulgent and mild father, who receives into his open arms a wayward son who returns, without upbraiding him for his former life (Luke 15:20).

"7. From the condition of the godly. For they are described as those who are not to be judged (John 3:17), who will not come into judgment (John 5:23), for whom there is no condemnation (Rom. 8:1) as washed, sanctified, justified (1 Cor. 6:11), whom none can accuse or condemn (Rom. 8:33), as without spot of wrinkle or any such thing (Eph. 5:27).

"8. From the norm of the judgment." (See below, 16.)

15. Will the godly recall their sins on the Day of Judgment?

If so, it will not be to their shame and confusion, or punishment, but to the praise of the grace of God that has forgiven them.

> "The fouler was the error,
> The sadder was the fall,
> The ampler are the praises
> Of Him who pardoned all."

> Luke 7:47. "To whom little is forgiven, the same loveth little."

The Norm of the Judgment: the Gospel for believers, the Law for unbelievers

16. According to what norm or rule will judgment be pronounced?

God's Word (John 12:48). But this Word is either Law or Gospel. He who rejects the Gospel will be judged according to the Law. He who accepts the Gospel will be judged according to the Gospel.

> Rom. 2:12. "As many as have sinned under the law, shall be judged by the law."

> "The sentence of acquittal to be published by the Judge with respect to the godly will not be another and a new acquittal, but the solemn publication, promulgation and confirmation of the absolution proclaimed on earth through the ministry of the Gospel, as is inferred from the words of Christ, 'He that believeth is not condemned Whatsoever ye shall loose on earth, shall be loosed in heaven.' The sentence against the godless will not be another and a new condemnation, but the solemn attestation, publication and ratification of the condemnation announced to them on earth through the law. There will not, therefore, be a different rule of judgment on the Last Day from that which is applied today in the ministry of the preached Word" (Gerhard).

17. But is it not expressly said that the godless also will be judged according to the Gospel?

In 2 Thess. 1:8, it is said that Christ will return to render vengeance "to them that obey not the Gospel So also:

> Rom. 2:16. "In the day when God shad judge the secrets of men according to my Gospel by Jesus Christ."

This means the Law, as illumined and interpreted by the Gospel. To the guilt of all other offenses, is added that of the rejection of Christ and His message of salvation (see above, 11).

> John 16:9. "He shall convict the world of sin, because they believe not on me."

> John 15:22. "If I had not come and spoken unto them, they had not had sin; but now have they no cloak for their sin."

So Matt. 11:23, 24 declares that it shall be more tolerable for Tyre and Sidon in the Day of Judgment, than for the cities which rejected the Gospel which Christ had proclaimed and attested by miracles in their midst.

The Examination and "Books"

18. In how far are the details of the examination to be figuratively interpreted?

Not so as to make of the judgment itself a pictorial representation of what occurs within the consciences of men, or a declaration of a separation made already in this life, but only in so far as the apparatus of human courts is employed as figures of matters that are suggested, but are not fully explained. Such, for example, is the statement concerning the opening of the books.

> Rev. 20:12. "And the books were opened; and another book was opened, which is the book of life; and the dead were judged out of the things which were written in the books, according to their works."

19. What is meant by "the Books"?

The Formula of Concord repeatedly interprets "the book of life" as Christ.

> "The Word of God leads us to Christ, who is the Book of Life, in whom all are written and elected who are to be saved"' (525).
>
> "God's Word presents Christ to us as the Book of Life" (527).
>
> "Christ Jesus, who is the true Book of Life" (652).
>
> "The entire Holy Trinity, Father, Son and Holy Ghost, direct all men to Christ, as to the Book of Life" (661).
>
> "They should seek eternal election in Christ and His Holy Gospel, as in the Book of Life" (665).
>
> "In the Holy Scriptures, a book is ascribed to God, after a human figure, to express His supreme knowledge of all things. The figure is taken from earthly rulers who have their annals and records of the affairs in their government. In this sense, the book is nothing but the knowledge of God" (Baldwin, on Phil. 4:3).

Gerhard has applied this thought in various relations:

> "There is 1. The Book of Life, in which, by eternal predestination, believers are written (Rev. 20:12).
>
> "2. The Book of Divine Omniscience containing a record of all that men have done on earth (Ps. 56:8; 139:16; Mal. 3:16).
>
> "3. The Book of Holy Scripture" (see above, under 16, 17).
>
> "4. The Book of Conscience. This will be opened on the Day of Judgment; because all that is hidden and secret in each one's conscience will then be made manifest.
>
> "5. The Book of Human Testimony. For they who are benefited by the godly in this life will publicly proclaim their works (Luke 16:9), while complaint will be made also of the unbelief of the godless (Matt. 12:41, 42).

"6. The Book of Accusations by Satan. As he accuses men day and night (Rev. 12:10), he will present on the Day of Judgment, an extended catalogue of the deeds wrought by the godless at his instigation.

"7. The Book of Divine Justice. This volume is closed during this life, because the godly sometimes suffer adversity, while the wicked prosper; but, on the Day of Judgment, it will be opened, when, in the public gaze of angels and men, rewards will be allotted the good, and punishment, the wicked."

All this may be briefly summarized in the statement that the memory of the Omniscient Judge will not need the process of a protracted inquisition, in order to ascertain the facts upon which to base his verdict and sentence.

20. With what two things has the decree of the Judge to do?

First, with the question of the guilt or innocence of those brought into judgment; and secondly, with the assignment of rewards and punishments.

Doctrine of Rewards to be guarded

21. Against what must the doctrine of rewards for the godly on the Day of Judgment be carefully guarded?

It must always be remembered that Justification before God, salvation and eternal life are never, properly speaking, the rewards of the life or the love or the labors of any believer, but are bestowed gratuitously solely because of the merits of Christ. The rewards assigned the godly presuppose that, without any merit or worthiness of theirs, and, indeed, with that in them which, on the contrary, if regarded apart from Christ, merits nothing but God's judgment, God, as a gift of pure grace, distributes to them various blessings; and that these blessings are proportioned to various degrees of fidelity, and in recognition of what has been accomplished in and through them, by God's own renewing and sanctifying power. (See above, under 12; also more amply in Chapter 23, 39-44). They are awarded because such is God's order and promise.

22. But is the awarding of these rewards postponed until the Day of Judgment?

Some of these rewards are given, indeed, already in this life, as the promise of the Fourth Commandment shows. But these are only the pledges or earnests of the future reward. Such rewards are not associated in Scripture with the state of bliss into which the believer is introduced at death. It is not until the return of Christ and the Day of Judgment, that what is called "the reward" of believers is received.

> 2 Tim. 4:8. "The crown, of righteousness, which the Lord, the righteous judge, shall give to me at that day; and not to me only, but also to all them that loved his appearing."
>
> 1 Peter 5:4. "When the Chief Shepherd shall be manifested, ye shall receive the crown of glory that fadeth not away."
>
> Matt. 25:34. "Then" (compare verse 31) "shall the King say unto them on his right hand, Come ye blessed of my Father, inherit the kingdom prepared for you from the foundation of the world."
>
> 1 Cor. 4:5. "Judge nothing before the time, until the Lord come, who will both bring to light the hidden things of darkness, and make manifest the counsels of the hearts; and then shall each man have his praise from God."
>
> Rev. 22:12. "Behold, I come quickly; and my reward is with me, to render to each man, according as his work is."

Difference in Rewards

23. Will there be differences, then, in the rewards?

This is taught in numerous places in Holy Scripture; especially in the Parable of the Talents (Matt. 25:21-23), and of the Pounds (Luke 19:16-19). The differences in reward bear a certain relation to the degree in which the believer has been an organ for the workings of divine grace and the progress of the Kingdom of God. Nevertheless, while, according to God's order, there is this proportion, the reward will be far in excess of the labors and sufferings which are recognized when they are bestowed (Rom. 8:18; 2 Cor. 4:17). The pounds well administered on earth are replaced by cities, at Christ's coming (Luke 19:17, 19).

Salvation "without reward"

24. Will any be saved who will be without reward?

As before said, salvation itself is the reward of the active and passive obedience of Christ; and the lowest place in the world of glory will be one of inexpressible bliss. Nevertheless, there will be those, who, although resting all their hopes of salvation upon Christ, have wasted privileges and opportunities in this life, and have in their weakness but not willfully, failed to fulfill the possibilities of their calling as Christians. Either in whole or in part, "according to their works," they lose their reward.

> 1 Cor. 3:13-15. "The fire itself shall prove each man's work of what sort it is. If any man's work shall abide which he built thereon, he shall receive a reward. If any man's work shall be burned, he shall suffer loss; but he himself shall be saved; yet so as through fire."

Incompleteness of Record at death

25. Are the works which are judged completed with the death of the person judged?

No. They continue to extend their influence throughout all time, as a stone thrown into the water creates successive and ever widening circles, until they reach the distant shore. Paul was indeed bound, but the word which he had preached was not bound (2 Tim. 2:9). He was executed as a criminal, but his influence is a thousand times more extensive in the Twentieth, than in the First Century. Every testimony given, every word spoken, every effort made, every sacrifice endured, every prayer offered, remains as a factor that contributes to the shaping of the world's history, and the progress of the Kingdom of God, until the sign of the returning Son of Man is seen in the heavens (Heb. 11:4; 12:1; Rev. 14:13). While man's labors cease when he enters into his rest, his work goes on and is never over until he rises from his grave. God's omniscience knows the whole record from all eternity; but it is only at the Judgment Day that the man himself is permitted to see it, or his fellow-men are made acquainted with its entire contents.

Degrees of Punishment and Incompleteness of Record of Wicked at death

26. In what will the sentence of the wicked agree with, and in what will it differ from that of the godly?

As there will be blessedness for all found in Christ, so there will be misery for all not so found. But as upon the basis of this common blessedness, there will be degrees of glory as the reward of varying degrees of fidelity among those, all of whom are saved out of pure grace for Christ's sake, so, among those whose portion is endless woe, there will be degrees of punishment proportioned to various degrees of guilt.

> Luke 12:47, 48. "That servant that knew his lord's will, and made not ready, nor did according to his will, shall be beaten with many stripes; but he that knew not, and did things worthy of stripes, shall be beaten with few stripes. And to whomsoever much is given, of him shall much be required."

> Luke 10:14. "It shall be more tolerable for Tyre and Sidon in the day of judgment than for you."

27. Is it true also of the godless that their works are not completed with their death?

Their influence also continues to work until the end of time. The measure of their iniquity is not full, when they are laid in their graves, but they continue to treasure up wrath against the day of wrath (Rom. 2:5).

> 1 Tim. 5:24. "Some men's sins are evident, going before unto judgment; and some men also they follow after."

It is only at the Last Day, that they will learn to know the desolation that their words and deeds, as perpetuated through succeeding generations, have accomplished, and to apprehend the measure of their guilt.

No third class

28. Beside the godly and the godless, do the Scriptures permit us to admit the suggestion of any third class?

Scripture knows of only two classes, and between them, it draws a very clear and sharp line, as believers and unbelievers, those on the right hand and those on the left, sheep and goats, blessed and cursed, those who have shown their faith by the exercise of merciful love to their fellow-men, and those who have been indifferent to all their appeals.

The Sentence

29. What important difference in the qualifications attending the sentence?

> Matt. 25:34. "Inherit the kingdom prepared for you."
>
> Matt. 25:41. "Depart into the eternal fire, prepared for the devil and his angels."

In these words, the Judge protests that the condemned have only themselves to blame for their sad lot, and that they perish not by His will, but by their deliberate choice and their obstinate adherence to that choice of the portion that was prepared not for them, but for their very greatest enemy.

Events succeeding Judgment, particularly End of World, Final Conflagration and Change of Heaven and Earth

30. What will immediately follow the execution of the sentence?

The end of the Mediatorial Office of Christ (1 Cor. 15:24-28. See Chapter 15. 18; also Lutheran Commentary, 8:129-134).

31. What then?

The end of the world. The entire visible creation, like man's body in consequence of sin, is hastening towards a crisis in which it shall be dissolved.

> Ps. 102:26. "The heavens shall perish; yea, all of them shall wax old like a garment; as a vesture shalt thou change them, and they shall be changed."
>
> Matt. 24:35. "Heaven and earth shall pass away."
>
> 1 Cor. 7:31. "The fashion of this world passeth away." The mode of its destruction, it is distinctly foretold, will be by fire.
>
> 2 Pet. 3:7, 10. "The heavens that now are, and the earth, by the same word, have been stored up for fire, being reserved against the day of judgment... The heavens shall pass away with a great noise, and the elements shall be dissolved with fervent heat, and the earth and the works that are therein shall be burned up."
>
> Is. 34:4. "And all the host of heaven shall be dissolved, and the heavens shall be rolled together as a scroll; and all their host shall fade away, as the leaf fadeth from off the vine, and as a fading leaf from the fig tree."

32. For what purpose will the world be destroyed?

That another world may take its place. As man's body is resolved into dust, to the end that, at last, a glorified resurrection body may come forth, so the world which has been the scene, the witness and the victim of man's sin (Rom. 8:22), will vanish that another may appear in its stead.

> 2 Pet. 3:13. "But, according to his promise, we look for new heavens and a new earth, wherein dwelleth righteousness."
>
> Rev. 21:1. "And I saw a new heaven and a new earth; for the first heaven and the first earth are passed away; and the sea is no more."
>
> Is. 65:17. "For, behold, I create new heavens and a new earth; and the former things shall not be remembered or come to mind."

> Is. 66:22. "For as the new heavens and the new earth, which I will make, snail remain before me, saith the Lord, so shall your name and your seed remain."

This is termed in Acts 3:21 "the restoration of all things."

33. Will this be accomplished by the complete annihilation of the present world, and the substitution of a new creation, or simply by the purification of this present world by fire and its transformation into "new heavens and a new earth"?

Those who teach the absolute annihilation of the world regard this as the necessary teaching of such expressions in the passages cited under 31, as "perish," "pass away," "burned up," "dissolved." But that this does violence to their meaning, may be inferred from the fact that 2 Peter 3:6 declares that the antediluvian world "perished" by water, although the flood did not affect the substance of the world, but only changed its outward form and inhabitants. In describing man's renewal, in 2 Cor. 5:17, it is said:

> "Old things are passed away; behold they are become new."

But it was the error of Flaeius that maintained that the renewal, as well as regeneration, implied a "substantial," instead of an accidental change in man. The burning up of the world does not require annihilation; since combustion does not annihilate, but only redistributes and rearranges particles of matter. If the vapor and gases released by the burning of a pound of wood could be collected and be added to the weight of its ashes, it would be found that not a grain of it is lost. There is, therefore, no scriptural testimony to compel this meaning, as most of our old Lutheran dogmaticians thought. On the other hand, the analogy of the flood and of man's renewal, suggests, although it does not teach in so many words, a thorough transformation, a change of qualities, instead of a change of substance. Such, too, was the opinion of Luther;

> "The heavens," (he said,) "have now their working-day clothes on; but then they will put on their Sunday robes." "The sun is nowhere as beautiful and bright, as when it was created; on man's account, it has become half darkened. But on that day, God will cleanse it by fire, so that it will be brighter and clearer than it was in the beginning."

To the same effect, Brentz:

> "Will heaven and earth pass away that nothing of them shall remain? By no means. They will not pass away entirely, but will be changed. They will cast aside the garment of corruption, and put on the new garment of incorruption; there will be indeed a change of heaven and earth, but not a total abolition."

Philip Nicolai:

> "The present world shall burn up and be entirely consumed with fire; nevertheless not materially, by the annihilation of its essence, but formally, according to its present fashion and accidental condition."

34. How has the other side been stated?

Gerhard says:

> "The opinion concerning the substantial destruction of the world we do not maintain as an article of faith, absolutely necessary to be known and believed for salvation, but we regard it more in harmony with emphatic statements of Scripture concerning the end of the world."

He quotes Heerbrand as saying:

> "Whether the world will perish according to accidents and inherent properties, or according to substance, is not to be curiously investigated by the array of human talent, for this has been placed in the power and judgment alone of God the Father."

So also Hutter and others.

35. What, however, is fixed?

That there will be a new heaven and a new earth, whether this be by transformation or by an absolutely new creation; and that on this new earth, men will dwell with bodies restored at the resurrection. Luther says that 2 Peter 3:13 "sounds as though we shall then live upon the earth" (Erlangen ed., 52:270). Glorified bodies will be at home on a glorified earth.

39. Eternal Death

This topic is discussed at much length on Klieforth's "Christliche Escatologie," Leipzig, 1886.

Defined

1. What is Eternal Death?

It is the final stage of death, which began, at the fall, with spiritual death, or the separation of the soul from God, advanced into bodily death, or the separation of the soul from the body; and culminates in eternal death, or the eternal separation of soul and body from God, with all the miseries connected with being beneath His condemnation. (See Chapter 8, 17.) It is sometimes known as "the second death" (Rev. 2:11; 20:6, 14; 21:8), in distinction from bodily or temporal death.

Both Place and State

2. Is it a place or a state to which the godless are to be consigned?

The literal interpretation of Scripture demands both. Neither is there an obvious reason for insisting that the scriptural references to a place must be figurative, since they are to be consigned thither, not simply in soul, but also in body.

Important distinction

3. What care must be taken in the understanding of terms employed?

> "As in Rev. 20:14 Death and Hades are said to be cast into 'the lake of fire' at the Day of Judgment, we must distinguish 'Hades' from 'the lake of fire,' since it could not be cast into itself. The former refers to something that precedes, the latter to something that follows the Judgment. It is described in Rev. 20:10 as 'a lake of fire and brimstone,' and the place of final punishment for the devil, and Antichrist and the false prophet. Here 'the destruction' and 'perdition' (Rom. 9:22; Phil. 3:19; 1 Tim. 6:9; 2 Peter 3:7:1 Thess. 5:3: Heb. 10:39), which begin in this life (John 3:18) and continue after death (Luke 16:18), culminate (2 Cor. 5:10)" (Rohnert).

Literal or figurative "Fire"

4. When the place of punishment is described as "a lake of fire," is this to be understood literally or figuratively?

Here the words of Gerhard are to be commended:

> "Whether the fire be truly corporeal, material and visible, or incorporeal, immaterial and invisible, we leave unsettled (although we incline to the latter), and we earnestly pray God not to reveal this to us by knowledge gained from experience. It is better for us with all earnestness to be anxious to escape the infernal fire, than to contend with passion and at leisure as to its nature."

The facts that to it will be consigned the fallen angels who are pure spirits, and that it will burn without consuming, have always been difficulties to those who were disposed to consider it literal fire. The element in the description to be tenaciously held, is that it stands for a dreadful reality, and not merely for something entirely subjective. Whatever it means, back of it all is the wrath of God, who is "a consuming fire" (Heb. 12:29).

5. How have the punishments been classified?

Some are negative; others, positive. The negative consist in separation from God, and all that this implies. The positive, in the internal punishments of grief and anguish; and external, to the bodily and mental tortures inflicted from without.

Classification of punishments

6. Will there be an end to these punishments?

> Matt. 25:46. "And these shall go away into eternal punishment; but the righteous into eternal life."
>
> Rev. 20:10. "And they shall be tormented day and night for ever and ever."
>
> John 3:36. "He that obeyeth not the Son, shall not see life; but the wrath of God abideth on him."
>
> 2 Thess. 1:9. "Who shall suffer punishment, even eternal destruction from the face of the Lord and from the glory of his might."
>
> Dan. 12:2. "And many of them that sleep in the dust of the earth shall awake; some to everlasting life and some to shame and everlasting contempt."
>
> Mark 9:43. "It is good for thee to enter into life maimed, rather than having thy two hands, to go into hell, into the unquenchable fire."

These passages are sufficient to dispel all thoughts of the annihilation of the wicked, or their ultimate conversion, or the mitigation or relief of their punishment after a long period.

"What sort of inference would it be,"' asks Augustine (*De Civitate Dei*, 21, 23):

> "...to regard 'eternal punishment' as only fire of long duration, and to believe 'eternal life' to be without end, when Christ embracing both, has said in one and the same sentence: 'These shall go into eternal punishment, but the righteous into life eternal If both are eternal, both must refer either to long duration with an end, or to perpetuity without an end. They are parallels; on the one hand, 'eternal punishment,' on the other, 'eternal life.'

> But to say in one and the same sense that eternal life will be without end, and eternal death will have an end, is extremely absurd. Wherefore seeing that the eternal life of the saints shall be without end, so therefore, it is a consequence that likewise without end will be eternal punishment."
>
> "Just as the elect will reign in heaven for ever and ever (Rev. 22:5), as holy souls desire that God may be glorified for ever and ever (1 Tim. 1:17; Heb. 13:21), as Jesus risen from the dead is alive for evermore (Rev. 1:18), as in His glory He shall reign for ever and ever (Rev. 11:15), as the very life of God is described by saying that He liveth for ever and ever (Rev. 4:9, 10; 5:14; 10:6), so is this same measure applied to the punishment of lost souls... Modern skepticism has tampered with the word 'eternal,' just as it has emptied 'salvation,''atonement,''grace,' of their natural meaning. But 'everlasting' means nothing more nor less than that which lasts for ever... Where that word is applied to our home in heaven, the hopes and longings of men gladly do justice to the natural force of human language. But it is noteworthy that no stronger expressions are applied anywhere to the Eternal Life of the Blessed in Heaven, within the New Testament, than are here used to describe the endlessness of the pains of hell" (Liddon).

Such questions are to be decided not by our subjective feelings, as we contemplate what is involved in eternal punishment, but solely by the revealed Word of God.

Punishments, without end; doctrine state, and objections answered

7. But will (here not be, according to this statement, a disproportion between sins as committed in a brief period of time, and their punishment throughout all eternity?

[A.] But sin is not limited to "a brief space of time."

Eternal sin belongs to the future; and eternal sin and eternal death go together.

[B.] Augustine in his "*De Civitate Dei*" (XXI, 11), asks, What Code of Laws has ever proposed to punish offenses by penalties of the same length of time as the act which is to be judged?

> "Is one condemned to lie in prison no longer than he was in doing his villainy? A servant who has but violently touched his master is awarded many years imprisonment."

A deed committed in a moment is often followed by a penalty for life. Such is the principle upon which even earthly justice acts. Esau's sale of his birthright was the thought and work of a moment. Its consequences affected both him throughout life and his posterity for many centuries. So with Adam's sin.

[C.] Beside this, we estimate the degree of guilt of an offense not by the time needed for its commission, but by the character and relation of the one against whom it is committed.

A wrong to a man is more serious than a wrong to a beast; a wrong to a benefactor is a greater crime, than one to other men; parricide or matricide is more heinous than other forms of murder; but the greatest of all sins is that which is against God, the Highest Good.

[D.] Still further, the degree of man's guilt may be estimated in that it required a sacrifice of no less importance than the Son of God Himself in order to deliver those who are saved from its consequences.

On the contrary, the greatness of the punishment is intended to help us to estimate the greatness of the guilt of sin. It is just in proportion as the significance of sin is minimized, that a worldly age protests against the teaching of eternal punishment. The love of God is never to be so preached, that His justice is forgotten; since it is through His justice, that His love is magnified.

8. But must not allowance be made for the qualitative use of the word "eternal"?

By this is meant, as we understand, the interpretation of the word in passages which declare that believers "have eternal life" already in this world, as in I John 5:13:

> "These things have I written unto you, that ye may know that ye have eternal life."

Upon the basis of this, it is argued that as believers have eternal life here, so the godless have eternal death in this world, and, therefore, that it is not to be apprehended in the world to come. But the reasoning is unfair. The believing children of God have, indeed, eternal life in this world, yet, only as the feeblest beginning, the pledge, the earnest of that which is yet to come. If the passage had read: "I have written unto you that ye may know that ye have all of your eternal life already," there might be some place for the suggestion that the punishment of the wicked may be no more than their bondage to sin in this world. But such is not the declaration; and beyond the text itself, Scripture is full of promises that what will be revealed to us at Christ's return, and the blessings then to be received far surpass our thought on this side of the grave.

9. What qualification, however, should always attend the preaching of this doctrine?

That not all the punishments threatened can be regarded as necessarily pertaining to all the condemned. There are degrees of punishment, proportioned to degrees of light and knowledge. Every one will be judged "according to his works"; and, as we have learned (Chapter 38, 26), these works will be estimated according to the degrees of light and knowledge.

> "Nevertheless, we should note in regard to this diversity of punishments:
>
> "1. That all the punishments of all the condemned will be eternal; and hence, there will be no diversity with respect to duration.
>
> "2. That there will be no diversity with respect to different places, as some wish, but that this inequality has reference entirely to distinct degrees" (Gerhard).

40. Eternal Life

Defined

1. What is Eternal Life?

As Eternal Death has been shown to be the culmination of the spiritual death, which began with the fall, so Eternal Life is the culmination of the spiritual life, imparted in regeneration, developed in renovation, advanced to a higher stage after the death of the body, but not reaching its fullness until the resurrection and the final judgment. Hence it is sometimes called simply "life," as in Matt. 18:8; 7:14, and "the life which is life indeed" (1 Tim. 6:19). As natural life is "the state of an animal or plant, in which its organs are in actual performance of their functions, or are capable of performing their functions" (Century Dictionary), so Eternal Life brings with it the realization of the ideal in God's mind in man's creation and redemption, and the highest exercise of all the functions with which man was naturally endowed and with which grace has enriched him, to the glory of his Creator and Redeemer.

Its three elements: 1. Complete Deliverance; 2. Perfection of the work of Grace; 3. Realization of the possibilities before Adam and their transcendence

2. What three things are included in the conception?

1. Man's complete deliverance from sin and all its consequences.
2. The bringing to perfection of the work of grace begun in this life.
3. the attainment of all the divine purposes in man's creation.

3. Explain the first?

Not only will the godly be beyond the power to sin (Matt. 22:30), for they will have reached this stage immediately after death, but, with the resurrection and judgment, they will reach a state, in which none of the consequences of sin can hereafter affect them. "Blessed" as they will be prior to the resurrection, the state of bodiless existence, is unnatural and abnormal, and a consequence of sin, which prevents their full enjoyment of what has been provided in Christ's redemption. But the restored body will also be entirely free from all the consequences of sin that enfeebled it and made it capable of suffering. There will be a bodily life, without tears and pain, poverty and want, hunger and thirst, cold and heat, night and darkness; all imperfections and limitations that come from sin will have ended.

> Rev. 21:4. "And he shall wipe away every tear from their eyes: and death shall be no more; neither shall there be mourning nor crying nor pain any more; for the former things have passed away."

> Rev. 7:16. "They shall hunger no more, neither thirst any more; neither shall the sun strike upon them, nor any heat."

> Rev. 22:5. "And there shall be night no more: and they need no light of lamp, neither light of sun."

> 1 Cor. 13:12. "For now we see in a mirror darkly; but then face to face: now I know in part; but then shall I know fully, even as also I was fully known."

Further, they will be completely separated from all persons defiled by sin, who have not been made subjects of regeneration.

> Rev. 22:15. "Without are the dogs and the sorcerers and the fornicators and the murderers and the idolaters and every one that loveth and that maketh a lie."

> 1 Cor. 6:9; Gal. 5:19-21.

The sight and conversation between the godly and the godless narrated in Luke 16 belongs to the period before the resurrection.

The world also, as we learned above in Chapter 38, 32-35, will bear traces no longer of the reign of sin.

4. Explain the second.

It is the uniform testimony of Holy Scripture, that the gifts of grace received in this life, are only "first-fruits," that pledge the full harvest that is to come at Christ's return.

> Rom. 8:23. "Ourselves also who have the first-fruits of the Spirit, even we ourselves groan within ourselves, waiting for our adoption, to wit, the redemption of the body."

> Eph. 1:13, 14. "Ye were sealed with the Holy Spirit of promise, which is an earnest of our inheritance, until the redemption of God's own possession."

> 1 John 3:2. "Beloved, now are we children of God, and it is not yet made manifest what we shall be. We know that if he shall be manifested, we shall be like him."

God's Predestination, that His elect shall "be conformed to the image of His Son" (Rom. 8:29), will then reach its goal. This pertains, first of all, to the perfection of spiritual endowments (Gal. 5:22, 23), the manifold forms of the love, that abides for ever (1 Cor. 13:8, 13); and also to the superior endowments of the resurrection bodies of believers (Phil. 3:21).

5. Explain the third.

Man was created, in order by the use of his free will to develop capacities with which he was endowed. As he came from the hand of God, his perfections were like those of the acorn, not like those of the oak. It was within his choice to advance from a state of possibility to one of impossibility of sinning; from one of possibility to one of impossibility of dying. As his liberty, so also his knowledge and holiness were to be developed. Although in the image of God, his chief significance lay in the possibilities before him, throughout all eternity, in his free choice to abide in the path in which God had placed him. (See Chapter 7, 28, 32.)

Redemption restores to man not only what he had lost in Adam, but brings the full realization of all the possibilities before Adam in case he had remained faithful. If this were not the case, the blot and blight of sin would still remain; and Satan would actually prevent the destiny of humanity from being attained by any of our race. Paradise Regained must be more than Paradise Lost, or it could not be said:

> "Where sin abounded, there did grace abound more exceedingly."

This has been traced already in regard to the obedience of Christ, in that He not only paid the penalty of sin by His sufferings, but also, by His perfect obedience to the Law, earned for man infinite merit, such as Adam never had or could have had in Eden (Chapter 14, 21-23); and in regard to justification which is not only the non-imputation of sin, but the imputation of what Adam never had, viz., the righteousness of Christ (Chapter 18, 3, 4, 6, 9). So in the Life Eternal, Renovation will also reach, and even more than reach the standard that was attainable by Adam's best use throughout eternity of his concreated knowledge and holiness, as well as of all his physical endowments.

"Salvation" and "Glory" distinguished; the former for the individual; the latter for the community of "the Blessed"

6. What distinction has been made by some of our theologians?

Between salvation and glory. It is based upon:

> 2 Tim. 2:10. "That the elect may obtain the salvation which is in Christ Jesus with eternal glory."

"Salvation" designates the relation of the individual who is in Christ to God, and the consequences resulting from this relation to the personal life. It is the life-communion of the individual with God. i.e., the complete realization of all that we attempt to express by the word "religion." "Glory" stands for what belongs to the saved in common; since they are regarded as not isolated, but as constituting a community or society of glorified humanity, "the general assembly and Church of the firstborn who are enrolled in heaven" (Heb. 12:23), "the people of God" (Rev. 21:3), "a kingdom" (1 Thess. 2:12; 2 Thess. 1:552 Tim. 4:18; 2 Peter 1:11, etc.), and as such each one is allotted his appropriate place, with ranks and degrees varying, as in every organized State.

7. What relation do these two conditions have to each other?

Salvation is the condition of glory. Glory always presupposes salvation.

8. But is salvation peculiar to the period after the General Judgment?

No. But it is then that salvation reaches its highest stage. It is, then, also that although long hidden, it is made manifest, and seen to be absolutely beyond the danger of any change. Most of all, it is then that the body at last shares in the blessedness and the activity, into which the soul had previously entered.

The Beatific Vision: its effects and attendants

9. What is a most prominent element of the blessedness of Heaven?

The Beatific Vision of God.

> Matt. 5:8. "Blessed are the pure in heart; for they shall see God."
>
> 1 Cor. 13:13. "For now we see in a mirror darkly, but then face to face."
>
> 1 John 3:2. "For we shall see him even as he is."
>
> John 17:24. "Rather, I desire that they also whom thou hast given me be with me where I am, that they may behold my glory."
>
> Rev. 22:4. "And they shall see his face."
>
> Ps. 17:15. "As for me, I shall behold thy face in righteousness; I shall be satisfied when I awake with beholding thy form."
>
> Matt.:8:10. "In heaven, their angels do always behold the face of my father who is in heaven."

10. What does this mean?

With much that we cannot comprehend, it tells clearly of a higher and deeper knowledge of God than is possible in this life (John 17:3; 1 Cor. 13:12). It will be an immediate knowledge, as contrasted with that of this world, which is imparted through the Means of Grace. It will be a direct knowledge, as contrasted with that acquired here by means of reflection and processes of reasoning. It will be relatively complete, and, while of course not exhausting the mysteries of God's being, will be elevated above the very fragmentary knowledge we have in this world. 2 Cor. 5:7, "For we walk by faith, not by sight."

We would miss the meaning, if we regarded only the intellectual side of the vision. It refers especially to that close intimacy that can be enjoyed only "face to face." Paul repeatedly expresses his great desire to be face to face with the people, beloved in Christ, to whom he writes (Rom. 1:11; 2 Thess. 2:17; 3:10). The joy of the •child to look into its father's eyes, the delight of the mother to gaze upon the features of her returning child, are feeble figures of what is meant by this vision of God. It is living within the light of His countenance (Num, 6:25; Ps. 67:1).

11. But does this mean that with their bodily eyes the godly shall behold God?

Why should it be impossible for the eyes of a glorified body to see God? The spiritual body will be adapted to whatever new offices God may have for it to discharge (Chapter 36, 17). It is not right to understand 1 Tim. 6:16 as teaching the impossibility of such a sight of God, as it refers only to present conditions. But Augustine correctly says:

> "I say they shall in the body see God: but whether they shall see Him by means of the body, as we now see the sun, moon, stars, sea, earth, and all that is in it, that is a difficult question" (*De Civitate Dei*, XXII, 29).

It is enough, however, to know that Christ, who is "the image of the invisible God" (Col. 1:17), and who is, thus, God Himself, will be clearly visible in His glorified human nature.

> Rev. 21:23. "And the city hath no need of the sun, neither of the moon to shine upon it; for the glory of God did lighten it, and the Lamb is the light thereof."

12. What will be the effect of this sight of God?

To transform those admitted to it, still more completely into God's image.

> 1 John 3:2. "We shall be like him; for we shall see him as he is."

It will be as when Moses beheld the glory of God. His face became so radiant with its reflection, that, as he went forth to converse with his people he had to be veiled, lest its brilliancy should overpower them (Ex. 34:29-35; 2 Cor. 3:7, 13). If the Apostle could say (2 Cor. 5:18), "We all with unveiled face beholding as in a mirror the glory of the Lord, are transformed into the same image, from glory to glory," what will it be when we no longer see "as in a mirror," but "face to face," and that too, no longer merely "the glory of the Lord," but the Lord Himself?

13. What will accompany the sight of God?

The fruition of God, i.e., the admiring contemplation of all God's attributes and deeds in Providence and in Grace; and with this, the joyful appropriation of it all as the personal possession of every man, to whom God has given Himself as his Lord and God. Only then will God's love be fully realized and experienced. It is a great thing, we are told, that by grace we are able to love God here, without seeing Him.

> 1 Pet. 1:8. "Whom, having not seen, ye love; on whom, though now ye see him not, yet believing, ye rejoice."

But this has as its goal, the beatific sight of Christ, "that the love wherewith thou lovedst me may be in them, and I in them" (John 17:24), where we shall not only know as' we are known, but love as we are loved, and "God will be all in all" (1 Cor. 15:28). The Revelation of John seems to exhaust the imagery of earth, in its employment of all that can charm the eye or impress the imagination, in order to convey some faint idea of what this means. If the eye lingered with inexpressible admiration upon the earthly Temple, as the highest achievement then attained of man's art. in the New Jerusalem the gaze is transferred from the Temple to its Lord and God.

> Rev. 21:22. "And I saw no temple therein; for the Lord God the Almighty and the Lamb are the temple thereof."

The Community of the Blessed

14. Is the communion of the blessed with God one that isolates them from one another?

In the state between death and the resurrection the blessed are referred to generally as mere individuals; but after the Judgment, while the individual is not entirely absorbed by the community, the fact that the saved constitute a society is particularly prominent. They are "a people"[21] (Rev. 19:4; 21:3; cf. Rom. 9:25; 2 Cor.

21 *Laos*, viz, those inwardly united by the bond of common ancestry and a common nature and common interests, not *ethnos*, referring to external relations, or *ochlos* a mere aggregate of atoms constituting an unorganized crowd.

6:16; Heb. 4:9:1 Peter 2:9, 10); "a general assembly" (Heb. 12:23); "an assembly*' or "church" (Eph. 5:27); "a kingdom" (Rev. 1:6, "And he made us to be a kingdom"), or the common heirs of a kingdom (Matt. 25:34), to judge and to reign (Rev. 22:5). Heaven will be no place of monastic seclusion, but a city (Heb. 11:10, 16:12:22; 13:14: Rev. 3:12; 21:2), planned and organized beyond the highest ideals of man's art. Beside communion with God, there will be close association with the godly of all ages and the holy angels.

> Heb. 12:22. "But ye are come unto Mount Zion, and unto the city or the living God, the heavenly Jerusalem, and to innumerable hosts of angels, and to the general assembly and church of the first-born who are enrolled in heaven."
>
> Matt. 8:11. "Many shall come from the east and the west, and shall sit down with Abraham and Isaac and Jacob in the kingdom of heaven."
>
> John 14:3. "In my Father's house, are many mansions."
>
> Rev. 20:11-27. The description of the New Jerusalem,
>
> Rev. 20:24. "And the nations shall walk amidst the light thereof; and the kings of the earth bring their glory into it."

15. In what form is this social life of the blessed described as especially expressing itself?

In their united worship (Rev. 4:8; 5:9, 10; 7:4-1 1); and joyful service (Rev. 22:3). The details of this service are are not revealed. Gerhard (IX, 379), upon the basis of Matt. 17:3, says:

> "As Moses and Elias at the Transfiguration conversed with Christ concerning His impending suffering, so, in life eternal, there will be perpetual and most joyful conversations concerning the fruit of the Lord's suffering."

Scripture abounds in similar suggestions, doubtless intended to excite our inquiry, and to stimulate to speculations concerning what may be, although, in order to exercise our faith, deferring precise information until the reality of the eternal world, in all its fulness, becomes ours. 1 Thess. 2:19 gives us ground for believing that the faithful will find part of their eternal bliss in the fruits of their faith as seen in the godly men and women, they will there meet, who, through their instrumentality have been brought to Christ, or been efficient in advancing the Kingdom of God on earth.

16. Will all have the same glory?

Each individual will have the same salvation, which, like justification, will be equal. But the glory will vary with individuals. It belongs to the entire community of the saved; but as in all societies, some are higher, and others lower. "*Omnibus una salus Sanctis, sed gloria dispar*" (Gerhard).

> Dan. 12:3. "They that are wise shall shine as the brightness of the firmament; and they that turn many to righteousness as the stars for ever and ever."
>
> 1 Cor. 15:41, 42. "One star differeth from another star in glory; so also is the resurrection of the dead."
>
> Matt. 19:28. "Verily I say unto you, that ye who have followed me, in the regeneration, where the Son of Man shall sit on the throne of his glory, ye also shall sit upon twelve thrones, judging the twelve tribes of Israel."
>
> Matt. 5:19. "Least in the kingdom of heaven;" "great in the kingdom of heaven.' (See also Chapter 37, 23.) Here the"Communion of Saints" will be realized in its fullest extent. While there will be differences, there will be no envy.
>
> "Qui Scientem cuncta sciunt, quid nescire nequeunt?
> Nam et pectoris arcand penetrent alterutrum,
> Unum volunt, unum nolunt, unitas est mentium.
> Licet cuiquam sit diversum pro labore praemium,
> Caritas hoc facit suum quod amat in altero.
> Proprium sic singulorum fit commune omnium." (Peter Damianus.)

To avoid misunderstanding we have changed "meritum" at close of line 4 to "praemium." (See above Chapter XXlll:41, 42.)

This passage from the great hymn: "Ad perennis vitae fontem," we have roughly paraphrased:

"Knowing Him who all things knoweth, what from them can be withheld? \
"Brother lives within his brother, none have secrets to conceal; \
"Heart and mind and will and purpose, one throughout and one

within. \
"What though diverse are their honors, as their labors were on earth? \
"Each his own esteems the glory which he sees his brother wear; \
"Every individual token, common gift and joy for all."

The Home of the Blessed

17. What will be the home of the Blessed after the Final Judgment?

The "New Heavens and New Earth" (2 Peter 3:13; Rev. 21:i; Is. 65 117; 66:22; see Chapter 38, 35); particularly "the new earth" (Matt. 5:5), into which John saw the New Jerusalem descending, from above, where the saints had dwelt as pure spirits (Rev. 21:2). The new home will be one in which the glorified will dwell in the bodies restored to them at the resurrection. The new earth and the new body will be fitted for the new existence into which they will then enter. If physical science is constantly making new discoveries concerning the properties of matter, showing how little it had previously known concerning them, it certainly is incompetent to determine anything concerning the new properties that will then be added. Although Scripture is often forced, from the poverty of human language, to resort to figurative terms to communicate its truths, not everything is figurative, but beneath the words there are the most real of all realities, which no reasoning can explain away.

18. What argument concerning the nature of this abode has been made from the blessings of the present life?

In one of the most eloquent passages in Christian literature, Augustine recounts at length the blessings that belong to this life, notwithstanding the fact that it is under a curse, and, then, reasoning from the less to the greater, asks what must be the rewards in the abode of the blessed! We quote a brief extract:

> "Shall I speak of the manifold and various loveliness of sky and earth and sea; of the plentiful supply and wonderful quality of the light; of sun, moon and stars; of the shade of trees; of the colors and perfume of flowers; of the multitude of birds, all differing in plumage and song; of the varieties of animals, of which the smallest in size are often the most wonderful? Shall I speak of the sea, which itself is so grand a spectacle, when it arrays itself as it were in its vesture of various colors, now running through every

> shade of green, and again becoming purple or blue? How grateful is the alternation of day and night! how pleasant the breezes that cool the air! how abundant the supply of clothing furnished us by trees and animals! Who can enumerate all the blessings we enjoy? If I were to attempt to detail and unfold only these few which I have indicated in the mass, such an enumeration would fill a volume. And all these are but the solace of the wretched and condemned, not the rewards of the blessed! What, then, shall these rewards be, if such be the blessings of a condemned state! 'He that spared not his own Son, but delivered him up for us all, shall he not with him also give us all things?" (*De Civitate Dei*, XXII, 24).

> "In the description of these heavenly things, the Holy Spirit employs various earthly figures far surpassing human understanding. But these figures should by no means be volatilized into what is purely spiritual; on the contrary it is to be firmly maintained that they all are images and shadows of the heavenly, and that, in the future world, they will find their complete realization. Just as certain as our resurrection body will be an actual body of a glorified nature, will the new earth be an actual earth, but, together with its creatures (Rev. 21:5) completely glorified. All in and on it will correspond to its new nature. According to Scripture, neither the animal, nor the vegetable, nor the mineral kingdom will be wanting there. For otherwise what meaning would there be in the precious stones of Rev. 21, or the Tree of Life of Rev. 22? Add to this what the Lord says of drinking of the fruit of the vine anew in His Father's kingdom (cf. Luke 13:29), what Paul writes of the deliverance of the creature from its corruption into the glorious liberty of the children of God (Rom. 8:19 sqq.), and the prophetic predictions concerning the peaceful dwelling together of the wolf and the lamb, etc. (Is. 11:6-1 1; 60:17-22; 62:8, 9; 65:17-25). It is absolutely impossible for us to interpret these as entirely spiritual" (Rohnert).

19. Will the rest of heaven be inaction?

Wherever this rest is referred to, it is in contrast to the labor and effort, the trial and trouble of this life, where we have a constant struggle to maintain, and where every movement prompted by the Holy Spirit and directed towards God, encounters resistance (2 Thess. 1:7; Heb. 4:1, 6, 9, 11). But just as God's rest is not inaction (cf. Gen. 2:2 with John 5:17), and declares only a change in the mode of His activity, so with that of the redeemed in their new life.

> "We shall stand in a state of unfettered vitality. The somatic-psychical organism will be the absolutely adequate means for the action of the spirit, all mortality and passivity of the body shall have vanished. The new spiritual body also is raised into fullness of spiritual energy. Man will be free from the possibility of sin, not through the loss of freedom, but through the indestructible energy of love springing from union with God" (Dorner).

It is the life of angels that men will live in their restored bodies. But it will be more. They will not only all serve, but not until then will their kingship be fully realized. However they who know of ruling and reigning only from a distance may deem it a life of indolence, they who are competent to judge know that it is the very highest form of activity.

> 2 Tim. 2:12. "If we endure, we shall also reign with Him."

> Rev. 22:5. "They shall reign for ever and ever."

Only then will every sanctified power and capacity and attainment of the believing reach its goal in the service of God, or rather in the rule and direction of every faculty and possession to His glory.

> "So far from life being done, when this portion of it is accomplished, we should rather say, that life is now only so far advanced that it may truly be said to begin; all this temporal and partial work, all the commotions and agitations of history, and the long conflict of the Church on earth, prepares only for this beginning; because herein the creation of man is only now at length fully accomplished" (Martensen).

> 1 Tim. 6:19. "The life which is life indeed."

41. The Divine Purpose As Interpreted By Its Contents And Results

Order of Treatment

1. What is the sum and substance of God's revelation of Himself to man?

His Grace and Mercy in Jesus Christ (see Chapter 9), This is shown in the devising and execution of a Plan of Redemption, the various stages of which have now been successively traced, according to what has been stated in Chapter 9, 20. The time has now come according to the order observed by Paul in the Epistle to the Romans (Chapter 9, 22, 23) for the treatment of Predestination.[22] All the provisions of the Gospel in detail go to make up what Predestination includes. For whatever God does in time He has purposed to do from all eternity. Unlike man, His plans are not modified by circumstances that had not been anticipated.

22 It is an interesting fact that even Calvin postpones the treatment of this subject to the very close of the Third of the Four Books into which he divides his "Institutes," viz., until after he has discussed Justification.

This order was adopted also by our Lutheran theologian, Conrad Dietrich, in his *Institutiones Catecheticae* of 1613, who treats of Predestination after his exposition of the last article of the Apostles' Creed; and by Hutter in his Loci of 1619, who puts it at the close of Soteriology.

Predestination defined, and definition explained clause by clause. Different senses of term, "Out of grace," "Out of Human Race," "Each Individual," Relation of Foreknowledge, In what senses "Absolute" and "Conditional," Condition presupposed in Decree, "In Christ," Is Faith a cause of Election, Parallel of Justification.

2. What is the meaning of "Predestination"?

Generally speaking, an act by which something is predetermined or foreordained.

> "The particle '*pre*' denotes the priority of time that intervenes between the decree of Predestination and the men who are said to be predestinated; so that there is a destination of men to eternal salvation, before they were or began to be" (Bechmann).

3. In what two senses is the word used?

> "The term is taken in:
>
> "(a) a more general sense, with respect to both the believing and the unbelieving, as the destination of both the former and the latter to a particular end; and thus Predestination is the destination to eternal salvation of those who believe unto the end, and to eternal damnation of those unbelieving unto the end; in which sense Predestination comprises also Reprobation. This, however, is not the meaning of the term in this article,
>
> "(b) Predestination is taken in the language of Scripture, in so far as it is opposed to Reprobation, and denotes only the destination or ordination of those who finally believe to eternal life, and that this has been done before those who believe were, viz., from eternity" (ibid.).

4. What synonym is there for Predestination?

Election. They refer to the same act of God, but connote different relations.

Predestination connotes the priority of the act to the existence of those with whom it has to do; Election connotes the particularity of the act and indicates that it is not universal.

5. Define Predestination or Election.

It is the eternal decree, purpose or decision of god, according to which, out of pure grace, He determined to save out of the fallen, condemned and helpless human race each individual who, from eternity He foresaw, would, by his grace, be in Christ unto the end of life.

6. What is the force of the expression, "out of pure grace"?

That this decree was in no respect or degree whatever determined or influenced by the consideration of anything existing within those who were elected. The motive for the election is found entirely within God.

> Eph. 1:5. "Having foreordained us unto adoption as sons through Jesus Christ unto himself, according to the good pleasure of his will."
>
> Rom. 11:5, 6. "There is a remnant according to the election of grace. But it it is by grace, it is no more of works; otherwise grace is no more grace."

7. What is meant by God's determination "to save out of the human race"?

It means that Election is not, as Huber strangely taught, universal. The very term "Election" declares this, and so, also the results show; for not all are saved.

8. What is declared by the words "out of the fallen, condemned and helpless human race"?

That man's fall, condemnation and sinful estate are not in consequence of the decree of Predestination, but that it assumes or presupposes all this. It is lost and fallen men whom Predestination is to eternally save. Predestination is God's determination to provide a remedy for the consequences of the fall.

9. Why do you say "each individual"?

Because Election deals with men, not as a class, but as individuals. Each and every man, woman and child who will be saved" eternally, was separately and individually the object of God's election from all eternity. As we are born and die and must give an account to God as individuals, as we are regenerated, justified and sanctified, as individuals, as we are baptized and receive the Lord's Supper as individuals; so also Election or Predestination is an act of God's will with respect to each person and each case individually, and to a class only because constituted of such individuals.

> "In his counsel, purpose and ordination, he prepared salvation not only in general, but in grace considered and chose to salvation each and every person of the elect, who shall be saved through Christ" (Formula of Concord, 653).

10. What is the force of the words "who from eternity he foresaw"?

To affirm, first, that the decree is as the word Predestination itself implies, prior to the existence of the persons, with whom God's mind and will were thus occupied; secondly, that Predestination is not identical with foreknowledge; and, thirdly, that, speaking of course anthropomorphically, but nevertheless in accordance with Holy Scripture and, therefore, with absolute truth, foreknowledge is not dependent upon Predestination, but Predestination upon foreknowledge.

11. Why cannot Predestination be identified with foreknowledge?

> "Because foreknowledge extends to all creatures, good and bad. He foresees and foreknows everything that is or will be, that is occurring or will occur, whether it be good or bad, since before God all things, whether they be past or future, are manifest and present... But Predestination pertains not at the same time to the godly and the wicked, but only to the children of God who were elected and appointed to eternal life before the foundation of the world was laid (Eph. 1:4, 5)" (Formula of Concord, 650).

12. In what sense is Predestination dependent upon Foreknowledge?

Since God has not predestinated all that He has foreknown ("for all that the perverse, wicked will of the devil and of men purposes and desires to do and will do, God sees and knows before," ibid.), but, in His inexplicable will, has allowed a certain measure of freedom and contingency in His creatures, and afforded them a degree of moral responsibility, knowing from all eternity what will be the result of their use of this trust, He also has determined how in every case their decision and activity will be treated. The divine foreknowledge unerringly records all the future, and the divine will acts with reference to all thus recorded without destroying the freedom of the will of the creature with respect to those things which He has left to this freedom (see Chapter 5, 18). When, therefore, God has willed that He will be determined in a certain decision by the free decision of a creature, that freedom of the creature will certainly be guaranteed in the result; but what in the exercise of this freedom, the decision of the creature will be, as well as the determination of His will concerning it He knows from all eternity, and makes His plans accordingly.

> "Thus there is no doubt that God most exactly and certainly saw, before the time of the world, and still knows who, of those who are called will believe or will not believe; also who of the converted will persevere in faith and who will not; who after a fall will return and who will perish in their sins" (Formula of Concord, 659).

13. Is the decree of Predestination, therefore, absolute?

The answer to this question depends upon the meaning of "absolute." If it means "fixed," "irrevocable," "including no conditions," it is absolute. The decree of election contains no proviso. Its formula is not: "Mary Magdalene shall be saved, in case, by God's grace, she be in Christ unto the end of life."

The fulfillment or non-fulfillment of the proviso or condition is contained in the foreknowledge which determined the predestination. That Mary Magdalene is in Christ, by God's grace, at the end of her earthly life, is foreseen and foreknown from all eternity; and this being foreknown, she is an elect child of God whose salvation is irrevocably predestinated.

If, however, "absolute" mean that no condition be admitted in the divine foreknowledge, and that there is no order established with respect to which the election is determined, and outside of which there is no election, its application is incorrect.

> "This eternal election or appointment of God to eternal life is not to be considered in God's secret, inscrutable counsel in such a manner as though it comprised in itself nothing further than that God foresaw who and how many would be saved, and who and how many would be damned, or that he only held a review, and would say: 'This one shall be saved, that one shall be damned; this one shall remain steadfast, that one shall not remain steadfast'" (Formula of Concord, 651).

14. Is it conditional?

This must be answered in the same way. In the decree there is no condition or proviso. But the difference between the persons elected and those who are non-elect is determined not by any unwillingness of God to provide for the salvation of all, but upon a different relation and attitude which they bear towards the Order of Salvation provided in Christ.

> "For this reason, the elect are described thus: 'My sheep hear my voice and I know them, and they follow me, and I give unto them eternal life' (John 10:27 sq.). And (Eph. 1:11, 13): Who, according to the purpose, are predestinated to an inheritance, who hear the Gospel, believe in Christ, pray and give thanks, are sanctified in love, have hope, patience and comfort under the cross (Rom. 8:25); and although in them all, this is very weak, yet they hunger and thirst for righteousness (Matt. 5:6). Thus the Spirit of God gives to the elect the testimony that they are the children of God, and, when they know not for what to pray as they ought, He intercedes with groanings that cannot be uttered. Thus, also, Holy Scripture shows that God, who has called us, is so faithful that, when He has begun a good work in us, He also will preserve and continue it unto the end, if we do not turn ourselves from Him, but retain firmly to the end the work begun, for retaining which He has promised His grace" (Formula of Concord, 655).

All this is to the effect, that the elect, according to God's will, comply with a certain order, while the non-elect, not by God's will, are outside of that order.

> "By this particular election, God closed the door of salvation upon no one, when, according to His infallible foreknowledge, He elected not all, but only some to salvation. For this was done, not because He was unwilling to elect all, or because He is even now unwilling that all be saved, but because He knew beforehand that only a few, mid not all would receive His Word, and persevere in faith" (Quenstedt, III, 51)

15. What caution have our theologians shown in applying these terms?

They define the decree as "not absolute, but ordinate and relative; not conditionate, but categorical and simple." By "ordinate" they mean "that which is determined by a certain order of means"; since it is God's good pleasure through the foolishness of what is preached, i.e., through the entire series of agencies comprised in the Gospel, to save them that believe (1 Cor. 1:21). In saying that the decree is not conditionate, they distinguish between it and God's will. When "God willed, according to His immense goodness, to give salvation to all upon the condition of faith in Christ, this will was conditionate, while the decree of election was not conditionate" (Hollazius), since it was based on infallible foreknowledge and was, therefore, as stated under 13, irrevocable, and without a proviso.

16. State the condition upon which the decree which is not conditionate is based?

That the person, concerning whom the decree is made be "in Christ," and that too, "unto the end of life."

> Eph. 1:14. "Even as he chose us in him before the foundation of the world."

No one is elected unless he be and remain in Christ. His being in Christ is not the consequence, but the condition of his election. Nevertheless this "being in Christ" is not a consummation which man attains by his own powers, but as the definition further states (see above, 5) even this is "by the grace of God" (see Chapter, 9, 20). For it is "by the grace of God," that the Son of God became incarnate, and by His obedience procured that merit, in virtue of which alone our salvation and inheritance of eternal life are possible. The sole ground of election, therefore, is the merit of Christ.

17. But does not the expression "in Christ" declare even more than that the merits of Christ have been provided for mans salvation?

It affirms that what Christ has provided has also been applied and appropriated. Although Christ has died for all, not all are elect, since not all are to the end of life "in Christ." What it is "to be in Christ," Paul declares in Phil. 3:9:

> "And be found in him, not having a righteousness of mine own, even that which is of the law, but that which is through faith in Christ, the righteousness which is from God by faith."

"In" denotes "the cause of account of which." The decree of election therefore is in view of the righteousness of Christ, as by faith it belongs to the one who is predestined to eternal life. What distinguishes the nonelect from the elect, is that the former are without, and the latter have the faith which appropriates Christ's righteousness and makes it their own.

18. Does not this introduce a synergistic error into the statement of Predestination by making faith a cause of election, and thus denying that it is an act of God's free will?

No statement can be guarded with such care that it is not liable to be perverted when taken by itself. The relation of faith to Predestination is precisely the same as it has to Justification. Men are justified not on account of faith, but through faith on account of the merits of Christ; or on account of faith apprehending the merits of Christ. Precisely so, they are elected, not on account of faith, but through faith on account of the merits of Christ; or on account of faith apprehending the merits of Christ. The merits of Christ do not justify, unless apprehended by faith; neither does faith justify, if it apprehend any other object than Christ, or if it even apprehend Christ outside of His divinely-human person and the righteousness which He has acquired through His priestly office. Both Predestination and Justification, therefore, are on account of the merits of Christ apprehended by faith. Nothing can be ascribed to faith in the one sphere, that cannot be ascribed to it in the other; neither should anything be denied to it in the one sphere, that is not denied to it in the other. Justification is the record in time of God's eternal Predestination; Predestination is the record from all eternity of that which was to occur in our Justification. Hence such difficulties must always be solved by turning to the article of faith particularly involved. (See especially Chapters 17, 15-17; 18)

19. Can you cite the opinion of any Lutheran theologian generally recognized as worthy of consideration?

> "With loud voice we declare that, in electing man to eternal life, God found nothing good in man, and that He regarded neither good works nor the use of the free will, nor even faith itself, so as to elect these movements or

on account of them to elect some men; but we say that it was the only and sole merit of Christ, whose worth God regarded and out of pure grace made the decree of election. Nevertheless since the merit of Christ has a place in man only through faith, we teach that election was made with respect to the merit of Christ to be apprehended by faith. All those and they alone, we maintain, have been elected by God from eternity unto salvation, who, He foresaw, would, by the efficacy of the Holy Spirit through the ministry of the Gospel, truly believe in Christ as Redeemer, and persevere in faith unto the end of life. We will present, with utmost brevity, the arguments for this: (1) Election was made in Christ (Eph. 1:4). But it is only through faith that we are in Christ (Eph. 3:17). Therefore they 'who hereafter believe in him,' are elect (1 Tim. 1:16). (2) Election is a decree concerning justifying and saving men. But it is only by faith that God in time justifies and saves men (Rom. 3, 4; Gal. 2, 3; Eph. 2, etc.). Therefore God determined from eternity to justify and save only those who would believe; and, as a consequence, He has chosen all those and those alone who He has foreseen, would by faith remain in Christ. (3) Outside cf Christ none are elected. But sinful men, without regard to faith, are outside of Christ. Sinful men, therefore, are not elected without regard to faith. Accordingly, as Paul says (Eph. 1:4), that God has elected us in Christ, so 2 Thess. 2:13 says that He elected us in faith; since we could not have been elected in Christ except with regard to faith apprehending Christ... Justification which occurred in time, is a mirror of the Election which occurred before time" (Gerhard, II, 86).

"The things which God does in time are the manifestation of what He decreed to do in time. From this, we infer that the manner in which He justifies and saves men in time, is that of the eternal decree concerning their salvation, which is called election... But

John 6:40. "This is the will of my Father that every one that beholdeth the Son and believeth on him, should have eternal life."

...To sum up, the decree and the execution of the decree most exactly correspond. From this it is manifest that the decree neither of Election nor of Reprobation is said to be absolute, but that the decree of Election was made with respect to Christ as He is to be apprehended by faith, and that all they and they alone are elect of God, whom God foresaw would perseveringly believe, by the efficacy of the Holy Spirit through the ministry of the Word, in Christ the restorer of the human race. So, in turn, the decree of Reprobation was made with respect to final impenitence and unbelief" (ibid., II, 49).

20. Can this be reduced to a tabular form?

Yes.

Paul was	Justified Elected	In view of	The Merits of Christ accepted by faith; or, of Faith accepting the merits of Christ.

The formula of Justification and that of Election are one and the same. Nothing dare be admitted with respect to Justification which is rejected with respect to Election.

> *Est enim vera regula ilia usitata: Eaedem sunt causae Electionis quae sunt Justiticationis* (Hutter, L. T., 801).

The Four and the Eight Factors to be accounted in constructing the doctrine

21. What factors must always be kept clearly in mind in attempting to construct a satisfactory statement of this subject?

> "The following pillars standing, the Absolute Decree falls; the Absolute Decree standing, these pillars fall:
>
> "1. God seriously wishes all to be saved.
>
> "2. God created all in Adam according to His own image, a part of which is immortality.
>
> "3. Christ, by His obedience and sanctification, merited salvation for all.
>
> "4. The Holy Spirit in the Word offers the means of salvation to all.
>
> "No one, therefore, has been excluded from salvation by any absolute decree" (Gerhard, II, 81).

"We should accustom ourselves not to speculate concerning the pure, secret, concealed, inscrutable foreknowledge of God, but how the counsel, purpose and ordination of God in Christ Jesus who is the true Book of Life have been revealed to us through the Word, viz: ...

"1. That the human race should be truly redeemed and reconciled with God through Christ...

"2. That such merit and benefits of Christ should be offered, presented and distributed through His Word and Sacraments.

"3. That He would be active and efficacious in us by His Holy Spirit through the Word...

"4. That all who in true repentance, receive Christ by a true faith, He would justify...

"5. That those who are thus justified, He would sanctify...

"6. That He would defend them against the devil, the world and the flesh, and would rule and lead them in His ways, and when they stumble would raise them again, and under the cross and in temptation, would comfort and preserve them.

"7. That the good work He has begun He would support unto the end. ....

"8. That those whom He has elected, called and justified, He would eternally save and glorify in life eternal" (Formula of Concord, 653).

Faith sometimes a condition, sometimes a result

22. But is not faith the fruit and result of Predestination?

A confusion may readily result by using the word Predestination in two different senses. *Bene docet qui bene distinguit.* On the one hand, Predestination refers to God's determination to provide salvation for man and includes the entire series of agencies whereby this is to be accomplished, viz., the Incarnation of the Son of God, Redemption, the gift of the Holy Spirit, Calling, Illumination, Regeneration, Justification, Sanctification, the Means of Grace, the Church, the

Ministry, etc. In this sense, faith is a fruit and result of Predestination. But, on the other hand, Predestination is applied to that which makes a difference between men, i.e., the eternal Election whose effect is to produce two distinct classes, the elect and the non-elect. This is the sense in which it is being treated here. Faith is not the result of Predestination in this sense, but enters into the condition, viz., as joined with the merit of Christ which it apprehends. Even the merit of Christ is in the one sense of Predestination, a result, for the gift of Christ was the result of foreordination; but in the other, and that the usual sense of the term, it is the condition.

Important caution concerning Faith

23. Is there no need of caution, however, in stating the relation of faith to election?

Certainly. For faith is too frequently regarded a result of man's own powers, and the words of the Catechism forgotten:

> "I believe that I cannot, of my own reason and strength, believe in Jesus Christ, my Lord or come to Him."

There is a strong tendency to make of it a ground instead of a mere organ for receiving mercy. (See Chapter 17, 11-13.) It is to this that the Formula of Concord refers when it says (665):

> "It is false and wrong, when it is taught that not alone the mercy of God and the most holy merit of Christ, but that there is also in us a cause of God's election, on account of which God has chosen us to eternal life."

The Elect: Are all who believe elect; can the elect fall; can one know whether he be elect.

24. Are all who believe elect or predestinated to life?

It has been shown (Chapter 17, 36), that faith can be lost, and that too, so as never to be restored (Chapter 17, 37; 8, 59, 60). Not all, therefore, who are regenerate are elect; but they only who, at the end of life, believe in Christ. For the promise is:

> Rev. 2:10. "Be thou faithful unto death, and I will give thee the crown of life."

25. Can the Elect fall from God's grace?

Yes; but only for a time. For if they were to be permanently alienated from God, they could not be elect, since the divine foreknowledge is infallible (see Chapter 5, 17, 18).

26. Can one know whether he be elect?

He can know that he is regenerate and justified (Chapter 17, 38-40), and that no means or effort will be lacking on God's part, that he be retained in this grace.

> John 10:28. "No man shall snatch them out of my hand." Phil. 1:6.

But as man, by his own will, can abandon this grace at any time during his earthly career, his certainty of election is "not absolute, but conditionate and ordinate." Hence Paul apprehends,

> "...lest that, by any means, after that I have preached to others, I myself should be rejected," 1 Cor. 9:27.

But at the close of life, he is so absolutely sure of his election, that, with the greatest confidence, he exclaims:

> 2 Tim. 4:7, 8. "I have fought the good fight, I have kept the faith, I have finished my course; henceforth, there is laid up for me the crown of righteousness which the Lord, the righteous Judge, shall give me at that day."

> "Between the Scylla of perpetual doubt and the Charybdis of absolute security, the ship of our faith, following the pole-star of God's Word, makes its way. We trust God on account of the rich and infallible promises which He has given us; yet, at the same time, we fear God, on account of the weakness and temptations of our flesh; and, therefore, with most earnest entreaties, pray Him for the gift of perseverance, and trust that we will obtain it, but yet, to avoid all carnal security, ask that our faith be confirmed by meditation upon the Word and the use of the Sacraments, and earnestly strive to advance daily in the path of godliness" (Gerhard, II, 105).

27. What is the remedy for doubt as to whether one be in the number of the Elect?

> "If faith be weakened in temptations, 'and the sense of faith be almost extinguished, we ought to regard the general promises in which God offers His grace to all; the merit of Christ which concerns all; the ministry of the Word and Sacraments, in which God offers the blessings of His Son to all; Baptism, the answer of a good conscience towards God; we must resort to the use of the Lord's Supper, in which Christ offers the very body for us to eat, which He gave to death for us, and the very blood for us to drink which He shed for us on the altar of the cross. From all this we ought to infer that God sincerely wishes that, knowing our sins, we believe in Christ, and by faith become partakers of eternal salvation" (ibid.).

The Non-elect: Meaning of "Reprobation," Why Predestination is particular, Rom. 9:15 sqq explained.

28. What of the disposition of God towards the Non-elect?

They are said to be "reprobate" (1 Cor. 9:27; 2 Cor. 13:5), i.e., "disapproved," "abandoned," "rejected." 29. Is Reprobation exactly the reverse of Predestination or Election?

No. For Reprobation simply leaves fallen man to the consequences of his sin, while Predestination or Election introduces a new order, viz., that of Redemption by which salvation from sin is provided.

30. Is the state of the Reprobate precisely the same as though Christ had not died and the offers of the Gospel had not been made them?

No. Their guilt and punishment are increased.

> John 15:22. "If I had not come and spoken unto them, they had not had sin; but now they have no excuse for their sin." 3:18. "He that believeth not hath been judged already, because he hath not believed on the name of the only-begotten Son of God."

John 16:9. "He will convict the world of sin, because they believe not on me."

31. What then is Reprobation?

It is the divine decree according to which, God, in the exercise of His justice, leaves those who to the end of life reject the offers of divine grace to the consequences of their sins, and particularly to those of the increased guilt incurred by not believing in Christ.

32. Why is Predestination particular instead of universal?

The answer for this question is not to be found in the absolute will of God. For "from eternity he determined to so concur with His Word and the preaching of the Gospel, that no one would lack faith except those who, to the end of life, would despise the means of conferring faith and grace itself."[23] All passages of Scripture in which God declares that it is not His will that any perish, clearly prove this (Ez. 33:11; 2 Peter 3:9; Matt. 23:37; see Chapter 9, 10-16). Predestination becomes particular, therefore, through the free will of man repudiating and opposing, until the end of life, God's purposes of love.

33. But is not this contrary to Rom. 9:15 "I will have mercy on whom I will have mercy," "Whom he will he hardeneth'?

This passage is entirely misunderstood when it is interpreted as though it taught that God created some for wrath, as well as some for mercy. Paul is doubtless wrestling with doubts and difficulties which often met him in the consideration of this question. The "old man" in Paul questions God's justice with respect to the different destinies of men, and the argument of the "new man" in Paul in reply, is to the effect, that the difference rests not upon justice, but upon pure mercy; and yet that, in this exercise of mercy, even though it would be restricted, there would be no violation of justice. Where all deserved eternal death, there could be no complaint of injustice no difference how many or how few were included in the Plan of Redemption. The question as to the extent of this provision is clearly answered in other passages.

23 "*Omnibus hominibus sufficiens gratia datur; iniidelibus, ut credant; fidelibus, ut perseverent.*" — (Hutter, L. T. 798.)

"Since it was the Apostle's purpose to vindicate the justice of God from the tongues of Jewish objectors, he demonstrates that God is everywhere just, whether, out of mercy, He save men, or, by His just judgment, He harden and condemn them. As an example of hardening, he cites Pharaoh, the greatest persecutor of the Church. But upon whom He wishes to have mercy, and whom He wishes to harden, the Apostle does not determine in this passage. All Scripture, however, shows that God in His beloved Son wills to have mercy upon all who believe, and that He wills to harden those who contumaciously strive against His Word, in order in them to declare His justice, as is shown by the example of Pharaoh."

"The application is not to be made that, as the potter from the same mass makes some vessels for honor and others for dishonor; so God, by an absolute decree creates some predestinated to salvation, and, by an absolute decree, creates others rejected to condemnation and destruction. For this would be in conflict with:

"1. The Context. The Apostle does not say that God prepares vessels of wrath, but that 'with much long-suffering he endureth vessels of wrath fitted unto destruction.'"What God endures with much long-suffering, He does not Himself make. Augustine has beautifully said: 'God does not make vessels of wrath, but finds them; He does not find vessels of grace, but makes them.'

"2. With Scripture, which so interprets this long-suffering of God, that by it God invites to repentance' (Rom. 2:4). How, therefore, can He fit them for destruction, who wishes that they should no longer be vessels of wrath?

"3. With the very words of the Apostle. They are called 'vessels of wrath'; but there can be no wrath of God, where no iniquity of man has preceded.

"4. With the rules of illustrations. As Chrysostom says: 'Illustrations must not be taken throughout.'" The potter deals with senseless clay which does not resist his will. Can this be said of men some of whom resist the Holy Spirit, despise the counsel of God, and repel the Word? With neither class of vessels, whether fitted for honor or for shame, is the potter angry. But of men. fitted for destruction, the Apostle says that they are 'vessels of wrath.'

"5. With the article of Creation. For man was created in the image of God, of which immortality was the chief part. With the article of Redemption; for the Son of Man came to save that which was lost. With the very nature of God, who is not angry with his own work (Wis. 11:25, etc.)" (Gerhard, II, 63 sqq.).

The doctrine of Predestination not to be ignored.

34. As this article contains so many difficulties, would it not be better to entirely ignore it?

By no means. Only, as before stated, care must be taken that it be treated at the proper place, and upon the basis of all the other articles.

Cf. the Latin axiom: *Omne simile claudicat.*

> "For the doctrine concerning this article, if presented from and according to the pattern of the divine Word, neither can nor should be regarded as useless or unnecessary, much less as causing offense or injury, because the Holy Scriptures not only in but one place and incidentally, but in many places, thoroughly discuss and explain the same. Therefore, on account of abuse or misunderstanding, we should not neglect or reject the doctrine of the divine Word, but precisely on that account, in order to avert all abuse and misunderstanding, the true meaning should and must be explained from the foundation of Scripture" (Formula of Concord, 649).

35. What consolation does the consideration of this doctrine in its true place and order afford?

[A.] It shows most effectually "that we are justified and saved without all works and merits of ours, purely out of grace, alone for Christ's sake.

For before we were born, yea before the foundation of the world was laid, when we could do nothing good, we were chosen, according to God's purpose, out of grace and in Christ, to salvation."

[B.] It shows that God was so solicitous concerning this salvation, that before the world began, He deliberated concerning it and ordained how to bring it to pass.

Beautifully expressed in a familiar hymn of Paul Gerhardt:

> "From all eternity, with Love
> Unchangeable, Thou hast me viewed.
> Ere knew this beating heart to move,
> Thy tender mercy me pursued."

So also J. A. Rothe:

> "Now I have found the ground wherein
> Sure my soul's anchor may remain; The wounds of Jesus, for my sin,
> Before the world's foundation slain;
> Whose mercy shall unshaken stay,
> When heaven and earth are fled away."

[C.] It shows that He was so earnest concerning my salvation, that He has put its accomplishment in the hands of one no less powerful than the Son of God Himself, and that from these hands no one can wrest us (John 10:28: Rom. 8:38, 39).

[D.] It shows also the part which the cross, i.e., the sorrows, afflictions and temptations of this life, performs in contributing to the attainment of the divine purpose.

Through them, as Paul teaches in Rom. 8:29, the elect are fashioned after the image of the Son of God (see Formula of Concord, 657, 658).

How to be guarded

36. In what does the special peril lie in its treatment?

> "Our curiosity always has much more pleasure in investigating those things that are hidden and abstruse than what God has revealed in His Word.'"

However far we proceed in our treatment, we have no sooner solved one difficulty, than another meets us. Mystery crowd's upon mystery, like summit upon summit upon the traveler in a mountainous region, who finds each mountain height only the opening to other heights beyond. No human terminology can be devised to adequately express the doctrine, or to be beyond the need of qualifications and explanations, so as to avoid being misunderstood. These difficulties, the Formula of Concord declares, "we cannot harmonize," and what is more, "we have not been commanded to do so," i.e., God has not called us to such task. Here, as in every other article of divine revelation,

> Deut. 29:29. "The secret things belong unto Jehovah our God; but the things that are revealed belong unto us and to our children forever."

Like John, in the Apocalypse (Rev. 4:1), we see in this doctrine a door opened in heaven, and are permitted to look through and get a faint glimpse of what is beyond. Let us beware of penetrating farther than to the utmost limit of that for which we have God's call. As in the doctrine of the Trinity, and of the Incarnation of the Son of God, we must be content to stand there. Faith begins, where reason ends.

Appendix: On The Spiritual Priesthood Of Believers. By Dr. Philip J. Spener (1677).

Translated From The Bibliothck Theologischer Klossiker, Vol. XXI, Gotha, 1889.

1. What is the Spiritual Priesthood?

The right which our Savior Jesus Christ has purchased for all men and for which He has anointed with His Holy Spirit those who believe on Him, in virtue of which they bring acceptable sacrifices to God, pray for themselves and others, and should edify, each himself and his neighbors.

2. Is there any scriptural testimony concerning it?

Yes; Rev. 1:5, 6; 5:10; 1 Peter 2:9.

3. Why is it called a Spiritual Priesthood?

Because it brings no bodily, but only spiritual sacrifices, and, in its office, has to do only with spiritual functions (1 Peter 2:5).

4. Whence is this Spiritual Priesthood derived?

From Jesus Christ, the true High Priest, according to the order of Melchisedek (Ps. 110:4), who, since He has no successor in His priesthood, but remains alone to all eternity a High Priest, has also made Christians priests before His Father, whose sacrifices have their holiness and are accepted before God solely because of His (Heb. 8:1-6; 7:23-28; cf. Question 2; 1 Peter 2:5).

5. How do Christians become priests?

As in the Old Testament, priests were not elected, but were born to the office, so it is regeneration in baptism that gives us the divine right of children of God, and therefore puts us into the spiritual priesthood which is combined with this (James 1:18).

6. Does not anointing also pertain to the Priesthood?

Yes; and just as priests of old were set apart with holy ointment (Ex. 28:41), and just as Christ was anointed (Ps. 451-7) with the most holy oil of gladness, the Holy Ghost, and, on this: account, is called Christ, "the Anointed One"; so out of grace (John 1:16) has He made those who believe on Him partakers, although in a less degree (Ps. 45:7; Heb. 1:9), of the same anointing.

7. Are all believers, then, partakers of the anointing?

Yes. All have received and continue to possess it, as long as they persevere in the divine order (1 John 2:19, 26).

8. But for what purpose was Christ anointed?

As King, High Priest and Prophet, since it was customary in the Old Testament to anoint such persons.

9. For what are those who believe on Him anointed?

Likewise as Kings, Priests and Prophets, since the office of prophet is included under that of priest (see Q. 2).

10. Who are such spiritual priests?

All Christians without distinction (1 Peter 2:9); old and young, man and woman, bond and free (Gal. 3:28).

11. But does not the name "priest" belong only to the preachers?

No. Preachers, according to their office, are not properly priests. They are nowhere so called in the New Testament, but are "ministers of Christ" "stewards of the mysteries of God," "bishops," "ciders," "ministers of the Gospel," "of the Word" etc. On the contrary, the name "priest," is a general name of all Christians, and does not belong to preachers in any other sense than to other Christians (1 Cor. 4:1; 3:5; 1 Tim. 3:1, 2; 5:17; Eph. 3:6, 7; Acts 26:17; Luke 1:2).

12. But are not preachers the only "spiritual" ones?

No. This part also belongs to all Christians (Rom. 8:5, 9).

13. What are the duties of the Spiritual Priesthood?

They are of various kinds. But we may distribute them into three chief functions: 1. That of sacrifice; 2. that of praying and blessing, and 3. that of the divine Word. Of these, the former 'has always been known as the proper office of the priesthood, while the last is also called the prophetic office.

14. What have spiritual priests to offer?

First of all, themselves, with all that belongs to them, so that they desire no more to serve themselves, but only Him who has purchased and redeemed them (Rom. 6:13; 14:7, 8; 2 Cor. 5:15; 1 Cor. 6:20; Ps. 4:5; 110:3; I Peter 3:18). Therefore, as the sacrifices in the Old Testament were separated from other animals (Ex. 12:3-6), so they must separate themselves from the world and its defilements (Rom. 12:2; 2 Cor. 6:14-18; James 1:27).

For this reason, they were called "an elect race" (Lev. 20:26; 1 Peter 2:9).

15. How have we to offer our bodies and their members to God?

By devoting our bodies not to sin, but only to God's glory and service (Rom. 12:1; 6:13; cf. Q. 14); and, therefore, keeping it under discipline (1 Cor. 9:27), and by suppressing the wicked lusts which attempt to work through our members. This lust is known in Scripture as "cutting off" our members (Matt. 5:29, 30; 18:8, 9; 19:12).

16. Hew should we offer our souls to God.

To the end that, with our bodies, they be the holy temples and dwelling-places of God (1 Cor. 3:16, 17); that our reason be brought into captivity to the obedience of Christ (2 Cor. 10:5); that our will submit to the divine will with true resignation and prompt compliance (1 Sam. 15:22; Matt. 6:10, 26, 39; Heb. 10:5-7); that our spirit and heart in true penitence be an acceptable offering to God (Ps. 51:17, 18).

17. How have we, further, to offer ourselves as a sacrifice to God?

By being willing to accept every cross from His hand; by offering ourselves for Him to send upon us whatever pleases Him (2 Sam. 15:26); and being ready, also, to surrender our life according to His will, for His glory (Phil. 2:17, 18; 2 Tim. 4:6).

18. Should we not also sacrifice our old Adam to God?

Just as "the devoted thing" (Lev. 27:28, 29) which was killed, as consecrated and thus sacrificed to God; so, in the same sense, should we put to death and sacrifice our old Adam (Rom. 6:6; Gal. 5-24; Col. 3:6).

19. What else have we to offer?

Our hearts and tongues for prayer, praise and thanksgiving (Ps. 141:2; 50:14, 23; 69:30, 31; Heb. 13:15; Ps. 27:6; 107:22; 116:17, 18; Hos. 14:3); as well as our bodily possessions, if we see that His glory is thereby promoted, and there be occasion to show mercy to those in distress, especially to the members of Christ (Heb. 13:16. Matt. 25:40; Acts 24:17; Phil. 4:18; Luke 21:1-4).

20. Is there nothing still further for us to offer?

Yes; especially the doctrine of the Gospel, and with it our fellowmen, who are thereby converted and sanctified to God (Mai. 1:11; Rom. 15:16; Is. 60:7; Phil. 2:17, 18; cf. Q. 17).

21. But have we not also to bring such offering to God, in order to atone for our sins?

No; for Christ alone, by His sacrifice, has made satisfaction for us; and whoever adds his own sacrifice for satisfaction, disparages and contemns that of Christ

(Heb. 10:14).

22. But are the above-mentioned sacrifices which we bring to God, entirely pure?

Of themselves, they would not be perfectly pure, but, in virtue of the holy sacrifice of Jesus, ours are also pure, and please God, for His Son's sake (1 Peter 2:5).

23. How often and when should we offer such sacrifices?

Always; throughout our entire lives; for while we devote and consecrate ourselves, once for all, with body and soul, when we first give our hearts to His service, such resolution should not only be often repeated, but also daily, yea hourly, such sacrifices should be offered the Lord.

24. Beside the sacrifices, what else belonged to the office of Christ, as Priest?

As the High Priest of the Old Testament blessed (Num. 6:23-27) and prayed for the people (Num. 16:47; 2 Chron. 30:27); and Christ, also, as a true High Priest of the New Testament has given us His blessing (Mark 10:16; Luke 24:50; Acts 3:25, 26; Eph. 1:3), and prayed (John 17:9, 20; Luke 22:31, 32; 23:24) and still prays for us (Rom. 8:34; 1 John 2:1; Heb. 9:24; 7:25; see Q. 4); it is the duty of Christians to offer to God prayers not only for themselves, but for their fellowmen (1 Tim. 2:1-3; James 5:14-16; Eph. 6:18, 19; Acts 12:5), and to bless them (Matt. 5:44; Rom. 12:14; 1 Peter 3:9). This prayer and blessing, for Christ's sake, is not useless, but is effectual (Matt. 18:19, 20; James 5:16; 1 Tim. 2:3).

25. What is, then, the third office of priest?

As priests were occupied with God's Law (Mai. 2:7), so also it is the office of spiritual priests that the Word of God should dwell richly among them (Col. 3:16). This is known otherwise as the Prophetic office.

26. Are all Christians, then, preachers, and have they to devote themselves to the office of the ministry?

No; but in order to fulfill this office publicly, in the Church, and before and over all, a special call is necessary. Whoever, then assumes this right above others or attempts to force himself into the ministry, thereby sins (Rom. 10:15; Heb. 5:4). Hence the teachers are one, and the hearers another class (1 Cor. 12:28-30), as to their reciprocable duties the Haustafel (i.e., Table of Duties appended to the Catechism) gives explicit information.

27. But what, then, have they to do with the Word of God?

To use it for themselves, and alongside of and with others.

28. How have they to use it for themselves?

Not only by hearing it when preached in the church, but also by diligently reading or having it read.

29. Is it. then, the duty of all Christians to diligently read the Scriptures?

Yes. Since it is a letter of the Heavenly Father to all His children, no child of God is excluded, but all have the right and command to read it (John 5:39).

30. But would it not be better, if they would simply believe all that they hear from their pastor?

No; but they are to search the Scriptures, in order to test the doctrine of their pastor, so that their faith may rest not upon their regard for and confidence in a man, but upon divine truth (Acts 17:11).

31. Are the Scriptures, therefore, not too difficult for simple persons who are without education?

No. For even in the Old Testament, the divine Word was given, in order to make wise the simple (Ps. 19:7; 119:130), and that fathers might teach it diligently to their children (Deut. 6:6, 7). But the New Testament is still clearer (Rom. 13:12; 1 John 2:8). Accordingly Christ did not direct His teaching to the wise and prudent of this world, but to the simple (Matt. 11:25, 26). Every one also who wants to understand Jesus, must put aside all worldly wisdom and become a child (Matt. 18:3; Luke 18:17). Paul, therefore, and all other Apostles did not discourse in high words but in the power of God, which was hidden from the wise, but revealed to infants, in accordance with the unsearchable wisdom of God, which "by foolish preaching" has brought to naught the wise of this world (1 Cor. 1:18-24; 2:1-5; 2 Cor.

1:12; 10:4, 5). Hence the Apostles have written their epistles mostly to unlearned and simple men, w? ho could not have understood them, from, heathen arts or sciences, but who, without them, by the grace of God, could understand them to their salvation (1 Cor. 1:2; 2:6-10).

32. But is there not in the Scriptures much that is obscure, and. therefore, too high for the simple?

The Scriptures themselves are not obscure, as they are not darkness, but a light (Ps. 119:105; 2 Peter 1:19). Nevertheless there is much in them, too high not only for the simple, but also for the most learned, and which, because of our darkened eyes, appears to us as dark (1 Cor. 13:9, 10).

33. Would it not, therefore, be better if plain persons would not read them?

No. As the learned should not be hindered from searching them by the fact that they frequently fail to understand many passages, so also we should not interfere with their study by simple, godly souls who seek in them a confirmation of their faith.

34. Can they then, in their simplicity, learn to understand them?

Yes, of course. As, first of all, the chief points of doctrine and rules of life are so clearly taught in the Scriptures, that every simple person as well as the learned, can learn and comprehend them; where godly minds have received and applied with obedience the first truths which are offered them, and continue, with meditation and prayer, to read the Scriptures, God the Holy Ghost will open to them their meaning more and more, so that they can also learn and understand that in Scripture which is higher and more difficult, so far as it be necessary for the strengthening of their faith, instruction in life, and consolation (Matt. 13:12; John 14:21; 2 Tim. 3:15-17).

35. But as they do not have the assistance of foreign languages and of sciences of various kinds, how is it possible for them to understand the Scriptures?

It would be desirable if all Christians could diligently devote themselves to the study of the Hebrew and Greek languages, in which the Scriptures were written, as they are accustomed to do with other foreign languages needed for secular pursuits, and thus, as far as possible, could learn from the Holy Spirit in His own language. But since, by God's grace, the Scriptures are now translated into other languages, so that every one may find therein enough for his necessary knowledge of Christianity, the want of acquaintance with foreign languages does not hinder godly Christians from such true knowledge of that which God regards profitable for their edification. Much less is the want of acquaintance with other sciences a hindrance, since, even in the case of the learned, they are not properly means for the saving knowledge of the truth, but, when rightly used, only serve to explain further the truth that has been learned by the soul, and to properly state it, and to establish and vindicate it against the attacks of others.

36. Whence, then, do simple, godly Christians have the ability to understand the Scriptures?

By the illumination of the Holy Spirit, at whose prompting they were first committed to writing, so that, without His light, they cannot be understood (2 Peter 1:21; 1 Cor. 2:12). But God has promised the Holy Spirit to all who call upon Him, and, therefore, not merely to the learned (Luke 11:13; James 1:5; 1 John 5:14. 15). From His anointing and illumination, therefore, they understand according to the measure of grace allotted each one. everything in Scripture which is needed for their salvation and growth in the inner man (1 John 2:20; Eph. 1:17, 18).

37. But what have they to do in the reading of the Scriptures, in order to be assured of their truth?

1. That they never come to the Scriptures without earnest prayer for the gift of the Holy Spirit, and with the purpose to accept its power and efficacy, and not only to learn to know, but also to obediently apply what they learn, to the glory of God.
2. That they do not allow their reasons to be masters, but that they most carefully attend to the words of the Holy Ghost, as they are written, and compare these words with what precedes and follows; that they ponder and

believe its meaning, and therefore regard every word of the Holy Ghost with the closest consideration, and examine whatever is read in the light also of other passages of Scripture.

3. That they read everything with a personal application to themselves, so far as it concerns them and is profitable for their edification.
4. That they, first of all, take to themselves whatever they find clear therein, and base their faith upon it. and immediately order their lives according to the obligation which they recognize.
5. That what in the beginning they find too difficult to be understood, they pass over and reserve, until gradually after much reading and prayer, if they continue faithful to the truth they have previously known, they obtain more light in regard to passages previously not understood.
6. That they always in humility, receive and put into practice all the knowledge which God gives them, and be content with His grace.
7. That they be ready and willing to converse concerning Scripture with godly preachers and other Christian persons, and if they be perplexed, take counsel of such advisers, and be willing, where, by God's grace they show them the true meaning of a passage, to receive it humbly and in the fear of God.

38. Is it necessary, then, to the salutary and living knowledge of Scripture, that we should seek to be improved thereby?

Yes, of course; for otherwise we read it not as the Word of the great God, which it, nevertheless, is. Regard for this should not only produce in us profound reverence, but also obedience. What we hear from His Word and mouth, we should do immediately and much more zealously than if a great earthly potentate had enjoined it upon us. He who does not read the Scriptures in this way, and who does not read them as the Word of God, and thus confines their power to himself, does not attain to their true spiritual knowledge (John 7:17; Ps. 111:10; 2 Peter 1:8, 9; 3:16; 2 Cor. 4:3, 4; 2 Thess. 2: io; ii; 1 John 2:3, 4; 4:7, 8).

39. But How can readers hinder this use of Scripture and thus do themselves injury?

1. When, against the rules above given, they read the Scriptures without earnest prayer and without the purpose of divine obedience, but only from motives of personal ambition and to satisfy their curiosity.

2. When they follow the judgments of their reason, and give them more weight than the words of the Holy Ghost.
3. When they consider not w r hat is profitable for their edification, but only what they may use for their glory or in controversy with others.
4. When they despise the simple passages, and those easily understood, but
5. Apply themselves only to those that are more difficult, and concerning which there has been much controversy, in order to find in them something that is out of the ordinary range of thought, and may make them more conspicuous.
6. When they use what they learn with pride, and so as to serve their own honor.
7. When they think that they alone are wise, selfishly resist better instruction, take pleasure in controversy, and receive nothing with modesty and discretion.
8. But especially when they lead a carnal life, so that the Holy Spirit cannot abide in the them. In such persons, the reading of the Holy Scriptures effects nothing. They receive only a natural knowledge of the letter of the Scriptures, without the inner power of the Spirit, and, by God's judgment, can, therefore, become only the more hardened and incapable (2 Tim. 3:7-9; Titus 1:15, 16; Jude 5:10). Compare passages under Q 38.

40. But would it not be better to leave the more diligent investigation of the Scriptures to the preachers, and for the rest to abide by their simplicity?

All Christians are bound to simplicity, i.e., not to desire to investigate what God has not revealed, so that their reasons should not be masters in regard to matters of faith. But if by abiding by simplicity, it be meant that they who are not preachers should not endeavor always to grow in knowledge, this is contrary to God's will, shameful ignorance, indolence and ingratitude towards the riches of divine revelation; since it is our duty to endeavor not to be simple but to be wise and intelligent, and. by means of practice, to have our senses exercised to distinguish good and evil (Heb. 5:14; Rom. 16:19; 1 Cor. 14:20; Eph. 1:15-19; 4:14; Col. 1:9-12, 28).

41. What, then, would one do who would commend such simplicity to the people?

He would thereby directly contradict God's command and will, detract from His glory, obstruct the progress of His Kingdom, and hinder all the good which can and should arise by such growth in knowledge, to the greatest danger of the souls of others, and to his own condemnation.

42. But where all would so diligently study the Scriptures, would not confusion result?

If such study proceed only from curiosity and carnal science, from which the attempt is made to derive ambitious theories and to engage in controversy with others, no good can result. But if conducted according to the above rules, a divine and salutary wisdom follows, which prevents rather than creates all confusion (James 3:17, 18).

43. But are Christians always to be occupied with God s Word, so as no longer to attend to their worldly business?

It is indeed their greatest joy to be occupied with their God and His Word rather than with their own necessities (Ps. 119:103). But since they live in the world, and, therefore, both need labor for the support of their bodily life, and, for the general good, have been placed 'by God in particular callings, where they have bodily labor and business, they discharge these also, according to the power which God has given them, with conscientious diligence, avoid all idleness, and? in such service, show their fidelity towards God and their love of their fellow-men (Luke 10:39-42; 1 Cor. 7.20 sq.; 1 Thess. 4. 11 sq.; 2 Thess. 3:11 sq.).

44. But have Christians to treat God's Word only for their own good?

No, but they should act in this with and by others for their edification. Compare Questions 25-27; 1 Peter 4:10; 2:9; 1 Thess. 5:11.

45. What is the preaching of which Peter speaks (1 Peter 2:9)?

That they speak with others concerning it and praise the grace, kindness and fidelity of our Father in heaven, who has redeemed us men from the power of darkness, from sin, death, the devil and hell, and, by the Holy Ghost, has called us to the marvelous light of righteousness and blessedness; and, on this account, that they should no more walk in darkness, but in the light. This summary comprises all that they are to preach.

46. Has the Christian, then, an obligation with respect to the salvation and edification of others?

Yes, of course. This is indicated again and again in the Word of God, and all the parts of the Catechism teach it.

47. How is it shown in the Ten Commandments?

We have in the Second Table the general command to love our neighbor as ourselves. His life, i.e., all his welfare is entrusted to us in the Fifth Commandment. If then I so love myself, as, first of all, to care for my soul and its temporal and eternal welfare, I am under obligation to show the same love towards my fellow men. Again, if, out of love, I am under obligation to protect him from all danger to life and body, this love obliges me still more to help him, as I am able, from not suffering any peril of soul (James 5:19, 20).

48. What is taught us on this point in the Apostles' Creed?

Since in it we confess that there is a communion of saints, this refers not only to a fellowship of heavenly blessings which we enjoy in and with one another, but also in the fellowship of a fraternal love that is directed towards a spiritual end (1 Cor. 12:25, 28).

49. What concerning this duty do we find in the Lord's Prayer?

Since we acknowledge and call upon a common Father, we should be charitably and fraternally disposed towards all; such brotherly . love includes care for the welfare of our neighbor.

Further, since, in this prayer, we pray not only for ourselves but also for our brethren, we are also in duty bound to endeavor, with all our powers, that God's name may be sanctified by and in our fellow-men, and that God's Kingdom may be founded and established, and His will in and concerning them be done. For whenever I pray for anything with real earnestness, I try also, so far as I can, to advance it.

50. How does our Baptism refer to this?

Since it is that whereby we are incorporated with Christ, and, therefore, all become members of one spiritual body, such communion requires that every member according to his power advance the highest interest of every other member (1 Cor. 12:13; Eph. 4:15 sqq.).

51. Is the Lord's Supper directed towards the same end?

Yes since it is a meal of love, and (as we are all partakers of one bread), signifies that we are one body; the duty above mentioned is further confirmed (1 Cor. 10:17).

52. But how have believing Christians to use the divine Word among their fellow-men?

Since the Scriptures have been given for doctrine, for reproof, for correction, for instruction in righteousness (2 Tim. 3:16), and besides for consolation (Rom. 15:4); believing Christians should use the Scriptures for all these purposes, and, therefore, should teach, convert from error, admonish, reprove and comfort, as the Scriptures repeatedly show.

53. Is this then for all Christians?

Yes, according to the gifts, which God has given every one; and with observance of the rule that this should not be done publicly before the entire congregation, but privately at every opportunity, and, therefore, without any hindrance of the regular, public office of the ministry.

54. How have Christians to teach?

By endeavoring, when they meet with uninformed people, to instruct them in simplicity of faith, and to lead them to the Scriptures. Besides, when Christians are together and read with one another the Scriptures, that, for the edification of the rest, each one modestly and in love, states what God has enabled him to see in the Scriptures and what he deems serviceable for the edification of the rest (1 Cor. 14:31; Col. 3:16; A. 25).

55. How can they convert the erring?

By showing them their error plainly out of God's Word, and admonishing them to receive the truth (James 5:19, 20; see Q. 47).

56. What have they to do in admonition?

By frequently, and at every opportunity, admonishing and encouraging each other, by God's aid, to carry into effect what they recognize as necessary; by such admonitions hearts are greatly strengthened in that which is good (1 Thess. 5:14; Heb. 3:13; 10:24 sq.; Rom. 15:14) .

57. How do they exercise the office of reproving?

That when they see their brethren sin, they kindly and tenderly reprove them for it, point out the wrong and seek to persuade them to amend their course (Lev. 19:17; Prov. 24:24, 25; Matt. 18:15; Gal. 6:1, 2; Eph. 5:11; 1 Cor. 14:24, 25).

58. How in consoling?

That when they are with the afflicted, they declare to them the divine consolations and encourage them according to their ability (1 Thess. 4:18). Also that, in case of necessity,' where no regular preacher can be had, that they give the consolation of the forgiveness of sins or absolution (Luke 17:3, 4; 2 Cor. 2:10).

59. Do the offices mentioned belong to all Christians?

Yes; and not merely that fathers and mothers of families, in their houses, diligently train their children and servants, but that every Christian also has the right and authority to so do with respect to his brother and sister as the above mentioned passages prove (compare Q. 31; Deut. 6:6, 7; Eph. 6:452 Tim. 3:15).

60. But do Christian women have any share in such priestly offices?

Yes, of course; for here there is neither Jew nor Greek, neither bond nor free, neither man nor woman, but they are all one in Christ Jesus (Gal. 3:28). In Christ, therefore, the distinction between man and woman, as to what is spiritual, is removed. Since God also favors believing women with His spiritual gifts (Joel 2:28, 29; Acts 21:9; 1 Cor. 11:5), their use of these gifts, in the proper order, dare not be forbidden. The Apostles mention the godly women who co-labored with them in edifying others; and so far are they from finding fault with them on this account, that they, on the contrary, praise them for it (Acts 18:26; Rom. 16:1, 2, 12; Phil. 4:2, 3; Titus 2:3-5).

61. But are not women forbidden to teach?

Yes, in the public assembly of the Church. But that outside of such public assembly, they are allowed to teach, is clear from the above passages and Apostolic examples (i Cor. 14:24 sq.; 1 Tim. 2: it, 12).

62. But in what way have Christians to exercise such offices?

According to the opportunity which God and Christian Love offer, so that they do not violently obtrude themselves upon any one, but only deal with those who are ready to accept such offices in love.

63. Is it proper for assemblies to be held for such purposes?

Just as in other respects, they may edify one another according to opportunity, so also it cannot be improper for a few well known friends to come together occasionally expressly for the purpose of going over the sermons with one another and recalling what they have heard, reading the Scriptures and conferring in the fear of the Lord as to how they may apply to practice what they read. This provision only being made, that there be no large assemblies, which may have the appearance of a separation and a public meeting; in order, thereby, not to neglect the public service and to bring it into disesteem, or to disparage the regular preachers, and so as otherwise to keep within their limits, and not to neglect their necessary work and what pertains to their callings; nor so as to act contrary to the will of parents, but to willingly give an account of what they do, and thus avoid every appearance of evil.

64. But should one be appointed in such assembly as a teacher of the others?

No; for such priesthood is common to all alike, and, according to it, one must learn from the rest, as he is ready in the divine order to teach.

65. But is it right for those who have not studied to devote their attention to intricate questions and dark passages of Scripture, and to be intent upon discussing them?

No. This would be officious, since such a matter cannot be readily done except by preachers endowed with extraordinary gifts. It is the office of spiritual priests only to search from God's Word as to how they all may be established in the foundations of the faith, and be edified to a godly life (see Q. 37, No. 5).

66. Are any duties with respect to the Sacraments included in their office?

Since we are in duty bound to furnish the means of grace to children, whom according to His promise, He wishes to be saved, any godly Christian may administer baptism, in case of necessity, where no preacher is to be had; and such baptism in so far as the divine order has been observed, is a right, true and valid baptism. But as to the Holy Supper, a case of necessity cannot ordinarily occur, since, where a regular preacher cannot be had, one desiring consolation may be directed to the spiritual partaking of Christ by faith; hence this Sacrament is not of equal necessity with baptism.

67. But are not disgraceful confusion and disorder in the Church to be apprehended from this?

Where proper care is not taken to keep everything within its limits, this, as well as everything else that is good, may, by man's fault, be perverted to evil. But this is not to be feared where both, viz., the office of the ministry as well as the spiritual priesthood discharge their duties according to Christ's rules.

68. What, then, has the ministry to do, in order that all disorder be avoided?

Ministers should instruct their people frequently concerning this spiritual priesthood, and not hinder the exercise of its functions, but rather guide them. They should note how their hearers do their part, and sometimes demand of them an account. Where they proceed wisely they should support and strengthen them; but where they have failed from ignorance, they should correct them with love and tenderness. Especially they should avoid falling into erroneous speculations, controversy or false doctrine, and proceeding further than is profitable for

Christian edification; and thus throughout to retain the control and Christian guidance of the work.

69. But how have Christian priests to conduct themselves so as to avoid disorder?

By aiming from pure love in all things at their own edification and that of their neighbor, and doing nothing for their own glory, or other carnal purposes; by not undertaking what is too high for them; and, therefore, by their confidential intercourse with godly preachers, asking for their counsel, accepting their aid and affording them every possible facility for the discharge of the duties of their office; cordially giving an account for whatever they do, and following their advice; and especially, by refraining from all detraction and censures of the same and injuring no one in his office, considering that any discord which may result thence will do more damage, than their best efforts can repair.

70. But have not spiritual priests the power to judge their preachers?

Yes; by diligently testing their doctrine as to whether it be according to the divine Word, and when they find it based upon Scripture, following it; but when they find it to be false, and, when without heeding any protests in private conference, they persevere in their error, by avoiding from thence such false doctrine (Acts 17:11; see Q. 30; 1 Thess. 5:20, 21; 1 John 4:1; Matt. 7:15).

About the Author

HENRY EYSTER JACOBS (November 10, 1844 – July 7, 1932) was an American educator and Lutheran theologian. Jacobs was born in Gettysburg, Pennsylvania, the son of professor Michael and Juliana M (Eyster) Jacobs. His sister Julia Jacobs Harpster became a missionary in India; his brother Michael William Jacobs became a judge. He graduated from Pennsylvania College in 1862 and from the Lutheran Theological Seminary at Gettysburg in 1865. Between 1870 and 1883, he was professor at Pennsylvania College. He was then appointed professor of systematic theology in The Lutheran Theological Seminary in Mount Airy, where he also assumed the office of dean in 1894. In 1920, he became President of the Seminary when the office of dean was abolished.

He served as president of his church's board of foreign missions (1902–07), of the General Conference of Lutherans (1899, 1902, 1904), of the American Society of Church History (1907–08), and of the Pennsylvania German Society (1910–11). He also translated various German theological works and editing the Lutheran Church Review (1882–96), and Lutheran Commentary (1895-98). Henry Eyster Jacobs, working with John A.W. Haas, published The Lutheran Cyclopedia in 1899.

Selected Bibliography

- First Free Lutheran Diet in America, Philadelphia, December 27–28, 1877 (1878)
- The Lutheran movement in England during the reigns of Henry VIII and Edward VI, and its literary monuments (1890)
- History of the Lutheran Church in America (1893)
- Elements of Religion (1894)

- Annotations on the Epistles of Paul to the Romans and I. Corinthians (1896)
- Annotations on the Epistles of Paul to I. Cortinthians VII-XVI, II. Corinthians and Galatians (1897)
- Martin Luther, the hero of the reformation (1898)
- The German Emigration to America, 1709- 40 (1899)
- Summary of the Christian Faith (1905)

How Can You Find Peace With God?

The most important thing to grasp is that no one is made right with God by the good things he or she might do. Justification is by faith only, and that faith resting on what Jesus Christ did. It is by believing and trusting in His one-time *substitutionary* death for your sins.

Read your Bible steadily. God works His power in human beings through His Word. Where the Word is, God the Holy Spirit is always present.

Suggested Reading: *New Testament Conversions* by Pastor George Gerberding

Benediction

Now unto him that is able to keep you from falling, and to present you faultless before the presence of his glory with exceeding joy, To the only wise God our Savior, be glory and majesty, dominion and power, both now and ever. Amen. (Jude 1:24-25)

Encouraging Christian Books for You to Download and Enjoy

Devotional

- *The Sermons of Theophilus Stork: A Devotional Treasure*
- Simon Peter Long. *The Way Made Plain*

Theology

- Matthias Loy. *The Doctrine of Justification*
- Henry Eyster Jacobs. *Summary of the Christian Faith*
- Theodore Schmauk. *The Confessional Principle*

Novels

- Edward Roe. *Without a Home*
- Joseph Hocking. *The Passion for Life*

Essential Lutheran Library

- The Augsburg Confession with Saxon Visitation Articles
- Luther's Small Catechism
- Luther's Large Catechism
- Melanchthon's Apology
- The Formula of Concord

The full catalog is available at LutheranLibrary.org. Paperback Editions of some titles at Amazon.

Made in the USA
Monee, IL
28 July 2022